MAN, MYTH & MAGIC

INDEX & BIBLIOGRAPHY

Editor-in-Chief
Richard Cavendish

Editorial Board
C. A. Burland; Professor Glyn Daniel;
Professor E. R. Dodds; Professor Mircea Eliade;
William Sargant; John Symonds;
Professor R. J. Zwi Werblowsky;
Professor R. C. Zaehner.

New Edition edited and compiled by
Yvonne Deutch, B.A. University of Exeter;
M.A. University of Kansas, Lawrence, Kansas.

MARSHALL CAVENDISH
NEW YORK, LONDON, TORONTO

Library of Congress Cataloging in Publication Data

Main entry under title:

Man, myth, and magic

Bibliography: p.
1. Occult sciences. 2. Psychical research.
I. Cavendish, Richard. II. Deutch, Yvonne.
BF1411.M25 1983 133 82-13041
ISBN 0-86307-041-8 (set)
ISBN 0-86307-068-X (v.12)

British Library Cataloguing in Publication Data

Man, myth and magic.
1. Mythology - Dictionaries
2. Religion - Dictionaries
I. Cavendish, Richard
291.1'3'0321 BL303

ISBN 0-86307-041-8 (set)
ISBN 0-86307-068-X (v.12)

Reference Edition Published 1983

Printed and Bound in Italy by L.E.G.O. S.p.a. Vicenza.

Published by Marshall Cavendish Corporation,
147 West Merrick Road,
Freeport, Long Island
N.Y. 11520

Distributed in India by Standard Literature.

INDEX

The main articles which appear throughout the set are detailed in bold type in the index. Other text references are in roman with all illustrations in italics. The volume that the entry is featured in is shown in bold type before the relevant page number.

The abbreviation 'f' has been used to indicate that the text reference appears on that page and a following page; 'ff' denotes that it appears on that page and consecutive pages.
The quotations in ruled boxes have not been indexed.

A

Aarne, Antti, 4: 1009
Aaron, rod of, **11:** 2986–7
Abadie, Jeannette d' (witch), **4:** 1047, **9:** 2447
Abbots Bromley, horn dance of, **1: 62, 2:** 589, *591,* **4:** *1345,* 1352, **10:** *2689*
Abbot of Unreason, 1: 242, **2:** 480
Abduh, Muhammad, 6: 1472
Abdul-Baha (Bahai leader), **1:** *224,* 225, *255*
Aberdeen witches, 1: 62–3, 110
Abhidharma schools (Buddhism), **10:** 2726
Abode of Love (Spraxton, Somerset), **7:** *1827,* 1828f, **8:** *2257,* 2258f
abominable snowman (yeti), **1: 64**
see also sasquatch
aborigines, Australian, *see* Australia
Abracadabra, 1: 64, 7: 1728
Abracax (demon), **1: 64**
Abraham (Old Testament patriarch):
God on ladder and, **10:** *2696*
promised land and, **3:** 798, **5:** 1322
sacrifice of Isaac and, **4:** 976, *976,* **9:** *2455,* 2556, **11:** 2897
Abra-Melin, *see Sacred Magic of Abra-Melin*
Abrams, Dr Albert, 9: 2331–2
Abrams' Box (Black Box, Oscilloclast), **9:** 2332
Abraxas (god), **1:** 16, **4:** *1118*
Abu Gurob (Egypt), temple of Re at, **9:** 2364
Abulafia, Abraham (Jewish mystic), **7:** 1941–2, **10:** 2833
Accad (Mesopotamia), *see* Akkad
Achaemenids (Persian dynasty), **8:** 2048
capital of, *see* Persepolis
Zoroastrianism and, **11:** 3100, 3103
Acheron (river), **2:** 448
Achilles, 1: 65–6
Agamemnon and, **1:** 65
father of, *see* Peleus
Hector and, **1:** 65
horses of, **5:** 1212
mother of, *see* Thetis
Patroclus and, **1:** 65
Penthesilea and, **1:** 66, 119
as type of the Homeric hero, **1:** 65f
Acholi (Nilotic people), **7:** 2000
acorn, 5: 1368, **8:** 2034, 2035
Acropolis (Athens), **9:** *2357*
Actaeon, Artemis and, **3:** 630, **10:** 2687, *2689, 2690–1*
acupuncture, 1: 67–9
AD (Anno Domini), **5:** 1323
Adad (god), *see* Baal
Adam (first man), **1:** 69, **2:** 538
bisexuality of, original, **8:** 2070
in Cabala, *see* Adam Kadmon
Eve and, **3:** 859f, **4:** *978,* 979f, **7:** *1706,* **10:** 2539–40, **11:** 3057
apple and, **1:** 142
Gypsy myth of, **5:** 1195
as hermaphrodites, **5:** *1288*
Manichean view of, **4:** 982, **6:** 1624, 1712–13, 1721
see also Eden, garden of
Lilith and, **6:** 1631
the Lord passing judgement on (Blake), **10:** *2835*
Martinists and, **7:** 1746
meaning of the name, **1:** 333, **4:** 979
Adamites (heretics), **4:** 982, **8:** *2017,* 2019
Adam Kadmon (Cabala), **6:** 1675, 1712
Luria and, **6:** 1668, 1712
Adam's Peak (Ceylon), sacred footprint on, **8:** 2196
adderwort (plant), *see* bistort
Adena Indians, 8: 2007
Adonai (name of God), **11:** 3063
Adonis, 1: 69, 137–8, **3:** 739–41
Aphrodite and, **1:** 138
as dying god, **3:** 739–41
Good Shepherd symbol and, **4:** 1137
by Michelangelo, **3:** *739*
myrrh tree and **1:** 137
Persephone and, **1:** 138
as vegetation god, **1:** 138, **3:** 739
Adrasteia (Greek goddess), *see* Nemesis
Adventure, An (Moberly and Jourdain), *see Versailles adventure*
A.E., *see* Russell, G. W.
Aeetes (King of Colchis), **2:** 485
Aegus (legendary king of Athens), **10:** 2818, 2820
Aegisthus (Greek mythology), **4:** 1055
Aelian (Elian), St, cursing well of, **2:** 581, **10:** 2685–7
Aeneas (Trojan hero), **4:** 1025f
Aphrodite and, **1:** 136, **11:** 2943
Harpies and, **5:** 1213
as a Lar, **6:** 1609
see also Aeneid
Aeneid (Virgil), **2:** 602f, **4:** 1025
divination by, **1:** 265
Hades in, **6:** 1545
purgation of souls in, **9:** 2305
Sibyl of Cumae in, **10:** 2574–5
Aeschylus, *Eumenides* of, **4:** 1055f
Aesculapius (Roman god), **1: 69, 5:** 1246
Asclepios identified with, **5:** 1245
Aesir (Scandinavian deities), **4:** 1051, 1052
Aesop, 4: 896
Aeternitas (Roman personification of time), **11:** 2848
Aetherius Society, 1: 69, 3: *821,* **4:** 1003–4, *1004*
aetiological myths, distinguished from ritual creation myths, **2:** 523, 533
Africa, 1: 70–83
ancestor worship in, *see* ancestor worship, in Africa
burial in, **1:** 79
Christianity in **1:** 75–6, **3:** 778, **7:** 1957ff, 1980–1
Congo, **2:** 503
Ethiopia, **3:** 841, 842, 843ff, 846
Zulus, **11:** 3106
see also African Orthodox Churches
cicatrization in, *see* cicatrization, in Africa
circumcision in, *see* circumcision, in Africa
creation myths of, **1:** 82
Ashanti, **1:** 161
death in, **1:** 79, **3:** 612f, 614f
see also reincarnation *below*
disease in, **3:** 648
see also medicine-man, African; witch-doctor
drum in, *see* drum, in Africa
fertility and **4:** 931, 936, *936*
fetishes of, **4:** 938, *938, 939,* **10:** *2632*
hyena in, **5:** 1378
initiation rites of, *see* initiation, in Africa
Islam in, *see* Islam, in Africa
life after death, beliefs concerning, **1:** 73f
lion in, **6:** 1634
magic, black and white, in, **1:** 81
masks in, **7:** 1756–7, *1757, 1758*
menstruation, beliefs concerning, **7:** 1800
nature worship in, **1:** 72f
new religious movements in, **7:** 1831ff, 1977ff, **9:** 2522
see also Church of the Cherubim and Seraphim; Church of the Lord, Aladura
phallic symbolism in, **4:** *931*
reincarnation, beliefs concerning, **1:** 73–5
rock paintings in, *see* rock paintings, in Africa
secret societies in, **1:** 81, **2:** 510
see also Leopard Societies; Mau Mau
snake in **1:** 72–3
Congolese myth, **2:** *508*
Ethiopia, **3:** 844
spirits in, *see* spirits, in Africa
taboo in **1:** 78
Bushmen, **2:** 380
Congo, **10:** 2770
thunderbird in, **10:** 2837
witchcraft in, **1:** 76–7, 81f, **4: 951ff, 8:** 2051, **10:** 2631ff, **11:** 3045
Azande, **1:** 211, 212–3, **4:** 869, 952f, *954–5,* **11:** 3041–2
Cewa, **11:** 3042, 3045
Congo, **2:** 509f, **7:** 1978
familiars of witches, **11:** 3045
Nilotes, **8:** 2003
sorcery distinguished from witchcraft, **1:** 211, **11:** 3041–2, 3105
Zulus, **11:** 3105–6
see also witch-doctor
see also Ashanti; Azande; Berbers; Bushmen; Congo; Dahomey; Dogon; Ethiopia; Kikuyu; Masai; Ndembu; Negroes; Nigeria; Nilotes; pygmies; Swazi; Touareg; Zulu
African Orthodox Churches, 11: 2989–90
afterlife, *see* life after death
Aga Khan, 6: 1470, 1472
Agamemnon, 5: 1168
Achilles and, **1:** 65
dragon and, **3:** 693
sceptre of, at Chaeronea, **9:** 2351
agape (Christian love feast), **1:** 84
Eucharist and, **7:** 1768
Agapemonites (messianic sect), **7:** *1827,* 1828–30
see also Prince, Henry James
Agar, Margaret (witch), **10:** 2626
agate, 6: 1511
Agatha, St, 3: 648, **9:** 2464
Agave (Greek mythology), **3:** 635f
Agdistis (monster; later Cybele), **2:** 583
Agla, 1: 112, **7:** 1942
Aglaia (Greek mythology), **4:** 1145
Agni (Indian fire god), **2:** 365, **5:** 1435, **7:** 1908
Agoué (spirit; Voodoo), **10:** *2588–9*
Agricola, Michael (Finnish church reformer), **4:** 958

agriculture, 1: 84
dance and, **2:** 589f
fertility in, **4:** 931f, 935
Greek goddess of, *see* Demeter
its origin not established, **11:** 2938
in Roman religion, **9:** 2414–15
see also corn; harvest; vegetation spirits
Agrippa, Heinrich Cornelius, 1: 84–5
on astral travel, **1:** 173
magic and, **1:** 84f, **2:** 387, **5:** 1182, **6:** 1685
magic circle, **6:** *1687*
magic squares, **6:** 1691f
on man as microcosm, **1:** 84, **6:** 1712
on talismans, **1:** 300, **9:** 2374
witchcraft and, **4:** 916–17
Ahasuerus, *see* Wandering Jew
ahimsa, **11:** 3072–3
Ahmad, Ghulam (Mahdi), **6:** 1700
Ahriman (Zoroastrianism), **1: 86–89, 11:** 3100
Angra Mainyu and, **8:** 2048
Ohrmazd and, **1:** 86ff, *87,* **3:** 729f, **6:** 1624, **8:** 2048, **11:** 3103, 3107
Ahura Mazdah (Zoroastrianism), **1:** 86, **89, 8:** 2048, *2048,* **11:** 3100, *3101,* 3102f
Azhi Dahaka (dragon) and, **3:** 691
Ohrmazd and, **1:** 86, **8:** 2048
Aidoneus, *see* Hades
Ainu (Japan), **1:** 244, 246, **8:** 2098
Aion (child of Isis), **3:** 742
air, 1: 89
as element, **3:** 801f
see also breath; *pneuma*
Airavata (elephant of Indra), **3:** 804, **4:** *993*
Aisai (Greek mythology), *see* Fates
Aix-en-Provence nuns, 1: 90–2
see also Demandolx de la Palud, Madeleine de
Aiyetoro Community (Nigeria), **2:** 502
Aizen-e (Japanese religious sect), **6:** 1496
Ajax (Greek hero), Athene and, **1:** 186
Ajello, Elena (stigmatist), **10:** 2698
Akasha (occultism), *see* Astral Light
Akashic Records (occultism), *see* Cosmic Memory
Akhenaten (pharaoh), *see* Ikhnaten
Akhetaten (El Amarna; Egyptian city), **3:** 790, 793, **5:** 1402
Akkad (Accad; Mesopotamia), **1:** 223, **7:** 1818
see also Sargon, King
also Babylonia
Aksobhya (Buddha), **2:** 360
Aksum (Ethiopian city), **3:** *840,* 842
al–. *For Islamic names beginning with al–, see under the following part of the name*
Alaca Hüyük, burial at, **2:** 570
Alalu (Alalus; Hittite god), **5:** 1324
al-Alawi, Ahmad (Sufi), **10:** 2716
Alba Longa (city), **4:** 1026
albedo (alchemical process), **8:** 2178
Albertus Magnus:
on the eagle, **3:** 746
on the houseleek, **5:** 1369
on divisions of the skull, **8:** 2189
on succubi, **3:** 862
Albigenses, Albigensian heresy, **2:** 422, 423–4, **5:** 1283
alchemy, 1: 93–99
Boehme and, **1:** 302
in China, **1:** 97, **3:** 809
diamond and, **6:** 1514
dragon and, **3:** *693*
four elements theory and, **1:** 97, **3:** *803*
Goethe and **4:** 1127
gold in, **1:** 93ff, **3:** 809, 811f, **4:** 1129
hermaphrodite in, **8:** 2069, *2069*
Hermetica and, **5:** 1291
hexagram in, **5:** 1300
Jung and, **1:** 99, **6:** 1550f
lead in, **6:** 1613
Lull and, **5:** *1291,* **6:** 1667
macrocosm and microcosm in, **6:** 1675
marriage, allegorical, in, **7:** 1808, **8:** 2069
mercury (metal) in, **1:** 94, 112, **3:** *803,* **4:** 1129, **7:** 1807f, **8:** 2069
ourobouros in, **1:** 94
Paracelsus and, **1:** 94f, **3:** 809, 810f, **7:** 1807f, **8:** 2127–8
planets and, **1:** 97–8
psychokinesis and, **1:** 97
Rosicrucians and, **9:** 2429, 2430, *2432*
salt in, **7:** 1807f, **9:** 2475
silver in, **10:** 2577
staircase symbolism in, **10:** 2697
sulphur and mercury theory in, **4:** 1129, **7:** 1807f, **10:** 2716
Sun in, *see Splendor Solis*
in Tantrism, **10:** 2780
unicorn in, **11:** 2910
water in, **11:** 3002
see also distillation; elixir of Life; Emerald Tablet; Flamel, Nicholas; homunculus; Philosophers' Stone
alcohol, 11: 2998
Aldebaran (star), Dakota Indian legend of, **8:** 2010
Alecto (Greek mythology), **4:** 918, 1054
alectromancy (divination), **8:** 2065
Alexander, Bishop Daniel William, 11: 2989
Alexander III (pope), **11:** 2980, *2982*
Alexander VI (pope), **9:** 2370
Alexander the Great, 1: 100–4
Amazons and, **1:** 103, 119
his horse Bucephalus, **1:** 104, **11:** *2952*
lunar eclipse as good omen for, **3:** *772*
yogis and, **10:** 2523
see also Gordian knot
Alexandria (Egypt):
Eleusinian cult at, **7:** 1925
temple of the Muses at, **7:** 1905
alexandrite, 6: 1511
Algazel, *see* Ghazali
Algol (star) **1: 104**
Algonquin Indians, 1: 105–7
culture-hero of, *see* Kuloskap
death, myth of origin of, **3:** 614
High God of, **5:** 1302
reincarnation belief of, **2:** 333
shamans of, **1:** 105f
see also Chippewa; manitou
Ali (cousin of Mohammed), **6:** 1469, 1699
Ali, Mirza Hussain, *see* Baha-Ullah
Ali, Muhammad (Cassius Clay), **1:** 280
Alice in Wonderland (Carroll), **6:** *1451,* **7:** 1908, *1909*
alicorn (horn of unicorn), **11:** 2909–10
Allah (Islam), **1:** 107, **6:** *1465,* **7:** 1871
Alleyn, Edward (actor), **3:** 865
All Hallows' Eve (Hallowe'en) **1: 109–10**
ashes ritual on, **1:** 166
bonfires and **1:** 109
divination on, **3:** 672, **6:** 1660, **10:** 2620
fairies and, **1:** 109–10
Sir James Frazer on, **1:** 109
mumming plays of, **4:** 1004
snail and, **10:** 2620
witches and **1:** 110, **3:** 853
alligator, in Mexican myth, **1:** 217
All Souls' Day, palm tree and, **8:** 2116
almond tree, origin of, in agdistis myth, **2:** 583
aloes, 1: 110
alphabet, 1: 111–14
divination by (alectromancy), **8:** 2065
Hebrew, *see* Hebrew alphabet
incense and, in Islamic incantation, **5:** 1428
North American Indians, first alphabet of, **8:** 2012
see also gematria; hieroglyphics; magic squares; O; runes; S; T; writing
alrunes (amulets), **6:** 1718
Alrutz, S., magnetism and, **6:** 1695
Altamira (Spain), cave art of, **2:** 363, *432*
altar, 1: 115–17, 10: 2707
Aztec, **1:** 117
Chinese, **1:** 117
Christian **1:** *116,* 117, **10:** *2824*
Egyptian, **1:** 116
Greek, **1:** 116f
Hindu, **1:** 117
Japanese, **1:** 117
Jewish, **1:** 116
Mesopotamian, **1:** 116, **8:** 2245
Nigerian, **1:** *117*
Persian, **1:** 117, *117*
prehistoric, **1:** 116
Roman, **1:** 116f, **9:** 2418
on a ship, **10:** 2569
Alur (Nilotic people), **7:** 2000f
Amalthea (nymph), Zeus and, **2:** 518, **8:** 2032
Amana Society (Community of the Truly Inspired), **2:** 497, 500–2
Amanita muscaria, *see* fly agaric
Amaterasu-Omikami (Japanese sun goddess), **10:** 2562
Amazons, 1: 118–19
Alexander the Great and, **1:** 103, 119
Hercules and **1:** 119, **5:** *1277,* 1279–80
Theseus and, **1:** 119, **10:** 2819
see also Penthesilea
amber, 6: 1511
ambergris, 11: 3014
Ambika (Indian goddess), **7:** *1893*
ambrosia (Food of the gods), fly agaric mushroom identified as, **7:** 1908
Amduscias (demon), **3:** *860,* **11:** *2909*
Amen (Egyptian god), *see* Amun
Amen (end of prayer or incantation), **7:** 1942
Amenhotep/Amenophis (pharaoh):
II, **6:** *1567*
III, **5:** 1420
IV, *see* Ikhnaten
Amenta (Egypt), **2:** 334, *335*
America, discovery of, **2:** 337, 338, 339
American Indians, North, *see* North American Indians
amethyst, 6: 1511f, *1512*
Amish sect, 2: 497
Amida, Amidaism (Japanese Buddhism), **1: 119–21, 6:** 1486, 1489, 1492
Amitabha identified with Amida, **2:** 360
Amitabha (Amitayus; Buddhism), **2:** 360, **8:** 2004
Ammonius (philosopher), **7:** 1967, **8:** 2207
Amor (Roman god), *see* Cupid
A.M.O.R.C. (Ancient and Mystic Order Rosae Crucis), **9:** 2433, *2433*
Amorites, 1: 168, 222
Amos (Old Testament prophet), **9:** 2266–7
Amphiaraus, dream cures of, **7:** 1852
Amphibalus, St, 11: 2907
Amphion and Zethus (Greek mythology), **11:** 2904
Amphitrite (nereid), **3:** 670, **9:** *2417*
Amritsar (India), **10:** *2575, 2576,* 2577
amulets, 1: 121, **10:** 2772–3
cowrie-shell, **2:** 525
eagle (Germanic), **4:** *1086*
ear-ring, **3:** 748
Egyptian, **10:** 2766, 2772, 2774–5
in Tutankhamen's tomb, **6:** 1454
see also scarab
Eskimo, **3:** 837
in Ethiopia, **3:** 846
mandrake, **7:** 1718f
Maori, *see tiki*
phallic, Greek, **10:** *2538*
Phoenician, **10:** 2766
Polynesia, *see tiki*
as protection against the evil eye, **4:** 890
talismans distinguished from, **10:** 2772
see also fetish; Gnostic gems
Amun (Egyptian god), **2:** 535, **3:** 794
Ikhnaten and, **3:** 790, **5:** 1402
ram and, **3:** *788,* **9:** 2556, *2558*
Re and, **3:** 789, **5:** 1402, **9:** 2556
temple of, at Karnak, **9:** *2356*

An (Anu, Anum; Mesopotamian god), **3:** 745, 750, **7:** 1818f, **10:** 2604
Alalu and Kumarbi and, **5:** 1324
horned cap of, **5:** 1347
Ishtar and, **6:** 1459
Anabaptists, 1: 121, 2: *499,* **3:** 825f, **5:** 1376, **9:** 2520, *2521*
Anahita (Iranian goddess), **7:** 1896, **11:** 3103
analogies, in magic, **8:** 2214–15
see also correspondences
analytical psychology, Jung's adoption of the phrase, **6:** 1548–9
Ananai-kyo (Japanese religious sect), **6:** 1496
Anandamayi Ma (Indian sage), **1: 121–2**
Ananse (spider-trickster), **1: 122, 10:** 2653
Ananta (serpent; Hinduism), **10:** *2614*
Anaon (Breton hell), **2:** 347
anaphrodisiac, 6: 1657–8, 1661
camphor as, **8:** 2167
Anat (Phoenician goddess), **1:** 168f
Astarte identified with, **8:** 2182
Baal and, **1:** 169, 223, **8:** 2182–3, **10:** 2761f, **11:** 2940–1
as Mother Goddess, **7:** 1895, 1896
anathema (excommunication ceremony), **2:** 582
Anaxagoras (Greek philosopher), **5:** 1282
Anaximander (Greek philosopher), **10:** 2718
ancestor worship, 1: 122, 2: 572–6, **4:** 1093f
in Africa, **2:** 573f, **7:** 1958
Ashanti, **1:** *162,* 163, **2:** 572, 573, 574, **3:** 726
Dahomey, **2:** 584f
Kikuyu, **6:** 1561f
Nilotes, **7:** 2002
Zulus, **11:** 3105
in China, **2:** 457, 459, 573
in Laos, **10:** 2646
in Micronesia, **8:** 2233
in New Guinea, **7:** 1757f, 1974
in Papua, **2:** *568*
anchor, 1: 122
anchorite, 1: 122
Julian of Norwich, **6:** 1548
Andaman Islands, 9: 2351, **10:** 2601
Andras (demon), **8:** *2098*
Andreae, Johann Valentin, 9: 2429–30
Andrew, St, 7: *1986,* 1989
androgyne, *see* hermaphrodite
Andromeda (Greek mythology), **3:** 693, *694,* **5:** *1295*
anemone, 5: *1274*
Adonis and, **1:** 138, **5:** 1271
Angad (Sikh leader), **10:** 2576–7
angel (touchpiece), **6:** 1573, *1573*
Angela of Foligno, Blessed, 11: 2963
angelica (herb), **5:** 1271–2
angels, 1: 124–6
in the Bible, **1:** 124ff
Daniel, **2:** 602, **5:** 1187
Revelation, **11:** 2897
John Dee and **3:** 618f
in dome of St Saviour (Constantinople), **9:** *2363*
fairies and fallen angels, **4:** 905–6
Fall of the Rebel Angels:
by Breughel, **2:** *342–3,* 344
by Le Brun, **10:** *2598*
guardian angels, **5:** 1187, **6:** 1721
harps and, **5:** 1212
Jesus ministered to by (Tissot), **11:** *3017*
of Mons, **1:** 145, *145,* **11:** *2963*
Moslem, **1:** 126, **5:** 1187, **10:** *2603*
soul weighed by, at Last Judgement, **1:** 124–5, **11:** 3007
trumpets and, **11:** 2897, *2897*
wings of, **11:** 3033
Zoroastrian, **1:** 126
see also cherub; Gabriel; Lucifer; Michael; Raphael; seraph; Uriel; Watchers
Angkor Wat, 10: *2647*
Angra Mainyu (Zoroastrianism), **8:** 2048
animal magnetism, *see* magnetism
animals, 1: 127–31
in African rock paintings, **9:** 2407–8
in astrology, **1:** 131
banished by poets, **8:** 2212–14
in cave art, **2:** 431
Celts and, *see* Celts, animals and
in Christian symbolism, *see* Christianity, symbolism in, animals
Dionysus and, **1:** 130
bull, **5:** 1348
dolphin, **3:** 670
goat, **4:** 1120, *1121*
dances, animal, **2:** 589, **5:** *1345*
see also Abbots Bromley
divination by, omens from, **8:** 2064
entrails of, *see* haruspicy
hare, **5:** 1210
horse, **5:** 1357
in Mesopotamia, **7:** 1826
in Egypt:
dog, **3:** 664
pig, **3:** 2191, *2191*
see also Egypt, animal gods of
Eskimos, spirits of animals and, **3:** 834
extra-sensory perception and, **3:** 883f
in Finland, **4:** 958
ghosts of **4:** 1097
hare, **5:** 1355f
in magic, **1:** 131
medieval lore of, *see* bestiary
moon and, **7:** 1880
in phallic symbolism, **8:** 2175
sacrifice of **1:** 130
bear, **1:** 116, 245–6, **8;** 2243, 2856
bull, **1:** 230, **3:** 742, **7:** *1861,* 1862, 1863f, **8:** 2261
at Carthage, **8:** *2181*
cat, **4:** 915
by Etruscans, **3:** 849–50
horse, **4:** 1052, **5:** 1353, 1410, 1435
in Malta, **6:** 1700
by the Nuer, **8:** 2022–3
in Polynesia, **8:** 2231
ram, **9:** 2556
in ritual magic, **9:** 2400
Rome and, **9:** 2418
in the *Veda,* **5:** 1435
saints and, **9:** 2465–71
white animals, **11:** 3018
see also alligator; anteater; ass; bat; bear; boar; buffalo; bull; cat; crab; crocodile; dog; dolphin; East Indian humped zebu; elephant; ferret; fox; frog; goat; hare; hedgehog; horse; hyena; jackal; jaguar; lion; lizard; llama; monkey; mouse; ocelot; opossum; oyster; panther; pig; polecat; rabbit; rat; reindeer; rhinoceros; scorpion; seal; serpent; sheep; shrew; snail; spider; stag; tiger; toad; tortoise; unicorn; whale; wolf
also birds; fish; insects; monsters
also horns; hunting magic; shape-shifting; totemism
animism, 1: 132
in Borneo, **1:** 312ff
Eskimos and **3:** 833
in Ethiopia **3:** 841
fairies and, **4:** 906
soul and, **1:** 132, **10:** 2636
ankh (Egyptian symbol), **2:** 550, *551,* **3:** *785, 792,* **5:** *1413*
Christian use of (*crux ansata*), **2:** 550
Ankou (Breton deity), **2:** 347
Anne, Queen, King's Evil and, **6:** 1573
Anne, St, 2: 349, **10:** 2685
Annunciation, festival of the, **2:** *336,* **6:** *1632,* **7:** 1750
Annwn, cauldron of, **1:** 154, **2:** 428, **4:** 1149
anointing, *see* unction
anorexia, religious inedia compared with **10** 2701
ant (insect), **6:** 1446
Antaei, of Arcadia, shape-shifting by, **9:** 2551–2
anteater, 1: 80, **2:** 329
Anteros (Greek mythology), **3:** 830
Anthesteria (Greek festival), **11:** 3035
Anthony, St, 1: 133, **9:** 2464
lion and, **9:** 2468
St Paul the Hermit and, **6:** *1601,* **9:** 2468
pig and **8:** 2192
St Anthony's fire and, **9:** 2464
temptation of, **1:** 133
by Bosch, (1), **1:** 320f, *321;* (2), **1:** 133, 321
by Breughel, **2:** 341
by Grünewald, **9:** *2525*
Anthony of Padua, St, 9: 2464, 2470–1
Anthroposophy, Anthroposophical Society, **10:** 2693ff
Antichrist, 1: 134
Beast of Revelation and, **4:** 1157
Rome as, **4:** 1157
anting (bird behaviour) **8:** 2186
Antiochus IV Epiphanes (Syrian king), **1:** 134, **3:** 609
Antiochus of Ascalon (Platonist), **7:** 1966
Antiope (Amazon), **1:** 119, **10:** 2819
antisemitism, 1: 134, 9: 2328–30
in the Middle Ages, **5:** 1328–9, **6:** *1531*
in Modern Europe, **5:** *1384,* **7:** *1966,* **8:** 2329–30
Germanen Order, **4:** 1081f
National Socialism, **9:** *2329,* 2330
volkisch movement, **7:** 1964
Anu (Celtic goddess), *see* Danu
Anu (Mesopotamian god), *see* An
Anuak (Nilotic people), **7:** 2000f, 2003
Anubis (Egyptian god), **1: 134, 3:** 616, *792*
Nefertiti and, **5:** *1378*
Osiris and, **3:** *740*
Anum (Mesopotamian god), *see* An
Anzu (Mesopotamian deity), *see* Zu
Apep (Egyptian serpent), *see* Apophis
aphrodisiac, 6: 1657ff
ambergris, **11:** 3014
honey, **5:** 1340
love potion (philtre), **6:** *1656,* 1657
mandrake, **6:** 1657, 1718
oyster, **4:** 987, **6:** 1658
perfumes, **8:** 2167
Roman, **6:** 1658
Aphrodite, 1: 135–8
Adonis and, **1:** 138
Aeneas and, **1:** 136, **11:** 2943
Ares and, **1:** 137
Astarte and, **1:** 168
birth of, **1:** 135
Cnidian (Praxiteles), **1:** 138
copper and, **2:** 522
Cyprus, her cult derived from, **1:** 135, **2:** 522
dove and, **2:** 522, **3:** 680
Eros and, **1:** 135f, **3:** 829, 830
goose and, **4:** 1138, *1140*
green and, **2:** 522
Hephaestus and, **1:**136f, **5:** 1268
Hera and, **1:** 136
Hermaphroditos and, **5:** 1287
meaning of the name, **1:** 135
myrtle sacred to, **11:** 2946
Pan with, **1:** *138*
Philommedes, **1:** 135
prostitution and, **1:** 137, **9:** 2272
sanctuaries of, **1:** 135
sparrow sacred to, **2:** 522
Trojan War and, **1:** 136
Venus identified with, **1:** 135, **11:** 2943
Zeus and, **1:** 136, 137, 138
see also Judgement of Paris
Apis (Egyptian god), **1: 138**
bull and, **1:** 138, **2:** *364,* 365, **3:** 790, **5:** 1347
moon and, **2:** 365
Osiris and, *see* Serapis
Aplu (Etruscan god), Apollo identified with, **3:** 849
Apocalypse, 1: 138, 9: 2378

Great Beast of the, *see* Great Beast
horsemen of the, **2:** 379
by Traini, **3:** *818–19*
by Turner, **5:** *1353*
by G. F. Watts, **10:** *2376–7*
of St John, *see* Revelation, book of
see also Daniel
apocalypses, apocryphal, 7: 1986, 1992
Apocrypha (Bible) **1:** 265
giants in, **4:** 1102
wisdom literature of, **11:** 3040
see also New Testament, Apocrypha
Apocryphon of John (Gnostic text), **4:** 1117
Apollinaire, Guillaume, 1: 148
Apollinaris (Christian heretic), **5:** 1282
Apollo (Greek god), **1: 139–40, 5:** *1170, 1395,* **6:** *1709,* **10:** *2822*
Apulunas identified with, **1:** 139
Artemis and, **3:** 630
Cassandra and, **1:** 141, **10:** 2574
Chiron and, **5:** 1246
Coronis and, **2:** 556, **5:** 1246
Crete and, **5:** 1171
Cupid and, **3:** 831
Daphne and, **3:** 831, **6:** 1610, *1610*
Dionysus and, **3:** 635, 638
dolphin and, **3:** 670
hawk sacred to, **5:** 1227
as healing god, **5:** 1246
Hermes and, **5:** 1289
Hyperboreans and, **1:** 139
Midas and, **1:** 140
mother of, *see* Leto
Muses and, **7:** 1905
Niobe and **1:** 140
nude priestess of, at Epirus, **8:** 2019
oracles of, **8:** 2073, 2077f
see also Delphi, oracle of Apollo at
Orestes and, **4:** *918,* 1055f
serpent killed by, at Delphi, **1:** 139, **9:** 2529
sibyls and, **10:** 2574
Stonehenge and, **3:** 721
summer associated with, **11:** 3035
sun and, **1:** 139
wolf and, **1:** 129, 139, **11:** 3047
Apollonia, St, toothache and, **3:** 648, **9:** *2464*
Apollonius of Tyana, 1: 140–1, **6:** 1510, **8:** 2502
Apophis (Apep, Apop; legendary monster, Egypt), **3:** 690
apostles (of Jesus), **11:** 2898
Acts of the, **8:** 2148–9
apocryphal acts of the, **7:** 1989–92
see also Andrew, St; James, St; John, St; Judas Iscariot; Peter, St; Simon, St
also Pentecost
Apostles' Creed, 2: 539
apotheosis, 1: 141
Appaliunaas (Hittite god), *see* Apulunas
apparition, 1: 141
astral body and, **1:** 172
collective, **11:** 2966
'crisis', **8:** 2275, **11:** 2961
religious, *see* visions
Society for Psychical Research and, **8:** 2275, **11:** 2962
see also ghosts; phantasms of the living
apple (tree and fruit), **1: 141–2**
Adam and Eve and, **1:** 142
Avalon and, **1:** 141
of the Hesperides, **1:** *141,* 142, **5:** 1280, *1281*
immortality and, **1:** 141
in Judgement of Paris, **1:** 142, *142*
mistletoe and, **7:** 1859
Volsung and, **4:** 1051
of youth, in Scandinavian mythology, *see* Idun
apportation (teleportation), **7:** 1789, **10:** 2812
Apsu (Mesopotamian mythology), **2:** 536, **7:** 1822
Ea and, **3:** 745, **7:** 1819, 1821
Tammuz (Dumuzi) and, **10:** 2776
Apuleius (author of *The Golden Ass*), **6:** 1473–4
Apulunas (Appaliunaas; Hittite god), Apollo identified with, **1:** 139
aquamarine, 6: 1511, *1512*
aquarius (the Water-carrier; zodiac sign, in astrology), **1: 143,** 175, 181
Aquila of Pontus (Christian writer), **1:** 142
Aquinas, St Thomas, 5: 1415–16, **9:** 2462
on fate, **4:** 921
on the pelican, **8:** 2158
on possession, **3:** 873
on predestination, **8:** 2242
on visions, **11:** 2962
Aradia (goddess of witches), **6:** *1474,* 1476
Aradus (Phoenician city), **8:** 2180
Arapaho Indians, medicine pipes of, **4:** 1164
Arbatel of Magic (grimoire), **5:** 1182
arbutus, as maypole, in America, **7:** 1773
Arcadia (Greece), **8:** 2031
Artemis and, **8:** 2031
Pan and, **8:** 2124
Zeus born in, **5:** 1168
archangel, 1: 126
Archer, the (zodiac sign, in astrology), *see* Sagittarius
archetypes, Jung's concept of, **6:** 1549f
architecture, religious, 1: 144, 9: 2362–8
Buddhist, **8:** 2112, **9:** 2366–7
see also stupa; Tooth, Temple of the
at Catal Hüyük, **9:** 2362
Celtic, **5:** 1237f
Christian, **9:** *2360,* 2365, *2368,* 2372
cathedrals, *see* Canterbury; Chartres; Kremlin, Cathedral of the Assumption in; St Peter's, Rome; Salisbury
churches facing east, **3:** 640
Egyptian, **3:** 793f, **9:** *2356,* 2363–4
see also pyramids, Egyptian
Etruscan, **3:** 849
Greek, **9:** *2357,* 2364
Hindu, **9:** 2366, *2366,* 2456
erotic carvings of, **4:** *933,* **5:** *1317, 1318–19,* **10:** *2722, 2777*
Islamic, *see* mosque
Jewish, **6:** 1531, *1534*
see also Jerusalem, temple of Yahweh at
lotus in, **6:** 1650
of Malta, **6:** 1700ff
Mesopotamian, **9:** 2362–3
Mexican, *see* pyramids, Mexican
Parsee, **8:** 2138–9, **11:** *3099*
Phoenician, **10:** 2763, *2765*
Polynesian, **8:** 2231, *2232*
Roman, **9:** *2357,* 2364
sacrifice and, **9:** 2456
sexual symbolism in, **8:** 2175–7
Zoroastrian fire temple, **11:** *3098*
Arch of Titus (Rome), **11:** 3078
arcosolium (catacombs), **4:** 1137
Ares (Greek god), **1:** 144
Amazons and, **1:** 118
Aphrodite and, **1:** 137
Eros and, **3:** 829f
Mars identified with, **1:** 144, **7:** 1744
Arethusa (Greek mythology), **4:** 1028–9
Argonauts (Greek mythology):
Argo built of oak, **8:** 2033
eyes on prow of *Argo,* **4:** *891*
Orpheus and, **8:** 2082, 2590
Phineas and, **5:** 1212–13
see also Golden Fleece
Argus (Greek mythology), **4:** *893,* **8:** 2153
Ariadne (Greek mythology), **10:** 2818, 2819
Aries (the Ram; zodiac sign, in astrology), **1: 144,** 175, *180,* 181
Arinitti (Hittite goddess), **5:** 1323f
Arion (Greek mythology), **3:** 670, *671*
Ariosophie (esoteric system), **7:** 1983
Aristides, Aelius, 5: 1246
Aristotle, 8: 2240
Hermetica and, **5:** 1290, 1392
Aritimi (Etruscan goddess), Artemis identified with, **3:** 849
Arius, Arian heresy, **2:** 470–1, **5:** 1282
Arjun (Sikh leader), **10:** 2577
ark, of Noah, *see* Noah, his ark
Ark, of Yahweh, 8: 2070–1, **11:** 3064f
Arkona (Slav religious centre) **10:** 2610–11
Arlecchino (commedia dell'arte), **5:** 1212
Armanen sect, 6: 1636
armies, 1: 144–5
see also war
Arminianism, 3: 800
Arminius, Jacobus, 3: 800
Armstrong, Anne (witch), **10:** 2825
Arnim, Joachim von, 5: 1174
Arnold, Eberhart; Arnoldites, **5:** 1377
Arnold of Villanova, 5: 1338, 1418
Arnquagssaq (Eskimo sea spirit), *see* Sedna
Arp, Hans (Jean), **1:** 147f
arrow, 1: 145, **4:** 1060–1
Cheyenne Indians and, **5:** 1164
see also elf-bolts
Ars, curé of (J.-M.-B. Vianney), *see* Curé of Ars
Arsacid dynasty (Persia), **8:** 2143f
Arsenius (hermit), **11:** 3057
art:
automatic, *see* automatic art
modern, **1: 146–151**
see also Beardsley, Aubrey; Chagall, Marc; Dali, Salvador; Duchamp, Marcel; Ensor, James; Ernst, Max; Redon, Odilon
prehistoric and primitive, *see* cave art
see also Blake, William; Bosch, Hieronymus; Breughel, Pieter; Dadd, Richard; Doyle, Richard; Rossetti, D. G.
Artemidorus (Greek writer), on dreams, **3:** 693, 705
Artemis, 1: 151, 3: 630ff, **5:** *1170*
Actaeon and, **3:** 630, **10:** 2687, *2689, 2690–1*
Amazons and, **1:** 118
Apollo and, **3:** 630
Arcadia and, **8:** 2031
bears and **1:** 246, **3:** 630, **8:** 2031
at Brauron, **1:** 246, **8:** 2031
Callisto and, **1:** 246. **3:** 630f, **8:** 2031
in Crete, **2:** 542
the daughter of Zeus and Leto, **3:** 630
Diana identified with, **1:** 151, **3:** 630
at Ephesus, **3:** 632
Hecate and, **3:** 632, **5:** 1256, 1257
lesbianism and, **3:** 632
moon and, **3:** 632
as mother goddess, **3:** 630
nymphs and, **8:** 2031
trees and, **11:** 2876
Artha (Hinduism), **5:** 1315
arthame (athame; magic knife), **1:** 151, **7:** 1866
Arthur, 1: 152–9, **4:** *1112,* **5:** 1298, *1350,* **9:** *2396*
St Brendan and, **2:** 337
Brittany and, **2:** 347
Celtic legends of, **1:** 153–4, **4:** 1149, **6:** 1672, 1674
not dead but sleeping, **10:** 2614, 2614–15
fairies and, **4:** 901, 905
giant of St Michael's Mount slain by **6:** 1478
Glastonbury and, **1:** 159, **2:** 391, **4:** 1109, 1110, 1112
knights of, *see* Round Table *and* Bedivere; Bors; Galahad; Gareth; Gawain; Kay; Lancelot; Mordred; Parsifal; Tristan, in Arthurian legend
Merlin and, **1:** 154, 158, **7:** 1810f
sword of, *see* Excalibur
Tudors and, **1:** 155, *159,* **2:** 396
Wild Hunt associated with, **11:** 3022
see also Camelot; Forest Perilous; Grail; Guinevere; Morgan le Fay
Arunachala (Tiruvannamalai; Indian holy mountain), **9:** 2336
Arundale, Dr George S. (Theosophist), **10:** 2814–15, 2815, *2815,* 2816

Arval Brothers (Roman priesthood), **7:** 1743
Aryans (early invaders of India), **5:** 1434ff, **11:** 3098–9
Arya Samaj (Hindu reformist sect), **5:** 1316
asafoetida, 1: 160, 8: 2166
Asallukhi (Mesopotamian god), Marduk equated with, **7:** 1820
asanas (bodily positions; yoga), **11:** 2935, 3073, *3074, 3075*
lotus position, **11:** *2933, 3071, 3073*
Ascension (of Christ), **6:** 1507
in Cypriot paintings, **9:** *2290, 2334*
in 15th cent. miniature, **6:** *1416*
asceticism, self-denial, **1:** 160, **10: 2523–6**
abnormality or madness and, **6:** 1678–9
in Buddhism, **8:** *2004,* **9:** 2523, 2526
in Christianity, **6:** 1678–9, **9:** 2523, 2524, 2526
see also Anthony, St; fasting; Simeon Stylites
dualism and, **9:** 2524
Graeco-Roman, **9:** 2523, 2526
Hindu, **9:** 2523, 2524f
see also sadhu
in Islam, *see* fakir
Asclepios (Greek healing god), **1:** 173, **5:** 1171–2, 1245–6, **7:** 1852f
Aesculapius identified with, **5:** 1245
cock and, **2:** 491
in Crete, **5:** 1171
Epidaurus and, **5:** 1172, 1245f, **9:** 2351
Pergamum and, **5:** 1246
snake and, **5:** 1171–2, 1246, **9:** 2529
Ascoli, Cecco d' (magician), **3:** 640
ash (tree), **1: 160**
oak and, **8:** 2035
in Scandinavian mythology, *see* Yggdrasill
snakes and, **1:** 160
warts cured with, **1:** 160
Ashanti (Africa), **1:** 160–3
ancestor worship in, **1:** 162, *162,* **2:** 572, 573, 574, **3:** 726
charms and amulets of, **1:** 162f
creation myths of, **1:** 161
dreams in **3:** 725f
gods of, **1:** 161–2, **10:** 2601
human sacrifice in, **2:** 361
nature spirits of, **1:** 162, 163
priests in, **1:** 163
al-Ashari, 6: 1469
Asherah (Canaanite goddess), **1:** 168f
Athirat identified with, **10:** 2762
ashes, 1: 163–6
of cremated bodies, **2:** 541
divination by, **1:** 166, **5:** 1255
in fertility rites, **1:** 163–4
in weather magic, **1:** 164
Ashikaga Period (Japan), **6:** 1492
Ashkenazim (Jews), **6:** 1530
Ashtart (Phoenician goddess), **1:** 168
Ashtoreth (demon), *see* Astaroth
Ashur (Assyrian city), **6:** 1460
Ashur (Assur; Assyrian god), **1: 166, 7:** 1820
winged sun disc symbol of, **5:** 1395
Asmodeus (demon), **1:** 167
Jewish tales of, **1:** 167
Madeleine de Demandolx and, **1:** 170
in *The Magus* (Barrett), **1:** *167*
Asoka, Emperor, Buddhism and, **2:** 358
ass, 1: 167
Assassins, the, 6: 1472
Assemblies of God (Pentecostalism), **8:** 2161
Assenden Spring (Oxfordshire), **10:** 2684
Association of Invisible Aryans, 9: 2441
Association for Rune Research, 9: 2441
Assumption of the Blessed Virgin Mary, *see* Mary, the Virgin, Assumption of
Assur (Assyrian god), *see* Ashur
Assyria (Mesopotamia), **1: 167, 7:** 1818
clay figurine from, **7:** *1894*
death in, **3:** 616
Gilgamesh and, **4:** 1105
gods of **7:** 1818ff
Ishtar, **6:** 1460
Marduk, **7:** 1734
see also Ashur
hunting magic in, **5:** *1370*
Israel invaded by, **6:** 1644
kingship in, **6:** 1570
Astaroth (Ashtoreth; demon), **1:** *168–9,* 169, *170*
Astarte (goddess), **1: 168–70, 4:** *932*
Anat identified with, **8:** 2182
animals sacred to, **1:** 170
Aphrodite identified with, **1:** 168
Asherah, Ashtart, and Ishtar identified with, **1:** 168
Astaroth and, **1:** 170
castration in worship of, **1:** 170, **7:** 1915
Etruscans and, **3:** 849
moon and, **1:** 170
as Mother Goddess, **7:** 1895
prostitution and, **1:** 170, **8:** 2271
Tanit and **8:** 2184
astasia (hysterical ailment), **7:** 1854
astragalomancy, *see* lots
astragyromancy, *see* lots
astral body (body of light), **1: 171–3, 6:** 1630
apparitions and, **1:** 172
ghosts, **4:** 1101
dreams and, **1:** 173
physical body, connection with, *see* plexus
physical body, failure to return to, **8:** 2284
pneuma and, **1:** 173
soul distinguished from, **1:** 171
yoga and, **1:** 172
Kundalini, **6:** 1586
see also aura
astral light (Akasha), **6:** 1630
Madame Blavatsky and, **1:** 291
Eliphas Levi on, **9:** 2284
astral plane, 6: 1630, **8:** 2283f
astrology, 1: 174–82
in Egypt, **10:** 2692
Goethe and, **4:** 1127
Jung and, **1:** 176, **6:** 1552
macrocosm/microcosm theory and **6:** 1675
in Mesopotamia, **7:** 1826, **10:** 2692
'mutable' signs in **11:** 2957
National Socialism and, **7:** 1944, 1945ff
Paracelsus and, **8:** 2127
planets in, **1:** 175ff, **4:** 1020, **10:** 2692
Jupiter, **1:** 175, 180, **6:** 1554
Mars, **1:** 175, 180, **7:** 1744
Mercury, **1:** 175, 180, **7:** 1806–7
moon, **1:** 175, 180, **7:** 1882
Neptune, **1:** 175, 181, **7:** 1970
Pluto, **1:** 175, 181, **8:** 2209
Saturn, **1:** 175, 181, **9:** 2480
sun, **1:** 175ff, 181, **10:** 2725
Uranus, **1:** 175, 181, **11:** 2921
Venus, **1:** 175, 181, **1:** 2947
seasonal changes and, *see* 'mutable' signs *above*
at 16th cent. confinement, **8:** *2241*
see also horoscope; zodiac
Asuka Period (Japan), **6:** 1488
Asvins (Indian twin gods), **5:** 1435, **11:** 2903, 3047
Atar (Zoroastrian god), **3:** 691
***ataraxia*, 9:** 2524
Atargatis (goddess), **3:** 680, **5:** 1213
atavism, 1: 183–4
Ate (Greek deity), **1: 184**
Aten (Aton; Egyptian sun disc), **1: 184, 3:** 790, *794,* **5:** 1402
temple of, at Akhetaten, **3:** 793, **6:** 1402
athame (magic knife), *see* arthame
Athanasius, St:
on St Anthony, **1:** 133
Arian heresy and, **2:** 470–1, **5:** 1282
on the Virgin Mary, **7:** 1749
Athena (Greek goddess), *see* Athene
Athenagoras (Christian Platonist), on immortality, **5:** 1415
Athene (Athena), **1: 185–7**
Athens and, **1:** 186f, **8:** 2060
birth of, **9:** *2260*
cap of darkness worn by, **8:** 2209
cock and, **2:** 490
in Crete, **2:** 542
Delphi, her temple at, **1:** *186*
Minerva identified with, **1:** *187*
olive and, **8:** 2060
Orestes and, **4:** 1056
in Orphism, **1:** 187
owl and, **1:** *185,* 187, **8:** 2098
Perseus and, **5:** 1441f
Poseidon and, **8:** 2060
Prometheus and, **8:** *2262*
statue of, by Pheidias, **5:** 1396
Stoicism and, **1:** 187
Trojan War and **1:** 142, 186, **11:** 2890
Zeus and, **1:** 185f
see also birth *above*
see also Judgement of Paris
Athens (Greece):
Athene and **1:** 186f, **8:** 2060
Dionysus and, **3:** 638
Eleusis and, **3:** 804ff
olive and, **8:** 2060
ox sacrifice (*bouphonia*), **1:** 210
Pan and, **8:** 2125
Theseus and, **9:** 2351, **10:** 2817f, 2821
see also Acropolis
Atholl, earls of, **11:** 3028
Athos, Mount, skulls of monks on, **9:** *2351*
Athirat (Phoenician goddess), **10:** 2762–3
Athtar (Ethiopian morning star), **3:** 842
Atkinson, R. J. C., Stonehenge and, **10:** 2704
Atlantic Ocean, early exploration of, **2:** 337ff
Atlantic, 1: 188–91
Madame Blavatsky and, **6:** 1614
bull cult in, **1:** 189
Crete and, **1:** 190
Plato on, **1:** 188ff, **8:** 2207
Poseidon and, **1:** 189
Santorin as, **1:** 190
Atlas (Greek giant), **1: 192**
atlas (maps), first use of term, **1:** 192
Atlas Mountains, 1: 192
Atman (Indian religion), **1: 192,** 323, **5:** 1309
Brahman and, **1:** 192, 323, **11:** 2931f
union with (yoga), **11:** 2932
see also Mahatmas; Ramana Maharshi
Aton (Egyptian sun disc), *see* Aten
atonement, 1: 192
in Christianity, **1:** 192, **6:** 1708
Jewish day of (Yom Kippur), **1:** 192, **6:** 1536, **9:** 2458
repentance and, **1:** 192
sacrifice as, **1:** 192
see also scapegoat
Atropos (Greek mythology), **4:** 918, *919*
Attale, St, hand of, at Strasbourg, **9:** *2353*
Attila (leader of the Huns), **1: 193**
in the *Nibelungenlied,* **1:** 193, **7:** 1999
Pope Leo I and, **1:** 193
Attis (god), **1:** 193, **2:** 583
boar and, **2:** 583, **3:** 742
bull and, **3:** 742, **10:** 2805
castration of, **2:** 583, **3:** 742
Cybele and, **1:** 193, **2:** 583, **3:** 742, **4:** 967, **11:** 2941
as dying god, **3:** 742
Roman cult of, **3:** 742, **10:** 2678
as vegetation god, **1:** 193, **2:** 583, **4:** 967, **11:** 2941
attribute (in mythology), **1: 193**
Atum (Egyptian god), **1:** 229, **2:** 533
Re and, **1:** 305, **2:** 533, **3:** 789f
temple of, at Heliopolis, **3:** 793
Audumulla (cow; Scandinavian mythology), **3:** 530, *537*
Augean stables, cleansed by Hercules, **5:** 1279
augury, 1: 194
birds in, **1:** 194, **2:** 557, 566, **3:** 657f, 747, 844

in Borneo, **1:** 316
comets in, **1:** 194
in Ethiopia, **3:** 844
Etruscans and, **1:** *194,* **3:** 652, **11:** 3004–5
Hittites and, **5:** 1325
omens, various, in, **1:** 194
Romans and, **1:** 194, **3:** 657f, 747, **6:** 1637, **8:** 2065, **9:** 2417, 2418
thunder and lightning in, **1:** 194, **3:** 848, **11:** 3004–5
Augustine, St (of Hippo), **9:** 2462
on the animals in Noah's ark, **11:** 2906
on the antiquity of Christianity, **9:** 2370
by Botticelli, **1:** 256
his conversion to Christianity, **2:** 515
on dualism, **3:** 733
on evil, **3:** 733
on heaven, **8:** 2135
on hell, **1:** 227
on incubi, **3:** 862
on the just war, **2:** 472
original sin and, **4:** 982, **7:** 1749
on the peacock, **8:** 2154
on predestination, **3:** 800, **4:** 921, **8:** 2242
on the Satanic pact, **8:** 2110
on the six days of creation, **10:** 2592
on time, **11:** 2845
Augustine, St (missionary to England), **10:** 2685
Augustus (Roman emperor):
Lares and, **6:** 1608f
Mars and, **7:** 1744
Auldearne witches, 1: 195
see also Gowdie, Isabel
Auliya, Nizam-ud-din, Thugs and, **10:** 2836
aura, 1: 195, 3: 677f, **6:** *1630,* **9:** 2331, *2331*
halo and, **1:** 195, **3:** 678
aureole (halo), **3:** 678
Aurésku (Basque dance), **2:** 414
Aurobindo, Sri, 5: 1317
aurochs (animal), **2:** 363
unicorn (Re'em) and, **11:** 2909
aurora, 1: 195
Eskimo and, **1:** 195, **3:** 835
Australia, aborigines of, **1: 196–204**
black magic among, **1:** 204
see also bone-pointing
body-painting and, **10:** 2804
cave and bark paintings of, **1:** *202,* 203, **6:** *1709,* **8:** *2145*
creation myths of, **2:** 333, *538*
culture heroes of, **1:** 201f
dancing and, **1:** 200, **11:** 2860
imitative magic, **5:** *1409*
death, beliefs concerning, **1:** 204, **2:** 576, **3:** 614, 615
disease, beliefs concerning, **1:** 204
flood legend of, **4:** 1054
frost, myth of origin of, **1:** 3039
initiation rites of, **1:** *198, 199*
lightning spirit of, **11:** *3003*
lizard and, **6:** 1638
medicine-men of, **1:** 201, 204
Melanesia compared with, **7:** 1799
meteors and, **7:** 1836
mutilation in, **7:** 1915
phallic symbolism and, **9:** *2541*
Pleiades and, **11:** 3039
quartz and, **9:** 2316
rainbow and, **9:** 2333
snakes and, **1:** 203, *203*
soul, beliefs concerning, **2:** 576, **8:** *2145,* **11:** 2860
sun and moon myth of, **10:** 2719–20
totemism among, **1:** 198ff, **11:** 2859–60
dingo, **11:** *2859*
wallaby, **1:** 128, 198
whale, **11:** *2859*
witchety grub, **4:** 1012
auto de fe, 1: 205, 5: 1283, *1286*
Autolycus, 1: 205
automatic art, 1: 205–9, 7: *1784, 1785*
see also Gill, Madge
automatic music, 1: 209
automatic writing, 1: 205ff
see also cross-correspondences
automatisms, 8: 2090
see also automatic art; automatic writing; mediums
Auxonne nuns, 1: 209
Avalokitesvara (Bodhisattva), **2:** 359, **10:** *2838*
Dalai Lama and, **9:** 2348
Avalon (Celtic paradise), **1:** 212, **8:** 2132
apple trees and, **1:** 141
Arthur and, **1:** 153, 159, 210
Glastonbury as, **1:** 210, **4:** 1109, 1110, 1112
Morgan le Fay and, **7:** 1884
avatara (incarnation; Hinduism), **5:** 1420
Aventine Hill (Rome), **3:** 630, **6:** 1552
Avesta (Zend-Avesta; Zoroastrian sacred texts), **4:** 1070, **8:** 2048, 2138, **11:** 3098, 3100, 3101–3
Avicenna (Arab physician), **1:** 298
Avitus (bishop), on the Devil, **3:** 629
Avvakum, Archpriest, Old Believers and, **8:** 2058
axe, 1: 210
in Athenian *bouphonia,* **1: 210**
in Crete, *see* double axe
divination and, **1:** 210
Donar and, **4:** 1086
Parthians and, **8:** *2143,* 2144
prehistoric, as amulet, **4:** 1086
in witchcraft, **1:** 210
Azad, Abul Kalam, 6: 1472
Azande (African people), **1: 211–13**
birth ceremony of, **1:** 272
blood-brotherhood ritual of, **2:** 581
circumcision of, **1:** *212, 213*
E. Evans-Pritchard on the, **1:** 211, **11:** 3041
oracles of, **1:** 212, **4:** 952f
witchcraft among, **1:** 211, 212–3, **3:** 869, **4:** 952f, *954–5,* **11:** 3041–2
Azazel, 4: 1121, **9:** 2487
Azhi Dahaka (Zoroastrian dragon), **3:** 691
Aztecs, 1: 214–21
calendar of, **1:** 219–20
creation myths of, **1:** 216ff
end of the world, beliefs concerning, **3:** *816,* 817
gods of, **1:** 215ff
see also Chalchihuitlicue; Coatlicue; Huitzilopochtli; Tezcatlipoca; Tlaloc; Tlazolteotl
history of **1:** 214ff, 221
human sacrifice and, **1:** 216, *217,* 218, **9:** *2454,* 2457
jade and, **6:** 1478
peyote and, **3:** 714–15
priests of, **1:** 220
rain and, **1:** 220
skull (?Tezcatlipoca) of, **1:** 217
soldiers of, ocelot and eagle groups of, **11:** 2861
see also Tenochtitlan

B

ba (Egypt) **3:** 791
Baal (Adad, Hadad; Phoenician god), **1:** 169, **222–3, 8:** 2182–3, **10:** *2602, 2763, 2766*
Amorites and, **1:** 222
Anat and, **1:** 169, 223, **8:** 2182–3, **10:** 2761f, **11:** 2940–1
in the Bible, **1:** 222–3
bull and **1:** 222
cedar tree and, **1:** 222
Dagon and, **8:** 2182, **10:** 2763
as demon, **1:** 223
as dying god, **8:** 2183, **10:** 2762
in Egypt, **1:** 222–3
Hercules and, **1:** 223
Mot and, **1:** 222, **8:** 2182, **10:** 2762, **11:** 2940–1
sea-monster and, **10:** 2761
temple of, in Tunisia, **10:** *2765*
as vegetation god, **1:** 222, 223, **8:** 2182–3, **10:** 2762, **11:** 2940–1
as weather god, **8:** 2182
as storm god, **1:** 222, **10:** 2604, 2762
Zeus and, **1:** 223
see also Baal Hammon; Tanit Pene Baal
Baal Hammon (Carthaginian deity), **8:** 2184, **10:** *2764*
Baal Shem Tov, *see* Eliezer, Israel ben
Bab (Bahai title), **1:** 224
Baba Yaga, 11: 3024
baboon, in Egypt, **1:** 129
Babylonia (Mesopotamia), **1: 223, 7:** 1818
bull in, **5:** 1347, **10:** 2805
Chaldeans and, **2:** 446
creation myth of, *see Enuma elish*
death and, **3:** 616
divination in, **3:** *658,* **6:** 1637, **8:** *2064*
dragon in, **3:** 690
eclipse cycle discovered in, **3:** 772
end of the world and, **3:** 817
flood legend of **3:** 817, **4:** 992f
forty and, **4:** 1023
gods of, **7:** 1818ff
monotheism in, **7:** 1821
see also An; Ea; Marduk; Shamash
hero myth of, *see* Gilgamesh
Hittites and **5:** 1324, **7:** 1733
Jerusalem captured by, **6:** 1644
kingship in, **6:** 1570
last king of, *see* Nabonidus
maze in, **7:** 1774
moon and, **7:** 1876, 1881
new year festival of (Sacaea), **2:** 537, **3:** 690, 838, **4:** 935, **7:** 1733, 1734, **11:** 3035
see also Hammurabi
Bacchae (Bacchantes; worshippers of Bacchus), **1:** 223
ivy and, **5:** 1329
Orpheus and, **8:** 2083
Bacchanalia, 1: 223
Bacchantes, *see* Bacchae
Bacchus, 1: 223, 9: 2482
Agdistis and, **2:** 583
Dionysus identified with, **1:** 223, **9:** 2482
fig tree and, **4:** 940
see also Bacchae
Bachelard, Gaston, on the four elements, **3:** 802
bachelor, origin of the world, **6:** 1610
backbone, *see* spine
Bacon, Francis (artist), **1:** 149, 151
Bacon, Francis (writer and politician), **7:** 1769
on the earth's virtues, **3:** 752
on flying ointment, **4:** 998
as one of the Masters, **7:** 1769
Bacon, Roger, 3: 622, **8:** 2112
Baghdadi Jews (Indian Jews), **8:** 2081
Bahais, 1: 224–5
Baha-Ullah (Mirza Hussain Ali; Bahai leader), **1:** 224f
Baigas (Indian tribe), tattooing and, **10:** 2800
Bailey, Alice (occult author), **7:** 1769
Baker, George, *see* Father Divine
baker's dozen, 10: 2825
balance, concept of:
in magic, **8:** 2070
in New Guinea, **7:** 1973f
six and, **10:** 2592
Balder (Scandinavian god), **1: 226, 6:** *1641,* **7:** 1860, **9:** 2483, 2486
Balfour, Arthur, Catherine Mary Lyttelton and ('Palm Sunday' case), **11:** 3030
Balfour, Gerald W., cross-correspondences and, **10:** 2776, **11:** 3030
Bali, 2: *541,* **4:** 1089
Balius (horse of Achilles), **5:** 1212
Ball, Hugo (artist), **1:** 147f
ballads, Scottish, *see* Scottish and Border

ballads
ball games, 4: 1061ff
Balmung (sword of Siegfried), **10:** 2744
Balor (Irish king), eye of **4:** 894
Bali Plá (dance), **2:** 413
Bamberg witches, 1: 227–8, 3: 629, 855, **4:** 1079, **10:** 2632
Banerjee, Prof. Hemendra, reincarnation investigated by, **9:** 2350
Bangkok (Thailand), temple of the Emerald Buddha at, **2:** *354*
Banneux, Virgin Mary at, **11:** 2965
banshee, 4: 901
banyan tree, 4: 940, **1:** *2876*
Banyard, John, Peculiar People and, **8:** 2157
Baphomet (idol), **1: 229**
Crowley as, **2:** 561
Knights Templar and, **1:** 229, **6:** 1576
baptism, 1: 229–32
Christian, **1:** 229, 230, 231–2, 275, 276, **9:** 2449f, **11:** 2998f
in Bolivia, **2:** *513*
eight and, **3:** 795
exorcism and, **3:** 872f
Gypsies and, **5:** 1197
of the Holy Spirit, Pentecostalist movement and, **8:** 2159f, 2162, **10:** 2652
Jehovah's Witnesses and, **1:** *232,* **6:** *1499*
of Jesus, **1:** 231, **2:** *471,* **6:** *1505,* **11:** *3000*
Mennonite, **2:** *498*
Mormons and, **7:** *1888,* 1889
St Paul on, **1:** 231–2, **11:** 3001
thumb in, **4:** 1089
torches in early ceremony of, **6:** 1629
unbaptized infants, fate of, **8:** 2242
see also Anabaptists; Dunkers; font
Mircea Eliade on, **11:** 3001
in Judaism, **1:** 230
see also John the Baptist
Barabbas, 6: 1509f
baraka (spiritual power):
in Berber belief, **1:** 256
dervishes and, **3:** 624
Barcelona, Church of the Holy Family (Gaudi) at, **9:** *2367*
Barclay, Margaret (witch), **5:** 1408, **10:** 2712
bards, 1: 233
Celtic, **3:** 719, **8:** 2210ff
modern, in Cornwall, **3:** 723
see also Eisteddfod
bark painting, in Australia, *see* Australia, cave and bark paintings of
Barlaam and Joasaph, Saints, **9:** 2357, **11:** 2907
Barnabas, epistle of, **7:** 1985
barnacle goose, 1: 233, **4:** 1139–40, *1140*
Barnsdale (Yorks), Robin Hood and **9:** 2404
Baron Samedi, 11: *2971,* 2976
Barratt, T. B., Pentecostalism and, **8:** 2160, **10:** 2651
Barrett, Francis (author of *The Magus*), **1: 233**
demons drawn by, **1:** *167, 170, 234*
on magic squares, **6:** 1691, 1693
Barrett, Sir William, 8: *2274*
on Kathleen Goligher, **7:** 1790–4
magnetism and, **6:** 1695
poltergeists and, **9:** 2275
Society for Psychical research and, **7:** 1919, **9:** 2274
basil (herb), **5:** 1272, **9:** 2502
Basil, St, Proterius saved by, **8:** 2110
Basilides, 1: 64, **2:** 333, **3:** 730
basilisk, 2: 490, **3:** 873, 888, **11:** 2856
Basque witchcraft, 1: 233–7
see also Lancre, Pierre de
Bassain (Nepalese festival), goat sacrificed at, **9:** *2457*
Bast (Egyptian cat goddess), **1:** 128, **2:** 417, *419,* **3:** 790, **7:** *1901*
bat (animal), **1: 238–40**
vampires and, **11:** 2924
Bathcat, Elizabeth (witch), **5:** 1358
bay (tree), **5:** 1368
laurel of mythology identified with, **6:** 1610
Bayeux Tapestry, 8: 2071
Bayts, Margaret (witch), **8:** 2247
BC (Before Christ), **8:** 1323
beads, *see* necklace; rosary; wampum beads
Beaker people, 10: 2704
Beale, Mgr Herbert, 11: 2987
bean, 1: 242
Harranian taboo on eating, **5:** 1213
head and, in invisibility formula, **6:** 1453
Pythagoras and, **1:** 242
see also Jack and the Beanstalk
bear, 1: 243–6
Ainu and, **1:** 244, 246, **4:** 935
Artemis and, **3:** 630, **8:** 2031
Astarte and, **1:** 170
bees and, **1:** 243
Beowulf and, **1:** 245, 254
Berserkers and, **7:** 1908
Bodvar, **8:** 2045–6, **9:** 2556
Celts and **1:** 246
St Columban and, **9:** 2468
in Crete, **8:** 2031–2
Eskimo and spirit of, **3:** 834
in fertility cults, **1:** 246
in Finland, **4:** 958
in Greece, **1:** 246
Gypsies and, **5:** *1199*
in Lapland, **6:** 1605–7, 1608
North American Indians and, **1:** 244, *245,* **2:** 589, **4:** 935, **8:** 2042
Odysseus and, **1:** 245
Pelasgian bear goddess, **8:** 2031
sacrifice of:
Gilyaks (northern Asia), **11:** 2856
Neanderthal, **1:** 116, 245, 246, **8:** 2243
shape-shifting and, **6:** 1668, **8:** 2045–6, **10:** 2556
Slavs and, **10:** 2612
unicorn and, **1:** 243
Bear (constellation), *see* Great Bear
beard:
in Mesopotamia, **2:** 365
Parsees and, **8:** 2140
Peter the Great and, **5:** 1204
Sikhs and, **10:** 2577
of St Uncumber, **11:** 2907
St Wulfstan and, **5:** 1204
Beardsley, Aubrey, 1: 146, **4:** *990,* **6:** *1656,* **1:** *2888*
Beast, 3: *666,* **4:** 1157, 1158, **6:** 1691–2
Crowley as, **2:** 559
beating the bounds, 8: 2035
Beauraing, Virgin Mary at, **11:** 2965, 2966
Becket, Thomas, 1: 247–8, **8:** 2198
bed, celestial, of James Graham, **5:** 1204
Bedford, Mirabel (witch), **10:** 2655
Bedivere (Arthurian knight), **1:** 154, 155, *156*
bee, 1: 248
bear and, **1:** 243
in Cretan cave, Zeus and, **8:** 2032
as Ethiopian symbol of royalty, **3:** 844
as omen, **8:** 2064
see also honey
beech (tree), **1: 248**
Beelzebub, 1: *92,* **249**
beetle, 6: 1446f
dung-beetle, *see* scarab
Re and, *see* scarab, Re and
Befana (Italian Christmas fairy), **2:** 483
Beghards, 3: 826, **9:** 2318
Beguines, 3: 826, **9:** 2318
Behemoth (book of Job), **11:** 3013
Behrens, Henry (dwarf), **3:** *738*
Bekker, Balthasar, 3: 866
Belial (Beliar; demon), **1: 249, 3:** 627
Belkis, Queen (Queen of Sheba), **9:** 2316–17
Bell, Arthur L, Mankind United and, **7:** 1725f
bell, book and candle, 2: 582, *582*
Bell, John (18th cent, clergyman), on witches' marks, **8:** 2247
Bellerophon (Greek hero), **2:** 454f
Bellona (Anatolian mother goddess), *see* Ma
bells, 1: 250–2
burial and, **1:** 251
Easter and, **3:** 784
evil eye averted by, **4:** 922
harvest and, **5:** 1218
of lost lands, submerged villages, **1:** 252, **9:** 2513
necromantic bell of Giradius, **7:** *1954*
shamans and, **4:** *962*
of ships, **10:** 2571
storms and, **1:** 251
witches and, **1:** 251
Beltane (Celtic festival), **1:** 109, **2:** 441
modern Druids and, **3:** 722
Benares (India), **11:** *2935*
Buddhism and, **2:** 354, 359, **4:** 1071
pilgrimage to, **8:** 2195, *2198*
Benedict XIV (pope), on supernatural phenomena attributed to saints, **10:** 2697
Benedict XVI (pope), on miraculous cures, **4:** 909
Bene Israel (Saturday Oilmen; Indian Jews), **8:** 2081
Benin, mask from, **7:** *1757*
Bennett, Allan, 2: 336
bennu (Egyptian mythical bird), **8:** 2185
Bensozia (goddess of witches), **1:** 237
Beowulf, 1: 253–4, 5: 1297–8, **7:** 1999
bear and, **1:** 245, 254
sword and, **10:** 2744, 2746, 2748
Béraud, Marthe (medium), *see* C. Eva
Berbers (African people), **1: 255–6**
Islam and, 1: 256
jinn, belief in, **1:** 256
women, treatment of, **1:** 255
Berbiguier, Alexis Vincent Charles (bottler of demons), **5:** 1417
Bergelmir (Nordic giant), **4:** 1103
Berkeley, Bishop George, 7: 1849
Bermuda Triangle, the, 1: 257
Bernadette, St (Marie-Bernard Soubirous), **6:** 1650, 1652–3, **10:** 2701
Bernard, St, 7: 1750, **9:** 2526
Bernard, Emile (artist), **1:** 146
Bernières, Jean de (Quietist), **9:** 2319
berserkers, 8: 2045–6, **11:** 3009
bear goddess and, **7:** 1908
drugs perhaps used by, **3:** 714, **7:** 1908
shape shifting and, **8:** 2045–6, **11.** 3009
Bertin, St, His soul carried up to god (Simon Marmion), **10:** *2636*
Bertrand (werewolf), **1: 257**
Bertrand, A. (physician), **6:** 1695
beryl, 6: 1511, **9:** 2506
Bes (Egyptian god), **3:** 791, **4:** 886, **10:** *2774–5*
Besant, Annie, 1: 257–9, *292*
hand of, **8:** *2122*
reincarnation, her belief in, **9:** 2348
Theosophy and, **1:** 258, **1:** 2814, 2815, 2816
Besold, Christoph, Rosicrucians and, **9:** 2430
bestiary, 1: 259, **8:** 2158, 2186
caladrius in, **3:** *644*
elephant in, **1:** 131
panther in, **1:** 259
peacock in, **8:** 2154
pelican in, **8:** 2158, *2158*
phoenix in, **8:** 2186
whale in, **1:** 259, **11:** 3013
Bethel ('house of God'), **10:** 2697
Bethel College (Topeka, Kansas), Pentecostalist movement and, **8:** 2159
betony (herb), **5:** 1272, *1274*
Bettiscombe Manor (Dorset), skull at, **5:** 1226, 1367, **10:** 2595
Buekels, John (John Bockelson, John of Leyden), **3:** 826, **9:** *2521*
Beuno, St, 10: 2685
Bev, R. Dov, 5: 1219, 1220
bewitchment, 1: 259
see also psychic attack

Beyrevra (Indian demon), **3:** *865*
Bhagavad Gita, **1: 260–5, 5:** 1313, **7:** 1936, **11:** 2960
sacrifice in, **5:** 1307, **9:** 2456
Bhagavata Purana, **5:** 1314, **6:** 1580, 1583f
Bhaiji (Indian holy man), **1:** 121, 122
Bhairava (Shiva), **10:** *2783*
bhakti (Hinduism), **1: 265, 5:** 1314, 1316, **6:** 1583f
Christianity and, **6:** 1560
see also bhakti yoga
bhakti yoga, 11: 2932–3, 3070
Bhavani (Kali), Thugs and, **10:** 2835f
Bible, the, **1:** 265, **5:** 1323, **7:** 1850–2
angels in, **1:** 124ff
divination by, *see* bibliomancy
divination in, **3:** 657, 705
dogs in, **3:** 664
eagle in, **3:** 746, **8:** 2158
eye in, **4:** 886
fig tree in, **4:** 939f
forty in, **4:** 1023f
giants in, **4:** 1102–3
Gog and Magog, **4:** 1127
interpretation of, *see* exegesis
Judaism and, **6:** 1532
light associated with God in, **6:** 1623
lily in, **6:** 1631
oak in, **8:** 2033
olive in, **8:** 2060
scorpion in, **9:** 2502
seven in, **9:** 2534
see also Revelation, seven in
sexual references in, **8:** 2175
unicorn in, **11:** 2909
vulture in, **8:** 2158
witches weighed against, **3:** 854
see also Apocalypse; Apocrypha; mystery plays; New Testament; New Testament Apocrypha; Old Testament
Bible Christians, *see* Walworth Jumpers
bibliomancy (divination by a book), **1: 265, 6:** 1647
Biddenden cakes, 3: 763
Bifrost (rainbow bridge, Scandinavian mythology), **9:** 2333–4, 2484
bile, 3: 801
Binsfeld (demonologist), **3:** 864
birch (tree), **1: 265, 9:** 2548
birds, 1: 266–71
in augury, **1:** 270, **8:** 2065
Borneo, **1:** 316
Ethiopia, **3:** 844
Etruscans, **1:** 194
Romans, **1:** 194, **8:** 2065
in Borneo, **1:** 314f
in cave art, **1:** 267, **2:** *433*
Celts and, **2:** 443f
colours of, **1:** 271
in creation myths, **1:** 268
in Crete, **5:** 1171
mythical, **see** bennu; Garuda; halcyon; phoenix; Roc; thunderbird
weather and, **10:** 2836f
see also barnacle goose; blackbird; brahminy kite; cock; crossbill; crow; cuckoo; diver; dove; eagle; falcon; goose; hawk; hoopoe; hornbill; ibis; kite; magpie; nightingale; ostrich; owl; partridge; peacock; pelican; petrel; raven; robin; rook; sparrow; stork; swallow; swan; turkey; vulture; woodpecker; wren; wryneck
also feather
birth, 1: 272–6
Bushmen and, **2:** 380
Gypsies and, **5:** 1197
harvest and, **5:** 1216f
knots and, **10:** 2710
of twins, **1:** 275, **11:** 2902
see also caul; *couvade;* footling; horoscope; umbilical cord; virgin births
Birth Number, 8: 2023
bisexuality, *see* hermaphrodite
Bishop, Ann (witch), **10:** 2626
Bishop, Bridget (witch), **4:** 914, **5:** 1408, **9:** 2472
al-Bistami, Abu Yazid (Sufi), **10:** 2715
bistort (adderwort, Easter Ledger, snakeweed), **5:** 1272
bitter-sweet (woody) nightshade, 8: 2203
bitumen, in mummification, **7:** 1903
black, 1: 277, **2:** 494f
black deities, **6:** 1556
Kali, **6:** 1554f
crow and, **2:** 556
lead and, **2:** 522, **6:** 1613
Morris dances and, **7:** 1890, 1891
Saturn and, **2:** 522
see also black magic; black mass
blackberry (bramble), **5:** 1272–3, *1274*
blackbird:
St Kevin and, **9:** 2468
as witches' familiar, **4:** 914
Black Box (radiesthesia), *see* Abrams' Box
Black Death, 10: 2634
'Black Fast' (Judaism), **6:** 1536
black fast (magic), **1: 277, 8:** 2282
Blackfoot Indians, 3: 615, **4:** 1161, 1164
Black Jews (Cochin Jews), **8:** 2081
Australian aborigines and, **1:** 204
black mass in, **1:** 277
distinguished from white magic, **1:** 115, **3:** 617
in Africa, **1:** 81f
distinguished from witchcraft, **1:** 115
Gurdjieff on, **5:** 1188–9
Kikuyu and, **6:** 1562
as the left-hand path, **6:** 1614
see also black fast
black mass, 1: 277–9, 3: 853, **4:** 1047
Black Muslims, 1: 279–81
Black Pagoda, *see* Konarak
Black Power (Negro movement), Black Muslims and, **1:** 280
Black Stone (in the Kaaba at Mecca), **7:** 1776, 1836
Mohammed and, **10:** *2708*
Blake, William, 1: 206, **282–9, 8:** 2268
creation of man, **4:** *981*
Druids and, **3:** 721, 722
Golden Dawn influenced by, **1:** 284, **4:** 1131
Great Red Dragon and the Woman Clothed with the Sun, **9:** *2379*
Hecate, **5:** *1256*
the Lord passing judgement on Adam, **10:** *2835*
Satan Before the Throne of God, **9:** 2478
Satan in Council, **3:** *626*
Satan smiting Job with boils, **6:** *1523*
Swedenborg and, **1:** 284, **10:** 2741
Thomas Taylor and, **10:** 2808
Valley of Dry Bones, **4:** *895*
visions of, **1:** 283ff, **11:** 2963
When the Morning Stars Sang Together, **10:** *2807*
Yeats and, **11:** 3067
Blavatsky, Helena Petrovna, 1: 290–3, 10: *2815*
Atlantis and, **6:** 1614
Mrs Besant and **1:** 258
J. W. Keely and, **11:** 2950
Lemuria and, **6:** 1614
Mahatmas and, **1:** 291ff, **6:** 1698
on the moon, **7:** 1876
on the sapphire, **6:** 1512
Society for Psychical Research's report on, **1:** 293
Spiritualism and, **1:** 290f
theosophy and, **1:** 258, 291ff, **10:** 2814
vibration and, **1:** 2949f
writings of, **1:** 291ff
Blocula (Sweden), witches of, **3:** 855, **4:** 998, **9:** *2447,* **10:** 2743
Blodeuwedd (wife of Lleu), **6:** 1639
blood, 1: 294–6, 300
birth and, **1:** 273
elder tree and, **3:** 796
four humours, blood in theory of, **3:** 801
Furies and, **4:** 1054
homunculus and, **5:** 1338
of Jesus, **1:** 295, **4:** 1150f, *1150–1*
Lapps and, **6:** 1606–7
of Nessus, Hercules and, **5:** 1280
in New Guinea initiation rites, **7:** 1975
oath-taking and, **8:** 2037
see also blood-brotherhood
pact with the Devil signed in, **8:** 2110f
of the pelican, **1:** *267,* **8:** 2158
red and, **2:** 495
robin, **9:** 2402
rose and, **9:** 2421
sacrifice and, **1:** 295, **9:** 2457
soul and, **1:** 294
stigmata and, **10:** 2698
taboos and **1:** 294f
witchcraft and **1:** 296f, **4:** 916
see also menstruation; vampire
blood-brotherhood, Azande ritual of, **2:** 581
bloodstone (jewel), **6:** *1512*
bloodwort (plant), *see* yarrow
Bloxham, Arthur (hypnotist), **1: 296, 9:** 2350
blue, 1: 296, 2: 496
fairies and, **4:** 902
green and, **3:** 813
Jupiter and, **2:** 522
tin and, **2:** 522
Bluebeard, 1: 296, 4: 1107
Bluejay (trickster), **10:** 2881
Blue Mosque (Istanbul), **6:** *1466–7, 1468,* **9:** *2362*
boar, 1: 297
Adonis killed by, **3:** 739
on Anglo-Saxon helmets, **1:** 254, **4:** 1051
Attis killed by, **2:** 583, **3:** 742
in Arthurian legend, *see* Twrch Trwyth
of Ben Gulban (Irish legend), **4:** 966
Celts and, **1:** 130, **2:** 443
see also Arthurian legend *above;* Ben Gulban *above*
of Erymanthus, Hercules and, **5:** *1278,* 1279
fertility and, **1:** 297
William Firmat and, **9:** 2468
in New Guinea, **7:** *1975*
in Scandinavia, **1:** 297, **3:** 737, **4:** 1051f
Vishnu as, **1:** *130,* **9:** *2349,* **11:** 2960
Boban, Claudine (witch), **2:** 350
Bockelson, John (Anabaptist), *see* Beukels, John
Boddy, Rev. Alexander A., 8: 2160, **10:** 2651
Bodhidharma (Zen monk), **11:** 3083–4
Bodhisattva (Buddhism), **1: 301,** 359, *360,* **4:** *1088,* **4:** 2841
in Ceylon, **10:** *2586,* 2587
in Tibet, **6:** 1589, **10:** *2838, 2839,* 2841
in Zen, **11:** 3081
see also Maitreya; Manjusri
bodhi tree (Buddhism), *see* bo-tree
Bodin, Jean (witch-hunter), **2:** 350, **4:** 1047
Bodvar Bjarki (Scandinavian champion), **8:** 2045–6, **9:** 2556
body, 1: 298–300
five and, **4:** 988
omens from, **8:** 2064
orifices of:
in Kikuyu oath-taking ceremony, **6:** 1562
penetrated by demons, **10:** 2625
preservation of, after death, *see* dried bodies; mummification
in yoga, *see* hatha yoga
see also blood; bones; breast; ear; entrails; eye; fingers; foot; hair; hand; head; heart; kidneys; liver; moles; navel; nose; penis; spittle; testicles; urine
also birth; cannibalism; corpses; death; faceless goddesses; mutilation; nudity; out-of-the-body experiences; physiognomy; sex; shadow
body of light, *see* astral body

body-painting, 2: *526,* **10:** 2796, 2804
in Australia, **10:** 2804
in Melanesia, **10:** 2804
  New Guinea, **10:** *2801*
North American Indians and, **8:** *2008*
in South America, **10:** 2804
  Brazil, **2:** *526*
body-snatching, feared by tinkers, **11:** 2854
Boehme, Jacob (mystic), **1: 301–2, 6:** 1629
alchemy and, **1:** 302
Cabala and, **1:** 387
on the Fall of Man, **4:** 982
on man as microcosm, **1:** *301,* 302
on opposites, **1:** 302
on predestination, **1:** 301–2
Boër, Walter (astrologer), **1:** 180
Boethius, on free will, **8:** 2242
bogey beasts (fairies), **4:** 901
boggarts (fairies), **4:** 901, 903
Puck related to, **9:** 2297
Boghaz Koi, *see* Hattusas
bogies (Scottish spirits), Puck related to, **9:** 2297
Bogomils, 1: 303–4
Cathars and, **2:** 522
Boguet, Henri (witch-hunter), **1:** 249, **4:** 1047
Bohr, Niels, 6: 1680
Bois, Jules, 1: 241
Boleyn, Anne, six fingers of, **4:** 957
Bombay (India), Parsees and, **8:** 2137
bomos (Greek altar), **1:** 116
Bon (pre-Buddhist religion of Tibet), **10:** 2839
Bonaventure, St, 8: 2242, **9:** 2462
bone-pointing (Australian magic), **1:** 204, **5:** 1410
bones, 1: 304
divination by:
  Bushmen, **2:** 378
  Congo, **2:** 509
  of sheep, **9:** 2559–60
in Ezekiel, **4:** 895
of Sir Charles McCarthy, Ashanti and, **4:** 1012
as relics, **9:** 2351f
see also bone-pointing; skeleton; skull; spine; wish-bone
bonfire:
Balder and, **7:** 1860
at Easter, **3:** 764
at Hallowe'en, **1:** 109
on St John the Baptist's Day, or Eve, **9:** 2461, **11:** 2948, 3039–40
at Midsummer, **1:** 163–4, **7:** 1845, 1860
at onset of winter, **8:** 2166, **11:** 3035
Book of Change(s), *see* I Ching
Book of Creation, *see Sefer Yetsirah*
Book of Days, The (Chambers), **9:** 2384
Book of the Dead (Egypt), **1: 305–9**
Thoth and, **9:** 2376–7
weighing of the heart in, **5:** *1251*
Book of the Dead (Tibet), **1: 310, 5:** 1266, **10:** 2844
Book of James, *see* Protoevangelium
***Book of the Spirits,* 6:** *1681*
Book of Splendour (Cabala), *see Zohar*
Book of the Two Ways (Egypt), **1:** 307
Book of the Yellow Emperor, *see Nei Jing*
Booth, William (founder of Salvation Army), **5:** 1328
al Borak (Mohammedan winged horse), **5:** 3032
Border Redcaps (fairies), **4:** 901
Borley Rectory, 1: 310–12, 8: 2223
Borneo, 1: 312–16
headhunting in, **1:** 312, 313, *315, 316,* **5:** *1232,* 1233
Bors (Arthurian knight), **4:** 1059, 1153
Bosch, Hieronymus, 1: 317–21
Adoration of the Magi, The, **8:** *2163*
Breughel and, **2:** 340ff
Crowning of Thorns, The, **5:** *1228*
Death of a Miser, **9:** *2391*
Garden of Delight, The, **1:** *320,* **4:** *1028*
Temptation of St Anthony, The, **1:** 133
Bosco, St John 10: 2702
Bosdeau, Jane (witch), **2:** 400
Bossuet, Jacques, Fénélon and, **9:** 2320
Boston (Mass.), Christian Science church at, **2:** 477, *479,* **3:** 780
Bosworth Hall, haunting of, **5:** *1221*
Bothwell, Francis Hepburn, Earl of, North Berwick witches and, **8:** 2013ff
bo-tree (Bodhi tree, sacred fig; Buddhism), **1: 322, 4:** 940, *940,* 1071, **10:** 2587
Bottadio, John (Wandering Jew legend), **11:** 2991
Botticelli, his *Primavera,* **9:** 2374, *2374*
bottle, demon in a, **5:** 1417
Boullan, Joseph-Antoine, **1:** 240f, *240*
bouphonia (Athenian ox sacrifice), **1:** 212
Bourignon, Antoinette, 1: 322
Bourne, Hugh (Primitive Methodist), **3:** 828
Boxing Day (St Stephen's Day), **2:** 483
wren hunt on, **8:** 2026, **11:** 3061
boxwood, true cross and, **10:** 2773
Bra (Jutland), cauldron of, **2:** 428
bracken, *see* ferns
Bradlaugh, Charles, Mrs Besant and, **1:** 257f
Bragi (Scandinavian god), **9:** 2483
Brahma (Hindu god), **1:** 324, *324,* **11:** 2960
in Buddhism, **2:** 357, 359
goose and, **4:** 1138, *1139*
Rod of, **6:** 1586
wife of, *see* Sarasvati
brahmacharya (yoga), **11:** 3073
Brahman (Hinduism), **1:** 264f, **323–4, 5:** 1309ff, **11:** 2958f
Atman and, **1:** 192, 323, **11:** 2931f
Brahma (god) and, **1:** 324
Buddhism and, **1:** 323
hearth and, **5:** 1435
threefold concept of, **10:** 2832–3
union with, *see* yoga
see also Brahmins (caste)
Brahmanas (Hindu sacred texts), **5:** 1307–8
Brahmins (caste; Hinduism), **1:** 324, **2:** 415f
brahminy kite (bird), in Borneo, **1:** 314, 316
Brahmo Samaj (Hindu reformist sect), **5:** 1316
Braid, James (surgeon), **6:** 1695, **7:** 1815
brainwashing, 2: 515
Brak, eye temple of, **4:** 888
bramble (wild blackberry), *see* blackberry
Bran (Celtic mythology), **1: 324, 2:** 396
Bran, son of Febail, voyage of, **1:** 324
Bran the Blessed, **1:** 324
  cauldron of, **2:** 428, **4:** 1149
  Fisher King and, **4:** 1149
  head of, **1:** 324, **5:** 1239
  in the *Mabinogion,* **1:** 324, **6:** 1673
  raven and, **1:** 324
Brandan, St, *see* Brendan, St
Branwen, daughter of Llyr *(Mabinogion),* **1:** 324, **6:** 1673
Brauron (Attica), Artemis and, **1:** 246, **8:** 2031
Brazil, 2: 325–30
anteater and, **2:** 329
burial in, **5:** *1414*
cannibalism in, **2:** 325f, 327
carnival in, **10:** *2681,* 2681–2
Christianity in, **10:** 2641f, 2645
cult of the dead in, **2:** 325f, *327, 569, 571*
culture hero of, *see* Maira
ecstatic cults of coastal cities of, **3:** 778
female figurine from **7:** *1894*
hallucinogenic plants in, **3:** 711f
hunting and taboo in, **5:** 1374
incest taboo in, **2:** 326, 327f
initiation rites in, **2:** 326f, **5:** *1437*
jaguar and, **2:** 326, *326,* 329, 330, *526,* **5:** *1407,* 1480
masks in, **7:** *1802*
moon and, **2:** 327f
new religious movements in, **7:** 1978, 1981, **8:** 2162, **10:** 2639ff, 2660, **11:** *2974, 2975*
opossum and, **2:** 329
sexual myth of snake in, **2:** 327
shamanism in, **2:** 329f
souls, beliefs concerning, **2:** 329f
twins in (Mikur myth), **2:** 329
see also Conselheiro
bread, 2: 331–2
see also unleavened bread
breast, St Agatha and, **3:** 648, **9:** 2464
breath, 2: 333–6
in acupuncture, **1:** 68
in Australian creation myth, **2:** 333
control of, in yoga, *see pranayama*
Egyptian beliefs concerning, **2:** 334, 335
Fijian beliefs concerning, **2:** 333
in Hinduism, *see prana*
the Virgin Mary and, in legend, **2:** 333–4
soul and, **2:** 333, **10:** 2636
  in Tibet, **2:** 336
see also air; animism; *orenda; pneuma;* Psyche
Brendan (Brandan), St, 2: 337–9
Arthurian cycle and, **2:** 337
Atlantic voyage of, **2:** 337ff
discovery of America and, **2:** 337, 338, 339
earthly paradise and, **2:** 337ff, **8:** 2132
Judas met by, **6:** 1538
Brentano, Clemens, 5: 1174
Brer Rabbit, 1: 105, **2: 345, 11:** *2882,* 2883
Breton, André (artist), **1:** 148
Breuer, Josef, Freud and, **4:** 1049, **8:** 2228
Breughel, Pieter, the Elder, 2: 340–4
Battle between Carnival and Lent, **4:** *1010–11*
Bosch and, **2:** 340ff
Children's Games, **2:** *450–1*
witches, **4:** *914*
breviary, 2: 345
Brian (Celtic god) **2:** 443
Bride, St, *see* Bridget, St
bridges, 2: 345
in children's games, **2:** 454
over hell:
  in Islam, *see Sirat*
  in Zoroastrianism, **2:** 345, **6:** 1545, **8:** 2138, 2141, **11:** 3100
rainbow as a bridge, **9:** 2333ff, 2484
Roman rite on Tiber bridge, **2:** 345
sacrifice at, **2:** 361, 454
Bridges, William (founder of Plumstead Peculiars), **2:** 492, **8:** 2157
Bridget, St (St Bride), **2:** 400
Bridget, St (of Sweden), **11:** 2965
Brieg, St, 2: 349
Brigantia (Celtic goddess), **2:** 345, *345,* 443
Brigge, Mabel, 1: 277, **8:** 2282
Brigit, 2: 345–6
Danu and, **2:** 443
Brigit, St (of Kildare), **2:** 345, 346
Brisingamen (necklace of Freyja), **4:** 1051
British Association of Progressive Spiritualists (1865–8), **10:** 2659
British Israelites, 6: 1645f, **9:** 2314
British National Association of Progressive Spiritualists, *see* London Spiritualist Alliance
Britomartis (Cretan deity), **2:** 542, **6:** 1631
Brittany, 2: 346–9
Arthurian legends and, **2:** 347, **6:** 1594
Bluebeard legend of, **4:** 1107
Druids in, **3:** 723
life after death, beliefs concerning, **3:** 347
lost land legends of, **2:** 349, **4:** 996
saints of, **2:** 349
springs in, **3:** 349, **10:** 2685
standing stones of, **2:** *348,* 348–9, 572, **3:** *718*
Brocken (Harz Mountains), **2: 349, 10:** 2653
Brodie-Innes, J. W., 6: 1687
Brome, Theophilus, skull of, **4:** 1126
broom (plant), as herb, **5:** 1273
broomstick, 2: 350–1
made of birch, **1:** 265

made of heather, **5:** 1256
superstitions concerning, **2:** 351
broomstick wedding, **2:** 350–1
witchcraft and, **2:** 350f, **3:** 853, **4:** 915, **5:** *1417*
Goya, **4:** *1145*
Alice Kyteler, **2:** 350, **6:** 1588
Teniers, **2:** *351*
Brosses, Charles de, 9: 2357
Brown, Rosemary (automatic musician), **1:** 209
Browne, Sir Thomas, on the human body, **1:** 298
brownies (fairies), **4:** 901, 902, 903
Browning, Robert (cunning man), **7:** 1954
Browning, Robert (poet), D. D. Home and, **5:** 1335
Browsers (ascetics), **6:** 1678
Bruno, Giordano, 2: 351–2, 9: 2374f
Brut (Brute, Brutus; legendary king of Britain), **1:** 154, **2: 352, 4:** 1103
Brynhild (Valkyrie), **5:** 1298
bryony (herb), **5:** 1273, **6:** 1720
Buber, Martin (Jewish mystic), **5:** 1220, **7:** 1937
bucan (Scottish spirit), Puck related to, **9:** 2297
bucca (Cornish fairy), **2:** 519
Bucephalus, 1: 104, **11:** *2952*
Buchman, Dr Frank Nathan Daniel, 7: 1882ff, *1883*
Buchmanism, *see* Moral Rearmament
Bucke, R. W., cosmic consciousness and, **7:** 1932
buckie (Scottish spirit), Puck related to, **9:** 2297
Buda (Ethiopian spirit), **3:** 845
Buddha, 2: 352, 354ff, **4: 1070–1, 11:** 3081–2
conception of, by Queen Maya, **4:** 1070, **11:** 2953, *2953*
death of, **7:** *1934–5*
iconography of, **5:** *1396,* **7:** *1777*
as ascetic, **8:** *2004,* **9:** *2523*
in Ceylon, **10:** 2587, *2587*
with Confucius and Lao Tze, **10:** *2785*
in Kamakura, **11:** *3079*
from Katmandu, **2:** *353*
Tibetan, **5:** 1397
as incarnation of Vishnu, **11:** 2960
life of, **4:** 1070f
lotus and, **6:** 1650
more than one Buddha, belief in, **2:** 356, 359f
personal description of **1:** 299
relics of, **8:** 2196, **9:** 2351
see also stupas; Tooth, Temple of the
ritual gestures of, **4:** 1089
Silent Sermon of, **11:** 3082
as tree spirit, **11:** 2875
see also bo-tree
also Buddhism
Buddhaghosa (Buddhist writer), **10:** 2585–6
Buddh Gaya (Buddhist pilgrimage centre), **8:** 2196
Buddhism, 2: 353–60
architecture of, **8:** 2112, **9:** 2366–7
see also stupas; Tooth, Temple of the
ascetism in **8:** *2004,* **9:** *2523,* 2526
in Ceylon, *see* Sinhalese Buddhism
in China, **2:** 360, 457, 459f, 463, **3:** 616, **6:** 1650, **9:** 2348
see also Zen Buddhism
death and, **3:** 858, 861
death personified in, **3:** 616
end of the world and, **3:** 817
evil and, **3:** 858, 861
guardian spirits in, **2:** *354*
Hinduism and, **2:** 360
Bhagavad Gita, **1:** 261
Brahma, **2:** 357, 359
Brahman, **1:** 323
Indra, **2:** 357, 359
Vedanta, **2:** 360
incarnation in, **5:** 1420
in Japan, **6:** 1486ff, **9:** *2164,* 2563, **9:** 2564
Chinese influence on, **6:** 1486, 1488
judgement of the dead in, **3:** *614,* 616, **6:** *1544*
see also Amida; Jizo; Kwannon; Zen
judgement of the dead in, in Japan, **3:** 616, **6:** *1544*
lotus and, **6:** 1513, 1650
man, Buddhist view of, **6:** 1709
mandalas in, **6:** 1714, *1715*
medieval ignorance of, **9:** 2357
meditation in, **2:** 355, 359, **7:** 1779
monks in, **2:** 355, *356,* 357
in Ceylon, **10:** 2586–7
in Southeast Asia, **10:** 2648
see also lamas
mysticism in, *see* mysticism, Buddhist
paradise and, **8:** *2129,* 2134
pilgrimage in, **8:** 2195f, *2198*
reincarnation in, *see* reincarnation, in Buddhism
relics in, *see* Buddha, relics of
rosary in, **9:** 2420
saints in, **2:** 355f
selfhood in, **6:** 1709
see also Nirvana, in Buddhism
sin and, **10:** 2582
in Southeast Asia, **10:** 2646f, 2648
Tantric, **2:** 360
in Tibet, **10:** 2839ff
see also lamas, Tibetan
see also Bodhisattva; Buddha; Mahayana; prayer wheel
Buer (demon), **3:** *866*
buffalo, Great Plains Indians and, **4:** *1160,* 1161, *1163*
'Buffalo Bill' (William Frederick Cody), **11:** *2912, 2916*
bug-a-boo (Scottish spirit), **9:** 2297
Buganda (Africa), drums in, **3:** 725
builders' rites, 2: 361–2
human sacrifice and, **2:** 361
in Hawaii, **8:** 2231
orientation, **2:** 361
shadow and, **2:** 361, **9:** 2543
Bulcock, John and Jane (witches), **6:** 1593
Bulgaria, 1: 303f
bull, 1: 129–30, **2: 363–7**
Astarte and, **1:** 170
in Atlantis, **1:** 189
Attis and **3:** 742, **10:** 2805
Baal and, **1:** 222
in Babylonia, **5:** 1347, **10:** 2805
in burial at Maikop in Russia, **2:** 570
at Catal Hüyük, **1:** 116
in cave art, **2:** 363f, 433
Celts and, **2:** 442, **5:** 1350f
in Crete, **2:** *363,* 365–7, 544, *545,* **5:** 1171, 1348
captured by Hercules, **5:** *1169,* 1279
Zeus and, **5:** 1167, 1271
see also Minotaur
Cybele and, **1:** 230, **3:** 742, **10:** 2805
Earth Mother and, **11:** 2939
in Egypt, *see* Apis; Mnevis
El (Phoenician god) and, **3:** 795, **8:** 2180
fertility and, **2:** 364, **5:** 1346, **11:** 2939
in greece, **5:** 1348
Prometheus and, **8:** 2261
see also Minotaur; Zeus *below*
Hebrews and, **5:** 1347–8
horns of, **5:** 1346
India, bull gods of, **2:** 365, **5:** 1346–7
Shiva, **10:** 2572, 2573
in Malta, **6:** 1702
Mithras and, **7:** *1861,* 1862, 1863f
in Sumer, **2:** 365, **5:** 1347
Zeus and, **5:** 1167, 1271, 1348, **11:** 3090
see also Europa
zodiac sign, *see* Taurus
see also ox
Bulwer, Dr John, 6: 1670
Bulwer Lytton, *see* Lytton
bundling, 7: 1737
Bungan Malan, 1: 316
Burgoyne, W. H., (dowser), **3:** 683
Buri (Scandinavian god), **2:** 530
burial, 2: 368–77
in Africa, **1:** 79
Bushmen, **2:** 378
anointing and, **8:** 2050
in Brazil, **5:** *1414*
cannibalism in lieu of, **2:** 374
Celtic, **2:** 439, *570*
in China:
shadow and, **9:** 2543
of Shang dynasty, **2:** 570–1
Christian, **2:** 370–1, *373*
bells and, **1:** 251
in churches, **9:** 2306–7
weather at, **10:** 2604–5
see also catacombs
cremation and, **2:** 539f
in Crete, **2:** 544, 572
at crossroads, **2:** 374, 555
curses as grave-protection, **2:** 581
in Egypt, *see* Egypt, cult of the dead in
Eskimo, **3:** 836
see also Ipiutak
first, in new cemetery, **4:** 977
ghosts and, **2:** 374, **4:** 1096
Gypsies and, **5:** 1197
of the heart, **5:** 1253
Parsees and, **2:** 374, **8:** 2139, 2140–1
Parthians and, **8:** 2144
prehistoric, **2:** *369,* 372, 569f, **3:** 641, 643, **10:** 2594
Neanderthal, **2:** 569, **5:** 1343–5
religious beliefs cannot be inferred from, **5:** 1413
see also dolmen
premature, Lytton's fear of **6:** 1670
as a rite of passage, **9:** 2391
Scythian, **2:** 572, **5:** 1413
in ships, *see* ship-burial
Veddas and, **11:** 2936
see also coffin; corpses; cult of the dead; grave goods; life after death; urn, funerary; wake
Burma, 10: 2646–8
Burne-Jones, Edward, 1: 146
Burnet, Thomas, on the end of the world, **3:** 822
Burney relief (Mesopotamian terracotta), **6:** 1460
burning, 2: 378
sacrifice and, *see* sacrifice, burning as method of
see also cremation; fire
burning bush, Moses and, 11: 3063–4, 3064
mistletoe and, **7:** 1860
Burning the Clavie (New Year custom), **5:** 1255, **7:** 1997
burnt offerings, *see* sacrifice, burning as method of
Burton Agnes (Yorks), skull and ghost of Anne Griffith at, **5:** 1225–6, 1227
burying-beetle, 6: 1447
bushido (Japan), **6:** 1557
Bushmen (Africa), **2: 378–80**
jackal and, **6:** 1478
rock paintings of, **2:** 380, **5:** *1375,* **9:** 2407, *2408,* 2409
buttercup, 2: 380
butterfly, 2: 380, 6: *1446,* 1447f
see also caterpillar
Buvée Barbara, Auxonne nuns and, **1:** 209
Buxton (Derbyshire), St Anne's Well at, **10:** 2685
buzzard, in augury, **1:** 194
Byblos (Phoenician city), **8:** 2180, **10:** *2766*

C

C, Eva (Marthe Béraud; medium), **3:** 779, **7** 1791, **8:** 2277
C., Stella (medium), **7:** 1791–2
Cabala (Cabbala, Kabbalah, Qabbalah; Jewish mystical system), **2: 381–7**
Boehme and, **2:** 387
Cathars and, **2:** 383
Christianity and, **2:** 386
creation/emanation in, **1:** 112, **2:** 383ff, **3:** 813, **7:** 1941f
see also sefiroth
first man myth of, *see* Adam Kadmon
Fludd and, **2:** 386, **4:** 998
Freud and, **4:** 1049
gematria and, **4:** 1074
Gnosticism and, **2:** 383, 384
Hasidism and, **2:** 383, 386, **5:** 1219f
Hebrew alphabet and, **1:** 112, **2:** 383, **7:** 1941f
light, imagery of, in, **6:** 1629
Lull and, **6:** 1667
magic and, **2:** *386,* 387
meditation in, **7:** 1778
Neoplatonism and, **2:** 384, **7:** 1968
origin of, **2:** 382f
Papus and, **8:** 2125
sefirotic tree in, *see* tree of Life, Cabalist
Shekhinah in, **2:** 385
A. E. Waite and, **2:** 387, **11:** 2979
see also Luria, Isaac; *Sefer Yetsirah*
Cabiri, 2: 523, **11:** 3073
Cabrini, St Frances, 9: 2462
Cadbury Castle (Somerset), Arthur and, **2:** 390f, *392, 393,* 396, **11:** 3022
Cader Idris, 388
Cadmus (king of Thebes), Dionysus and, **3:** 635, 636
caduceus, 2: 335–6, **388**
Caeneus, battle of centaurs and Lapiths and, **2:** *445*
Cagliostro, Count Alessandro, 2: 388–9, 6: 1476
Cahagnet, A., 7: 1817
Cailleach (Scottish monster), **2:** 557, **4:** 902
Caindia (Irish god), *see* Fothad Canainne
cairns, 10: 2706–7
Hermes and, **5:** 1289, **10:** 2706
Calabrese, Hayyim Vital (disciple of Luria), **6:** 1668
Caladbolg (sword), **3:** 867
caladrius, in the bestiary, **3:** *644*
Calcutta, origin of the name, **6:** 1556
calendar:
astrological, medieval, **3:** *838*
Aztec, **1:** 219–20
Druids and, **3:** 720
lunar, **7:** 1876f
Maya, **7:** 1770, 1772
Parsees and, **8:** 2137
Peruvian, **3:** *839*
Roman civil, **9:** 2415–16
Caliburnus (sword of Arthur), *see* Excalibur
caliph (Islamic title), **6:** 1469
Callimachus, Drusiana and (Christian legend), **7:** 1989–92
Calliope (Muse), **7:** 1905
Callisto (Kallisto; Greek mythology), **1:** 246, **3:** 630f, **8:** 2031
Calusari (Rumanian dancers), **7:** 1890, 1891
Calvin, John, 3: *852*
on predestination, **3:** 800, **8:** 2242
Servetus and, **5:** 1286
witchcraft and, **3:** 851, 854
Cambrai (France), possessed nuns at, **5:** 1381
Camelot and Arthurian Britain, 2: 390–6
Camisards (Cévenols; French Protestants), **2: 397–8, 10:** 2651
Shakers and, **2:** 499, **9:** 2545
camphor, 2: 398
as an aphrodisiac, **8:** 2167
Camulos (Celtic god), **2:** 443
Canaan, as promised land of the Israelites, **3:** 798f, **5:** 1322, **11:** 2992, 3064f
Canaanites, *see* Phoenicians and Canaanites
Cancer (the Crab; zodiac sign, in astrology), **1:** 175, 181, **2: 398, 8:** 2157
candle, 2: 399–400
hand of glory and, **5:** 1207f
Judaism and, **2:** 399
witches and, **2:** 400, **8:** *2015*
see also Paschal Candle
Candlemas, 2: 400, 483
candomblés (Brazil), **7:** 1981, **10:** 2642
Canewdon (Essex), **1:** 252, **2: 401–2, 4:** 1097
cannabis, 3: 714
cannibalism, 2: 402
in Brazil, **2:** 325f, 327
instead of burial, **2:** 374
in Kwakiutl initiation rite, **5:** 1440
among the Maori, **7:** 1731–2
in Melanesia, **7:** 1796
New Guinea **2:** 374, **7:** 1974
Canon Episcopi, 3: 632, 853, **4:** 998, **9:** 2552
canonization, 2: 402, 9: 2465
Canopic jars, 7: 1903
Canterbury cathedral:
Becket's tomb in, **1:** 247
foliate heads in, **11:** *2939*
cantharides, *see* Spanish fly
Capeau, Sister Louise (possessed nun), **1:** 90ff
Capitoline Hill (Rome), temple of Saturn on **9:** 2479
capnomancy (divination by smoke from sacrifice), **8:** 2066
Capricorn (the Goat; zodiac sign, in astrology), **1:** 131, 175, 181, **2: 402**
placed in sky by Zeus, **2:** 518
Cardan, Jerome, personality judged from lines on forehead by, **8:** *2188*
Cardiac, Jean (child prodigy), **9:** 2348
cards, playing, 2: 403–8
fortune-telling with (cartomancy), **2:** 403ff, 414
superstitions associated with, **4:** 1064
see also Tarot
cargo cults, 2: 409–12, 7: 1800, **11:** 3043
Carington, Whately (psychical researcher), S. G. Soal and, **9:** 2278
Carlisle (Cumberland), origin of the name, **6:** 1640
Carmel, Mount (Israel):
Bahai shrine on, **1:** 224, 225, *225*
cave burial on, **2:** 569
see also Carmelite Order
Carmelite Order, 10: 2812f
Carnac (Brittany), standing stones at, **2:** *348,* 349
Carneades (Greek philosopher), **8:** 2240
carnelian, 6: *1513*
carnival, 10: 2679–82
and Lent, Battle between (Breughel), **4:** *1010–11*
Mexican, **4:** 1018
see also Mardi Gras
carol (seasonal song), **2:** 414
carole (dance), **2: 412–14,** *590*
Caroline of Brunswick (wife of George IV), imitative magic allegedly practised by, **5:** 1408
carp (fish), in Japan, **4:** *987*
Carrica, Tia (wise woman), **11:** 3019
Carrington, Hereward (psychical researcher), **8:** 2113, 2114, 2227
Cartaphilus (Wandering Jew legend), **11:** 2990f
Carter, Howard and John (Pentecostalists), **8:** 2162
Carteret, Lady Louisa, ghost of, **5:** 1225
Cartesian philosophy, *see* Descartes, René
Carthage, Carthaginians, **2: 414, 8: 2180, 2183–4**
animal sacrifice and, **8:** *2181*
child sacrifice and, **4:** 976, **8:** 2184, **10:** 2764
gods of, **8:** 2183, 2184
Rome and, **8:** 2180, 2184
cartomancy, *see* fortune-telling, by cards
Carus Karl (physician), on the unconscious, **4:** 1049
Casanova, Giacomo, 2: 414
Cassandra (Trojan princess), **1:** 140, **10:** 2574
cassock, 2: 528
castle, 2: 415–16, 5: 1315
Indian Jews and, **8:** 2081
in Sinhalese Buddhism, **10:** 2586–7
see also Brahmins; untouchables
Castelmellano (Italy), white magic at, **11:** 3019
castle:
in Grail legend, **4:** 1146, 1149, 1153
symbolism of, **6:** 1603
see also Cadbury castle; Krak des Chevaliers; Tintagel
Castle Dore (Cornwall), King Mark and, **2:** 391
Castor and Polydeuces (or Pollux), *see* Dioscuri
castration, 7: 1915
of Attis, **2:** 583, **3:** 742
of *castrati,* **7:** 1915
castration complex (psychological theory), **11:** 3051
of Origen, **7:** 1915, **10:** 2593
Skoptsy and, **7:** 1915, **10:** 2593, 2594
of Uranus, **1:** 135
in worship of Astarte, **1:** 170, **7:** 1915
cat, 2: 417–21
in Arthurian legend (demon cat of Losanne), **1:** 153, 154
in Egypt, as goddess, *see* Bast
mummified, in Egypt, **7:** *1901*
as omen, **8:** 2064
sacrifice of, **4:** 915
in witchcraft:
as familiar, **2:** 420, *420,* **3:** 755, 866, **4:** 914ff, **8:** 2282, **10:** 2626
in shape-shifting, **2:** 419, **9:** 2552
in storm-raising, **8:** 2014
catacombs, 2: 421
of Rome, **2:** 421, **5:** 1396f
Christ in, **5:** 1398
Good Shepherd symbol in, **4:** 1137, **5:** 1398
Jonah in, **5:** 1398, **6:** 1528
of Sicily, **2:** 370
Catal Hüyük, Neolithic settlement at, **9:** 2362
female figurines from, **6:** *1393,* 1394, **7:** *1894*
fertility rites at, **1:** 116
headless figures at, **5:** 1245, *1245*
shrine of mother goddess at, **8:** 2244–5
caterpillar, 2: 421, 6: 1450
in *Alice in Wonderland,* **6:** *1451,* **7:** 1908, *1909*
Cathars, 1: 279, **2: 422–4, 5:** 1283, **9:** 2477–9
Basque witchcraft and, **1:** 234
Bogomils and, **2:** 422
Cabala and, **2:** 383
dualism of, **2:** 422f
French witchcraft and, **4:** 1043
cathedrals, Christian, *see* Canterbury; Chartres; Kremlin, Cathedral of the Assumption in; St Peter's, Rome
Catherine of Alexandria, St, 9: 2464
Catherine of Genoa, St, 9: 2307, 2318, **10:** 2700
Catherine of Ricci, St, 10: 2701, 2965
Catherine of Siena, St, 2: 425–7
incombustibility of, **10:** 2701
by Sodoma, **10:** *2699*
stigmata of **2:** 426
by Veronese, **7:** *1931*
catherine wheel, 9: 2464
Catholic Apostolic Church (Irvingites), **6:** 1458f
Catholic church, *see* Roman Catholic church
catoptromancy, *see* mirror, divination by
cat's cradle (string game), **2: 427, 10:** 2710

cat's eye (jewel), Sun and Leo associated with, **6:** 1511
Caucasus, earthquake myth of **8:** 2262
caul (hallihoo, holy hood), **1:** 275, **2: 427**
cauldron, 2: 427–8
of Annwn (Arthurian cycle), **1:** 154, **2:** 428, **4:** 1149
of Bran the Blessed, **2:** 428, **4:** 1149
Celts and, **2:** 427f, **4:** 1147f
in Crete, **11:** 3089
of Goibniu, **4:** 1147
of Gundestrup, **2:** 427f, *428, 440,* **3:** *772,* **5:** 1350, **11:** *3017*
of Tyrnoc, **4:** 1149
causation, cause and effect, **7:** 1850, **8:** 2240
Jung's principle of synchronicity and, **6:** 1552, 1648
Cavalier, Jean (Camisard), **2:** 398
cave art, 2: 429–34, 4: 935
of Africa, *see* rock paintings
of Australia, *see* Australia, cave and bark paintings of
dating of, **2:** 429f, 431f
of Paleolithic Europe, **2:** 363f, 430ff, 435, **5:** 1394, **8:** 2243–4
animals in, **2:** 431
birds in, **1:** 267, **2:** *433*
as fertility cult, **2:** 432
fish in, **2:** *430*
horns in, **5:** 1345
as imitative magic, **2:** 432f
of post-Paleolithic Europe, **2:** 430
caves, 2: 435
of Cappadocia, early Christians in, **2:** *435, 467*
in Crete, as sanctuaries, **2:** 435, 545
dwarfs and, **3:** 738
Mithras and, **9:** 2364–5
subterranean race and, **10:** 2712f
symbolism of, **6:** 1603
in Tristan legend, **11:** 2888
Zeus born in a cave, **2:** 435, 523, **8:** 2032, **9:** 2482, **11:** *3094*
see also cave art; Choukoutien; Guattari cave; Teshik-tash
Cayce, Edgar, 2: 436
Cecilia, St, 9: *2468*
cedar (tree):
Baal and, **1:** 222
cross of Jesus and, **8:** 2060, 2116, **10:** 2773
Ea and, **11:** 2878
Cefalu (Sicily), Aleister Crowley at, **2:** 562f
Celeus (Greek mythology), **11:** 3060
celibacy:
of Christian monks, **2:** 472
of Christian priests, **2:** 473
among communistic religious movements, **2:** 499ff
Shakers, **2:** 499, **9:** 2544
Walworth Jumpers, **11:** 2984
Cellini, Benvenuto, magical ceremony described by, **6:** 1476
Celtic cross, 2: *437,* 551
Celts, 2: 437–44
animals and, **2:** 443
boar, **1:** 130, **2:** 443
bull, **2:** 442, **5:** 1350f
horse, **1:** *128,* 130, **2:** 347, **5:** 1352, 1357
ram, **2:** 443, **5:** 1350f
ram-headed serpent, **1:** 129, **2:** 443, **5:** 1350
stag, **1:** 129, **2:** 443, **5:** 1350f, **10:** 2687–9
see also horns *below*
Arthurian legends of, **1:** 153–4, **4:** 1149, **6:** 1672, 1674
birds and, **2:** 444
crane, **2:** 444, 532
burial among, **2:** 439
cauldron and, **2:** 427f, *440,* **4:** 1147f
Christianity of, **2** 393f
Celtic cross, **2:** *437,* 441
see also Brendan, St; Columba, St; Patrick, St
festivals of, **2:** 441
see also Beltane; Imbolc; Lugnasad; Samain
glass and, in myth, **4:** 1110
Glastonbury and, **4:** 1109, 1110
gods of, **2:** 442–3
triple gods, **2:** 345, 443, **4:** 966, **5:** 1239
see also Bran; Brigit; Cernunnos; Epona; Goibniu; Lugus; Matunus; Rhiannon; Teutates
head cult of, **2:** 324, *441,* **3:** *722,* **5:** 1237ff
heroes of, **2:** 565, 566, **5:** 1298
cauldron and, **2:** 428
see also Arthur *above;* Cu Chulainn; Finn mac Cumail; Furbaide the Horned; Gwydion
horns and, **2:** *442,* **5:** 1348–52
human sacrifice by, **2:** 428, *428,* 441f
life after death, beliefs concerning, **2:** 439, 440
oak and, **6:** 1639
priests of, *see* Druids
stones and, **10:** 2706, 2788
story-telling and, **6:** 1674
three and, **2:** 443, **4:** 965–6, **6:** 1639
see also gods, triple gods, *above*
Urnfield culture and, **2:** 437
vessels of plenty and, **5:** 1147f
wells and, **5:** 1240
see also Brittany; *Mabinogion*
censer, from Ramsey Abbey, **8:** *2165*
Census of Hallucinations (S.P.R.), **8:** 2275
centaurs, 2: 445
Lapiths and, **2:** 445, **5:** *1354–5,* **10:** 2819
Theseus and, **10:** 2819
see also Chiron; Nessus
centaury (herb), **5:** 1273
Centini, Giocinto, Urban VIII and, **6:** 1476
Central America, modern, *see* Mexico and Central America
Central America, Pre-Columbian, *see* Aztecs; Maya; Mixtecs; Olmecs; Toltecs; Zapotecs
centre, the:
pentagram and, **8:** 2158
symbolism of, **10:** 2758
see also world mountain; world tree
see also navel
Cerberus (three-headed dog; Greek mythology), **3:** 669, *669,* **5:** *1258,* 1266, 1280, **8:** 2208
Cercyon (Greek mythology), **10:** 2818
Cerealis (plant), *see* vervain
Ceres (Roman goddess), **2: 445, 3:** 631f, **9:** 2412
acorn and, **8:** 2034
Demeter identified with, **3:** 621, **9:** 2412
Janus and, **6:** 1484
Cerialia (festival of Ceres), **3:** 621
Cerne Abbas giant (Dorset), **4:** *930*
Cernunnos (Celtic god), **1:** 129, **2:** 443, **5:** 1350, **10:** 2687
Ceryneian hind, captured by Hercules, **5:** 1279, **10:** 2687
Cetshwayo (Cetewayo; Zulu chief), **1:** 3103, 3105
Cévenols, *see* Camisards
Crewa (Central African people), witchcraft among, **10:** 2634, **11:** 3042, 3045
Ceylon, 2: 445
Buddhism in, *see* Sinhalese Buddhism
indigenous tribe of, *see* Veddas
Chac (Maya rain god), **7:** 1772
Chagall, Marc, 1: 151
Bouquet with Flying Lovers, **10:** *2667*
The Dream, **3:** *704*
Time is a River without Banks, **10:** *2757*
The Vision, **11:** *2964*
chain of being, *see* great chain of being
chain dances, 2: 412ff, 594f
Chaka (Zulu chief), *see* Shaka
chakras, 6: *1585,* 1586, **10:** 2780
lotus and, **6:** 1650
Chalcedon, Council of AD 451, Jesus's dual nature defined by, **2:** 471, **5:** 1420, **7:** 1749
chalcedony, 6: 1512f
Chalchihuitlicue (Aztec goddess), **11:** *3003,* 3006
Chaldean Oracles, 7: 1968, **10:** 2821f
Chaldeans (Mesopotamia), **2: 446**
chalice, 2: 576
Grail as chalice of the Last Supper, **4:** 1150f
Chalice Well (Glastonbury), **4:** 1114
Chamberlain, Houston Stewart, 7: 1964
chamber tomb, *see* dolmen
Chambre Ardente case, 8: 2218–19
chance:
divination by chance happenings, *see* cledonomancy
ESP and, **3:** *876–7,* 878
see also luck
Chan Chan (Peru), **5:** 1424
changeling, 1: 275, **2: 446, 4:** 902
in Cornwall, **2:** 519
foxglove and, **5:** 1275
Changing Woman (Navaho Indian deity), **7:** 1949
Channel Islands, 2: 350, **447–8**
Chantal, St Jeanne Françoise de, 9: 2319
chaos, 2: 448, 3: 816
in Babylonian mythology, *see* Tiamat
in Genesis, **2:** 537
in Sumerian mythology, *see* Zu
water or sea and, **1:** 223, **3:** 690, **4:** 1157, **11:** 3001
Charcot, Jean Martin (neurologist), Lourdes and Asclepios compared by, **7:** 1854
Chariot (Tarot card), **8:** 2147, *2207,* **10:** 2792, *2792*
charismatic movement (Christianity), **10:** 2653
Charites (Greek mythology), *see* graces
Charlemagne, 2: 448, 5: 1298, **11:** 3037
legendary ring of his mistress, **9:** 2387
sword of (Joyeuse), **10:** 2748
Charles I, King's Evil and, **6:** 1573
Charles II:
King's Evil and, **3:** *642,* **6:** 1573
oak and, **8:** 2035
Charles Martel, 11: 2993
charms, 2: 449, 10: 2730–1
Ashanti, **1: 162f**
hare's foot as, 3: 641, **5:** 1210
in love magic, **6:** 1657ff
sleep induced by, **10:** 2613–14
vervain and, **11:** 2948
see also amulet; *cimaruta;* hand of glory; milpreve
Charmouth (Dorset), haunted house at, **3:** 688
Charon (Greek mythology), **2: 448–9, 6:** *1603*
Charta Borgiana (magical papyrus), **6:** 1689
Chartres Cathedral, 9: *2366,* **11:** *2906*
Charun (Etruscan god), **2:** 449, **3:** 850
Chaudron, Michelle (witch), **8:** 2246
Chavannes, Puvis de (artist), **1:** 146
Chavin de Hvantar (Peru), **5:** 1423
Chelmsford (Essex), witches and, **3:** 753, 755f, *757,* **4:** 913
see also Francis, Elizabeth
Cherokee Indians, 8: 2011
cherub, cherubim, **2: 449, 11:** *3033*
in the Old Testament, **1:** 125, **8:** 2070–1
chess, 4: 1064
Chester, mystery play cycle of, **7:** 1922, 1923, 1924
Cheyenne Indians, 4: 1161, 1164
Chichen Itza, 7: 1772
chicken:
in augury, **1:** 194
as oracle among the Azande, **4:** 952–3
wishbone of, **4:** 1139
see also cock
chicory, 5: 1273, *1275*
Childermas (feast of the Holy Innocents), **3:**

607
child prodigies, 9: 2348–50
Children of God, *see* Walworth Jumpers
Children of Light (associates of George Fox), **4:** 1030
Children of the Resurrection (Agapemonites), **8:** 2259
children's games, 2: 449–54
death and, **2:** 449f, 599
fertility as theme of, **2:** 454
marriage and, **2:** *452, 453,* 453f
singing games, dance origin of, **2:** 414
soul and, **2:** 454
chimaera, 2: 454–5
chimney, 5: 1255
Chimu culture (Peru), **5:** 1424, *1426–7*
China, 2: 456–64
alchemy in, **1: 97, 3:** 809
altars in, **1:** 117
ancestor worship in, **2:** 457, 459, 573
Buddhism in **2:** 360, 457, 459f, 463, **3:** 616, **6:** 1650, **9:** 2348
see also Zen Buddhism
burial in:
shadow and, **9:** 2543
Shang dynasty, **2:** 570–1
Communism in, **2:** 463f, **11:** *2942*
couvade in, **5:** *1412*
crane in, *2:* 532
creation myths in **2:** 538, **3:** 781
demons in, **2:** 460ff
dragon in, **3:** *692,* 693ff, **8:** 2188
eclipses and, **3:** 772
divination in, *see* I Ching
eclipses in, **3:** 772, **10:** 2725
elements, five, theory of the, **2: 457, 3:** *802*
emperor of, **6:** 1572
fate, beliefs concerning, **4:** 921–2
four spiritual creatures of, **3:** 693, **8:** 2188
see also dragon *above;* phoenix *below;* unicorn *below*
gods of, **2:** *456,* 457, 460ff, *464,* **8:** *2136,* **10:** *2786*
guardian spirit of, **5:** *1186*
hell, beliefs concerning, **2:** *462, 463,* **3:** 616
horse in, **1:** 128
Islam in, **2:** 463
jade in, **6:** *1478, 1479,* 1480
Jews in, **8:** 2080f
lotus in, **6:** 1650
man, view of, **6:** 1712
medicine in, **2: 463**
see also acupuncture
meditation in, **7:** 1778
messianic movements in, **2:** 463
see also Taiping rebellion
owl in, **8:** 2098
peacock in, **8:** 2153
philosophers of, *see* Confucius; Lao Tze; Tsou Yen
phoenix in, **3:** 693, **4:** 929, **8:** *2186–7,* 2188
religions of, *see* Buddhism *above;* Confucianism; gods *above;* joss-stick; Tao, Taoism
secret societies of, **2:** *461,* 463, **10:** 2787, 2858
shadow in, at funerals, **9:** 2543
soul, beliefs concerning, **2:** 459, 460
thunderbird in, **10:** 2837
Tibet and, **10:** 2838, 2843
tortoise in, **3:** 693, **8:** 2188
unicorn *(ki-lin)* in, **3:** 693, **8:** 2188, 2910
universe, Chinese view of, **6:** 1712
see also Yin and Yang
see also Fo-hi; Peking
Chintamani (wishing-gem), **6:** 1514
Chippewa (Ojibway; Algonquin Indian tribe), **1:** 106, **8:** *2011*
chi-rho monogram (Christian symbol), **2:** 550
Chirico, Giorgio de, 1: 149, *151*
chiromancy, *see* palmistry
Chiron (centaur), **2:** 445
Asclepios and, **5:** 1246, *1247*
betony and, **5:** 1272
centaury and, **5:** 1273
Choctaw Indians, 8: 201
cholera, origin of the name, **3:** 802
Chons (Egyptian moon god), **10:** 2692
chorea, convulsive, St Vitus and, **2:** 600
chosen people, *see* election
Choukoutien caves (China), **2:** 435, 569
Chrétien de Troyes (French poet):
Arthurian legend and, **1:** 156
Camelot, **2:** 390
Gawain, **4:** 1071
Grail, **4:** 1149f, 1153
Lancelot, **6:** 1594
Morgan le Fay, **7:** 1884
Perceval (Parsifal), **4:** 1149, **8:** 2141–2
Christ, meaning of the word, **2:** 466, **8:** 2050
Jesus Christ, *see* Jesus
Christadelphians, 3: 824, **9:** 2521
Christian Israelites (Southcottian sect), **10:** 2646
Christianity, 2: 466–76
absurdity of, as reason for belief, **6:** 1680
in Africa, *see* Africa, Christianity in
altars in, **1:** 116, 117, **10:** *2824*
angels in, **1:** 124ff
see also guardian spirits *below*
Apollonius of Tyana and, **1:** 141
architecture of, **9:** *2360,* 2365, *2368,* 2372
cathedrals, *see* Canterbury; Chartres; Kremlin, Cathedral of the Assumption in; St Peter's, Rome; Salisbury
churches facing east, **3:** 640
ascetism and self-denial in, **6:** 1678–9, **9:** 2523, 2524, 2526
see also Anthony, St; fasting; Simeon Stylites
baptism in, *see* baptism, Christian
burial and, **2:** 370f, *377*
bells and, **1:** 251
in Sicily, **2:** *376*
see also catacombs
Cabala and, **2:** 386
Celtic, **2:** 393f
chastity, celibacy, and, **2:** 472, 473, **9:** 2524
Constantine and, **2:** 470
creation as expression of the will of God in, **4:** 1159
cross in, *see* cross, Christian
death and, **3:** 617, 859f
see also dance of death
dying god myth and, **3:** 743f
election and, **3:** 797, 799f
end of the world in, **3:** 815, 818ff
see also Second Coming
eternal return myth contrasted with, **3:** 838, 839
evil and, **3:** 859f
see also Devil
exorcism and, *see* exorcism, Christian
fasting and, **4:** 918
first man myth of, *see* Adam
Good Shepherd symbol in, **4:** 1137
guardian spirits and, **5:** 1187, **6:** 1721
see also angels *above*
heaven and, *see* paradise, Christianity and
heresy in, *see* heresy, Christian
Hinduism and, **5:** 1316, **9:** 2360–2
history and, **5:** 1322f, **11:** 2850
iconography in, **5:** *1395,* 1396ff
Iconoclastic Controversy, **2:** 472, **5:** 1399
incense and, **5:** 1428
Jerusalem and, *see* Jerusalem, Christianity and
Judaism and, **2:** 466, **3:** 767f, **5:** 1322
judgement of the dead in, **6:** 1546
see also Last Judgement, in Christianity
life after death, beliefs concerning, *see* hell, in Christianity; immortality, in Christianity; judgement of the dead *above;* limbo; paradise, Christianity and; purgatory; *refrigerium*
love feast of, *see agape*
man, Christian view of, **6:** 1708
marriage and, **2:** 470
as a sacrament, **9:** 2450, 2451–2
martyrs of, *see* martyrs, Christian
meditation and, **7:** 1779–80
missionaries of, *see* missionaries, Christian
monasticism in, **2:** 472f
mountains and, **7:** 1900
music and, **7:** 1911f
Mystery religions of Rome and, **7:** 1929
St Paul and, **8:** 2151f
mysticism in, *see* mysticism, Christian
Neoplatonist influence on, **7:** 1968
in New Zealand, **7:** 1732–3
omniscience of God in, **8:** 2242
opus anglicanum and **8:** *2070,* 2071
origins of, **2:** 466, **3:** 767f
Jesus and, **6:** 1504ff
St Paul and, **2:** 469, **3:** 799f, **6:** 1507f, **8:** 2148ff
palm tree and, **8:** 2116
peyote cults and, **8:** 2172
pilgrimage and, *see* pilgrimage, Christian
predestination in, *see* predestination and free will, in Christianity
priests in, **8:** 2256
prophecy and, **8:** 2267f
reincarnation and, **9:** 2346
relics and, **3:** 649, **8:** 2196f, **9:** 2351–3
Renaissance and, **9:** 2370f
resurrection in, **6:** 1708
see also Jesus, resurrection of
revelation and, **9:** 2377f
see also Revelation, book of
rose and, **9:** 2421–2
sacraments in, **9:** 2449–52
see also baptism, Christian; Extreme Unction; marriage; Mass; penance
sacrifice and, **9:** 2458
salvation of the individual in, **8:** 2242
science and, **2:** 474f
separation of Eastern (Byzantine) and Western (Roman) churches, **2:** 473
sin and, *see* sin, Christianity and
soul in, **5:** 1415f, **6:** 1708
see also life after death *above*; mysticism, Christian
in Southeast Asia, **10:** 2646
spiritual healing and, *see* faith healing, Christian attitudes to
symbolism in, **10:** 2758
animals, **1:** 130–1, **9:** 2471
ass, **1:** 167
fish, **4:** *983,* 985
lion, **1:** 130, **5:** *1398,* **6:** 1634, **9:** 2471
mouse, **9:** 2471
pig, **9:** 2471
stag, **10:** 2687
unicorn, **11:** 2909
cock, **2:** 491
crow, **10:** 2758
dove, *see* dove, in Christian symbolism
evangelists, symbols of, **5:** *1398*
Good Shepherd, **4:** 1137, **9:** 2559, **10:** 2756
heart, **5:** 1250
key, **10:** 2756
the Mass, **10:** 2756
net, **7:** 1970, **10:** 2756
peacock, **8:** 2154
pelican, **1:** 267, **8:** 2158
pomegranate, **8:** 2233
shell, **9:** 2560
ship, **9:** 2565
white (colour) **4:** 1059, **11:** 3017
see also anchor; chi-rho; crook; hand of God; IHS
war, Christian attitudes to, **2:** 470, 472, **11:** 2993–5
see also crusade
see also Antichrist; Aquinas; Augustine, St; Bible; Christmas; creed; Dead Sea Scrolls, Christianity and; Easter; Epiphany; friars; grace; Grail; Holy

Ghost; Jesus; Mary, the Virgin; miracles; monasticism, Christian; papacy; Paul, St; Pentecost; sabbath (Christian); saints, Christian; speaking in tongues; Trinity; Whitsun
also Anabaptists; Arnoldites; Camisards; Christadelphians; Christian Science; Cokelers; convulsionaries; Copts; Divine Principles; Doukhobors; Dunkers; Ebionites; Elkesaites; Exclusive Brethren; Holiness movement; Huguenots; Hutterian Brethren; Irving, Edward; Jehovah's Witnesses; Jezreel, James Jershom; Maronites; Melchiorites; Methodism; Peculiar People; Pentecostalist movement; Pietism; Plymouth Brethren; Protestantism; Quakers; Quietism; Reformation; Roman Catholic Church; Shakers; Taborites; Walworth Jumpers; wandering bishops
Christian Science, 2: 476–9
animal magnetism and, **2:** 476, 478, **7:** 1817
Mrs Eddy and, **2:** 476ff, **3:** 779f
healing and, **2:** 476, 478, **3:** 779, 780, 909
P. P. Quimby and, **7:** 1993f
Christmas, 2: 480–3, 11: *3037*
formerly called Midwinter Feast, **2:** 480
holly and, **5:** 1329, 1330
ivy and, **5:** 1329, 1330
laurel and, **6:** 1611
mistletoe and, **2:** 481, **7:** 1860
origins of, **2:** 480
twelve days of, **11:** *2898, 2899,* 2900, *2900*
see also carol; Christmas tree; Lord of Misrule; mummers; plough plays; Saturnalia; Twelfth Night; Yule
Christmas tree, 2: 481, **4:** 968
Christopher, St, 8: 2116
Christ's Church of the Golden Rule, 7: 1726
chrysolite, sun associated with, **6:** 1511
chthonian deities, 2: 484, 3: 751
Hades as, **8:** 2209
serpents and, **3:** 751, **9:** 2528f, 2532
church ales, 3: 763
Church of the Ark of the Covenant (Clapton, London), **7:** 1830, **8:** 2259
Church of the Carmel (sect), **1:** 240
Church of the Cherubim and Seraphim (West Africa), **2:** 502, **3:** 778, **7:** 1981
Church of God of Prophecy, 5: 1332
Church of God (Tomlinson), 5: 1332, **8:** 2161
churching of women, 1: 276
Church of the Lord, Aladura, 3: 778, **7:** 1981
Church of the Nazarene (Holiness sect), **5:** 1329
Churchward, Colonel James, Mu and, **6:** 1614f
churinga (Australia), **11:** 2860, *2860*
Ciaran, St, 4: 2470
ciborium (container of the host), **4:** 1147
Grail as, **4:** 1147, *1148*
cicada, 6: 1450
cicatrization, 2: 484, 10: 2796, 2800f
in Africa, **1:** 71
Bushmen, **2:** 380
Chad, **5:** *1442*
Ibo, **5:** 1386f
Kikuyu, **6:** 1563
Sudan, **7:** *1914*
in Australia, **1:** 198, **10:** *2804*
in Brazil, **10:** *2804*
Cicero, on divination, **3:** 657
cimaruta (charm), **3:** 648
Cinderella, 2: 484–5, 4: 1006, **11:** *3056*
cinema, *see* films
cinnamon, 2: 522
cinquefoil, creeping (five leaf grass), **5:** 1273–4, **8:** 2202
Cinteotl (Mexican god), **1:** 219
ciphers, John Dee and, **3:** 618
Circe, 2: 485–6, 9: *2553*
Circe's Plant, *see* mandrake
circle, 2: 486–7
in Celtic cross, **2:** 551
see also cycles of time; magic circle; mandala; ourobouros; ring; spheres; stone circles
circle dances, *see* ring dances
circumcision, 2: 487, 7: 1915f
in Africa, **1:** 79–81, **9:** 2390–1, 2392–3
Azande, **1:** *212, 213*
Bushmen, **2:** 380
Kikuyu, **6:** 1563, 1564
Masai, **7:** 1754
in Judaism, **6:** *1530*
psychoanalytical explanation of, **9:** 2392
circumpolar stars, in the Pyramid Texts, **3:** 792, **10:** 2692
city, symbolism of the **6:** 1602
Jerusalem, **6:** 1502
Civil War, English:
adventist groups among Puritans, **9:** 2520–1
ghosts and, **1:** 145
portents and marvels associated with, **1:** 145–6, **4:** 916
witchcraft and, **4:** 916
clairaudience, 2: 487
clairvoyance, 2: 487, 3: 875, 880, 881f, **10:** 2665
E. Osty and, **9:** 2278
Charles Richet and, **9:** 2286
telepathy and, **3:** 878
see also object reading
Clarke, Elizabeth (witch), **1:** 295, **3:** 755
Clark-Kennedy, Dr A. E., 4: 907f
Claros, oracle of Apollo at, **8:** 2077f
Claver, St Peter, 9: 2462
Clay, Cassius, *see* Ali, Muhammad
cledonomancy (divination by chance happenings), **3:** 658f
Clement, St, 7: 1985, **10:** 2618, *2618*
Cleopatra, 8: 2157, **11:** *3059*
cleromancy (divination by dice, etc.), **3:** 659
see also dice, divination by
Clifton Hampden (Oxfordshire), ghost at, **5:** 1225
Climax (Climacus), St John, 6: *1547,* **10:** 2695
Clio (Muse of history), **7:** 1905
Clophill (Bedfordshire), **2: 488–9**
Closed Brethren *see* Exclusive Brethren
clothes, *see* costume
Clotho (Greek mythology), **4:** 918, *919*
***Clouds of Unknowing,* 2: 488–90, 3:** 634
clove, 2: 552
clover, 2: 490, 8: 2204
Clovis (French king), **8:** 2050
Clyack (Scottish feast), **9:** 2388
clyack chief (corn sheaf), **2:** 518
Clymer, Dr R. Swinburne (writer on Rosicrucianism), **9:** 2433
Clytemnestra, 4: 1055f
Cnossus (Knossos; Crete), **4:** *1017*
excavation of, by Sir Arthur Evans, **5:** 1167
labyrinth at, **1:** 212, **5:** 1271, **7:** 1774–5
coal, 2: 490
Coatlicue (Aztec goddess), **1:** *221,* **3:** *751,* **11:** *2940*
cocoa (drug), **3:** 714
cocaine, Freud and, **3:** 714
Cochin Jews (Indian Jews), **8:** 2081
cock (bird), **2: 490–1**
in Christian symbolism, **2:** 491
St Colman and, **9:** 2470
Dionysus and, **10:** *2754*
divination by (alectromancy), **8:** 2065
in Ethiopia, **3:** 844
Leto and, **11:** 3090
at Ragnarok, **9:** 2486
Slavs and, **10:** 2612
sun and, **2:** 490f
Zeus and, **11:** 3090f
see also chicken
cockchafer (insect), **6:** 1446–7
cock-fighting, 2: 491
Cockie, Isobel (witch), **1:** 63
'cocking a snook', 4: 1089
cockle-shell (or scallop-shell; pilgrims' emblem), **2: 492, 9:** 2513
Cody, William Frederick, *see* 'Buffalo Bill'
coffins:
Egyptian, **1:** 306f, **3:** *786–7,* **7:** 1903–4
see also Coffin Texts
Parthian, **8:** 2144
Coffin Texts (Egypt) **1:** 305, 306ff, **2: 492, 3:** 615–16, **6:** 1540f
Cokelers (Society of Dependants; Puritanical sect), **2: 492**
Colas, Aritide (witch), **4:** 1047
Coleridge, Samuel Taylor, 2: 493–4
on dreams, **2:** 494
on the imagination, **2:** 494
laudanum taken by, **3:** 713
as Platonist, **2:** 493f
on reason, **2:** 494
Thomas Taylor and, **10:** 2808
collective unconscious, 6: 1549
Yeats and, **11:** 3068
Colman, St, 9: 2470
colobrium (Christian iconography), **11:** 2907
Colossians, St Paul's epistles to, **8:** 2148
colours, 2: 494–6
of fairies, **4:** 902
metals associated with, **2:** 522
planets associated with, **2:** 522
see also black; blue; green; red; white; yellow
Columba, St, 9: 2462
crane and, **2:** 532
St John's wort and, **9:** 2461
St Ronan buried by, **2:** 361
Columban, St, 9: 2468
Columbus, Christopher, 2: 339
eclipse and, **3:** 772
Columcille, St, oak wood of Derry saved by, **8:** 2034
Comanche Indians, 4: 1161, 1164
comets, 2: 496, 8: 2064, 2066
in augury, **1:** 194
in the Bayeux Tapestry, **8:** 2071
Julius Caesar and, **2:** 496
pestilence and, in Anglo-Saxon belief, **3:** 647
commendation ninepence, 6: 1660
Communism, Chinese, 1: 463f, **11:** *2942*
communistic religious movements, 2: 497–502
see also Anabaptists; Shakers; Taborites; Walworth Jumpers
Community for Germanic Beliefs, 7: 1964
Community of the Truly Inspired, *see* Amana Society
comparative religion, 2: 502, 9: 2354–60
Compendium Maleficarum (Guazzo), **1:** 62, **5:** 1382, **6:** *1475,* **7:** *1956,* **8:** 2280, 2446, **9:** 2447, *2448,* **11:** *3046*
Compitalia (Roman festival), **6:** 1608
complex (psychology), **6:** 1548
Compostela (Spain), pilgrimage to shrine of St James at, **2:** 492
concentration:
meditation distinguished from, **7:** 1777
in yoga, *see dharana*
Condwiramurs (Arthurian legend), **8:** 2143
confession, *see* sin, confession of
confetti, 7: 1739
confirmation (Christian sacrament), **9:** 2450, 2451
Confucianism, 2: 457ff
Confucius (Kung Fu-tze), **2:** 457, **502, 10:** *2784, 2785*
I Ching and, **5:** 1390
on Lao Tze, **10:** 2784
see also Confucianism
Congo, 2: 503–10
divination in, **2:** 509
gods of, **2:** 504f
initiation rites in, **2:** *506–7*

life after death, belief in, **2:** 509
magic in, **2:** 509
myth of origin of death of, **3:** 615
new religious movements in, **7:** 1978–9
Salvation Army in, **7:** 1979
secret societies in, **2:** 510
spirits and ghosts in, **2:** 505f
taboo in, **10:** 2770
witches and witch-doctors in, **2:** 509f, **7:** 1978
Conn of the Hundred Battles (Irish hero), **4:** 1150, **10:** 2787
consciousness, psychology of, **9:** 2292ff
Conselheiro, Antonio ('the Counsellor'; Antonio Maciel), **2: 511–12**
Constantine (Roman emperor), **2:** 470, 550
Constantinople:
First Council of (381 AD), **5:** 1282
Second Council of (553 AD), **9:** 2346
sacked by crusaders, **11:** 2995
constellations, 2: 512
see also Dolphin; Great Bear; Orion; Pleiades; zodiac
contagious magic, Frazer's use of term, **3:** 642f, **3:** 1409
contemplation, 2: 512
meditation distinguished from, **2:** 489f
Contrapás (Spanish dance), **2:** 413
control (Spiritualism), **7:** 1783ff
conversion, 2: 513–15
Convulsionaries (Jansenist group), **2: 516**
dancing mania and, **2:** 600
see also Paris, François de
Conway Bay (Wales), lost land legend of, *see* Tyno Helig
Cook, Florence (medium), Sir William Crookes and, **2:** 548
Cook, Captain James, death of, **8:** 2230
Cook Islands (Polynesia), **8:** 2230, 2232
Coombe, George (phrenologist), **8:** 2189
Coombe Tennant, Mrs Charles, *see* Willett, Mrs
Cooper, Joe (statistics in astrology), **1:** 182
Copernican theory, Bruno and, **2:** 352
Copertino, Joseph of, *see* Joseph Mary Desu, St
copper (metal), **2:** 522
Copts, Coptic Christianity, **2:** 471, **8:** *2250*
Egyptian influence on, **3:** 788, 792
coral, 6: 1514, **9:** 2341–2
Coraule (Swiss dance), **2:** 414
Corinthians, St Paul's epistles to, **8:** 2148, 2151
Cormelian (giant), **6:** 1478
corn (wheat), **2: 517–18**
dogs and, **3:** 669
in Egyptian tombs, *see* corn-mummies
Eleusis and, **3:** *806,* 807
Greek goddess of, *see* Demeter
hare and, **5:** 1210
last sheaf of, **2:** *517,* 518, **5:** 1214ff, **11:** 2942
Roman goddess of, *see* Ceres
see also corn-springs; maize
corn dolly (corn sheaf), **2:** *517,* 518, **5:** 1217, **11:** *3018*
Cornely, St, 2: *348,* 349
corn-mummies (Egypt), **11:** 2939–40
corn-springs (levants), **10:** 2684
cornucopia, 2: 518
Cornwall, 2: 519–20
bards and Druids in, **3:** 723
corn dolly (neck) in, **2:** 518
fairies of, **2:** 519, **4:** 906
mines of, **2:** 519
mystery plays in, **7:** 1923
rocking stones (logans) of, **2:** 519–20
standing stones of, **2:** 520, *520,* **10:** *2706*
wells in, **10:** 2684, 2685
witches and, **2:** 520
see also Helston furry dance; Lyonesse; Mark (king of Cornwall); Padstow Old Hoss; St Michael's Mount
Coródes (Belgian dance), **2:** 414
coronation:
anointing and, **6:** *1572,* **8:** 2050
of King Arthur (15th cent. MS), **9:** *2396*
crown and, **2:** 564
oath, **8:** *2038*
sceptre and, **11:** 2987
Coronis (nymph), Apollo and, **2:** 556, **5:** 1246
corposant, *see* St Elmo's Fire
corpse candle, *see* will-o'-the-wisp
corpse light, *see* will-o'-the-wisp
corpses:
divination by (necromancy), **7:** 1953ff
healing powers of, **3:** 649
relics from, **9:** 2351f
on a ship, **10:** 2570
see also dried bodies; hand of glory; mummification; vampire; zombies
***Corpus Hermeticum,* 5:** 1290f, **10:** 2692
correspondences, 2: 522, 6: 1684f
Cabala and, **2:** 522
of colours, **2:** 522
of days, **2:** 522
of jewels, **6:** 1510ff
land and sea, **4:** 986
macrocosm/microcosm and, **6:** 1675
of metals, **2:** 522
of planets, **2:** 522
see also forces; Law of Correspondences
Corybantes (Greek mythology), **2: 522–3, 9:** 2482
cosmetics, 2: 523
see also body painting; cicatrization; tattooing
cosmic consciousness, 7: 1932f
Cosmic Memory (Akashic Records; occultism), **1: 204, 6:** 1630
cosmic order, 3: 861
Egyptian view of, *see* Maat
in Zoroastrianism, *see* Truth, in Zoroastrianism
cosmogony, 2: 523
see also creation myths
cosmos, *see* universe
Costa Rica, 7: 1838f
costume, clothes, dress, robes, **2: 524–9, 3: 711, 9: 2401**
amuletic, Zoroastrian, **10:** 2772–3
dance and, **2:** 596
Easter and, **3:** 763
magical associations of, **2:** 523f
North American Indians and, **8:** *2008*
nudity and, **2:** 527
priestly, **2:** 528
opus anglicanum, **8:** 2070f
reasons for wearing, **2:** 524ff
in representations of the Crucifixion, **11:** 2907
royal, **2:** 528
see also cosmetics; garter; head-dress; stockings
Cotta, John (writer on witchcraft), **3:** 672, **7:** 1954
Coubertin, Baron Pierre de, modern Olympic Games and, **4:** 1067
Coulomb, Mme., Mme. Blavatsky and, **1:** 293
councils of the church, *see* Chalcedon; Constantinople; Nicaea; Toledo; Trent; Vienna
'Counsellor, the' (Brazil), *see* Conselheiro, Antonio
counter-charm, 2: 529
couvade (birth custom), **1:** 275
in China, **5:** *1412*
coven (of witches), **10:** 2825
in modern witchcraft, **7:** 1866
Coventry:
Lady Godiva and, **4:** 1122
mystery play cycle of, **7:** 1922, 1924
cow, 2: 530–1
in Egypt:
Hathor as, **1:** 128, *309,* **2:** 530, *530,* **3:** 790
Isis and, **6:** 1460
Nut as, **2:** 530
Hera and, **5:** 1271
in India, **2:** 530–1, **5:** *1306*
in Scandinavian mythology, *see* Audumulla
cowrie shell:
as fertility amulet, **2:** 525
in Paleolithic period, **8:** 2244
Cox, Edward, W. Stainton Moses and, **7:** 1790
Cox, Julian (witch), **2:** 350, **10:** 2626
Coyote (trickster), **3:** 730, **4:** 1161, **9:** 2302, **10:** 2881, 2882, 2883
crab, 2: 531
in Tarot card, *see* Moon (Tarot card), crab in
zodiac sign, *see* Cancer
Craik, Henry (of Plymouth Brethren), **3:** 867
Cramignon (Belgian dance), **2:** 414
cramp-rings, 2: 531, 9: 2386, *2387*
Crandon, Margery (medium), **7:** *1789,* **8:** 2277, *2277*
crane (bird), **2: 532**
Celts and, **2:** 444, 532
in China, **2:** 532
dance of, **2:** 532
sun and, **2:** 532
Crawford, Dr W. J., Kathleen Goligher and, **7:** 1790–1
creation:
as expression of will of God, **4:** 1159
six days needed for **10:** 2592
creation myths, 2: 533–8
African, **1:** 82
Ashanti, **1:** 161
Australian, **2:** 333, *538*
Babylonian, *see Enuma elish*
birds in, **1:** 268
Cabalist, *see* Cabala, creation/emanation in
central Asian, **4:** 1053–4
Chinese, **2:** 538, **3:** 781
eggs in, **1:** 267–8, **3:** 781, *783,* **4:** 960
Egyptian, **1:** 229, **2:** 533ff, **3:** 781, **4:** 886f, 1053, **6:** 1706, **7:** 1941
end of the world and, **3:** 815ff
Eskimo, lack of, **3:** 833
Etruscan, **3:** 849
Finnish, **4:** 960
frogs in, **4:** 1053–4
giants in, **4:** 1102, 1103
Ymir, **4:** 1103, **9:** 2484
Gnostic, **10:** 2692
Greek, **1:** 135, **2:** 538
Prometheus and, **4:** *981,* **8:** 2262, *2262,* 2263
see also Deucalion and Pyrrha
Gypsy, **5:** 1195f
Hittite, **5:** 1325
Indian, **2:** 415f, 538, **3:** 781, **6:** 1650, **11:** 2960
Japanese, *see* Shinto *below*
Jewish, **2:** 537f
Lapp, **6:** 1607
Mexican, **1:** 216ff, **2:** *538*
Micronesian, **8:** 2232
North American Indian, **8:** 2010
Algonquin, **1:** 106
Kwakiutl, **8:** 2104
Navaho, **7:** 1899, 1949
trickster in, **10:** 2882
opposites in, **8:** 2069
Peruvian, *see* Viracocha
Polynesian, **8:** 2230
Scandinavian, **4:** 1103, **6:** 1623, **9:** 2484
Shinto, **10:** 2562
sky and earth in:
Egypt, **2:** 534
Greece, **10:** 2601
Polynesia, **2:** 2230
Sumer, **3:** 750
Sumerian, **2:** 535f, **3:** 750, **7:** 1821
trickster in, **10:** 2882
two types of, distinguished, **2:** 523, 533

water in, **1:** 229, **2:** 533, 535, 536
Zoroastrian, **8:** 2048, **11:** 3100, 3107
see also eternal return; first man
creed (Christianity), **2: 538**
Cree Indians, 1: 106, **4:** 1164
Creek Indians, 8: 2011
Creeping to the Cross, *see* Veneration of the Cross
cremation, 2: 539–41
burial and, **2:** 539f
in India, **4:** *972*
see also suttee
crescent 2: 542
Crete, 2: 542–5
Apollo and, **5:** 1171
Atlantis and, **1:** 190
bear in, **8:** 2031–2
birds in, **5:** 1171
bull in, **2:** *363, 365,* 365ff, 544, *545,* **5:** 1171, 1348
  see also Minotaur
burial in, **2:** 544, 572
cave sanctuaries of, **2:** 435, 545
dance in, **2:** 544
dying god in, **5:** 1167
goddess of, **2:** 542, **5:** 1167, 1168f, *1171,* 1395
Greece and, **2:** 545, **5:** 1166f, 1168ff, **11:** 3089ff
Hera and, **2:** 542, **5:** 1271
Hermes and, **5:** 1289
horns in, **5:** 1348, **10:** *2820*
initiation in, **11:** 3090
labyrinth in, *see* Cnossus, labyrinth at
Leto and, **5:** 1171, **11:** 3090
lily in, **6:** 1631
marriage of sun and moon in, **5:** 1271
moon in, **2:** 377, **3:** 613, **5:** 1271
Mycenae and, *see* Greece *above*
snake in, **2:** *544,* 545, **5:** 1171
Zeus born in, **2:** 435, 523, **5:** 1167, **8:** 2032, **9:** 2482, **11:** *3094*
see also Cnossus; Curetes; double axe; Minos
cricket (insect), **6:** 1450
in Borneo, **1:** 312
Crockett, Davy, 8: 2100, **11:** 2919, 2920
crocodile:
in Egypt, *see* Sebek; Taurt
in New Guinea shape-shifting myth, **9:** *2553*
Croiset, Gerard, object reading and, **8:** 2039ff, *2042*
Cromwell, Oliver, 2: 474, **4:** 916
Cronus (Greek god), **2: 546–7, 3:** 751
Golden Age myth and, **2:** 546, **8:** 2132, 2851
Saturn and, **9:** 2479
Uranus and, **1:** 135, **2:** *546,* **11:** 2921
crook, shepherd's, as Christian symbol, **2: 547**
Crookes, Sir William, 2: 547–8
D. D. Home and, **2:** 547, **5:** 1334, 1790
with Mrs Leonard, **8:** *2276*
Spiritualism investigated by, **2:** 547f, **8:** 2274
cross, 2: 549–52
Christian, **2:** 550ff
  of St Andrew, **7:** *1986*
  Bogomils and, **1:** 304
  Celtic, **2:** *437,* 551
  of Jesus, *see* Crucifixion; Judgement of the Cross; stations of the cross; True Cross; Veneration of the Cross
  symbolism of, **10:** 2758
  see also T-shaped cross
and the four directions, as symbol of the world, **4:** *1029,* **10:** 2758
pre-Christian, **2:** 550
prehistoric, **2:** 550
rose and, *see* Rose Cross
Touareg and, **11:** 2863
see also swastika
crossbill (bird), Crown of Thorns and, **10:** 2736
crossbow, in Abbots Bromley horn dance, **5:** 1352
cross-correspondences, 1: 208–9, **2: 553–4, 7:** 1787, **9:** 2275f, **11:** 3030
crossroads, 2: 374, **555**
croton (Greek city), Sybaris and, **9:** 2526
crow, 2: 556–7
Apollo and, **2:** 556
in augury, **1:** 194, **2:** 557
Cu Chulainn and, **2:** 557
owl and, **2:** 557
raven and, **2:** 556f
storms and, **2:** 556
as witch's familiar, **4:** 914
Crow Indians, 11: 2858, 2881
Crowley, Aleister, 2: 558–63, 6: 1687–8, **7:** *1870,* **9:** *2350*
Beelzebub invoked by, **1:** 249
Cabala and, **2:** 387, 522
at Cefalu, **2:** 560f
Choronzon summoned by, **9:** 2399
Christianity and, **2:** 559, 562, **9:** 2477
episcopal status of, **11:** 2988–9
Dion Fortune and, **4:** 1022
Gnostic Catholic Mass of **11:** 2977
God defined by, **6:** 1685
Golden Dawn and, **2:** 559f, **4:** 1132f
as the Great Beast, **3:** 666, **2:** 559
Iao (name), his comments on, **7:** 1944
Liber Samekh ritual of, **5:** 1418–19
magic defined by, **6:** 1682
Mathers and, **2:** 237, 559f, **4:** 1132f
names of his daughter, **7:** 1940
Victor Neuburg and, **9:** 2540–1, **11:** 2869
Papus and, **8:** 2126
Theodor Reuss and, **2:** 560f, **11:** 2988
Sacred Magic of Abra-Melin and, **9:** 2452
Serpent of Wisdom and Tree of Life drawn by, **9:** *2400*
sexual magic and, **2:** 560f, **4:** 1133, **8:** 2239, **9:** 2540–1
Tarot and, **2:** *562–3,* **8:** *2068*
trance and, **11:** 2868–9, 2869
Wagner and, **11:** 2977, 2978–9
weapons, magical, listed by, **9:** 2398
crown, 2: 564, 5: 1241–2
see also coronation; Crown of Thorns; Iron Crown of Lombardy
Crown of Thorns (of Jesus), **5:** *1228,* 1229, **10:** 2736
stigmatization in the form of, **10:** 2697, 2698
crozier, 2: 547
crucifixion (of Jesus), **2:** 552, **5:** 1398–9
by Antonello da Messina, **10:** *2755*
catacombs, not depicted in, **5:** 1398
clothed and unclothed representations of, **11:** 2907
by Dali, **6:** *1525*
magpies in legend of, **6:** 1696
St Paul on, **6:** 1508, **8:** 2151f, **10:** 2693
by Raphael, **2:** *552*
reasons for, **2:** 467
relics of, *see* True Cross
in 16th cent. woodcut, **3:** *744*
skull in representations of, **4:** 980
swallows in legends of, **6:** 1696, **10:** 2736
tree as the cross, **2:** 552
  boxwood, **10:** 2773
  cedar, **8:** 2060, 2116, **10:** 2773
  cypress, **2:** 584, **8:** 2060, 2116
  elder, **3:** 796
  mistletoe, **7:** 1860
  oak, **10:** 2773
  olive, **8:** 2060, 2116
  palm, **8:** 2060, 2116
  pine, **10:** 2773
  rowan, **9:** 2437
  Tree of Life, **2:** 552, **6:** *1707*
by Velazquez, **4:** *988*
see also Crown of Thorns; deposition from the cross; Pontius Pilate; Wandering Jew
crucifixion (of persons other than Jesus):
St Andrew, **7:** *1986*
St Peter, **7:** *1987*
St Uncumber, **11:** 2907
Zealot leaders, **11:** 3077–8
crusade, 2: 564, 11: 2993–5
Islamic, *see jihad*
Knights Templar and, **6:** 1574, 1575
the People's Crusade (1076), **8:** *2193,* **11:** 2993
sword and, **10:** 2748, *2752*
***crux ansata,* 2:** 550
crux commissa, *see* T-shaped cross
crux decussata, *see* X-shaped cross
crux immissa, *see* Latin cross
crux quadrata, *see* Greek cross
crystal-gazing *see* scrying
Cu Chulainn (Celtic hero), **2: 565–6**
cauldron of Mider and, **2:** 428
dog and, **2:** 566
Finn compared with, **4:** 964
Lugh and **6:** 1640
spear of, **2:** 565
as type of the Celtic hero, **2:** 565
cuckoo, 2: 566–7, 11: *2848*
wryneck and, **11:** 3063
Culhwch and Olwen *(Mabinogion),* **4:** 966, 1147f, **6:** 1671, 1672, 1674
Cullenden, Rose (witch), **3:** 756
Culpeper, Nicolas, 5: 1271
on basil, **5:** 1272
on betony, **5:** 1272
on the houseleek, **5:** 1369
cult of the dead, 2: 568–76
in Brazil, **2:** 325f, *327, 569, 571*
in Egypt, **1:** 231, **2:** 570, **4:** *1017*
  see also ankh; Book of the Dead; Coffin Texts; corn-mummies; mummification; Pyramid Texts; ushabti
fairies and **4:** 906
harvest and, **5:** 1215–16
in Papua, **2:** *568*
in Peru, **5:** 1423
in Phoenicia, **10:** 2764
prehistoric, **2:** 569f
in Uganda, cursing and, **2:** 581
Slavs and, **10:** 2612
see also ancestor worship; life after death; sin eater
culture hero:
Australian, **1:** 201f
Brazilian, *see* Maira
Celtic, *see* Gwydion
North American Indian (raven), **2:** 556
  Algonquin, *see* Kuloskap
Prometheus as, **8:** 2262
of the Shilluk (Nyikango), **7:** 2001
Siberian, **2:** 556
Cumae, Sibyl of, **10:** 2574–5
Cumall (Umall; Irish legend), **4:** 965
Cummins, Geraldine, 1: 206, **11:** 3030
cunning men, 3: 754f, 757, **5:** 1203, **11:** 3019
see also Browning, Robert; Murrell, James
cup, 2: 576
see also Grail
Cupid (Amor; Roman god), **1:** 145, **2: 576, 3:** 830f
Apollo and, **3:** 831
Eros identified with, **2:** 576, **3:** 830
Psyche and, **3:** *830,* 831, **8:** 2273, **9:** *2413*
Venus and, **3:** 831
curandera (Mexican wise woman), **7:** 1842
Curé of Ars (St Jean-Marie-Baptiste Vianney), **2: 577–9, 8:** *2223*
spontaneous flight of the host and, **10:** 2702
cures, magical, *see* healing
Curetes (Greek mythology), **2:** 552f, 542, **6:** 1614, **10:** 2842
curfew bell, 1: 252
Curran, Mrs J. H. 1: 206, **8:** 2277
curse, 2: 579–82
cursing well of St Aelian, **2:** 581, **10:** 2685–7
as grave-protection, **2:** 581
in Greece, **2:** 581f
Kikuyu and, **6:** 1563
lead and, **6:** 1613

in magical papyri, **6:** 1690
words sanctified by christianity used as, **8:** 2279
see also Mass, in magic
see also excommunication
Custer, General George A., 11: *2913*
Cuthbert, St, 5: 1242
Cutlerites (Mormon sect), **7:** 1889
Cuzco (Peru), **5:** 1423, 1424, 1425, **10:** 2712
Cybebe (Lydian goddess), **2:** 583
Cybele (goddess), **2: 583**
Agdistis and, **2:** 583
Attis and, **1:** 193, **2:** 583, **3:** 742, **4:** 967, **11:** 2941
bull and, **1:** 230, **3:** 742, **10:** 2805
as the Great Mother, **2:** 583, **3:** 742, **7:** 1896
keys of the earth held by, **11:** 3038
pine tree sacred to, **4:** 967
prostitution and, **8:** 2272
Rhea identified with, **2:** 522
Roman cult of, **2:** 583, **3:** 742, **7:** 1896
cycles of time, 3: 838f, **11:** 2848–50
Aztecs and, **1:** 217
in Eastern thought, **5:** 1323
India, **11:** 2848
Etruscans and, **3:** 849
in Greece, **11:** 2850
see also seasons
cyclopean buildings, giants and, **4:** 1103
Cyclops, 2: 584, 4: 886
cylicomancy (method of scrying), **9:** 2506
Cynon *(Mabinogion),* **5:** 1350–1, **11:** 3029
Cynopolis (Egypt), dogs and, **3:** 664
cypress, 2: 584
cross of Jesus and, **2:** 584, **8:** 2060, 2116, **10:** 2773
as symbol of Ohrmazd, **11:** 2875
Cyprus, Aphrodite and, **1:** 135, 137
Cyrene (Libya), faceless goddess from, **4:** 896
Cyrus (king of Persia), **6:** 1644

D

Da (Dahomean spirit), *see* Dan
Dactyls, Idaean (Greek mythology), **2:** 523
Dada (art movement), **1:** 147ff
Dadd, Richard, fairy paintings by, **4:** *900,* **9:** *2296*
Daedalus (Greek mythology), **2:** 365, **5:** 1271
see also Icarus, fall of
Dagan (Phoenician god), *see* Dagon
dagger, exorcizing, Tibetan, **11:** *3021*
Dagon (Dagan: Phoenician god):
as corn god, **8:** 2182, **10:** 2763
fish and, **4:** 985, **5;** 1242
Dahn, Felix (historical novelist), **7:** 1964
Dahomey, 2: 584–6, 11: *2972*
ancestor worship in, **2:** 584f
divination in, **2:** 586
drumming to summon spirits in, **8:** *2077*
fetishes in, **4:** *939*
human sacrifice in, **2:** 576
lizard myth of, **6:** 1638
possession, spirit, in, **2:** 584
serpent deity of (Dan), **2:** 586, **9:** 2529
Voodoo and, **2:** 584, **10:** 2882–3
yam cultivation in, magic and, **3:** *752*
Dakota Indians, 4: 1164, **8:** 2010
Dalai Lama, 6: 1589, 1590, *1590,* **9:** *2350,* **10:** 2842, 2843
as incarnation of Avalokitesvara, **9:** 2348
meaning of 'Dalai', **10:** 2843
Dali, Salvador, 1: 147, **6:** *1598–9*
Dalton, Michael, on the Devil's mark, **8:** 2246
Damascius (Neoplatonist), **7:** 1968
Damballa (Voodoo), **9:** 2529
Dame Habonde (goddess of witches), **3:** 853
Damian and Cosmas, saints, miracle of, **7:** *1853*
Damocles, sword of, **10:** 2744
Dan (Da; Dahomean spirit), **2:** 586, **9:** 2529
Danal, Zeus and, **10:** *2604,* **11:** *2954*
Dana o'Shee (Irish fairies), **4:** 901, 904
dance, 2: 587–97
in Africa, **1:** *78, 79,* **2:** *588, 592, 593, 594*
Congo, **2:** *505, 508*
Nigeria, **2:** *587*
Zulu, **11:** *3104, 3105, 3106*
agriculture and, **2:** 589f
animal dances, **2:** 589, **5:** *1345*
see also Abbots Bromley
Australian aborigines and, **1:** *200,* **5:** *1409,* **11:** 2860
in Bali, **4:** 1089
in Brazil, **2:** *327*
chain and circle dances, *see* chain dances; ring dances
costume in, **2:** 596
crane dances, **2:** 532
in Crete, **2:** 544
dervishes and, *see* Mevlevi dervishes
fertility and, **5:** 1352
see also Morris dances
gesture in, **2:** 592f
Hindu, **4:** 1089
in greece, **2:** 412f
Dionysus and, **3:** 647ff
healing dances, **2:** 588f, 597
horn dance, *see* Abbots Bromley
as hunting magic, **2:** 589
in India, **4:** *957,* 1089
in initiation rites, **2:** 588, *588*
in Japan (Tensho Kotai Jingu-kyo sect), **1:** 175
madness and, **6:** 1679
see also dancing mania
masks in, **2:** 596, **7:** 1756ff
maze and, **7:** 1775
Muses and, **7:** 1905
music and, **2:** 595f, **7:** 1911
of North American Indians:
Algonquin, **1:** 105, *107*
Great Plains Indians, **4:** 1162f
Iroquois, **2:** 589, 591, **6:** 1457f
Pueblo, **9:** *2298–9,* 2300–2, 2303, 2304
see also Ghost Dance
pattern in, **2:** 592
Shakers and, **9:** 2544
shamans and, **1:** 105
Shiva and, **10:** 2572
stilt dance, Nigerian, **2:** *587*
Sufis and, **10:** 2714
see also Mevlevi dervishes
war dance, African, **2:** *593, 594,* **11:** *3105*
witches and, **2:** 414, **6:** 1476, **9:** 2446–7
see also Corybantes; dance of death; Helston furry dance; Morris dances
dance of death, 2: 598–9, 4: *1128*
dancing dervishes, *see* Mevlevi dervishes
dancing mania, 2: 599–600, 6: 1679
hysteria and, **2:** 600
St John the Baptist and, **2:** 599f
release from tension in conversion compared **2:** 515
tarantula and, **2:** 600
St Vitus and, **2:** 600
danewort (elder tree) **3:** 796
Daniel (Old Testament prophet), **2: 600–2**
angels and, **2:** 602, **5:** 1187
beast of Revelation and, **4:** 1157
Dante Alighieri, 2: 602–4, 9: 2307
Dantza Khorda (Basque dance), **2:** 414
Dantza Prima (Spanish dance), **2:** 414
Danu (Anu; Celtic goddess), **2:** 443
Daphne (nymph), Apollo and, **3:** 831, **6:** 1610, *1610*
Darazi (Druze), **3:** 727, 728
Darby, John Nelson (founder of the Exclusive Brethren), **3:** 867f, *868*
Dardanus (Greek mythology), **4:** 995
ad-Darqawi, Arabi (Sufi), **10:** 2716
Darius the Great (Persian king), **11.** 3103
darkness:
cap of (Greek myth), **8:** 2209
evil and, **6:** 1622ff
invisibility and, **6:** 1453
see also black; night
Darling, Thomas (bewitched boy), **5:** 1380
darshan (Hinduism), **6:** 1697
Darwin, Charles, Sir William Crookes and, **2:** 574f
Das, Amar (Sikh leader), **10:** 2577
Das Ram (Sikh leader), **10:** 2577
Dashwood, Sir Francis, 7: 1794, *1795*
Davenport, James (revivalist), **3:** 828
Davenports (mediums), **3: 605–6**
Davey, S. J., 8: 2275
David, King, tomb of, at Jerusalem, **8:** *2194*
David, Father Pierre, nude nuns and, **8:** 2019
Davies, William, grave of, **1:** 294
Davis, Andrew Jackson (seer), **7:** 1817
Davy Jones, 3: 606
Dayananda (Hindu reformer), **5:** 1316
Day of Judgement (Tarot card), *see* Judgement
days, 3: 606–7
finger-nails cut on various, **4:** 957
planets associated with, **2:** 522, **3:** 606
see also Friday; Sunday; Thursday; Tuesday
Dazhbog (Slav god), **10:** 2608
dead, cult of the, *see* cult of the dead
deadly nightshade, 8: *2202,* 2203–4
deadman's fingers (plant), *see* foxglove
Dead Sea Scrolls, 3: 608–11
on the angel of darkness, **3:** 625
Christianity and, **3:** 611, 767
on the baptism of Jesus, **1: 230**
the Bible and, **3:** 611
Essenes and, **3:** 611
Judaism and, **3:** 609ff
death, 3: 612–17
in Africa, **1:** 79, **3:** 612f, 614f
Bushmen, **2:** 378
in Australia, **1:** 204, **2:** 576, **3:** 614, 615
in Buddhism, **3:** 616
in children's games, **2:** 449f
Christianity and, **3:** 617, 859f
dove and, **3:** 682
in Egypt, **3:** 615, **6:** 1704–6
Eskimos and, **3:** 835ff
in Greece, **3:** 617, **6:** 1706
Hebrews and, **6:** 1706
in Hinduism, **3:** 616
house and, **5:** 1365f
initiation and, **5:** 1437, 1443
maze and, **7:** 1774f
in Mesopotamia, **3:** 616, **6:** 1706
night and, **7:** 1999
North American Indians and, **3:** 614, 615
in Oceania, **3:** 613, 615, **7:** 1799
origin of, **2:** 337, **3:** 612ff, 858ff
African myths, **3:** 612ff
Melanesian myths, **7:** 1799
moon and, **2:** 377, **3:** 613
Polynesian myth, **3:** 613
personified, **3:** 615–17
by Breughel, **2:** *340,* 344
as fourth horseman of the Apocalypse, **3:** *818–19,* **5:** 1353, **9:** *2377, 2379*
as skeleton, **3:** *612,* 617
see also dance of death
rose and, **9:** 2422
salt and, **9:** 2475
in South America, **3:** 612f
Stoicism and, **3:** 858
white and **11:** 3018
will-o-the-wisp as warning of, **11:** 3031
willow and, **11:** 3031–2
in Zoroastrianism, **3:** 616, **8:** 2048
see also burial; cult of the dead; dying god; judgement of the dead; immortality; life after death
Death (Tarot card), **3:** *660,* **8:** 2147, **10:** 2793, *2793,* 2825
death masks, 7: 1760–3
death wish (Freudian term), **4:** 1049

Decker, Frank (medium), **9:** *2277*
Dee, John, 3: 617–20
Golden Dawn and **4:** 1134
scrying by, **3:** 618f, **7:** 1858, **9:** 2506
deer (animal), *see* stag
Defoe, Daniel, on the plague, 1: 64
Deianeira (wife of Hercules), **5:** 1280, **9:** *2537*
Deir-el-Bahari (Egypt), *see* Hatshepsut, temple of
deism, 3: 620, 7: 1849
***déjà vu,* 9:** 2350
Dekanawida (Iroquois law-giver), **6:** 1455f
Delaage, Henri, 8: 2126
De la Warr, George, 9: 2332f
Deleuze, J. P. F., 6: 1693
Delhi (India), as the centre of the earth, **7:** 1952
Delort, Catherine (witch), **4:** 1043, 1118
de Paradiso, Venerable Domenica, 10: 2701
Delphi (Greece), **3: 620**
Athene's temple at, **1:** *186*
Dionysus cult at (*oreibasia*), **3:** 638f
oracle of Apollo at, **1:** 139, **3:** 620, **8:** 2076
  as the centre of the earth, **7:** 1952
  Christianity and, **8:** 2078
  chthonian aspects of, **3:** 751
  colonizers and, **1:** 140
  Dodona and, **8:** 2077
  foundation of, **1:** 139, **3:** 670
  hawk and, **5:** 1227
  laurel and, **6:** 1610, **11:** 2867
  omphalos at, **1:** 139, **7:** 1952
  priestess of (Pythia), **1:** 139, **9:** 2529
  python and, **1:** 139, **9:** 2529
  rock of the sibyl at, **8:** *2073*
  trance and, **11:** 2867
Delphic Amphictyony, 11: 2996
Del Rio, Martin, on the Devil's mark, **8:** 2246
Deluge, *see* Flood
Demandolx de la Palud, Madeleine de (possessed nun), **1:** 90ff, 170, **9:** 2446
Demeter (Greek goddess), **3: 621–2, 5:** *1170*
Carthaginian cult of, **8:** 2184
Ceres identified with, **3:** 621, **9:** 2412
Cretan origin of, **2:** 542, **5:** 1171
Demophon and, **3:** 805
as earth goddess, **3:** 751
as mother goddess, **7:** 1896
mysteries of, **3:** 621
  see also Eleusis
Persephone and, **3:** 621, 804, **8:** 2168, 2170, **11:** 2941–2
pine tree and, **4:** 968
Plutus and, **3:** 621
Triptolemus and, **3:** 621, *804, 806,* **7:** 1909
Demetria (plant), *see* vervain
demiurge, 3: 622
in Gnosticism, **3:** 622, 730, **4:** 1116, 1117
Manichean, **6:** 1721
demons, 3: 622, 861–6
Baal as, **1:** 223
Francis Barrett and, **1:** *167, 170,* 230
bodily orifices penetrated by, **10:** 2625
casting out, *see* exorcism
at Chartres cathedral, **11:** *2906*
disease and, **8:** 2280ff
of the four directions, **3:** 640, 864
Krishna and, **6:** 1580, *1581*
sexual, *see* incubus and succubus
summoning, *see* ritual magic
see also Abracax; Amduscias; Andras; Asmodeus; Astaroth; Beelzebub; Belial; Belphegor; Hind Etin; Lilith; Mephistopheles
also asafoetida; evocation; ghoul; imp
Demophon, Demeter and, **3:** 805
Denck, Hans (mystic), **6:** 1624f
Dendrites (ascetics), **6:** 1678
Dengyo Daishi (Saicho; Japanese priest), **6:** 1489
Denis, St, 3: 633, *633*
Denis, Maurice (artist), **1:** 146
deosil (clockwise), **2:** 487
de Quincey, Thomas, 3: 713, **5:** 1416
Deren, Maya, Voodoo and, **11:** 2868
dervish, 3: 622–4
dancing dervishes, *see* Mevlevi dervishes
hemp used by, **7:** *1932*
howling dervishes, *see* Rufai dervishes
origin of the word, **3:** 622, **10:** 2714
river crossed on prayer mat by a, **9:** *2463*
Desana (South American tribe), **5:** 1374
Desbarolles, Adolphe (palmist), **6:** 1619
Descartes, René, 7: 1849
desert, wilderness, symbolism of, **6:** 1597, *1601*
dessounin (Voodoo rite), **11:** 3096
destiny, *see* Fate; predestination
determinism, *see* Fate; predestination
Deucalion and Pyrrha (Greek mythology), **4:** 995, **8:** 2262, **10:** *2705*
Deuson, Edmund van, (statistics in astrology), **1:** 182
Devi, Shanti, 9: 2350
Devi, Shrimati Rukmini, 10: 2815, *2816*
Device, Alizon (witch), **6:** 1592f
Device, Elizabeth (witch), **4:** 915, **6:** 1592ff
Device, James (witch), **6:** 1592, 1593
Device, Jennet (witch), **6:** 1592, 1593
Devil, the (Lucifer; Satan; Christianity and Judaism), **3: 625–9,** 862
Belial and, **3:** 627
defined at Council of Toledo, **5:** 1348
as dragon, **3:** 628f, *682,* 691, *820*
not a dualist concept, **3:** 733
at Fairford, in stained glass, **9:** *2342*
Levi and, **1:** 229, *229*
Lucifer, **3:** 677f, **6:** 1662
Milton on, **7:** 1846ff
in the New Testament, **9:** 2477
in the Ozarks, **8:** 2100
pact with, *see* pact, Satanic
as Satan, **3:** 627f
two and, **11:** 2906
Wild Hunt led by, **11:** 3022
witches and, **1:** 278, **3:** 629, 852ff, *856,* **9:** 2477
  animal forms of, **3:** 629, 853, *856,* **4:** 1047, 1118, *1119*
  Basque witches, **1:** 233, 234, **9:** 2446
  French witches, **4:** 1043, 1046f, 1118
  Gowdie and, **5:** 1144
  phallus, artificial, of, **5:** 1144, **9:** 2447
  Swedish witches, **10:** 2742f
  see also Devil's Mark; familiars; pact; Satanic, witches and; pricking of witches; sabbath
wolf and, **11:** 3049
see also Satanism
Devil (Tarot card), **3:** *627,* 886, **4:** 939, **8:** 2147, **10:** *2792,* 2793
Devil's Bane (plant), *see* St John's wort
Devil's-bit scabious, 5: 1274
devil's coach-horse beetle, 6: 1447
Devil's mark:
Grandier and, **4:** 1155
witches and, **3:** 853, 854, **4:** 1044
  see also pricking of witches
Devil-worship, *see* Satanism
dew, on May Day, **7:** 1774
de Wohl, Louis (astrologer), **7:** 1946, *1947*
dharana (concentration; yoga), **7:** 1777, **11:** 2935, 3074
***dharma,* 5:** 1307
in Buddhism, **2:** 354, 355, 357, 358
in Hinduism, **5:** 1307, 1315, **11:** 2934
in Jainism, **6:** 1481f
symbol of, in flag of India, **2:** 360
Dhat Himyam (Shams; Ethiopian sun god), **3:** 842
dhyana (meditation; yoga), **7:** 1777, **11:** 2935, 3074
origin of the word 'Zen', **11:** 3080
dhyana yoga, 11: 3070–1
diamond, 6: *1512,* 1513–14
in alchemy, **6:** 1514
Saturn associated with black diamond, **6:** 1512
sun associated with yellow diamond, **6:** 1511
in Tantric Buddhism, **6:** 1513
diamond necklace (of Marie Antoinette), affair of the, **2:** 389, **6:** 1514
Diana (goddess of witches), **1:** 237, **3:** 632, **6:** 1476
Basque counterpart, 'la Dama', **1:** 233, 237
in Canon Episcopi, **3:** 632, 853
Margaret Murray and, **3:** 632
Roman Diana and, **3:** 632
Diana (Roman goddess), **3: 630–2**
Artemis identified with, **1:** 151, **3:** 630
by Cranach the Elder, **3:** *631*
at Ephesus, **3:** 632
moon and, **3:** 630, 632, *801*
sacred grove of, at Nemi, **3:** 630, **7:** 1964, **11:** 2942
water and, **3:** *801*
see also Diana (goddess of witches)
Diarmait mac Duinn (Irish legend), **4:** 964
Diarmuid and Grania (Irish legend), rowan and, **9:** 2437
Dibble, Jennet (witch), **4:** 915
Dicaearchus (Greek philosopher), **11:** 2851
dice:
divination by, **3:** 659, **4:** 1064, **6:** 1647
  Hittites, **5:** 1325
fall of, mental influence on, *see* psychokinesis, dice and
gambling with, **4:** *1061,* 1064
Dickens, Charles, Christmas and, **2:** 481
Didache (Christian text), **7:** 1985
Didyma, temple of Apollo at, **8:** *2074–5,* 2077, 2078
Digambaras (Jain sect), **6:** 1481
Digby, Sir Kenelm, sympathetic powder of, **1:** 296
Diggers (Puritan group), **9:** 2520–1
Diktynna (Cretan deity), **2:** 542
Dilbat (Venus; Mesopotamia), **6:** 1460
dill (herb), **4:** 1274
Dindyma (Dindymum), Mount (now Gunusu Dagh), Cybele and, **2:** 583
Dinka (Nilotic people), **7:** 2000ff
Diomedes (Greek hero), Aphrodite and, **1:** 136
Dione (Greek goddess), Aphrodite and, **1:** 136
Dionysia (Greek festival), **11:** 3035
Dionysius of Alexandria, 9: 2381
Dionysius the Areopagite, 3: 633–4
Dionysus (Greek god), **3: 634–9, 5:** 742f, **5:** 1168, **7:** *1928,* **8:** 2079, **10:** *2568, 2754*
animals and, **1:** 130
  bull, **5:** 1348
  dolphin, **3:** 670
  goat, **4:** 1120, *1121*
Apollo and, **3:** 635, 638
Athens and, **3:** 638
Bacchus identified with, **1:** 223, **9:** 2482
birth of, **3:** 635, 650
dance and, **3:** 637ff
dismemberment of, **3:** 635, 742, **8:** 2085
drama and, **3:** 638, 696f, **4:** 2482
as dying god, **3:** 742
Eleusis and, **3:** 742f
flagellation in cult of, **3:** *636, 989*
ivy and, **5:** 1329, **10:** 2837
Lycurgus and, **3:** 635
mushroom and, **7:** 1908
Mysteries of, **7:** 1925f, **8:** 2086
  see also Villa of the Mysteries (Pompeii)
nymphs and, **8:** 2032
Olympian gods contrasted with, **3:** 636–7
Orphism and, **3:** 859, **8:** 2085f
Osiris identified with, **8:** 2086
Pan and, **8:** *2124*
pine tree and, **4:** 968, **10:** 2837
at Pompeii, cult of, *see* Villa of the

Mysteries
satyrs and, **9:** 2481f
Silenus and, **3:** 635, **7:** *1926–7,* **10:** 2577
spring festival of, **10:** 2678
Thebes and, **3:** 635f
Titans and, **3:** 742, 859, **8:** 2085
underworld and, **8:** 2168
wine and, **3:** *634,* 635
winter festivals and, **11:** 3035
Zeus and, **3:** 635, 650, 859, **5:** 1167, 1168, 1329
see also maenads
diopet (from Ephesus), **3:** 632, **7:** 1836
Dioscorides, 5: 1271, **6:** 1658
Dioscuri (Castor and Polydeuces (or Pollux); greek mythology), **3: 639, 11:** *2902,* 2093
daughters of Leucippus and, **5:** *1165*
St Elmo's Fire and, **11:** 2904
Gemini and, **4:** 1075, **11:** 2903, 2904
hatched from egg laid by Leda, **3:** *782*
Theseus and, **10:** 2820
dirae (omens), **1:** 194
directions, 3: 640
cross and, as symbol of the world, **4:** *1029,* **10:** 2758
demons associated with, **3:** 640, 864
jade and, in china, **6:** 1480
mountains and, **7:** 1899
pentagram and, **8:** 2158
see also east; left; widdershins
Dis (Roman god), *see* Pluto
disc, *see* disk
disease, illness, sickness, **3: 641–9**
African view of, **3:** 648
Ethiopia, **3:** 845, 846
Zulus, **11:** 3105
Australian aborigines and, **1:** 204
demons and, **8:** 2280f
dowsing and, **3:** 683
Eskimo view of, **3:** 835
forty and, **4:** 1024
four humours theory and, **3:** 647
magic as cause of, **3:** 641f
palmistry and, **8:** 2118f
treatment of, medicine, *see* healing
see also epilepsy; leprosy
also poisoning
disk (disc; sun-symbol), **3: 650**
in Egypt:
winged, **5:** 1395, **11:** 3014, *3034*
see also Aten
in Mesopotamia, winged, **5:** *1398*
Stone Age, **11:** 3014
see also wheel, as symbol of the sun
dismemberment, 3: 650
of Dionysus, **3:** 635, 742, **8:** 2085
of Lycurgus, **3:** 635
of Pentheus, **3:** 636
of shamans, **3:** 650, 714, **9:** 2546f
of Zagreus, **3:** 650
dispensation, 3: 650
Dispensationalism, 3: 867
displacement (psychical research), **3: 650,** *876–7,* **8:** 2278
distillation (alchemy), **3: 650**
Distinctionists (Buddhist sect), *see* Vibhajyavadins
diver (loon; bird), **3: 651, 10:** 2837
divination, 3: 652–60, 8: 2214–15
on All Hallows' Eve, **3:** 672, **6:** 1660
in Babylonia, *see* Mesopotamia *below*
in the Bible, **3:** 657
in Dahomey, **2:** 586
Etruscans and, *see* Etruscans, divination and
Hittites and, **5:** 1325
Bulwer Lytton and, **6:** 1670
in Mesopotamia, **3:** *658,* **6:** 1637, **7:** 1826, **8:** *2064*
methods of, **3:** 658
arrows, **4:** 1060
ashes, **1:** 166, **5:** 1255
axe, **1:** 210
birds, *see* augury
books, *see* bibliomancy
bones:
Bushmen, **2:** 378
Congo, **2:** 509
of sheep, **9:** 2559–60
chance happenings, *see* cledonomancy
comets, **1:** 194
corpses, *see* necromancy
crystal-gazing, *see* scrying
the dead, spirits of, *see* necromancy
dice, **3:** 659, **4:** 1064, **6:** 1647
dreams, *see* oneiromancy
drums, **3:** 725
earth, pebbles, etc., *see* geomancy
eggs, **3:** 783
entrails, *see* haruspicy
fingernails, **4:** 957
forehead, **3:** *655,* **8:** *2188*
ghosts, *see* necromancy
hand, *see* palmistry
hare, **5:** 1210
hazel nuts, **5:** 1230
horses, **5:** 1357
I Ching, **5:** 1389, 1390f
ivy, **5:** 1330
liver, *see* liver, divination by
lots, *see* lots, divination by
mirror, **7:** 1858, **9:** 2506
moles on the body, **3:** *654*
shadow, **9:** 2543–4
smoke, *see* capnomancy; empyromancy
sortilege, *see* lots, divination by
stars (and planets), *see* astrology
thunder and lightning (augury), **1:** 194, **3:** 848
wedding rings, **9:** 2388–9
willow, **11:** 3032
Navaho Indians and, **7:** 1952
Phoenicians and, **10:** 2763
prophecy distinguished from, **8:** 2266, 2268
Romans and:
augury, **1:** 194, **3:** 657f, 747, **6:** 1637, **8:** 2065, **9:** 2417, 2418
Cicero on, **3:** 657
haruspicy, **6:** 1637, **9:** 2418
sortes (lots), **6:** 1647, **9:** 2418–19
Scandinavian, *see seidr*
see also fate; fortune-telling; omens; oracles
Divine Life Society, 10: 2591
Divine Principles (millenarian sect), **3: 661–3**
see also Moonies
divine right (of kings), **3: 663, 6:** 1566
Divine Science (philosophical group), **7:** 1994
Dixon, Jeane, 8: 2269
Docetists (Christian heretics), **5:** 1282
Dodona (oracle of Zeus at), **1:** 248, **3: 663, 8:** 2076–7
destruction of, **8:** 2077, 2078
founded by a dove, **3:** 680–1
laurel and, **6:** 1610
oak tree and, **3:** 663, **8:** 2033, 2076–7
dog, 3: 664–9
in the Bible, **3: 664**
corn and, **3:** 669
of Culann, slain by Cu Chulainn, **2:** 566
in Egypt, **3:** 664
in Eskimo myth, **3:** 833
ghosts of, **4:** 1097
Gypsies and, **5:** 1198
Hebrews and, **3:** 664
Hecate and, **5:** 1257
Hinduism and, **3:** 667f
Islam and, **3:** 664f
mandrake and, **6:** *1717,* 1718, *1718, 1719*
in Mesopotamia, **3:** 664
as omen, **8:** 2064
Parsees and, **8:** 2140
in Persia, **3:** 666f
of Sango (Nigerian god), **5:** *1371*
in Scandinavian mythology, *see* Garm
three-headed:
Greek, *see* Cerberus
Parthian, **8:** *2143,* 2144
two-headed, **1:** *274*
as witches' familiar, **3:** 755, *757,* **4:** 915, **6:** 1592, 1593
see also Wild Hunt
dogma, 3: 669
Dogon (Sudanese tribe), **3: 669**
dualism among, **3:** 731
masks and, **7:** 1756
dog star, *see* Sirius
Dol, St, 10: 3061
dolls, 3: 670
Kachinas, of Pueblo Indians, **8:** *2012, 2303*
in magic, *see* image magic
see also Heraut, Henri
dolmen (chamber tomb; prehistoric burial), **2:** *372,* **8:** *2244,* **10:** *2706*
dolphin (animal), **3: 670–1**
Dolphin (constellation), origin of, **3:** 670
Dome of the Rock (Jerusalem), **6:** 1502, *1502*
Dominic, St (Dominic Guzman), **2:** *423,* 423–4
Dominican Order (friars), founded by Dominic Guzman, **2:** 424
Domovoy (Slav spirit), **10:** *2608,* 2612
Donar (Germanic god), **4:** 1086
Don Juan, 3: 671
Donn of Cualnge (Irish mythical brown bull), **5:** 1351
Doom of the Gods (Scandinavian mythology), *see* Ragnarok
Dooms, Doom paintings (Last Judgement), **6:** 1546
Virgin Mary in, **7:** 1750
see also Last Judgement
door, doorway, *see* threshold
Doppelgänger, 3: 672
Dorn, Gerhard (alchemist), **3:** 809
Dornheim, Prince-Bishop Gottfried von (the 'Witch Bishop'), **1:** 227, 228
double, 3: 672–8
animal, in New Guinea, **5:** 1374
Finnish beliefs concerning, **4:** 959
various names for, **3:** 672
in occultism, *see* astral body
in out-of-the-body experiences, **8:** 2093ff
shadow and, **3:** 672
soul and, **3:** 672, **10:** 2636
in witch trials (spectral evidence), **3:** 672, **11:** 3043
see also ka; phantasms of the living
double axe (Cretan; *Labrys*), **1:** 210, **2:** 545
Dougga (North Africa):
Dionysus mosaic from, **10:** *2568*
Odysseus and the Sirens (mosaic) from **11:** *2950*
Roman temple at, **9:** *2357*
Doukhobors (religious sect), **2:** *501,* 502, **3: 679–80**
dove (pigeon), **3: 680–2**
in alchemical symbolism, **8:** 2178
Aphrodite and, **2:** 522, **3:** 680
Astarte and, **1:** 170
in Babylonian flood legend, **4:** 993
in Christian symbolism, **3:** 682
as the Holy Ghost, **1:** 268, **2:** 334, **3:** 682
in Cypriot mural, **6:** *1505*
by El Greco, **2:** *336,* **3:** *824*
in English 13th cent. MS, **3:** *682*
in Ethiopian MS, **2:** *471*
in French 15th cent. Book of Hours, **10:** *2652*
by Giotto, **7:** *1989*
death and, **3:** 682
Dodona founded by **3:** 680–1
Jesus (alpha and omega) as **4:** 1074
Noah and, **3:** *680,* 682, 992
Venus and, **3:** *681,* 682
dowsing, 3: 683–6
extra-sensory perception and, **3:** 686, 876
hazel used in **3:** 683, **5:** 1229, *1230*
illness and, **3:** 683
radiesthesia and, **3:** 686
Doyle, Arthur Conan, 3: 686–8, 10: 2659

Doyle, Richard (artist):
fairy paintings by, **4:** *897, 902, 906,* **7:** *1906–7,* **11:** *2871*
Jack the Giant-Killer, **4:** *1104*
Dracula (vampire), **3: 688, 11:** 2922, 2923f, 2924
film, **4:** *944,* 946, **11:** *2926, 2927*
dragon, 3: 689–95, 4: 972
in alchemy, **3:** *693*
in Babylonia, *see* Musrussu dragon; Tiamat
Beowulf and, **1:** 253
in China, **3:** *692,* 693ff, **8:** 2188
the Devil as, **3:** 628f, *682,* 691, *820*
in Egypt, **3:** 690
eye of, **3:** 690
in Greek mythology, **3:** 693
in Hindu mythology, **3:** 691
in Hittite mythology, **5:** 1325
in Iranian mythology, **3:** 691
in Japan, **3:** 695
Midsummer and, **7:** 1845
Perseus and, **3:** 693
serpent and, **3:** 690
St Simeon Stylites and, **9:** 2471
sun gods and, **3:** 690
from Sutton Hoo, **1:** 253
treasure and, **3:** 693
Tristan and, **11:** 2886
water and, **3:** 690
wings of, **11:** 3033
Yahweh and, **3:** 691
see also George, St; Taresque; wyvern
dragonfly, 6: *1446,* 1450
Drake, Sir Francis, 10: 2571
his drum, **3:** *725,* **10:** 2571
Wild Hunt associated with, **11:** 3022
drakos (modern Greek folklore), **3:** 693
drama, 3: 696–9
comedy, origin of, **3:** 697
earliest known play, **3:** 696
Greek, **3:** 696f, **7:** 1764, **9:** 2482, **10:** 2678
Dionysus and, **3:** 638, 696f, **9:** 2482
imitative magic and origin of, **3:** 696
in Japan, **6:** *1488*
Saturnalia and, **3:** 697
spring and, **10:** 2678
tragedy, origin of, **3:** 697
see also folkplays; mummers; mystery plays; Plough Monday
Draupnir (ring of Odin), **3: 699,** 737
Dravidians, 3: 699, 5: 1309
Dreaming (Australian aborigines' myth), *see* Dreamtime
Dream of Macsen Wledig *(Mabinogion),* **6:** 1672
Dream of Rhonabwy *(Mabinogion),* **6:** 1672, 1674
Dream of the Rood (Anglo-Saxon poem), **2:** 551
dreams, 3: 701–11
in the Bible, **3:** 705
in Canaan, **3:** 704
Coleridge on, **2:** 494
divination by, *see* oneiromancy
extra-sensory perception and, **3:** 875, **8:** 2278, **10:** 2666, 2669–70, 2672, 2673–5, 2675f
Greeks and, **3:** 705
see also healing gods, Graeco-Roman
Hebrews and, **3:** 704f
healing by, *see* healing gods
in Mesopotamia, **3:** 704, **7:** 1826
modern study of, **3:** 706ff
out-of-the-body experiences and, **8:** 2095
astral body and, **1:** 173
in Polynesia, **8:** 2231
psychology of, **3:** 708ff
Freud and, **3:** 708ff, **4:** 1049
Romans and, **3:** 705
see also healing gods, Graeco-Roman
visions compared with, **11:** 2962
Wundt on, **6:** 1679
see also nightmare
Dreamtime (Dreaming; Australian aborigines' myth), **1:** 198ff, **11:** 2859f
dress, *see* costume
dried bodies (other than Egyptian mummies):
of North American Indians, **8:** *2009*
at Palermo, **7:** *1901*
in Peru, **5:** 1423
drink, *see* food and drink
Drown, Dr Ruth, 9: 2332, 2333
drugs, 3: 711–16
in Mexico, **3:** 711, **7:** 1842
North American Indians and, **8:** 2010
see also peyote cults
shamanism and, **3:** 712f, 714
trance and, **11:** 2867
yoga powers compared with drug-state experience, **11:** 3076
see also soma; tobacco
Druids, 3: 717–23
Celtic priests, **2:** 439, 440, 441f, **3:** 719ff
astronomical knowledge of, **3:** 720
Stonehenge and, **3:** 722, **10:** 2703
Blake and, **3:** 721
human sacrifice and, **2:** 441f, **3:** 720
in Ireland, **3:** 719
life after death, beliefs concerning, **3:** 720
mistletoe and, **3:** 719, **7:** 1859f
oak and, **2:** 441, **3:** 719
'snake's egg' badge of, **2:** 520
standing stones and, **3:** *718*
Stonehenge, **3:** 721f
modern, **3:** 719, *720,* 721, 722f
Blake and, **3:** 722
in Brittany, **3:** 723
colours of robes of, **2:** *494*
Glastonbury and, **3:** 722
in London, **3:** 721, 722, 723
midsummer (summer solstice) and, **3:** 722, **7:** *1845*
oak and, **8:** *2034*
Stonehenge and, **3:** *717,* 721, 722, **7:** *1845,* **8:** *2034,* 2703
drum, 3: 724–6, 7: 1911
in Africa, **3:** 725, **7:** 1911
Ashanti, **3:** 725f
Buganda, **3:** 725
Dahomey, **8:** *2077*
Nigeria, **3:** *724*
divination by, **3:** 725
Drake's **3:** *725,* **10:** 2571
in Ethiopian wall painting, **7:** *1912*
in initiation rites, **3:** 725
in Lapland, **6:** 1605, *1607,* 1608
in New Guinea, **3:** 725
shamans and, **3:** 725, 837, **4:** *962, 963,* **6:** 1605, *1607,* **9:** 2548, *2548*
Tibetan, **3:** 726
see also Drummer of Tedworth; Drumming Well
Drummer of Tedworth (poltergeist), **3: 726, 8:** 2224
Drumming Well (Oundle), **10:** 2684
Drummond, Henry (Irvingite), **6:** 1459
Drusiana, Callimachus and (Christian legend), **7:** 1989–92
Druzes (Moslem sect), **3: 727–8**
dryads (Greek tree spirits), **3: 728, 8:** 2031
Dryope (mother of Pan), **8:** 2124–5
dualism, 3: 729–33, 859
asceticism and, **9:** 2524
Bogomils and, **2:** 304, **3:** 730
Cathars and, **2:** 422f
in China, **3:** 731, 859
Christianity and, **3:** 733, 859
Dogon and, **3:** 731
ethical, **3:** 733
Gnosticism and, **3:** 730, 731, 859, **4:** 1116
in Greece, **3:** 731, 859, **6:** 1708
in India, **3:** 731, 859
Manicheans and, **3:** 730, 859, **6:** 1721
Parsees repudiate, **8:** 2138
Yezidi and, **3:** 730
in Zoroastrianism, **1:** 86ff, **3:** 729–30, 859, **11:** 3099–3100, 3100, 3103, 3107
Dubus, Edouard, 1: 241
Duchamp, Marcel, 1: 148, 151, **10:** *2770*
Duguid, David (automatic painter), **1:** 206
Duke, Alice (witch), **10:** 2626
Duke University, 3: 878ff, *881,* **8:** 2278, 2286ff
du Mont, Colette (witch), **2:** 447
Dumuzi (Mesopotamian god), *see* Tammuz
Duncan, Gilly (witch), **8:** 2013, 2014
Duncan, Helen (medium), **10:** 2660
Dundhi, King, horse of (Indian mythology), **5:** *1356*
dung-beetle, *see* scarab
Dunkers (Christian sect), **3: 733**
Dunmow Flitch, 3: 733, 7: 1740
Dunne, J. W. 8: 2269
Dunstan, St, 4: 1110, **10:** 2619
Duny, Amy (witch), **3:** 756
Dupuis, Charles-François, 9: 2357
Durandal (sword of Roland), **10:** 2748
Durga (wife of Shiva; Hinduism), **5:** 1314, **7:** *1897,* **10:** 2573
goat sacrificed to, **9:** *2457*
Kali and, **6:** 1556
durian fruit (Borneo), **1:** 316
Durkheim, Emil, on totemism, **9:** 2358
Dutugamunu (king of Ceylon), **10:** 2585
Dvaraka Mayi (mosque of Sai Baba), **9:** 2459
dwarfs, **3:** 734–8
in Greece, **3:** 734
origin of belief in, **3:** 737f
Scandinavian and Teutonic, **3:** 734ff
smiths and, **10:** 2620
treasure and, **3:** 735f
Vishnu as, **11:** 2960
Dyaus (Indian god), **1:** 129, **6:** 1434, **10:** 2601
bull and, **2:** 365
dying god, 1: 269ff, **3: 739–44**
Adonis as, **3:** 739–41
Attis as, **3:** 742
Baal as, **3:** 2183, 2762
Christianity dissociated from the myth, **3:** 743f
in Crete, **5:** 1167
divine king and, **3:** 739
Dionysus as, **3:** 742f
Osiris as, **3:** 741, **8:** 2088
Tammuz as, **3:** 739, 10: 2776
Zeus as, **5:** 1167, 1168
dynasties, Egyptian, dates of, **3:** 788
Dyrnawg (giant), *see* Tyrnoc

E

Ea (Enki; Mesopotamian god), **2:** 535f, **3: 745, 7:** 1818f, 1941
Apsu and **3:** 745, **7:** 1819, 1821
cedar and, **11:** 2878
creation myth and **7:** 1821, 1822
Enki identified with, **3:** 745, **4:** 993
flood legend and, **4:** 992f
form of, **4:** 983
forty and, **4:** 1023
Inanna and, **7:** 1822
in magical incantation, **7:** 1824
eagle, 3: 745–7
Astarte and **1:** 170
Aztecs and, **1:** 131, **11:** 2861
in the Bible, **3:** 746, **8:** 2158
in divination, **1:** 194, **3:** 747
in India, **3:** 746
in Mesopotamia, **3:** 746
lion-headed (Imdugud), **4:** *1820*
Odin and, **4:** 1086
Pawnee Indians and, **4:** 1164
Prometheus and, **4:** 2262
Pueblo Indians, eagle dance of, **9:** *2298–9*
serpent and, **3:** 746
storms and, **3:** 746
as symbol of St John, **5:** 1398
Wodan and, **4:** 1086

Zeus and, **3:** 746, **11:** 3090, *3092,* 3093, *3093*
see also griffin
Eannatum (of Lagash; Sumerian ruler), **11:** 2992
ear (body), **1:** 299, **3: 748**
ear-ring, 3: 748
earth, 3: 748–52
Ashanti spirit of, **1:** 162
Aztec alligator myth of, **1:** 217
Aztec goddess of, *see* Coatlicue
as element, **3:** 801f
first man and, **4:** 979
four and, **4:** 1029
Greek gods and, **3:** 751
see also Ge
Maori goddess of, *see* Papa
as mother goddess, **3:** 748f, **4:** 936, **7:** 1894, **11:** 2939
in Finland, **4:** 958
Neolithic, **8:** 2244f
Roman god of, *see* Tellus
in Scandinavia, **4:** 1051, **10:** 2825
sky and, **3:** 750, **11:** 2921
in creation myths, **2:** 534, **3:** 750, **8:** 2230, **10:** 2601
Dahomean spirits of, **2:** 586
in serpent myths, **9:** 2529f
Slavs and, **10:** 2612
as symbol of female body, **6:** 1603
treasure buried in, **11:** 2870ff
see also agriculture; chthonian deities; fertility
earthquakes, 3: 751
Caucasian myth of, **8:** 2262
Poseidon and, **3:** 751, **8:** 2234f
east, 3: 640, **752**
churches, etc. facing, **2:** 361, **3:** 640
East Anglian and Essex witches, 3: 753–9
flying by, **2:** 350
James Murrell and, **7:** 1904
see also Canewdon; Chelmsford witches
Easter, 3: 760–6
bonfires and, **3:** 764
eggs and, **3:** 763, *766, 781,* 784
hare and, **5:** 1210
lamb and, **3:** 760
Maltese procession at, **2:** *469*
Virgin Mary in Sicilian procession at, **7:** *1748*
Mexican fiesta at, **4:** 1018
origins of, **3:** 744
rabbit and, **9:** 2320
water and, **3:** 763
Easter Island, 8: 2229, *2229,* 2231
Easter ledger (plant), *see* bistort
East Indian humped zebu, in Indian cow-worship, **2:** 530
Ebenezer (Amana Society settlement), **2:** 500
Ebertin, Reinhold (astrologer), **1:** 182
Ebionites (Nazarenes; Christian sect), **3: 767–8, 6:** 1721
Ecce Homo, 3: 768
Eccles, Solomon (prophet of doom), **4:** 975
Echo (Greek mythology), **3: 769**
Eckhart, Meister, 3: 769–71, 6: 1624, **9:** 2318
Pseudo-Dionysius and, **3:** 634, 770
eclipse, 3: 771–2
Chinese and, **3:** 772, **10:** 2725
Urban VIII and, **6:** 1686
Economy (Harmony Society colony), **2:** 500
ecstasy, 3: 773–8, 6: 1678
Christian, **3:** 773ff
St Catherine of Siena, **2:** 425
Curé of Ars, **2:** 579
Roman Catholic use of the term, **3:** 773, 775
in Hinduism, **3:** 775f
in Judaism, **3:** 776f
levitation and, **10:** 2703
mysticism and, **3:** 773ff, **11:** 2697–8
orgies and, **8:** 2079
priests and, **8:** 2252
shamans and, **8:** 2251, 2548–9
spirit possession and, **3:** 778
in Sufism, **3:** 775, 778
trance and, **3:** 778, **10:** 2697–8
visions and, **11:** 2962
ectoplasm, 3: 779, 7: *1788, 1789,* **8:** *2277, 2278*
Edda (Poetic Edda and Prose Edda), **3: 779**
Poetic Edda, end of the world in, **3:** 817, **9:** 2484f
Prose Edda, **9:** 2483
Balder in, **1:** 226
giants in, **4:** 1103
Eddy, Mary Baker, 2: *477, 479,* **3: 779–80**
P. P. Quimby and, **3:** 779, **7:** 1817, 1993f
Eddy, William and Horatio, 1: 290, *291*
Edelin, Guillaume (witch), **2:** 350
Eden, garden of, 2: 538, **4:** 979, **8:** 2129f
by Bosch, **1:** *320*
by Jan Breughel, **8:** *2130–1*
by Cranach the Elder, **10:** *2581*
by Goes, **2:** *536*
in 13th century MS, **11:** *2877*
in the *Très Riches Heures du Duc de Berry,* **6:** *1596,* 1597
Edessa, Atargatis cult at, **5:** 1213
Edgehill, battle of, ghosts and, **1:** 145
Edict of Nantes, 2: 397, **5:** 1369
edim (*etimmu;* Mesopotamia), **6:** 1706
Edric, Wild, *see* Wild Edric
Edward III, Order of the Garter founded by, **4,** 1070, **10:** 2825
Edward the Confessor, King's Evil and, **3:** *642,* **6:** 1573, *1573*
Edwards, Harry (faith healer), **4:** *907,* 909
Edwards, Jonathan (revivalist), **3:** 828
Edwards, Susanna (witch), **4:** 889
Eeman, L. E., 9: 2332
Egeria (nymph), **8:** 2034
egg, 3: 781–4
in alchemy, *see* Philosophers' Egg
Castor and Pollux hatched from, **3:** *782*
Concert in the Egg (Bosch), **1:** *317*
in creation myths, **1:** 267–8, **3:** 781, *783*
Chinese, **3:** 781
Egyptian, **1:** 267, **2:** 335, 534, **3:** 781
Finnish, **4:** 960
Hindu, **3:** 781
Dionysus and, **10:** *2754*
divination by, **3:** 783
Easter and, **3:** 763, *766, 781,* 784, **9:** 2320
as fertility symbol, **3:** 781
Helen of Troy hatched from, **3:** *782*
Mithras and, **3:** *783,* **7:** 1864
of ostrich, **8:** 2088
of owl, **8:** 2098
as protection against the evil eye, **3:** 784
witches' use of, for transport, **3:** 783
egg rolling (Easter game), **3:** 784
Eglinton, William (medium), **8:** 2275
ego (Freudian term), **4:** 1049
Egypt, 3: 741, **785–94**
altars in, **1:** 116
amulets in, **6:** 1454, **10:** 2766, 2772, *2774–5*
see also scarab
animal gods of, **1:** 127, 128–9, **3:** 790f
astrology in, **10:** 2692
ba, **3:** 791
Baal in, **1:** 222–3
bull in, **1:** 138, **2:** 365, **3:** 790, **5:** 1347
burial in, *see* cult of the dead *below*
cat goddess of, *see* Bast
creation myths of, **1:** 229, **2:** 533f, **3:** 781, **4:** 886f, 1053, **6:** 1706, **7:** 1941
cult of the dead in, **3:** 794
coffins used in, **1:** 306f
eye and, **4:** 886
food for the dead, **4:** *1017*
Osiris and, **3:** *740,* 790
water in, **1:** 229, *231,* **9:** 2345, *2346*
see also Amenta; Book of the Dead; Coffin Texts; corn-mummies; judgement of the dead *below*; letters to the dead; mummification; pyramids, Egyptian; Pyramid Texts; ushabti
death in, **3:** 615, 794
see also life after death *below*
dogs in, **3:** 664
dragon in, **3:** 690
dreams of kings in, **3:** 701f
dynasties of, dates of, **3:** 788
election in, **3:** 797
emerald in, **3:** 813
eye in, **4:** 886f, *889, 894*
falcon in, **1:** 271, **4:** 912, **5:** 1359, *1360*
gesture, ceremonial, in, **4:** 1089
gods of, **3:** 790f
healing gods, **5:** 1248, 1405
see also Serapis
iconography of, **5:** 1394
see also Amun; Anubis; Aten; Bast; Bes; Chons; Geb; Hathor; Horus; Isis; Khnum; Maat; Nephthys; Nut; Osiris; Ptah; Re; Sekhmet; Seth; tefnut; Thoth
Greece and, **6:** 1461, 1689, **8:** 2086f, **9:** 2527–8
harvest in, **5:** 1216, *1216*
head-dress in, **5:** 1241
holy war in, **11:** *2991,* 2991–2
ib, **3:** 791
immortality and, **7:** 1904
incense in, **5:** 1428
judgement of the dead in, **3:** 791, **5:** 1259, **6:** 1539–41
Anubis and, **1:** 134
heart weighed in, **4:** 929, **5:** *1251,* **6:** 1541, *1542–3,* 1671, **9:** 2489
Maat and, **4:** 929, **6:** 1671
Osiris and, **4:** 929, **6:** 1541, **8:** 2088
Thoth and, **3:** 791, **6:** 1541
ka, **3:** 791
kings of, *see* pharaoh; Ptolemy
see also dreams of kings *above*
life after death, beliefs concerning, **1:** 229, **3:** *790–1, 792,* 794, **5:** 1259, **6:** 1706, **11:** 2846
see also cult of the dead *above;* judgement of the dead *above;* soul *below*
lotus in, **6:** *1649,* 1649–50
magic in **3:** 792f
man, Egyptian view of, **6:** 1704–6
see also creation myths *above;* death *above*
maze in, **7:** 1774
moon and, **2:** 365, **7:** 1877, **10:** 2692
music in, **3:** 794, **7:** *1910*
new year and, **6:** 1461
ointments in, **8:** 2049
owl in, **8:** *2096*
path symbolism in, **8:** 2146
perfume in, **8:** 2164–5
phallic symbolism in, **8:** 2174
phoenix in, **8:** 2185
pig in, **8:** 2191, *2191*
priests of, **3:** 793, **8:** *2254*
Sirius and, **6:** 1460–1
soul beliefs concerning, **3:** 791, **5:** 1413, **6:** *1704,* **9:** *2346,* **10:** *2637*
see also life after death *above*
stars in, **10:** 2692
see also circumpolar stars; Great Bear, in Egypt; Orion, Osiris and; Sirius, in Egypt
steps and ladders in, **10:** 2695–7
sun and, **3:** 788f, **4:** 886f, **5:** *1418,* **10:** 2722, *2723,* 2723–5
Apophis and, **3:** 690
Horus and, **3:** 789, *789,* **5:** 1360, **6:** *1625*
Mnevis and, **2:** 365
pharaoh and, **10:** 2723
see also Aten; disk, in Egypt; Re
tattooing in, **10:** 2797
temples of, *see* architecture, religious, Egyptian
tombs of, **9:** 2364
see also pyramids, Egyptian
tree spirits in, **9:** *2346,* **11:** 2874
women at their toilet in, **11:** *3051*
see also ankh; execration texts; hieroglyphs

Egypt, Islamic, **6:** 1470, 1699
eight, **1:** 114, **3: 795,** **8:** 2025
Christian baptism and, **3:** 795
888 as number of Jesus, **4:** 1158
eight-legged horse of Odin, *see* Sleipnir
eight-pointed star as symbol of Ishtar, **6:** *1459*
four and, **3:** 795
names adding to, **8:** 2024
Sunday and, **3:** 795
Eightfold Path (Buddhism), **2:** 354f
Eilithyia, *see* Ilithyia
Eire (Ireland), origin of the name, **3:** 748
eiresione (Greece), **8:** 2060, **11:** 2877
Eisai (Zen teacher), **11:** 3085
Eisteddfod, **1:** 233, **3:** 721, 723, **795,** **8:** *2210*
El (Phoenician god), **1:** 168f, **795,** **8:** 2180–2, **10:** 2761, 2762, 2763, *2763*
bull and, **3:** 795, **8:** 2180
dreaming by, **3:** 704, **10:** 2762
Elaine (Arthurian legend), **4:** 1059
Elam (Mesopotamia), Babylon and, **7:** 1733
El Amarna (Egypt), *see* Akhetaten
Eldad, lost tribes of Israel and, **6:** 1645
elder (tree), **3: 795–6,** **8:** 2203
Elders (Sthaviras; Buddhist sect), **2:** 357ff
El Dorado, **3: 796**
election, **3: 797–800**
in Christianity, **3:** 797, 799f
in Egypt, **3:** 797
Jehovah's Witnesses and, **6:** 1500
in Judaism, **3:** 797ff, **6:** 1535, **11:** 3064ff
in Mesopotamia, **3:** 797
predestination and, **3:** 800, **8:** 2242
elementals, **3:** 802f
artificial, magically created, **6:** 1687, **8:** 2283
elements and, **3:** 802f
fairies as, **4:** 906
Paracelsus on, **3:** 802f
see also gnomes; sylphs
elements, **3:** 647, **801f**
in alchemy, **1:** 97, **3:** *803,* **7:** 1807f
Chinese theory of, **2:** 457f, **3:** *802*
elementals and, **3:** 802f
fifth element, *see* quintessence
four humours and, **3:** 801f
Neoplatonists and, **3:** 802
pentagram and **8:** 2158
elephant, **3: 804**
in bestiary, **1:** 131
conception of Buddha and, **4:** 1070, **11:** 2953, *2953*
in Ghana ceremonial, **1:** 80
hare and, **7:** *1878–9*
Indra and, *see* Airavata
Kama and, **6:** 1556
Krishna and, **6:** *1583*
Mohammed's enemies mounted on, **6:** *1471*
moon and, **7:** *1878–9*
see also Ganesha
Eleusis, Eleusinian Mysteries, **3:** 621, **804–7,** **7:** 1896, 1925
at Alexandria, **7:** 1925
bathing as purificatory rite of, **1:** 229–30, **3:** 807
chief priest of, *see* hierophant
corn revelation at, **3:** 807, **11:** 2942
Cretan origin of, **5:** 1171
Demeter and, **3:** 621, 804ff, **11:** 2941–2
Dionysus and, **3:** 742f
Hades and Persephone and, **3:** 807, **8:** 2209, **11:** 2941–2
Orphism and, **8:** 2083, 2085
sacramental drink in, **9:** 2449
sacred marriage and, **3:** 807
sexual symbolism in **8:** 2175
Zeus and, **3:** 807
eleven, **3: 808**
elf, **3: 808**
elf-boats, elf-arrows, **1:** 145, **4:** 904, **10:** 2707
Isabel Gowdie and, **4:** 1144
elf light, *see* will-o'-the-wisp
Elguin, G. H., magnetism and, **6:** 1695
Elian, St, *see* Aelian, St
Eliade, Mircea:
on baptism, **11:** 3001
eternal return theory of, **3:** 838
Eliezer, Israel ben (the Baal Shem Tov), **5:** 1219f
Elijah (Old Testament), **6:** 1644, **7:** *1849,* **8:** 2266
fed by ravens, **2:** 557, *557,* **8:** *2265*
Elijah of Chelm, Rabbi, golem and, **4:** 1136
Eliot, T. S., *Waste Land* of, **4:** 1152
Elixir of Life, **3: 809–12**
as the panacea, **3:** 809f
Philosophers' Stone and, **3:** 809, **8:** 2178
'Elizabeth' (stigmatic), Dr Adolph Lechler and, **10:** 2698–9
Elizabeth I, **6:** 1573, **9:** 2386, 2388
Elkesaites (Christian sect), **1:** 126
Elliot, Mrs Warren (medium), **7:** 1788
Elliotson, John, **8:** 2274
elm, **3: 813**
Elmo, St, **9:** 2469, **11:** 3031
Elohim (name of God), **3: 813,** **10:** 2814, **11:** 3063
El Shaddai (name of God), **11:** 3063
Elysium (Elysian Fields), **3: 813,** **8:** 2132, *2134*
emanation(s) **3: 813**
in Cabala (sefiroth), **2:** 383ff, **3:** 813
embalming, in mummification, **7:** 1900ff
Embla (Teutonic mythology), **3:** 813
emerald, **3: 813,** **6:** 1511, *1512*
Emerald Buddha, temple of, **2:** *354*
Emerald Tablet (alchemy), **3:** 813
Emerson, Ralph Waldo, New Thought and, **7:** 1993
Emico, Count of Leiningen, **9:** 2518
Emma-O (judge of the dead; Japanese Buddhism), **3:** *614,* 616, **6:** *1544*
Emmerich, Anne Catherine (stigmatic), **10:** 2698, 2699, **11:** 2965
Empedocles (Greek philosopher), **3:** 731
four elements theory advanced by **3:** 801
reincarnation, his belief in, **9:** 2348, 2850
Emperor (Tarot card), **8:** 2147, **10:** *2791, 2792*
Empress (Tarot card), **8:** 2147, **10:** *2791,* 2792
empyromancy (divination by smoke from burning incense or plants), **3:** 659
Encausse, Dr Gérard, *see* Papus
end of the world, **2:** 409, **3:** 814–22
Aztecs and, **3:** *816,* 817
Babylonians and, **3:** 817
Buddhism and, **3:** 817
Christianity and, **3:** 815, 818ff
see also Second Coming
creation and, **3:** 815ff
fire and, **3:** 815, 818, 822, **9:** 2486
Greek myths of, **3:** 817–18
Hinduism and, **3:** 817
in Judaism, **3:** 818f
in Scandinavian mythology, *see* Ragnarok
water and **3:** 815
sea, **9:** 2486
winter and, **11:** 3035–7
see also Fimbul winter
in Zoroastrianism, **8:** 2048
see also Apocalypse; eschatology
Endymion (Greek mythology), **7:** *1876,* **9:** 2522
Engel, Leopold (reviver of the Illuminati), **5:** 1404
English Shakers, *see* Walworth Jumpers
Enki (Mesopotamian god), *see* Ea
Enkidu (Mesopotamian mythology), **3:** 616, **4:** 1106, **11:** 3057
Enlil (Mesopotamian god), **3:** 690, **7:** 1818f
in creation myth, **3:** 750
flood legend and, **4:** 992f
Marduk and, **7:** 1820
as ox, **1:** 129, **2:** 365
sack of Ur and, **10:** 2604
Eno (Zen master), *see* Hui-Neng
Enochian (language), John Dee and, **3:** 620
Ensor, James (artist), **1:** 151, **3: 822–3**
enthusiasm (religious), **3: 824–8**
Camisards and, **2:** 397
entrails, divination by, *see* haruspicy
Entremont, Celtic temple at, **5:** 1239
Enuma elish (Babylonian creation myth), **2:** 536f, **3:** 690, 838, **7:** 1733, 1822–3, **10:** 2692
emphemerides (astrology), **1:** 176
Ephesus (Greece), **3:** 632, **7:** 1836
Sleepers of, *see* Seven Sleepers of Ephesus
epic poetry, Greek, **11:** 2890
Epictetus (Stoic philosopher), **6:** 1707
Epicurus (Greek philosopher), **4:** 921, **8:** 2240
Epidaurus (Greece), Asclepios and, **5:** 1172, 1245, **9:** 2351
epilepsy, **6:** 1678
Epimetheus, Pandora and, **8:** 2262, **11:** 3056
Epiphanius (bishop of Salamis), on the Virgin Mary, **7:** 1750
Epiphany (Christianity), **6:** 1680
Isis and, **3:** 742
episcopi vagantes, *see* wandering bishops
Epistle to Diognetus (Christian text), **7:** 1985
epistles, apocryphal, **7:** 1986, 1992
epistles of St Paul, *see* Paul, St, epistles of
epitaph of Shakespeare, **2:** 581, *581*
epitaphion (Byzantine embroidery), **8:** 2071
Epona (Celtic goddess), **1:** 128, *130,* **5:** 1352
Rhiannon equated with, **6:** 1673, 1674
Erato (Muse), **7:** 1905
Erech (Uruk; Mesopotamian city), **4:** 1106, **6:** 1459, 1460, **7:** 1821
eremite, *see* hermit
Ereshkigal (Mesopotamian goddess), **6:** 1706, **7:** 1820, 1821f
Eridu (Mesopotamian city), **7:** 1821, **8:** 2245
Erin (Ireland), origin of the name, **3:** 748
Erinyes (Greek mythology), *see* Furies
Eriu (Irish goddess), **3:** 748
Ernst, Max, **1:** 148
Of this men shall know nothing, **1:** 150
The robing of the bride, **1:** 266
Eros (Greek god), **1:** 135f, **3: 829–31,** **9:** *2542*
Aphrodite and, **1:** 135f, **3:** 829, 830
Ares and, **3:** 829f
Cupid identified with, **2:** 576, **3:** 830
dolphin and, **3:** 670
Hermes and, **3:** 829
Plato's myth of the birth of **8:** 2206
Zeus and, **3:** 829, 830
Erra (Mesopotamian pestilence god), **7:** 1823
Erto, Pasquale (medium), **7:** *1793,* **8:** *2277*
Erythrae, Sibyl of, **10:** 2574
Eryx, Mt (Sicily), goddess of, **11:** 2943f
eschara (Greek altar), **1:** 116
eschatology, **3: 831**
see also end of the world; judgement of the dead
Eschenbach, werewolf of, **11:** *3010*
Eshmun (Phoenician god), **8:** 2183, 2184, **10:** 2763, *2766*
Eskimo, **3: 832–7,** **8:** 2008
amulets of, **3:** 837
animism and, **3:** 833
aurora and, **1:** 195, **3:** 835
burial among, **3:** 651, 836
creation myths lacking among, **3:** 833
death, beliefs concerning, **3:** 615, 835ff
disease, beliefs concerning, **3:** 835
dog myth of, **3:** 833
drum, of shamans of, **3:** 837
ghosts and, **3:** 835f
gods and spirits of, **3:** 833f
see also Sedna
ill-wishing among, **2:** 580
incest myth of sun and moon, **3:** 833, **5:** 1428
mammoth, legends perhaps referring to, **8:** 2007

marriage and, **7:** 1737
masks and, **3:** *835,* **7:** 1760, *1765*
moon and, **3:** 833, 834, **5:** 1428
seal and, **9:** 2515f
sea spirits of, **3:** *832,* 833f
see also Sedna
shamans of, **3:** 833f, 835, 836, 837, **6:** 1630, **7:** 1760, **9:** 2548
soul, beliefs concerning, **3:** 834f
string figures made by, **3:** *837*
sun and, **3:** 833, *837,* **5:** 1428
taboos of, **3:** 833–4, 835, **9:** 2515f
whale and, **11:** 3014
ESP, *see* extra-sensory perception
Espagnet, Jean d' (alchemist), **3:** 811
Essenes (Jewish sect), **3:** 611, **837, 4:** 1115
secret lore of, **2:** 383
Essex, witchcraft in, *see* East Anglian and Essex witches
Estan (Hattic sun god), **5:** 1323
Esus (Celtic god), **2:** 442, 443
eternal return, 3: 838–9, 4: 935
Ethiopia, 3: 840–7
amulets in, **3:** 846
animism in, **3:** 841
augury in, **3:** 844
bee in, **3:** 844
Christianity in, **3:** 841, 842, 843ff, 846
Adam and Eve, **9:** *2407*
baptism of Jesus, **2:** *471*
the flood, **4:** *995*
St George and the Dragon, **5:** *1297,* **9:** *2470–1*
Massacre of the Innocents, **2:** *580*
disease, Ethiopian view of, **3:** 845, 846
drum in, **7:** *1912*
gods of, **3:** 842
gravestones in, **10:** *2707*
Islam in, **3:** 841
Judaism in, **3:** 841
magic in, **3:** 844ff
Nilotes of, **7:** 2000ff
possession in, **3:** 845, **8:** 2239
Queen of Sheba and, **3:** 843, **9:** 2316, 2317
Ras Tafari movement and, **7:** 1832ff
snake and, **3:** 844
Solomon and, **3:** 843
spirits in, **3:** 845f
etimmu (Mesopotamia), *see edim*
Etna (volcano):
Hephaestus and, **5:** 1269, 1270
saints invoked against eruptions of, **3:** *645,* **7:** *1854*
Etruscans, 3: 848–50
creation myth of, **3:** 849
divination and:
augury, **1:** 194, **3:** 652, **11:** 3004–5
haruspicy, **3:** 652, **6:** 1637, **9:** *2419*
hepatoscopy, **3:** 848, **6:** 1637, *1637*
gods of, **3:** 849
Saturn, **9:** 2479
see also Charun
life after death, beliefs concerning, **3:** 848, *849,* 850
music and, **9:** *2416*
phallic symbolism and, **8:** *2173, 2174*
Roman religion influenced by, **9:** 2414f, 2418
Roman gods identified with Etruscan, **3:** 849
sacrifice and, **3:** 849f
satyr, **9:** *2481*
temples of **3:** 849
Eucharist, *see* Mass
euhemerism, 3: 850, 9: 2354–6
Eumenides (Greek mythology), *see* Furies
Euphrates aspen (tree), **11:** 3031
Euphrosyne (Greek mythology), **4:** 1145
eurhythmy, 10: 2694
Europa, 2: 365, **10:** 2805, **11:** 3090
Hera identified with, **5:** 1271
European witchcraft, 3: 852–6, 8: 2279ff, **10:** 2631ff, **11:** 3042ff
All Hallows' Eve and **1:** 110, **3:** 853
axe and, **1:** 212
bells as protection against witches, **1:** 251
Bible, witches weighed against, **3:** 854
black magic distinguished from witchcraft, **1:** 115
black mass and, **1:** 278, **3:** 853
blood and, **1:** 295f
broomstick in, **2:** 350f, **3:** 853, 915
Teniers, **2:** *351*
in Bulgaria, **3:** *862*
candles and, **2:** 400
cat and, *see* cat, witchcraft and
in the Channel Islands, **2:** 350, 447, 448
dancing by witches, **2:** 414, **6:** 1476, **9:** 2446–7
the Devil and, *see* Devil, witches and
disease caused by, **3:** 865, **8:** 2280f
dolls and wax images used by, *see* image magic, witches and
double (spectral evidence) and, **3:** 672
dragon and, **3:** *695*
eggs used for transport, **3:** 783
elder (tree) and, **3:** 795f, **8:** 2203
in England, **3:** 851f, 854, **10:** 2632
in Cornwall, **2:** 520
last conviction, *see* Wenham, Jane
witchcraft laws in, **3:** 753, 757, **6:** 1660, **11:** 2871–2
see also East Anglian and Essex witches; Hopkins, Matthew; Lancashire witches; Malmesbury witches; Somerset witches; Warboys, witches of
evil eye and, **4:** 889
finding of witches, **3:** 853–4, **4:** 951, 953ff
see also pricking of witches
in Finland, **4:** 962
flying by witches, **3:** 853, **10:** 2446
see also broomstick *above;* Canon Episcopi; flying ointment
in France, *see* French witchcraft
frogs and, **4:** 914, 1054
in Germany, *see* German witchcraft
goat and, **1:** 278, **3:** 629, 853, *856*
Eliphas Levi, **1:** 229, *229*
goddess of, *see* Diana
hailstorm created by, **11:** *3006*
hair and, **5:** 1203
hare and, **5:** 1210
heart and, **5:** 1251
herbs and, **5:** 1272, 1273, 1274
heresy and, *see* Inquisition, witchcraft and
horse and, **5:** 1354
horseshoe and, **5:** 1358
hysteria and, **5:** 1380ff, **8:** 2280
impotence caused by, **5:** 1380f, **6:** 1453
Inquisition and, *see* Inquisition, witchcraft and
in Ireland, **3:** 851f
St Patrick and, **3:** 873
see also Kyteler, Alice
in Italy, *see* Italian witchcraft
in Lapland, **6:** 1605
lead, witches immune to, **6:** 1613
mandrake and, **6:** 1718
at Midsummer, **7:** 1845
persecution of witches, **3: 851–6, 4:** 1077f
see also finding of witches *above;* floating of witches; *Malleus Maleficarum;* torture of witches; trials *below*
plants as protection against, **8:** 2202f
possession and, **3:** 873, **5:** 1379–85
primitive societies compared with, **4:** 951, 953ff, **10:** 2631ff, **11:** 3042ff
psychology of witches and witchcraft accusations, **5:** 1379
mental disorder as a characteristic of witches, **5:** 1379ff, **8:** 2053ff, 2280, **10:** 2634
sexual repression and, **5:** 1381
social tension relieved by accusations, **4:** 954f, **8:** 2053ff, **10:** 2631ff, **11:** 3043, 3045–6
red as protection against witches, **4:** 890
rowan and, **9:** 2437
in Scotland, **3:** 851f
in ballads, **9:** 2504–5
goddess of witches, **3:** 632
silver bullet, **6:** 1613
Weir and, **11:** 3007, 3008
see also Aberdeen witches; Auldearne witches; North Berwick witches
sexual disabilities induced by witches, *see* impotence *above*
sexual repression and, **5:** 1381
shape-shifting and, **2:** 419, **11:** 3010f, 3049
silver bullets and, **5:** 1210, **6:** 1613
in Spain, **1:** 233ff
in Sweden, *see* Swedish witchcraft
trials of witches, **3:** 853, **4:** 1077–9
spectral evidence in, **3:** 672, **11:** 3043
white magicians and, **11:** 3021, 3042
wolf and, **11:** 3049
see also coven; hex; sabbath; Walpurgisnacht; witch bottle
Euryale (Gorgon), **4:** 1141
Eurydice, Orpheus and, **5:** 2082
Eurylochus, Circe and, **2:** 485
Eurynome (demon), **3:** *861*
Eurystheus (Greek king), Hercules and, **5:** 1278ff
Eurytion (centaur), **2:** 445
Euterpe (muse), **7:** 1905
Evans, Sir Arthur, Cretan excavations of, **5:** 1167
Evans, Frederick (Shaker Evans), **10:** 2544, *2545*
Evans, Jane, 1: 296
Evans-Pritchard, E. E.:
on the Azande, **1:** 211, **11:** 3041
on the Shilluk, **6:** 1567
Eve (first woman), **3: 856**
Adam and, *see* Adam, Eve and
meaning of the name, **4:** 979
Evening Star:
Ishtar and, **10:** 2692
in Mexican myth, *see* Xolotl
North American Indians and, **7:** 2000
evergreens (trees and shrubs):
Christmas and, **2:** 480, **6:** 1611
see also Christmas tree; holly
First Foot and, **5:** 1330
in Renaissance symbolism, **9:** *2369*
Saturnalia and, **5:** 1330
see also cypress; fir; ivy; laurel; myrtle; pine; yew
Everyman (morality), **7:** 1924
evil, 3: 857–61
Buddhism and, **3:** 858, 861
Christianity and, **3:** 859f
see also Devil
darkness and, **6:** 1622
death and, **3:** 858ff
Hinduism and, **3:** 860f, **11:** 2932
Judaism and, **3:** 859f
the left and, **3:** 640
in Mesopotamia, **3:** 859
owl and, **8:** 2096f
transcended by magic, **6:** 1688
two and, **1:** 113, **8:** 2068, **11:** 2905f
woman, evilness of, **4:** 980, **11:** 3050ff
in Zoroastrianism, *see* Ahriman
see also demons; dualism; evil eye; sin
evil eye, 4: 888–94, *890, 891,* **8:** 2282f
in Ethiopia, **3:** 845
pig and, **4:** 890
protection against:
amulets, **4:** 890
bells, **4:** *922*
egg, **3:** 784
gestures, **4:** 890
iron, **6:** 1454, *1454*
lemon, **6:** *1454*
mirror, **7:** 1858–9
owl, **8:** 2098
plants, **4:** 890
red, **9:** 2341–2

spell, **11:** 3019
spittle, **4:** 890, **10:** 2664
wolf's skin, **11:** 3049
toad and, **4:** 889
witchcraft and, **4:** 889, **8:** 2282f
evil spirits, *see* demons; Devil; keres
evocatio(Roman rite), **3:** 870
evocation (magic), **3:** **867,** **6:** 1686
invocation and, **6:** 1454, 1687
evolution, Teilhard de Chardin on, **10:** 2811f
Ewen, C. L'Estrange, on diseases caused by witches, **8:** 2280–1
Excalibur (Caliburnus; sword of Arthur), **1:** 155, *157,* 158, **3:** **867,** **10:** 2744
sword in the stone distinguished from, **10:** 2748
Exclusive Brethren (Closed Brethren), **3:** **867–8**
excommunication, **2:** 580, 582, **3:** **869**
execration texts (Egypt), **2:** 582
exegesis, **3:** **869**
Exodus (Jewish history), **11:** 3064
see also Passover
exogamy, **5:** 1428f
exorcism, **3:** **869–73,** **6:** 1678
Christian, **3:** 865, 870ff
of Aix-en-Provence nuns, **1:** 90f
baptism and, **3:** 872, 873
in Brittany, **2:** 347–8
foul smells used in, **8:** 2166
of Jeanne de Anges, **4:** 1156
Judaism and, **3:** 870
in Tibet, dagger used in, **11:** *3021*
exstispicy (divination), in Mesopotamia, **7:** 1826
extra-sensory perception (ESP), **3:** **874–84**
animals and, **3:** 883f
mice, **9:** 2291
chance and, **3:** *876–7,* 878
classification of ESP experiences, **10:** 2665ff
the dead, active part played by, in ESP, **10:** 2675f
dowsing and, **3:** 686, 876
dreams and, **3:** 875, **8:** 2278, **10:** 2666, 2669–70, 2672, 2673–5, 2675f
Freud and, **4:** 1049f
hallucination and, **3:** 875, **4:** 2666–9, 2675
intuition and, **3:** 875, **10:** 2666, 2668–9
mediums and, **3:** 878
psychical research and, **3:** 875, **9:** 2278f
psychokinesis and, **3:** 875, 879ff, **9:** *2285,* 2287, 2290f, 2675
religion and, **3:** 876
Spiritualism and, **3:** 877
seen as a unitary process, **10:** 2673
see also clairaudience; clairvoyance; object reading; second sight; telepathy
extravert, introvert distinguished from, by Jung, **6:** 1549
Extreme Unction, **8:** 2050, **9:** 2450, **11:** 2907
eye, **1:** 299, **4:** **885–94**
in the Bible, **4:** 886
black diamond and, **6:** 1512
of dragons, **3:** 690
in Egypt, **4:** 886–7, *889, 894*
of Atum, **4:** 886–7
of Bes, **4:** 886
of Herus, **4:** 886, **5:** 1359, **9:** *2488*
of Re, **1:** *306–7,* **3:** 791
of the Fates, **4:** 920
Gorgons, eyes of **4:** 1141f
St Lucy and diseases of, **3:** 648, *885,* **9:** 2464
of Marduk, **4:** 886, **5:** 1395
multiplicity of, significance of, **4:** 886
of Odin, sacrificed, **4:** 1029
in the peacock's tail, **4:** *892, 893,* 894, **8:** 2153
stars and, **4:** 886
sun and, **4:** 886f
third eye, in Hindu belief, **4:** 886
see also evil eye
eyebright (herb) **5:** 1274, *1275,* **8:** 2205
eye idols, eye goddess, **4:** 888, *888–9*
Eysenck, Hans (psychology and astrology), **1:** 182
Ezekiel, **1:** 195, **4:** 886, **895,** **8:** 2267, **10:** 2834, **11:** 3016–17

F

Fa (Dahomey), **2:** 586
fable, **4:** **896**
faceless goddesses, **4:** **896**
Greek, **4:** 896
Paleolithic (Venus figures), **1:** 272, **4:** 896, 936, **8:** 2243, **9:** 2360
of Laussel, **4:** 896, **5:** *1343,* 1345, 1393, **9:** 2360
of Malta, **6:** 1701, *1702*
of Willendorf, **1:** 276, **4:** 896
Fafnir (dragon; Teutonic mythology), **3:** 693
Fahrenkrog, Prof. Ludwig, **7:** 1964, 1965, *1965,* 1966, **10:** 2739
fairies, the 'Little People', **4:** **897–906,** **6:** **1636**
on All Hallows' Eve, **1:** 109–10
of Arthurian legends, **4:** 901, 905
classification of, **4:** 901–2
colours of, **4:** 902
of Cornwall, **2:** 519, **4:** 906
explanations of fairy beliefs, **4:** 905–6
hawthorn and, **5:** 1228, 1229
of Ireland, **4:** 901, 902, 903, 904
see also leprechauns
plants associated with, **8:** 2204
Scandinavian, *see* troll
of Scotland, **4:** 901, 902, 903, 904
Isabel Gowdie and, **5:** 1144
in Scottish and Border ballads, **9:** 2503f
tinkers and, **11:** 2854
wings of, **11:** 3033, *3034*
see also changeling; Dadd, Richard, fairy paintings by: Doyle, Richard, fairy paintings by; elf; elf-bolts; fairy rings; Puck
fairy fire, *see* will-o'-the-wisp
fairy midwife, **4:** 902
fairy rings, **4:** **907,** **8:** 2204, *2389*
faith, **4:** **907**
faith healing, spiritual healing, **4:** **907–10,** **7:** 1855
Christian attitudes to, **4:** 909
Christian Science, **2:** 476, 478, **3:** 779, 780, **4:** 909
Curé of Ars, **2:** 578
Jansenists, **2:** 516
Jesus and his disciples, **4:** 908–9
miracles and, **7:** 1854f
pilgrimage and, **3:** 648–9, **8:** 2198
see also Lourdes
saints and, **3:** 648, **4:** 909
New Thought and, **7:** 1993
psychosomatic medicine, **4:** 909
scientific attitudes to, **4:** 909
Spiritualism and, **4:** 909
in Brazil, **10:** 2644
by touch **4:** 908, 956
see also king's evil
see also Cayce, Edgar; Greatrakes, Valentine; healing gods; namapathy; Philippe, Nizier
fakir, **3:** *778,* **4:** **910–12**
Indian, *see* sadhu
Islamic, **4:** 910
origin of the word, **10:** 2714
Falasha (Ethiopian Jews), **3:** 841
falcon, **4:** **912**
in Egypt, **1:** *271,* **4:** **912,** **5:** 1359, *1360*
Falconi, Juan (Quietist), **9:** 2319
Falling Tower (Tarot card), *see* Tower Struck by Lightning
fall of man (Christianity), **4:** **912**
by Blake, **1:** 285
see also Adam
False Face society (Iroquois), **5:** *1217,* **6:** 1455, 1457, 1458
Fama Fraternitas (Rosicrucian text), **9:** 2426–9, *2433*
familiars (witches' imps), **2:** 401, **3:** 866, **4:** **913–17,** **8:** 2283, **11:** *3043*
in Africa, **11:** 3045
blackbird as, **4:** 914
cat as, **2:** 420, *420,* **3:** 755, 866, **4:** 914ff, **8:** 2282, 2626
crow as, **4:** 914
dog as, **3:** 755, *757,* **4:** 915, **6:** 1592, 1593
in East Anglia, **3:** 755, *757*
ferret as, **3:** *757*
fish as, **4:** 986
frog as, **4:** 914
hedgehog as, **10:** 2626
of Alice Kyteler, **4:** 914, **6:** 1588
lamb as, **3:** 866
of Lancashire witches, **6:** 1592, 1593
mouse as, **2:** 401, *420,* **5:** 1417
owl as, **2:** *420*
polecat as, **3:** 755
rabbit as, **3:** 755
of Somerset witches, **10:** 2626
spider as, **10:** 2655
toad as, **3:** 755, 866, **4:** 914, **10:** 2626, 2855
see also witches' mark
fan, **4:** **917**
fana (Sufism), **8:** 2004
fanatic, origin of the word, **7:** 1898
Farandole (dance), **2:** 413f
Fard, Wallace D. (Farrad Muhammad; Black Muslim), **1:** 280
Faria, Abbé, **6:** 1695
Farquhar, John Nicol, on Christianity and Hinduism, **9:** 2361
fascination (enchantment), **8:** 2282f
fasting, **4:** **917–18**
Christianity and, **4:** 918
in eastern religions, **4:** 918
in Islam, **4:** 918, **6:** 1466–7
Judaism and, **4:** 918, **6:** 1536
see also inedia
Fata Morgana (mirage), **7:** 1886
fate, **4:** **918–22**
Greek view of, **6:** 1707
see also Fates; Nemesis
Isis and, **6:** 1462
providence distinguished from, **8:** 2273
see also fortune telling; luck; predestination and free will
Fates, the (Aisai, Moirae, Parcae; Greek mythology), **4:** 918f, **7:** 1874, **10:** *2710–11*
in astrological MS, **4:** *919*
eye of, Perseus and, **4:** 920
in 15th cent. tapestry, **10:** *2830–1*
Hittite forerunners of, **5:** 1325
Father Christmas, **2:** 480, *480,* 481, 483, **4:** 1004
Father Divine (George Baker), **7:** *1830,* 1830–1, *1831*
Father Time, **3:** 617, **11:** 2850
Fátima, Virgin Mary and, **7:** 1752, **11:** 2965, 2966
Fatimid Caliphate of Egypt, **6:** 1470, 1699
Faunus (Roman god), Pan identified with, **4:** 1120
Faust, **1:** *298,* **4:** **922–7,** **8:** 2110, 2112
Goethe and, **4:** *924, 925,* 925f, *1124,* 1124–5, 1127, **8:** *2111*
grimoire attributed to, **6:** 1613
Mephistopheles and, **4:** 924, **7:** 1805
Simon Magus and, **10:** 2580
fay (fairy), **4:** 897
Fay, Annie Eva, **7:** *1786, 1787,* 1789
Feast of Booths (Judaism), *see* Feast of Tabernacles
Feast of Dedication (Judaism), *see* Hanukkah
Feast of Fools, **3:** 697
Feast of Orthodoxy (Greek Orthodox Church), **5:** 1399

Feast of Tabernacles (Succoth, Feast of Booths; Judaism), **1:** 222, **5:** 1214, **6:** 1536, **11:** 2998
Feast of Trumpets (Judaism), **11:** 2897
Feast of the Visitation (of the Virgin Mary), **6:** 1633
feather, 4: 929
in Egypt, in judgement of the dead, **4:** 929, *929,* **6:** 1671
in Mexican festival, **7:** *1837*
of the peacock, **8:** 2153
Prince of Wales and, **4:** 929
shamans and, **4:** *962*
Feathered Serpent (Plumed Serpent), **9:** 2529
in Mexico, *see* Quetzalcoatl
February, in *Les Très Riches Heures,* **11:** *3036*
Feilding, Hon. Mrs Everard (medium), *see* Tomzcyk, Stanislawa
Felkin, Dr R. W., Golden Dawn and, **4:** 1132–3, **9:** 2431–3
Female Pope (Tarot card), *see* High Priestess
Fénelon, Abbé de, Madame Guyon and, **5:** 1191, 2320
feng (feng-hwang; Chinese mythical bird), **4: 929, 8:** 2188
Fenian Cycle, **4:** 964, 966
fennel (herb), **5:** 1274–5
Prometheus and, **8:** 2261–2
Fenris wolf (Scandinavian mythology), **11:** 3047
bound by Tyr, **4:** 1084, **11:** *3048*
Loki the father of, **4:** 1103
Odin killed by, **3:** 817, **9:** *2485,* 2486
ferns (bracken), rain and storm and, **10:** 2604
ferret, as witch's familiar, **3:** *757*
Ferrete, Bishop Julius, 11: 2988
fertility, beliefs and rites concerning, **4: 930–7**
in Africa, **4:** *931,* 936, *936*
of animals, **4:** 931ff
bear, **1:** 246, **4:** 935
ashes and, **1:** 163–4
Brigit and, **2:** 346
Canaanites and, **1:** 222
at Catal Hüyük, **1:** 116
cave art and, **2:** 432f, **4:** 935
in children's games, **2:** 454
cowrie shell amulet, **2:** 525
dance and, **2:** 589f, **5:** 1352
see also Morris dances
divine king or dying god and, **3:** 739
egg as symbol of **3:** 781
fir and pine as symbols of, **4:** 968
fountains and, **4:** 1029
Greek goddess of, *see* Demeter
harvest and, **5:** 1216f
high gods and, **4:** 935, 936
king and, **6:** 1566ff, **11:** 2941
in Malta, **6:** 1702
Mars and, **6:** 1743
maternity and, **4:** 937
see also Mother Goddess
modern witchcraft and, **7:** 1866
phallic symbolism and, **4:** 936, **8:** 2174, 2177
of plants, agriculture, **4:** 931f, 935
boar and, **1:** 297
bull and, **2:** 364, **5:** 1346
dance and, **2:** 589f
see also harvest *above*
plants and, **8:** 2204–5
pomegranate and, **8:** 2233
prostitution and, **9:** 2270ff
sacred marriage and, **4:** 935
Scandinavian deities of, *see* Vanir
sex and, **4:** 936f, **9:** 2538
see also phallic symbolism *above;* prostitution *above;* sacred marriage *above*
spirits and, **4:** 931ff
water and, **4:** 936
woodpecker and, **11:** 3060
see also vegetation spirits
Festival of Lights (Judaism), *see* Hanukkah
fetch (double), **3:** 672, 674f
fetch candle, *see* will-o-the-wisp
fetch light, see will-o-the-wisp
fetish, 4: 938–9, 10: *2632*
Fian, John (Scottish wizard), **5:** 1204, **8:** 2013f
Ficino, Marsilio, 4: 939, 9: 2370, 2374
Fiddler's Green, 10: 2571
Fides Publica (Roman deity), **9:** 2412, 2413
fifteen, 4: 939
Fifteen Men For Sacrificing (Roman priests), *see* Ten Men For Sacrificing
Fifth Monarchy Men, 2: 602, **9:** 2521, *2522*
fig (tree and fruit), **4: 939–40**
in the Bible, **4:** 939f
Adam and Eve and, **4:** 939–40
Buddha and, **4:** 940
see also bo-tree
Roman myths of, **4:** 940
Romulus and Remus and, **4:** 1026, 1027
on seals from Mohenjo-daro, **5:** *1435,* 1436
in sexual symbolism, **8:** 2174
Fiji, 2: 333, 409
filbert (hazel), origin of the name, **5:** 1230
Filippov, Danila (founder of the Khlysty), **10:** 2594
films, 4: 941–51
Dracula in, **4:** *944,* 946, **11:** *2926, 2927*
science fiction in, **4:** 949ff, **9:** *2497, 2500,* 2501
Fimbul winter (Scandinavian mythology), **3:** 817, **11:** 3035
finding of witches, 4: 951–5
in Africa, **4:** 951ff
in Europe, **3:** 853–4, **4:** 951, 953ff
see also pricking of witches
fingernails, 4: 957
fingers, 4: 956–7
crossed for luck, **4:** 1087
Evil Eye averted by, **4:** 1087f
of God, in art, **4:** 1087
healing by, **4:** 956
mutilation of, **4:** 957
to nose, **4:** 1089
in palmistry, **5:** 1201
pointing of, **4:** 957
wedding ring and, **9:** 2389
see also thumb
Finland, 4: 958–64
gods of, **4:** 958
see also Ukko
mountains and, **7:** 1900
Finney, Charles G. (revivalist), **3:** 828, **5:** 1328, 1331
Finn mac Cumaill (Irish hero), **1:** 324, **4: 964–7**
Cu Chualainn compared with, **4:** 964
father of, **4:** 965
head and, **5:** 1239
salmon and, **4:** 966, **9:** 2474
shadow of Cuirrech and, **9:** 2543
shape-shifting by, **1:** 127
fir (tree), **4: 967–8**
fire, 4: 969–75
Celtic festivals of, *see* Beltane; Samhain
as element, **3:** 801f
end of the world and, **3:** 815, 818, 822, **9:** 2486
houseleek as protection against, **5:** 1369
immunity to, of saints, *see* incombustibility
Indian god of, *see* Agni
meteors and, **7:** 1836
Norse festival of, **11:** 3076
oak tree and, **4:** 971
Parsees and, **1:** 117, **4:** 970, **8:** 2138
at Pentecost, **3:** *824*
in Persian religion, **1:** 117
phoenix and, **4:** *972,* **8:** 2185f, 2188
robin and, **9:** 2402, 3061
sacred:
of Brigit at Kildare, **2:** 346
at Dvaraka Mayi, **9:** 2459
of Parsees, **8:** 2138
sacrifice and, **1:** 116f, **2:** 378, **4:** 970
Shetland festival of, *see* Up-helly-aa
Slavs and, **10:** 2608–10
stolen from the gods, **8:** 2261–2
by Prometheus, **4:** *970,* **8:** 2261
by trickster, **11:** 2882
wren and, **11:** 3061
Zoroastrian fire temple, **11:** 3098
see also ashes; bonfire; cremation; fire-fly; Fire of Heaven (Tarot card); fireworks; hearth; need fire; will-o-the-wisp; Yule
fire-fly, 6: 1450
Fire of Heaven (Tarot card) *see* Tower struck by Lightning
fireworks, 4: 968
see also catherine wheel
firmament, 4: 975
Firmat, William, boar and, **9:** 2468
first, 4: 976–7
first-born, sacrifice of, **4:** 976
Janus as god of beginnings, **6:** 1484
in new year customs, **4:** 977
see also First Foot; first fruits; first man; first woman
Firstborn Church of Christ, 8: 2172
First Foot (new year custom), **4:** 977, **7:** 1997
evergreens and, **5:** 1330
salt and, **9:** 2475
first fruits, 4: 976, **9:** 2391
Swazi ceremonies of, **9:** 2393
first man, creation of man, **4: 978–82**
African myths of, **3:** 614
in Cabala, *see* Adam Kadmon
in Christianity, *see* Adam
earth and, **4:** 979
in Gnostic beliefs, **4:** 982
Greek myth of Prometheus, **4:** *981*
Indian myth of, *see* Yama, as first man
Melanesian myths of, **7:** 1799
Sumerian myth of **2:** 535f, **7:** 1821
in Zoroastrianism, *see* Gayomart
first woman:
in Christianity, *see* Eve
in Greece, *see* Pandora
in Teutonic mythology, *see* Embla
Fischer, Doris, 8: 2277
fish, 4: 983–7
as aphrodisiac, **6:** 1658
Astarte and, **1:** 170
Atargatis and, **5:** 1213
in cave art:
Australian, **1:** 203
European, **2:** *430*
as Christian symbol, **4:** *983,* 985
gods as, **4:** 983f
Vishnu, **11:** 2960
imitative magic used to obtain, in Mauritius, **11:** *3019*
Jonah and, **6:** 1527
on Mesopotamia altar, **8:** 2245
mitre and, **5:** 1242
sex and, **4:** 987
as witch's familiar, **4:** 986
zodiac sign of the Fishes, *see* Pisces
see also herring; mermaids and mermen; salmon; trout
Fisher King (Maimed King; Grail legend), **4: 987,** 1146f, 1149, 1152f, **8:** 2141f
Bran and, **4:** 1149
Joseph of Arimathea and, **4:** 1150f, 1153
Waste Land of, **4:** 1147, 1152f
Fishes, the (zodiac sign, in astrology), *see* Pisces
five, 1: 113, **4: 988, 8:** 2025
body and, **4:** 988
fingers, **4:** 956
fifteen and, **4:** 939
five-pointed star, *see* pentagram
the five senses, **4:** 988
names adding to, **1:** 113, **8:** 2024
in Pythagoreanism, **9:** 2316

sex and, **4:** 988
five leaf grass (herb), *see* cinquefoil
flabellum, **4:** 917
Flagellants, 4: *990,* 991, **9:** 2523
flagellation, 4: 988–91
in cult of Dionysus, **3:** *636,* **4:** *989*
medieval Christian sect, *see* Flagellants
in modern witchcraft, **4:** *990*
as purification, **4:** 991
sex and, **4:** 991
Flamel, Nicholas (alchemist), **4: 991**
flamen (Roman priest), **4: 991, 8:** 2256, **9:** 2417
Flamen Dialis, **4:** 991, **6:** 1552–3, **8:** 2019
flea, 6: 1450, **8:** 2116
Fletcher, Sarah, ghost of, **5:** 1225
fleur-de-lis, **6:** 1633
Fliess, Wilhelm, Freud and, **5:** 1288
flight into Egypt, the (Holy Family):
in Bulgarian mural, **6:** *1504*
fig tree and, **4:** 940
flint, 10: 2707
see also elf-bolts; Grimes Graves
floating (swimming) of witches, 4: 854, *951*
flood, deluge, **4: 992–6**
Australian legend of, **4:** 1054
in Genesis, *see,* Noah, his Ark
Greek legends of, **4:** 995, **8:** 2262, **10:** *2705*
Indian legends of, **4:** 995
Mesopotamian legends of, **3:** 817, **4:** 992–4, 1106, **9:** 2456
North American Indian legends of, **2:** 556, **4:** 1054, **8:** 2010–11
see also lost lands
Floralia (Roman festival), **10:** 2678
Flora's Day, 5: 1268
Flower, Joan (witch), **2:** 331, **8:** 2036, 2281–2
Flower, Margaret and Philippa (witches), **4:** 915
flower arrangement, Japanese, 11: *3084, 3085*
flowers, *see* plants and flowers
Fludd, Robert, 2: 386, *386, 387,* **4: 997–8**
blood distilled by, **5:** 1338
Cabala and, **2:** 386, **4:** 998
macrocosm/microcosm and, **1:** 298, **4:** 997, 998, **6:** 1675, *1712*
Rose Cross and, **9:** *2426*
on the ruby, **6:** 1511
on the universe, **2:** *382,* **11:** *2950, 2951*
flute (musical instrument):
of Marsyas, preserved at Sicyon, **9:** 2351
in Roman religion, **9:** 2412
sacred, in Brazil, **2:** 327, *330*
fly (insect), **6:** 1451
St Colman and, **9:** 2470
fly agaric *(Amanita muscaria;* hallucinogenic mushroom), **3:** 711, 714, **7:** 1908, *1908*
flying ointment (witchcraft), **4: 998–9**
Francis Bacon on **4:** 998
Basque witches and, **1:** 234, 235, 236
bat's blood used in **1:** 239
broomstick and, **2:** 350
Canon Episcopi on, **4:** 998
French witches and, **4:** 998, 1043
Isabel Gowdie and, **4:** 1144
physiology of, **4:** 998
Reginald Scot on, **4:** 998
Flying Roll, 6: 1514f
flying saucers (unidentified flying objects, UFOs), **4: 1000–4**
Fo-hi (legendary founder of Chinese empire), **11:** 2953
foliate heads, in medieval churches, **5:** 2035, *2939,* 2943
folkplays, 3: 698f, **4: 1004–6,** 1017
see also mummers; Plough Monday
folktales, 4: 1006–9
lion in, **6:** 1634
see also Cinderella; fable; Grimm; Jack; *Märchen*
font (Christianity), **3:** 795, **4: 1009**
food and drink, 3: 711, 4: 1010–17
as aphrodisiacs, **6:** 1657, 1658–9
honey, **5:** 1340
oyster, **4:** 987, **6:** 1658
Celts and, **4:** 1147
cauldron and, **2:** 427, **4:** 1147f
fish as, **4:** 985
Gypsies and, **5:** 1198
imitative magic used to obtain, **4:** 1012f
Islamic dietary rules, **4:** 1016
Jewish dietary rules, **4:** 1015–16
see also kosher
marriage and, **7:** 1737–9
peacock as, **8:** 2154
pig as, **8:** 2191f
Roman household spirits of, *see* Penates
taboos concerning, **4:** 1013ff
at witches' sabbath, **9:** 2446
see also alcohol; bread; corn; fasting; harvest; honey; kava; libation; mushroom; rice; salt; sin eater; wine
fool, 4: 1017–20
in Abbots Bromley horn dance, **5:** 1352
of Finn, *see* Lomna
in folkplays, **4:** 1005, 1017
North American Indians and, **4:** 1018–19
Pueblo, **4:** 1018, **9:** 2302, 2304
Fool (Tarot card), **2:** *334,* 335, **4:** *1020,* **8:** 2146, 2147, **10:** *2790,* 2791, 2792
foolish fire ***(ignis fatuus),*** *see* will-o-the-wisp
foot (body), **1:** 299
divination by; *see* foot reading
see also toe
football, 4: 1062–4, *1062, 1063*
footling, 6: 1611
footprint, sacred, on Adam's Peak, **8:** 2196
foot reading (solistry; divination), **8:** 2118
forces, 4: 1020–1
see also correspondences
ford, symbolism of, **6:** 1602
forehead, lines on, as key to personality, **3:** *655,* **8:** *2188*
forest, in Finland, **4:** 958
see also Forest Perilous; wildwood
Forest Perilous (Arthurian legend), **11:** 3025
Forgione, Father Pio (Padre Pio), **10:** 2698, **10:** 2700, *2701*
Forman, Simon, 8: *2217,* 2219–22
Fortuna (Roman goddess of fortune), **9:** 2419, **11:** 3015
Isis and, **6:** 1461, 1462
Fortunate Isles, *see* Isles of the Blest
Fortune, Dion (Violet Mary Firth), **4: 1021–3**
on artificial elementals, **6:** 1687
Crowley and, **4:** 1022
on the Devil, **3:** 629
Fraternity of the Inner Light founded by, **4:** 1022
Golden Dawn and, **4:** 1022
on the magic circle, **2:** 487
psychic attack and, **4:** 1022, **8:** 2284
fortune, wheel of, 11: 3015
in fortune-telling (cards), **2:** 404–5
in medieval symbolism, **11:** 3015, *3016*
Tarot and, *see* Wheel of Fortune
fortune-telling, 4: 1023, 6: 1664f
by cards (cartomancy), **2:** 403ff, 414
Tarot cards, **2:** 406–7, **10:** 2789, *2794*
Gypsies and, **5:** 1201
by scrying, **9:** 2506, 2508
see also palmistry; tea-leaf reading
forty, 4: 1023–4, 8: 2026
Forwald, Haaken (PK researcher), **9:** 2289–90
Fothad Canainne (Caindia, Fair God; Irish god), **5:** 1239
founding of Rome, 4: 1025–8, 7: 1744
see also Palilia; Romulus and Remus
fountain, 4: 1028–9
symbolism of **4:** 1028f, **6:** 1602
of youth, **4:** 1029, **11:** 2997
four, 1: 113, **4: 1029, 8:** 2025, **10:** 2831
earth and **4:** 1029
eight and, **3:** 795
four directions, *see* directions
four elements, *see* elements
four humours, theory of, *see* humours
kuphi and, **5:** 1428
names adding to, **1:** 113, **8:** 2024
in Pythagoreanism, **4:** 1029, **9:** 2316
Four Holy Truths (Buddhism), **2:** 354f
Fournet, St Andrew, 10: 2702, 2703
fourteen, 4: 1030
fox, 5: 1378
jackal and, **5:** 1378
in Japan, **6:** *1493,* **8:** *2089*
Samson and, **7:** 1909–10
Fox, George (founder of the Quakers), **4: 1030–1,** 1629
Fox, Oliver, out-of-the-body experiences and, **8:** 2095
Fox family (Spiritualism), **10:** *2656,* 2656–8
fox fire, *see* will-o'-the-wisp
foxglove (deadman's fingers), **5:** 1275, **8:** 2204
Frances of Rome, St, 11: 2965
Francis, Elizabeth (Chelmsford witch), **4:** 916, **8:** 2218
Francis I (of France), as hermaphrodite, **9:** *2370*
Francis of Assisi, St, 4: 1031–3, 4: 2470
by Bellini, **4:** *1032,* **6:** 1597
by Giotto, **9:** *2465*
stigmata of, **4:** *1031,* 1032, **10:** 2698, *2700*
wolf of Gubbio and **11:** *3047,* 3049
Francis de Sales, St, 4: 1033, 7: 1930, **9:** 2319
Francis of Paola, St, 10: 2701
Frankenstein (novel) **5:** 1338, **9:** 2496f
film of, **4:** 943ff
frankincense, 5: 1428
Fraternity of the Inner Light, 4: 1022
Fraudulent Mediums Act (1951), **7:** 1867
Frazer, Sir James George:
on divine king and dying god, **3:** 739
folktales, his theory of origin of, **4:** 1009
on Jewish pig taboo, **4:** 1016
magic, his classification of, **3:** 642, **5:** 1409, **10:** 2760
on the threshold, **10:** 2833
see also Golden Bough, The
Frederick II, Emperor (of Sicily), **6:** 1475
Frederick the Great, Freemasonry and, **4:** 1038
Freemasonry, 4: 1034–40
Cagliostro and, **2:** 388
Christianity and, **4:** 1035, 1036, *1040*
French Revolution and, **4:** 1038, 1133
Golden Dawn and, **4:** 1131
Illuminati and, **5:** 1402ff
Mormonism and, **7:** 1890
National Socialism and, **7:** 1944
Papus and, **8:** 2126
Rosicrucians and, **9:** 2430
Free Spirit, Brethren of the, **3:** 826
free will, *see* predestination and free will
French Revolution, 4: 1041–3
Freemasonry and, **4:** 1038, 1133
French witchcraft, 1: 278, **3:** 851, **4:** 998, **1043–7,** 1118
in Basque region, **1:** 233, 236, **4:** *1044–5,* 1047
Freud, Sigmund, 4: 1048–50
bisexuality and, **5:** 1288
Breuer and, **4:** 1049, **8:** 2228
Cabala and **4:** 1049
cocaine taken by, **3:** 714
death wish defined by, **4:** 1049
on dreams, **3:** 708ff, **4:** 1049
extra-sensory perception and, **4:** 1049f
Fliess and, **5:** 1288
ghosts and, **4:** 1100
hypnosis and, **4:** 1049
hysteria and, **4:** 1049, **8:** 2228
id, ego, and superego defined by, **4:** 1049
Jung and, **6:** 1548f, 1550
libido defined by, **4:** 1049

'oceanic feeling' named by, **7:** 1932
Oedipus complex and, **4:** 1049, **5:** 1429, **9:** 2392
origin of religion, his view of, **9:** 2358
on the Satanic pact, **3:** 714, **11:** 2972
on sex, **4:** 1048, 1049
on the unconscious, 1048ff
Freyja (Scandinavian goddess), **4: 1051–2**
her chariot drawn by cats, **2:** 417
Frigg and, **4:** 1051
meaning of the name, **4:** 1051
as mother goddess, **7:** 1898
necklace of, *see* Brisingamen
Freyr (Scandinavian god), **4: 1051–2, 9:** 2483
boar of, see Gollinborsti
horse and, **1:** 130, **4:** 1052
meaning of the name, **4:** 1051
at Ragnarok, **9:** 2486
ship of, *see* Skipbladnir
friars, origin of, **4:** 1031, 1033
begging friars, **7:** 1800
friar's lantern, *see* will-o'-the-wisp
Friday, 3: 606f, **4:** 1052
emerald and, **3:** 813
see also Good Friday
Friends, Society of, *see* Quakers
Friends of Truth (associates of George Fox), **4:** 1030
Frigg (Scandinavian goddess)), **4: 1051–2**
Frija (Germanic goddess), **4:** 1051
Fritsch, Theodor, 4: 1081
Frod, King (of Denmark), **4:** 1052
frog, 4: 1053–4
in trial by ordeal (in Kenya), **8:** *2036*
witches and, **4:** 914, 1054
frost, 11: 3038–9
frumenty (food), **5:** 1214
Fufluns (Etruscan god), Bacchus identified with, **3:** 849
Fu Hsi, I Ching and, **5:** 1390, *1391*
Fu-Hsing (Chinese god), **8:** *2136*
Fulda (Germany), witches burnt at, **3:** 853
Fuji, Mount (Japan), **6:** *1485*
Full Gospel Business Men's Fellowship International, 10: 2653
fumigation, in medicine, **8:** 2166
funeral, *see* burial; cremation
Furbaide the Horned (Celtic hero), **5:** 1351
Furies (Erinyes, Eumenides, the 'kindly ones', Maniai), **4:** 918, **1054–6**
Fuseli, Henry:
Nightmare, **5:** *1430–1,* **7:** *1999*
future, the, *see* divination; fate; predestination and freewill
fye (double), **3:** 672
fylgya (double), **3:** 672–3
Fyzee, Asaf A. A., 6: 1472

G

Gabbaras (giant), **4:** 1103
Gabble Ratchets (Wild Hunt), **11:** 3022
Gabley, Mother (witch), **3:** 783, **8:** 2282
Gabriel (angel), **1:** 125f, **4: 1057**
Koran dictated by, **8:** 2268, **9:** 2378
south and **3:** 640
Gabriel Hounds (Wild Hunt), **11:** 3022
Gaia (Greek goddess), *see* Ge
Galahad (Arthurian knight), **4: 1057–9**
Grail and, **4:** 1057f, 1153
Lancelot and, **4:** 1057, 1059, **6:** 1594f
Parsifal and, **4:** 1057, 1059, **8:** 2142
sword in the stone and, **4:** 1057
Galatians (mummers), **4:** 1004
Galatians, St Paul's epistles to, **8:** 2148, 2149–50
Galen, 1: 298
four humours theory and, **3:** 801
on frogs, for toothache, **4:** 1054
incantations rejected by, **3:** 647
Galgani, St Gemma, 7: 1971, **9:** *2464,* **10:** 2699
Gall, Franz Joseph (phrenologist), **8:** 2188ff
Galop Infernal (French dance), **2:** 414
Galton, Sir Francis:
apparitions, visions, and, **11:** 2961, 2962
Sir William Crookes and, **2:** 547f
games, 4: 1060–7
psi ability in games of chance, **9:** 2286
Roman, **6:** 1553–4, **9:** 2412f, 2416
see also children's games; Olympic Games
Ganapati (Hindu god), *see* Ganesha
Gandhi, Mahatma, 5: 1371f, *1320,* **6:** *1697,* 1698
Mme Blavatsky and, **6:** 1698
fasting and, **4:** 918
relics of, **9:** 2351
Gan Eden (rabbinic paradise), **8:** 2135
Ganesha (Ganapati; Hindu god), **3:** 804, **5:** *1310,* **6:** *1697*
Ganga (Indian deity), **4:** 1068f
Ganges (river), **4: 1068–9**
pilgrimage to, **4:** 1069, **7:** *1996,* **8:** 2195, *2198*
Ganymede (Greek mythology), **11:** *3092, 3093*
garden, 5: 1368, **6:** *1596,* 1597ff
Biblical, olive and, **8:** 2060
Japanese, **1:** *3080, 3081*
as paradise, **8:** 2129
Venus and, **11:** 2943
see also Eden, garden of
Gardner, Gerald, 7: *1870*
modern witchcraft and, **7:** 1869
Gareth (Arthurian knight), **1:** 154
garlic, 4: 1069, 8: 2202–3
Hecate and, **4:** 1069
as protection against vampires, **11:** 2924, 2926
Garm (hound of death; Scandinavian mythology), at Ragnarok, **3:** 817, **9:** 2486
garnet (jewel), **6:** *1512,* **10:** 2773
Garnier, Gilles (werewolf), **11:** 3010, 3011
garter, 4: 1070
in modern witchcraft, **7:** 1866
Order of, *see* Order of the Garter
Garuda, 1: 268, *269,* **5:** *1310,* **10:** 2837
Garvey, Marcus (Negro leader), **7:** 1832
Gasparetto, Luiz (psychic artist), **1:** 206
gate, gateway:
Janus and, **6:** 1483f
Mycenae, Lion Gate at, **10:** *2834*
see also threshold
Gathas (Zoroastrian sacred texts), **4: 1070, 8:** 2048, **11:** 3100, 3101, 3102, 3107
Gaudi y Cornet, Antoni, his Church of the Holy Family, Barcelona, **9:** *2367*
Gaufridi, Father Louis, 1: 90ff, **8:** 2246–7
Gauguin, Paul, 1: 146f
Gaule, Rev. John, Matthew Hopkins attacked by, **3:** 756
Gauquelin, Michel (statistics in astrology), **1:** 182
Gautama Buddha, *see* Buddha
Gawain (Arthurian knight), **1:** 154f, **4: 1071–4**
Grail and, **4:** 1057, 1071f, 1150, **11:** 3025
Green Knight and, **4:** 1072–4, **5:** 1245, **8:** 2035
sword not drawn from stone by, **4:** 1057
Gayomart (first man; Zoroastrianism), **1:** 89, **4:** 979, *982,* **8:** 2048
Ge (Gaia; Greek goddess), **3:** 750, *751,* **11:** 2921
Geb (Egyptian god), 2: 534, *534–5,* **3:** 790, **5:** 1359
Geber (Jabir ibn Hayyan), **4:** 1129
Gee, Donald (Pentecostalist), **8:** 2162
geesers, *see* mummers
Gefion (giantess; Scandinavian mythology), **4:** 1051
Gehenna, 5: 1260f
Geirrod (giant; Scandinavian mythology), **6:** 1642, **10:** 2826
Geller, Uri, 3: 875, **4: 1074, 7:** 1726, **8:** 2278, **9:** 2291
gematria, 2: 387, **4: 1074,** 1158
Gemini (the Twins; zodiac sign, in astrology), **1:** 175, 181, **3:** 639, **4: 1075**
Castor and Pollux and, **4:** 1075, **11:** 2903, 2904
emerald and, **3:** 813
Mercury (planet) and, **4:** 1075
Genesis, book of:
creation of man described in, **4:** 979f
creation of the world described in, **2:** *533,* 537f
Flood story in, **4:** 992
twelve tribes of Israel in, **6:** 1643
Geneva gown (Calvinist garb), **2:** 528
genius, 4: 1075, 5: 1186, **9:** 2418
genius loci, **5:** 1186–7
Lares and, **6:** 1608f, *1609,* **9:** 2418
Genshin (Japanese priest), **1:** 119–20
Geoffrey of Monmouth (historian):
on King Arthur, **1:** 154ff, **2:** 396
Gawain, **4:** 1071
Merlin, **7:** 1810
Morgan le Fay, **7:** 1884
on Gog and Magog, **4:** 1103
geomancy (divination), **4: 1075–7**
Bulwer Lytton and, **6:** 1670
George, St:
dragon and:
in Ethiopian MS, **5:** *1297*
in Ethiopian mural, **9:** *2470–1*
in mumming plays, **4:** 1004f, 1006
Georgel, Anne-Marie de (witch), **1:** 278, **4:** 1043, 1118
Gerald of Wales, *see* Giraldus Cambrensis
Gereint, son of Erbin *(Mabinogion),* **6:** 1672, 1674
Germanen Order, 4: 1081–2, 6: 1636
antisemitism of, **4:** 1081f
National Socialism and, **4:** 1081, 1082, **7:** 1945
runes and, **9:** 2441
Germanic Belief Fellowship, 7: 1964
Germanic (or Teutonic) mythology, 4: 1083–7
Anglo-Saxon mythology related to, **4:** 1083
dwarfs in, **3:** 734ff
first woman myth of, *see* Embla
giants in, **4:** 1103
gods of, **4:** 1083ff
see also Heimdall; Holda
Grimm brothers and, **5:** 1176
heroes of, *see* Siegfried; Wolfdietrich
Scandinavian mythology related to, **4:** 1083
spear in, **4:** 1086
German Order (O.S. Reuter), **7:** 1965
German Religious Fellowship (O.S. Reuter), **7:** 1964
German witchcraft, 3: 851, 855, **4: 1077–80**
see also Bamberg witches; Brocken
Germany, *see* Germanen Order; Germanic mythology; German witchcraft; List, Guido von; National Socialism; neo-pagan German cults; New Templars
Gerovit (Herovit; Slav god), **10:** 2611
Gertrude, St, mice and, **9:** 2471
Geryon, cattle of, Hercules and, **5:** 1280
gesture, 4: 1087–9
Buddha and, **4:** 1089
in dance, **2:** 592f, **4:** *957,* 1089
in Egypt, **4:** 1089
in magic, **4:** 1089
in the Mass, **4:** 1089
mimicry and, **5:** 1409–10
as protection against the evil eye, **4:** 890
in yoga, **11:** 3073
see also kiss
Gethsemane, garden of, **8:** 2060
Gévaudan, werewolf of, **11:** *3011*
Ghana (Africa), *see* Ashanti
al-Ghazali (Algazel), **3:** 622, **4: 1090, 6:** 1452, 1469, 1629
Ghost Dance (of North American Indians),

4: 1091–2, 1163, **4:** 2171, *2172,* **11:** 3043
ghosts 4: 1093–1101, 9: 2383
animal, **4:** 1097
horses, **5:** 1355f
astral travel and, **4:** 1101
burial and, **2:** 374, **4:** 1096
Bushmen and, **2:** 378
of Civil War (English), **1:** 145
divination by (necromancy), **7:** 1953ff
Eskimo beliefs, **3:** 835f
explanations of, **4:** 1100f
in films, **4:** 949
Jacobite Rebellion and, **1:** 145
Japanese, **4:** *1094–5*
Navaho Indians and, **7:** 1950
in New Guinea, **7:** 1974
Nuer and, **10:** 2638
in the Ozarks, **8:** 2100–1
perfume and, **8:** 2167
psychical research and, **4:** 1100f
Pueblo Indians and, **9:** 2302f
at Reculver (Kent), **2:** 361
Roman, *see* Lemures
in Scottish and Border ballads, **9:** 2504f
of ships, **9:** 2512, **10:** 2571
in Southeast Asia, **10:** 2647–8
see also ancestor worship; haunts, haunted houses; phantasms of the living; poltergeists
also apparition
ghoul (demon), **4: 1101**
origin of the word, **6:** 1516
ghul (jinn), **6:** 1516
giants, 4: 902, **1102–5**
Babylonian, *see* Humbaba
in the Bible, **4:** 1102–3
Watchers and, **3:** 628, **4:** 1102
British, *see* Cerne Abbas giant; Gog and Magog; Idris; Tyrnoc
in creation myths, **4:** 1102, 1103
Scandinavian, **4:** 1103, **9:** 2484
cyclopean buildings and, **4:** 1103
in Germanic mythology, **4:** 1103
in Greek mythology, **4:** 1103
see also Atlas; Cyclops; Orion; Titans
heroes and, **4:** 1102, 1103, 1105
Guy of Warwick, **5:** 1191
Hercules, **4:** 1103
Jack, **4:** *1104,* **6:** 1477, 1478
in Hittite mythology, *see* Upelluri
Indian, **4:** *1102*
Iroquois myth of, **6:** 1458
in Lapland (Stallo), **6:** 1607–8
Persian, **10:** *2686*
of St Michael's Mount, *see* Cormelian
in Scandinavian mythology, **4:** 1103
at Ragnarok, **9:** 2486
Thor and, **4:** 1103, 1205, **6:** 1642, **10:** 2826–8
see also Gefion; Hrimthursar; Jotunheim; Vafthrudnir; Ymir
treasure and, **6:** 1477, 1478
volcanoes as burial places of, **4:** 1103
Gifford, George (writer on witchcraft), **3:** 754f
Gifford, Elmer (New Thought minister), **7:** 1994
Gifford, Robert Swain (automatic painter), *see* Thompson-Gifford case
Gigantes (Greek giants), **4:** 1103
Gildas (historian), **1:** 153
Gilgamesh, 3: 616, **4: 1105–6**
flood legend in Epic of, *see* Utnapishtim
giant Humbaba and, **11:** 3029
Hittites, Hurrians, and, **5:** 1324
Ishtar and, **4:** 1106
serpent and, **3:** 860, **4:** 1106
Gill, Madge (psychic artist), **1:** 206, 208, **10:** *2668*
Gilles de Rais, 292, **4: 1107–8**
Gillingham (Kent), Jezreelites at, **6:** 1514f
gimmal (ring), **9:** 2388
Giradius, necromantic bell of **7:** *1954*
Giraldus Cambrensis (Gerald of Wales):
on barnacle geese, **4:** 1140
on Morgan le Fay, **7:** 1884
poltergeist phenomena described by, **8:** 2223
Girling, Mary Anne (founder of Walworth Jumpers), **4:** 1108, **11:** 2984, *2984*
Girlingites, *see* Walworth Jumpers
Giuliani, St Veronica, 10: 2701
Glamis castle, 5: *1222–3*
glamour, 9: 2283
Glanvil, Joseph, 10: 2626
on the Drummer of Tedworth, **9:** 2224
seances conducted by, **7:** 1956
on witchcraft, **5:** 1380, **10:** 2626
Glasgow, arms of, **9:** 2402, 2474, *2474*
Glass Mountain, 4: 1108
Glastonbury (Somerset) **4: 1109–14**
Arthurian legends and, **1:** 159, **2:** 391, **4:** 1109, 1110, 1112
as Avalon, **1:** 159, 210, **4:** 1109, 1110, 1112
Celts and, **4:** 1109, 1110
Chalice Well at, **4:** 1114
Christianity at, **4:** 1109, 1110ff
Druids and, **3:** 722
St Dunstan and, **4:** 1110
Grail and, **4:** 1109, 1111
Joseph of Arimathea and, **4:** 1109, 1111, 1114
St Michael and, **4:** *1109,* 1110
St Patrick and, **4:** 1109, 1111
relics at, **9:** 2353
holy thorn of, **4:** *1113,* 1114, *1114,* **5:** 1229
William of Malmesbury on, **4:** 1111
Gleipnir (Scandinavian mythology), **3:** 737
glossolalia, *see* speaking in tongues
gloves, Easter and, **3:** 763
glow-worm (insect), **6:** 1450f
gnomes (elementals), **3:** 802f, **4: 1115**
gnosis, **4:** 1115
Gnostic gems (amulets), **4:** *1116, 1117*
Gnosticism, 4: 1115–18
Cabala and, **2:** 383, 384
Christianity and, **4:** 1115ff
creation of man and, **4:** 982, **10:** 2692
demiurge in, **3:** 622, 730, **4:** 1116, 1117
dualism and, **3:** 730, 731, 859, **4:** 1116
Hermetica and, **5:** 1290
Jesus and, **2:** 470, **4:** 1116, 1117, **9:** 2477
Judaism and, **4:** 1115f
light and darkness in, **6:** 1624
Manicheans and, **6:** 172ff
St Paul and, **8:** 2151–2
Satanism and, **9:** 2477f
self, selfhood, in, **6:** 1713
Simon Magus and, **4:** 1115, **10:** 2578ff
soul in, **4:** 1116f
goat, 4: 1118–21
the Devil as:
Eliphas Levi on, **1:** 229, *229*
Tarot card, **4:** 939
witches and, **1:** 229, 230, 278, **3:** 629, 853, *856,* **4:** 1047, 1118f, *1119*
Dionysus and, **4:** 1120, *1121*
Good Shepherd symbol and, **4:** 1137
Lupercalia and **4:** 1120
in Mesopotamia, **10:** *2761*
Pan and, **4:** 1120
sacrificed, in Nepal, **9:** *2457*
sheep and goats (Christian metaphor), **4:** 1121
in Valhalla, *see* Heidrun
zodiac sign, *see* Capricorn
see also chimaera; scapegoat
goblins, 4: 901, **1122**
Godiva, Lady, 4: 1122–3, 8: 2018f
Godric, St, 3: 862
God Save the King, **10:** 2631
Goessen, Claire (witch), **4:** 998
Goethe, Johann Wolfgang von, 4: 1124–7
Faust and, **4:** *924, 925,* 925f, *1124,* 1124–5, 1127, **8:** *2111*
Goetheanum (Dornach, Switzerland), **10:** 2694, *2695*
Gog and Magog (giants), **4:** 1103, **1127**
Goibniu (Celtic smith god), **4:** 1147, **10:** 2620
Gokhale, G. K., Gandhi and, **6:** 1698
gold, 4: 1128–9
in alchemy, **1:** 93ff, **3:** 809, 811f, **4:** 1129, **6:** *1628*
sun and, **2:** 522, **4:** 1129, **6:** *1628*
yellow and, **2:** 522
see also El Dorado; Golden Age
Golden Age, 8: 2132f, **11:** 2851–2
Cronus's reign as, **2:** 546, **8:** 2132, 2851
Golden Ass, The (Apuleius), **6:** 1473
Golden Bough, The (Frazer), **3:** 630, **11:** 2942
on animism, **1:** 132
on divine king and dying god, **3:** 739, **6:** 1566f
on Hallowe'en, **1:** 109
magic classified in, **3:** 642, **5:** 1409, **10:** 2760
on meteors, **7:** 1836
on mistletoe, **7:** 1859, 1860, **11:** 2942
on Nemi, sacred grove of Diana at, **3:** 630, **7:** 1964, **11:** 2942
religion defined in, **9:** 2358
on tree spirits, **11:** 2942–3
golden calf, worship of the (Israelites), **2:** *366–7*
Golden Dawn, Order of the, **4: 1130–4**
Blake and, **1:** 284, **4:** 1131
Cabala and, **4:** 1134
Crowley and, **2:** 599f
Dion Fortune and, **4:** 1022
Freemasonry and, **4:** 1131
holy guardian angel invoked by, **9:** 2401
invisibility ritual of, **6:** 1453
Levi and, **4:** 1131–2
magic and, **4:** 1131ff
Mathers and, **4:** 1131ff, **7:** 1769, 1770, **11:** 3067
pentagram and, **8:** 2158, 2159
Rose-Cross symbol of, **1:** *300*
Rosicrucians and, **4:** 1131, 1132, 1134, **9:** 2430–3
Theosophical society and, **4:** 1131, 1132
Vault of the Adepts of, **4:** *1022, 1023*
vibration of divine names by, **11:** 2951
A. E. Waite and, **4:** 1131, 1132, **11:** 2979
Yeats and, **1:** 284, **4:** 1131, 1132, **11:** 3067
Golden Fleece, 4: 1134, 9: 2556
Jason's expedition to obtain, *see* Argonauts
golden temple (Amritsar), *see* Amritsar
Golem, 4: 1135–6
film, **4:** 943, *1135*
Goliath (Biblical giant), **4:** 1103, **5:** *1294*
Goligher, Kathleen (medium), **7:** 1790—1, *1793*
Gollinborsti (mythical boar), **1:** 297, **3:** 737, **4:** 1051
Goll mac Morna (Irish legend), **4:** 964
Gonds (Indian tribe), **10:** 2637f, 2800
gong, 4: 1134
Good Friday, 3: 764f
bread and, **2:** 331
Spanish penitents on, **3:** *762*
Good Shepherd, 4: 1137, 10: *2556,* 2756
in Christianity, **4:** 1137, **9:** 2559, 2756
Hermes as, **4:** 1137
Hittite version of, **4:** 1137
'good wine needs no bush', 5: 1329
goose, 4: 1138–40
see also barnacle goose
Gopal, Ram (Hindu dancer), **4:** *957*
Gopastami (Indian cow festival), **2:** 531
Gordian knot, cut by Alexander the Great, **1:** 104, **10:** 2710, 2744
Gordon, General, 6: 1700, **7:** 1827, 1828
Goretti, St Mary, 9: 2462
Gorgons (Greek mythology), **4: 1141–2**
Gosforth Cross (Cumberland), **2:** 551f, **6:** 1642, **9:** *2483*
gospel, 4: 1143, 6: 1507, **7:** 1852
apocryphal, **7:** *1985,* 1986ff
Gospel according to the Hebrews

(apocryphal text), 7: 1986
gospel oak, 8: 2035
Gospel of Truth (Gnostic text), 4: 1115
Gosvami, Rupa, 6: 1584
Gottfried von Strassburg, 11: 2885, 2886
Gottschalk of Orbais, 8: 2242
Gouranga (Krishna Chaitanya; Indian saint), 5: 1208f
Gowdie, Isabel (witch), 1: 145, 195, 4: **1143–5**
broomstick and, 2: 350, 4: 1144
covens and, 4: 1143
cow's milk magically stolen by, 10: 2712
Devil and, 4: 1144, 9: 2446
elf-bolts and, 4: 1144
fairyland visited by, 4: 1144
flying and, 4: 1144, 9: 2446
image magic and, 4: 1144
grace (Christianity), 4: **1145**, 8: 2242
bhakti and, 6: 1560
Graces (*Charites;* Greek mythology), 4: **1145**
in Botticelli's *Primavera,* 9: 2374, *2374*
Graham, Billy (evangelist), 2: *469, 514*
Graham, James (quack-doctor):
celestial bed of, 5: 1204
earth-baths of, 3: 752
Temple of Health of, magnetic cures at, 7: 1854
Grail, Holy, 1: 153, 2: 391, 393, 396, 4: **1146–53**
appears to knights of Round Table, 4: 1057
Celtic vessels of plenty and, 4: 1147f
chalice from Last Supper as, 4: 1150f
Galahad and, 4: 1057f, 1153
Gawain and, 4: 1057, 1071f, 1150, 11: 3025
Glastonbury and, 4: 1109, 1111
four Hallows seen by seekers of 10: 2750
Joseph of Arimathea and, 4: 1109, 1111, 1150f, 1153, 1528
Lancelot and, 4: 1153, 6: *1594,* 1594f
Parsifal and, 4: 1059, 1149f, 1152, 8: 2141ff
sword and, 4: 1071f, 1146, 10: 2750
see also Fisher King
Grand Grimoire (Red Dragon), 4: 1182
on the magic circle, 2: 487, *487*
on the magic wand, 9: 2398
on pact with a demon, 8: 2112
Grandier, Urbain, 1: 164, 4: **1154–7**, 8: 2112
granny-wells, 10: 2685
Gratiadei, Domenica (witch), 6: 1476
grave goods:
Eskimo, 3: 836
ghosts and, 4: 1096
Neolithic, 2: 570
Paleolithic, 2: 372, 569f
Parthian, 8: 2144
gravestone, *see* tombstone
Great Bear (Charles's Wain, Plough; constellation):
Charlemagne and, 2: 448
in Egypt, 9: 2533, 10: 2692
Greek myth of, 1: 246, 3: 630
Mexican myth of 1: 217
Great Beast (of Revelation), 4: **1157–8**
Antichrist as, 4: 1157
Crowley as, 2: 559
Daniel and, 4: 1157
666 as number of, 4: 1157, 1158
sun and, 6: 1691–2
great chain of being, 4: **1159**
Greater World Christian Spiritualist League, 10: 2660
Great Plains Indians, 4: **1160–4**, 7: 2011
buffalo and, 4: *1160,* 1161, *1163*
dance and, 4: 1162f
buffalo dance, 4: *1160, 1163*
Sun Dance, 4: 1162f, 10: 2721
see also Ghost Dance
gods of, 4: 1161, 1163f
magic and, 4: 1164
medicine-men of, 4: 1162
peyote used by, 3: 714
skulls and, 4: *1164*
talismans of, 4: 1164
tobacco and, 11: 2858
trickster of, *see* Coyote
visions sought by, 3: 775, 4: 1162f
see also Blackfoot; Cree; Dakota; Pawnee; Sioux
Greatrakes, Valentine, 4: 908, 956, 6: 1573
Great Schism (papacy), 2: 427
Greece, 5: 1165–72
altars in, 1: 116
bears in, 1: 246
Bronze Age in, *see* Mycenaean Greece *below*
bull in, 5: 1348
Hercules, 5: *1169,* 1279
Zeus, 5: 1167, 1271
see also Minotaur
chronology of, 11: 2891
creation myths of, 1: 135, 2: 538
Prometheus and, 4: *981,* 8: 2262, *2262,* 2263
see also Deucalion and Pyrrha
Crete and, 2: 545, 5: 1166f, 1168ff
see also Minotaur
cursing in, 2: 581f
death and, 3: 617, 6: 1706
dice in, 4: *1061*
dragon and, 3: 693
drama of, 3: 638, 696f, 7: 1764, 9: 2482
dreams and, 3: 705
see also gods, healing gods *below*
dualism in, 3: 731, 859, 6: 1708
dwarfs in, 3: 734
Egypt and, 6: 1461, 1689, 8: 2086f, 9: 2527–8
end of the world and, 3: 817–18
epic poetry of, 1: 2890
see also Homer
fate and, 6: 1707
see also Fates; Nemesis
fertility goddess of, *see* Demeter
first woman, myth of, *see* Pandora
flood legends of 4: 995, 8: 2262, 10: *2705*
fountains and, 4: 1028f
giants in, 4: 1103
see also Atlas; Cyclops; Orion; Titans
gods of, 5: 1167ff
Dionysus contrasted with Olympians, 3: 636–7
earth and, 3: 751
food and drink of, *see* ambrosia; nectar
healing gods, 5: 1245ff, 7: 1852
home of, *see* Olympus, Mount
iconography of, 5: 1395–6
light and darkness associated with, 6: 1624
triple deities, 10: 2832
see also Fates; Furies; Gorgons; Graces
twelve Olympians, 5: 1168, 11: 2898
twin gods, *see* Dioscuri
victory of Olympians over Titans, 3: 751
wolves and, 11: 3047
see also Adonis; Aphrodite; Apollo; Ares; Artemis; Ate; Athene; Cronus; Demeter; Dionysus; Eros; Hades; Hecate; Helios; Hephaestus; Hera; Hermes; Hestia; Hypnos; Iris; Muses; Pan; Persephone; Poseidon; Selene; Uranus; Zeus
hawthorn in, 5: 1228
head-dress in, 5: 1241
heresy in, 5: 1282
hermaphrodite deity in, 5: 1287
heroes of, 1: 65, 66, 5: 1295, 1296–7
see also Achilles; Argonauts; Bellerophon; Diomedes; Dioscuri; Hercules; Jason; Odysseus; Perseus; Prometheus; Theseus
Hittite parallels with Greek mythology, 1: 135, 2: 546, 5: 1324
holy war in, 11: 2996
initiation rites in, 5: 1168
see also Eleusis
judgement of the dead and, 6: 1545
kingship in, 6: 1572
laurel and, 6: 1610, 1611, 8: 2202
life after death, beliefs concerning, 3: 859, 5: 1259
see also Charon; Elysium; Hades; judgement of the dead *above;* soul *below*
lotus-eaters, legend of, 6: 1650
man, view of, 6: 1706ff
see also life after death *above*
Mycenaean Greece, 5: 1166ff
Cretan influence on, 2: 545, 5: 1166ff
see also Trojan War
Mystery religions of, 7: 1925ff
see also Eleusis
Nature spirits of, *see* nymphs; satyrs
olive and, 8: 2060
oracles of, *see* oracles, Graeco-Roman
paradise and, 3: 813, 8: 2132f, 2134
peacock in, 8: 2153
perfume in, 8: 2165
philosophy in, 7: 1966f
Hermetica derived from, 5: 1290, 1292
see also Anaxagoras; Anaximander; Aristotle; Empedocles; Epicurus; Heraclitus; Plato; Pythagoras; Sceptics; Socrates; Stoicism; Xenophanes
priests in, 8: 2073
relics in, 9: 2351
religion appraised in, 9: 2354–6
see also euhemerism
seal (animal) in, 9: 2517
soul, beliefs concerning, in, 5: 1413
Orphic myth of Dionysus and, 3: 859
Plato on, 1: 172–3, 5: 1413
see also pneuma; Psyche; reincarnation, in Greece
spring festivals of, 10: 2677–8
swallow in, 10: 2735
swastika in, 10: *2739*
temples of, 9: *2357,* 2364
tree spirits, tree worship, in, 11: 2876f, 2878–9
see also dryads
wheel in, 11: 3015
winter festivals of, 11: 3035
wryneck in, 11: 3063
see also Alexander the Great; Amazons; Athens; Corybantes; Oedipus; Olympic Games; Orpheus and Orphism
Greek cross (*crux quadrata,* equal-armed cross), 2: 487, 550
green, 2: 496, 5: **1173**
Aphrodite and, 2: 522
blue and, 3: 813
copper and, 2: 522
fairies and, 4: 902
spring and, 5: 1173
water and, 3, 813
see also emerald; Green Knight; Green Man
'green geese', 4: 1138
Green George, 5: 1173
Green Knight, Sir Gawain and the, 4: 1072–4, 5: 1245, 11: 3025
Green Man (Jack in the Green), 4: 968, 5: 1173, 6: *1477*
hawthorn and, 5: 1228
at Knutsford (Cheshire), 1: 2942–3
oak and, 8: 2035
Green Thursday, *see* Maundy Thursday
Gregory, W., on magnetism, 6: 1694
Gregory VII (pope), 2: 473
Gregory IX (pope), 11: *2982*
Inquisition founded by, 2: 422, 5: 1283
Waldenses and, 1: 2980
Gregory XI (pope), 2: 426f
Gregory of Nyssa, mystical experience and, 3: 775
gremlin, 5: **1174**
Grendel (monster), 1: 253
Grenier, Jean (werewolf), 5: **1174**, 11: 3011
Gresham, Sir Thomas, pearl drunk by, 8: 2157
grey (colour), Mercury and, 2: 522
Grey, Lady Jane, her ghost at Tower of London, 5: *1224*

Grierson, Isobel (witch), **2:** 419
griffin (griffon, gryphon), **11:** 3033
Alexander the Great and, **1:** *102*
Griffith, Anne, head of, preserved at Burton Agnes, **5:** 1225–6, 1227
Grimes Graves (Neolithic flint mine), **3:** 750
Grimm, Jacob and Wilhelm, 5: 1174–80
folktales and, **5:** 1174ff
Cinderella, **2:** 484f
Grimoire of Honorius the Great, **1:** 115, 299, **5:** 1182
frontispiece of, **9:** *2398*
incantations from, **1:** 300, **3:** 640
grimoires (magical texts), **1:** 115, 299, 300, **5: 1181–2, 5:** 2397ff
demons described in, **9:** 2374
Satanic pact not important in, **8:** 2112
see also Grand Grimoire; Grimoire of Honorius the Great; Grimorium Verum; Key of Solomon; Lemegeton; Picatrix; Sacred Magic of Abra-Melin, the Mage
Grimorium Verum (grimoire), **5:** 1182,
invisibility formula in, **6:** 1453
on names of power, **7:** 1942
Grinsett, Abre, accused of witchcraft, **3:** 757, **4:** 915, 916
Griselda, 5: 1182
Groddeck, Georg, psychosomatic medicine and, **4:** 909
grove, 5: 1182
see also Nemi
Gruzewski, Marjan (automatic painter), **1:** 206
gryphon, *see* griffin
Guaita, Stanislas de (Rosicrucian), **1:** 241, **9:** 2433
Papus and, **8:** 2125f
Gualter, Catherine (possessed girl), **5:** 1382
Guarayo Indians (Bolivia), path symbolism and, **8:** 2146
guardian spirits, 5: 1183–7
in Africa, **5:** 1183–6
Buddhist, **2:** *354*
Chinese, **5:** *1186*
Christian, **5:** 1187, **6:** 1721
Golden Dawn and, **9:** 2401
Martinists and, **7:** 1746, 1747
in Melanesia, **7:** 1796
in New Guinea, **5:** *1236,* **7:** *1797*
Parsee, **8:** 2138
in *Sacred Magic of Abra-Melin,* **9:** 2452
Valentinus and, **4:** 1115
see also ancestor worship; genius
Guatemala, 7: 1842–3
Guattari cave, prehistoric skull from, **2:** 435, 569
Guazzo, *see Compendium Maleficarum*
Gudea (of Lagash), **9:** 2377
Guest, Lady Charlotte, 6: 1671, 1674
Guinevere (Arthur's queen), **1:** 153ff, **5: 1188, 6:** 1594f
guisers (guizards), *see* mummers
Gulval (Cornwall), Holy Well of, **10:** 2684
Gundestrup (Jutland), cauldron of, **2:** 427f, *428, 440,* **3:** *722,* **5:** 1350, **11:** *3017*
Gungnir (spear of Odin), **3:** 737, **4:** 1086, **8:** 2047
Gunusu Dagh (mountain), *see* Dindyma
Gurdjieff, George Ivanovitch, 5: 1188–9
Ouspensky and, **5:** 1188, 1189, **8:** 2092, 2093
Gurney, Edmund, 5: 1190
cross-correspondences and, **2:** 553f, **7:** 1787, **11:** 3030
hypnotism/magnetism and, **5:** 1190, **6:** 1695, **8:** 2275
phantasms of the living and, **5:** 1190, **8:** 2275
Society for Psychical Research and, **5:** 1190, **7:** 1919, **8:** 2274
Guyon, Madame, 5: 1191, 9: *2319,* 2320
Guy of Warwick, 5: 1191
Guzyk, Jan (medium), **8:** 2277
Gwenole, St, 2: *346,* 347
Gwydion, 5: 1192, 6: 1639, 1674
Gwyn ap Nudd (Welsh legend), **4:** 966, 1110
Gypsies, 5: 1193–1201
tinkers and, **11:** 2853, 2854

H

Habakkuk (Old Testament prophet), **8:** 2266, 2267
Hadad (god), *see* Baal
Haddock, Dr J. 7: 1817
Hades (Aidoneus, Plouton), **5: 1201, 8:** 2208f
as god, **3:** 751, **5:** 1259, **8:** 2208f
cap of darkness and, **8:** 2209
Hercules and, **8:** 2209
horses and **8:** 2209
Persephone and, **3:** 621, 807, **5:** *1258,* **8:** 2168, 2209, **11:** 2941–2
Pluto identified with, **3:** 751, **8:** 2208
as the subterranean Zeus, **8:** 2208, 2209
as underworld, **5:** 1259f, **6:** 1545, 1706
entrances to, **8:** 2209
Hercules and, **5:** 1266, 1280
Orpheus and, **8:** 2082
Theseus and, **5:** 1266, **8:** 2168–70, **10:** 2819
see also Cerberus
Hadleigh (Essex), James Murrell at, **7:** 1904
Haeckel, Ernst, Lemuria and, **6:** 1614
Haggadah (Judaism), **6:** *1533,* 1536
hagging (projection of astral body; West Indies), **1:** 171
Hagiographa, 6: 1532
hagiography, 5: 1201
Hahnemann, Samuel Christian Friedrich (founder of homoeopathy), **5:** 1336f, *1337*
Haigh, John (the 'vampire of London'), **11:** *2924*
haiku (Japanese verse form), **11:** 3081
hair, 5: 1201–4
18th cent. style, **5:** 1243–4
Sikhs and, **10:** 2577
witches and, **5:** 1203
see also beard
hajj (Islam), **6:** 1468, **7:** 1775f
Hakim (founder of Druzes), **3:** 727f
Halberstadt, 'scapegoat' at, **9:** 2488
halcyon (bird), **5: 1205**
Hallaton (Leics), hare pie at, **5:** 1210, *1210*
Hallett, James (quack doctor), **6:** 1573
hallihoo, *see* caul
Hallowe'en, *see* All Hallows' Eve
Hallstatt (Celtic culture), **2:** 439
hallucination, 10: 2672
apparitions as, **11:** 2961, 2962
ghosts, **4:** 1100f
phantasms of the living, **5:** 1190, **8:** 2275
Census of Hallucinations, **8:** 2275
drugs and, **3:** 711, 714–15
see also peyote cults
ESP and, **3:** 875, **10:** 2666–9, 2675
mushroom and, **3:** 711, **7:** 1908f
halo, 5: 1205
in Buddhist art, **1:** 120, *120*
in Christian art, **3:** 678
hamadryads (Greek tree spirits), **3:** 728, **8:** 2031
hammer, 5: 1205
Hephaestus and, **5:** 1205
Lapps and, **5:** 1205, **6:** *1606*
in Scandinavia, **5:** 1205
Thor and, **3:** 737, **5:** 1205, **6:** 1641–2, **10:** 2826, *2827*
sickle and, Communist symbol of, **5:** 1205
Sucellos and, **5:** 1205
Hammurabi (king of Babylon), **9:** 2377
Hamza (Druze), **3:** 727, 728
Hanafi school (Islam), **6:** 1465
Hanbali school (Islam), **6:** 1465
hand, 1: 299
bronze, Roman, **4:** *956*
Buddha, ritual hand gestures of, **4:** 1089
in cave art, **2:** 430, 431
in Hindu dance, **4:** 1089
in the Mass, **4:** 1089
Nigerian altar of, **1:** 117
in salute, **4:** 1087
yoga, hand gestures in, **11:** 3073
see also fingers; hand of glory; hand of God; palmistry; thumb
handfasting (Scottish trial marriage), **7:** 1737
hand of glory (charm), **2:** 399–400, **5: 1206–8, 10:** 2613
Handsel money, 4: 976, **10:** 2664
Handsome Lake (Iroquois prophet), **6:** 1457
Hanged Man (Tarot card), **8:** 2147, **10:** 2793, *2793*
Hanifa, Abu, 6: 1465
Hannahanna (Hittite goddess), **5:** 1325
Hansel and Gretel, 11: 3024
Hanukkah (Feast of Dedication, Festival of Lights; Judaism), **2:** 399, **6:** 1536
Hanuman (Hindu monkey god), **5: 1208,** *1314*
fiery tail of, **5:** *1308*
in Katha Kali dance, **3:** *696*
haoma (sacred plant; Zoroastrianism), **11:** 3102
hara-kiri, 5: 1208
Haranath, Sri, 5: 1208–9
Harappa (city; India), **5:** 1436, **8:** *2245*
Hardedef (Egyptian sage), 1405
Hardinge-Britten, Emma (medium), **10:** 2660
hare, 5: 1210–11
corn and, **5:** 1210
divination and, **5:** 1210, **8:** 2064
Easter and, **3:** 764, 784, **5:** 1210
elephant and, **7:** *1878–9*
its foot as a charm, **3:** 641, **5:** 1210
in Hottentot myth of origin of death, **3:** 613
lion and, **6:** 1634
March and, **5:** 1210
moon and, **5:** 1210, **7:** *1878–9*
North American Indians and, **11:** 2881, 2882, 2884
Pan and, **8:** 2125
rabbit and, **5:** 1210
tortoise and, **5:** *1211*
as trickster, **11:** 2881, 2882
witches and, **5:** 1210
hare pie, scrambling for, **5:** 210, *1210*
harlequin, 5: 1212, 11: *2885*
dervish source of, **3:** 624
Harmakhis (Re), **3:** 704
Harmony Society (Rappites; religious sect), **2:** 499f
harp, 5: 1212
angels and, **5:** 1212
of Jews, hung on 'willow' trees in exile, **11:** 3031
Harpies (monsters; Greek mythology), **5: 1212–13, 11:** 3032–3
harpist, song of the (Egypt), **3:** 794
Harpocrates, *see* Horus, Harpocrates
Harranian religion, 5: 1213
harrowing of hell, 5: 1213, 1265–6
in Christianity, **3:** *616,* **5:** 1213, 1265, *1265*
other myths of, **5:** 1265–6
Hartmann, Dr Franz, 6: 1686–7, **9:** 2433
haruspicy (divination by entrails):
Etruscans and **3:** 652, **6:** 1637, **9:** *2419*
Hittites and, **5:** 1325
Romans and, **6:** 1637, **9:** 2418
harvest, 5: 1214–18
bells and, **5:** 1218
birth and, **5:** 1216f
the dead and, **5:** 1215–16
in Egypt, **5:** 1216, *1216*
fertility and, **4:** 935, **5:** 1216f
first fruits of, **4:** 976
hare and, **5:** 1210
harvest festival, **2:** 518, **4:** 1013, **5:** 1214, *1218,*
in Greece, **8:** 2060, **11:** 2877
Khond sacrifice and, **5:** 1217–18

last sheaf of corn, **2:** *517,* 518, **5:** 1214ff, **11:** 2942
ritual marriage and, **5:** 1216
in Shetland Isles, **5:** 1215, 1218
in Tibet, **5:** 1218
in Trobriand Islands, **5:** *1215*
water and, **2:** 518, **5:** 1214, 1215, 1217
rain, **2:** 517–18
harvest knots, 5: 1217
Harvest May, 11: 2942
harvest queen (corn sheaf), **5:** 1217
al-Hasan (imam), **6:** 1469
Hasidism (Jewish mysticism), **2:** 383, 386, **5: 1219–20, 6:** 1532
Buber and, **5:** 1220
Cabala and, **2:** 383, 386, **5:** 1219f
golem and, **4:** 1136
tsaddikism in, **5:** 1220
hatha yoga, 2: 335, **11:** 3071–5
Hathor (Egyptian goddess), **3:** 790
as cow, **1:** 128, *309,* **2:** 530, *530,* **3:** 790
creation of man and, **2:** 535
Edfu, her annual journey to, **3:** 793
as the eye of Re, **3:** 791
as hippopotamus, **1:** *309*
moon and, **7:** 1877
as mother of Horus, **5:** 1359
Hatshepsut, temple of (Deir-el-Bahari), **1:** 116
Hatti, land of, **5:** 1323
Hattusas (modern Boghaz Koi; Hittite capital), **5:** 1323
Hauffe, Frederica (seeress), **7:** 1817
Hauhau (Maori religious movement), **7:** 1732
haunts, haunted houses, 4: 1097ff, **5: 1221–7,** 1365f
see also Borley Rectory; Charmouth; Versailles adventure
Hawaii (Polynesia), **3:** 695, **8:** 2230f, *2231, 2232*
Hawaiki (Polynesian afterworld), **8:** 2231
hawk, 5: 1227
Egyptian hawk-headed god, *see* Seker
see also falcon
Hawker, Rev. Robert, 7: 1812
Hawkins, G. S., Stonehenge and, **10:** 2704
hawthorn, 5: 1228–9, 8: 2203
Christ's crown of thorns and, **5:** *1228,* 1229
fairies and, **5:** 1228, 1229
in Greece, **5:** 1228
Green Man and, **5:** 1228
holy wells and, **5:** 1229
last load of harvest and, **11:** 2942
May Day and, **5:** 1228, **7:** 1773
hawthorn globe, 5: 1229
hazel, 5: 1229–30
divination by, **5:** 1230
in dowsing, **3:** 683, **5:** 1229, *1230,* **7:** 1846
magic wands and, **5:** 1229f
Midsummer and, **7:** 1846
St Philibert and, **5:** 1230
as protection against lightning, **8:** 2203
head, 5: 1231–40
beans and, in invisibility formula, **6:** 1453
brazen speaking head of Sylvester II, **8:** 2112
carved, in medieval churches, *see* foliate heads
Celts and, **1:** 324, **2:** *441,* **3:** *722,* **5:** 1237ff
of Bran, **1:** 324, **5:** 1239
Finn and, **5:** 1239
of Anne Griffith, preserved at Burton Agnes, **5:** 1225–6
head-pot (Voodoo), **11:** 3096
of John the Baptist, **5:** *1238*
Knights Templar and, **1:** 229
of Medusa, **4:** 1141f
Odin and, **5:** 1240
of Orpheus, **8:** 2083
in Polynesia, **10:** 2769
in South America, **5:** *1233,* 1237
three heads of Thracian Rider god, **10:** 2828
yoga, headstand in, **11:** 3073
see also ear; eye; forehead; hair; head-dress; headhunting; headless spirits; nose; phrenology; scalping; skull
head-dress, 5: 1241–4
see also crown; hood; mitre
headhunting, 5: 1231ff
in Borneo, **1:** 312, 313, *315, 316,* **5:** 1231, *1232,* 1233
as holy war, **11:** 2996
in Melanesia, **7:** 1796
Nagas and, **5:** 1232–3, **7:** 1939, **10:** 2799
in Peru, **5:** *1425*
in the Philippines, **5:** 1233ff, 2799
tattooing and, **10:** 2799
headless spirits, 5: 1245
at New Year, **7:** 1994
see also Green Knight, Sir Gawain and the
healing, medicine:
buttercup in, **2:** 380
cat in, **2:** 420–1
caterpillar in, **2:** 421
in China, **2:** 463
see also acupuncture
cramp-rings in, **2:** 531
dance in, **2:** 588f, 597
eagle in, **3:** 747
elder tree in, **3:** 796
frog in, **4:** 1054
fumigation in, **8:** 2166
garlic in, **4:** 1069
herbs in, **5:** 1271ff, **8:** 2166
houseleek in, **5:** 1369
hypnotism in, **4:** 908
jade in, **6:** 1478f, **10:** 2773
knots in, **10:** 2711
laurel in, **6:** 1610f
lizard in, **6:** 1639
magical, **3:** 642ff, **11:** 3018ff
magnetism in, **6:** 1693, **7:** 1815
mandrake in, **6:** 1717
North American Indians and:
Iroquois, **6:** 1458
Navaho, **2:** 589, **7:** 1950, 1951–2
Pacific North-West, **8:** 2108–9
Paracelsus and, **8:** 2126ff
peacock in, **8:** 2153
pearl in, **8:** 2157
poisoning confused with, **8:** 2216ff
red in, **9:** 2341
rings in, **9:** 2386f
see also cramp-rings
runes in, **9:** 2411
St John's wort in, **9:** 2461
serpent in, **9:** 2532
shamans and, **9:** 2549
sheep in, **9:** 2560
shrinking charms in, **1:** 64
skull in, **10:** 2596
snail in, **10:** 2620
spider in, **10:** 2653–5
spiritual, *see* faith healing
spittle in **10:** 2656
stork in, **10:** 2709
swallow in, **10:** 2735
talismans in, **10:** 2773f
tobacco in, **11:** 2858
urine and, **2:** 380, **8:** *2128,* **11:** 2921
vervain in, **11:** 2948
wells, healing, **10:** 2684–5
willow in, **11:** 3032
see also Galen; healing gods; Hippocrates; homoeopathy; medicine-man; panacea; radiesthesia; warts, cure of
also disease
healing gods, 5: 1245–8
Graeco-Roman, **3:** 644f, **5:** 1245–8, **7:** 1852
see also Asclepios
Hermetica and, **5:** 1290
Imhotep as, **5:** 1248, 1405
Isis as, **5:** 1248
heart, 5: 1249–53
weighed in judgement of the dead (Egypt), **4:** 929, **5:** *1251,* **6:** 1541, *1542–3,* 1671, **9:** 2489
see also Heart Number
hearth, 5: 1253–5
chimney, **5:** 1255
Greeks and, **5:** 1254, 1300
house warming, origin of, **5:** 1253
in India, **5:** 1435
Romans and, **5:** 1254, **9:** 2418, **11:** 2949
see also Yule, Yule log
Heart Number, 8: 2023
heather, 5: 1256
heaven, *see* paradise
Hebat (Hittite/Hurrian goddess), **5:** 1324
Hebrew alphabet:
Cabala and **1:** 113, **2:** 383, **7:** 1941f
numerology and, **1:** 114
Tarot cards and, **1:** 113, **2:** 406, **10:** 2789
see also Tau; Tetragrammaton
Hebrews, *see* Jews. *For the religion of the Hebrews, see* Judaism
Hecate (goddess), **5: 1256–7**
Artemis and, **3:** 632, **5:** 1256, 1257
by Blake, **5:** *1256*
crossroads and, **2:** 555
dog and, **5:** 1257
garlic and, **4:** 1069
Jason and, **5:** 1257
moon and, **5:** 1257
Persephone and, **8:** 2168
threefold aspect of, **5:** 1257
Zeus and, **5:** 1256f
Hector (Trojan hero), Achilles and, **1:** 65
Hecuba 11: 2890–1
Heddle, Bishop William (of the Peculiar People), **8:** 2157
hedgehog as witch's familiar, **10:** 2626
Hedley Kow (fairy) **4:** 901
Hedrickites (Mormon sect), **7:** 1889
Hegira (Islam), **5: 1257, 7:** 1775, 1872
Heian Period (Japan), **6:** 1486, 1489
Heidrun (goat; Scandinavian mythology), **9:** 2346
Heilsgeschichte (salvation-history), **9:** 2377–8
Heimdall (Scandinavian and Teutonic god), **9:** 2483
Bifrost defended by, **9:** 2334
at Ragnarok, **9:** 2486, **11:** 2897
ram and, **5:** 1346
hei-tiki (Polynesian amulet), *see tiki*
Heket (Egyptian goddess), **4:** 1053
Hel (Scandinavian mythology), **5:** 1266
Balder and, **1:** 226
Loki the father of, **4:** 1103
Helena, Empress:
churches built at Jerusalem by, **3:** 764
true cross discovered by, **2:** 550f
Helen of Troy, 5: 1257
hatched from egg laid by Leda, **1:** 226, **3:** *782*
by Moreau, **11:** *3058*
Theseus and, **10:** 2819–20
Heliopolis (Egypt):
Atum-Re and, **2:** 533f, **3:** 789f, 793
as the centre of the earth, **7:** 1952
creation myth of priesthood of, **2:** 533f, **4:** 886f
phoenix and, **8:** 2185
Pyramid Texts and, **1:** 305, **2:** 533
Helios (Greek sun god), **10:** *2720*
Circe the daughter of, **2:** 485
hell, 5: 1258–66
in Breton folk belief, *see* Anaon
Chinese beliefs concerning, **2:** *462, 463,* **5:** 1266
in Christianity, **5:** 1259, 1261–5, *1266*
Dante on, **2:** 602ff
by Giotto, **5:** *1262–3*
mouth of (in Christian art), **1:** 249, **4:** *1157,* **5:** *1264*
by Orcagna, **6:** *1539*
by Signorelli, **2:** *604*
in Torcello Cathedral, **6:** *1541*
Egyptian beliefs concerning, **5:** 1259
Greeks and, **5:** 1259f

see also Hades
Hinduism and, **5:** 1266, **6:** 1558–9
Islam and, **5:** 1266
see also Sirat
Jews and, **5:** 1260–1
Mesopotamian beliefs concerning, **5:** 1259
in Scandinavian mythology, *see* Hel
Tibetan beliefs concerning, **5:** 1266
in Zoroastrianism, **5:** 1261, **11:** 3100–3101
Parsees, **8:** 2141
see also harrowing of hell
Hell-Fire clubs, 7: 1794
helmets, 5: 1243
Helston furry dance, 5: 1267–8
hemlock (plant), **8:** *2202*
hemp, dervishes and, **7:** *1932*
henbane (plant), **8:** *2202,* 2204
henotheism (definition), **8:** 2233
Henry II, 1: 247, **4:** 1112
Henry IV, consecrated oil and, **8:** 2050
Henry VII (Henry Tudor), **1:** 155, **2:** 396
King's Evil and, **6:** 1573
Henry VIII, King's Evil and, **6:** 1573
Hensley, George Went (snake-handler), **10:** 2623, 2623–4
hepatoscopy, *see* liver, divination by
Hephaestus, 5: 1268–70
Aphrodite and, **1:** 136f, **5:** 1268
Hera and, 5: 1268
Orion and, **5:** 1269
Prometheus and, **5:** 1268, 1269, **8:** 2262
thunderbolts made by, **5:** 1205
volcanoes and, **5:** 1268, 1269f, **10:** 2620
Etna, **5:** 1269, 1270
Vulcano, **5:** 1270
Vulcan (god) and, **5:** 1270
Zeus and, **5:** 1205, 1268f
***Heptameron (Magical Elements*; grimoire), 5:** 1182, **9:** 2397
Hera, 5: *1167, 1170,* **1270–1**
Aphrodite and, **1:** 136
Argus and, **4:** *893*
cow and, **5:** 1271
Cretan origin of, **2:** 542, **5:** 1271
Dionysus and, **3:** 635
Echo and, **3:** 769
fountain of Kanathos and, **4:** 1029
Hephaestus and, **5:** 1268
Hercules and, **5:** 1270, 1271, 1278, 1279, 1280, 1281
Juno identified with, **5:** 1271
lily and, **6:** 1631
moon and, **5:** 1271
as mother goddess, **5:** 1270, 1271
in Mycenaean Greece, **5:** 1270
Olympia and, **5:** 1270
peacock and, **8:** 2153
Samos and, **5:** 1270
Semele and, **3:** 635
virginity of, annually restored, **4:** 1029
Zeus and, **2:** 523, 635, **5:** *1270,* 1271, **8:** 2049
see also Judgement of Paris
Heracleon (Gnostic), **4:** 1116, 1117f
Heraclitus (Greek philosopher), end of the world and, **3:** 817, 818
Herakles (Greek hero), *see* Hercules
heraldry, rune occultism and, **9:** 2441
Heraut, Henri (artist), **3:** *678*
Herbert, Benson, 5: *1227*
herb Paris, 8: 2203
herb Robert, 5: 1275
herbs, 5: 1271–6, 8: 2202f
in medicine, **5:** 1271ff, **8:** 2166
as protection against the Evil Eye, **4:** 890
in ritual magic, **8:** 2167
see also anemone; moly; soma; springwort; tansy
Hercle (Etruscan god), Hercules identified with, **3:** 849
Hercules (Herakles), **5: 1277–81**
Amazons and, **1:** 119, **5:** *1277,* 1279–80
Augean stables cleansed by, **5:** 1279
Baal assimilated to, **1:** 223
boar of Mount Erymanthus and, **5:** *1278,* 1279
cattle of Geryon and, **5:** 1280
Cerberus and, **3:** *669,* **5:** 1266, 1280
Cerne Abbas giant and, **4:** *930*
Ceryneian hind captured by, **5:** 1279, **10:** 2687
Chiron and, **2:** 445
Christ compared with, **5:** *1169,* 1279
Cretan bull captured by, **5:** *1169,* 1279
Deianeira and, **4:** 1086
Donar and, **4:** 1086
dwarfs and, **3:** 734
Eurystheus and, **5:** 1278ff
giants slain by, **4:** 1103
Hades and, **5:** 1266, **8:** 2209, **10:** 2819
Hera and, **5:** 1270, 1271, 1278, 1279, 1280, 1281
Hesione saved from sea-monster by, **5:** 1280
Hesperides and, **1:** 142, **5:** 1280, *1281*
Hydra and, **5:** 1279
Iolaus and, **5:** 1278, 1279
Iphicles his twin brother, **5:** 1279
Labours of, **5:** 1278, 1279–80, **11:** 2897–8
lion of Cythaeron killed by, **5:** 1279
lion of Nemea killed by, **5:** 1279, *1279*
mares of Diomedes and, **5:** 1279
Megara and, **5:** 1279
Nessus and, **5:** 1280, **9:** *2537*
Olympic Games and, **5:** 1270
Prometheus and, **8:** 2262, 2263
Romans and, **5:** 1281
Stymphalian lake and, **5:** 1279
Telephus his son, **10:** 2689
Theseus and, **10:** 2819
Zeus his father, **5:** 1279
Herder, J. G., 4: 1126
heresy, 5: 1282–6
Christian, **5:** 1282, 1282–6
enthusiasm and, **3:** 825
Gnosticism and, **4:** 1115
Joan of Arc accused of, **6:** 1518f
Knights Templar accused of, **6:** 1575f
nudity and, **8:** 2019
see also Adamites; Arius; Bogomils; Cathars; Jansenists; Judaizers; Lollards; Modalism; Monophysites; Monothelitism; Nestorianism; Paulicianism; Valentinus; Waldenses
also Inquisition, heresy and
in Egypt, **5:** 1282
in Greece, **5:** 1282
Islamic, **5;** 1282
Hereward the Wake, 5: 1287
Herla, King, 4: 905
Herlequin (jester), **5:** 1212
herm, 8: *2175*
hermaphrodite (androgyne), **5: 1287–8, 8:** 2069–70
Adam and Eve as, **5:** *1288*
in alchemy, **8:** 2069, *2069*
in Dahomey, *see* Mawu-Lisa
Francis I (of France) as, **9:** *2370*
Freud and, **5:** 1288
in Greece, **5:** 1287
Plato and, **8:** 2206
moon and, **5:** 1287
North American Indians and, **5:** 1287–8
Shiva as, **5:** 1288, **10:** 2573
Hermaphroditos (Greek god), **5:** 1287, *1287*
Hermes (Greek god), **5:** *1170,* **1289, 9:** 2529
Apollo and, **5:** 1289
cap of darkness worn by, **8:** 2209
Crete and, **5:** 1289
the dead guided to Hades by, **2:** 448
Eros and, **3:** 829
Hermaphroditos and, **5:** 1287
lyre invented by, **5:** 1289
Mercury and, **7:** 1805, 1806
Odysseus and, **2:** 485
Pan and, **8:** 2124, 2125
Persephone and, **8:** 2168
Perseus and, **4:** 1141
phallic symbolism and, **3:** 829, **8:** *2175*
serpent and, **9:** 2529
see also caduceus
shepherds and, **4:** 1137, **5:** 1289
stones and, **5:** 1289, **10:** 2706
Thoth identified with, **5:** 1290
trickster compared with, **11:** 2883
see also Hermes Trismegistus
Hermes Trismegistus, 1: 97, **5:** 1290
Thoth identified with, **3:** 791, **5:** 1290
Hermetica, 5: 1290–2
planets in, **10:** 2692
Hermetick Romance, The (Rosicrucian text), **9:** 2429
Hermetic Society, founded by G. W. Russell, **9:** 2442
hermit (eremite), **5: 1292**
see also anchorite; Anthony, St; Arsenius
Hermit (Tarot card), **8:** 2147, **10:** *2792,* 2793
Hermopolis (Egypt):
creation myth of priesthood of, **2:** 534
Thoth and, **3:** 791
Herne the Hunter, 5: 1293
hero, 5: 1294–1300
Celtic, **2:** 428, 565
see also Arthur, Celtic legends of; Cu Chulainn; Finn mac Cumaill; Furbaide the Horned; Gwydion
Christian, *see* Charlemagne; George, St
dragons and, **3:** 693
see also serpents *below*
English, *see* Arthur; Beowulf; Drake, Sir Francis; Guy of Warwick; Hereward the Wake; Orfeo, Sir; Robin Hood
Finnish, *see* Lemminkäinen; Väinämoinen
giants and, **4:** 1102, 1103, 1105
see also Jack the Giant-Killer
Greek, **1:** 65, 66, **5:** 1295, 1296–7
see also Achilles; Argonauts; Bellerophon; Diomedes; Dioscuri; Hercules; Jason; Odysseus; Perseus; Prometheus; Theseus
Grimm brothers and, **5:** 1174, 1177
Jungian view of, **10:** 2759
in the Old Testament, *see* Samson
Persian, *see* Rustem
Polynesian, **8:** 2232
Russian, **5:** 1298–9
Scandinavian, *see* Volsungs
serpents slain by, **9:** 2529, *2530–1*
see also dragons *above*
sleeping, **10:** 2614–15
Teutonic, *see* Siegfried; Wolfdietrich
in United States folklore, **11:** 2919f
in the Ozarks, **8:** 2100
see also culture hero
Herodiade, Herodias (goddess of witches), **1:** 237, **3:** 853
Herovit (Slav god), *see* Gerovit
herring, 4: 986, *1010*
Hesiod (Greek poet), **5:** 1167
Hesione (princess of Troy), saved from sea-monster by Hercules, **5:** 1280
Hesperides (Greek nymphs), **1:** *141,* 142, **5:** 1280, *1281*
Hess, Rudolf (National Socialist), **7:** 1942, 1947
Hestia (Greek goddess), **5:** 1254, **1300**
Vesta identified with, **5:** 1300, **11:** 2949
Hewit, Katherine (witch), **6:** 1593
hex (charm), **5: 1300**
hexagram, 5: 1300, 11: 2592
in alchemy, **5:** 1300
in ritual magic, **5:** 1300, **9:** 2400
see also Star of David
Hexateuch (Bible), **7:** 1852, **11:** 3064f
Israel's election described in, **3:** 798f
Hiawatha (Iroquois hero), **5:** *1296,* **6:** *1455,* 1455f
Longfellow and, **1:** 105, **6:** *1455*
Hierapolis (Syria), Atargatis worshipped at, **3:** 680
hieroglyphs (Egyptian), **1:** 111, **5: 1301**
hierophant, 5: 1301, **8:** 2256

Tarot card, *see* Pope
High Gods, 4: 935, 936, **5: 1301–2**
Babylonian, *see* Marduk
Eskimo, *see* Sila
Andrew Lang and, **5:** 1301
Nilotic, **7:** 2000
North American Indian, **5:** 1302
sky phenomena and, **5:** 1302, **10:** 2601
Sumerian, *see* An
Yahweh as, **5:** 1302
Zeus as, **5:** 1302, **10:** 2601
Zulu, **11:** 3105
High Priestess (Female Pope; Tarot card), **8:** 2147, *2234,* **10:** *2791,* 2792, **11:** 2906
Hilaria (Roman festival), **10:** 2678
Hilarion, St, 8: 2164
Hildegard of Bingen, St, 5: 1302–3, 11: 2965
hill-billies, 8: 2099, **11:** 2912
Hill Reddi tribe (India), **8:** 2249–50
hills, *see* mountains
Hilton, Walter (mystic), **2:** 489, 490, **5: 1304, 6:** 1548
Pseudo-Dionysius and, **3:** 634
Himeros (Greek mythology), **3:** 830
Himmler, Heinrich (National Socialist), **7:** 1942, 1948, 1966
Hina (Hine; Polynesian goddess), **8:** 2230, 2232
Hinayana (Buddhism), **2:** 359, **5: 1304**
Hind Etin (demon), **5:** 1230
Hinduism, 5: 1305–21
altars and, **1:** 117
ancestor worship and, **2:** 573
asceticism in, **9:** 2523, 2524f
  see also sadhu
breath and, *see prana*
Buddhism and, **2:** 360, **5:** 1309
Christianity and, **5:** 1316, **9:** 2360–2
cow and, **2:** 530f, **5:** *1306*
creation myths in, **2:** 416, **3:** 781, **6:** 1650, **11:** 2960
dance, sacred, in, **4:** 1089
death personified in, **3:** 616
dogs and, **3:** 667f
dragon and, **3:** 691
dualism in, **3:** 731, *732*
elephant in, **3:** 804
  Kama and, **6:** 1556
  Krishna and, **6:** *1583*
  see also Airavata; Ganesha
end of the world and, **3:** 817
evil and, **3:** 860f, **11:** 2932
fakirs of, *see* sadhu
fate and, **4:** 921
God, Hindu concepts of, **11:** 3070
gods of, **5:** 1307, 1313ff
  iconography of, **5:** 1396
  see also Agni; Brahma; Hanuman; Indra; Kali; Rudra; Shiva; Surya; Varuna; Vishnu
heaven and, *see* paradise *below*
hell and, **5:** 1266, **6:** 1558–9
incarnation (*avatara*) in, **5:** 1420
  see also Vishnu, incarnations of
Indian Jews and, **8:** 2081
Islam and, **5:** 1316
lotus in, **5:** *1305,* **6:** 1650
love in, *see Bhagavad Gita*
man, Hindu view of, **6:** 1709
mandala in, **6:** 1714
mysticism in, *see* mysticism, Hindu
Nirvana in, **1:** 264f, **7:** 1935, 1936, 2004
phallic symbolism in, *see* lingam
paradise and, **6:** 1558–9, **8:** *2132,* 2134
pilgrimage in, **8:** 2195f
rainbow in, **9:** 2333
reformist sects of, **5:** 1316ff, **9:** 2361
  see also Ramakrishna
rivers, sacred, of, **8:** 2195
  see also Ganges
rosary in, **9:** 2420, **10:** *2930,* 2932
sacred texts of, *see Bhagavad Gita; Vedas*
self, selfhood, in, *see* Atman; Brahman
serpent and, *see* Ananta; Nagas; Shesha; Visvarupa
sexual abstinence and, **9:** 2524
Sikhs and, **10:** 2575ff
six recognized systems of, **11:** 3070
  see also Vedanta; yoga
  see also karma; reincarnation, in Hinduism
in Southeast Asia, **10:** 2646
temples of, **9:** 2366, *2366,* 2456
  erotic carvings of, **4:** *933,* **5:** *1317, 1318–19,* **10:** 2722, *2777*
third eye and, **4:** 886
time in, **11:** 2846–7, 2848
trinity (Brahma, Vishnu, Shiva) in, **1:** 324, **1:** 2960
widows, suicide of, in, *see* suttee
woman, place of, in, **11:** 3050
see also bhakti; caste; *kama;* Kundalini; Mahatmas; Tantrism
also India
Hippocrates (Greek doctor):
aphrodisiac recipe of, **5:** 1340
four humours theory of, **3:** 801
herbs listed by, **5:** 1271
hippogriff, 11: 3033
Hippolyta (Amazon), **1:** 119, **5:** 1279–80, **10:** 2819
Hippolytus (Greek mythology), **3:** 630, **10:** 2819, 2820
hippopotamus, in Egypt, *see* Hathor, as hippopotamus; Taurt
Hissarlik, excavation of, **11:** 2891, 2894
history, 5: 1322–3
Christianity and, **5:** 1322f, **9:** 2377–8, **11:** 2850
Judaism dependent upon, **5:** 1322
Muse of, *see* Clio
origins of myths found in, *see* euhemerism
see also cycles of time; end of the world; eternal return
Hitler, Adolf, 2: *514*
astrology and, **7:** 1944, 1945, *1945,* 1947
Adolf Lanz and, **7:** 1982, 1983
Hito no Michi (Japanese religious sect), **6:** 1497
Hittites, 5: 1323–5
Babylonia and, **5:** 1324, **7:** 1733
creation myth of, **5:** 1325
divination and, **5:** 1325
dragon myth of, **5:** 1325
gods of, **5:** 1323ff
  Mithras, **7:** 1861
  see also Apulunas; Kumarbi; Teshub
Good Shepherd symbol and, **4:** 1137
Greek mythology, Hittite parallels with, **1:** 135, **2:** 546, **5:** 1324
Hurrians and, **5:** 1323, 1324
stag and, **10:** 2687
Hobbes, Thomas, on miracles, **7:** 1849
hobby-horse, 4: 1004f, **5: 1326–7**
at Abbots Bromley, **5:** 1352
Morris dances and, **7:** *1890,* 1892
hobgoblin, 9: 2297
see also Robin Goodfellow
Hobthrush, *see* Robin Goodfellow
hockey (game), **4:** 1064
Hodening Horse, 5: 1355
Hoder (Scandinavian god), Balder and, **1:** 226
Hodgson, Dr Richard (psychical researcher), **8:** *2275*
Society for Psychical Research and, **8:** 2274, 2275
  Eusapia Palladino, **8:** 2113
  Mrs Piper, **8:** 2199f, 2275
Hoenir (Scandinavian god), 9: 2483, 2486
Hofmann, Melchior (founder of Melchiorites), **3:** 825
hog, *see* pig
Hogmanay, 5: 1327, 7: 1997
Hohenlohe-Waldenburg-Schillingfürst, Prince Alexander, 7: 1855
Holda (Germanic goddess), **5: 1327, 11:** 3038
Holda-Perchta (goddess of witches), 853
Holiness movement, 2: 502, **5: 1328–9**
enthusiasm and, **3:** 824–5, 827
Holy Rollers and, **5:** 1329
Methodism and, **5:** 1328
Pentecostalist movement and, **5:** 1328, 1332, **8:** 2159f
Pietism and, **5:** 1328
Salvation Army and, **5:** 1328
see also snake-handling cults
Holland, Mrs (Mrs Fleming), cross-correspondences and, **2:** 553
Hollandus, Johannes Isaac (alchemist), **8:** 2178
holly, 5: 1329–30
holy (definition), **5: 1330**
holy places, *see* pilgrimage
Holy Celtic Church (of Archbishop Tugdual), **11:** 2987
Holy Communion, *see* Mass
Holy Face of Lucca, 11: 2907
Holy Ghost (Holy Spirit; Christianity), **5: 1330**
dove as symbol of, **1:** 268, **2:** 334, **3:** 682
  in Cypriot mural, **6:** *1505*
  by El Greco, **2:** *336,* **3:** *824*
  in English 13th cent. MS, **3:** *682*
  in Ethiopian MS, **2:** *471*
  in French 15th cent. Book of Hours, **10:** *2652*
  by Giotto, **7:** *1989*
enthusiasm and, **3:** 826ff
see also Holiness movement; Holy Rollers; Pentecostalist movement
Holy Innocents, feast of, *see* Childermass
Holy Innocents, massacre of, *see* Massacre of the Innocents
Holy Office, *see* Inquisition
holy orders (Christian sacrament), **9:** 2450, 2451
Holy Rollers, 3: *827,* **5: 1331–2**
Holy Spirit (Christianity), *see* Holy Ghost
Holy Spirit (Zoroastrianism), **11:** 3100f
see also Ahura Mazdah; Ohrmazd
holy war, 11: 2991ff
Christian, **11:** 2993–5
  see also crusade
in Egypt, **11:** 2991–2, 2992
in Greece, **11:** 2996
headhunting seen as, **11:** 2996
in Islam, *see jihad*
Jews and, **11:** 2992–3
  see also Jericho, fall of; promised land
in Sumeria, **11:** 2992
Holy Week (Christianity), **3:** 764f
Holywell (Wales), medicinal well at, **10:** 2685
Home, Daniel Dunglas (medium), **5: 1333–5, 7:** *1793,* **10:** 2658–9
accordion of, **5:** *1334*
Robert Browning and, **5:** 1335
Sir William Crookes and, **2:** 547, **5:** 1334, **7:** 1790
levitation of, **5:** 1334, *1335*
Bulwer Lytton and, **5:** 1335
table-tilting and, **5:** 1333f
Homer, 5: 1167, 1296, **8:** 2085, **11:** 2890
homoeopathic magic, Frazer's use of the term, **3:** 642f
homoeopathy, 5: 1336–7
homosexuality, 5: 1338
of shamans, **1: 105, 5:** 1338
see also lesbianism
homunculus (artificial human being; alchemy), **4:** *1136,* **5: 1338**
Honen (Japanese priest), **1:** 120
honey, 5: 1339–42
as aphrodisiac, **5:** 1340
marriage and, **5:** 1340
in Samson's riddle, **9:** 2384
of Zeus, stolen by Celeus, **11:** 3060
see also bee
'Honi soit qui mal y pense', 4: 1070
Honorius I (pope), Monothelitism

and, **2:** 472
hood (head-dress), **5: 1342**
hoodoo, 5: 1342
Hoomi, Koot (Mahatma), Mme Blavatsky and, **1:** 292f, **6:** 1698
hoopoe, 1: 271
in Philomela myth, **7:** 2000, **10:** 2735
springwort and, **11:** 3060
Hope, William (spirit photographer), **10:** 2663
Hope Diamond, 6: 1513–14, **10:** 2773
Hopewell Indians, 8: 2007
Hopi Indians (Pueblo), **9:** 2300f, 2530
Hopkins, Matthew (Witchfinder General), **3:** 755f, *757, 852,* 854, **8:** 2247
Hop Scotch (children's game), **2:** 454
hora (ring dance), **2:** 413, 590, *590,* **3:** 763
Horites (Biblical people), Hurrians identified with, **5:** 1323
Horkey Supper (harvest), **5:** 1214
hornbill (bird), in New Guinea, **7:** *1974*
horn dance, *see* Abbots Bromley
horns, 5: 1343–52
on altars, **1:** 116
Celts and, **2:** *442,* **5:** 1348–52
crescent moon as, **2:** 542
in Crete, **5:** 1348, **10:** *2820*
cuckoldry and, **4:** 1089
in Egypt, **5:** 1347, **7:** 1877
as fertility symbols, **2:** 542
in Greece, **5:** 1348
Hebrews and, **5:** 1347–8
of Herne the Hunter, **5:** 1293
horn dance, *see* Abbots Bromley
horned gods, **5:** 1346ff
in India, **5:** 1346–7
in Mesopotamia, **5:** 1347
in Neolithic period, **5:** 1345–6
in Paleolithic period, **5:** 1343–5
of reindeer, Thermes and, **6:** *1606*
in Scandinavia, **5:** 1346
sexuality and, **5:** 1343
of unicorn, **11:** 2908f, 2909–10
see also cornucopia; *mano cornuta;*
also bull; ram; stag
horoscope, 1: 175ff, 273, **5: 1352**
of Elizabeth I, by John Dee, **3:** 617
of Hitler, **7:** 1945, *1945,* 1947
of Karl Ernst Krafft, **1:** 178–9, 181–2
horse, 5: 1352–7
of Achilles, **5:** 1212
of Alexander the Great (Bucephalus), **1:** 104, **11:** *2952*
Celts and, **1:** 128, 130, **2:** 347, **5:** 1352, 1357
in China:
jade, **6:** *1479*
stone, at Nanking, **1:** 128
controlled by toadmen, **11:** 2856
divination by, **5:** 1357
Freyr and, **1:** 130, **4:** 1052
Hades and, **8:** 2209
Mars and, **7:** 1743
of Odin (Sleipnir), **6:** 1642, **8:** 2043, *2044*
phantom, **4:** 1097, **5:** 1355f
Poseidon and, **5:** 1352, **8:** 2235
sacrifice of, **4:** 1052, **5:** 1353, 1410, 1435
sun and, **10:** 2720
vampires detected by, **11:** 2926
Vishnu incarnate as, **9:** *2550–1*
in Voodoo (metaphorical), **7:** 1961
winged, **11:** 3032
see also Pegasus
witches and, **5:** 1354
see also Apocalypse, horsemen of the; centaur; hobby-horse; horseshoe; kelpies; Thracian Rider god; white horse of Uffington; Wild Hunt
horseshoe, 5: 1358
horse whisperers, 5: 1357
***hortus conclusus,* 6:** 1601
Horus, 3: 790, **5: 1359–60**
eye of, **4:** 886, **5:** 1359, **9:** *2488*
falcon and, **5:** 1359, 1360
Geb as father of, **5:** 1359
Harpocrates, **3:** 742, **8:** 2087
Hathor as mother of, **5:** 1359
Isis and, **5:** *1359,* 1359f, **6:** 1460, 1461
Osiris and, **4:** 886, **5:** 1359, **8:** 2086, 2087
Re and, **3:** 789, *789,* **5:** 1360, **6:** *1625*
Seth and, **3:** 790, **5:** 1359, **8:** 2087, 2533
as sky god, **5:** 1359, **10:** 2602
sun and, *see* Re *above*
thoth and, **5:** 1359
Hosea (Old Testament prophet), **8:** 2266f, **9:** 2458
Hospitallers (Knights of Rhodes, of Malta), **5: 1360, 6:** 1576, **11:** 2995
host (Christianity), **5: 1360, 7:** 1768
in trial by ordeal, **8:** 2036
Hottentots, their myth of origin of death, **3:** 613
Houdini, Harry, 10: *2659*
houri, 5: 1360
hours, 3: 607, **5: 1360**
house, 5: 1361–8
Lares and, **6:** 1608
see also builders' rites; chimney; haunts, haunted houses; hearth; house warming; threshold
House of God (Tarot card), *see* Tower Struck by Lightning
houseleek (Jupiter's beard, thunder-beard; plant), **5: 1369**
houses of eternity (Parthian tombs), **8:** 2144
house warming, origin of, **5:** 1253
Howard, Peter (leader of Moral Rearmament), **7:** 1884
Howarth, Mgr Arthur, 11: 2987
howling dervishes, *see* Rufai dervishes
Hrimthursar (frost giants; Scandinavian mythology), **11:** 3038
Hrungnir (giant), Thor and, **10:** 2826
Hrunting (sword of Beowulf), **10:** 2746, 2748
Hsi Wang Wu (Chinese deity), **10:** *2786*
Huang Ti (the Yellow Emperor), **10:** 2786
Hubert, St, mad dogs and, **3:** *665*
***hubris* 4:** 921
Hudson, Frederick (spirit photographer), **10:** 2663
Hudson, Henry (explorer), mermaid seen by, **7:** 1811
Huelsenbeck, Richard (artist), **1:** 147
Hugh of St Victor:
on the number five, **4:** 988
mysticism and, **7:** 1933, 1937
on the number two, **11:** 2906
Huguenots, 2: 397, **5: 1369**
Hui-Neng (Eno; Zen master), **11:** 3079
Huitzilopochtli (Aztec god), **1:** 131, 215, 216
humanism, in the Renaissance, **9:** 2370ff
human sacrifice, 2: 576
Abraham and Isaac, **4:** 976, *976,* **9:** *2455,* 2556, **11:** 2897
ancestor worship and, **2:** 576
blood and, **1:** 295, **9:** 2457
in building rites, **2:** 361, 454
Carthaginians and, **4:** 976, **8:** 2184, **10:** 2764
Celtic, **2:** 428, *428,* 441f, **3:** 720
children's games and, **2:** 454
Etruscans and, **3:** 850
in Greece, **1:** 246
at harvest, by Khonds, **5:** 1217–18
Kali and, **6:** 1556
in Melanesia, **7:** 1796
in Mexico, **1:** 216, *216, 217,* 218, **7:** 1772, **9:** *2454,* 2457
nursery rhymes and, **8:** 2026
Odin and, **8:** 2045
by Pawnee Indians, **8:** 2008–10, 2457
Phoenicians (Canaanites) and **4:** 976
see also Carthaginians *above*
in Polynesia, **8:** 2231
prehistoric, in Denmark, *see* Tollund, hanged man of
at Rome, **9:** 2419
the sea and, **9:** 2510
Slavs and, **10:** 2611
in Sweden, **8:** 2045, **9:** 2457
Humbaba (Huwawa; Babylonian giant), **11:** 3029
Hume, David, 7: 1849–50
humours, theory of the four, **3:** 801f
Saturn and, **9:** 2480
Hung Hsui-chuan, 7: 1827, *1834*
Huns, *see* Attila
hunting magic, 5: 1370–5
Assyrian, **5:** *1370*
cave art and, **2:** 432f, **5:** 1374
dance and, **2:** 589
of Ndembu of Zambia, **5:** 1374f
Nigerian, **5:** *1371*
taboo and, in Brazil, **5:** 1374
of Zuni Indians (Shalako), **8:** 2304
Hurayrah, Abu, 10: 2715
Hurrians (Mesopotamian people), **10:** 1323, 1324
al-Husayn (imam), **6:** 1469–70, **7:** 1873f
Husk Faces (Iroquois), **6:** 1457, 1458
Huss, John (Christian preacher), **2:** 473, **5:** 1286
Hut, Hans, 5: 1376
Hutter (Huter), Jacob, 5: 1376
Hutterian Brethren, 2: 499, **5: 1376–7, 9:** 2520
Huwawa (giant), *see* Humbaba
Huysmans, Joris-Karl, 1: *240,* 241, **9:** 2343
Hydra (water-snake), Hercules and, **5:** 1279
Hydromancy, *see* water, divination by
Hyena, 5: 1378
Hymir (giant), Thor and, **10:** 2826
hymn, 5: 1379
Peculiar People and, **8:** 2157
in Pentecostal churches, **10:** 2631
Hyperboreans, Apollo and, **1:** 139
Hypnos (Greek god of sleep), **3:** *706–7, 710*
hypnotism, 5: 1379
in medicine, **4:** 908, **7:** 1815ff, 1854, 1855
Freud and, **4:** 1049
psychical research and, **5:** 1190, **8:** 2275
in research into reincarnation, **9:** 2350
see also magnetism
Hypsisterians (4th cent. sect), **4:** 1127
Hyslop, Prof. J. H., Mrs Piper and, **8:** 2199
hysteria, 7: 1854
dancing mania and, **2:** 600
disease and, **7:** 1852f
Freud on, **4:** 1049, **8:** 2228
inedia and, **10:** 2701
poltergeists and, **8:** 2227f
stigmata and, **10:** 2698, 2700, 2701
witchcraft and, **5:** 1380ff, **8:** 2280

I

Iacchus procession (from Athens to Eleusis), **3:** 807
Iamblichus (Neoplatonist), **7:** 1968, **8:** 2260, **10:** 2822, 2823
Iao (variant of Tetragrammaton), **7:** 1942
ib (Egypt), **3:** 791
Ibadites (Islam), **6:** 1470
Iban people (Sarawak), **1:** 312ff
ibis, Thoth and, **3:** 791
Iblees (Islamic devil), **6:** 1516
Ibn Anas, Malik (Sunnite), **6:** 1465
Ibn Arabi (Islamic mystic), **5: 1385–6**
Ibn Gebirol (Jewish thinker), **7:** 1968
Ibn Hanbal, Ahmad (Sunnite), **6:** 1465
Ibn Idria al-Shafii, Mohammed (Sunnite), **6:** 1465
Ibn Tumart (Mahdi), **6:** 1699
Ibo (Nigerian tribe), **5: 1386–8**
Icarus, fall of, **10:** *2724,* **11:** 3033
ice, 11: 3039
in Scandinavian creation myth, **4:** 1103
Iceland, poets of, **8:** 2212
Iceland spar, 6: 1511
I Ching (Yee King. Book of Change), **5:**

1389–91
atavistic experience with, **1:** 183
in Japan, **6:** 1648
icon, 5: 1399
Byzantine, **5:** *1392*
Iconoclastic Controversy, 2: 472, **5:** 1399
iconography, 5: 1392–9
see also idol
***iconostasis*, 9:** 2365
id (Freudian term), **4:** 1049
idol, 5: 1400
Idomeneus (Greek myth), **11:** 3090
Idris (giant), **2:** 388
Idun (Norse mythology), **3:** 734, **4:** 1051, **6:** 1642
Iemanja (Nigerian/Brazilian goddess), **10:** 2639ff, 2644, 2645
ifreet (jinn), **6:** 1516
Ifugao tribe (Philippine Islands), **9:** 2253
Ignatius, epistle of, **7:** 1985
***ignis fatuus*,** *see* will-o'-the-wisp
IHS (IHSV, IHV; Christian symbol), **2:** 550
Ikhnaten (Akhenaten, Amenhotep IV; pharaoh), **3:** 790, *793,* **5:** 1282, **1400–2**
***Iliad*, 11:** 2890
see also Homer
Ilion (Ilios), *see* Troy
Ilithyia (Greek goddess), Hera and, **5:** 1271
Illuminati, Order of the, **5: 1402–4**
ill-wishing, 2: 580
see also evil eye
Ilmarinen (Finnish god), *see* Ukko
Ilmuqah (Ethiopian moon god), *see* Sin
image magic (witch dolls, wax images, etc.), **5:** 1407–9
in Brittany, **2:** 348
in the Congo, **2:** 510
witches and, **2:** *582,* **5:** 1407ff, **8:** 2281, **11:** *3042*
Gowdie, **4:** 1144
Lancashire witches, **5:** 1407
North Berwick witches, **5:** 1409, **8:** 2014
in the Ozarks, **8:** 2100
Somerset witches, **10:** 2626
imagination, the, 10: 2806
Coleridge on, **2:** 494
in magic, **6:** 1686f
imam (Islam), **6:** 1466
Imamites (Islam), **6:** 1469f
see also Imams, the twelve
Imams, the twelve (Islam), **6:** 1469–70, 1699
Bahais and, **1:** 224
Imbolc (Celtic festival), **2:** 346, 441
modern Druids and, **3:** 722
Imdugud (Mesopotamia), **7:** *1820,* 1821
Imhotep (Imouthes), **5:** 1248, **1404–5**
imitative magic, 5: 1406–12
in Australia, **5:** *1409*
cave art as, **2:** 432f
with dolls and wax images, *see* image magic
origin of drama and, **3:** 696
to obtain food, **4:** 1012f, **11:** *3019*
see also leaping and jumping
Immaculate Conception, 5: 1412, 7: 1752, **11:** 2956
St Bernadette of Lourdes and, **6:** 1653
Feast of the, **5:** 1412
pilgrimage to Lourdes on, **6:** 1650
immanent (definition), **5: 1412**
immortality, 5: 1413–16
apple and, **1:** 141
Christianity and, **5:** 1413ff
shell as symbol of, **9:** 2560
in Egypt, **7:** 1904
see also Egypt, life after death
in Greece, **5:** 1413
in Polynesia, **8:** 2231
Walworth Jumpers' belief in, **11:** 2984
see also life after death
Imouthes (healing god), *see* Imhotep
imp (demon), **5: 1417**
witches' imps, *see* familiars
impotence:
Evil Eye and, **8:** 2283
knot-tying and, **10:** 2710
witchcraft and, **5:** 1380f, 1453, **8:** 2281
Inanna (Innin; Sumerian goddess), **5:** 1266, **6:** 1460, **7:** 1819
Ea (Enki) and, **7:** 1822
Ishtar identified with, **6:** 1459f, **7:** 1819
as Mother Goddess, **7:** 1895–6
Tammuz and, **7:** 1820, 1822, **10:** 2776
underworld visited by, **7:** 1821–2, 1895–6, **10:** 2776
Venus equated with, **7:** 1819
incantation, 5: 1418–20
in Mesopotamia, **7:** 1824f
poetry and, **8:** 2210ff
in ritual magic, **5:** 1418ff, **9:** 2400f
incarnation, 5: 1420–1
in Buddhism, **5:** 1420
in Christianity, **2:** 469, **5:** 1420, **9:** 2452
in Egypt, **5:** 1420
in Hinduism, **5:** 1420
see also Vishnu, incarnations of
Incas, 5: 1422–7
creation myth of, *see* Viracocha
long ears of, **2:** 295
sun god and, **5:** *1411,* 1424f
woman and, **5:** 1425
***incendium amoris*, 10:** 2700
incense, 2: 335, **5: 1428**
burnt sacrifice and, **8:** 2164
censer, from Ramsey Abbey, **8:** *2165*
Christianity and, **5:** 1428
in Egypt, **5:** 1428, **8:** 2165
Islam and, **5:** 1428
Judaism and, **5:** 1428
Romans and, **5:** 1428
incest, 5: 1428–9
Eskimo myth of sun and moon, **3:** 833, **5:** 1428
Rumanian myth of sun and moon, **7:** 1877
taboo in Brazil, **2:** 326, 327f
see also Oedipus
incombustibility, 10: 2700–2701
incorruptibility of the body, saints and, **10:** 2701
incubus and succubus, 3: 862, **5: 1430–4, 10: 2713**
Index (of prohibited books), **5:** 1286
India, 5: 1434–6
animal gods of, **1:** *129,* 130
bull gods, **2:** 365, **5:** 1346–7
animal sacrifice in, **5:** 1307f, 1435
horse, **5:** 1410, 1435
Aryan invaders of, **5:** 1434ff, **11:** 3098–9
ashes, ritual use of, in, **1:** *164, 165, 166*
Mrs Besant and, **1:** 258, **10:** 2814, 2815, 2816
the British in, **5:** 1316, 1321
Gandhi, **5:** *1320,* 1321, **6:** 1698
Parsees, **8:** 2137
Punjab, **10:** 2577
cow in, **2:** 530–1
creation myths of, **2:** 415f, 538, **3:** 781, **6:** 1650
cremation in **4:** *972*
dance in, **3:** *696,* **4:** 1089
demons of, **3:** *864, 865*
early inhabitants of, *see* Dravidians; Indus civilization *below*
erotic temple carvings of, **4:** *933,* **5:** *1317, 1318–19*
fakirs of, *see* sadhu
first man myth of, *see* Yama, as first man
flag of, *dharma* symbol in, **2:** 360
flood legends of, **4:** 995
giants in, **4:** *1102*
gods of, **5:** 1434ff
of the dead, *see* Yama, as god of the dead
of fire, *see* Agni
Mother Goddess, **7:** *1893,* 1895
of the sky, **5:** 1434f, **10:** 2601–2
of the sun, **5:** *1306, 1315,* 1435, **10:** 2720, 2722
twin gods, *see* Asvins
see also Hinduism, gods of
headless spirits in, **5:** 1245
Hill Reddi tribe of, **8:** 2249–50
Indus civilization of, **5:** 1436
see also Harappa; Mohenjo-daro
Islam in, **5:** 1316
Jews in, **8:** 2080f
kingship in, **6:** 1572
Mithras and, **7:** 1861
nudity in, **8:** 2017f
path symbolism in, **8:** 2145–6, 2146
peacock in, **8:** 2153
phallic symbolism in, **8:** 2174, *2176*
see also lingam
pilgrimage in, **8:** 2195–6
possession in, **8:** 2239
prostitution in, **8:** 2272
saints and holy men of, *see* Anandamayi Ma; Haranath; Mahatmas; Ramana Maharshi; sadhu; Sai Baba; Sivananda; swami
Saora tribe of, **8:** 2250
snake-charmer of, **10:** *2621*
spring festival in, **10:** *2682, 2683*
tattooing in, **10:** 2800
time, beliefs concerning, **11:** 2846–7, 2848
tree spirits or gods of, **1:** 132, **5:** 1436, **8:** *2243,* **11:** 2875
see also Ajanta caves; Buddhism; Ganges; Gonds; Hinduism; Jains; *Mahabharata;* mantra; Nagas; Nayars of Malabar; Parsees; Sikhs; soma; Taj Mahal; *Vedas*
individuation, Jung's concept of, **6:** 1550, **8:** 2069
Indra (Indian god), **5:** 1434, **10:** 2601–2, **11:** 2958
in Buddhism, **2:** 357, 359
bull and, **2:** 365
elephant and, *see* Airavata
flood legend and, **4:** *993*
peacock and, **8:** 2153
rainbow and, **9:** 2333
indulgences (Christianity), **2:** 474, **8:** 2196
Indus civilization (India), **5:** 1436
see also Harappa; Mohenjo-daro
inedia, 10: 2701
Ineffable Name of God, 7: 1942
infancy gospels, 7: 1988
initiation, 5: 1437–44
in Africa, **1:** 79f, **7:** 1802
Bushmen, **2:** 380
Congo, **2:** *506–7*
Dahomey, *vodun* cult, **2:** 584
Kikuyu, **5:** 1440
in Australia, **1:** *198, 199*
in Brazil, **2:** 326f, **5:** *1437*
in Crete, **11:** 3090
death and, **5:** 1437, 1443
in Greece, **5:** 1168
see also Eleusis
of Irish heroes, **4:** 964
to magic, **6:** 1684
in Melanesia, **5:** 1440, **7:** 1797
to Mysteries of Isis, **6:** 1461–2
Ndembu and, **9:** 2394–5
in New Guinea, **3:** 725, **7:** 1974–5
of North American Indians, **5:** 1444, **8:** 2107
to priesthood, **8:** 2252–3
in Christianity, *see* holy orders
rebirth and, **5:** 1437
in Roman rites of Mithras, **7:** 1862ff
sex and, **5:** 1443f
see also circumcision
of shamans, **9:** 2546ff
to Voodoo, **11:** 2972ff, 3096
see also rites of passage
Innin (Sumerian goddess), *see* Inanna
Innocent III (pope), **2:** 422, 423–4, **5:** 1283, **10:** 2631
Innocent IV (pope) **5:** 1283
Innocent VIII (pope), **3:** 853, **5:** 1286
Inquisition (Holy Office), **5: 1444**
founding of, **2:** 422, **3:** 853, **5:** 1283, 1444

heresy and, **5:** 1282, 1444
Holy Office, adoption of the title, **5:** 1286
Reformation and, **5:** 1286
witchcraft and, **3:** 852, 853, 1286, 1444, **10:** 2631–2
see also auto da fe; Spanish Inquisition
insects, 6: 1445–51
Peruvian demon, **6:** *1448–9*
see also bee; beetle; butterfly; cricket; flea; mantis; witchety grub
inspiration, 6: 1451, 8: 2215
Institoris, Heinrich, *see* Kramer, Heinrich
Institute of Psychophysical Research, 8: 2093f
International Institute of Universal Research and Administration, 7: 1725
International Legion of Vigilantes, 7: 1725
International New Thought Alliance, 7: 1994
Interplanetary Parliament, 4: 1003
interrogation of the dead (Islam), **6: 1452**
see also Sirat
introvert, extravert distinguished from, by Jung, **6:** 1549
intuition, ESP and, **3:** 875, **10:** 2666, 2668–9
inverted symbols, 6: 1453, 10: 2756
invisibility, 6: 1453
quartz and, **6:** 1510
Invisibles, the (Voodoo), **11:** 2972
invocation, 6: 1454, 1686
evocation and, **6:** 1454, 1687
Io (Greek myth), **5:** 1271, 1461
Iolaus, Hercules and, **5:** 1278, 1279
Iphicles (twin brother of Hercules), **5:** 1279
Ipiutak (Alaska), Eskimo burial at, **3:** 651
Iqbal, Sir Muhammad, 6: 1472
Irenaeus (Christian writer), on the Ebionites **3:** 767
iris (flower), **6:** 1633
Iris (Greek goddess of rainbow), **5:** 1212, 1213, **6: 1454, 9:** 2333
iron (metal), **6: 1454, 10:** 2616
Evil Eye averted by, **6:** 1454
Mars and, **2:** 522
meteors and, **6:** 1454, **10:** 2616
as protection against jinn, **6:** 1516
red and, **2:** 522
smiths and, **10:** 2616
Iron Crown of Lombardy, 2: 551, 564
Iroquois (North American Indians), **6: 1455–8, 8:** 2007, 2011
dances of **2:** 589, 591, **6:** 1457f, **9:** 2538
disease and, **6:** 1458
giant, myth of a, **6:** 1458
masks and, **6:** 1455, *1457,* 1457f
tobacco and, **11:** 2858
see also Hiawatha
Irving, Edward; Irvingites, **6: 1458–9, 10:** 2651
Isaac (son of Abraham), **3:** 798
sacrifice of, *see* Abraham, sacrifice of Isaac and
Isaiah (Old Testament prophet), **8:** 2266f, **10:** 2834
Ishtar (Mesopotamian goddess), **6: 1459–60**
Akkad and, **6:** 1459
Assyria and, **6:** 1460
Astarte identified with, **1:** 168
Gilgamesh and, **4:** 1106
Inanna identified with, **6:** 1459f, **7:** 1819, 1820
moon and, **7:** 1877
as Mother Goddess, **7:** 1895
prostitution and, **6:** 1460, **8:** 2271
ritual marriage of, **6:** 1460
Sin the father of, **5:** 1213
star symbol of, **6:** *1459,* **10:** 2692
Tammuz and, **7:** 1820, **10:** 2776
underworld visited by, **7:** 1821–2, **10:** 2776
Venus (planet) and, **6:** 1460, **10:** 2692
Isis (Egyptian goddess), **3:** 790, **6: 1460–3, 7** *1925*
birth of, in Heliopolitan myth, **2:** 534
cow and, **6:** 1460
Epiphany and, **3:** 742
fate and, **6:** 1462
Greeks and, **6:** 1461
as guardian of the dead, **3:** *786–7*
healing and, **5:** 1248
Horus and, **5:** *1359,* 1359f, **6:** 1460, 1461
Io and, **6:** 1461
moon and, **7:** 1877
Mysteries of, **6:** 1461f, **7:** 1928, **8:** 2088, 2272
Nile and, **6:** 1460, **10:** 2692
Osiris and, **3:** 741, **6:** 1460, 1461, **8:** 2086f, 2088
as Providence, **6:** 1461, 1462
Re and, **3:** 791, **7:** 1941
Romans and, **3:** 741–2, **6:** 1461f, **7:** 1896–7, 1928, **8:** 2088
Sirius (Sothis) and, **6:** 1460, **10:** 2692
Isis Unveiled (Blavatsky), **1:** 291f
Islam, 6: 1464–72
in Africa, **1:** 75, **6:** *1472*
  Egypt, **6:** 1470, 1699
  Ethiopia, **3:** 841
  see also Berbers; Touareg
alsmgiving in, **6:** 1466
angels in, **1:** *126,* **5:** 1187
in China, **2:** 463
dietary rules of, **4:** 1016
divisions of, **6:** 1464–5, 1469f
  see also Shia; Sunnites
dogs and, **2:** 664f
election in, **3:** 800
fakirs in, **4:** 910
fasting and, **4:** 918, **6:** 1446–7
god of, *see* Allah
hell and, **5:** 1266
  see also Sirat
Hinduism and, **5:** 1316
holy war in, *see jihad*
incense and, **5:** 1428
Jerusalem and, **6:** 1502
judgement of the dead in, *see* interrogation of the dead; last judgement *below*
last judgement in, **6:** 1708
man, view of, **6;** 1708
meaning of 'Islam', **6:** 1708
mysticism in, *see* Sufism
paradise and, **8:** 2133, 2135f
  see also houri
pilgrimage in, **6:** 1468, **7:** 1775f, **8:** 2195
predestination and freewill in, **3:** 800, **4:** 921, **6:** 1469, 1470
no priesthood in, **8:** 2256
prophecy in, **8:** 2268
  see also Mohammed
resurrection in, **6:** 1708
revelation in, **9:** 2378
  see also Koran; Mohammed
rosary in, **9:** 2420
saints in, **6:** 1469
Sikhs and, **10:** 2575ff
sin and, **10:** 2580
soul in, **6:** 1708
in Southeast Asia, **10:** 2646, 2648
Touareg and, **11:** 2863
worship in, **6:** 1465f, *1472*
  see also mosque; muezzin
see also Bahais; Black Muslims; Druzes; jinn; Mahdi; Moharram
Isles of the Blest (Fortunate Isles), **6: 1472, 8:** 2132f
Pythagoreans and, **9:** 2305–6
Ismailis (Ismailites; Islam), **3:** 727, **6:** 1470, **1472**
Israel (biblical country), Judah and, **6:** 1643, 1644, **11:** 3065
Israel (modern country), **6:** 1535
Israelites (biblical), *see* Jews
Issberner-Haldane, Ernst (palmist), **7:** 1945
Istanbul, Blue Mosque at, **6:** *1466–7, 1468*
Istanu (Hittite sun god), **5:** 1323
Italian witchcraft, 6: 1473–6
ithyphallic, *see* phallic symbolism
Ittoen (Japanese religious sect), **6:** 1496
luchar (Celtic god), **2:** 443
lucharba (Celtic god), **2:** 443
ivy, 5: 1329–30, 6: 1476, 8: *2202*
Christmas and, **5:** 1329, 1330
Dionysus and, **5:** 1329, **10:** 2837
divination and, **5:** 1330
holly and, **5:** 1329f
ivy doll (corn sheaf), **5:** 1217
Ixion, 2: 445, **11:** 3015
Izana-gi (Shinto god), **9:** 2562
Izana-mi (Shinto goddess), **9:** 2562

J

Jabir ibn Hayyan, *see* Geber
Jack, 6: 1477–8
in the Ozarks, **8:** 2100
jackal, 5: 1378, 6: 1478
Jack and the Beanstalk, 1: *242,* **6:** 1477
Jack of the Bright Light, *see* will-o'-the-wisp
Jack Frost (by Arthur Rackham), **11:** *3038*
Jack the Giant-Killer, 4: *1104,* **6:** 1477, 1478
Jack in the Green, *see* Green Man
Jack and Jill, 6: 1477, **7:** 1877
jack-o-lantern, *see* will-o'-the-wisp
Jacob (Old Testament patriarch), **8:** 2049, **10:** 2697
Jacobite rebellion, ghosts and, **1:** 145
Jacobites (Monophysite sect), **2:** 471
jade, 6: 1478–80, 10: 2773
jaguar, 6: 1480
in Brazil, **2:** 326, *326,* 329, 330, *526,* **5:** *1407,* **6:** 1480
in Mexico, **1:** 131, **7:** *1838*
shape-shifting and, **6:** 1480, 1668
Jahenny, Marie-Julie (stigmatic), **10:** 2699, 2701
Jains, 6: 1480–3
dharma and, **6:** 1481f
Nirvana and, **6:** 1483
soul and, **6:** 1481f
  reincarnation and, **5:** 1309, **6:** 1483
wheel as symbol of time among, **11:** 3014f
Jamaica, Ras Tafari movement in, **7:** 1832–5
James, St (brother of Jesus), **3:** 767, 768, *768*
James, William (psychologist), **8:** 2274
on automatic writing, **1:** 206
on ghosts, **4:** 1100f
on opposites, **8:** 2068
Mrs Piper and, **8:** 2199, 2200
James I (James VI of Scotland):
King's Evil and, **6:** 1573
on tobacco, **8:** 2166
witchcraft and, **3:** 853–4, **8:** 2013ff, **9:** 2446
James II, King's Evil and, **6:** 1573
Jansenists (Christian heretics), **2:** 516
January, Janus and, **1:** 143, **6:** 1483f
Janus (Roman god), **1:** 143, **6: 1483–4**
japam (Hinduism), **11:** *2930,* 2932
Japan, 6: 1485–98
altars in, **1:** 117
Buddhism in, **6:** 1486ff, **8:** *2164,* **9:** 2563, 2564
  Chinese influence on, **6:** 1486, 1488
  judgement of the dead in, **3:** *614,* 616, **6:** *1544*
  see also Amida; Jizo; Kwannon; Zen
carp in, **4:** *987*
dragons in, **3:** 695
emperor of, **6:** *1570–1,* 1572, **9:** 2564
flower arrangement in, **11:** *3084, 3085*
fox in, **6:** *1493,* **8:** *2089*
ghosts in, **4:** *1094–5*
I Ching in, **6:** 1648
modern religious sects of, **6:** 1494–8
  Divine Principles, **3:** 663
pine tree in, **4:** 968, *968*
snow personified in, *see* Yuki-onne
spider in, **10:** *2654, 2655*
Tea ceremony of, **6:** 1492, *1494, 1498*
theatre of, **6:** *1488,* **7:** 1764
wrestlers of, **6:** 1486–7

see also Ainu; hara-kiri; kamikaze; Samurai; Shinto; Silver Pavilion
Jason (Greek hero), **5:** 1257, **7:** 1776, **8:** *2282*
folktale parallels with, **4:** 1007
see also Argonauts; Golden Fleece
jaundice, yellow in cure of, **3:** 642
Java, mask from **5:** *1236*
Jeanne des Anges (Loudun nun), **4:** 1154ff
Jeffreys, George and Stephen (Pentecostalists), **8:** 2162
Jehovah, *see* Yahweh
Jehovah's Witnesses, 3: 826, **6: 1499–1500**
baptism and, **1:** 232, **6:** *1499*
not enthusiasts, **3:** 824
Second Coming and, **6:** 1499, **9:** 2521–2
Jekyll, Dr, and Mr Hyde, 4: *945,* 946, **11:** *3009*
Jenkyn, William, on names, **7:** 1941
Jenny Green Teeth, 7: 1812
Jerah (Canaanite moon goddess), **7:** 1877
Jeremiah (Old Testament prophet), **8:** 2267
Jericho:
fall of (biblical), **9:** 2534, *2896,* **11:** 2897, 2992
origin of the name, **7:** 1877
sanctuaries of, **9:** 2362
skull from, **8:** *2245*
Jeroboam (Israelite leader), **6:** 1643
Jerome, St, 2: 472
on guardian angels, **5:** 1187
lion and, **6:** 1634, **9:** 2471
on reincarnation, **9:** 2346
on the soul, **5:** 1415
on virginity, **7:** 1749–50
Jerusalem, 6: 150–2
Babylonian capture of, **6:** 1644
Christianity and, **3:** 767f, **6:** 1502, 1508, **8:** 2149ff, 2152, **11:** 2993f
entry of Jesus into, **6:** 1508, *1509,* **8:** *2115,* 2116, *2116*
Knights of the Hospital of St John of, *see* Hospitallers
pilgrimage to, **8:** *2194,* 2196
siege of, *11: 2994–5*
15th cent. view of, **11:** *2993*
Islam and, **6:** 1502
temple of Yahweh at, **9:** 2364
built by Solomon, **10:** 2626, **11:** 2906, 3065
cherubim in, **2:** 449
destroyed by Nebuchadnezzar, **11:** 3066
destroyed by Romans, **9:** 2328, **11:** 3066, 3078
see also Zion, hill of
Jesse, tree of, *see* tree of Jesse
jester, medieval, **4:** 1017, *1019*
dervishes perhaps associated with, **3:** 624
see also Herleqin
Jesus, 6: 1503–10
anointing of, **8:** *2049,* 2050
baptism of, **1:** 231, *471,* **6:** *1505,* **11:** *3000*
blood of, **1:** 295, **4:** 1150f, *1150–1*
Bogomil view of, **1:** 304
cross and, *see* Crucifixion; Judgement of the Cross; stations of the cross; True Cross; Veneration of the Cross
888 the number of, **4:** 1158
his entry into Jerusalem, **6:** 1508, *1509,* **8:** *2115,* 2116, *2116*
Gnostic view of, **2:** 470, **4:** 1116, 1117, **9:** 2477
Good Shepherd symbol and, **4:** 1137, **9:** 2559, **10:** 2756
healing by, **4:** 908f
see also Lazarus
Hercules compared with, **5:** 1281
iconography of, **5:** *1395,* 1396ff
see also Lamb of God *below*
as the Lamb of God, **3:** *760,* **4:** 886, 887, **6:** 1591, **9:** 2458, 2556, *2557*
life of, **2:** 466ff, **6:** 1504ff
apocryphal gospel accounts of, **7:** 1986ff
see also Last Supper
as Light of the World (Holman Hunt), **6:** *1623,* 1624
magi and, **6:** 1680, **10:** *2833*
as the Messiah, **2:** 467, **6:** 1507ff, **8:** 2150ff
miracles of, **7:** 1852, 1855
see also Lazarus; marriage at Cana
his mother, *see* Mary, the Virgin
name of, *see* Pentagrammaton
Nativity of, **6:** *1504,* **11:** *2956*
nature of, **2:** 470, 471f, **5:** 1282, **7:** 1749
Osiris compared with, **8:** 2088
St Paul and, **2:** 469, **3:** 768, **6:** 1507f, 1510, **8:** 2150–2
pelican as symbol of, **1:** *267,* **8:** 2158
as prophet, **8:** 2268
in Ravenna mosaic, **11:** *2992*
relics of, *see* Shroud, Holy, of Turin; True Cross; Veronica, St, veil of
resurrection of, **2:** 469, **6:** 1507, 1708
Jonah as symbol of, **6:** 1528
by Mantegna, **6:** *1626–7*
see also Ascension; Easter
in Revelation, **9:** 2378ff
as the son of God, *see* incarnation, in Christianity
St Thomas as twin of, **11:** 2903
water turned to wine by, *see* marriage at Cana
Zealots and, **2:** 467, **6:** 1508ff, **11:** 3077, 3078
see also apostles; Ecce Homo; harrowing of hell; Mass; Pontius Pilate; Second Coming; soteriology; stigmata
jet (mineral), **10:** 2773
jewels, precious stones, **6: 1510–14**
see also emerald; garnet; pearl; quartz; sardonyx
Jewish Gnosticism, 4: 1115
Jews (Hebrews, Israel, Israelites):
as the chosen people, *see* Judaism, election and
exclusiveness of, Jonah and, **6:** 1527f
harps of, hung on 'willow' trees in exile, **11:** 3031
history of, **11:** 3064ff
see also Old Testament; Rome *below;* twelve tribes *below*
kingship among, **6:** 1570–1
origins of, in Judah, **6:** 1643, 1644
palm tree and, **8:** 2114f
religion of (biblical and modern), *see* Judaism
Rome and, **2:** 466, **9:** 2328, 2458, **10:** 3066, 3077–8
in Spain, converted to Christianity, *see* Marranos
Star of David and, **5:** 1300, *1300,* **6:** *1538*
twelve tribes of, **11:** 2898
see also Lost Tribes of Israel
see also antisemitism; Israel (modern country); Moses; oriental Jewish communities; Wandering Jew
Jezreel, James Jershom, 6: 1514–15, 10: 2646
jihad (Islam), **6:** 1470f, **1516, 11:** 2993
Jinarajadasa, C. (Theosophist), **10:** 2814, *2815,* 2816
jinn (genie; spirit), **6: 1516–17**
Berber belief in, **1:** 256
Jivaro Indians, shrunken heads of, **5:** *1233,* 1237
jnana yoga, 11: 2933–4, 3071
Joachim of Fiore, 9: 2518–20
Joan of Arc, 6: 1518–22
Job, 3: 627, **6: 1522–3, 11:** 3066
Jodo (Pure Land) sect (Japan), **1:** 119, **7:** 2004, 2134
Joel (Old Testament prophet), **8:** *2267*
John, Abbot, of Rila, **9:** *2524*
John, St (evangelist), **11:** 2898
apocryphal acts of, **7:** 1989–92
eagle the symbol of, **5:** *1398*
Revelation and, **9:** 2381–3
John XXII (pope), witchcraft and, **5:** 1286
John XXIII (anti-pope), Huss excommunicated by, **5:** 1286
John the Baptist, St, 1: 230–31, **2:** *471*
bonfires and, **9:** 2461, **11:** 2948, 3039–40
Breton relic of, **2:** 349
dancing mania and, **2:** 599f
by El Greco, **1:** 230
head of, **5:** *1238*
midsummer festival and, **2:** 599, **7:** 1845, **9:** 2461, **11:** 3015–16
as last Old Testament prophet, **8:** 2267–8
John of the Cross, St, 3: 775, **6: 1524–6, 9:** 2318–19, 2538
John of Damascus, St, 8: 2242
John of Leyden (Anabaptist), *see* Beukels, John
John of Nottingham, image magic used by, **5:** 1408
John of Salisbury, 3: 873, **9:** 2371
Johnson, Alice, Society for Psychical Research and, **8:** 2275, 2276
Johnson, Douglas (medium), **7:** *1793*
Jonah, 6: 1526–8
book of, **8:** 2267
in catacomb art, **5:** 1398, **6:** 1528
as Christian symbol of Jesus' resurrection, **6:** 1528
Jewish exclusiveness typified by, **6:** 1527f
'whale' and, **4:** *984,* **6:** 1526, *1526,* 1527, *1527,* 1528, *1528,* **11:** 3013, *3013*
Jordan (river), symbolism of, **6:** 1602
Joseph (father of Jesus), 11: 2952, 2954, 2956
apocryphal accounts of, **7:** 1988–9
wedding of (Giotto), **7:** *1989*
Joseph (Old Testament), dream of Pharaoh and, **3:** *702–3,* 705
Joseph, R. Jacob (Hasidism), **5:** 1220
Joseph of Arimathea, 6: 1528
Fisher King and, **4:** 1153
Glastonbury and, **4:** 1109, 1111, 1114
Grail and, **4:** 1109, 1111, **5:** 1150f, 1153, **6:** 1528
holy thorn and, **4:** 1114
Joseph Mary Desu, St (Joseph of Copertino), **10:** 2702f
Josephus (Jewish historian):
on Jesus, **6:** 1507
on John the Baptist, **1:** 231
on Pontius Pilate, **8:** 2233f
Zealots and, **11:** 3077
Joshua (Old Testament), **11:** 2992
joss-stick, 6: 1528, 9: *2562*
Jotunheim (Scandinavian mythology), **9:** 2484
journey, as symbol, *see* path symbolism
Jove (Roman god), *see* Jupiter
Joyeuse (sword of Charlemagne), **10:** 2748
Judah (biblical country), **6:** 1643, 1644, **11:** 3065
Judaism (Jewish religion), **6:** 1522, 1523, **1529–38**
altars and, **1:** 116
angels and, **1:** 124ff
Atonement, Day of (Yom Kippur), **1:** 192, **6:** 1536, **9:** 2458, 2487
Baal and **1:** 222, 223
baptism in, **1:** 230
see also John the Baptist
Bible and, **6:** 1532
see also Old Testament
bull and, **5:** 1347–8
candles, use of, *see* Hanukkah; menorah
circumcision and, **6:** *1530*
creation myths of, **2:** 537f
Dead Sea Scrolls and, **3:** 609ff
death and, **3:** 616, **6:** 1706
see also life after death *below;* Sheol
the Devil in, **3:** 625ff, 733
dietary rules of, **4:** 1015–16
see also kosher
dogs and, **3:** 664
dreams and, **3:** 704f
dualism in, **3:** 859

dying god myth rejected by, **3:** 743
election and, **3:** 797ff, **6:** 1535, **11:** 3064ff
embroidery in, **8:** 2070–1
end of the world in, **3:** 818f
eternal return myth contrasted with, **3** 838, 839
in Ethiopia, **3:** 841
evil and, **3:** 859f
exorcism and, **3:** 870
fasting and, **4:** 918, **6:** 1536
festivals of, **6:** 1535, 1536
see also Feast of Tabernacles; Hanukkah; Passover
Gnosticism and, **4:** 1115f
hell and, **5:** 1260–1
history and, **5:** 1322
holy war and, **11:** 2992–3
see also Jericho, fall of; promised land
iconography forbidden in, **5:** 1396
incense and, **5:** 1428
judgement of the dead and, **6:** 1523, 1545
Last Judgement, **6:** 1545, 1609, **8:** 2135
life after death in, **6:** 1522, 1535
see also judgement of the dead *above*
mysticism in, *see* mysticism, Jewish
New Year in, **6:** 1536
origin of the word Judaism, **6:** 1643
original sin and, **4:** 980
origins of Christianity and, **2:** 466, **3:** 767f, **5:** 1322, **8:** 2149ff
paradise and, **8:** 2133, 2134, 2135f
pig not eaten by Jews, **4:** 1016, **8:** 2191
priesthood in, **6:** 1531
prophecy and, **8:** 2267, 2268, **9:** 2377, prophetic books, **6:** 1532
ram and, **5:** 1348, **9:** 2556
resurrection of the body and, **6:** 1535, 1545, 1708
sacrifice and, **9:** 2458
see also atonement, Jewish day of
soul in, **6:** 1535, **8:** 2135
Trinity rejected by, **6:** 1531
trumpet and, **11:** 2897
see also mezuzah; Moses; Pharisees; rabbi; sabbath; Sadducees; Torah; Yahweh
Judaizers (Russian heretical sect), **3:** 679
Judas of Galilee, 11: 3077
Judas Iscariot, 6: 1538
St Brendan and, **6:** 1538
suicide of, **6:** 1538
elder tree and, **3:** 796, *796*
fig tree and, **4:** 940
Judas Maccabaeus, 3: 609, **8:** 2306
Jüdel (double; Germany), **3:** 672
Judge, W. Q. (Theosophist), **1:** *292*
Judgement (Day of Judgement; Tarot card), **8:** 2146, **10:** *2793,* 2794
Judgement of the Cross (judicial procedure), **8:** 2036–7
judgement of the dead, 6: 1539–47
in Christianity, **6:** 1546
see also Last Judgement, in Christianity
in Egypt **3:** 791, **5:** 1259, **6:** 1539–41
Anubis and, **1:** 134
heart weighed in, **4:** 929, **5:** *1251,* **6:** 1541, *1542–3,* 1671
Maat and, **4:** 929, **6:** 1671
Osiris and, **4:** 929, **6:** 1541, **8:** 2088
Thoth and, **3:** 791, **6:** 1541
Greece and, **6:** 1545
in Islam, *see* interrogation of the dead; Last Judgement, in Islam
in Japanese Buddhism, **3:** 616, **6:** *1544*
in Judaism, **6:** 1523, 1545
Last Judgement, **6:** 1545, 1609, **8:** 2135
paradise as reward after, **8:** 2133ff
in Zoroastrianism, **2:** 345, **6:** 1545–6, **11:** 3100–3101
Parsees, **8:** 2138, 2141
see also hell
Judgement of Paris (Greek mythology), **1:** 142, *142,* **9:** *2371,* 2374
juggernaut, 8: 2196
Juggler (Tarot card), *see* Magician
Julia Domna (Roman empress), **1:** 140, 141
Julian the Apostate (Roman emperor), **1:** 141, **10:** *2821,* 2822
Julian of Norwich (mystic), **2:** 489, **6: 1548**
Pseudo-Dionysius and, **3:** 634
Julianus the Chaldean, 10: 2821
Julius Caesar, 4: 1028
comets and, **2:** 496
on the Druids, **2:** 439, **3:** 719, 720, 721
Venus and, **11:** 2944
Jumala (Finnish god), *see* Ukko
Jumna (river), **4:** 1068, 1069
Junayd of Baghdad (Sheikh of the Sheikhs), **10:** 2713
Jung, Carl Gustav, 6: 1548–52
alchemy and, **1:** 99, **6:** 1550f
analytical psychology, his adoption of the term, **6:** 1548–9
archetypes, his concept of, **6:** 1549f
astrology and, **1:** 176, **6:** 1552
city seen as maternal symbol by, **6:** 1602
collective unconscious, his concept of, **6:** 1549
complex defined by, **6:** 1548
dragon and, **3:** 695
on dreams, **3:** 710
extravert and introvert distinguished by, **6:** 1549
Ezekiel and, **11;** 3017
Freud and, **6:** 1548f, 1550
on ghosts, **4:** 1100
on God, **7:** 1780
on the I Ching, **5:** 1390f
individuation, his concept of, **6:** 1550, **8:** 2069
libido and, **6:** 1548
on opposites, in creation myths, **8:** 2069
paranormal powers of, **6:** 1550
religion studied by, **9:** 2358
on symbolism, **10:** 2759
synchronicity, his principle of, **6:** 1552, 1648, **11:** 2950
on trickster, **11:** 2885
on the unconscious, **11:** 3002
see also collective unconscious *above*
vision experienced by, **11:** 2962
Jung-Stilling, Dr J. H., 6: 1693
Junius, Johannes (witch), **1:** 228
Juno (Roman goddess), **6: 1552, 9:** 2412
Hera identified with, **5:** 1271, **6:** 1552
Jupiter (planet):
in astrology, **1:** 175, 180, **6:** 1554
blue and, **1:** 296, **2:** 522
jewels associated with, **6:** 1511–12
Pisces and, **6:** 1554, **8:** 2200
Sagittarius and, **6:** 1554
tin and, **2:** 522
Jupiter (Jove; Roman god), **6: 1552–4, 9:** 2412, **11:** *3089*
Etruscans and, **6:** 1553
as High God, **5:** 1302
priest of, *see* flamen, Flamen Dialis
sky and, **6:** 1552f, **10:** 2601
thunderbolt and, **10:** *2602*
Zeus and, **6:** 1552
Jurieu, Pierre, 2: 397
Jurupari (Brazilian spirit), **2:** 327
Justice (Tarot card), **8:** 2147, **10:** 2792–3, *2793*

K

ka (double; Egypt), **3:** 791
Kaaba (Islam), **7:** 1775, 1776, *1776,* 1871
pilgrimage to, **6:** 1468
prayer directed to, **6:** 1465
Mohammed and, **7:** 1872, **10:** *2708*
Kabbalah (Jewish mystical system), *see* Cabala
kachina (dancers, dolls), *see* Pueblo Indians, kachina dancers/dolls of
Kadesh, battle of, **11:** 2992
Kadmis (Parsee sect), **8:** 2137
Kai Ka'ns (Persian legend), **3:** *745*
Kailasa, Mount (Indian mythology), **8:** *2132*
Kalanga (of Botswana), guardian spirits of, **5:** 1183–5, 1185f, *1187*
Kalbhairab (Indian demon), **3:** *864*
Kalevala (Finnish poem), **4:** 958ff
Kali (Indian goddess), **1:** 123, **3:** *614,* 616, **4:** 937, **6: 1554–6, 10:** *2778, 2779*
Anandamayi Ma and, **1:** 121–22
blackness of, **6:** 1554f
Durga and, **6:** 1556
as Great Mother, **6:** 1554
iconography of, **5:** 1396, **11:** 2847
lotus held by, **6:** 1650
sacrifice and, **6:** 1556
time personified by, **11:** 2847
see also Thugs
Kaliya (serpent; Hinduism), **9:** *2528*
Kalkin (incarnation of Vishnu), **11:** 2960
Kallisto (Greek goddess), see Callisto
kama (Hinduism), **5:** 1315, **6: 1556**
Kamakura Period (Japan), **6:** 1486, 1489f
kamikaze, 6: 1557
Kamwana, Elliot (African religious leader), **9:** 2522
Kandinsky, Vasily, on colour, **2:** 494
Kanphata ('ear-torn' yogis), **1:** 299
Kaourintin, St, 2: 349
Karbala, battle of, **6:** 1470, **7:** 1873
Kardec, Alain; Kardecists, **7:** 1981, **10:** 2642ff
Karens (Burmese people), rainbow and, **9:** 2333
***karma*, 6: 1558–60,** 1709, **11:** 2934
caste dependent on, **5:** 1315
sin and, **10:** 2582
in Sinhalese Buddhism, **10:** 2587
karma yoga, 1: 2934, 3071
Karttikeya (Hindu god), **5:** *1310*
Katha Kali (Indian danced drama), **3:** *696*
Kaustubha (Indian gem), **6:** 1514
kava (Polynesian drink), **6: 1560**
Kay (Arthurian knight), **1:** 154, 155
Kayan people (Borneo), **2:** 316
Keely, John Worrell, 11: 2949–50
Kelabit people (Borneo), **1:** 316
Kelley, Edward, John Dee and, **3:** 618f
kelpies (Scottish water spirits), **4:** 902, **4: 1560, 7:** 1814
Kempe, Margery, on Julian of Norwich, **6:** 1548
Kempe, Ursula (witch), **3:** 866
Kentigern, St, 9: 2402, 2474
Kenya, Mount, 6: *1561*
Kepler, Johann, his imaginary account of the moon, **9:** 2494
keres (Greek spirits), **4:** 920, **6: 1561**
Keres Indians (Pueblo), **9:** 2300ff
Ker-Is (Breton lost land legend), **4:** 996
kern baby, kern doll (corn sheaf), **2:** 518, **5:** 1217
Kerry, Great White Horse of (hobby-horse), **5:** 1327
Kevin, St, blackbird and, **9:** 2468
key, 5: 1364, **6: 1561, 10:** 2756
Key of Solomon (grimoire), **1:** 299, **5:** 1181, *1181, 1182,* **6:** *1687,* **7:** *1941*
arthame in, **1:** 151
magic circle in, **9:** 2399
planets in, **3:** 607
purification of magician prescribed in, **9:** 2398
sacrifice in, **9:** 2400
Sunday, rituals appropriate to, in, **2:** 522
white recommended in, **9:** 2399
Khakists (Congolese movement), **7:** 1979
Khan, Sir Sayyid Ahmad, 6: 1472
Kharijites (Islam), **6:** 1470
Khlysty (Men of God), **9:** 2338, 2523, **10:** 2594
Khnum (Khnemu; Egyptian god), **5:** *1344,* **9:**

2556
creation of man and, **2:** 535, **4:** 1053
Khomeini, Ayatollah Ruhollah, 6: 1472
Khonds (Bengali tribe), harvest sacrifice of, **5:** 1217–18
Khunrath, Heinrich (alchemist), **8:** 2178
Ki (Sumerian goddess), **3:** 750
kidneys, jade used for disorders of, **6:** 1478f
Kikuyu (African tribe), **5:** 1440, **6: 1561–5**
see also Mau Mau
ki-lin (Chinese unicorn), *see* unicorn, in China
killer whale, Pacific North-West Indians and, **8:** *2106, 2107*
Kilner, W. R., aura and, **3:** 677f
Kimbangu, Simon (Congolese religious leader), **7:** 1978, **9:** 2522
Kinabalu, Mount (Borneo), **11:** 312
Kinderhook plates (Mormonism), **7:** *1888*
'kindly ones', the (Eumenides; Greek mythology), *see* Furies
king, 6: 1566–72
anointing of, **6:** *1572,* **8:** 2049–50
in China, **6:** 1572
costume, royal, **2:** 528
dying god and divine king, **2:** 739
Egyptian, *see* pharaoh; Ptolemy
fertility and, **6:** 1566ff, **11:** 2941
in Greece, **6:** 1572
in India, **6:** 1572
in Ireland, **2:** 439, **10:** 2787, 2788
in Israel, **6:** 1570–1
in Japan (emperor), **6:** *1570–1,* 1572, **10:** 2564
killing of, **6:** 1566ff, **11:** 2941
in Mesopotamia, **6:** 1570
Nilotes and, **7:** 2001
in Persia, **6:** 1571–2, **7:** 1862
  see also Achaemenids; Sassanians
in Phoenicia, **10:** 2762
in Rome, **6:** 1572
  emperor, **6:** 1572, **7:** 1928–9, **9:** 2418
  Mystery religions and, **7:** 1928–9
Swazi and, **9:** 2393
as vegetation god, **6:** 1566
see also coronation; divine right; Fisher King; King's Evil
King's Bench, Court of, medieval, **8:** *2037*
King's Evil (scrofula), **3:** *642,* 644, **6: 1573**
Kirlian photography, 6: 1573
kiss, 6: 1574
caulking, **10:** 2568
mistletoe and, **2:** 481, **7:** 1860
obscene (*osculum infame*):
  Knights Templar and, **6:** 1576
  Luciferans and, **6:** 1663
  witches and, **3:** 853, *856,* **4:** 1118, **9:** 2446
Kissos (nymph), **5:** 1329
kiswa (Islam), **7:** 1776
Kitamura Sayo (Japanese religious leader), **6:** 1495
kite (bird), **5:** 1227
see also brahminy kite
kite flying, 6: 1574
Klee, Paul, 1: 149
Kloppenburg, Bonaventura (Franciscan priest), **10:** 2645
Kluski, Franek (medium), **8:** 2277
knackers (knockers; mine fairies), **2:** 519
Knigge, Adolph, 5: *1403,* 1403f
knights, knighthood, **11:** 2995
of the Round Table, *see* Arthur, knights of
sword and, **10:** 2749
see also Hospitallers; Knights Templar; Order of the Garter; vigil
Knights of Malta, *see* Hospitallers
knight's milfoil (plant), *see* yarrow
Knights of Rhodes, *see* Hospitallers
Knights Templar, 6: 1574–6, 11: 2995
Baphomet and, **1:** 229, **6:** 1576
knockers (mine fairies), *see* knackers
Knorr, Nathan (leader of Jehovah's Witnesses), **6:** 1500
Knossos (Crete), *see* Cnossus
knot, 6: 1576, 10: 2710–12
in childbirth, **10:** 2710
in love magic, **10:** 2710
in medicine, **10:** 2711
as Odin's symbol, **8:** 2045, 2047
Shinto, symbolic, **10:** *2564*
in white magic, **11:** 3019
wind controlled by, **10:** 2712
in witchcraft, **10:** 2712
in zombification rite, **11:** 3096
Knott, Elizabeth, image magic used by, **5:** 1408
koan (Zen riddle), **11:** 3085–6
Kobo Daishi (Kukai; Japanese priest), **6:** 1489
Koerner, Bernhard, runes and, **9:** 2441
Kolo (Yugoslav ring dance), **2:** 413
Konarak, Indian temple at (the Black Pagoda), **5:** *1318–19,* **10:** 2722, *2777*
Kono (tribe of Guinea), masks and, **7:** 1756–7
Koran (Islamic sacred text), **6:** 1465, 1468, **1576, 7:** 1871
belief and submission distinguished in, **6:** 1464
eternity of, **6:** 1469
dictated by Gabriel, **8:** 2268, **9:** 2378
jihad and, **11:** 2993
jinn in, **6:** 1516
judgement of the dead in, **6:** 1452
light and darkness in, **6:** 1624
Medina suras of, **7:** 1872–3
Mohammed as God's messenger in, **9:** 2378
Queen of Sheba in, **9:** 2316
Sufism and, **10:** 2714
Korsch, Dr Hubert (astrologer), **7:** 1945, 1947–8
kosher (Judaism), **6: 1576**
Kostka, St Stanislaus, 10: 2700
Kothmann (witch-hunter of Lemgo), **4:** 1080
Kowalski, Michael, 11: 2988
Kozlowska, Maria, 11: 2988
Kozma (Bulgarian priest), on the Bogomils, **1:** 303, 304
Krafft, Karl Ernst (astrologer), **7:** *1947*
horoscope of, **1:** 178–9, 181–2
National Socialism and, **7:** 1946, 1947, **8:** 2017
Kräger, Professor Heinrich, 4: 1081
Krak des Chevaliers, 6: *1575*
kraken (sea-monster), **4:** 985, **6: 1577**
Kremlin, Cathedral of the Assumption in, **9:** *2365*
Kretschmer, Ernst (psychologist), **8:** 2190
Krishna (Hindu god), **1:** 260ff, *269,* **5:** *1311,* 1313f, **6: 1578–84,** 1629, **7:** *1930,* 1936, **8:** 2195, **11:** 2958, 2960
cow and, **2:** 531
demons and, **6:** 1580, *1581*
flood legend and, **4:** *993*
hell and, **5:** 1266
Kaliya and, **9:** *2528*
Radha and, **5:** 1314, **6:** 1584
sexuality and, **5:** 1314
see also Gouranga
Krishna Chaitanya (Indian saint), *see* Gouranga
Krishnamurti, Jeddu, 1: 258, 259, **5:** *1321,* **10:** 2815–6
kriya yoga 11: 3071
Kshatriyas (caste; Hinduism), **2:** 415f
Ku (Hawaiian god), *see* Tu
Kukai (Japanese priest), *see* Kobo Daishi
Ku Klux Klan, 5: *1244*
Kukulcan (Maya god), **9:** 2529
Kulibangan (city; India), **5:** 1436
Kullervo (Finnish myth), **4:** 961
Kuloskap (Algonquin culture-hero), **3:** 651
Kumarbi (Kumarbis; Hittite/Hurrian god), **2:** 546, **5:** 1324
Kummer, Siegfried Adolf (rune occultist), **9:** 2441
Kundalini (Hinduism), **2:** 335f, **6: 1585–7,** 1629, **10:** 2780, 2934, **11:** 3071
European counterpart of, *see* Vril Society
Kung Fu-tze, *see* Confucius
kuphi, in worship of Re, **5:** 1428
Kuz'ma-Dem'yan, 10: 2619
Kwakiutl Indians, 8: 2105
flood legend of, **2:** 556
initiation rites of, **5:** 1444
masks of, **8:** *2005*
raven and creation myth of, **8:** 2104
salmon and, **9:** 2474
totemic carving of, **10:** *2862*
winter and, **11:** 3038
Kwannon, 4: *987,* **11:** 3081
Kypris (Cypriot goddess), Aphrodite and, **1:** 135
Kyteler, Alice (witch), **6: 1588**
broomstick and, **2:** 350, **6:** 1588
familiar of, **4:** 915, **6:** 1588

L

Labrys, see double axe
labyrinth, *see* maze
Lachesis (Greek mythology), **4:** 918, *919*
Lacombe, Father, 5: 1191
ladder, *see* steps and ladders
Lady of the Beasts (Mediterranean goddess), **2:** 486, **4:** *922*
ladybird, 6: 1446f
Lady of the Fountain *(Mabinogion),* **5:** 1350–1, **6:** 1672, 1674, **11:** 3027
Lafitau, Joseph, 9: 2357
Lagarde, Paul de, 7: 1965
laibon (Masai medicine-man), **7:** 1754
Lailoken (Scottish legend), **7:** 1810, **11:** 3028
lakes:
Lady of the Lake, Excalibur and, **1:** 159, **3:** 867, **10:** 2748
Lancelot and, **6:** 1594
symbolism of, **6:** 1602
Lakshmi (wife of Vishnu; Hinduism), **4:** *920*
riding Garuda, **1:** 269, **5:** *1310*
lotus and, **6:** 1650
lamas, 6: 1589–90
Nepalese, **8:** *2250*
Tibetan, **6:** 1589–90, **8:** *2256, 2782,* **10:** 2841ff
  see also Dalai Lama
Lamashtu (Mesopotamian spirit), **7:** 1824
lamb, 6: 1591
Easter and, **3:** 760f
Jesus as the Lamb of God, **3:** *760,* 886, **4:** *887,* **6:** 1591, **9:** 2458, 2556, *2557*
Pythagoras and, **9:** 2556
as witches' familiar, **3:** 866
Lamb, Dr, 8: 2222
La Mercuria (witch), **6:** 1476
Lamets (Laotian tribe), **10:** 2646
Lammas (1 August), meaning of the name, **4:** 1013
Lancashire witches, 5: 1382f, **6: 1591–4**
image magic used by, **5:** 1407
see also Device, Elizabeth; Whittle, Anne
Lance, Holy, Grail quest and, **4:** 1059, 1071f, 1146, 1150, 1152f
Lancelot (Arthurian knight), **1:** 154, **6: 1594–5**
Brittany and, **2:** 347, **6:** 1594
Elaine and, **4:** 1059
in the enchanted forest, **11:** *3026–7*
Galahad and, **4:** 1057, 1059, **6:** 1594f
Grail and, **4:** 1153, **6:** 1594f
Guinevere and, **4:** 1153, **6:** *1594,* 1594f
Morgan le Fay and, **7:** 1886
Venus and, **6:** *1595*
Lancre, Pierre de (witch-hunter), **1:** 236–7, 249, 278, **4:** *1044–5,* 1047, **9:** 2446
landscape symbolism, 6: 1596–1603
On landscape generally and on its symbolism, see also castle; caves; earth;

fountain; garden; lakes; mountains; rivers; sea; springs; wells
Lang, Andrew, **4:** 1007, **5:** 1301
Lango (Nilotic people), **7:** 2000
language, *see* words
Lanz, Adolf (Dr Jörg Lanz von Liebenfels), **6:** 1636, **7:** 1982f, *1983*
Lao Tze (Chinese philosopher), **8:** 2004, **10:** 2784, *2784,* 2785
Laparelli, Sister Veronica, **10:** 2701
lapis lazuli, **6:** 1511
lapiths, centaurs and, **2:** 445, **5:** *1354–5,* **10:** 2819
Lapland, **6: 1604–8**
hammer sacrifice in, **5:** 1205
mountains and, **7:** 1900
shamanism in **3:** 725, **6:** 1605f, *1607,* **9:** *2548*
Lares (Roman deities), **6: 1608–9,** **9:** 2418
Las Casas, Sebastian de, Martinists and, **7:** 1747
Lascaux (cave), **1:** 267, **2:** 363, *429, 433*
Last Judgement, **6: 1609**
in Christianity, **6:** 1545, 1546, 1609, **8:** 2135
by Fra Angelico, **3:** *730–1*
in Autun cathedral (12th cent. relief), **9:** *2307*
Blake's view of, **1:** 289
in Ethiopian MS, **3:** *842–3*
in 14th cent. Italian painting, **3:** *797*
by Giotto, **5:** *1262–3*
in *Mappa Mundi,* **7:** 1750
Virgin Mary and, **7:** 1750
serpents and the damned at (Cypriot wall painting), **9:** *2532*
by Signorelli, **1:** *296,* **2:** *604*
souls weighed by angel at, **1:** 124–5, **11:** 3007
trumpet and, **11:** 2895
see also Dooms
in Islam, **6:** 1708
in Judaism, **6:** 1545, 1609, **8:** 2135
in Zoroastrianism, **6:** 1546, **11:** 3101
Last Supper, **6: 1609,** **10:** 2580
by Damaskinos, **10:** *2825*
Grail as chalice used at, **4:** 1150f
in Turkish wall painting, **3:** *808*
see also Mass
Lateau, Louise (stigmatic), **7:** 1971, **10:** 2698
La Tène (Celtic culture), **2:** 439
Druids and, **3:** 719
Latin cross *(crux immissa),* **3:** 550
Latter Day Saints, Church of Jesus Christ of the, *see* Mormons
laurel (tree), **6: 1610–11,** **8:** *2202*
Christmas and, **6:** 1611
Daphne and Apollo and, **6:** 1610, *1610*
Egyptian mummy and, **7:** *1903*
footling and, **6:** 1611
frenzy induced by, **8:** 2202
in Greece, **6:** 1610, 1611, **8:** 2202
magpie and, **6:** 1611
oracles and, **6:** 1610, **11:** 2867
in Rome, **6:** 1610f
wreaths of, **6:** 1610
see also camphor
Laurence, St, **9:** 2464
Lavater, Johann Kaspar, **6: 1611–12,** **8:** 2188, 2190
La Vey, Anton Szandor, **9:** 2477
Law, William (mystic), **6: 1612,** 1629
laya yoga, **11:** 3071
Lazarus, raising of, **11:** *3020*
Lea, H. C., on witchcraft, **4:** 1046
lead (metal), **2:** 522, **6: 1613**
Leadbeater, C. W., **11:** 2990
on the aura, **6:** *1630,* **9:** *2331*
Mrs Besant and, **1:** 258f, **10:** 2816
on elementals in psychic attack, **8:** 2283
Krishnamurti and, **10:** 2815
on the subterranean race, **10:** 2712–13
Leaf, Walter, Society for Psychical Research and, **8:** 2274
Leah, Frank (psychic artist), **1:** 206
leaping and jumping, **6: 1614**
Curetes and, **2:** 522, **6:** 1614
Midsummer bonfires and, **7:** 1845
Lechler, Dr Adolph, stigmata and, **10:** 2698–9
le Clerc, Gentien (witch), **4:** 1047
leconomancy (method of scrying), **9:** 2506
Le Corbusier, church at Ronchamp by, **9:** *2368*
Leda (Greek mythology), **1:** 270, **3:** *782,* **10:** *2737, 2738*
Lee, John D., Mormonism and, **7:** *1887*
Lee Penny (Scottish talisman), **10:** 2774
Lefébure, Dr Francis, astral body and, **1:** 171f
left, **6: 1614**
evil and, **3:** 640, **6:** 1614
left-hand path (black magic), **3:** 640, **6:** 1614
Leftwich, Robert (dowser), **3:** 685f
Legba (Dahomean spirit), **2:** 586, **11:** 2882–3
Leibnitz, Gottfried, **7:** 1849
Lekganyane, Edward (messianic leader), **7:** 1831f
Leland, Charles (writer on witchcraft), **6:** *1474,* 1476
Lemegeton (Lesser Key of Solomon; grimoire), **1:** 299, **5:** 1181–2
incantations in, **9:** 2400
on the kings of the four quarters, **3:** 640
names of power in, **7:** 1942, **9:** 2400
on the pentagram, **8:** 2158
spirits and demons described in, **8:** 2374, 2400
Asmodeus, **1:** 167
on triangle and magic circle, **9:** 2399
Lemminkäinen (Finnish hero), **4:** 958
lemon, Evil Eye averted by, **6: 1454**
Lemures (ghosts; ancient Rome), **1:** 242, **10:** 2678
Lemuria, **6: 1614–15**
Lenaea (Greek festival), **11:** 3035
Lenshina, Alice (Zambian religious leader), **7:** 1979, *1979*
Lent (Christianity), **3:** 761f
Battle between Carnival and Lent (Breughel), **4:** *1010–11*
Leo (the Lion; zodiac sign, in astrology), **1:** 131, 179, 181, **6: 1616**
cat's eye (jewel) and, **6:** 1511
Leo, Alan (astrologer), **1:** 176
Leo I (pope), Attila and, **1:** 193
Leon, Moses de (Spanish cabalist), **2:** 383
Leonard, Mrs Gladys Osborne (medium), **1:** 207, **6: 1616–17,** **7:** 1786, 1788, **8:** *2276,* 2276–7
Leonardo da Vinci, on human proportion, **1:** 298
leopard, shape-shifting and, **6:** 1668
Leopard Societies, West African, **1:** 81, 127
leprechauns, **4:** 901, **6: 1617**
leprosy, **6: 1617**
Lesa, Mwana (African religious leader), **9:** 2522
lesbianism:
Artemis and, **3:** 632
rarity of, in church history, **1:** 209
Leshy (Slav spirit), **10:** 2612
lesser celandine (plant), **8:** 2203
Lesser Key of Solomon, see Lemegeton
Les Trois Frères (cave), **5:** 1345, 1394, *1394,* **8:** 2243–4
Leto (Titaness), **1:** 139
Crete and, **5:** 1171, **1:** 3090
frogs and, **4:** *1053*
Letter of Lentulus, **5:** 1396, **7:** 1992
letters to the dead (Egypt), **6: 1618**
Leucippus (Greek mythology), **11:** 3090
levants, *see* corn-springs
Levi, Eliphas (Abbé Louis Constant), **5:** 1418, **1618–19,** 1683f
Apollonius of Tyana invoked by, **6:** 1618, **7:** 1956, **8:** 2159
on the astral light, **8:** 2284
on Baphomet, **1:** 229, *229*
on breath, in sexual conquest, **2:** 335
Cabala and, **2:** 387
Adolphe Desbarolles and, **6:** 1619
Golden Dawn and, **4:** 1131–2
Bulwer Lytton and, **6:** 1618, 1619
'mystery of universal equilibrium', **9:** *2398*
necromancy and, **7:** 1954, 1956
Papus and, **8:** 2125, 2126
on the pentagram, **8:** 2158, 2159
Tarot and, **6:** 1619
on the Trinity, **10:** 2830
Wronski and, **6:** 1618, **11:** 3063
Lévi-Strauss, Claude, on incest, **5:** 1429
levitation, **6: 1620,** **10:** 2663, 2701, 2702–3
by a brahmin, **9:** *2288*
ecstasy and, **10:** 2703
Kathleen Goligher and, **7:** 1709–1
by D. D. Home, **5:** 1334, *1335*
by St Joseph of Copertino, **10:** 2702f
W. Stainton Moses and, **7:** 1790
Lewis, H. Spencer (Rosicrucian), **9:** 2433
Lew Trenchard (Devon), ghost at, **5:** 1224–5
libation, **6: 1620**
Liberal Catholic Church, **11:** 2990
Liberata, Santa, *see* Uncumber, St
libido (psychology):
Freud's concept of, **4:** 1049
Jung and, **6:** 1548
Libra (the Scales; zodiac sign, in astrology), **1:** 175, 181, **3:** 813, **6: 1620**
lice, **6:** 1450
Lidwine of Schiedam, St, **11:** 2965
Liebenfels, Dr Jörg Lanz von, *see* Lanz, Adolf
African beliefs concerning, **1:** 73f, **2:** 509
Aztec beliefs, **2:** 347
Breton beliefs, **2:** 347
Celtic beliefs, **2:** 439, 440
Christian beliefs, *see* Christianity, life after death
coolness as feature of, *see refrigerium*
Egyptian beliefs, *see* Egypt, life after death
Etruscan beliefs, **3:** 848, *849,* 850
Finnish beliefs, **4:** 960
ghosts and, **4:** 1093ff, 1101
in Judaism, **6:** 1522
Melanesian beliefs, **7:** 1799–1800
Mesopotamian beliefs, **5:** 1259, **6:** 1706
Phoenician beliefs, **10:** 2764–6
psi as evidence of, **10:** 2675–6
see also cult of the dead; hell; immortality; judgement of the dead; paradise; reincarnation; spiritualism
light, **6: 1621–30**
ghosts and, **4:** *1098,* 1099
see also astral light; aura; aurora; candle; halo; sun; will-o'-the-wisp
lightning, *see* thunder and lightning
Liguori, St Alphonsus, **10:** 2703
Lilith (demoness), **5:** 1434, 1469, **6: 1631**
Lill, John, (automatic musician), **1:** 209
lily, **6: 1631–3**
Limbo (Christianity), **6: 1633,** **8:** 2242
Limpias (Spain), prodigies recorded of statue of Christ at, **11:** 2963–5
lingam (phallic symbol; Hinduism), **4:** *934,* 936, **5:** 1288, **6: 1633,** **8:** *2050, 2175,* **10:** 2573, 2782–3
lion, **6: 1634–5**
in Africa, **6:** 1634
St Anthony and, **9:** 2468
Astarte and, **1:** 170
in Christian symbolism, **1:** 130, **5:** *1398,* **6:** 1634, **9:** 2471
of Cythaeron, killed by Hercules, **5:** 1279
eagle, lion-headed, in Mesopotamia (Imdugud), **7:** *1820*
in Egypt, *see* Sekhmet
in folktales, **6:** 1634
hare and, **6:** 1634
Hercules and, **5:** 1279
St Jerome and, **6:** 1634, **9:** 2471

of Judah, Christ as, **3:** *844,* **6:** 1634
Emperor of Ethiopia, **3:** *844,* **9:** 2317
St Mamas and, **6:** 1635
man-lion, Vishnu as, **11:** *2959,* 2960
Mohammed and, **6:** *1470*
Mycenae, Lion Gate at, **10:** *2834*
Nemean, killed by Hercules, **5:** 1279, *1279*
in Parsifal's vision, **8:** *2141*
on Phoenician ivory plaque, **8:** *2182*
in Samson's riddle, **9:** 2384
topaz and, **6:** 1511
unicorn and, **11:** 2909, *2910*
zodiac sign, *see* Leo
see also chimaera; griffin
Lisa (Dahomean spririt), *see* Mawu-Lisa
Lisgar, Lady, ghost of, **5:** *1221*
List, Guido von, 6: 1636, 7: *1946*
Armanen sect founded by, **6:** 1636
Germanen Order and, **4:** 1082, **6:** 1636
National Socialism and, **6:** 1636
runes and, **6:** 1636, **9:** 2441
swastika and, **6:** 1636, **10:** 2739
Little Big Horn, battle of, **11:** *2913*
Little People (fairies), *see* fairies
liturgy (definition), **6: 1636**
lituus (augur's emblem), **1:** 194
liver, 6: 1637
divination by (hepatoscopy), **6:** 1637
in Babylonia, **3:** *658,* **6:** 1637, **8:** *2064*
Etruscans and, **3:** 848, **6:** 1637, *1637*
Phoenicians and, **10:** 2763
lizard, 6: 1638–9
Maori and, **3:** 693
llama (animal), **5:** 1425
Lleu (Welsh god), **5:** 1192, **6: 1639–40,** 1674
Lloyd, Temperance (witch), **8:** 2282
Lludd and Llefelys *(Mabinogion),* **6:** 1672
Loathly Damsel (Arthurian legend), Parsifal and, **8:** 2141, 2143
Loch Ness Monster, 3: *691*
Locke, John, 7: 1849
locust, 6: *1445,* 1450
Lodge, Sir Oliver, 8: *2274*
Society for Psychical Research and, **8:** 2274
cross-correspondences and, **11:** 3030
Eusapia Palladino and, **8:** 2113
Spiritualism and, **10:** 2659
Loew, Rabbi Judah, Golem and, **4:** 1136
logans, *see* rocking stones
Logrono, trial of witches at, **1:** 235f
Loki (Scandinavian god), **6: 1641–3**
Balder and, **1:** 226, **6:** *1641*
father of Fenris wolf, World Serpent and Hel, **4:** 1103
giants and, **4:** 1103, **6:** 1642
Idun and, **6:** 1642
at Ragnarok, **9:** 2486
Thor and, **6:** 1641, 1642, **10:** 2826–8
as trickster, **6:** 1643, **11:** 2883
Lollards, 2: 473, **5:** 1286
Lombards (Langobards, Longbeards), origin of the name, in Wodan legend, **4:** 1051
Lomna (Finn's fool), **5:** 1239
London Spiritualist Alliance (formerly the British National Association of Spiritualists), **10:** 2659
Longbeards, *see* Lombards
Longleat (Wilts), haunting of, **5:** 1224, 1225
Longue Dance (Belgian dance), **2:** 414
Lono (Hawaiian god), *see* Rongo
loon (bird), *see* diver
Lord of Misrule, 1: 242, **2:** 480, **6: 1643**
Duke of Wellington as, **4:** *1018*
Lord's Prayer:
warts cured by, **5:** 1418
witches unable to repeat, **10:** 2626
Lord's Supper, *see* Mass
Lorelei, 6: 1643
Losanne, demon cat of, **1:** 153, 154
lost lands, submerged towns and villages, **9:** 2513
bells of, **1:** 252, **9:** 2513
Breton legends, **2:** 349, **4:** 996
Cornish legends, **4:** 996
Welsh legends, **4:** 995f
see also Atlantis; Lemuria; Mu
lost tribes of Israel, 6: 1643–6
Bene Israel and, **8:** 2081
Mormons and, **7:** 1888
Persia, myth of their living in, **9:** 2306
see also British Israelites
lots, 6: 1647–8
divination by (sortilege), **6:** 1647f, **10:** 2636
at Dodona, **8:** 2076–7
at Rome *(sortes),* **6:** 1647, **9:** 2418–19
runes as lots, in ancient Germany, **9:** 2441
scapegoat chosen by, **9:** 2487
lotus, 6: 1649–50, 8: *2202*
Buddhism and, **6:** 1513, 1650
in Egypt, **6:** *1649,* 1649–50
female principle symbolized by, **6:** 1649, 1650, **8:** 2174–5
Greek myth of lotus-eaters, **6:** 1650
Hinduism and, **5:** *1305,* **6:** 1650, **10:** *2720,* **11:** 2960
lotus position (yoga), **11:** *2933, 3071,* 3073
Lou (Louwrens van Voorthuizen), **7:** 1828, *1828*
Loudun nuns, 4: 1154ff, **6: 1650**
Louis IX (of France), King's Evil and, **6:** *1573*
Louis XIV (of France):
Fénélon and, **9:** 2320
King's Evil and, **6:** 1573
witches reprieved by, **4:** 1047
see also Montespan, Madame de
loup-garou, *see* werewolf
Lourdes, 3: *646–7,* **4:** 909, **6:** *1650–5,* **7:** 1854, 1855
love-apple (mandrake; tomato), **6:** 1718
'love feast', Christian, *see agape*
love magic, 6: 1656–61
knots in, **10:** 2710
see also aphrodisiac
love potion, *see* aphrodisiac, love potion
Lovers (Tarot card), **8:** 2147, **10:** *2592,* 2792, *2792*
Lowes, John (witch), **3:** 756
Lowland Hundred (Welsh lost land legend), **4:** 995
Loxwood (Sussex), Cokelers at, **2:** 492
Loyola, St Ignatius, 9: 2462, **11:** 2963
LSD (drug), **11:** 3076
Lua (Roman goddess), **9:** 2479
Lubeck, Infant of (child prodigy), **9:** 2348
Lucian of Antioch, St, 3: 671
Lucidus (5th cent. priest), **8:** 2242
Lucifer, 3: 627f, *860,* **6: 1662–3**
Luciferans (German Satanists), **6:** 1662–3
luck, 6: 1664–5
Japanese gods of, **10:** *2569*
thirteen and, **10:** 2824–5
three and, **10:** 2830, 2831
see also fate; predestination and free will
Lucretius (Roman poet), **6:** 1658, **9:** 2356
Lucy, St, eye disorders and, **3:** 648, **4:** *885,* **9:** 2464
Lugh (Irish god), **6:** 1640
Leu identified with, **5:** 1192, **6:** 1639
Lugnasad (Lughnasa; Celtic festival), **2:** 441, **6:** 1640
modern Druids and, **3:** 722
Lugus (Celtic god), **2:** 443
festival of, *see* Lugnasad
Leu identified with, **5:** 1192, **6:** 1639
Lu-Hsing (Chinese god), **8:** *2136*
Luke, St, 6: 1507
on the symbol of, **5:** *1398*
Lull (Lully), Raymond, 3: 622, **5:** *1291,* **1666–7**
Lumière brothers, 4: 942
Luminous Lodge, *see* Vril Society
Lumpa Church (of Zambia), **7:** 1979
lunacy, *see* madness
Luo (Nilotic people), **7:** 2000, *2002*
Lupercalia (Roman festival), **4:** 1026f, 1028, 1120, **10:** 2678
Luperci (Roman priests), **9:** 2417
Luria, Isaac (Cabalist), **2:** 383, 386, **5:** 1219f, **6: 1668**
Luther, Martin, 2: 473f
Christmas tree and, **2:** 481
music and, **7:** 1911
pilgrimage to Rome by, **8:** 2198
predestination and, **8:** 2242
Lyangombe (Congolese god), 2: 504–5
Lycaeon (Greek mythology), **11:** 3008
lycanthropy, *see* shape-shifting
Lycurgus (King of Thrace), Dionysus and, **3:** 635
Lyonesse (Cornish lost land legend), **4:** 996, **9:** 2513
Lyons (France):
origin of the name, **6:** 1640
Poor Men of, *see* Waldenses
lyre:
invented by Hermes, **5:** 1289
Orpheus and, **8:** 2082, *2082–3,* 2084
Lytton, Sir Edward Bulwer, 6: 1669–70
D. D. Home and, **5:** 1335
Eliphas Levi and, **6:** 1618, 1619
Wagner influenced by, **11:** 2977

M

Ma (Bellona; Anatolian mother goddess), **3:** 742, **7:** 1898
Maat *(maat,* Mat, Mut; Egyptian deity), **2:** *333,* 335, **3:** 794, **4:** 929, *929,* **6: 1671**
Mabinogion (medieval Welsh tales), **6: 1671–4**
Arthur in, **6:** 1672, 1674
see also Culhwch and Olwen
Bran the Blessed in, *see* Branwen, daughter of Llyr
Gwydion in, *see* Math and Mathonwy
Lleu in, *see* Math and Mathonwy
see also Lady of the Fountain
Macarius, St, 9: 2524
Maccabaean War, 11: 2993
McDougall, William (psychologist), ESP and, **3:** 878, **8:** 2278
McGee, John and William (revivalists), **3:** 828
McGready, James (revivalist), **3:** 828
McGuire, Bishop George Alexander, 11: 2989
Macha (Celtic goddess of war), **5:** 1239
Machen, Arthur, Angels of Mons and, **1:** 145
Machu Pichu (Inca city), **5:** *1422*
Maciel, Antonio, *see* Conselheiro, Antonio
Mackenzie, Kenneth (Masonic Rosicrucian), Eliphas Levi and, **6:** 1619
Maclean, Euphemia (witch), **8:** 2013, 2014, 2015
McPherson, Aimée Semple (revivalist), **8:** *2160,* 2161
macrocosm and microcosm, 6: 1674–5, 1684f, 1686, 1712, **7:** *1845,* **9:** 2371–2
in alchemy, **6:** 1675
in astrology, **6:** 1675
Boehme's doctrine of, **1:** *301,* 302
correspondences and, **6:** 1675
Fludd on **1:** 298, **4:** *997,* 998, **6:** 1675, *1712*
great chain of being and, **4:** 1159
magic and, **6:** 1674f, 1684f
pentagram and, **8:** 2158
Macumba (Brazil), *see* Umbanda
Madanotsava (Hindu festival), **6:** 1556
Madhyamika school (Buddhism), **10:** 2726
madness, 6: 1675–80
asceticism and, **6:** 1678–9
dancing and, **6:** 1679
see also dancing mania
dreaming as, **6:** 1679
French asylum inmates unchained, **5:** *1381*
moon and, **6:** *1676–7,* **7:** 1881

shamanism and, **6:** 1675f, **8:** 2247
shiva and, **6:** 1678, **10:** 2573
Madyan, Abu, 5: 1385
maenads (worshippers of Dionysus), **3:** 635, *639,* **6: 1680**
Magharians (Jewish sect), **4: 1116**
magi, 6: 1680
Jesus and the three, **6:** 1680, **10:** *2833*
Parthians and, **8:** 2144
magic, 6: 1681–8
in Africa, **1:** 81
Ethiopia, **3:** 844
Zulus, **11:** 3105
Agrippa and, **1:** 84f, **2:** 387, **5:** 1182, **6:** 1685
analogies in, **8:** 2214f
see also correspondences
animals in, **1:** 131
balance in, **8:** 2070
books of, *see* grimoires
Bruno on, **2:** 352
Cabala and, **2:** *386,* 387
Cagliostro and, **2:** 388
disease caused and cured by, **3:** 641ff
in Egypt, **3:** 792f
in Finland, **4:** 958, 962–3
Frazer's classification of, **3:** 642, **5:** 1409, **10:** 2760
gesture used in, **4;** 1089
Golden Dawn and, **4:** 1131ff
good and evil transcended by, **6:** 1688
Great Plains Indians and, **5:** 1164
imagination in, **6:** 1686f
initiation to, **6:** 1684
inspiration and, **8:** 2215
Bulwer Lytton and, **6:** 1670
macrocosm and microcosm as basis of, **6:** 1674f, 1684f
mandala in, **6:** 1714–16
in Melanesia, **7:** 1797–9
in Mesopotamia, **7:** 1824f
names and, **7:** 1940ff
numbers in, **3:** 643f
see also magic squares
origin of the word, **6:** 1680
Paracelsus on, **6:** 1684
poetry and, **8:** 2210ff, 2214–15
power as goal of, **6:** 1683, 1688
priest and magician compared, **8:** 2248ff
psychic attack in, **8:** 2283–4
religion distinguished from **3:** 641, **4:** 935, **6:** 1691
in the Renaissance, **9:** 2374f
science and, **6:** 1682–3
secrecy in, **6:** 1683–4
self, magic as search for, **6:** 1687–8
serpent in, **9:** 2530–2
sex and, *see* sex, in magic
smiths and, **10:** 2619–20
sound as foundation of, **7:** 1727
in Tantrism, **10:** 2779
trance in, **11:** 2868f
Voodoo and, **11:** 2967ff
witch persecutions seen as attempt to exclude, **4:** 1079
see also incantation; mantra; names *above;* poetry *above*
see also black magic; hunting magic; imitative magic; love magic; ritual magic; treasure magic; weather magic; white magic
also charm; correspondences; Crowley, Aleister; Faust; forces; hexagram; hoodoo; Levi, Eliphas; magical papyri; magic circle; magic wand; pentagram; Simon Magus; theurgy
Magical Elements (grimoire), *see Heptameron*
magical papyri, 6: 1689–91
Seth in, **9:** 2533
magic circle, 2: 487, *487,* **9:** 2399f
of Agrippa, **6:** *1687*
arthame used to draw, **1:** 151, **7:** 1866
lead as material of, **6:** 1613
names of power inscribed in, **7:** *1941,* **8:** 2158, **9:** 2399
in necromancy, **7:** 1954
pentagram and, **8:** 2158, **9:** 2400
triangle used with, **9:** 2399
witches' use of, **4:** *916*
modern witches, **7:** 1866f
Magician (Juggler; Tarot card), **8:** 2147, **10:** *2790,* 2792
magic squares, 6: 1691–3
of Abra-Melin, **6:** 1693, **9:** 2452
in Dürer's *Melancolia,* **3:** 644, **6:** *1692*
as protection against jinn, **6:** 1516
see also palindrome
magic wand, 11: 2986
of Aleister Crowley, **2:** *560*
Grand Grimoire's specifications for, **9:** 2398
hazel and, **5:** 1229f, **9:** 2398
see also caduceus
magloire, *see main-de-gloire*
magnetism, animal magnetism, **6: 1693–5**
Christian science and, **2:** 476, 478
disease treated by, **6:** 1693, **7:** 1815, 1855
electromagnetism distinguished from, **6:** 1693
Mesmer and, **6:** 1693, **7:** 1815
see also hypnotism
magpie, 6: 1696
in augury, **2:** 557
laurel and, **6:** 1611
in legends of Christ, **6:** 1696, **10:** 2736
Magritte, René:
Hardy Sleeper, **3:** *700*
La réproduction interdite, **3:** *673*
magus, *see* magi
Magus, The, *see* Barrett, Francis
Mahabharata (Indian epic), **1:** 260, *260, 262–3, 264,* 295, **2:** *415,* **5:** 1297, *1312,* **6:** 1580
anger condemned in, **11:** 3073
bhakti in, **6:** 1583
on woman, **11:** 3053
Maharishi Mahesh Yogi, 5: *1321,* **7:** *1779*
Mahasanghikas (Buddhist sect), **2:** 357, 359
Mahatmas, 6: 1697–8
Madame Blavatsky and, **1:** 291ff, **6:** 1698
see also Gandhi
Mahayana (Buddhism), **2:** 359, **6: 1698**
Nirvana and, **7:** 1935, 1937
sin and, **10:** 2582
in Tibet, **6:** 1589
see also Sunyavada; Zen Buddhism
Mahdi, 6: 1699–1700, 7: 1828, *1832, 1833*
Ismailis and, **6:** 1472
al-Mahdi, Mohammed, 6: 1700, **7:** 1828, *1832, 1833*
Mahomet (the prophet of Islam), *see* Mohammed
maiden (corn sheaf), **2:** 518
Maid Marian, 9: 2406
in Abbots Bromley horn dance, **5:** 1352
Maimed King (Grail legend), *see* Fisher King
Maimonides, Moses, 6: 1531ff
main-de-gloire (magloire), **6:** 1718
Maintenon, Madame de, Madame Guyon and, **5:** 1191
Maira (culture hero; Brazil), **2:** 326, 327, 329, 330
Maitreya (Bodhisattva), **2:** 356, 359, **11:** 3081
maize, 6: 1700
Iroquois mask of, **6:** 1457, *1457*
in Mexican myth, **1:** 219, **1:** *2941*
Ma-Kuh (Chinese fairy), **4:** *903*
Malachi (Old Testament prophet), **8:** *2267*
Malaval, François (Quietist), **9:** 2319
Malaya, 10: 2648
Malebranche, Nicolas de, 7: 1849
Maliki school (Islam), **6:** 1465
Malking Tower, witchcraft at, **6:** 1592
Malleus Maleficarum (Hammer of Witches), **3:** 853, **6: 1700**
on archery, **1:** 145
on disorders caused by the Devil, **8:** 2281
on the evil eye, **4:** 889
on the penis, **6:** 1453, **8:** 2281
on witches and the Devil, **8:** 2112
Malmesbury witches (17th cent.), **4:** 889
Malo, St, 2: 349
wren and, **9:** 2468, **11:** 3061
Malory, Sir Thomas, His *Morte d'Arthur,* **1:** 158f
Camelot, **2:** 390
Excalibur, **10:** 2748
Lancelot, **6:** 1595
Merlin, **7:** 1810
Malta, 6: 1700–3
knights of, *see* Hospitallers
temples of, **6:** 1700ff, **8:** *2072*
Venus figure from, **4:** *896*
woman-shaped sanctuaries of, **3:** 750, *750*
Mamas, St, 6: *1635*
Mamertini (Italian people), **7:** 1744
mammoth, Eskimo legends that may refer to, **8:** 2007
Mammoth Cave (Kentucky), **10:** 2712
man, 1: 300, **6: 1704–13**
as copy of the universe, *see* macrocosm and microcosm
see also body; double; first man; self; soul
Man, Andrew (witch), **1:** 63
mana, 6: 1713
in Melanesia, **6:** 1713, **7:** 1796
in Micronesia, **8** 2233
in Polynesia, **6:** 1713, **8:** 2230, **10:** 2769
Manasa (Bengali snake goddess), **9:** 2529
Manawydan, son of Llyr *(Mabinogion),* **6:** 1673–4
mandala, 6: 1714–17, 11: *3072*
in magic **6:** 1714–16
in meditation, **7:** 1778
of Shiva as Bhairava, **10:** *2783*
in Tantrism, **6:** 1716
Tibetan, **6:** *1551, 1716*
Mandan Indians, 4: *1160, 1164*
Mandeans, 6: 1721
dualism of, **3:** 730, **6:** 1721
Sabians and, **5:** 1213
mandrake (mandragora; Circe's Plant), **6: 1717–20, 8:** 2202
as aphrodisiac, **6:** 1657, 1718
Joan of Arc and, **6:** 1522
white bryony and, **5:** 1273, **6:** 1720
manes (spirits of the dead; Rome), **6: 1720**
Mani, 5: 1282, **6:** 1721ff
martyrdom of, **3:** *729*
twin self of, **4:** 1115, **11:** 2903
Maniai (Greek mythology), *see* Furies
Manicheans, 6: 1721–4
Adam, Manichean view of, **4:** 982, **6:** 1624, 1712–13, 1721
dualism of, **3:** 730, 859, **6:** 1721
gnosticism and **6:** 1721ff
light and darkness and, **6:** 1624
medieval Manichees and, **6:** 1724
see also Mani
maniple (Christian vestment), **2:** 528
manitou, 6: 1725
Manjusri (Bodhisattva), **2:** 359, **6:** *1709,* **11:** 3081
Mankind United, 6: 1725–6
manna, gathered by Israelites, **2:** *332*
Mannanan mac Lire (Celtic sea god), **1:** 324
Manning, Matthew (British psychic), **1: 206, 7: 1726, 8:** 2278, **9:** 2291
Mannington Hall (Norfolk), haunting of, **5:** 1223–4
Manoa (El Dorado), **3:** 796
mano cornuta, **4:** 890, 1087
mano fica, **4:** 890
mano pantea, **4:** 1089
Mansur al-Hallaj (Sufi), **5:** 1282
manti (insect), Bushmen and, **2:** 380
mantra, 7: 1727–8
Kundalini and, **6:** 1586–7
in Tantrism, **9:** 2540, **10:** 2780
mantra yoga, 11: 3071
Manu, code of (Hinduism), **2:** 416

ancestor worship in, **2:** 573
cow in, **2:** 530f
Maori (New Zealand), **7: 1728–33**
amulets of, *see tiki*
aurora and, **1:** 195
cannibalism and, **7:** 1731–2
Christianity and, **7:** 1732–3
gods of, **7:** 1730–1
lizard and, **3:** 693
mana and, **7:** 1713
priests of, **7:** *1730,* 1731
tapu (taboo) and, **7:** *1730,* 1731f, 1733
tattooing and, **10:** 2797
Mappa Mundi (Hereford cathedral), Virgin Mary in, **7:** 1750
Marby, Friedrich Bernhard, 9: 2441
Marcel, Gabriel, on immortality, **5:** 1416
March (month), **7:** 1742–3
Mars and, **7:** 1742, 1744
New Year and, **7:** 1742, 1994
see also March hare
***Märchen,* 7: 1733**
March hare, 5: 1210
Mardi Gras, 7: 1733, 10: *2680,* 2682–3
Marduk (Babylonian god), **2:** 536f, **3:** 690, **7: 1733–4,** 1820, 1821, 1822f
in Assyria, **7:** 1734
four eyes of, **4:** 886, **5:** 1395
horns and, **5:** 1347
stars and, **10:** 2692
mare (corn sheaf), **2:** 518
crying the mare, **5:** 1214
mares of Diomedes, Hercules and, **5:** 1279
Marett, R. R., on animism, **1:** 132
marga (India), **8:** 2145f
Maria of Agreda, Blessed, 11: 2965
Maria of Ituren (witch), **1:** 234
Mariavite Church, 11: 2988
marigold, 6: 1657
Marigrane, Marie d' (witch), **9:** 2447–8
Marilaha (Mesopotamian deity), **5:** 1213
Mari Lwyd (Welsh hobby-horse), **5:** 1327
Mark (King of Cornwall), **1:** 2885ff
Brittany and, **2:** 347
Castle Dore and, **2:** 391
Mark, St, 6: 1507, 1508, 1510, **7:** 1852
lion the symbol of, **5:** *1398*
Marley, Bob (Rastafarian musician), **7:** 1835
Marlowe, Christopher, Faust and, **4:** 924, 925
Maronites (Christian sect), **2:** 472
Marquesas Islands (Polynesia), **8:** 2230ff, **10:** 2797
Marranos (Jewish converts; Spain), **5:** 1286
marriage and betrothal, matrimony, wedding, **7: 1735–42, 11: 3007**
allegorical, in alchemy, **7:** 1808, **8:** 2069
banns, calling the, **7:** 1737
bundling, **7:** 1737
child brides, **7:** 1735
in children's games, **2:** *452, 453,* 453f
Christianity and, **2:** 470
as a sacrament, **9:** 2450, 2451–2
confetti and, **7:** 1739
Eskimos and, **7:** 1737
food and drink and, **7:** 1737–9
gifts and, **7:** 1737
Gypsies and, **5:** 1196f
honey and, **5:** 1340
Kikuyu and, **6:** 1564f
May unlucky month for, **3:** 606
oak and, **8:** 2034, 2035
Parsees and, **8:** *2138,* 2140
St Paul on, **11:** 3057
of priests, **8:** 2253f
sacred, as fertility rite, **4:** 935, **5:** 1271
in Crete, **5:** 1271
at Eleusis, **3:** 807
Ishtar and, **6:** 1460
six and, **10:** 2592
Slavs and, **10:** 2619
spiritual, of Saora shamans, **8:** 2250–1
termination of, St Uncumber as means to, **11:** 2907
trial marriage, **7:** 1737
Voodoo and, **11:** 2974f
see also Dunmow Flitch
marriage at Cana, 11: *2999*
Mars (planet):
in astrology, **1:** 175, 180, **7:** 1744
iron and, **2:** 522
jewels associated with, **6:** 1511
in Mesopotamia, **10:** 2692
red and, **2:** 522, **7:** 1744
Mars (Roman god), **7: 1742–4**
Ares identified with, **1:** 144, **7:** 1744
Augustus and, **7:** 1744
fertility and, **7:** 1743, **9:** 2412
founding of Rome and, **4:** 1026, 1027f, **7:** 1744
horse and, **7:** 1743
Janus and, **6:** 1483, 1484
March and, **7:** 1742f, 1744
Venus and, **11:** *2946*
war and, **7:** 1743f
woodpecker oracle of, **7:** 1744, **11:** 3060
Marston Moor, battle of, ghosts and, **1:** 145
Marsyas (satyr), **1:** 140, **9:** 2351
Martin of Arles, on witchcraft, **1:** 234, **4:** 1046
Martinists, 7: 1746–7
Papus and, **7:** 1747, **8:** 2126
martyrs, 7: 1747
St Andrew, **7:** *1986*
St Peter, **7:** *1987*
St Stephen, **7:** 1747
see also Thecla, St, martyrdom of
Mary, Queen of Scots, 8: *2041*
Mary, the Virgin, 7: 1747–52, *1984, 1992,* **11: 2956**
Annunciation of, Festival of, **7:** 1750
by El Greco, **2:** *336*
by Martini, **6:** *1632*
assumption of, **7:** *1913*
Festival of, **7:** 1750, 1752
St Bernadette and, **6:** 1653
see also Lourdes
birth of, **7:** *1988*
Bogomils and, **1:** 304
breath and, legends concerning, **2:** 333–4
St Brigit and, **2:** 346
dead body of Christ and, in art, *see* pieta
death of, by Duccio, **7:** *1990–1*
in dome of St Saviour (Constantinople), **9:** *2363*
garden as symbol of, **6:** 1601
Great Mother's attributes transferred to, **7:** 1898
lily and, **6:** 1631, *1632,* 1633
her mother not a virgin, **11:** 2956
Nativity of, Festival of, **7:** 1750
original sin, her freedom from, *see* Immaculate Conception
Purification of, Festival of, **7:** 1750
rose and, **9:** 2422, *2431*
taken to the Temple (Giotto), **7:** *1989*
Theophilus of Adana saved from the Devil by, **8:** 2110
Trinity, represented with, **7:** 1750
her virginity, **11:** 2952ff
seen in vision, **11:** 2965f, 2983
see also St Bernadette *above*
Mary Frances of the Five Wounds, St, 10: 2699, 2701
'Mary of the Gaels' (St Brigit of Kildare), **2:** 346
Mary of Jesus Crucified, Sister, 10: 2701
Mary Magdalen of Pazzi, 10: 2700
Masada, 11: 3077, 3078
Masaharu Taniguchi (Japanese religious leader), **6:** 1496
Masai (African people), **7: 1753–5**
smiths and, **10:** 2618
Maskelyne, J. N., 10: *2661*
masks, 7: 1756–67
in Africa, **7:** 1756–7
Benin, **7:** *1757*
Nigeria, **7:** *1758*
in Brazil, **7:** *1802,* **10:** *2681*
Celtic, horned, **2:** *442*
in dance, **2:** 596, **7:** 1756ff
death masks, **7:** 1760–3
in Dionysian mysteries, **3:** *637,* **7:** 1764
in drama, **7:** 1763f
Greek, **3:** *697,* **7:** 1764
Japanese, **6:** *1488,* **7:** 1764
James Ensor and, **3:** 822, *823*
Eskimo, **3:** *835,* **7:** 1760, *1765*
Iroquois, **5:** *1217,* **6:** 1455, *1457,* 1457f
Javanese, **5:** *1236*
Melanesian, **7:** 1756, 1757, 1796–7
New Guinea, **7:** 1757–8, *1972*
Mongolian, **5:** *1231*
Pacific Northwest Indians and, **7:** 1758–9, **8:** *2010, 2107*
Kwakiutl, **8:** *2005*
Peruvian, **5:** 1236, 1426–7
pumpkin, at Hallowe'en, **1:** 110
in Tibet, **7:** *1762,* 1763
Mass (Eucharist, Holy Communion, Lord's Supper), **2:** *331,* 470, **3: 850, 4:** *1013,* 1016–17, **7: 1768, 9:** 2449, 2450–1, *2452*
altar and, **1:** 117
gesture in, **4:** 1089
in magic **7:** 1768, **8:** 2279
see also black mass
as sacrifice, **9:** 2451, 2458
symbolism in, **10:** 2756
see also host; Last Supper; transubstantiation
Massacre of the Innocents in Ethiopian MS, **2:** *580*
mass of the dead, 1: 277
mass of the Holy Ghost, 1: 278
mass of St Secaire, 1: 277
Mastema (evil spirit), **3:** 627
Masters, 7: 1769
St-Germain as a Master, **9:** 2461
Mat (Egyptian goddess), see Maat
materialization (Spiritualism), **7:** 1789, 1791
Palladino and, **8:** 2113
see also ectoplasm
maté tea, as drug, in Brazil, **3:** 712
Math and Mathonwy *(Mabinogion),* **5:** 1192, **6:** 1639, 1674
Mather, Cotton, Salem witches and, **9:** 2473
Mathers, Samuel Liddell (Macgregor Mathers), **1:** 249, **2:** 559, **4:** *1133,* **7: 1770**
Crowley and, **1:** 249, **2:** 559f, **4:** 1132f
Golden Dawn and, **4:** 1131ff, **7:** 1769, 1770, **9:** 2430f, **11:** 3067
Key of Solomon and, **5:** 1181
magic circle and, **3:** 640
Rosicrucians and, **9:** 2431
Sacred Magic of Abra-Melin and, **6:** 1693, **9:** 2452
Yeats and, **11:** 3067
Mathew, Archbishop, 11: 2987–8, 2990
Mathijs, John (Anabaptist), **3:** 825f
Matswa, Andrew (Congolese religious leader), **7:** 1978
Matthew, St, 6: 1507
man the symbol of, **5:** *1398*
Matholwch (King of Ireland), in the *Mabinogion, see* Branwen, daughter of Llyr
matriarchy, 11: 3053
matrimony, *see* marriage
Matunus (Celtic bear god), **1:** 246
Maui (Polynesian hero), **8:** 2232
Mau Mau, 6: 1561, 1562, **7: 1770, 10:** *2633,* 2635
Maundy Thursday (Green Thursday), **3:** 766, 781
Maurice, St, 9: *2469*
Maury, Alfred, on dreams, **3:** 706, 707
Mawu-Lisa (Dahomean spirits), **2:** 586
Maximus, Emperor, 4: 1103
Maximum of Tyre, 9: 2356

May (month), **2:** 351, **3:** 606
see also May Day
may (tree), *see* hawthorn
Maya (Mexican people), **7: 1770–3, 8:** *2255,* **9:** 2529
Mu and, **6:** 1614f
Maya (Vedanta), **11:** 2932
Maya, Queen (mother of Buddha), **4:** 1070, **11:** 2953, *2953*
Mayo, Jeff (astrologer), **1:** 182
May Day, 3: 698, **7: 1773–4**
Green May (Jack in the Green) and, **5:** 1173, 1228, **6:** *1477,* **8:** 2035, **11:** 2942–3
Helston furry dance and, **5:** 1268
May King, May Queen, and, **4:** 935, **5:** 1173, **7:** 1773
at Minehead, **7:** *1758*
Morris Dances and, **7:** 1774, 1892
Robin Hood and, **5:** 1173, **7:** 1774, **9:** 2405–6
trees and, **11:** 2877–8
hawthorn, **5:** 1228, **7:** 1773
oak, **8:** 2035
rowan, **5:** 1228, **9:** 2437
see also maypole; Padstow Old Hoss
maypole, 3: 698, 4: *937,* **7:** 1773, **10:** *2679,* **11:** 2877–8, 2942
hawthorn and, **7:** 1773
Morris dances and, **7:** 1891
maze (labyrinth), **6: 1589, 7: 1774–5**
in children's games, *see* Hop Scotch
at Cnossus (Crete), **1:** 210, **5:** 1271, **7:** 1774–5
mead of inspiration, Odin and, **8:** *2045,* 2046
Mecca (Arabian city), **7: 1775–6**
Islamic worship performed facing, **6:** 1465
Mohammed and, **6:** 1464, **7:** 1775f, 1871f
pilgrimage to, **6:** 1468, **7:** 1775f
Mede, Joseph (theologian), **9:** 2520
Medea (Greek witch), **7: 1776**
Circe and, **2:** 485
Jason and, **5:** 1257, **7:** 1776, **8:** 2282
medicine, *see* healing
medicine-man, 7: 1776
African, **1:** 76, 82
Kenya **8:** *2251*
Masai, **7:** 1754
Australian, **1:** 201, 204
Corybantes as, **2:** 522
costume and, **2:** 526
of Great Plains Indians, **4:** 1162
see also obeah; shaman
Medina (Yathrib; Arabian city), **7:** 1776
Mohammed and, **5:** 1257, **6:** 1464, **7:** 1775, 1776, 1872f
meditation, 7: 1777–80
in Buddhism, **2:** 355, 359, **7:** 1779
in Ceylon, **10:** 2587
Cabala and **7:** 1778
in China, **7:** 1778
Christianity and, **7:** 1779–80
concentration distinguished from, **7:** 1777
mandala used in, **7:** 1778
rosary and, **9:** 2420
Sufism and, **7;** 1778
in yoga, **7:** 1777, **11:** 3074
mediums, 7: 1781–93, 8: 2277, **10:** 2662, 2663
cold breezes at sittings of, **7:** 1792
'controls' of, **7:** 1783ff
ESP testing and, **3:** 878
'sensitive' as alternative name for, **7:** 1782
sex and, **7:** 1792
Society for Psychical Research and, **8:** 2274–5
Eva C., **7:** 1791
Stella C., **7:** 1791–2
Eusapia Palladino, **8:** 2113f, 2275
Mrs Piper, **8:** 2199f
Schneider brothers, **9:** 2489ff
telepathy and, **7:** 1785ff
in theurgy, **10:** 2823f
trance and, **7:** 1783ff, **11:** 2869f
see also C. Eva; Cook, Florence; Davenports; Hardinge-Britten, Emma; Home, Daniel Dunglas; Leonard, Mrs; Palladino, Eusapia; Piper, Mrs; Schneider brothers; Willett, Mrs; Williams, Charles Edward
also materialization; seance
Medmenham monks, 7: 1794–5
Medusa (Gorgon), **4:** 1141f, **5:** *1202–3*
Megaera (Greek mythology), **4:** 918, 1054
megaliths, megalithic buildings:
burial and, **2:** 572
giants and, **4:** 1103
Maltese temples, **6:** 1700, *1701*
sun worship and, **10:** 2724–5
see also Stonehenge
Megara (wife of Hercules), **5:** 1279
Megiddo, stone altar found at, **1:** 116
Melanesia, 7: 1796–1800
Australia compared with, **7:** 1799
body-painting in, **10:** 2804
cannibalism in, **7:** 1796
cargo cults in, **2:** 409–12, **7:** 1800
death, myths of origin of, **7:** 1799
first man myths of, **7:** 1799
headhunting in, **7:** 1796
human sacrifice in, **7:** 1796
initiation in, **5:** 1440, **7:** 1797
life after death, beliefs concerning, **7:** 1799–1800
magic in, **7:** 1797–9
mana and, **6:** 1713, **7:** 1796
masks in, **7:** 1756, 1757, 1796–7
new religious movements in, **7:** 1981
see also cargo cults *above*
Polynesia compared with, **7:** 1799, **8:** 2229ff
spirits and, **7:** 1796, *1796, 1797*
totemism in, **11:** 2863
see also Fiji; New Guinea
Meleagant (Arthurian legend), **6:** 1594
Melwas identified with, **4:** 1112
Melchior, Nicholas (alchemist), **1:** 99
Melchiorites (religious sect), **3:** 825
Melissa (nymph), Zeus and, **8:** 2032
Melkart (Phoenician god), **8:** 2183, 2184
mell doll (corn sheaf), **5:** 1217
Melor, St, severed head of, **5:** 1240
Melpomene (Muse), **7:** 1905
Melwas (King of Somerset), **4:** 1112
see also Meleagant
memory, psychology of, object reading and, **8:** 2039f
Memphis (Egypt), **3:** 790
sacred bull of, *see* Apis
creation myth of priesthood of, **2:** 534
Imhotep and, **5:** 1405
Mendès, Catulle, 8: 2126
mendicants, 7: 1800
Menerva (Etruscan goddess), *see* Menrva
Men of God (Russian sect), *see* Khlysty
Meng P'o (Chinese goddess of the underworld), **9:** 2348
menhir, in Brittany, **2:** 572, **3:** *718*
Mennonites (Protestant sect), **2:** *498,* 499, **7: 1800**
Menorah (candlestick; Judaism), **2:** 379, **6:** 1536
Menrva (Menerva; Etruscan goddess), **3:** 849
Athene identified with, **1:** 187
Minerva identified with, **3:** 849
menstruation, 1: 273, 295, **7: 1800–5**
in Africa, **7:** 1800, 1802
Bushmen, **2:** 380
initiation and, **7:** 1801–2
moon and, **7:** 1877
Mentawei (Indonesian island), tattooing and, **10:** 2797–9
Mephistopheles (demon), **4:** 924, **7: 1805**
Mephisto's Ring, 10: 2773
Mercuria, la (witch), *see* La Mercuria
mercury (quicksilver; metal), **7: 1807–8, 9: 2318**
in alchemy, **1:** 94, **7:** 1807f, **8:** 2069
Azoth as the name of, **1:** 112
in *Splendor Solis,* **3:** *803*
sulphur and, **4:** 1129, **7:** 1808
unicorn as symbol of, **11:** 2910
grey and, **2:** 522
planet Mercury and, **2:** 522
Mercury (planet):
in astrology, **1:** 175, 180, **7:** 1806–7
Gemini ruled by, **4:** 1075
grey and, **2:** 522
jewels associated with, **6:** 1511
in Mexican myth, **1:** 218
quicksilver and, **2:** 522
Mercury (Roman god), **7: 1805–6,** *1807*
Mercury's Blood (plant), *see* vervain
Merkabah, *see* throne mysticism
Merlin (magician), **7: 1809–11**
Arthurian legends and, **1:** 154, 158, **7:** 1810f
Stonehenge moved by, **7:** 1810, 1811, *1811,* **10:** 2703
Vivien and, **2:** 347, **7:** 1810
mermaids and mermen, 7: 1812–14
in Dürer engraving, **9:** *2511*
Japanese, **9:** *2510*
in Scottish and Border ballads, **9:** 2505
seals and, **9:** 2516
Sirens and, **10:** 2591
whale changed into, **11:** 3014
see also Triton
Meru (Hindu world mountain), **9:** 2366, **10:** 2758
Merzbacher, Friedrich (writer on witchcraft), **4:** 1079
mescal, peyote distinguished from, **8:** 2170
Meshuararim (Cochin Jews), **8:** 2081
Mesmer, F. A. 5: 1379, **6:** 1693, **7: 1815–17, 8:** 2236
Spiritualism partly derived from mesmerism, **7:** 1817, **8:** 2273f
Mesopotamia, 7: 1818–26
altars in, **1:** 116
astrology in, **7:** 1826, **10:** 2692
beards in, **2:** 365
creation myths in, **2:** 535f, **3:** 750, **7:** 1821
see also Enuma elish
death and, **3:** 616, **5:** 1259, **6:** 1706
divination in, **7:** 1826
dogs in, **3:** 664
dreams in, **3:** 704, **7:** 1826
eagle in, **3:** 746
election in, **3:** 797
evil and, **3:** 859
eye idols of, **4:** 888
flood legends of, **3:** 817, **4:** 992–4, 1106
goat in, **10:** *2761*
gods of, **7:** 1818–23
iconography of, **5:** 1394–5
monotheism in, **7:** 1821
see also Ashur; Ea; Enlil; Ereshkigal; eye idols *above;* Inanna; Ishtar; Marduk; Nergal; Ningursu; Ninurta; Oannes; Shamash; Sin; Tammuz
hero in, *see* Gilgamesh
kingship in, **6:** 1570
magic in, **7:** 1824f
man, view of, **6:** 1706
Mother Goddess in, **7:** 1895–6
prostitution in, **8:** 2270f
Ishtar and, **6:** 1460, **8:** 2271
spirits in, **7:** 1823f
stars in, **10:** 2692
see also astrology *above*
temples of, **9:** 2362
Tower of Babel and, **11:** 2867
water in, *see* Apsu; Tiamat
see also Akkad; Assyria; Babylonia; Chaldeans; Harranian religion; Hurrians; Sumer
Messenia (Greece), Zeus born in, **5:** 1168
Messiah:
Jesus as, **2:** 467, **6:** 1507ff, **8:** 2150ff
in Jewish belief, **2:** 466, **6:** 1534–5
origin of the word, **6:** 1570
see also Mahdi; messianic movements

messianic movements, 3: 825, 828, **7: 1827–35**
in Africa, **7:** 1831ff, **9:** 2522
in China, **2:** 463, **7:** 1827
millennarian movements compared with, **7:** 1827
of North American Indians, *see* Ghost Dance
see also Tanchelm; Zevi; Sabbatai
metallotherapy, 7: 1854
metals, 7: 1835
colours associated with, **2:** 522
four races of man symbolized by, **11:** 2851
planets associated with, **2:** 522
see also gold; iron; lead; mercury; silver
metamorphosis, *see* shape-shifting
metempsychosis, *see* reincarnation
meteors, 7: 1836
iron of, **6:** 1454, **10:** 2616
Methodism:
Holiness movement and, **5:** 1328
William Law's influence on, **6:** 1612
see also Wesley, John
metoposcopy (divination by the lines on the forehead), **3:** *655*
Mevlevi dervishes (dancing dervishes), **2:** 589, **3:** 622, **9:** 2439, *2440,* 2441, **10:** *2716*
Mexico, pre-Columbian:
god of hunting in, **5:** *1372–3*
pyramids of, **1:** 214, 217, **7:** 1770, **10:** *2721*
see also Aztecs; Maya; Mixtecs; Olmecs; Toltecs; Zapotecs
Mexico and Central America (modern), **7: 1837–44**
carnival in, **4:** 1018
Easter fiesta in, **4:** 1018
hallucinogenic mushroom in, **7:** 1908f
New Year in, **7:** *1995*
shamanism in, **7:** 1840ff
Spanish invasion of, effects of, **7:** 1839ff
skulls from, **1:** 109, **4:** *1014,* **7:** *1844*
Mexico City (pre-Columbian), *see* Tenochtitlan
mezuzah (Judaism), **6:** *1537,* **7: 1844**
Mgijima, Enoch (African religious leader), **9:** 2522
Micah (Old Testament prophet), **8:** 2266f
Michael, St (archangel), **1:** 125f, **7: 1844**
by Breughel, **2:** *342–3*
dragons fought by, **5:** 1268
the Devil fought by, **5:** 1268
in revelation, **3:** 629, 691
Glastonbury and, **4:** *1109,* 1110
Helston furry dance and, **5:** 1268
pilgrim badge of, **8:** *2196*
soul weighed by, at Last Judgement, **1: 124–5, 11:** 3007
south and, **3:** 640
on touchpieces, **6:** 1573, *1573*
see also Michaelmas
Michaelmas (feast of St Michael), **7:** 1844
blackberry and, **5:** 1273
goose and, **4:** 1138
microcosm, *see* macrocosm and microcosm
Micronesia, 7: 1845, 8: 2229, 2232–3
Midas (Phrygian king), **1:** 140
Attis and, **2:** 583
Middle Kingdom (Egyptian history), **3:** 788
Midewiwin (society of shamans), **7:** 1725
Midgard Serpent (world serpent: Scandinavian mythology), **9:** 2529
Loki the father of, **4:** 1103
Thor and, **10:** 2826, *2827*
at Ragnarok, **9:** 2486
Midsummer, Midsummer Eve, **4:** 935, **7: 1845–6**
Balder and, **7:** 1860
bonfires and, **1:** 163–4, **7:** 1845, 1860
dancing mania and, **2:** 599, 600
dragons and, **7:** 1845
Druids and, **3:** 722, **7:** 1845
hobbyhorse and, **5:** 1327
St John the Baptist and, **2:** 599, **7:** 1845, **9:** 2461, **11:** 3015–16
plants and, **7:** 1846, **8:** 2205
mistletoe, **7:** 1860
St John's wort, **7:** 1846, **9:** 2461
wheel and, **11:** 3015f
witches and, **7:** 1845
midwinter, 4: 935
Christmas and, **2:** 480
halcyon breeding at, **5:** 1205
wren hunt at, **11:** 3061
Mihr (Parsee deity), **8:** 2138
mihrab (mosque), **9:** 2366
mikado (Japan), **6:** 1572
Milky Way, 8: 2146
millennarian religious movements:
Jehovah's Witnesses as, **6:** 1499f
messianic movements compared with, **7:** 1827
in the Middle Ages, **9:** 2518
see also cargo cults; Conselheiro; Divine Principles; Melchiorites; Montanists
millennium (Christianity), **9:** 2518, 2520
see also millennarian religious movements
Miller, William (prophet of the Second Coming), **6:** 1499, **9:** 2521
milpreve (Cornish charm), **2:** 520
Milton, John, 7: 1846–8, 9: 2494–6
Mimamsa (Hinduism), **11:** 3070
mimicry, magical, *see* imitative magic
Mimingus (sword of Hoder), Balder slain by, **1:** 226
Mimir (Scandinavian god), **9:** 2483, **10:** 2620
fountain of, **4:** 1029
head of, **5:** 1240
Min (Egyptian god), **5:** 1216
minaret (mosque), **7:** 1892, **9:** 2366
'mind over matter', *see* psychokinesis
mind-reading, *see* telepathy
Minehead (Somerset), May Day at, **5:** 1327, **7:** *1758,* 1774
Minerva (Roman goddess), **1:** 187, **7: 1848**
Athene identified with, **1:** 187
Brigantia and, **2:** 345
by Mantegna, **3:** *863*
Menrva identified with, **3:** 849
mines:
in Cornwall, **2:** 519
dwarfs and, **3:** 737
Neolithic, *see* Grimes Graves
Mineteda (Spain), headless figures at, **5:** 1245
Minguet, Barthélemy (witch), **4:** 1047
Mink (trickster), **11:** 2881
Minoan civilization of Crete, *see* Crete
Minos (Cretan king), **2:** 365f
labyrinth of, **5:** 1271, **7:** 1774
Theseus and, **10:** 2820
Zeus and, **5:** 1168
see also Minotaur
Minotaur, 1: 130, **2:** 365–6, **5:** 1271, **7: 1846**
labyrinth and, **5:** 1271, **7:** 1774f
Theseus and, **10:** 2818, *2818*
by G. F. Watts, **10:** *2817*
Zeus and, **11:** 3090
miracle plays, 7: 1921, 1924
miracles, 7: 1848–55
of Jesus, **7:** 1852, 1855
in childhood, apocryphal, **7:** 1988
see also Lazarus
faith healing and, **7:** 1854f
laws of nature and, **7:** 1848f
causality and, **7:** 1850
of the Old Testament, **7:** 1852
of saints, **9:** 2462
miracles of abundance, **10:** 2702
Miriam (biblical), **8:** 2264
mirror, 7: 1855–9
divination by (catoptromancy), **7:** 1858, **9:** 2506
double and, **3:** 672, 677
Evil Eye averted by, **7:** 1858–9
in Japanese imperial symbolism, **9:** 2563
reflection in, as the soul, **7:** 1855
as symbol of Tezcatlipoca, **8:** 2042
water used as, **7:** 1855f
witchcraft and, **4:** 1043
Miru (Polynesian deity), **8:** 2232
Misenus (Greek myth), **11:** 2897
miser:
from *Dance of Death* (Holbein), **4:** *1128*
Death of a miser (Bosch), **9:** *2391*
Mishna (Judaism), **2:** 383
missionaries:
Christian
in Africa, **7:** 1957ff
in the Congo, **2:** 503
apostolic, **2:** 469
in India, **9:** 2360ff
of Divine Principles sect, **3:** 662
mistletoe, 7: 1859–60
apple and, **7:** 1859
Balder and, **1:** 226, **7:** 1860
burning bush (Moses) and, **7:** 1860
Christmas and, **2:** 481, **7:** 1860
Druids and, **3:** 719, **7:** 1859f
Golden Bough on, **7:** 1859, 1860, **11:** 2942
kissing under, **2:** 481, **7:** 1860
Midsummer bonfires and, **7:** 1860
oak and, **7:** 1859, 1860, **8:** 2033
Mithras (Mithra), **7: 1861–4**
birth of, from an egg, **3:** *783,* **7:** 1864
bull sacrifice and, **7:** *1861,* 1862, 1863f
cave sanctuaries of, **9:** 2364–5
Christianity and, **7:** 1864
Hittites and, **7:** 1861
India and, **7:** 1861
ladder and, **10:** 2697
Mihr (Parsee deity) identified with, **8:** 2318
mystery cult of, **7:** 1862ff, 1928
Persia and, **6:** 1571, **7:** 1861f, *1863,* **11:** 3103
Rome and, **7:** 1861ff
sun and, **7:** 1862, 1863f
time and, **11:** 2848
Mitra (Indian sun god), **10:** 2722
Mithras and, **7:** 1861–2, **10:** 2722
mitre (Christian headgear), **2:** 528, **5:** 1242, *1244*
Mixtecs, 1: 216, **2:** *538,* **7:** *1842*
Mjölnir (hammer of Thor), **3:** 737, **5:** 1205, **6:** 1641–2, **10:** 2826, *2827*
Mnevis (Egyptian god), **2:** 365, **5:** 1347
Möbius, Paul, on woman's inferiority, **11:** 3053
***Moby Dick,* 11:** 3014
Mochica culture (Peru), **5:** 1423, 1424
Moctecuzoma (Montezuma; Aztec king), **1:** 216
modalism (Christian heresy), **2:** 471
modern witchcraft, 1: 115, **7: 1865–70, 9:** *2445,* **11:** *2986,* 3042
All Hallows' Eve and, **1:** 110, *110*
arthame in, **1:** 151, **7:** 1866
broomstick and, **2:** *350,* 351
coven and, **7:** 1866
as fertility cult, **7:** 1866
festivals of, **7:** 1866
flagellation in, **4:** *990*
garters and, **4:** 1070, **7:** 1866
magic circle and, **7:** 1866f
moon and, **7:** 1866, 1867
ring dance in, **2:** *412,* **7:** *1870*
sex and, **7:** 1867
wedding, **11:** *3041*
Mohammed (Muhammad, Mahomet; the prophet of Islam), **6:** 1464, *1470,* **7: 1871–3, 10:** *2603*
his ascension to heaven, **8:** *2133,* **11:** 3032
Jerusalem, his miraculous journey to, **6:** 1502
Jews and, **7:** 1872
Kaaba and, **7:** 1872, **10:** *2708*
Mecca and, **6:** 1464, **7:** 1775f, 1871f
Medina and, **5:** 1275, **6:** 1464, **7:** 1775, 1776, 1872
Moharram and, **7:** 1873
obscene idols destroyed by, **8:** 2174
Ramadan instituted by, **7:** 1873
Shiite view of, **7:** 1873
Sunnite view of, **7:** 1873

tomb of, **6:** 1468
winged horse of, **11:** 3032
Mohammed, Mirza Ali (founder of Bahai sect), **1:** 224
Mohammedanism, *see* Islam
Moharram, 7: 1873–7
Mohenjo-daro (city; India), **5:** *1434, 1435,* 1436, *1436,* **6:** 1650, **8:** *2245*
Mohra (Sweden), witches of, *see* Blocula
Moirae (Greek mythology), *see* Fates
Molech (Canaanite term), **4:** 976, **8:** 2184
moles on the body, divination by (moleosophy), **3:** *654*
Molinos, Miguel (Quietist), **9:** *2318,* 2319
moly (magic herb), **7: 1874**
Momoyama Period (Japan), **6:** 1492
monasticism, Christian:
early history of, **2:** 472f
see also Carmelite Order
Monday, 3: 606f
Mongan, King (of Ireland), **4:** 965
monism, in Islam, **5:** 1386
monkey, 7: 1875
head of, dried, in Nigeria, **8:** *2252*
Hindu monkey god, *see* Hanuman
see also baboon
monks, Buddhist, 2: 355, *356, 357*
in Ceylon, **10:** 2586–7
in Southeast Asia, **10:** 2648
see also lamas
monks, Christian, *see* monasticism, Christian
Monophysites (Christian sect), **2:** 471
in Ethiopia, **3:** 841
monotheism, 7: 1875
in Babylonia, **7:** 1821
as the earliest form of religion, **9:** 2358
in Zoroastrianism, **11:** 3099–3100
Monothelitism (Christian heresy), **2:** 472
Mons, Angels of, 1: 145, *145,* **11:** *2963*
monsters and mythical beasts, *see* abominable snowman; basilisk; Cailleach; centaurs; chimaera; dragon; Frankenstein; Golem; Gorgons; Great Beast; Grendel; griffin; Harpies; Jenny Green Teeth; Loch Ness monster; Minotaur; Questing Beast; sasquatch; Scylla and Charybdis; sea monsters; Typhon; Ullikummi; unicorn; vampire; wyvern
Montanists (Christian heresy), **3:** 825, **7: 1875**
Montespan, Madame de, 1: 170, 279, **2:** 400, **8:** 2218
Monte Ulmi, Antonius de, 5: 1409
Montezuma (Aztec king), *see* Moctecuzoma
Montgeron, Louis-Baptiste Carré de, Convulsionaries and, **2:** 516, **7:** 1854
Montgomery, William (attacker of witches), **2:** 419, **9:** 2552
Montparnasse cemetery (Paris), François Bertrand and, **1:** 257
Montségur (Cathar stronghold), **2:** 422, 424
Moody, Dwight L., 5: 1328, 1331, **8:** *2161*
moon, 7: 1876–82
amber and, **6:** 1511
animals and, **7:** 1880
Apis and, **2:** 365
Artemis and, **3:** 632
Astarte and, **1:** 170, *170*
in astrology, **1:** 175f, 180, **7:** 1882
in Babylonia, **7:** 1876, 1881
bisexuality and, **5:** 1287
Madame Blavatsky and, **7:** 1876
in Brazil, **2:** 327f
crescent shape of, **2:** 542
in Crete, **2:** 377, **3:** 613, **5:** 1271
death, origin of, moon and, **2:** 377, **3:** 613
eclipses and, **3:** 771f
elephant and, **6:** *1878–9*
Eskimo and, **3:** 833, 834, **5:** 1428
frog and, **4:** 1054
goddesses of, **7:** 1877
Carthaginian, *see* Tanit Pene Baal
Greek, *see* Artemis *above;* Hecate, moon and; Hera, moon and; Selene
Roman, *see* Diana, moon and
gods of:
Egyptian, *see* Chons
Ethiopian, *see* Sin
Japanese, **9:** 2562
Mesopotamian, *see* Sin
Peruvian, *see* Sin
hare and, **5:** 1210, **7:** *1878–9*
Jack and Jill and, **6:** 1477, **7:** 1877
Kepler's imaginary account of, **9:** 2494
madness (lunacy) and, **6:** *1676–7,* **7:** 1881
Virgin Mary and, **7:** *1984*
meteors and, **7:** 1836
in Mexican mythology, **1:** 217
modern witchcraft and, **7:** 1866, 1867
month, lunar, **7:** 1876f
Islamic, *see* Moharram
moon-calf, **7:** 1877
North American Indians and, **8:** 2007
at Palmyra, **10:** 2766
Paracelsus and, **7:** 1881
pearl and, **6:** 1511
plants and, **7:** 1880
quartz and, **6:** 1510
rabbit and new moon, **9:** 2320
rook crystal and, **6:** 1510
sea and, **9:** 2509
seven and, **9:** 2534–6
silver and, **2:** 522, **5:** 1210, **10:** 2577
soma identified with, **5:** 1272
sun and, **10:** 2719, 2720
in Australia, **10:** 2719–20
in Crete, **5:** 1271
in Eskimo incest myth, **3:** 833, **5:** 1428
in Rumanian incest myth, **7:** 1877
symbolism of, **10:** 2758
tides caused by, **10:** 1878f
water and, **11:** 3002
white and, **2:** 522
woman and, **7:** 1877
Moon (Tarot card), **7:** *1880,* **8:** 2146, **10:** *2793,* 2794
crab in, **2:** 531
Moonies, 3: 662–3, **7: 1882,** *see also* Divine Principles
moonstone, 6: 1511, *1512*
Moors, Christian converts from among, *see* Moriscos
Mora (Sweden), witches of, *see* Blocula
Moral Rearmament (Oxford Group, Buchmanism), **7: 1882–4**
Moravian Brethren (religious sect), **3:** 827f, **5:** 1328
Easter and, **3:** 760f
Morbidus and the sea-monster, **9:** *2530–1*
Mordred (Arthurian cycle), **1:** 153, 154, 159
More, Henry, 2: 386f
Moreau, Adèle, palmistry and, **8:** 2121
Moreau, Gustave, 1: 146, **5:** *1238*
Morgan, Nanny (witch), **4:** 889
Morgan le Fay (Arthurian legend), **7: 1884–6**
Morganwg, Iolo, *see* Williams, Edward
Moriscos (Moorish converts; Spain), **5:** 1286
Mormons (Church of Jesus Christ of the Latter Day Saints), **3:** 827, **7: 1886–90**
speaking in tongues and, **10:** 2651
Morning Star:
in Ethiopia, *see* Athtar
Ishtar and, **10:** 2692
Lucifer as, **6:** 1662
in Mexico, *see* Quetzalcoatl
North American Indians and, **8:** 2008f
Pawnee Indians, **4:** 1161, **8:** 2008–10
Morra, Don Sebastian (Spanish dwarf), **3:** *735*
Morrigans (Irish goddesses), **5:** 1239
Morris dances, 2: *591,* **7: 1890–2**
hobby-horse and, 7: *1890,* 1892
May Day and, **7:** 1774, 1892
origin of the name, **7:** 1890
sword dances compared with, **10:** 2751
Moses, 7: 1892
Maimonides on, **6:** 1531, 1532
rod of, **11:** 2986
striking water from a rock, **11:** *2985*
Yahweh and, **3:** 798, **9:** 2377, **11:** 3063ff
see also burning bush
Moses, Rev. W. Stainton, 1: 208, **7:** 1790, **10:** 2660
Moslem (definition), **6:** 1464
mosque (Islam), **6:** 1465–6, **7: 1892, 9:** 2366
see also Blue Mosque; Dome of the Rock; St Saviour (Constantinople)
mosquito (insect), **6:** 1451
Mot (Phoenician deity), Baal/Anat and, **1:** 223, **8:** 2182, **10:** 2762, **11:** 2940–1
mother:
city as symbol of, **6:** 1602
earth as, *see* earth, as mother goddess
garden as symbol of, **6:** 1601
see also birth; Mother Goddess; pregnancy
Mother Damnable (shrew of Kentish Town), **8:** *2053*
Mother Goddess (Great Mother), **7: 1893–8**
in Anatolia, **3:** 742
at Catal Hüyük, **1:** 116, **5:** 1394
Cybele, **2:** 583, **3:** 742, **7:** 1896
Ma (Bellona), **3:** 742, **7:** 1898
in Crete, **2:** 542, **5:** 1167, 1168f, 1171, *1171*
as earliest form of deity, **1:** 132
earth as, **3:** 748f, **4:** 936, **7:** 1894, **11:** 2939
in Finland, **4:** 958
Neolithic, **8:** 2244f
faceless goddesses as prototypes of, **4:** 896, **7:** 1895, **9:** 2360
in Greece:
Aphrodite as, **1:** 135, **7:** 1896
Artemis as, **3:** 630
Cretan, **5:** 1167, 1171
Demeter as, **7:** 1896
Hera as, **5:** 1270, 1271
in India, **7:** *1893,* 1895
Kali as, **6:** 1554
Virgin Mary and, **7:** 1898
in Mesopotamia, **7:** 1895–6
eye idols and, **4:** 888
Inanna as, **7:** 1895–6
Ishtar as, **7:** 1896
in Phoenicia/Canaan, **1:** 168, **7:** 1895, 1896
at Rome, **7:** 1896f
in Scandinavia, Freyja as, **7:** 1898
mountain, hill, **7: 1899–1900**
Aetherius Society and, **1:** 69, **3:** 821, **4:** 1003
in Christian tradition, **7:** 1900
of Cronus, **2:** 547
of Cybele, **2:** 583
Hebrews and, **7:** 1899–1900
Lapps and, **7:** 1900
nymphs of, *see* Oreads
omphalos compared with, **7:** 1952
of paradise (Indian myth), **8:** *2134*
of the philosophers (alchemy), **9:** *2432*
primeval, in Egyptian creation myth, **2:** 533f, **7:** 1952
of Purgatory, Dante and, **2:** 602
seven and, **7:** 1899
symbolism of, **6:** 1602
see also Adam's Peak; Arunachala; Atlas; Brocken; Cader Idris; Carmel; Eryx; Fuji; Glass Mountain; Glastonbury; Kenya; Kinabalu; Montségur; Olympus; Parliament Hill; Parnassus; Primrose Hill; Raggedstone; Sinai; world mountain; Zion
also volcanoes
mountain ash (tree), *see* rowan
Mountain Meadows massacre, 7: *1887,* 1889
Mount Badon, battle of, **1:** 153
mouse:
banished by poets, **8:** 2212
St Colman and, **9:** 2470
as cure for whooping cough, **3:** 643
St Gertrude and, **9:** 2471
precognition in, **9:** 2291

as witches' familiar, **2:** 401, *420,* **5:** 1417
Mousterian man, *see* Neanderthal man
Moyes, Winifred (Spiritualist), **10:** 2660
Mpadi, Simon (Congolese religious leader), **7:** 1978f
MRA, *see* Moral Rearmament
Mu, 6: 1614f, *1615,* **7: 1900**
mudras (gestures; yoga), **11:** 3073
Muezzin (Islam), **6:** *1464*
mugwort (St John's herb), **5:** 1275–6
Muhammad (the prophet of Islam), *see* Mohammed
Muhammad, Elijah (Black Muslim), **1:** 280, *281*
Muhammad, Farrad (Black Muslim), *see* Fard, Wallace D.
mujtahids (Islam), **6:** 1470
Mukhtar (Islamic rebel), **6:** 1699
mukti (Hinduism), **2:** 335
Muldoon, Sylvan, astral body and, **1:** 172, 173, *173,* **8:** *2095*
Muller, G. E., on the psychology of memory, **8:** 2040
Müller, George (of Plymouth Brethren), **3:** 867
Müller, (Friedrich) Max, 9: 2358
on folktales as solar myths, **4:** 1007
on theosophy, **10:** 2814
mumia, **3:** 643
Mumler, William (spirit photographer), **10:** 2663
mummers (guises, guizards, geesers), **3:** 698f, **4:** 1004f, *1005,* **5: 1188, 7: 1900, 11:** *3037*
Father Christmas and, **2:** *480,* **4:** 1004
St George and, **4:** 1004f
Puck and, **9:** 2297
mummification (Egypt), **3:** *791,* **7: 1900–4**
of baboons, **1:** 129
origin of the word 'mummy', **3:** 643, **7:** 1903
of Rameses II, **3:** *741*
see also Opening of the Mouth; ushabti
For preservation of bodies in other cultures, see dried bodies
Münster (Germany), Anabaptists at, **1:** 121, **2:** 499, **3:** 825f, **9:** 2520, *2521*
al-Muntazar, Mohammed (imam), **6:** 1470
Murcia (Roman goddess), **11:** 2946
Murphy, Bridey, 9: 2350
Murray, Gilbert, telepathy and, **8:** 2277–8
Murray, Margaret, witchcraft theories of, **1:** 247–8, **3:** 632, **4:** 906, **7:** 1866, 1869, **8:** 2148, **10:** 2825, **11:** 3043
Murrell, James (cunning man), **7: 1904**
Murshilish I (Hittite king), Babylon sacked by, **7:** 1733
Muses (Greek mythology), **7: 1905**
museum, origin of the word, **7:** 1905
mushroom, 3: 711, **7: 1905–10**
music, 7: 1910–13
Christianity and, **7:** 1911f
dance and, **2:** 595f, **7:** 1911
in Egypt, **7:** 1910
Etruscan, **9:** *2416*
Indian goddess of, *see* Sarasvati
Muses and, **7:** 1905
Orpheus and, **8:** 2082
Pythagoras and, **8:** 2024, **9:** 2315
ritual and, **7:** 1910ff
of the spheres, **8:** 2024
United States, folk music of, **11:** 2912, 2918
words, holy, and, **7:** 1911
see also drum; flute; gong; harp; lyre; *shofar;* trumpet
also Arion; song
Musrussu dragon (symbol of Marduk), **7:** 1734, *1734*
Mut (Egyptian goddess), *see* Maat
'mutable' signs in astrology, 11: 2957
Mutazilitism (Islam), **6:** 1468f
mutilation (of the body), **1:** 300, **7: 1914–18**
of fingers, **4:** 957
see also castration; cicatrization; circumcision; tattooing
Mycenae:
excavation at, by Schliemann, **5:** 1167
Lion Gate at, **10:** *2834*
Mycenaean civilization, **5:** 1166ff
Crete and, **2:** 545, **5:** 1166f, **11:** 3089ff
see also Trojan War
Myers, F. W. H., 7: 1918–20, 8: *2275*
cross-correspondences and, **2:** 553f, **7:** 1787, **8:** 2275f, **11:** 3030
on ghosts, **4:** 1101
magnetism and, **6:** 1695
phantasms of the living and, **4:** 1190, **7:** 1919
scrying and, **9:** 2507
Society for Psychical Research and, **7:** 1919, **8:** 2274
Mrs Piper and, **8:** 2200
Eusapia Palladino and, **8:** 2113
subliminal, his doctrine of the, **7:** 1920
Myerscough, Thomas (Pentecostalist), **8:** 2162
Myrddin (bard), **7:** 1810
myrrh (gum resin; tree), **7: 1920**
phoenix and, **8:** 2185
sun and, **2:** 522
in worship of Re, **5:** 1428
see also Myrrha
Myrrha (Greek mythology), **1:** 137
myrtle (flower, shrub), **7: 1920**
Aphrodite/Venus and, **11:** 2946
Graces and, **4:** 1145
lover tested with, **8:** 2204
mystery plays, 3: 698, **7: 1921–4**
miracle plays distinguished from, **7:** 1921
mystery religions, 3: 838f, **7: 1925–9**
Christianity and, **7:** 1929
St Paul, **8:** 2151f
of Demeter, **3:** 621
see also Eleusis
of Dionysus, **7:** 1925f, **8:** 2086
see also Villa of the Mysteries (Pompeii)
of Isis, **6:** 1461f, **7:** 1928, **8:** 2088, 2272
of Mithras, **7:** 1862ff, 1928
mysticism, 7: 1930–8
Buddhist, **7:** 1932, 1933, 1934f, 1937
see also Nirvana
Christian, **3:** 773ff, **7:** 1930–1, 1936ff
14th-century movements, **3:** 634
see also Cloud of Unknowing; Hildegard of Bingen; Hilton, Walter; Julian of Norwich; Ruysbroeck
see also Boehme, Jacob; Bourignon, Antoinette; Catherine of Siena; Denck, Hans; Francis de Sales; John of the Cross; Law, William; Pseudo-Dionysius; Teresa of Avila
ecstasy and, **3:** 773ff, **10:** 2697–8
Hindu, **3:** 775f, **7:** 1933ff
see also Anandamayi Ma
Islamic, *see* Sufism
Jewish, **3:** 776f
see also Buber, Martin; Cabala; Hasidism; Shekhinah; throne mysticism
love and, **3:** 774, **7:** 1934, 1936ff
paranormal phenomena and the occult distinguished from, **7:** 1930
physical phenomena of, *see* stigmata
sex and, **3:** 774, **7:** 1934, 1936, **9:** 2538
Mystic Krewe of Comus, 2682
mystic ring, 10: 2697, 2699
Goethe and, **4:** 1126
see also creation myths; end of the world; eternal return; euhemerism

N

nabhi (Old Testament), **8:** 2264f, **9:** 2377
Nabis, the (group of artists), **1:** 146
Nabonidus (last king of Babylon), **5:** 1213
Nabus (Mesopotamian god), **7:** 1820
Nagarjuna (Buddhist teacher), **10:** 2726
Nagas (people), **7: 1939–40**
headhunting by, **5:** 1232–3, **7:** 1939, **10:** 2799
tattooing and, **10:** 2799
Nagas (serpent deities), **9:** 2528, 2529, *2529*
Nahum (Old Testament prophet), **8:** 2267
Naiads (nymphs of running water), **8:** 2031
see also Salmacis
Nakano Yonosuke (Japanese religious leader), **6:** 1496
Nakayama Miki (Japanese religious leader), **6:** 1495
nakedness, *see* nudity
namapathy, 10: 2591
names, 7: 1940–4
of God, **7:** 1941f
see also Adonai; Elohim; Pentagrammaton; Tetragrammaton
in magic, **1:** 300, **7:** 1940ff, **9:** 2400f
in Ethiopia, **3:** 845
Golden Dawn and, **11:** 2951
numerology and, **1:** 113f, **8:** 2023f
of ships, **10:** 2568–9
Nammu (Sumerian goddess), **2:** 535
Nanak (founder of Sikhism), **10:** 2575–6
Nandin (bull of Shiva), **10:** 2573
Nannar (Mesopotamian moon god), *see Sin*
Nao Deguchi (Japanese religious leader), **6:** 1496
Napi (Blackfoot trickster), **4:** 1161
Napier, Barbara (witch), **8:** 2013, 2014, 2015
napistu (Mesopotamia), **6:** 1706
Napoleon, in numerology, **1:** *113*
Naram Sin (king of Akkad), stele of, **7:** *1819*
Nara Period (Japan), **6:** 1486ff
Narayana (Hinduism), **5:** 1420, **10:** 2958
Narcissus (Greek mythology), by Dali, **1:** *147*
narmer (pharaoh), palette of, **5:** 1394, **11:** *2991,* 2991–2
Nasca (Peru), **5:** 1423, 1424
Natalis, St, people of Ossory cursed by, **9:** 2552–3
Natchez Indians, 8: *2009,* 2011
National Socialism (Nazi Party), **7: 1944–8**
antisemitism and, **9:** *2329,* 2330
astrology and, **7:** 1945ff
black magic and, **1:** 279
Freemasonry and, **7:** 1944
Germanen Order and, **4:** 1081, 1082, **7:** 1945
Guido von List and, **6:** 1636
neo-pagan German cults and, **7:** 1966
New Templars and, **7:** 1983
Nostradamus and, **7:** 1946, **8:** 2017
sleeping hero myths and, **10:** 2615
swastika and, **2:** 550, *551,* **10:** 2739, *2739*
see also Hitler
Native American Church, 8: 2172
Nativity (birth of Jesus), **6:** *1504,* **11:** *2956*
nats (Burmese spirits), **10:** 2647
nature mysticism, 7: 1932–3
Navaho Indians, 7: 1949–52
bisexuality and, **5:** 1288
creation myth of, **7:** 1899, 1949
disease and, **2:** 589, **7:** 1950, 1951–2
divination and, **7:** 1952
ghosts, belief in, **7:** 1950
peyote and, **8:** 2172
sand-paintings of, **7:** *1949, 1950, 1951,* 1952
swastika and, **10:** 2739
taboos of, **7:** 1952
navel, 7: 1952
see also omphalos; umbilical cord
Navsari (India), Parsees and, **8:** 2137
Navy (Slav spirits), **10:** 2612
Nayars of Malabar, 7: 1802
Nayler, James (Quaker), **3:** 826
Nazarenes (early Christian sect), *see* Ebionites
Nazareth Baptist Church (African messianic sect), **7:** *1829,* 1832
Nazi Party, *see* National Socialism
Ndembu (of Zambia):
guardian spirits of, **5:** 1183, 1185
hunting magic of, **5:** 1374f

initiation ceremony of, **9:** 2394–5
Ndengei (Fijian snake god), **1:** 129
Neanderthal (Mousterian) man:
bear sacrifice of, **1:** 116, 245–6, **8:** 2243
burial and, **2:** 569, **5:** 1343–5
skull of, on Guattari cave, **2:** 435, 569
Nebuchadrezzar I (king of Babylon), **7:** 1733
Nebuchadrezzar II (king of Babylon), **7:** 1734
Nechepso (fictitious Egyptian king), **10:** 2692
neck (corn sheaf), **2:** 518
crying the neck, **5:** 1214–15
necklace:
diamond necklace (of Marie Antoinette), **2:** 389, **6:** 1514
of Freyja, *see* Brisingamen
in Japanese imperial symbolism, **9:** 2563
necromancy, 7: 1953–6
Rome and, **10:** 2824
Nectanebus (pharaoh), **1:** 103
nectar (drink of the gods), **7: 1956**
fly agaric mushroom identified as, **7:** 1908
need fire, 5: 1254, **8:** 2035
Nefertiti (Egyptian queen), **11:** *3058*
Anubis and, **5:** *1378*
Ikhnaten and, **3:** 790, **5:** 1400, *1401*
Negroes, 7: 1957–63
Christianity and, **7:** 1957ff
in the Congo, **2:** 503ff
race myths concerning, **9:** 2322ff
slavery and, **1:** 279f
in the United States, **7:** 1959, **11:** 2917–18
see also Black Muslims
see also hoodoo; Voodoo
Nehalennia (Germanic goddess), **4:** 1086
Nei Jing (Book of the Yellow Emperor), **1:** 68
Nekhebet (Egyptian goddess), vulture and, **1:** 271
Nelson, Horatio, 5: *1299*
Nemesis (Adrasteia; Greek goddess), **4:** 918, **11:** 3033
Nemi (sacred grove of Diana), **3:** 630, **7: 1964, 11:** 2942
Nennius, on King Arthur, **1:** 153
Neolithic (New Stone Age) period, **8:** 2244–5
cult of the dead in, **2:** 570
horns in, **5:** 1345–6
see also Catal Hüyük; Grimes Graves
neo-pagan German cults, 7: 1964–6
National Socialism and, **7:** 1966
swastika and, **10:** 2739
Neoplatonism, 7: 1966–8
Cabala influenced by, **2:** 384, **7:** 1968
Christianity influenced by, **7:** 1968
elements and, **3:** 802
exorcism and, **3:** 873
great chain of being and, **4:** 1159
Pseudo-Dionysius and, **3:** 634
soul, Neoplatonist view of, **7:** 1967f
theurgy and, **7:** 1968, **8:** 2259, 2260, **10:** 2821ff
see also Plotinus; Porphyry; Proclus; Taylor, Thomas
Nepal:
goat sacrifice in, **9:** *2457*
lama of, **8:** *2250*
prayer wheel in, **5:** *1419*
stupa in, **10:** *2840*
trumpet in, **10:** *2840*
Nephilim (Biblical giants), **4:** 1102
Nephthys (Egyptian goddess), **2:** 534, **8:** 2086, **9:** 2533
Neptune (planet), in astrology, **1:** 175, 181, **7:** 1970
Neptune (Roman god), **7: 1969–70**
Amphitrite and, **9:** *2417*
Nereids (sea nymphs), **8:** 2031
seals and, **9:** 2517
with sea-monster (Roman mosaic), **9:** *2414–15*
see also Amphitrite; Thetis
Nergal (Mesopotamian god), **6:** 1706, **7:** 1734, 1820, **10:** 2692
Neri, St Philip, 9: 2462, **10:** 2700
Nero (Roman emperor), **4:** 1157, 1158
Nerrivik (Eskimo spirit), *see* Sedna
Nerthus (Scandinavian deity), **4:** 1051, **10:** 2678
Nessus (centaur), Hercules and, **5:** 1280, **9:** *2537*
Nestorianism, 2: 471, **5:** 1282, **7:** 1749
net, 7: 1970, 10: 2756
Neuburg, Victor, Aleister Crowley and, **10:** 2540–1, 2869
Neumann, Teresa, 7: 1971, 10: 2698
Neuri (Scythian tribe), shape-shifting by, **9:** 2552
neurosis, poltergeists and, **8:** 2228
Nevillon, Silvain (witch), **4:** 1047
Newcomb, Prof. Simon, 8: 2274
New Guinea, 7: 1972–6
ancestor worship in, **7:** 1757f, 1974
animal double in, **5:** 1374
ashes used to prevent snake-bite in, **1:** 164–6
balance, concept of, **7:** 1973f
boar in, **7:** *1975*
body-painting in, **10:** *2801*
cannibalism in, **2:** 374, **7:** 1974
earth as symbol of victory in, **3:** *749*
ghosts in **7:** 1974
hornbill in, **7:** *1974*
initiation rites of, **3:** 725, **7:** 1974–5
marriage in, **7:** *1740, 1742*
masks in, **7:** 1757–8, *1972*
mud and mourning in, **10:** *2802–3*
pig in, **8:** *2192*
shape-shifting myth of, **9:** *2553*
skull in, **7:** *1975,* **10:** *2595*
spirits and, **5:** *1236,* **7:** *1797,* 1974, 1976
tattooing in, **10:** *2796*
New Harmony (Harmony Society settlement), **2:** 500
New Kingdom (Egyptian history), **3:** 788
New and Latter House of Israel (Jezreelites), **6:** 1514, **10:** 2646
Newman, Cardinal, William Law and, **6:** 1612
new religious movements, 7: 1977–81
in Africa, **7:** 1977ff
see also Church of the Cherubim and Seraphim
in Brazil, **7:** 1978, 1981, **8:** 2162, **10:** 2639ff
in Melanesia, **7:** 1981
see also cargo cults
see also Pentecostalist movement
News [Newes] from Scotland (witchcraft pamphlet), **8:** 2013, *2013, 2014–15, 2015*
New Templars, 7: 1982–3
New Testament, 1: 265, **5:** 1323
angels in, **1:** 125f, **5:** 1187
Dead Sea Scrolls and, **3:** 611
the Devil in, **9:** 2477
dreams in, **3:** 705
hell in, **5:** 1265
lots in, **6:** 1646
speaking in tongues in, **10:** 2649
three in, **10:** 2832
see also apostles, acts of the; gospel; Revelation
New Testament Apocrypha, 7: 1984–92
New Thought, 7: 1993–4
Newton, Benjamin Wills (leader of Plymouth Brethren), **3:** 867
Newton, Sir Isaac, 7: 1849
New Year, 4: 977, **7: 1994–7**
Babylonian festival of (Sacaea), **2:** 537, **3:** 690, 838, **4:** 935, **7:** 1733, 1734, **11:** 3035
coal and, **2:** 490
in Egypt, **6:** 1461
headlessness and, **7:** 1994
Iroquois and, **6:** 1458
in Judaism, **6:** 1536
March and, **7:** 1742, 1994
in Mexico, **7:** *1995*
pilgrimage and, **8:** 2194
vegetation god in festivals at, **11:** 2941
water and, **7:** 1995–7
see also Burning the Clavie; First Foot; hawthorn globe; Hogmanay
New Zealand, *see* Maori
Ngai (Kikuyu sky god), **6:** 1561
***Nibelungenlied,* 5:** 1298, **7:** *1997–9*
Attila in, **1:** 193, **7:** 1999
Wagner and, **7:** 1999, **11:** 2978
Nicaea, First Council of (AD 325):
Arianism rejected by, **2:** 471, **5:** 1282
castration forbidden by, **7:** 1915
Nicaea, Second Council of (AD 787), on relics, **9:** 2353
Nicene Creed, 2: 539
Nichiren (Japanese Buddhist sect), **6:** 1486, *1490–1,* 1492, 1497f
Nicholas, St, 4: 893
as Santa Claus, **4:** 483
Nicholas of Cusa, Eckhart and, **3:** 769
Nider, John (author of *Formicarius),* on witches, **8:** 2112
Nigeria:
altar of the hand in, **1:** *117*
Christian churches in, **7:** 1981
see also Church of the Cherubim and Seraphim; Church of the Lord, Aladura
criminals not buried in, **2:** *371*
dried monkeys' heads in, **8:** *2252*
drum in, **3:** *724*
hunting magic in, **5:** *1371*
masks in, **7:** *1757, 1758*
owl in, **9:** 2098
sacrifice in, **9:** 2488
twins in, **11:** 2902, *2905*
Yoruba of, **10:** 2639–40
see also Ibo
night, 7: 1999–2000
see also darkness; nightmare
nightingale, 7: 2000
Philomela and, **7:** 2000, **10:** 2735
nightmare, 5: 1432f, **7:** 2000
by Fuseli, **5:** *1430–1,* **7:** *1999*
nightshade (plant), *see* bitter-sweet nightshade; deadly nightshade
nigredo (alchemical process), **8:** 2178
Nile (river), **3:** 741, **11:** *2997*
Isis and, **6:** 1460, **10:** 2692
Nilotes (African people), **7: 2000–3**
see also Nuer; Shilluk
Nimrod, Tower of Babel built by, **11:** 2867
nimbus (halo), **3:** 678
nine, 1: 114, **7: 2003, 8:** 2025, 2026
names adding to, **1:** 114, **8:** 2023
nine heads of Hydra, **5:** 1279
ninety-nine, Amen (prayer) and, **7:** 1942
Ningursu of Lagash (Mesopotamian god), **3:** 746, **11:** 2992
Ninhursag (Sumerian goddess), **4:** 888
Ninmah (Sumerian goddess), **2:** 536
Ninurta (Sumerian god), **7:** 1820
Saturn (planet) and, **9:** 2480
Zu (Anzu) slain by, **3:** 690, **7:** 1821
Niobe, Apollo and, **1:** 140
Nirvana, 7: 2004
in Buddhism, **1:** 261, **2:** 354, 355, 356, **5:** 1309, **6:** 1712, **7:** 1932, 1935, 1937, 2004
in Ceylon, **10:** 2587
in Hinduism, **1:** 264f, **7:** 1935, 1936, 2004
in Jainism, **6:** 1483
Nisaba (Sumerian goddess), **7:** 1820
Nishkuntu (John Wilson), peyote cults and, **8:** 2171, 2172
nixies (German water spirits), **7:** 1811
niyama (yoga), **11:** 2935, 3072–3
Niyamen (Ras Tafari group), **7:** 1834
Njörd (Scandinavian god), **4:** 1051, **9:** 2483
Noah (Old Testament):
his Ark, **4:** 992, **11:** 3001–2
animals in pairs and sevens, **11:** 2906
dove sent out from, **3:** *680,* 682
in Ethiopian MS, **4:** *995*
in Mogul miniature, **4:** *994*

rainbow and, **8:** 2064, **9:** 2333
sacrifice and, **9:** 2456
his sons, **11:** 3064
Noah of Washington Mud Flats, 3: *821*
Nobili, Roberto de, 9: 2361
Noble, Michel de, 5: 1250
Noctiluca (goddess of witches), **1:** 237
non-jurors (Anglicanism), **6:** 1612
Nordic mythology, *see* Scandinavian mythology
Nordic Religious Working Community, 7: 1966
Nordungen Fraternity, 7: 1965
Nore, mutiny at the (1797), **8:** 2037–8
Norns (Scandinavian mythology), **4:** 904, 920
Norse mythology, *see* Scandinavian mythology
north, 3: 640
North American Indians, 8: 2005–12
first alphabet of, **8:** 2012
animals and, **4:** 935
bears, **1:** 244, 245, **2:** 589, **4:** 935, **8:** 2042
bisexuality and, **5:** 1287–8
creation myths of, **8:** 2010
flood legends of, **4:** 1054, **8:** 2010–11
fool and, **4:** 1018–19
hallucinatory drugs and, **8:** 2010
see also peyote cults
harvest mask of, **5:** *1217*
High Gods of, **5:** 1302
initiation and, **5:** 1444
moon and, **8:** 2007
owl and, **8:** 2098, *2098*
paradise and, **8:** 2133
priests of, **8:** 2011
salmon and, **9:** 2474
scalp dance of, **6:** *1679*
serpent and, **9:** 2530
stars and, **8:** 2008f
sun and, **8:** *2006*
see also Sun Dance
thunderbird and, **10:** 2836–7
tobacco and, **8:** 2010, **11:** 2858
totemism and, **8:** 2012, **11:** 2859, 2861, *2861, 2862*
trickster and, *see* trickster, North American Indians and
whale and, **11:** 3014
see also Algonquin Indians; Great Plains Indians; Iroquois; Navaho Indians; Pacific North-West Indians; Pueblo Indians
North Berwick witches, 2: 400, **5:** 1409, **8: 2013–15**
Norton, Thomas (alchemist), **1:** 93, 99
nose, 8: 2016
fingers to, **4:** 1089
phallic symbolism of, **4:** 1089
see also sneezing
Nostradamus, 8: 2016–17, 2268f
Nazi interpretations of, **7:** 1946, **8:** 2017
notarikon, 4: 1074
No theatre (Japan), **6:** *1488,* **7:** 1764
Notre Dame du Haut (Ronchamp, Le Corbusier), **9:** *2368*
Nouvelet, Father, Auxonne nuns and, **1:** 211
Noyes, John Humphrey (founder of Oneida Community), **2:** 502, **3:** 828, **5:** 1328
nudity, 2: 527, **8: 2017–19**
in Christian heresies, **8:** 2019
in India, **5:** 2017f
modern witchcraft and, **7:** 1867, *1868,* 1870
ploughing and, **7:** 2018
see also Adamites; Godiva, Lady
Nuer (Nilotic people), **7:** 2000ff, **2020–3**
ghosts and, **10:** 2638
twins and, **11:** 2902
Nuliajuk (Eskimo spirit), *see* Sedna
numbers, *see* numerology
numerology, 1: 113f, **8: 2023–6**
forces and numbers, **4:** 1020–1
gematria and, **4:** 1074
magic and, **3:** 643f
see also magic squares
male and female numbers, **8:** 2025
names and, **1:** 113f, **8:** 2023f
perfect numbers, **10:** 2592
Pythagoras and, **8:** 2024ff, **9:** 2315–16
see also one; two; three; four; five; six; seven; eight; nine; ten; eleven; twelve; thirteen; fourteen; fifteen; twenty-two; forty; ninety-nine
numinous, 8: 2026
Rudolf Otto on, **9:** 2359
Nun (Egyptian creation myth), **1:** 229, **2:** 533f, 535
nuns, possessed, *see* possession, of nuns
nursery rhymes, 8: 2026–30
Jack in, **6:** 1477, **7:** 1877
Ring A Ring O Roses, **10:** *2625*
Nusayrites (Islam), **6:** 1470
Nut (Egyptian sky goddess), **2:** 530, 534, *534–5*
nut (fruit), fertility and, **8:** 2205
Nutter, Alice (witch), **6:** 1593
Nyabingi (African movement), **7:** 1834
Nyame (Ashanti god), **1:** 161, 163
Nyaya (Hinduism), **11:** 3070
Nyikango (Shilluk culture hero), **7:** 2001
nymphs (Greek mythology), **8: 2031–2,** 2124
see also Amalthea; Amphitrite; Coronis; Daphne; Egeria; Hesperides; Kissos; Salmacis; Thetis

O

O (letter), eye and, **4:** 886
oak, 8: 2033–5
Argonauts and, **8:** 2033
ash tree and, **8:** 2035
in the Bible, **8:** 2033
Celts and, **6:** 1639
Druids, **2:** 441, **3:** 719
modern Druids, **8:** 2034
Charles II and, **8:** 2035
at Dodona, **3:** 663, **8:** 2033, 2076–7
Dryads and, **3:** 728
fire and, **4:** 971
need fire, **8:** 2035
Yule log, **8:** 2035
in Germany; Prussia, **8:** 2034, 2077
gospel oak, **8:** 2035
Green Man and, **8:** 2035
in Ireland, **8:** 2034
marriage and, **8:** 2034, 2035
May and, **8:** 2035
mistletoe and, **7:** 1859, 1860, **8:** 2033
as protection against lightning, **8:** 2034–5, **10:** 2604
Romans and, **8:** 2034
Praeneste (oracle) and, **6:** 1647
shrieking of, **8:** 2034
Thor and, **10:** 2826
True Cross made of **10:** 2773
see also acorn
Oak-Apple Day (Royal Oak Day, Shickshack Day), **8:** 2035, *2035*
Oannes (Mesopotamian god), **7:** 1810
oath, 2: 579, **8: 2036–8**
blood and, **8:** 2037
coronation, **8:** *2038*
Kikuyu and, **6:** 1562–3, **8:** 2037
Quakers and, **8:** 2038
obeah, 8: 2039, 11: 2967f
obelisk, 8: 2039
Oberammergau, passion play at, **3:** *699,* **7:** *1922*
object reading (psychometry, psychoscopy), **8: 2039–42, 2296**
obsidian, 8: 2042
occult (definition), **8: 2042**
ocean, *see* sea
Oceania:
myths of origin of death in, **3:** 613, 615
witchcraft and sorcery distinguished by writers on, **11:** 3042
see also Melanesia; Micronesia; Polynesia
Oceanides (nymphs of the ocean), **8:** 2031
ocelot (wild cat), Aztecs and, **11:** 2861
Od, Odic force (occultism), *see* Odyle
Odin, 8: 2043–7, 2483
Balder and, **1:** 226, **4:** *1083*
eagle and, **4:** 1086
eye of, scarificed, **4:** 1029
fire festival and, **11:** 3076
fountain of Mimir and, **4:** 1029
head of Mimir and, **5:** 1240
horse of, *see* Sleipnir
killed by Fenris wolf, **3:** 817, **9:** *2485,* 2486
knot symbol of, **8:** 2045, 2047
mead of inspiration won by, **8:** *2045,* 2046
meaning of the name, **4:** 1086
ravens and, **2:** 556f, **4:** 1086, **8:** *2043*
riddles and, **9:** 2386
ring of, *see* Draupnir
runes and, **1:** 111
sacrifice and, **8:** 2045
shape-shifting by, **9:** 2550, 2556
son of, *see Vidar*
spear of, *see* Gungnir
Vanir and, **4:** 1052
King Vikar and, **8:** 2045
wife of, *see* Frigg
Wild Hunt led by, **4:** 1086, **11:** 3022
Wodan and, **4:** 1084f
wolf and, **4:** 1086, **8:** *2043*
see also Valkyries
Odomankoma (Ashanti god), **1:** 161
odour of sanctity, 10: 2701
Odyle (Od, Odic force; aura), **1:** 195, **3:** 677, **6:** 1694, **9:** 2331
Odysseus (Ulysses; Greek hero), **8: 2047**
bear and, **1:** 245
Circe and, **2:** 485f, **7:** 1874
Sirens and, **10:** 2590, *2590*
see also Odyssey
***Odyssey,* 11:** 2890
see also Homer; Odysseus
Oedipus (Greek mythology), **5:** 1429, **8: 2047**
Sphinx and, **9:** *2385*
see also Oedipus complex
Oedipus complex (psychology), **4:** 1049, **5:** 1429, **9:** 2392
Og (Biblical giant), **4:** 1102–3
Ogg, Isobel (witch), **1:** 63
Ogg, Margaret (witch), **1:** 63
Ohrmazd (Ormuzd; Zoroastrianism, **8: 2048**
Ahriman and, **1:** 86ff, *87,* **3:** 729f, **6:** 1624, **8:** 2048, **11:** 3103, 3107
Ahura Mazdah and, **1:** 86, **8:** 2048
cypress symbol of, **11:** 2875
Parsees and, **8:** 2138
oil, 8: 2049–50
see also unction
ointment, *see* flying ointment; oil
Oisin (Irish legend), *see* Ossian
Ojibway Indians, *see* Chippewa
Olcott, Colonel Henry Steel, 1: 290ff, *292,* **9:** 2348
old age and witchcraft, 8: 2051–7
Old Believers, 8: 2058–9
Old Chattox (witch), *see* Whittle, Anne
Old Demdike (witch), *see* Sowthern, Elizabeth
Old Kingdom (Egyptian history), **3:** 788
Old Man (trickster), **11:** 2881
Old Man of the Sea, Sinbad and, **9:** *2514,* **10:** 2584
Old Stone Age, *see* Paleolithic
Old Testament, 1: 265, **5:** 1323
altars in, **1:** 116
angels in, **1:** 124ff, **5:** 1187
Baal in, **1:** 222f
books of, *see* Daniel; Hexateuch; Job; Pentateuch; Psalms; *also* prophecy *below*
Dead Sea Scrolls and, **3:** 609, 611
dreams in, **3:** 705

fountains in, **4:** 1028, 1029
leprosy in, **6:** 1617
lots in, **6:** 1647–8
miracles in, **7:** 1852
oil, ointment, in, **8:** 2049–50
promised land in, **3:** 798f, **5:** 1322, **11:** 2992
prophecy in, **8:** 2264–7
see also Elijah; Ezekiel; Hosea; Isaiah
prostitution in, **8:** 2271
Queen of Sheba in, **9:** 2316
sacrifice in, **9:** 2457–8
Abraham and Isaac, **4:** 976, *976,* **9:** *2455,* 2556, **11:** 2897
symbolism of, adopted by Christians, **10:** 2760
threshold in, **10:** 2833
trees in, **11:** 2874f, 2878
twins in, **11:** 2902–3
water in, **11:** 2998
wisdom literature of, **11:** 3040
see also Samson; Yahweh
Old Uppsala (Sweden), sacrifice at, **8:** 2045, **9:** 2457
olive (tree and fruit), **8: 2060**
in the Bible, **8:** 2060
cross of Jesus and, **8:** 2060, 2116
in Greece, **8:** 2060
oracle of Praeneste and, **6:** 1647
Yule-log and, **8:** 2060
Olmecs, 1: 219
Olympia (Greece)
Hera and, **5:** 1270
Zeus born at, **5:** 1168
see also Olympic Games
Olympic Games, 4: 1065–7, **8: 2060**
Endymion and, 9: 2522
Hercules and, **5:** 1270
Zeus and, **8:** 2060, **11:** 3093
Olympus, Mount (Greece), **5:** 1168, **7:** *1899,* **8: 2060**
om (mantra), **7:** 1728
see also om mani padme hum
Omar Khayyam, 8: 2061–3
omens, 8: 2064–7
animals as, **8:** 2064
Aztecs and, **1:** 220
body, aspects of, as, **8:** 2064
in the Ozarks, **8:** 2102
sneezing as, **10:** 2625
sky phenomena as, **8:** 2064
see also augury
For divination by various omens, see divination *or under specific headings*
Ometecuhtli (Mexican god), **1:** 216–7
om mani padme hum (Tibetan prayer), **6:** 1513
omniscience of God, in Christianity, **8:** 2242
Omoto (Japanese religious sect), **6:** 1496
Omphalos (Greek 'navel' stone), **1:** 139, **7:** 1952
one, 1: 113, **8:** 2025, **2068, 10:** 2830
names adding to, **1:** 113, **8:** 2023, 2068
the One, as divine principle, **4:** 1159, **7:** 1933f, **8:** 2068
in Hinduism, *see* Brahman
in Islam (monism), **5:** 1386
in Neoplatonism, **7:** 1967f, **8:** 2208, 2260
in pantheism, **8:** 2125
in Pythagoreanism, **9:** 2316
ten and, **8:** 2068
two and, **8:** 2068
Oneida Community (Perfectionists), **3:** 497, 502, **3:** 828
oneiromancy (divination by dreams), **3:** 704–5
onion, origin of, in Mohammedan legend, **4:** 1069
Onisaburo Deguchi (Japanese religious leader), **6:** 1496
Ono (Polynesian god), *see* Rongo
onychomancy (divination by finger-nails), **4:** 957
onyx (jewel), **6:** 1512
opal (jewel), **6:** 1511, *1513*
Open Brethren, *see* Plymouth Brethren
Opening of the Mouth (mummification), **9:** 2449, *2449*
ophitism (Gnosticism), **3:** 731
opium, 3: *712, 713,* 713f
opossum, in Brazil, **2:** 329
opposites, 8: 2068–70
in alchemy, **7:** 1808, 2069
black mass and, **1:** 278f
Boehme on, **1:** 302
in Chinese philosophy, *see* Yin and Yang
William James on, **8:** 2068
Jung on, **8:** 2069
in numerology (male and female numbers), **8:** 2025
Renaissance interest in, **9:** 2373f
sex as reconciliation of, **8:** 2070, **9:** 2539
three and, **9:** 2373
unicorn as symbol of, **11:** 2910
see also dualism
Ops (Roman goddess), **9:** 2413–14
optical illusions, *see* visual illusions
***opus anglicanum,* 8: 2070–1**
oracles, 8: 2072–9
Graeco-Roman, **8:** 2072–8
of Apollo, **8:** 2073, 2077f
see also Delphi, oracle of Apollo at
laurel and, **6:** 1610
of Mars (woodpecker), **7:** 1744, **11:** 3060
of Zeus, *see* Dodona
see also Praeneste
primitive, **8:** 2078–9
of Azande, **1:** 212, 260f
Tibetan, **11:** 2867
trees as, **11:** 2878
***Oracula Sibyllina,* 10:** 2575
orange (fruit and flower), **8:** 2205
orchid, as herb, **5:** 1276
Orc Treith (Irish legend), **4:** 966
Orcus (Roman god), *see* Pluto
ordeal, 8: 2079
see also trial by ordeal
Order of the Garter, 4: 1070, **10:** *2749,* 2825
Order of the Gold and Rosy Cross (Richter), **9:** 2430
Order of the Holy City, 7: 1747
Order of the Illuminati, *see* Illuminati
Order of the Templars of the East, 2: 561, **9:** *2397,* 2541
Oreads (Orestiads; mountain nymphs), **8:** 2031
oreibasia (Dionysian dance rite), **3:** 638
Oreithyia (Amazon), **1:** 119
***orenda,* 1:** 106, **11:** 2861
Orestes (Greek mythology), **4:** *918,* 1055f
Orestiads (mountain nymphs), *see* Oreads
Orexa, Maria Miguel de (witch), **1:** 235
Orfeo, Sir, 11: 3025
orgy, 8: 2079
Orias (spirit), **9:** 2400
oriental Jewish communities, 8: 2080–1
Origen:
castrates himself, **7:** 1915, **10:** 2593
Gnosticism and, **4:** 1117f
on guardian angels, **4:** 1187
on hell, **5:** 1265
on Jesus and the Roman empire, **7:** 1929
meaning of his name, **7:** 1941
on sin, **3:** 625
on the Song of Solomon, **7:** 1936
on the soul, **5:** 1415
original sin, 3: 860, **4:** 890f, **6:** 1708, **8: 2081**
Adam and, **4:** 980
St Augustine and, **4:** 982
not a dualist concept, **3:** 733
infant baptism and, **1:** 232
Judaism and, **4:** 980
Virgin Mary, her freedom from, *see* Immaculate Conception
St Paul and, **3:** 860, **4:** 980
virgin birth of Christ and, **7:** 1749
Orion, 8: 2081
constellation, **8:** 2081
Osiris and, **8:** 2081, **10:** 2692
giant, **8:** 2081
Hephaestus and, **5:** 1269
Ormuzd, *see* Ohrmazd
Oro (Polynesian god), **8:** 2230
Orobas (demon), **3:** *860*
Orolum (Nigerian god), **10:** 2639
Orpheus and Orphism, 8: 2082–6
Orpheus, **8:** 2082ff
Argonauts saved from Sirens by, **8:** 2082, **10:** 2590
Bacchants and, **8:** 2083
death of, **8:** 2082–3
Eurydice and, **8:** 2082
head of, **8:** 2083
as a Lar, **6:** 1609
lyre of, **8:** 2082, *2082–3, 2084*
relics of, preserved, **9:** 2351
Orphism, **7:** 1925, **8:** 2082ff
Athene and, **1:** 187
Dionysus and, **3:** 859, **8:** 2085f
Eleusinian Mysteries and, **8:** 2083, 2085
the Orphic poems, **8:** 2082, 2083
Plato and, **8:** 2083, 2084f
Pythagoreans and, **8:** 2083ff
reincarnation and, **6:** 1707–8, **11:** 2850
not an established religion, **8:** 2082
orpine (plant), **7:** 1846
Orthodox Church, Great Schism in, **8:** 2058
Orungan (Nigerian god), **10:** 2639–40
Oscilloclast, *see* Abrams Box
Osiris, 3: 741, 790, **8: 2086–8**
Abydos, Osiris play enacted at, **3:** 696, **8:** 2088
Apis and, *see* Serapis
birth of, in Heliopolitan myth, **2:** 534
Christ compared with, **8:** 2088
cult of the dead and, **3:** *740,* 790, **6:** *1567,* **7:** 1900, **8:** 2087–8
see also judge of the dead *below*
Dionysus identified with, **8:** 2086
as dying god, **3:** 741, **8:** 2088
in Graeco-Roman world, **8:** 2086ff
see also Isis, Romans and; Serapis
head of, **5:** 1245
Horus and, **4:** 886, **5:** 1359, **8:** 2086, 2087
iconography of, **8:** 2087
Isis and, **3:** 741, **6:** 1460, 1461, **8:** 2086f, 2088
as judge of the dead, **4:** 929, **6:** 1541, **8:** 2088
Orion and, **8:** 2081, **10:** 2692
in the Pyramid Texts, **1:** 305ff, **6:** 1540, **8:** 2086, 2087f
Seker identified with, **1:** 308
Seth and, **3:** 790, **8:** 2086, 2087, **9:** 2533
Tammuz and, **10:** 2776
as vegetation deity, **4:** 967, **8:** 2088, **11:** 2939
Ositelu, J. A. (founder of Church of the Lord, Aladura), **7:** 1981
Osmont, Anne (occultist), **1:** 171
osprey, in augury, **1:** 194
Ossian (Oisin), **4:** 964, 966, **10:** 2689
ostrich, 8: 2088
feathers of, **4:** 929
Otomi Indians (Mexico), **7:** 1842
Otshirvani (central Asian creator), **4:** 1053
Otto, Rudolf, 9: 2358–9
ouija boards, 7: *1781,* **8: 2089–92**
see also planchette
ourobouros (snake swallowing its tail), **1:** 94, **2:** 487, **9:** 2532
Crowley and, **8:** *2068*
Golden Dawn and, **4:** *1130*
Ouspensky, Peter Demianovich, 5: 1188, 1189, **8: 2092–3, 10:** 2790–1
out-of-the-body experiences, 8: 2093–6
methods of inducing, **8:** 2095
in primitive belief, **3:** 648, **9:** 2543
shamans and, **9:** 2549
two types of, **8:** 2093
see also astral body
outlaws, 11: 3029

see also Robin Hood
overlooking, 8: 2282
see also Evil Eye
Owen, Robert, Harmony Society and, **2:** 497, 500
Owen, Robert Dale, Spiritualism and, **1:** 290
owl, 8: 2096–8
in African witchcraft, **11:** 3045
Ainu and, **8:** 2098
Athene and, **1:** 185, 187, **8:** 2098
in augury, **1:** 194
birds' hostility to, **6:** 1640, **8:** 2098
in China, **8:** 2098
crow and, **2:** 557
eggs of, **8:** 2098
in Egypt, **8:** *2096*
evil and, **8:** 2096f
Evil Eye and, **8:** 2098
lightning and storms averted by, **8:** 2098
in Nigeria, **8:** 2098
North American Indians and, **8:** *2010,* 2098, *2098*
in Rome, **8:** 2096
in Sumer, **8:** 2096
as witch's familiar, **2:** *420*
wren and, **8:** 2098
owl corners, 8: 2098
ox:
Athenian sacrifice of, *see bouphonia*
Enlil as, **1:** 129, **2:** 365
as symbol of St Luke, **5:** *1398*
see also bull
Oxford Group (Buchmanism), *see* Moral Rearmament
Oxford Movement (Tractarians), Oxford Group (Moral Rearmament) distinguished from, **7:** 1882
oyster:
as aphrodisiac, **4:** 987, **6:** 1658
see also pearl
Ozarks, 8: 2099–2103
rain-making in, **2:** 518
witchcraft in, **8:** 2100

P

pace eggs, pace eggers (Easter), **3:** 784, **4:** 1004, *1006*
Pacific North-West Indians, 8: 2011–12, **2104–9**
dance societies of, **8:** 2107
initiation and, **8:** 2107
masks and, **7:** 1758–9, **8:** *2010, 2107*
myth of origin of death of, **3:** 615
potlatch ceremony of, **8:** 2107, **9:** 2526
raven and, **7:** 1758–9, **8:** 2104f, *2106,* **11:** 2881
shamans of, **8:** 2108–9
totemism and, **8:** 2012
see also Kwakiutl Indians
pact, Satanic, 8: 2110–12
St Augustine on, **8:** 2110
Roger Bacon and, **8:** 2112
Freud on, **3:** 714, **11:** 2972
Louis Gaufridi and, **1:** 91–2
Urbain Grandier and, **4:** 1155, *1156,* **8:** 2112
grimoires not greatly concerned with, **8:** 2112
Proterius and, **8:** 2110
signed in blood, **8:** 2110f
Pope Sylvester II and **8:** 2112
Theophilus of Adana and, **8:** 2110
witches and, **8:** 2110, 2112, 2246, **10:** 2626, 2632
see also Faust
Padma (Lakshmi), **6:** 1650
Padstow Old Hoss (hobby-horse), **5:** *1326,* 1326f, **7:** 1892
pagan (definition), **8: 2112**
pagoda, 8: 2112
Pahlavi (language), Parsees and, **8:** 2137
pain, origin of, **3:** 858ff
Palatine Hill (Rome), **4:** 1027
temple of Cybele on, **7:** 1896
Paleolithic (Old Stone Age) period, **8:** 2243–4
bull in, **2:** 363
burial in, **2:** 372, **5:** 1343–5
cave art of, *see* cave art, in Paleolithic Europe
cult of the dead in, **2:** 569f
headless figures at Mineteda from, **5:** 1245
see also faceless goddesses, Paleolithic; Neanderthal man
Palermo (Sicily), dried bodies in, **1:** *307,* **7:** *1903*
Palestine, 8: 2113. *For the Canaanites, see also* Phoenicians. *For the Jews and their religion, see also* Jews; Judaism. *For the modern state of Israel, see* Israel.
Palilia (Roman festival), **7:** 1863
palindrome, 8: 2113
magic squares and, **6:** 1693, **8:** 2113
Palladino, Eusapia (medium), **3:** *880,* **7:** 1790, *1793,* **8: 2113–14,** 2275
palm (tree), **8:** 2060, **2114–16,** 2180
see also Palm Sunday
Palmer (pilgrim), **8:** 2116, 2193
Palmer, John, image magic used by, **5:** 1408
palmistry (chiromancy), **3:** *656,* **8: 2117–23**
Adolphe Desbarolles and, **6:** 1619
Gypsies and, **5:** 1201
Palm Sunday, 3: 764, **8:** 2116
see also Jesus, his entry into Jerusalem
'Palm Sunday' case (Society for Psychical Research), **11:** 3030
Palmyra (Syria), **10:** *2765,* 2766
Pan (Greek god), **8: 2124–5**
Aphrodite with, **1:** 138
Arcadia and, **8:** 2124
Athens and, **8:** 2125
Dionysus and, **8:** *2124*
Faunus identified with, **4:** 1120
hare and, **8:** 2125
Hermes and, **8:** 2124, 2125
nymphs and, **8:** *2031,* 2124
panacea, 3: 809f
Panacea Society of Bedford, 10: 2645, 2646
J. J. Jezreel and, **6:** 1515
Panama, 7: 1839f, 1844
Panchen Lama, 6: 1590
Pandemonium, by John Martin, **7:** *1847*
Pandora (first woman; Greek mythology), **8: 2125, 11:** 3056–7, *3058*
created by Hephaestus, **5:** 1268
Prometheus and, **8:** 2125, 2262
P'an Ku (Chinese myth), **3:** 781
pantheism, 8: 2125
in Stoicism, **8:** 2240
Teilhard de Chardin and, **10:** 2812
Vedanta not pantheistic, **11:** 2931
panther, in the bestiary, **1:** 259
Papa (Maori earth goddess), **7:** 1731
papacy, 2: 472ff
see also Alexander III; Alexander VI; Benedict XIV; Benedict XVI; Gregory VII; Gregory IX; Gregory XI; Honorius I; Innocent III; Innocent IV; Innocent VIII; John XXII; Leo I; Paul III; Pius IX; Pius XII; Sylvester II; Urban II; Urban VI; Urban VIII; Zachary
also Great Schism; John XXIII; Pope Joan
Papias (Christian writer), **7:** 1875, 1985
Papini, Giovanni, on the Devil, **3:** 625
Papua, cult of the dead in, **2:** *568*
Papus (Dr Gérard Encausse), **8: 2125–6**
Martinists and, **7:** 1747, **8:** 2126
Theodor Reuss and, **8:** 2126, **11:** 2988
Tarot and, **8:** *2125,* 2125f, **10:** 2791
papyrus, 6: 1689
Paracelsus, 8: 2126–8
alchemy and, **1:** 94f, **3:** 809, 810f, **7:** 1807f, **8:** 2127–8, 2180
astrology and, **8:** 2127
at Basle, **8:** 2126–7
on beryl and familiar spirits, **6:** 1511
demon kept by, **5:** 1417
elementals and, **3:** 802f
gnomes, **4:** 1115
homunculus and, **5:** 1338
Jung on, **6:** 1550f
on magic, **6:** 1684
medicine and, **3:** 809, 810f, **8:** 2126ff
on the moon's connection with madness, **7:** 1881
Rosicrucians and, **9:** 2428
Paradise, heaven, **5: 1256, 7:** 1909, **8: 2129–36**
Buddhism and, **8:** *2129,* 2134
Celts and, **8:** 2132
St Brendan and, **2:** 337ff, **8:** 2132
see also Avalon
Christianity and:
earthly paradise, **8:** 2132
see also Eden, garden of
heaven, **5:** 1256, **8:** 2133, 2134ff
Dante on, **2:** 602ff
see also Last Judgement
drugs as route to, **3:** 711, **7:** 1909
garden as, **8:** 2129
see also Eden, garden of
Golden Age myth and, **8:** 2132f
Greeks and, **8:** 2132f, 2134
see also Elysium
Hinduism and, **6:** 1558–9, **8:** *2132,* 2134
Islam and, **5:** 1256, **8:** *2133,* 2135f
see also houri
Judaism and, **8:** 2133, 2134, 2135f
ladder to, **6:** *1547,* **10:** 2695f, *2696*
meaning of the word, **7:** 1909
North American Indians and, **8:** 2133
Parsees and, **8:** 2141
in Scandinavian mythology, *see* Valhalla
see also Isles of the Blest
Paradise Lost, *see* Milton, John
paranoia, witchcraft and, **5:** 1379f
paranormal powers:
in Buddhism, **2:** 355
Curé of Ars and, **2:** 579
Jung and, **6:** 1550
see also psi
parapsychology, 3: 875, **8: 2136**
see also extra-sensory perception; psi; psychical research; psychokinesis; spontaneous psi experiences
Parashurama (incarnation of Vishnu), **11:** 2960
Parcae, *see* Fates
parchment, 8: 2136
Parham, Charles F. (Pentecostalist), **8:** 2159, 2161
Parilia (Roman sheep festival), **10:** 2559, 2678
Paris, François de, 2: 516, **7** 1854
Paris, Judgement of, *see* Judgement of Paris
Parjanya (Indian god), bull and, **2:** 365
Parliament Hill (London), Druids and, **3:** 722, 723
Parnassus, Mount (Greece), Dionysian dance rite on, **3:** 638
Parr, J. Nelson (Pentecostalist), **8:** 2162
Parsees, 8: 2137–41
calendars of, **8:** 2137
the dead, disposal of, **2:** 374, **8:** 2139, *2139,* 2140–1, **11:** *3099*
dogs and, **8:** 2140
dualism repudiated by, **8:** 2138
festivals of **8:** 2139–40
fire and, **1:** 117, **4:** 970, **8:** 2138
guardian spirits of, **8:** 2138
haoma and, **11:** 3102
heaven and, **8:** 2141
hell and, **8:** 2141
judgement of the dead and, **8:** 2138, 2141
marriage and, **8:** *2138,* 2140
Persian origin of, **8:** 2137
priests of, **8:** 2137, 2140
soul and, **8:** 2141
Zoroastrianism of, **8:** 2137ff
Parsifal (Perceval, Parzival; Arthurian

knight), **4:** 1149f, **8: 2141–3**
enchanted island visited by, **8:** 2142
Fisher King and, **4:** 1149, **8:** 2141f
forest and, **11:** 3025
Galahad and, **4:** 1057, 1059, **8:** 2142
Grail and, **4:** 1059, **6:** 1149f, 1152, **8:** 2141ff
Loathly Damsel and, **8:** 2141, 2143
marriage of, **8:** 2143
Wagner and, **11:** 2978
parsley, 5: 1276
Parsva (Jain prophet), **6:** 1480f, *1482*
Parthenon (Athens), **1:** 187, **9:** *2357*
frieze from (detail), **10:** *2808–9*
Parthians, 8: 2143–4
partridge, as aphrodisiac, **6:** 1657
Parvati (wife of Shiva; Hinduism), **4:** *934,* **5:** *1310,* 1314, **10:** 2573, *2780*
Ganga identified with, **4:** 1068
yoni symbol of, **5:** 1288
Parzival (Arthurian knight), *see* Parsifal
Pascal, Blaise, 6: 1716, **9:** 2524
Paschal Candle, 3: 766
Paschal Lamb, Jesus as, **3:** 760
Pashley sarcophagus, 8: *2124*
Pasiphae (mother of the Minotaur), **2:** 365, **5:** 1271
Pasqually, Martinez de (founder of Martinists), **7:** 1746, 1747
Passion plays, 3: *699*
Passover (Jewish feast), **3:** 734f, **4:** *1015,* **6:** *1533,* 1536, **9:** 2458
Pasupati (Lord of the Beasts; India), **5:** 1436
Patanjali (writer on yoga), **11:** 3070
Patern, St, 2: 349
path symbolism (the road, the way, journey symbolism), **6: 1528, 8: 2145–7**
see also pilgrimage; sefiroth
Patrick, St, 9: 2462
Breastplate of (prayer), **10:** 2618
Fenians and, **4:** 966
Glastonbury and, **5:** 1109, 1111
witches, his disbelief in, **3:** 873
Patroclus (Greek hero), **1:** 65
Patterson, Charles Brodie, on New Thought, **7:** 1994
Paul, St, 2: 469f, **8: 2148–50**
on Adam, **4:** 980
apocryphal acts of, **7:** 1989, 1992
at Athens, **4:** 896, **5:** 1415
on baptism, **1:** 231–2, **11:** 3001
on the Crucifixion, **6:** 1508, **8:** 2151f, **10:** 2693
epistles of, **6:** 1507, **8:** 2148
see also Corinthians; Galatians
on the Eucharist, **7:** 1768
Gnosticism and, **8:** 2151–2
healing and, **4:** 909
heaven and purgatory, his allegory of, **9** 2306
on immortality, **5:** 1415
Jerusalem Christians and, **3:** 768, **6:** 1508, **8:** 2149ff, 2152
Jesus, his view of, **2:** 469, **3:** 768, **6:** 1507f, 1510, **8:** 2150–2
see also Last Supper, *below*
Jews and, **3:** 799f, **8:** 2150f, 2152
on the Last Supper, **7:** 1768
on marriage, **1:** 3057
Mystery religions and, **8:** 2151f
original sin and, **3:** 860, **4:** 980
origins of Christianity and, **2:** 469, **3:** 799f, **6:** 1507f, **8:** 2148ff
St Peter and, **8:** 2149, 2150
predestination and, **8:** 2242
on the resurrection of the body, **11:** 2949
on sacrifice, **9:** 2458
on salvation, **8:** 2242
Paul, St Francis de, 9: *2464*
Paul, St Vincent de, 9: 2462
Paul III (pope), Holy Office founded by, **5:** 1286
Paul the Hermit, St, 6: *1601,* **9:** 2468
Paulicianism (Christian heresy), **1:** 304
Pawnee Indians, 4: 1161
first man myth of, **4:** 979
High God of, **5:** 1302
human sacrifice and, **8:** 2008–10, **9:** 2457
Morning Star and, **4:** 1161, **8:** 2008–10
sex confusion myth of, **5:** 1288
'storm eagle' of, **4:** 1164
tobacco and, **10:** 2858
trickster of, *see* Coyote
peach, as Chinese symbol of immortality, **2:** *464*
peacock, 8: 2153–5
actors superstitious concerning, **4:** 894
eyes in tail of, **4:** *892, 893,* 894, **8:** 2153
pearl, 6: *1512,* **8: 2156–7**
moon and, **6:** 1511
pearlwort (plant), **8:** 2204
pearly queen, 8: *2157*
Pearson, Margaret (witch), **6:** 1593
peatbog, body found in, in Denmark, *see* Tollund, hanged man of
Peculiar People (Plumstead Peculiars), **8: 2157**
John Sirgood and, **2:** 492
Peeping Tom, Lady Godiva and, **4:** 1122
Pegasus (horse of Bellerophon), **2:** 455, **4:** 1141, **11:** 3032
Peking, as the centre of the earth, **7:** 1952
Peladan, Joséphin, **1:** 146, 241, **8:** 2126, **9:** *2425,* 2431, 2433, **11:** 2977
Pelagius, Pelagian controversy, **8:** 2242
Peleus (father of Achilles), **1:** 66, **8:** 2031
on Portland Vase, **3:** *830*
pelican, 1: 267, **8: 2158**
Pelletier, Blessed Marie, 10: 2701
Pelops, shoulder-blade of, preserved at Elis, **9:** 2351
penance, 8: 2158, 2450, 2451
on Good Friday, **3:** *762*
in Hinduism, **10:** 2582
Penates (Roman deities), **8: 2158, 9:** 2418
Pendle Forest, *see* Lancashire witches
Pendulum Institute, 7: 1948
penis:
bewitchment of, **5:** 1380, **6:** 1453, **8:** 2281
see also penis envy; phallic symbolism
penis envy (psychological theory), **11:** 3051
Penn, William (founder of Pennsylvania), **4:** 1052
pentacle, 8: 2159
pentagram, 8: 2158–9, 9: 2400
Pentagrammaton (name of Jesus), **7:** 1942, **8:** 2159
Pentateuch, 6: 1531, 1532
Pentecost (Christian festival)
by El Greco, **3:** *824*
in French 15th cent. Book of Hours, **10:** 2652
by Pinturicchio, **10:** *2649*
see also Whitsun
Pentecost (Jewish festival), **6:** 1536
Pentecostalist movement, 8: 2159–62
ecstasy and, **3:** 778
enthusiasm and, **3:** 828
Holiness movement and, **5:** 1328, 1332, **8:** 2159f
Holy Rollers and, **5:** 1332
hymns and, **10:** 2631
in South America, **8:** 2162
Brazil, **7:** 1981, **8:** 2162
speaking in tongues and, **8:** 2159, 2162, **10:** 2649, 2651ff
Spirit baptism and, **8:** 2159f, 2162
Penthesilea (Amazon), **1:** *65,* 66, 119
Pentheus (king of Thebes), Dionysus and, **3:** 635f
peony, 5: *1274,* 1276, **6:** 1718
Pepys, Samuel, hare's foot charm and, **3:** 641, **5:** 1210
Perceval (Arthurian knight), *see* Parsifal
Peredur (*Mabinogion*), **6:** 1672, 1674
Père-Lachaise cemetery (Paris), François Bertrand and, **1:** 257
perfectionism (Christianity), **3:** 826, 828, **5:** 1328
see also Oneida Community
perfect numbers, 10: 2592
perfume, 8: 2163–7
in ritual magic, **8:** 2167, **9:** 2400
see also incense; joss-stick; odour of sanctity
Pergamum, Asclepios and, **5:** 1246
peridot (jewel), **6:** *1513*
Periphetes (Greek mythology), **10:** 2818
Perkins, William (writer on witchcraft), **7:** 1954
Perpignan (France), procession of penitents of, **2:** *468*
Perrault, Charles, 2: 484
Persephone (Greek goddess), **8: 2168–70**
Adonis and, **1:** 137
Carthaginian cult of, **8:** 2184
Cretan origin of, **2:** 542
Demeter and, **3:** 621, 804, **8:** 2168, 2170, **11:** 2941–2
as faceless goddess, **4:** 896
Hades and, **3:** 621, 807, **5:** *1258,* **8:** 2168, 2209, **11:** 2941–2
Hecate and, **8:** 2168
pomegranate seed eaten by, **8:** 2168
Proserpina identified with, **3:** 622, **8:** 2168
by Rubens, **3:** *743*
Sirens and, **10:** 2590
Zeus and, **8:** 2168, 2170
Persephonion (plant), *see* vervain
Persepolis:
Ahura Mazdah relief from temple at, **8:** *2048*
Median nobles relief at, **11:** *3100*
sack of, **8:** 2048
Perseus (constellation), **1:** 104
Perseus (Greek hero):
Andromeda and, **3:** 693
by Cosimo, **3:** *694*
by Leighton, **5:** *1295*
Athene and, **4:** 1141f
Atlas and, **1:** 192
eye of the Fates and, **4:** 920
Gorgons and, **4:** 1141f, **8:** 2209
hermes and, **4:** 1141
Personality Number, 8: 2023
Personal Year Number, 8: 2023
Peru, 8: 2170
calendar from, on gold plate, **3:** *839*
insect demon from **6:** *1448–9*
masks from, **5:** *1236,* **6:** 1426–7
see also Incas
Perun (Slav god), **10:** 2608
Peten Itza (Maya city), **7:** 1770f
Peter, St, 2: 469f
apocryphal acts of, **7:** 1989
St Paul and, **8:** 2149, 2150
crucifixion of, **7:** *1987*
healing by, **4:** 909
Jerusalem community of Christians and, **3:** 767, **8:** 2149, 2150
keys of heaven and, **3:** *800*
St Paul and, **8:** 2149, 2150
Peter of Abano, on the basilisk, **3:** 873
Peter the Hermit, 11: 2993
Peter of Palermo (Italian sorcerer), **6:** 1476
***Peter Pan,* 11:** 3033–4
Petetin, J. H. 8: 2274
Petosiris (Egypt), **10:** 2692
petrel, 8: 2170
Petrus Cantor, on magical use of the Mass, **8:** 2279
peyote cults, 3: 714–16, **8: 2170–2, 11:** 3043
Christianity and, **8:** 2172
Pfenninger, Baron (alchemist), **1:** 94
Phaedra (Greek mythology), **10:** 2819, 2820
phallic symbolism, 4: 936, **1476, 8: 2173–7**
in Africa, **4:** *931*
animals in, **8:** 2175
in architecture, **8:** 2175–7
in Australia, **9:** *2541*
in the Bible, **8:** 2175
in Egypt, **8:** 2174
in the Eleusinian Mysteries, **8:** 2175

Eros and, **3:** 829
Etruscan, **8:** *2173,* 2174
fertility and, **4:** 936, **8:** 2174, 2177
Greek amulet, **9:** *2538*
Hermes and, **3:** 829, **8:** *2175*
in India, **8:** 2174, *2176*
see also lingam
maypole as, **3:** 698, **4:** *937*
of nose, **4:** 1089
plants in, **8:** 2174–5
of thumb, **4:** 1089
in Viking Age, **4:** 1051, *1051*
see also Cerne Abbas giant
phantasms of the living (wraiths), **5:** 1190, **8: 2177, 11: 3060**
Edmund Gurney and, **5:** 1190, **8:** 2275
F. W. H. Myers and, **5:** 1190, **7:** 1919
Mrs Sidgwick and, **8:** 2277
telepathy and, **5:** 1190
Phantom's Frenzy, The (Irish story), **4:** 1150, 1153
pharaoh, 3: 788–9, **6:** 1569–70
meaning of the title, **3:** 788
resurrection of, Osiris and, **8:** 2087–8
see also Egypt, cult of the dead
sun and, **3:** 788–9, **10:** 2723
Re incarnate as, **5:** 1420
symbols of, **10:** 2756
see also Amenhotep/Amenophis; Ikhnaten; Narmer; Nectanebus; Rameses II; Rameses VI; Thothmes III; Thothmes IV; Tutankhamen; Unas
Pharisees, 2: 466, 467, **8: 2177**
Pharmaceutical Society, Exclusive Brethren and, **3:** 868
Pheidias (Greek sculptor), **5:** 1396
Pheidippides (Greek runner), Pan and, **8:** 2125
Philadelphia experiment, 8: 2177
Philemon, St Paul's note to, **8:** 2148
Philibert, St, hazel and, **5:** 1230
Philip, St (apostle), apocryphal acts of, **7:** 1989
Philip IV (of France), Knights Templar and, **6:** 1575f
Philippe, Nizier, 8: 2126
Philippians, St Paul's epistles to, **8:** 2148
Philippine Islands:
headhunting in, **5:** 1233ff, **10:** 2799
Ifugao priests of, **8:** 2253
tattooing in, **10:** 2799
Philo the Jew of Alexandria, 7: 1967
Philomela (Greek mythology), **7:** 2000, **10:** 2735
Philosophers' Egg (alchemy), **3:** *783*
Philosophers' Stone (alchemy), **1:** 93ff, **7:** 1808, **8: 2178–80, 9:** 2341
descriptions of, **7:** 1808, **8:** 2180
Elixir of Life and, **3:** 809, **8:** 2178
as reconciliation of contradictions, **8:** 2069
see also Philosophers' Egg
Philosophers' Tincture, 3: 810f
Philostratus (Greek writer), **1:** 140f
philtre (love potion), *see* aphrodisiac, love potion
Phinehas (Book of Numbers), **11:** 3077
Phineus, King (Greek mythology), **5:** 1212f
phlegm (theory of the humours), **3:** 801
Phoenicians and Canaanites, 2: 398, 8: 2180–4, 10: 2761–6
amulets of, **10:** 2766
Canaanites identified with Phoenicians, **8:** 2180
cult of the dead and, **10:** 2764
divination and, **10:** 2763
dreams and, **3:** 704
gods of, **8:** 2180ff, **10:** 2763ff
Graeco-Roman gods assimilated to, **10:** 2766
see also Anat; Astarte; Baal; Dagon; El; Jerah
kingship and, **10:** 2762
life after death and, **10:** 2764–6
meaning of the name, **8:** 2180
prostitution and, **8:** 2271
sacrifice and, **10:** 2763–4
of children, **4:** 976
temples of, **10:** 2763, *2765*
see also Carthage
phoenix, 4: *972,* **8: 2185–8**
in China, **3:** 693, **4:** 929, **8:** *2186–7,* 2188
Phoroneus (Greek hero), **8:** 2261
Phouka (Irish spirit), Puck identified with, **8:** 2297
phrenology, 3: *654,* **5:** *1234–5,* **8: 2188–90**
phrenomagnetism, 8: 2190
physiognomy, 6: 1611f, **8: 2188, 2190**
Physiologus (bestiary), **8: 2158, 2186**
see also bestiary
pi (mathematics), in pyramidology, **9:** 2313, 2314
Picasso, Pablo, 1: 151
Picatrix (grimoire), **8: 2190**
love magic in, **6:** 1408
pickaxe, Thugs and, **10:** 2835f
Pickingale, George, 2: 401
Pico dell Mirandola, Giovanni, 9: 2370, 2373
Picquart, Mme Eugene (medium), **7:** *1789*
Picts, carved stones of, **2:** *551*
Piddington, J. G., Society for Psychical Research and, **8:** 2276
pieta, 8: 2191
***pietas,* 9:** 2412
Pietism (Christianity), **3:** 827, **5:** 1328
pig (hog, swine), **8: 2191–2**
St Anthony and, **8:** 2192
in Egypt, **8:** 2191, *2191*
in Eleusinian Mysteries, **1:** 229–30, **3:** 807
Evil Eye and, **4:** 890
as food, **8:** 2191f
Jews and, **4:** 1016, **8:** 2191
Gwydion and, **5:** 1192
in New Guinea, **8:** *2192*
Odysseus's men turned into pigs, **2:** 485
Orestes purified with, **4:** *918*
weather lore of, **8:** 2192
see also boar; Dunmow Flitch
pigeon, *see* dove
pilgrimage, 8: 2193–8
Buddhist, **8:** 2195f, *2198,* **10:** 2587
Christian, **8:** 2196–8
to Ars (tomb of Curé of), **2:** 578
to Becket's tomb at Canterbury, **1:** 247, **8:** 2198
cockle shell emblem in, **2:** 492
to Compostela, shrine of St James at, **2:** 492
cures sought by, **3:** 648–9, **8:** 2198
see also Lourdes
Gypsy, **5:** *1193, 1194,* 1196
to Jerusalem, **8:** *2194,* 2196
to Rome, **8:** *2195,* 2196, 2198
palm tree and, *see* palmer
to Walsingham, **11:** 2983–4
see also Pilgrim's Progress
Hindu, **8:** 2195f
Islamic, **6:** 1468, **7:** 1775f, **8:** 2195
New Year festivals and, **8:** 2194
Pilgrimage of Etheria, 3: 764
pilgrim festivals (Judaism), **6:** 1536
Pilgrim's Progress (Bunyan), **8:** 2145, *2147*
pillars, saints on, *see* stylites
pine (tree), **4:** 967f
true cross and, **10:** 2773
see also pine cone
pine cone, 4: *956*
Dionysus and, **4:** 968, **10:** 2837
as virginity symbol, **4:** 968
Pinel, Dr (psychiatrist), his treatment of lunatics, **5:** *1381*
Pio, Padre, *see* Forgione, Father Pio
pipe (tobacco), **4:** 1164, **10:** 2858
Piper, Mrs Leonora E. (medium), **1:** 207ff, **7:** *1793,* **8: 2199–200,** 2275
cross-correspondences and, 553f
Pirithous (Lapith), **8:** 2170, **10:** 2819
Pisces (the Fishes; zodiac sign, in astrology), **1:** 175, 181, **4:** *985,* **8: 2200**
Jupiter and, **6:** 1554, **8:** 2200
pitchfork, witches and, **2:** 350
Pius IX (pope), Immaculate Conception dogma promulgated by, **7:** 1752
Pius XII (pope), Assumption of the Virgin Mary dogma promulgated by, **7:** 1752
pixies, 3: 902–3
Puck identified with, **9:** 2297
PK, *see* psychokinesis
Plains Indians, *see* Great Plains Indians
planchette, 8: 2089, *2090,* **2200**
planets, 4: *1021,* **8: 2200**
in astrology, *see* astrology, planets in
Boehme on, **1:** 302
colours associated with, **2:** 522
days associated with, **2:** 522, **3:** 606
in Gnostic creation myth, **10:** 2692
Harranian worship of, **5:** 1213
hours associated with, **3:** 607
jewels associated with, **6:** 1510ff
magic squares of (Agrippa), **6:** 1510ff
metals associated with, **1:** 97–8, **2:** 522
in Mexican myth, **1:** 218
see also Jupiter; Mars; Mercury; Moon; Neptune; Pluto; Saturn; Sun; Uranus; Venus
also Ficino, Marsilio; spheres; zodiac
plaintain (herb) **5:** 1276
plants and flowers, 4: 996, 8: 2201–5
fertility of, **4:** 931f
see also agriculture
in fertility rites, etc., **8:** 2204–5
hallucinogenic, **3:** 711f, 714
language of flowers, Victorian, **8:** 2205
Midsummer and, **7:** 1846, **8:** 2205
moon and, **7:** 1880
in phallic symbolism, **9:** 2174–5
as protection against the Evil Eye, **4:** 890
as protection against lightning, **10:** 2604
as protection against witchcraft and sorcery, **8:** 2202f
psychokinesis as aid to growth of, **9:** 2290
of eternal youth, in Gilgamesh legend, **4:** 1106
see also aloes; anemone; bean; blackberry; broom; buttercup; clove; clover; corn; durian fruit; ferns; foxglove; garlic; haoma; heather; houseleek; iris; ivy; lily; lotus, maize; mandrake; marigold; mistletoe; mushroom; onion; orchid; peach; peony; poinsettia; poppy; potato; radish; rhubarb; rose; St John's wort; satyricon; soma; tea; tobacco; tomato; vervain; water-lily; yarrow
also flower arrangement, in Japan; garden; herbs; trees; wreath
Plato, 8: 2205ff
Atlantis and, **1:** 188f, **8:** 2207
cycles in world history, his theory of, **3:** 817f
on dreams, **3:** 705
dualism and, **3:** 731
Hermetica and, **5:** 1290, 1292
his myths, **8: 2205–7, 11:** 2851
of Er, **5:** 1260, **9:** 2348
of the birth of Eros, **8:** 2206
of the origin of the sexes, **8:** 2206
Orphism and, **8:** 2083, 2084f
Pythagoreanism and, **8:** 2084, **9:** 2315
on the soul, **1:** 172–3, **5:** 1413, **6:** 1708, **8:** 2207, **11:** 2850
see also Coleridge, as Platonist; Neoplatonism; Renaissance, Platonism in; Taylor, Thomas
play, *see* games
playing cards, *see* cards
Pleiades (Seven Sisters; stars):
Australian myth of, **11:** 3039
Iban of Sarawak and, **1:** 316
plexus (body), **1:** 300
P L Kyodan (Japanese religious sect), **6:** 1496–7

ploiaphesia (festival of Isis), **6:** 1462
Plotinus (founder of Neoplatonism), **7:** 1966ff, **8: 2207–8,** 2260
Gnosticism and, **4:** 1118, **7:** 1967
not a theurgist, **10:** 2822
plough, ploughing, **2:** 517
nudity and, **8:** 2018
woodpecker and, **11:** 3060
see also Plough Monday
Plough (constellation), *see* Great Bear
Plough Monday, plough plays, **3:** 698, **4:** 1004, 1005, 1017
Plouhinec (Brittany), standing stones at, **2:** 349
Plouton (Greek god), *see* Hades
Plumed Serpent, *see* Feathered Serpent
Plumpton Park, Robin Hood and, **9:** 2404
Plumstead Peculiars, *see* Peculiar People
Plutarch of Athens (Neoplatonist), **8:** 2259
Pluto (planet), in astrology, **1:** 175, 181, **8:** 2209
Pluto (Dis, Orcus; Roman god), **5:** *1258,* **8: 2208–9, 9:** 2412f
Hades identified with, **3:** 751, **9:** 2208
Plutus (Greek god, son of Demeter), **3:** 621, 807
Plymouth Brethren (Open Brethren), **3:** 867, **8: 2210**
pneuma, **1:** 173, **8: 2210**
in ophitism, **3:** 731
Po (Polynesian underworld), **8:** 2230, 2232
Pocahontas (Indian princess), **1:** 105
Podmore, Frank, 5: 1190, **8:** 2274, 2275
Poe, Edgar Allan, 9: 2500f
films based on, **4:** 942, **9:** *2497,* 2501
Poet Laureate, 6: 1610
poets, poetry, verse, **8: 2210–15**
animals banished by, **8:** 2212–14
Icelandic, **8:** 2212
  see also Edda, Poetic Edda
inspiration and, **8:** 2215
Irish, ancient, 2210ff; modern, *see* Russell, G. W.; Yeats, W. B.
magic and, **8:** 2210ff, 2214–15
Muses and, **7:** 1905
Sufis and, **10:** 2715
see also bards; Coleridge; Dante; Eliot; Goethe; Hesiod; Homer; Milton; Poet Laureate; Skelton; Virgil
also haiku
Pohl, Hermann, 4: 1081, 1082, **6:** 1636, **9:** 2441
Poimandres (Hermetic literature), **5:** 1290–1, **10:** 2692
poinsettia, Christmas and, **2:** 483
pointing, 4: 957
at rainbow and heavenly bodies, **9:** 2335
see also bone-pointing
poisoning, 8: 2216–22
witchcraft and, **6:** 1475, **8:** 2216ff
Pol, St, 2: 349
polecat, as witch's familiar, **3:** 755
Pole Star, 3: 640
Mexican god of, *see* Ueueteotl
sacred mountain and, **7:** 1899
pollution, 8: 2222
see also purification
Pollux, castor and, *see* Dioscuri
poltergeists, 4: 1099, **8: 2223–8**
Sir William Barrett and, **8:** 2275
at Borley Rectory, **1:** 310f, **8:** *2223*
Curé of Ars and, **2:** 579
hysteria and, **8:** 2227f
psychokinesis and, **3:** 883, **8:** 2226
see also Drummer of Tedworth
Polycarp, St, 9: 2465
epistle of, **7:** 1985
martyrdom of, **7:** 1875, **9:** 2353, 2465
Polydectes (king of Seriphos; Greek mythology), **4:** 1141
Polydeuces, Castor and, *see* Dioscuri
polygamy:
Kikuyu and, **6:** 1565
Mormons and, **7:** 1888f
Polyhymnia (Polymnia; Muse), **7:** 1905
Polynesia, 8: 2229–33
amulets of, *see tiki*
chiefs of, **8:** 2230
creation myths of, **8:** 2230
dreams in, **8:** 2231
gods of, **8:** 2230
head in, **10:** 2769
heroes in, **8:** 2232
life after death, beliefs concerning, **8:** 2231f
lizard in, **6:** 1638
mana in, **6:** 1713, **8:** 2230, **10:** 2769
Melanesia compared with, **7:** 1799, **8:** 2229ff
priests of, **8:** 2231
rainbow in, **9:** 2333
religion and magic in, **8:** 2230f
sacrifice in, **8:** 2231
soul, beliefs concerning, **8:** 2231f
taboo in, **8:** 2230f, **10:** 2769
tattooing in, **10:** 2797
temples of, **8:** 2231, *2232*
totemism not found in, **11:** 2861–3
see also Hawaii; kava
Polyphemus (Cyclops), **2:** 584, **4:** *886*
polytheism (definition), **8: 2233**
pomegranate, 8: 2233
Persephone and, **8:** 2168
Pompeii:
mosaic portrait of Alexander the Great from, **1:** 100
mysteries of Dionysus at, *see* Villa of the Mysteries
phallic symbolism at, **8:** *2177*
pontiffs (Roman priests), **8:** 2256, **9:** 2417
Pontius Pilate, 3: 768, **6:** 1504, 1508, 1510, **8: 2233–4, 11:** *2998*
Pooley, Thomas (Cornish blasphemer), **1:** 166
Poor Men of Lyons, *see* Waldenses
pope (Christianity), *see* papacy
Pope (Hierophant; Tarot card), **5:** 1301, **8:** 2147, **10:** *2791,* 2792
Pope Joan, 8: 2234
poppy, 8: 2234
Porenutius (Slav god), **10:** 2611
Porevit (Slav god), **10:** 2611
Porphyry (Neoplatonist), **1:** 173, **7:** 1967f, **8:** 2207f
Portland Vase, Peleus and Thetis on, **3:** *830*
Poseidon (Greek god), **5:** *1170,* **8: 2234–5**
Amphitrite and, **3:** 670
Athene and, **8:** 2060
Atlantis and, **1:** 188f
dolphin and, **3:** 670
earthquakes and, **3:** 751, **8:** 2234f
horse and, **5:** 1352, **8:** 2235
meaning of name not known, **8:** 2235
Neptune and, **7:** 1970
the sea and, **8:** 2234f
Posidonius (Stoic philosopher), **11:** 2851
posies (mottoes), **9:** 2388
possession, 6: 1678, **8: 2236–9**
in Dahomey, 2: 584
ecstasy and, **3:** 778
in Ethiopia, **3:** 845, **8:** 2239
hysteria and, **5:** 1380ff
in India, **8:** 2239
mesmerism and, **8:** 2236
of nuns, **5:** 1382, **8:** 2236
  at Aix-en-Provence, **1:** 90ff
  at Auxonne, **1:** 209
  at Cambrai, **5:** 1381
  at Loudun, **4:** 1154ff, **6:** 1650
  Sister Renata and, **9:** 2375
revivalism and, **3:** 828
sex and, **9:** 2539
trance and, **11:** 2867ff
among the Veddas, **11:** 2936
in Voodoo, **3:** 713, **7:** 1961, **8:** 2239, **11:** 2867f, 2870, 2973–4
Wesley and, **8:** 2236
witchcraft and, **4:** 873, **5: 1379–85**
see also exorcism
potato, 6: 1660
Pothos (Greek mythology), **3:** 830
potlatch (American Indian ceremony), **8:** 2107–8, **9:** 2526
power, as goal of magic, **6:** 1683, 1688
Poyen, Charles (mesmerist), **3:** 779
Praeneste, oracle at, **6:** 1647
Prajapati (Hinduism), **11:** 2958
prana (breath; Hinduism), **2:** 335, **11:** 3074
see also pranayama
pranayama (breath control; yoga), **2:** 335f, **6:** 1586, **11:** 2935, 3073–4
pratyahara (yoga), **11:** 2935, 3074
Praxiteles (Greek sculptor), Cnidian Aphrodite of, **1:** 138
prayer, 8: 2240
magical incantation distinguished from, **5:** 1419–20
rosary and, **9:** 2420
prayer wheel, 11: 3015
in Nepal, **5:** *1419*
in Tibet, **10:** *2843,* **11:** 3015
precession of the equinoxes, 1: 143
precognition, 3: 875, **8:** *2240,* **10:** 2665, 2673
in mice, **9:** 2291
psychokinesis and, **3:** 879ff, **9:** 2287
predestination and free will, 4: 918, 921, **6:** 1665, **8: 2240–2**
in the ancient world, **8:** 2240
in Christianity, **4:** 921, **8:** 2240–2
  Aquinas and, **8:** 2242
  St Augustine on, **3:** 800, **4:** 921, **8:** 2242
  Boehme on, **1:** 301–2
  Calvin and, **3:** 800, **4:** 921, **8:** 2242
  St Paul and, **8:** 2242
  Pelagius and, **8:** 2242
in Islam, **3:** 800, **6:** 1469, 1470
in Zoroastrianism, **1:** 86, **11:** 3100
Preece, Ruth, 8: 2259, *2259*
pregnancy, 1: 272f
Bushmen, **2:** 380
forty and, **4:** 1024
prehistoric religion, 8: 2243–5, 2354, 2359–60
see also cult of the dead, prehistoric; faceless goddesses, paleolithic
premonition, 8: 2246
Prentice, Joan (witch), **3:** *757*
Presbyterianism, Irvingites and, **6:** 1458f
pressing to death, 9: 2472
Prester John, 8: 2246
Preston, Jennet (witch), **6:** 1593, 1594
Prevotte, Catherine (witch), **9:** 2445
Price, Harry, 1: *310,* **8:** *2276, 2277*
Borley Rectory and, **1:** 310ff
Stella C. and, **7:** 1791f
Schneider brothers and, **9:** 2489–90, 2490, 2491
Price, Prof. H. H., on mediums, **7:** 1784–5
Price, James (alchemist), **1:** 94
Price, Dr William (advocate of cremation), **2:** *540,* 541
pricking of witches, 8: 2246–7
see also Devil's mark
pride, fall of Lucifer due to, **3:** 628
priests, 8: 2248–56
Ashanti, **1:** 163
Aztec, **1:** 220
Celtic, *see* Druids
Christian, **8:** 2256
ecstasy and, **8:** 2252
Egyptian, **3:** 793, **8:** *2254*
Greek, **8:** 2073, 2256
  of Eleusinian Mysteries, *see* hierophant
initiation to priesthood, **8:** 2252–3
  in Christianity, *see* holy orders
Islam, no priests in, **8:** 2256
in Judaism, **6:** 1531
magician and priest compared, **8:** 2248ff
Maori, **7:** 1731
marriage of, **8:** 2253f
Maya, **7:** *1771, 1772,* **8:** *2255*
in Micronesia, **8:** 2233

Mormon, **7:** 1890
North American Indian, **8:** 2011
nudity and, **8:** 2019
Parsee, **8:** 2137, 2140
in Philippine Islands, **8:** 2253
in Polynesia, **8:** 2231
Roman, **8:** 2256, **9:** 2413, 2416f, 2418
see also Arval Brothers; flamen; Salii; Vestal Virgins
Tibetan, *see* lamas, Tibetan
of the Veddas, **11:** 2936–8
in Voodoo, **11:** 2972ff
see also medicine-man; shaman
prima materia (alchemy), **8:** 2178
Primavera (Botticelli), **9:** 2374, *2374*
Primitive Methodists, 3: 828
Primrose Hill (London), Druids and, **3:** 721
Prince, Henry James (founder of Agapemonites), **7:** 1828f, **8: 2258–9**
Prince of Wales, ostrich feather crest of, **4:** 929
Priscillianism (Christian heresy), **5:** 1282
Proclus (Neoplatonist), **7:** 1968, **8: 2259–60, 10:** 2821, 2822
Procne, Philomela and (Greek mythology), **7:** 2000, **10:** 2735
Procrustes (Greek mythology), **10:** 2818
Prognometer, 11: 3063
Prometheus (Greek mythology), **8: 2261–3**
Athene and, **8:** *2262*
creation of man by, **4:** *981,* **8:** 2262, *2262,* 2263
as culture hero, **8:** 2262
fire stolen from heaven by, **4:** *970,* **8:** 2261
Hephaestus and, **5:** 1268, 1269, **8:** 2262
Hercules and, **5:** 2262, 2263
Oceanides and (in Aeschylus), **8:** 2031
Pandora and, **8:** 2125, 2262
Zeus and, **8:** 2261ff
promised land, Israelites and, **3:** 798f, **5:** 1322, **11:** 2992
prophecy, 8: 2264–9
Christianity and, **8:** 2267f
divination and prediction distinguished from, **8:** 2264, 2266, 2268
in Islam, **8:** 2268
see also Mohammed
Judaism and, **8:** 2264–7, 2268, 2377
in the Old Testament, **8:** 2264–7
see also Elijah; Ezekiel; Hosea; Isaiah
see also Blake; Nostradamus
see also cargo cults; Handsome Lake
Proserpina (Roman goddess), Persephone identified with, **3:** 622, **8:** 2168
prostitution, 8: 2270–2
Aphrodite and, **1:** 137, **8:** 2272
Astarte and, **1:** 170, **8:** 2271
in Canaan, **8:** 2271
Cybele and, **8:** 2272
as fertility rite, **8:** 2270ff
in India, **8:** 2272
Isis and, **8:** 2272
in Mesopotamia, **8:** 2270f
Ishtar and, **6:** 1460, **8:** 2271
Old Testament objections to, **8:** 2271
Shinto and, **9:** 2562–3
Proterius, Satanic pact and, **8:** 2110
Protestantism, 2: 474ff
pilgrimage and, **8:** 2198
see also Holiness movement; Huguenots; Methodism; Plymouth Brethren; Quakers; Reformation
Proteus, shape-shifting by, **9:** 2550–1
Protoevangelium (Book of James), **7:** 1749, 1988
providence, 8: 2273
fate distinguished from, **8:** 2273
Isis as, **6:** 1461, 1462
psalms, 8: 2273
Psamathe (nereid), **9:** 2517
Pseudo-Dionysius, 3: 633f
psi, 3: 875, 882ff, **8: 2273,** 2285, 2289, 2291
in games of chance, **8:** 2286
see also spontaneous psi experiences
***Psyche,* 3:** *830,* 831, **8: 2273, 9:** *2413*
psychical research, 8: 2273–9
apparitions and, **8:** 2275
ghosts, **4:** 1100f
phantasms of the living, **5:** 1190, **8:** 2275
extra-sensory perception and, **3:** 875, **8:** 2278f
hypnotism and, **5:** 1190, **8:** 2275
Spiritualism and, **8:** 2273f
see also cross-correspondences; Curé of Ars; displacement; Gurney, Edmund; mediums; Myers, F. W. H.; poltergeists; second sight; Society for Psychical Research
'psychic art', 1: 206
see also Gill, Madge
psychic attack, 8: 2279–84
Dion Fortune and, **4:** 1022, **8:** 2284
see also bewitchment; black fast; curse; Evil Eye; ill-wishing
psychoanalysis, 4: 1048
religious conversion compared with, **2:** 515
psychokinesis (PK, telekinesis, 'mind over matter'), **3:** 875, 883, **8:** 2278, **2285–91, 10:** 2665, 2666, 2670–2, **2812**
alchemy and, **1:** 97
'crisis' cases of, **10:** 2670ff
dice and, **3:** 879, *881,* **8:** 2278, 2286ff
extra-sensory perception and, **3:** 875, 879ff, **9:** 2285, 2287, 2290f, **10:** 2675
Jung and, **6:** 1550
as evidence of life after death, **10:** 2675f
Bulwer Lytton and, **6:** 1670
mediums and, **7:** 1789
plant growth influenced by, **9:** 2290
poltergeists and, **3:** 883, **8:** 2226
psi, PK as the only exclusive form of, **10:** 2672
saints and, **10:** 2702
psychology, 8: 2292–6
of dreams, **3:** 708ff
of memory, **8:** 2039f
of witchcraft, *see* European witchcraft, psychology of witches and witchcraft accusations
see also Freud; Jung; madness; parapsychology
psychometry, *see* object reading
psychons (ghost theory of), **4:** 1101
psychoscopy, *see* object reading
psychosomatic medicine, 4: 909
Ptah (Egyptian god), **3:** 790
Apis bull and, **1:** 129
as creator, **2:** 534, **9:** 2354
as father of Imhotep, **5:** 1405
Ptolemaeus (Gnostic), **4:** 1116, 1117
Ptolemy I (king of Egypt), **8:** 2088
puberty, 9: 2296
Puck, 9: 2296–7, 2403
Pueblo Indians, 8: 2007, **2298–304**
eagle dance of, **8:** *2298–9*
fool and, **4:** 1018, **9:** 2302, 2304
ghosts and, **9:** 2302f
gods and spirits of, **9:** 2302
kachina dancers of, **9:** 2300–2, 2303, 2304, **11:** 2861
kachina dolls of, **8:** *2012,* **9:** *2303*
rituals of, **8:** 2011, **9:** 2300ff
tobacco and, **11:** 2858
witches and, **9:** 2302f
woman, place of, among, **9:** 2300
see also Hopi Indians
Pug (small devil), Puck identified with, **9:** 2297
Pulotu (Polynesian afterworld), **8:** 2231
Puluga (sky god of Andaman Islands), **10:** 2601
Punch and Judy, 9: 2305, 11: *2884*
Punjab (India), Sikhs in, **10:** 2575ff
puppets:
in Japan, **6:** *1488*
see also Punch and Judy
Puranas (Hindu texts), **6:** 1580
see also Bhagavata Purana
Pure Land sect (Japan), *see* Jodo
purgatory, 6: 1546, **9: 2305–7**
Dante and, **2:** 602, 604
indulgences and, **8:** 2196
Luther and, **8:** 2198
purification:
alchemy and, **3:** 811, **8:** 2178, *2178, 2179*
flagellation as method of, **4:** 991
Ganges and, **4:** 1069
Kikuyu ritual of, **6:** 1563f
of Orestes, **4:** *918*
in Polynesia, **8:** 2230
see also Purgatory
Purim (Jewish festival), **6:** 1536
Puritanism (Christianity: in England), **2:** 474
names, uplifting, of Puritans, **7:** 1941
see also Cokelers; Fifth Monarchy Men
Purusha, Vedic creation myth of, **2:** 416
Pusan (Indian god), **5:** 1435
Puységur, Marquis de, 6: 1693, **7:** 1815
pwca (Welsh spirit), Puck identified with, **9:** 2297
Pwyll, prince of Dyfed *(Mabinogion),* **6:** 1672–3
pygmies, 9: 2308–12
pyramidology, 9: 2313–14
pyramids, 9: 2315
Egyptian, **6:** *1710–11,* **9:** 2364
obelisk and, **8:** 2039
at Sakkara, **5:** 1404, *1404,* 1405
see also Pyramid Texts
see also pyramidology
Mexican, **1:** 214, 217, **7:** 1770, **10:** *2721*
Pyramid Texts, 1: 305ff, **9: 2315**
creation myth in, **2:** 533f
human nature, physical and psychic components of, in, **1:** 132
judgement of the dead in, **6:** 1539f
land of the dead described in, **3:** 792
mummification and, **7:** 1900
Osiris in, **1:** 305ff, **6:** 1540, **8:** 2086, 2087f
Re in, **9:** 2489
river to be crossed by the dead in, **2:** 449
steps and ladders in, **10:** 2695–7
Unas (pharaoh) in, **9:** 2489
water, ritual use of, in, **1:** 229
Pyrenees, healing springs of, **6:** 1650
Pyrrhus (king of the Molossians), healing method of, **4:** 908
Pythagoras, 8: 2083, **9: 2315–16**
beans and, **1:** 242
Croton and Sybaris and, **9:** 2526
four elements theory and, **3:** 647
lamb and, **9:** 2556
music and, **8:** 2024, **9:** 2315
reincarnation and, **8:** 2083, **9:** 2315
see also Pythagoreanism
Pythagoreanism, 8: 2083, **9:** 2315f
Apollonius of Tyana and, **1:** 140
creation explained by, **9:** 2316
dualism in, **3:** 731
numbers and, **8:** 2024ff, **9:** 2315–16
forty, **4:** 1024
four, **4:** 1029, **9:** 2316
Orphism and, **8:** 2083ff
Plato and, **8:** 2084, **9:** 2315
soul and, **9:** 2305–6
Pythia (priestess of Delphi), **1:** 139, **9:** 2529

Q

Qabbalah (Jewish mystical system), *see* Cabala
al-Qadir al-Jilani, Abd (Sufi), **10:** 2716
Qadmon, Adam, *see* Adam Kadmon
Qat (Melanesian spirit), **7:** 1799
qibla (mosque), **9:** 2366
qiyas (Islam), **6:** 1465
Qonya (Anatolia), Rumi at, **9:** 2439, 2441
Quakers (Society of Friends), **4:** 1030f, **1052**

enthusiasm and, **3:** 826
oaths and, **8:** 2038
quarantine, 4: 1024
quartz, 6: 1510, **9: 2316,** 2506
Quedlinburg (Saxony), witches burnt at, **3:** 853
Queen of Sheba, 3: 843, **9: 2316–17**
Questing Beast (Arthurian legend), **11:** 3025
Quetzalcoatl (Feathered Serpent, Plumed Serpent, the Morning Star; Mexican deity), **1:** 215, 218, *218,* 220f, **9: 2318,** 2529
quick beam, quicken (tree), *see* rowan
quicksilver (metal), *see* mercury
Quietism, 5: 1191, **9: 2318–20**
meditation in, **7:** 1780
Quimby, Phineas P., 3: 779, **7:** 1817, *1993,* 1993f
Quin, Dr Frederick Foster Harvey, 5: 1336f
quintessence, 9: 2320
Quinzani, Blessed Stefana, 10: 2701
Quirinus (Roman god), **7:** 1743
Qumran community, 3: 609ff
quoits (standing stones; Cornwall), **2:** 520

R

Ra (Egyptian god), *see* Re
rabbi, 6: 1531, **9: 2320**
rabbit, 9: 2320
Easter and, **3:** 764, **9:** 2320
hare and, **5:** 1210, **9:** 2320
new moon and, **9:** 2320
as North American Indian trickster, **11:** 2881
see also Brer Rabbit
as witch's familiar, **3:** 755
Rabiah (Islamic saint), **10:** 2714
race myths, 9: 2321–30, 11: 3018
New Templars and, **7:** 1983
see also antisemitism
Radha, Krishna and, **5:** 1314, **6:** 1584
Radhakrishnan, Sir Sarvepalli, 5: 1317, 1321, **9:** 2362
radiesthesia, 3: 686, **9: 2331–3**
radionics, 9: 2331, 2332–3
radish, Easter and, **3:** 763
Raggedstone (Malvern Hills), **9:** 2544
Ragnarok (Doom of the Gods, Twilight of the Gods, end of the world; Scandinavian mythology), **3:** 817, **9: 2333,** 2334, 2484f
ragwort (St James's herb), **8:** 2204
Rahner, Karl, on death, **5:** 1416
rain, 9: 2333
Aztecs and, **1:** 220
ferns and, **10:** 2604
frog and, **4:** 1054
at funerals, **10:** 2604
Jupiter and, **6:** 1552
Maya god of, *see* Chac
peacock and, **8:** 2153
woodpecker and, **10:** 2837, **11:** 3060
see also rainbow; rain-making; St Swithin's day
rainbow, 9: 2333–5
in Australia, **9:** 2333
in Brazilian myth, **2:** 327
as bridge, **9:** 2333ff, 2484
Christ and, **9:** *2334*
in Dahomey, **2:** 586
Greek goddess of, *see* Iris
Karens (Burma) and, **9:** 2333
by Millais, **8:** *2066*
Noah and, **8:** 2064, **9:** 2333
in Scandinavian mythology, **9:** 2333–4, 2484
serpent and, **9:** 2529f
Zulus, **9:** 2333
unlucky to point at, **9:** 2335
weather lore of, **9:** 2335
Zulus and, **9:** 2333, **11:** 3105
rain-making, 2: 517–18, **2:** 2333
in Africa, **1:** 77
Congo, **2:** 509
birds and, **10:** 2837
woodpecker, **11:** 3060
in South America, **1:** 164
raja yoga, 11: 2934, 3071
ram (animal):
Amun and, **3:** *788,* **9:** 2556, *2558*
Celts and, **2:** 443, **5:** 1350f
ram-headed serpent, **1:** 129, **2:** 443, **5:** 1350
Heimdall and, **5:** 1346
Jews and, **5:** 1348, *1351,* **9:** 2556
Khnum and, **5:** *1344,* **9:** 2556
Re and, **5:** *1344,* **9:** 2556
sacrifice of, **9:** 2556
see also Abraham, sacrifice of Isaac and
Zeus and, **9:** 2556, **11:** 3090
zodiac sign of, *see* Aries
Ram, N. Sri (Theosophist), **10:** *2815,* 2816
Rama (Indian god, incarnation of Vishnu), **5:** *1307,* 1313, **11:** *2931, 2958,* 2960
see also Ramayana
Ramadan (Islamic fast), **4:** 918, **6:** 1466
instituted by Mohammed, **7:** 1873
Ramakrishna Paramahamsa, 5: 1316f, **9: 2335–6**
on sainthood, **6:** 1678
Ramakrishna Mission, **5:** 1317, **9:** 2361, **11:** *2929*
Ramana Maharshi, 9: 2336
Ramayana (Indian epic), **11:** 2960
giant demoness in, **4:** *1102*
Hanuman, fiery tail of, in, **5:** *1308*
Indra as peacock in, **8:** 2153
Rameses II (pharaoh), **3:** *741,* **11:** 2992
Rangi (Maori sky god), **7:** 1731
Ranken, Ruth, 8: 2259
Raphael (angel), east and, **3:** 640
Rapp, Frederick (Harmony Society leader), **2:** 500
Rapp, George (founder of Harmony Society), **2:** 499f, **9:** 2521
Rappites, *see* Harmony Society
Rashin Coatie (Scottish folktale), **2:** 484
Rashu (Parsee deity), **8:** 2138
Rasmussen, Anna (medium), **7:** 1792, *1793*
Rasputin, 9: 2337–40
Ras Shamra, *see* Ugarit
Ras Tafari (messianic movement), **7:** 1832–5
cannabis used by, **3:** 714
rat, banished by poets, **8:** 2212
Rata (Polynesian hero), **8:** 2232
Ratana (Maori church), **7:** 1733
raven, 2: 556f, **9: 2340**
in alchemical symbolism, **8:** 2178
in augury, **1:** 194, *194,* **2:** 557
in Babylonian flood legend, **4:** 993
Bran and, **1:** 324
in creation myth, **8:** 2104f
crow and, **2:** 556f
Elijah fed by, **2:** 557, *557,* **8:** *2265*
Mithras and, **7:** 1863
Noah and, **2:** 556, **4:** 992
North American Indians and, **2:** 556, **7:** 1758–60, **8:** 2104f, *2106,* **11:** 2881
Odin and, **2:** 556f, **5:** 1086, **8:** *2043*
St Paul the Hermit and, **6:** *1601*
storms and, **2:** 556
sun and, **7:** 1863
at Tower of London, **2:** 557
as trickster, **8:** 2105, *2106*
St Vincent and, **2:** 557
Raven, F. E., 3: 868
Re (Ra; Egyptian sun god), **1:** 305f, **3:** 789, **5:** 1402, **9: 2340, 10:** 2723
as Amun-Re, **3:** 789, **5:** 1402, **9:** 2556
Atum and (Re-Atum, Atum-Re), **1:** 305, **2:** 533, **3:** 789f
eye of, **1:** *306–7,* **3:** 791
as Harmakhis, **3:** 704
Horus and (Re-Horakhti), **3:** 789, *789,* **5:** 1360
incense in worship of, **5:** 1428
Isis and, **3:** 791, **7:** 1941
maat and, **6:** 1540
pharaoh the incarnation of, **5:** 1420
ram and, **5:** *1344,* **9:** 2556
scarab (dung-beetle) and, **3:** 789, *789,* **9:** 2488
secret name of, **7:** 1941
Tefnut and, **3:** 791
temple of, at Abu Gurob, **9:** 2364
reason:
Coleridge on, **2:** 494
French Revolutionary cult of, **4:** 1042
gnosis not a product of, **4:** 1115
magic and, **6:** 1684
mysticism and, **2:** 489
Nature seen as irrational, **6:** 1680
Reculver (Kent), ghost at, **2:** 361
red, 2: 495–6, **9: 2341–2**
birds and, **1:** 271
robin, **9:** 2402
the dead painted red, **2:** *368,* 372, 569f, **5:** *1414*
Easter eggs and, **3:** 784
Evil Eye, red as protection against, **9:** 2341–2
in healing, **9:** 2341
Holy Ghost, red as symbol of, **4:** 1059
iron and, **2:** 522
Mars and, **2:** 522, **7:** 1744
Philosophers' Stone and, **7:** 1808, **9:** 2341
'red sky at night, shepherd's delight', **6:** 1664
witches, red as protection against, **4:** 890, **9:** 2342
see also Border Redcaps
Red Book of Hergest (Welsh tales), **6:** 1672
Red Calf, the (Scottish folktale), **2:** 484
Redcap, Old Mother (witch), **9:** 2342
Red Dragon (grimoire), *see Grand Grimoire*
Redfearne, Anne (witch), **6:** 1592, 1593
Red Indians, *see* North American Indians
Redon, Odilon, 1: 146, **9: 2343–5**
Re'em, 11: 2909
Reformation (Christianity), **2:** 473f, **8:** 2198
see also Calvin, John; Luther, Martin; Protestantism
***refrigerium*, 9: 2345–6**
Regardie, Israel:
on the Fool of the tarot, **10:** 2791
Golden Dawn and, **4:** 1131, 1133, 1134, **8:** 2159
on triangle and magic circle, **9:** 2399
Rehoboam (Israelite leader), **6:** 1643
Reich, Wilhelm, aura and, **3:** 677
Reichenbach, Baron Karl von, 3: 677, **6:** 1694, **9:** 2331
Reilly, Margaret (stigmatic), **10:** 2701
Reinburg, Wenceslaus von (alchemist), **1:** 94
reincarnation (metempsychosis, transmigration of souls), **7: 1836, 9: 2346–50, 11: 2870**
in Africa, **1:** 73–5
Algonquin Indians and, **2:** 333
Mrs Besant and, **9:** 2348
in Buddhism *(samsara),* **1:** 261, **2:** 354, 355f, **5:** 1309, **6:** 1709, **9:** 2346
Bodhisattvas and, **2:** 359, **9:** 2348
in China, **9:** 2348
in Tibet, **6:** 1589f, **9:** 2348, **10:** 2481–2
Christianity and, **9:** 2346
in Greece, **6:** 1707–8, **9:** 2346
Empedocles, **9:** 2348, **11:** 2850
Orphism, **6:** 1707–8, **11:** 2850
Plato, **5:** 1413, **6:** 1708, **8:** 2207, **9:** 2348, **11:** 2850
Pythagoras, **8:** 2083, **9:** 2315, **11:** 2850
in Hinduism *(samsara),* **1:** 261, **5:** 1309, **6:** 1559f, 1709, **9:** 2346, 2347
as basis of caste system, **2:** 415
hypnosis in recent research into, **9:** 2350
in Jainism, **5:** 1309, **6:** 1483
Jews and, **9:** 2346
reindeer:
horns of, at Abbots Bromley, **5:** 1352
in Lapland, **6:** *1604, 1605, 1606,* 1607, 1608

Reisch, Gregor, on macrocosm and microcosm, **6:** *1675*
Reiyuka (Japanese religious sect), **6:** 1497
relics, 9: 2351–3
of the Buddha, **8:** 2196, *2198,* **9:** 2351
see also stupas
Christian, **3:** 649, **8:** 2196f, **9:** 2351–3
in Greece, **9:** 2351
religion, 9: 2354–68
extra-sensory perception and, **3:** 876
inspiration and, **8:** 2215
life after death the basic concern of, **11:** 2846
magic distinguished from, **3:** 641, **4:** 935, **6:** 1691
man's place in the universe the basic concern of, **6:** 1704
ritual in, **9:** 2396
see also architecture, religious; atonement; Buddhism; Christianity; communistic religious movements; comparative religion; conversion; cosmic order; cosmogony; deism; ecstasy; eschatology; faith; High Gods; Hinduism; immanent; immortality; incarnation; Islam; Jains; Judaism; messianic movements; millennarian religious movements; monotheism; mystery religions; mysticism; new religious movements; numinous; pantheism; pilgrimage polytheism; prayer; prehistoric religion; priests; revelation; sacrifice; Shinto; sin; soul; symbolism; syncretism; Taoism; theism; theurgy; visions; Zoroastrianism
religious liberty/pluralism, in Christian history, **2:** 473, 474
Religious Science (philosophical group), **7:** 1994
Remy, Nicolas, 4: 1046, 1047, **9:** 2445, 2446–7
Renaissance, 9: 2369–75, 2493f
Platonism in, **4:** 1159, **9:** 2370
three and, **9:** 2372–3, 2832
Renata, Sister Maria, 9: 2375
Renatus, Sincerus, *see* Richter, Sigmund
Renfaing, Elisabeth de, 3: 873
repentance, atonement and, **1:** 192
Rephaim (Biblical giants), **4:** 1102
repression (psychology):
object reading and, **8:** 2040f
ouija board and, **8:** 2091
sexual repression and witchcraft, **5:** 1381
Reshef (Canaanite god), **10:** 2763
resin, 4: 968
in worship of Re, **5:** 1428
resurrection (of the body):
in Christianity, **6:** 1708
of Jesus, *see* Jesus, resurrection of
St Paul on, **11:** 2940
peacock as symbol of, **8:** 2154
by Signorelli (detail), **10:** *2597*
in Egypt, **1:** 229
see also Egypt, cult of the dead
in Islam, **6:** 1708
in Judaism, **6:** 1535, 1545, 1706
in Zoroastrianism, **6:** 1712
Reuchlin, Johann (Christian Cabalist), **7:** 1942, **9:** 2370
Reuss, Theodor:
Crowley and, **2:** 560f, **11:** 2988
Illuminati and, **5:** 1404
Papus and, **8:** 2126, **11:** 2988
Wagner and, **11:** 2978
Reuter, O. S., 7: *1964,* 1964f
revelation, 9: 2376–83
see also Revelation, book of
Revelation, book of (Apocalypse of St John), **1:** 138, **3:** 821–2, **9:** 2378–83
angels with trumpets in, **11:** 2897
authorship of, **9:** 2381–3
date of, **9:** 2383
hell in, **5:** 1265
interpretations of, **9:** 2379–81
Jesus in, **9:** 2378ff
palm in, **8:** 2116
river of the water of life in, **9:** 2346
seven in, **3:** 822, 886, *887,* **9:** 2379, *2382,* 2534
summary of, **9:** 2378–9
twelve in, **11:** 2897, 2898–2900
war in heaven described in, **3:** 628–9, 691
woman as harlot in, **11:** 3053–7
see also Great Beast
revenant, 9: 2383
as werewolf, **11:** 3011
see also ghosts; vampire
revivalism, 2: 514, **5:** 1328, 1679
enthusiasm and, **3:** 826ff
spirit possession and, **3:** 828
see also Holy Rollers; McPherson, Aimée Semple; Moody, Dwight L.; Welsh Revival
Rhea (Greek mythology), **2:** 522f, 546
rheumatism, willow and, **11:** 3032
Rhiannon (Celtic goddess), **6:** 1672ff
Rhine, J. B., 3: 878, *879,* **8:** 2278
parapsychology defined by, **8:** 2136
telepathy in twins studied by, **11:** 2904
Rhine, Louisa E., 3: 878, *879,* **8:** 2278, 2279
rhinoceros, at Mohenjo-daro, **5:** *1435*
Rhodes, Anna (Californian heretic), **8:** 2019
rhubarb, in Zoroastrian creation myth, **1:** 89
Ricci, Paul (Cabalist), **2:** *384*
rice, 9: 2383
Richard of St Victor (Christian mystic), **7:** 1937, 1938
Richards, Dr Guyon, 9: 2332
Richelieu, Cardinal, Grandier and, **4:** 1155
Richet, Prof. Charles:
clairvoyance and, **9:** 2286
materialization and, **7:** 1791
Palladino and, **8:** 2113
table-tilting and, **8:** 2092
Richter, Sigmund (Sincerus Renatus: Rosicrucian), **9:** 2430
Rida, Rashid, 6: 1472
riddles, 9: 2384–6
in Zen Buddhism, *see* koan
Rider god, of Thrace, *see* Thracian Rider god
Ridvan Festival (Bahais), **1:** 224
Riedemann, Peter, 5: 1376
Rigdon, Sidney, Mormonism and, **7:** 1888
right (right-hand side), good associated with, **3:** 640
Rijrasva (Indian legend), **11:** 3047
Rila (Bulgaria), monastery of, **9:** *2524*
Second Coming depicted at, **2:** *475*
Rinck, Melchior (Anabaptist), **3:** 825
ring, 9: 2386–9
healing and, **9:** 2386f
see also cramp-rings
of Odin, *see* Draupnir
salmon and, **9:** 2474
stigmatization and, *see* mystic ring
see also fairy rings; Mephisto's Ring; ring dances; wedding ring
Ringatu Christian Church (New Zealand), **7:** 1732–3
ring dances (circle dances, wheel dances), **2:** 412ff, 590, 594f
of modern witches, **7:** *1870*
see also Ghost Dance
Rip van Winkle, 10: *2613*
Rissho Koseikai (Japanese religious sect), **6:** 1497–8
Rita of Cascia, St, 10: 2698
Ritchie, Isobel (witch), **1:** 63
rites of passage, 9: 2389–92
ritual, **9: 2392–6**
of Freemasonry, **4:** 1035ff
masks and, **7:** 1756ff
music and, **7:** 1910ff
in religion, **9:** 2396
see also initiation; rites of passage; ritual creation myths; ritual magic; sacraments
ritual creation myths, distinguished from aetiological myths, **2:** 523, 533
ritual magic, 9: 2397–2401
correspondences and, **2:** 522
herbs in, **8:** 2167
incantation in, **5:** 1418ff, **9:** 2400f
pentagram in, **8:** 2158f, **9:** 2400
perfume in, **9:** 2400
robes in, **9:** 2399
sacrifice in, **9:** 2400
see also evocation; grimoires; magic circle; magic wand
rivers, 9: 2401
Nilotes and, **7:** 2001
nymphs of, *see* Naiads
sacred, in Hinduism, **8:** 2195
see also Ganges
symbolism of, **6:** 1602
as water of life (in Revelation), **9:** 2346
see also Acheron; Nile; Sambatyon; Styx
road, as symbol, *see* path symbolism
Robert the Bruce (king of Scotland), **5:** 1253, **10:** 2615
robes, *see* costume
Robespierre, 4: 1042f
Robey, Isabel (witch), **6:** 1593
Robigus (Roman deity), **9:** 2414
robin (bird), **9: 2402–3**
blood and, **9:** 2402
Crown of Thorns and, **10:** 2736
fire and, **9:** 2402, **11:** 3061
St Kentigern and, **9:** 2402
red and, **9:** 2402
weather lore of, **9:** 2403
wren and, **9:** 2402, **11:** 3061
Robin Artisson (familiar of Dame Alice Kyteler), **4:** 915, **6:** 1588
Robin Goodfellow (Robin Roundcap, Hobthrush), **9:** 2296f, **2403**
herb Robert and, **5:** 1275
Robin Hood, 5: *1296,* **9: 2403–6, 11:** 3029, *3029*
May Day and, **5:** 1173, **7:** 1774, **9:** 2405–6
Robin Hood's Bay (Yorks), **9:** 2405
Robin Roundcap, *see* Robin Goodfellow
Roc (mythical bird), **1:** 268, **9: 2406, 11:** 3033
Rochas, A. de, magnetism and, **6:** 1695
rock crystal, 6: 1510–11, **9:** 2316, **10:** 2773
rocking stones (logans), of Cornwall, **2:** 519–20
rock paintings, in Africa, **9: 2407–11**
of the Bushmen, **2:** 380, **5:** *1375,* **9:** 2407, *2408,* 2409
Rod of Brahma, 6: 1586
Rogers, John (preacher), **9:** 2521
Rogie, Helen (witch), **1:** 63
Roland (knight of Charlemagne), **5:** 1298
sword of (Durandal), **10:** 2748
Rolle, Richard (mystic), **2:** 489, 490
Pseudo-Dionysius and, **3:** 634
Roman Catholic Church, 2: 474ff
ecstasy in, **3:** 773, 775
Freemasonry and, **4:** 1035, *1040*
French Revolution and, **4:** 1041ff
pilgrimage and, **8:** 2198
see also Lourdes
predestination and, **8:** 2242
relics and, **9:** 2353
rosary and, **9:** 2420
sacraments of, **9:** 2449ff
vestments in, **2:** 528
see also breviary; canonization
Romans, St Paul's epistle to, **8:** 2148
Romany (Gypsy language), **5:** 1196
Rome (ancient), **9: 2412–19**
agriculture in religion of, **9:** 2414–15
altars in, **1:** 116f, **9:** 2418
as Antichrist, **4:** 1157
aphrodisiacs used in, **6:** 1658
astrology not found in religion of, **9:** 2418
bridge rite in, **2:** 345
calendar, civil, of, **9:** 2415–16
Carthage and, **8:** 2180, 2184

cosmetics in, **8:** 2165
Cybele/Attis cult in, **2:** 583, **3:** 742, **7:** 1896, **10:** 2678
divination in:
augury, **1:** 191, **3:** 657f, 747, **6:** 1637, **8:** 2065, **9:** 2417, 2418
Cicero on, **3:** 657
haruspicy, **6:** 1637, **9:** 2418
sortes (lots), **6:** 1647, **9:** 2418–19
dreams in, **3:** 705
dualism in, **6:** 1708
eclipses and, **3:** 771
emperor of, *see under* kingship *below*
Etruscan influence on Roman religion, **9:** 2414f, **9:** 2418
fig tree and **4:** 940
flute in, **9:** 2412
food, spirits of, *see* Penates
games and, **6:** 1553–4, **9:** 2142f, 2416
gods of, **9:** 2412ff
domestic, **9:** 2418
see also genius; Lares; Penates
Etruscan gods identified with, **3:** 849
see also Aesculapius; Ceres; Cupid; Cybele *above;* Diana; Faunus; Fortuna; Isis *below;* Janus; Juno; Jupiter; Mars; Mercury; Minerva; Mithras, Rome and; mystery religions *below;* Neptune; Pluto; Saturn; Venus; Vesta; Vulcan
Greek influence on Roman religion, **9:** 2414f
Hercules and, **5:** 1281
hills of, *see* Aventine Hill; Capitoline Hill; Palatine Hill
incense used in, **5:** 1428
Isis cult in, **3:** 741–2, **6:** 1461f, **7:** 1896–7, 1928, 2088
Jews and, **2:** 466, **9:** 2328, 2458, **11:** 3066, 3077–8
kingship in, **6:** 1572
emperor, **6:** 1572, **7:** 1928–9, **9:** 2418
ladder and **10:** 2697
laurel and, **6:** 1610f
magic not found in Roman religion, **9:** 2418
magical papyri and, **6:** 1689, 1691
mystery religions in, **7:** 1925ff
see also Isis *above;* Mithras, mystery cult of
necromancy and, **10:** 2824
oak and, **8:** 2034
oracles of, *see* oracles, Graeco-Roman
owl and, **8:** 2096
Parthians and, **8:** 2143
priests of, **8:** 2256, **9:** 2413, 2416f, 2418
see also Arval Brothers; flamen; Salii; Vestal Virgins
rose and, **9:** 2421
sacrifice and, **9:** 2416, 2417–18, 2419
human, **9:** 2419
sheep festival of (*Parilia*), **9:** 2559
spring festivals of, **10:** 2678
see also Lupercalia
sun cult in, **10:** 2722
Mithras, **7:** 1862, 1863f
temples of, **9:** 2357, 2364
threshold, doorway, in, **6:** 1483f, **10:** 2833
time and, **9:** 2479, 2848
tree spirits, tree worship, in, **11:** 2876, 2878–9
witchcraft in, **6:** 1473f
see also evocatio; founding of Rome; Lemures; *manes;* sibyls
Rome (medieval and modern):
Christian pilgrimage to, **8:** *2195,* 2196
Luther, **8:** 2198
15th-cent. plan of, **4:** *1026*
papel cortège in, **8:** *2197*
see also papacy; St Peter's
Romuald, St, 10: 2697
Romulus and Remus, 4: 940, 1026ff, **11:** *2903,* 2904
by Rubens, **4:** *1025*
Ronan, St. 2: 349, 361
Rongo (Lono, Ono; Polynesian god), **8:** 2230
Ronwe (demon), **3:** *860*
rook, 6: 1696, 9: 2419
Rops, Felicien, 1: 146
Roquepertuse, Celtic temple at, **5:** 1237f
rosary, 9: 2420
in Hinduism, **9:** 2420, **11:** *2930,* 2932
rose, 9: 2421–4
cross and, *see* Rose Cross
as female symbol, **8:** 2174–5
Graces and, **4:** 1145
Rose, Antoine (witch), **4:** 1043, **8:** 2112
Rose Cross, 9: 2424
Fludd and, **9:** *2426*
Rosicrucians and, **9:** 2424, 2426ff
Rose of Lima, St, 9: 2462
rosemary (herb), **5:** *1275,* 1276, **8:** 2204, **2424**
Rosenkreutz, Christian, 7: 1769, **9:** 2426ff
Rosicrucians, 7: 1769, **9: 2425–33**
alchemy and, **9:** 2429, 2430, *2432*
Freemasonry and, **9:** 2430
Golden Dawn and, **4:** 1131, 1132, 1134, **9:** 2430–3
Stanislas de Guaita and, **1:** 241, **8:** 2126, **9:** 2433
Bulwer Lytton and, **6:** 1670
Paracelsus and, **9:** 2428
Péladan and, **1:** 146, 241, **9:** *2425, 2431,* 2433
Rudolf Steiner and, **9:** 2433
in the United States, **9:** 2433
Rossetti, Dante Gabriel, 9: 2434–7
Damozel of the Sanct Grael, The, **8:** *2167*
How They Met Themselves, **3:** *676*
Rothman, Bernard (Anabaptist), **3:** *825*
Round Table, King Arthur's, **1:** 153, **2:** 391f, **4:** *1148*
earliest surviving reference to, **1:** 155
Galahad and, **4:** 1057, 1059
Tudors and, **1:** 159
Roux, Georges, 7: 1828
rowan (mountain ash, quick beam, quicken, wicken, witch-wood), **5:** 1228, **9: 2437**
Roy, Ram Mohan, 5: 1316, *1321*
Royal Oak Day, *see* Oak-Apple Day
ruby, 6: 1511, *1513*
Rudra (Indian god), **5:** 1435
Brahman and, **5:** 1313
bull and, **2:** 365, **10:** 2572
crossroad offerings to, **2:** 555
end of the world and, **3:** 817
Shiva and, **5:** 1313, 1435, **10:** 2572
Rufai dervishes (howling dervishes), **2:** 589, 622
Rugievit (Slav god), **10:** 2611
Rumi, Jalalu'd-Din, 3: 637, **9: 2438–41**
Rumpelstiltskin, 9: *2384*
rune occultism, 9: 2441
runes, 1: 111, 112, **4:** 1083
on Ruthwell cross, **2:** 551
see also rune occultism
Rupprecht, Knight (Christmas gift-bringer), **2:** 483
Rusalki (Slav water spirits), **10:** 2612
Russell, Charles Taze, Jehovah's Witnesses and, **6:** 1499
Russell, G. W. (A. E.), **9: 2442–4**
Rustem (Persian hero), **3:** *857*
Rutherford, Judge Joseph (leader of Jehovah's Witnesses), **6:** 1499f
Ruthwell cross, 2: 551
Ruysbrook, Jan van, 1: 209, **3:** 634

S

S (letter), **7:** 1942
sabbath (Christian), **3:** 607
see also Seventh Day Adventists; Sunday
sabbath (Jewish), **3:** 607, **6:** 1535–6, **9:** 2534
sabbath (witchcraft), **1:** 278, **9: 2445–8**
by Baldung Grien, **8:** *2055*
of Basque witches, **1:** 233ff
by Franckens, **1:** *278,* 8: *2057*
French witches and, **4:** 1043, *1044–5, 1046,* 1046f
by Goya, **1:** 115
Italian witches and, **6:** 1474, 1476
Sabians, 5: 1213
Sacaea, *see* New Year, Babylonian festival of
sacramentism, 3: 825
sacraments, 9: 2449–52
Christian, **9:** 2449–52
incarnation of God in, **9:** 2452
see also baptism, Christian; Extreme Unction; marriage, Christianity and; Mass; penance
in Egypt, **9:** 2449
in the Eleusinian Mysteries, **9:** 2449
***Sacred Magic of Abra-Melin, the Mage, The Book of the,* 9: 2452**
magic squares in, **6:** 1693, **9:** 2452
sacrifice, 9: 2453–8
altars used for, **1:** 116f
ancestor worship and, **2:** 575
as atonement, **1:** 192
of bears, **1:** 116, 245–6, **8:** 2243, **11:** 2856
blood and, **1:** 295, **9:** 2457
of bulls, **1:** 230, **3:** 742, **7:** 1861, 1862, 1863f
burning as method of, **1:** 116f, **2:** 378, **4:** 970
divination by smoke from, *see* capnomancy
incense and, **8:** 2164
at Carthage, **8:** *2181*
of cats, **4:** 915
Christianity and, **9:** 2458
to chthonian powers, in Greece, **3:** 751
divination by smoke from, *see* capnomancy
Etruscans and, **3:** 849–50
in Greece, **3:** 751, **8:** 2261
of horses, **4:** 1052, **5:** 1353, 1410, 1435
Jewish, **9:** 2458
see also atonement, Jewish day of
in Malta, **6:** 1700
in Micronesia, **8:** 2233
in Nigeria, **9:** 2488
by the Nuer, **8:** 2022–3
in the Old Testament, **9:** 2457–8
see also Abraham, sacrifice of Isaac and
in Polynesia, **8:** 2231
of rams, **9:** 2556
see also Abraham, sacrifice of Isaac and
in ritual magic, **9:** 2400
Rome and, **9:** 2416, 2417–18, 2419
in Scandinavia, **9:** 2458, 2484
in Sweden, **8:** 2045, 2457
in the *Veda,* **5:** 1307f, 1435, **9:** 2456
see also human sacrifice
Sadducees, 2: 466, 467, **9: 2458**
sadhu (Indian fakir), **4:** 910f, **6:** 1678, **7:** *1780,* **9: 2458,** 2523
sado-masochism, 4: 991
Saehrimnir (boar; Scandinavian mythology), **1:** 297
saga (Roman witch), **6:** 1474
Sagbata (Dahomean spirit), **2:** 586
sage (herb), **5:** 1276
Sagittarius (the Archer; zodiac sign, in astrology), **1:** 175, 181, **9: 2459**
Jupiter and, **6;** 1554
placed in the sky by Zeus, **2:** 445
Sahajiya sect (India), **6:** 1584
Sahara desert, Touareg of, **10:** 2863–5
Sai Baba (Indian saint), **9:** 2459
Saicho (Japanese priest), *see* Dengyo Daishi
sailors, seamen, superstitions and traditions of, **9:** 2509–10, 2512, **10:** 2568ff, 2731
saining (Scots blessing), **1:** 275
St Andrew's cross, *see* X-shaped cross
St Anthony's cross, *see* T-shaped cross
St Augustine's Well (Cerne, Dorset), **10:** 2685
St Brendan's Isle, 2: 339
St Cuthbert vestments (Durham), **8:** 2071
Saint Denis, Hervey de, on dreams, **3:** 706, 707
St Edward's crown, 2: 564

St Elmo's Fire (corposant), **9:** 2512, **11:** 3031
Castor and Pollux and, **11:** 2904
Saintes-Maries-de-la-Mer (France), Gypsy pilgrimage to, **5:** *1194, 1195,* 1196
St-Germain, Comte de, 9: 2460–1
St Helen's Well (Rushton Spencer, Staffs), **10:** 2684
St James's herb, *see* ragwort
St John Ambulance Brigade, origin of, **5:** 1360
St John's Eve/Day, bonfires and, **9:** 2461, 2948, **11:** 3039–40
see also Midsummer, St John the Baptist and
St John's herb, *see* mugwort
St John's wort (Devil's Bane), **5:** 1276, **6:** 1657, **7:** 1846, **9: 2461**
St Mark's Eve, divinatory rite on, **1:** 166
Saint-Martin, Louis-Claude de, Martinists and, **7:** 1746, 1747
St Médard (Parisian cemetery), miraculous cures at, **2:** 516
St Michael's Mount (Cornwall), giant of, **6:** 1478
St Nun's spring (Pelynt, Cornwall), **10:** 2685
St Osyth (Essex), witches and, **3:** 754, 755, *755,* 758, 866
St Peter's (Rome), **9:** 2370
saints, 9: 2462–71
Buddhist, **2:** 355f
Christian, **9:** 2462–71
  animals and, **9:** 2465–71
  Breton, **2:** 349
  healing powers of, **3:** 648, **4:** 909
  miracles and, **9:** 2462
  Quietist tendencies of many, **9:** 2318f
  relics of, **9:** 2351f
  springs and wells and, **4:** 1029, **10:** 2685
  see also canonization; hagiography
  also the names of individual saints
Indian, *see* India, saints and holy men of
Islamic, **6:** 1469
Ramakrishna on the madness of, **6:** 1678
St Saviour (Constantinople), dome of, **9:** *2363*
St Stephen's Day, *see* Boxing Day
St Swithin's day, 10: 2605
Sakkara (Egypt), **5:** *1404,* 1404f
mummified baboons at, **1:** 128–9
see also Pyramid Texts
Saklon (Saklas; demiurge), **6:** 1721
Sakti (Hinduism), *see* Shakti
Sakyamuni, *see* Buddha
salamander (mythical creature), **3:** 802f, **4:** *973*
Salazar y Frias, Alonzo de, on Basque witchcraft, **1:** 236, 237
Salem witches, 4: 914, **5:** 1385, 1408, **9: 2472–4**
Salii (Salians; Roman priests), **9:** 2417
Mars and, **7:** 1742f
Saturn and, **9:** 2479
Salisbury cathedral, triple head in, **5:** *1236*
Sallust, 9: 2356, 2370
Salmacis (naiad), Hermaphroditos and, **5:** 1287
Salmon, 9: 2474
Eskimo spirit of, **3:** *835*
Finn and, **4:** 966, **9:** 2474
Salome, head of John the Baptist and (Moreau), **5:** *1238*
salt, 9: 2475–6
in alchemy, **7:** 1807f, **9:** 2475
death and, **9:** 2475
First Foot and, **9:** 2475
as protection against jinn, **6:** 1516
Salter, Mrs W. H., *see* Verrall, Helen
Salt Lake City (Utah), Mormon headquarters at, **7:** 1886, 1889
Salus (Roman deity), **9:** 2412, 2413
salvation (Christianity), **8:** 2242
see also soteriology
Salvation Army, 5: 1328, **7:** 1979
salvation-history, *see Heilsgeschichte*
samadhi (yoga), **2:** 335, **7:** 1777, **9: 2476, 11:** 2870, 2935, 3074f
Samain (Samhain; Celtic festival), **1:** 109, **2:** 440, 441
modern Druids and, **3:** 722
Samaria, Samaritans, 6: 1644
Sambatyon (legendary river), **6:** 1645
Samhain (Celtic festival), *see* Samain
Samhitas (Hindu sacred texts), **5:** 1307
Samkara (Vedantist), **2:** 360
Samkyha (Hinduism), **11:** 3070
Sammonicus, Quintus Serenus (Roman doctor), **1:** 64
Samoa (Polynesia), **8:** 2230f
Samos (Greece), Hera and, **5:** 1270
Sampson, Agnes (witch), **4:** 915, **8:** 2013, 2014, 2015
Samsara, *see* reincarnation (in Buddhism *and* in Hinduism)
Samskaras (Hinduism), **11:** 2934
Samson (Old Testament), **9: 2476**
riddle asked by, **9:** 2384
Samsun, St, 2: 349
Samurai (Japan), **5:** 1390, **6:** 1492
sanbenito (heretics' garment), **1:** 205, **5:** 1283
sanctuary, 9: 2476
Sandan (Cappadocian god), **4:** 970
Sanders, Alex, modern witchcraft and, **7:** *1868, 1869,* 1869f, *1870*
sand garden, Japanese, **11:** *3080*
sand-paintings, Navaho Indian, **7:** *1949, 1950, 1951,* 1952
Sangha (community; Buddhism), **2:** 355
Sango (Nigerian god), his piper and dog, **5:** *1371*
Sankara (Indian philosopher), **5:** 1310
Sankey, Ira David, 8: *2161*
Sannyasin (Hinduism), **5:** 1316, **11:** *2935*
Santa Claus (St Nicholas), **2:** 483
Santorin, Atlantis and, **1:** 190, 191
al-Sanusi, Mohammed Ali (Mahdi), **6:** 1699–1700
Saora tribe (India), **8:** 2250
sapphire 6: 1511, 1512, *1513*
Sara la Kali, 5: *1194, 1195,* 1196
Sarapis (Graeco-Egyptian god), *see* Serapis
Sarasvati (Indian goddess), **8:** *2154*
Sarasvati (river), **4:** 1068
Sarasvati, Swami Dayananda, 6: 1698
sarcophagi, early Christian, **5:** 1398
Sardana (Spanish dance), **2:** 413, *590*
sardonyx, 10: 2773
Sargant, Dr William, on conversion, **2:** 515
Sargon, King (of Akkad), **6:** 1459, 1570, **8:** 2270
Sargon II (king of Assyria), **6:** 1644
Sarn Cynfelin (supposed site of submerged town), **4:** 995
Saros cycle (of eclipses), **3:** 772
sasquatch, 9: 2476
Sassanians (Persian dynasty), **8:** 2048
Parthians overthrown by, **8:** 2143
Zoroastrianism and, **11:** 3100, 3103, 3107
Satan, 3: 627
Job and, **6:** 1522
see also Devil; Satanism
Satanism, 9: 2477–9
black mass and, **1:** 277ff
at Clophill, **2:** 488
Gnosticism and, **9:** 2477f
witches and, **1:** 115, **9:** 2448, 2479
see also Luciferans; pact, Satanic
sati, *see* suttee
satori (Zen Buddhism), **7:** 1932, **11:** 3079
Saturday, 3: 606f
Saturday Oilmen, *see* Bene Israel
Saturn (planet), **9:** 2480
in astrology, **1:** 175, 180, **9:** 2480
black and, **1:** 277, **2:** 522
jewels associated with, **6:** 1512–13
lead and, **2:** 522, **6:** 1613
melancholy and, **9:** 2374, 2480
Saturn (Roman god), **9: 2479–80**
devouring his son (Goya), **4:** *1012*
Ops and, **9:** 2413–14
Saturnalia (Roman festival), **3:** 697, **9:** 2479, 3035
Christmas and, **2:** 480, **3:** 696
evergreens and, **5:** 1330
satyricon (plant), as aphrodisiac, **6:** 1657
satyrs (Greek mythology), **3:** 697, **8:** *2032,* **9: 2481–2**
see also Marsyas; Silenus
Saul, King, 8: 2049–50, **11:** 2992–3
Savitri (Indian sun god), **10:** 2722
Savonarola, 9: 2526
Sawyer, Elizabeth (witch), **8:** 2247
Saxo Grammaticus, 1: 226, **9:** 2483
al-Sayyid, Mohammed Ahmad (Mahdi), **6:** 1700
Scales, the (zodiac sign, in astrology), *see* Libra
scallop-shell, *see* cockle-shell
scalping, 9: 2482
Scandinavia, Scandinavian (Norse, Nordic) mythology, **9: 2483–6**
ash tree in, *see* Yggdrasill
boar in, **1:** 297, **3:** 737, **4:** 1051f
Christian influence on, **3:** 817
cow in, *see* Audumulla
creation myths of, **4:** 1103, **6:** 1623, **9:** 2484
dwarfs in, **3:** 734ff
elder tree in, **3:** 795
end of the world in, *see* Ragnarok
Germanic mythology related to, **4:** 1083
giants in, *see* giants, in Scandinavian mythology
gods of, **9:** 2483
  fertility gods, *see* Vanir
  see also Balder; Heimdall; Hel; Hoenir; Loki; Mimir; Norns; Odin; Thor; Tyr
hammer in, **5:** 1205
  of Thor, *see* Mjölnir
heroes of, *see* Volsungs
horns and, **5:** 1346
paradise of, *see* Valhalla
rainbow bridge in, *see* Bifrost
rowan in, **9:** 2437
sacrifice in, **9:** 2458, 2484
  Sweden, **8:** 2045, **9:** 2457
sun and, **10:** 2720–1
Wagner and, **10:** 2978
wolf in:
  Odin and, **4:** 1086, **8:** *2043*
  sun and, **10:** 2721
  see also Fenris wolf
World Tree in, *see* Yggdrasill
see also Edda
scapegoat, 1: 192, **9:** 2458, **2487–8**
Azazel and, **4:** 1121, **9:** 2487
figs and, **4:** 940, **9:** 2488
by Holman Hunt, **1:** 192
in Peru, **5:** 1425
witches, etc., described as, **5:** 1379f
see also sin eater
scarab (dung-beetle), **3:** *733,* **6:** *1447,* **10: 2488–9**
Christ and, **6:** 1447
Re and, **3:** 789, *789,* **9:** 2488f
weighing of the heart and, **10:** 2489
scars on the body, deliberately induced, *see* cicatrization
Sceptics (Greek philosophers), **8:** 2240
Schimmel (Alpine hobby-horse), **5:** 1327
schizophrenia, witchcraft and, **8:** 2053ff
Schliemann, Heinrich, 5: 1167, **11:** 2894
Schmeider, K. C. (writer on alchemy), **3:** 811
Schmidt, Dr Helmut (ESP researcher), **8:** 2278–9, 2288, 2289
Schmidt, Wilhelm, on monotheism, **9:** 2358
Schneider brothers (Willi and Rudi), **8:** 2277, **9: 2489–91**
Rudi, **7:** *1793*
Schulte-Strathaus, Ernst (astrologer), National Socialism and, **7:** 1947
Schwenkfeld, Caspar von, 7: 1884

Schwenkfelders (Christian sect), **7:** 1884
science:
Christianity and, **2:** 474f
Teilhard de Chardin on, **10:** 2811f
Goethe and, **4:** 1124ff
magic and, **6:** 1682–3
science fiction, 9: 2492–2501
in films, **4:** 949ff, **9:** *2497, 2500,* 2501
Sciron (Greek mythology), **10:** 2818
Sclater, P. L., Lemuria named by, **6:** 1614
Scone, Stone of, **10:** 2707
Scorpio (the Scorpion; zodiac sign, in astrology), **1:** 175, 181, **9: 2502**
scorpion, 5: 1272, **9: 2502**
zodiac sign, *see* Scorpio
Scot, Reginald (writer on witchcraft), **3:** 754, 783, 855
on coral as protection against bewitchment, **9:** 2342
on flying ointment, **4:** 998
on poisoning, **8:** 2218
on shape-shifting, **11:** 3010
Scott-Elliot, W. (occultist), on Atlantis, **1:** 191
Scottish and Border ballads, 9: 2503–5
scrofula, *see* king's evil
Scrutten, Mary (witch), **5:** 1417
scrying (crystal-gazing), **2: 564, 7:** 1858, *1859,* **9: 2506–8, 10:** 2963
John Dee and, **3:** 618f, **7:** 1858, **9:** 2506
see also Dixon, Jeane
Scylla and Charybdis, 9: 2508
scythe, 9: 2508
Ankou and, **2:** 347
Father Time and, **3:** 617
in New Year symbolism, **7:** *1994*
as protection against witches, **2:** 350
Scythians:
burial among, **2:** 572, **5:** 1413
shape-shifting by, **9:** 2552
sea, ocean, 9: 2509–15
chaos and, **1:** 223, **3:** 609, **4:** 1157
end of the world and, **9:** 2486
Eskimo spirits of, **3:** *832,* 833f
see also Sedna
Greek god of, *see* Poseidon
human sacrifice and, **9:** 2510
in Mesopotamian mythology, *see* Nammu; Tiamat
moon and, **9:** 2509
Neptune and, **7:** 1969
nymphs of, *see* Nereids; Oceanides
Venice, Doge of, married to, **9:** *2513*
see also Atlantic Ocean; Davy Jones; dolphin; fish; lost lands; mermaids and mermen; seal; sea-monsters; shells; ships; whale
Seabrook, William, 1: 183
seal (animal), **9: 2515–17**
seamen, *see* sailors
sea monk, 4: 985
sea-monsters, 1: 222f, **9:** 2510, **11:** 3002
Baal and, **10:** 2761
Morbidus and, **10:** *2530–1*
Nereids with, **9:** *2414–15*
see also Andromeda; Hesione; kraken; sea monk
seance, 7: *1782,* **9: 2517**
seasons:
astrology and, **11:** 2957
cyclical character of, **4:** 932f
seasonal festivals as rites of passage, **9:** 2391
vegetation spirits and, **11:** 2939
see also harvest; Midsummer; New Year; spring; winter
Sebastian (king of Portugal), Antonio Conselheiro and, **2:** 511
Sebastian, St, 9: 2464
Sebek (Egyptian crocodile god), **1:** 128, **3:** 790
Sebottendorff, Baron Rudolph von, **4:** 1082
Second Coming, 3: 821, **9: 2518–22, 1:** 2990
Christadelphians and, **9:** 2521
Jehovah's Witnesses and, **6:** 1499, **9:** 2521–2
Plymouth Brethren and, **3:** 867
depicted at Rila monastery (Bulgaria), **2:** *475*
Seventh Day Adventists and, **9:** 2521, 2536
Shakers and, **9:** 2546
second sight, 9: 2522
Secretain, Françoise (witch), **4:** 1047
Secret Chiefs, 9: 2426
see also Mahatmas; Masters
Secret Doctrine, The (Blavatsky), **1:** 293
Secret of Secrets, The (grimoire), *see True Black Magic*
secret societies:
African, **1:** 81, **2:** 510
see also Leopard Societies; Mau Mau
Chinese, **2:** 461, 463, **10:** 2787, 2858
Indian, *see* Thugs
Secular Games (Rome), **9:** 2412, 2413
Sedna (Arnquagssaq, Nerrivik, Nuliajuk; Eskimo sea spirit), **3:** 833f, 837, **9:** 2515f
seer, in the Old Testament, prophet distinguished from, **9:** 2377
Sefardim (Jews), **6:** 1530
Sefer Yetsirah (Book of Creation; Jewish mystical text), **1:** 112f, **2:** 383, **4:** 1135–6
sefiroth (emanations; Cabala) **2:** 383ff
in magic, correspondences and, **2:** 522
forces and, **4:** 1020–1
meditation on, **7:** 1778
Tarot and, **8:** 2146–7
Seicho no Ie (Japanese religious sect), **6:** 1496
seidr (Scandinavian divination rite), **4:** 1052
Seker (Socharis; Egyptian god), **1:** *308*
Sekhmet (Egyptian goddess), **6:** *1634, 1649*
Selene (Greek moon goddess), **7:** *1876, 1882,* **9: 2522**
Seleucid dynasty (Persia), overthrown by Parthians, **8:** 2143
self, selfhood, **7:** 2004
Buddhism and, **6:** 1709
see also Nirvana, in Buddhism
in Gnosticism, **6:** 1713
Hinduism and, *see* Atman; Brahman
magic as search for, **6:** 1687–8
mystical experience and, **7:** 1932ff, 2004
self-denial, *see* asceticism
self-sacrifice, pelican as symbol of, **8:** 2158
Selivanov, Kondrati, 7: 1915, **10:** 2594, *2594*
Semele (mother of Dionysus), **3:** 635, **7:** 1908
Senchan (Irish poet), **8:** 2212
Serafino of Dio, 10: 2700
seraph, 9: 2527
in the Old Testament, **1:** 125
Serapis (Serapis; Graeco-Egyptian god), **1:** 138, **5:** 1248, *1248,* **6:** 1461, 1462, **8:** 2088, **9: 2527–8, 10:** 2848
serpent, snake, **1:** 129, **9: 2528–32, 10: 2620**
Adam and Eve and, **3:** 859, 860, **4:** 979f
by Goes, **2:** *536*
tarragon and, **5:** 1276
in Africa, **1:** 72–3
Congolese myth, **2:** *508*
in Ethiopia, **3:** 844
Apollo and, **1:** 139, **9:** 2529
Asclepios and, **5:** 1171–2, 1246, **9:** 2529
ash tree and, **1:** 160
bite of, cures for:
herbal, **5:** 1272, 1274, 1276
peacock, **8:** 2153
Brazilian sexual myth of, **2:** 327
Breton legend of, **2:** 348
caduceus and, **2:** 335–6, 388
chthonian deities, spirits, and, **3:** 751, **9:** 2528f, 2532
in Crete, **2:** *544,* 545, **5:** 1171
divination by, in Borneo, **1:** 316
dragon and, **3:** 690
eagle and, **3:** 746
earth and sky in myths of, **9:** 2529f
feathered or plumed, **9:** 2529
see also Quetzalcoatl
fennel and, **5:** 1274
Gilgamesh and, **3:** 860, **4:** 1106
in healing, **9:** 2532
Hermes and, **9:** 2529
see also caduceus
heroes and, **9:** 2529, *2530–1*
Hesperides and, **5:** 1280
in Hindu myth, *see* Ananta; Nagas; Shesha; Visvarupa
imaginary, seen by alcoholics, etc., **7:** 1909
at Last Judgement, the damned tormented by, **9:** *2532*
lizard and, **6:** 1639
in magic, **9:** 2530–2
in Malta, **6:** 1702
North American Indians and, **9:** 2530
in Parsifal's vision, **8:** *2141*
peacock and, **8:** 2153
rainbow and, **9:** 2529f
Dahomey, **2:** 586
Zulus, **9:** 2333
ram-headed, Celtic, **1:** 129, **2:** 443, **5:** 1350
swallowing its tail, *see* ourobouros
Tree of Life and, **5:** *1291*
Vishnu asleep on, **10:** *2614*
world serpent, cosmic snake, **9:** 2529
in Scandinavian mythology, *see* Midgard Serpent
in Hinduism, *see* Shesha
see also chimaera; Hydra; Kundalini; milpreve; ophitism; snake-handling cults; Typhon
Sertorius (Roman general), fawn and, **10:** *2688*
Sérusier, Paul (artist), **1:** 146
Servetus, Michael (Christian heretic), **5:** 1286
Sesha (cosmic serpent), *see* Shesha
Seth (Set: Egyptian god), **3:** 615, 790, **9: 2533**
birth of, in Heliopolitan myth, **2:** 534
dragon and, **3:** 690
Great Bear and, **9:** 2533, **10:** 2692
Horus and, **3:** 790, **5:** 1359, **8:** 2087, **9:** 2533
in the magical papyri, **9:** 2533
Nephthys and, **8:** 2086, **9:** 2533
Osiris and, **3:** 790, **8:** 2086, 2087, **9:** 2533
Typhon identified with, **3:** 790, **9:** 2529, 2533
Upper Egypt and, **9:** 2533
Sethlans (Etruscan god), Vulcan identified with, **3:** 849
seven, 1: 112, 114, **8:** 2025, 2026, **9: 2534–6, 10:** 2831
in angelology, **1:** 126
in the Bible, **9:** 2534
in Revelation, **3:** 822, 886, *887,* **9:** 2379, *2382,* **9:** 2534
calendar and, **7:** 1876–7
completeness of, **9:** 2536
Ismailis and, **3:** 728
moon and, **9:** 2534–6
mountains and, **7:** 1899
names adding to, **1:** 114, **8:** 2023, **9:** 2536
in Pythagoreanism, **9:** 2316
in Scottish and Border ballads, **9:** 2503f
Seven Champions of Christendom, **9:** 2536
seven halcyon days, **5:** 1205
seven planes of existence (Spiritualism), **10:** 2660
Seven Saints of Brittany, **2:** 349
seven seals (Revelation), **3:** 822
Tower of Babel and, **11:** 2867
twelve and, **11:** 2897
see also Seven Deadly Sins; Seven Sleepers of Ephesus; Seven Wonders of the World
Seven Deadly Sins, 9: 2536
by Bosch, **1:** 318, *318–19*
devils associated with, **3:** 864
13th cent. illustrations of, **8:** *2024–5,* **10:** 2582–3
Seven Sleepers of Ephesus, 9: 2536, 10: 2615
Seventh Day Adventists, 9: 2521, **2536**
Seven Wonders of the World, 9: 2536
Zeus, statue of, **5:** 1396, **11:** 3093
see also pyramids, Egyptian
sex, sexuality, **1:** 300, **9: 2537–42**

Adam and Eve and, **4:** 979, 980, **9:** 2539–40
demons, sexual, *see* incubus and succubus
fertility and, **4:** 936f, **6:** 2538
phallic symbolism and, **4:** 936, **8:** 2174, 2177
fifteen and, **4:** 939
fish and, **4:** 987
five and, **4:** 988
flagellation and, **4:** 991
Freud on, **4:** 1048, 1049
horns and, **5:** 1343
Indian erotic temple carvings, **4:** *933,* **5:** *1317, 1318–19*
initiation and, **5:** 1443f
Krishna and, **5:** 1314
in magic, **1:** 300, **6:** 1685, **8:** 2070, **9:** 2540ff
Crowley, **2:** 560f, **4:** 1133, **8:** 2239, **9:** 2540–1
mediumship and, **7:** 1792
mystical experience and, **3:** 774, **7:** 1934, 1936, **9:** 2538
opposites, reconciliation of, in, **8:** 2070, **9:** 2539
race myths concerning, **9:** 2324f
religious belief implanted or confirmed by, **9:** 2539
in Revelation, **11:** 3053–7
self-denial and, **9:** 2524
serpent and, **10:** 2621
in Brazil, **2:** 327
snake-handling cults, **10:** 2624
Shiva/Shakti and, **5:** 1314, **10:** 2778, 2781f
sinlessness and, religious beliefs concerning, **2:** 502, **3:** 826, 828
spring and, **10:** 2678
in Tantrism, **5:** 1314, **10:** 2778, 2780, 2782f
witchcraft and, **5:** 1381
impotence caused by witches, **5:** 1380f, **6:** 1453, **8:** 2281
modern, **7:** 1866
see also sabbath
vampirism and, **11:** 2928
Voodoo and, **11:** 2974f
yoga and, **11:** 3073
see also aphrodisiac; celibacy; hermaphrodite; homosexuality; incest; love magic; marriage; orgy; phallic symbolism; prostitution
Seymour, Alice (founder of the Panacea Society), **10:** 2646
Shabaka Stone, 9: 2354
Shackleton, Basil, S. G. Soal and, **8:** 2278
Shadhili, Abu 'l-Hasan ash- (Sufi), **10:** 2716
shadow, 9: 2543–4
builders' rites and, **2:** 361, **9:** 2543
in China, at funerals, **9:** 2543
divination by, **9:** 2543–4
Finn and, **9:** 2543
in Haiti, **10:** 2969
soul and, **3:** 672, **9:** 2543, 2636
Shafii school (Islam), **6:** 1465
Shaka (Chaka; Zulu chief), **11:** 3103, 3104–5
Shakers (religious sect), **2:** *498,* 499, **9: 2544–6**
Spiritualism and, **3:** 828, **9:** 2545
Shakespeare, William, epitaph of, **2:** 581, *581*
Shakti (Sakti; Hinduism), **5:** 1314, **6:** 1556, **10:** 2573
Kundalini and, **6:** 1587
in Tantrism, **5:** 1314, **10:** 2778, 2781f
Shaktism, *see* Tantrism
Shakyamuni, *see* Sakyamuni
Shalako (Zulu festival), **9:** 2304
shaman, 8: 2251–2, **9: 2546–9**
birch tree and, **9:** 2548
in Borneo, **1:** 314, 316
in Brazil, **2:** 329f
in central America, **7:** 1840ff
costume of, **2:** 526, **4:** *962*
death and resurrection of, **9:** 2548
dismemberment of, **3:** 650, 714, **9** 2547f
drugs and. **3:** 712f, 714
drum and, **3:** 725, 837, **4:** *962, 963,* **6:** 1605, *1607,* **9:** 2548, *2548*
ecstasy and, **8:** 2251, **9:** 2548–9
Eskimo, **3:** 833f, 835, 836, 837, **6:** 1630, **7:** 1760, **9:** 2548
in Finland, **4:** 958, *962, 963*
fir tree and, **4:** 968
healing and, **9:** 2549
homosexuality and, **1:** 104, **5:** 1338
in India, **8:** 2250
initiation of, **9:** 2546ff
in Lapland, **3:** 725, **6:** 1605f, *1607,* **9:** *2548*
light, illumination, and, **6:** 1630
madness and, **6:** 1675f, 2547
North American Indian, **3:** *649*
Algonquin, **1:** 104, 104f, **7** 1725
Pacific North-West, **8:** 2108–9
Siberian, **3:** 651, 725, **9:** 2546ff
soul and, **9:** 2549
world tree and, **9:** 2547, 2548
see also medicine-man; priest
Shamash (Utu; Mesopotamian sun god), **7:** 1819f, *1825*
Hammurabi and, **9:** 2377
Sin the father of, **5:** 1213
sun disc symbol of, **5:** 1398, **7:** *1825*
Shameer (alchemical symbol), **6:** 1514
Shams (Ethiopian sun god), *see* Dhat Himyam
shape-shifting, lycanthropy, metamorphosis, **6: 1668, 7: 1836, 9: 2550–6**
by the Antaei of Arcadia, **9:** 2551–2
bear and, **8:** 2045–6, **9:** 2556
berserkers and, **8:** 2045–6, **11:** 3009
Canon Episcopi condemns belief in, **9:** 2552
cats and, **2:** 419, **9:** 2552
Celts and, **2:** 443
Circe and, **2:** 485, **9:** *2553*
hyena and, **5:** 1378
in New Guinea, **9:** *2553*
by Odin, **9:** 2550, 2556
by Proteus, **9:** 2550–1
stag and, **10:** 2687–9
stork and, **10:** 2708–9
swan and, **10:** 2736–8
by vampires, **11:** 2924
in *Volsunga Saga,* **9:** 2553–6
by witches, **2:** 419, **11:** 3010f, 3049
wolf and, **9:** 2552, 2553f, **11:** 3049
see also werewolf
by Zeus, **9:** 2550
see also Vishnu, incarnations of
Sharruna (Hurrian god), **5:** 1324
Shaw, George Bernard, Mrs Besant and, **1:** 258
Sheba, Queen of, *see* Queen of Sheba
sheep, 10: 2556–60
goats and (Christian metaphor), **4:** 1121
see also Golden Fleece; Good Shepherd; lamb; ram
Shehenshais (Parsee sect), **8:** 2137
Sheikh of the Sheikhs, *see* Junayd of Baghdad
Sheila-na-gig, 8: 2177
Shekhinah (Judaism), **9: 2560**
in the Cabala, **2:** 385
Sheldon, William, 8: 2190
Shelley, Mary, *Frankenstein* written by, **5:** 1338
shells, 9: 2513–15, **2560**
see also cockle-shell; cowrie shell; wampum
Shellycoat (Scottish fairy), **4:** 901
Shema (Judaism), **6:** 1531
Shembe, John Galilee, 7: 1832
Shem Hameforash (Ineffable Name of God), **7:** 1942
Sheol (Old Testament land of the dead), **5:** 1260, 1413, **6:** 1545, **9: 2560**
shepherd, in religious symbolism, *see* Good Shepherd
Shepherd of Hermas (Christian text), **7:** 1985
Sherwood Forest, Robin Hood and, **9:** 2404f
Shesha (cosmic serpent; Hinduism), **9:** 2529, 2960
Shetland Isles:
diver in weather lore of, **3:** 651
fire festival of, *see* Up-helly-aa
harvest and, **5:** 1215, 1218
Shia, Shiites (Islam), **6:** 1469f, **9: 2560**
al-Husayn and, **7:** 1873f
Mahdi and, **6:** 1699
Mohammed, Shiite view of, **7:** 1873
Moharram and, **7:** 1873f
see also Ismailis
Shickshack Day, *see* Oak-Apple Day
Shiites (Islam), *see* Shia
Shilluk (Nilotic people), **6:** 1566f, 2000ff
Shimegi (Hurrian sun god), **5:** 1323
Shingon (Japanese Buddhist sect), **6:** 1486, 1489, 1492
Shinshu (Japanese Buddhist sect), **6:** 1492
Shinto, 9: 2560–4
Buddhism and, **6:** 1488, 1489, 1492, **9:** 2563, 2564
ship, 2565–71
of Freyr (Skipbladnir), **4:** 1051
ghost ships, **9:** 2512, **10:** 2571
see also St Elmo's Fire; ship-burial; Ship of Fools
ship-burial, 10: 2571
at Sutton Hoo, **1:** 254
of Viking Age, **4:** 1051, **10:** *2570*
Ship of Fools, 10: 2565
by Bosch, **1:** 318
by Oscar Laske, **10:** *2565*
Shirdi (India), Sai Baba at, **9:** 2459
Shiva (Siva; Hindu god), **5:** *1310,* 1313, 1314f, *1315, 1435,* 1436, **10: 2572–3, 11:** 2960
as Bhairava, **10:** *2783,* **11:** 2847
bisexuality of, **5:** 1288, **10:** 2573
bull and, **10:** 2572, 2573
consort of, various names of, **5:** 1314, **10:** 2573
see also Kali; Parvati; Shakti
as creator of the universe, **10:** 2573
dance and, **10:** 2573
as destroyer, **1:** 324, **3:** 616, **10:** 2573, **11:** 2847, 2960
Ganges and, **4:** 1068
heaven of, **8:** *2132*
Kundalini and, **2:** 335, **6:** 1586, 1587
madness and, **6:** 1678, **10:** 2573
mountain embodiment of, *see* Arunachala
Pasupati and, **5:** *1435,* 1436
phallic symbolism and, **4:** *934,* 936, **6:** 1633, **8:** *2176,* **10:** 2572–3
Rudra and, **5:** 1313, 1435, **10:** 2572
shofar (ram's horn), **5:** 1348, *1351*
Shomu, Emperor (of Japan), **6:** 1488
shooting stars, *see* meteors
Shotoku (Japanese ruler), **6:** 1488
Shou-Lao (Chinese god), **8:** *2136*
Shovel, Sir Cloudesley, 2: 520
shrew, folklore concerning, **1:** 160
Shroud, Holy, of Turin, **9:** 2353
Shrove Tuesday, 4: 1062, **10:** 2679
shrunken heads (of Jivaro Indians), **5:** *1233,* 1237
Shu (Egyptian sun god), **2:** 534
Si (Peruvian moon god), **5:** 1424
Siberia, shamanism in, **3:** 651, 725, **9:** 2546ff
Sibylline books, 2575
sibyls, 10: 2574–5
Sicily:
catacombs of, **2:** *370*
cave art in, **2:** *434*
Aleister Crowley in, *see* Cefalu
Easter procession in, **7:** *1748*
three saints of Trecastagni, **7:** *1854*
sickle:
hammer and, Communist symbol of, **5:** 1205
Uranus castrated with, **11:** 2921
sickness, *see* disease
siddhis (yoga), **11:** 3076
Sidgwick, Eleanor, 8: 2274, 2275, 2276, 2277

Sidgwick, Prof. Henry, **8:** *2275*
cross-correspondences and, **2:** 553, **7:** 1787
Society for Psychical Research and, **7:** 1919, **8:** 2113, 2274
Sidon (Phoenician city), **8:** 2114, 2180, 2183
Siegfried (Teutonic hero), **7:** 1997ff
Fafnir killed by, **3:** 693
sword of (Balmung), **10:** 2744
Sif (wife of Thor), **3:** 737, **10:** 2825
Sigmund (Scandinavian hero), **5:** 1298
Signatures, Doctrine of (magical principle), *see* Law of Correspondences
sign of the cross (magical protection), **2:** 552
Sigurd (Scandinavian hero), **5:** 1298
Sikhs, 10: 2575–7
Sila (Silap Inua; Eskimo god), **3:** 833
Silenus, 7: *1929,* **9:** 2481, **10: 2577**
Dionysus and, **3:** 635, **7:** *1926–7,* **10:** 2577
silver (metal), **10:** 2577
alchemy and, **10:** 2577
moon and, **2:** 522, **5:** 1210, **10:** 2577
white and, **2:** 522, **10:** 2577
see also silver bullet
silver bullet, 10: 2577
vampire and, **11:** 2926
werewolf and, **11:** 3012
witches and, **5:** 1210, **6:** 1613, **8:** 2100
Silver Pavilion (Kyoto), **9:** *2359*
Simeon Stylites, St, 6: 1679, **10: 2578**
dragon cured by, **9:** 2471
Simon, Father, 11: *2961*
Simon, St (Simon the Zealot), **11:** 3077, 3078
Simon Magus, 10: 2578–80
Faust and, **10:** 2580
Gnosticism and, **4:** 1115, **10:** 2578ff
homunculus and, **5:** 1338
Simon Stock, St, 11: 2965
simony, 10: 2578
Simurgh (Persian mythical bird), **1:** 268
sin, 10: 2580–3
Buddhism and, **10:** 2582
Christianity and, **3:** 858, 859f, **10:** 2580ff
  capital (mortal) and venial sins distinguished, **9:** 2306, 2581
  confession of sin, **9:** 2581f
  see also Fall of Man; original sin; Seven Deadly Sins; sin eater
confession of, **9:** 2581–2
evil and, **3:** 858, **10:** 2580
freedom from, excesses resulting from belief in the attainment of, **3:** 826, **5:** 1328
Islam and, **10:** 2580
karma and, **10:** 2582
see also judgement of the dead; penance
Sin (Ilmuqah; Ethiopian moon god), **3:** 842
Sin (Nannar; Mesopotamian mood god), **5:** 1213, **7:** 1819, **10:** 2565–6
Sinai, Mount, 10: 2584
St Catherine of Alexandria and, **9:** 2464
by El Greco, **6:** *1600*
Israelites and, **3:** 798, **6:** 1623, **7:** 1899, **9:** 2377, **11:** 3064
skulls of monks buried on, **2:** *571*
Sinbad, 10: 2584
Old Man of the Sea and, **9:** *2514,* **10:** 2584
Roc and, **9:** 2406
Sindri (dwarf), **3:** 737
sin eater, 2: 332, **10: 2584**
Singh, Gobind (Sikh leader), **10:** 2577
singing in the Spirit (Pentecostalism), **10:** 2652
Singreen ointment, 5: 1369
Sinhalese Buddhism, 2: 358, 445, **8:** 2196, *2198,* **10: 2585–7**
Sinis (Greek mythology), **10:** 2818
Sion, *see* Zion
Sioux Indians, 4: 1161, *1162*
Ghost Dance and, **4:** 1092, **8:** *2172*
High God of, **5:** 1302
al-Sirat (bridge over hell; Islam), **2:** 345, **6:** 1452, *1452,* 1470
Sirens (Greek mythology), **10: 2588–91**
Argonauts saved from, by Orpheus, **8:** 2082, **10:** 2590
bird form of, **10:** 2590, *2590,* 2591
mermaid form of, **10:** 2591
in Voodoo, **10:** *2588–9*
Sirgood, John (Cokeler), **2:** 492
Sirius (the dog star), in Egypt (Sothis), **3:** 664, **6:** 1460f, **10:** 2692
Sisyphus, cattle of, Autolycus and, **1:** 205
Sitting Bull (North American Indian leader), **4:** 1092
Siva (Hindu god), *see* Shiva
Sivananda, 10: 2591–2
six, 1: 114, **8:** 2025, **10: 2592**
balance and, **10:** 2592
Great Beast, **3:** 666, **4:** 1157, 1158, 1691–2
marriage and, **10:** 2592
names adding to, **1:** 114, **8:** 2023–4
in Pythagoreanism, **9:** 2316
see also hexagram
skeleton:
death personified as, **3:** *612*
  in dance of death, **2:** 598, *598–9*
  as fourth horseman of the Apocalypse, **3:** *818–19*
  in Tarot cards, *see* Death (Tarot card)
of St Osyth witch, **3:** *755,* 758
in Signorelli's *Resurrection of the Body* (detail), **10:** *2597*
see also skull
Skelton, John (poet), on the pelican, **8:** 2158
Skipbladnir (ship of Freyr), **4:** 1051
Skofnung (sword), **10:** 2748
Skoptsy (religious sect), **7:** 1915, **9:** 2523, **2593–4**
Skrymir (giant; Scandinavian mythology), **4:** 1103, **10:** 2828
skull, 10: 2594–7
Aztec, **1:** 217
burial and:
  Eskimo, at Ipiutak, **3:** 651
  of monks, on Mt Sinai, **2:** *571*
  prehistoric, **2:** 435, 570, **8:** *2245,* **10:** 2594
  separate from body, **5:** 1225ff
crossbones and, **10:** 2595–6
Crucifixion, skull depicted in, **4:** 980
as drinking cup, **10:** 2595
Great Plains Indians and, **4:** *1164*
healing and, **10:** 2596
Mexican, modern, **1:** 109, **4:** *1014,* **7:** *1844*
of monks, on Mt Athos, **9:** *2351*
in New Guinea, **7:** *1975,* **10:** *2595*
in Renaissance symbolism, **9:** *2369*
shape of, character told from, *see* phrenology
Shiva and, **5:** *1310*
Tibetan drum made of, **3:** *726*
see also head; head-hunting; skeleton
sky, 10: 2598–605
earth and, **3:** 750, **11:** 2921
  in creation myths, **2:** 534, **3:** 750, **8:** 2230, **10:** 2601
  Dahomean spirits of, **2:** 586
  in serpent myths, **9:** 2529f
gods of **10:** 2598ff
  of Andaman Islands, **10:** 2601
  Ashanti, **10:** 2601
  Babylonian, *see* An
  Egyptian, *see* Horus; Nut
  Finnish, **4:** 958
  in Germanic mythology, *see* Donar Tiwaz
  Greek, *see* Uranus; Zeus
  Indian, **5:** 1434f, **10:** 2601–2
  Kikuyu, **6:** 1561
  Maori, *see* Rangi
  Naga, **7:** 1940
  Neolithic, **8:** 2244, 2245
  Nilotic, **7:** 2001
  Polynesian, **8:** 2230
  Roman, *see* Jupiter
  Zulu, **4:** 3105
  see also High Gods
natural phenomena of, **10:** 2598, 2600
  High gods and, **5:** 1302, **10:** 2610
  as omens, **8:** 2064
  see also aurora; comets; eclipse; meteors; moon; planets; rain; rainbow; star; storm; sun; thunder and lightning; weather
supported by columns or mountains, in Eurasian mythology, **1:** 192, **8:** 2262
see also firmament; spheres
Slade, Henry (medium), **7:** 1792, *1793*
slapstick, origin of, **5:** 1212
Slavs, 10: 2606–12
vampire legend and, **11:** 2923ff
see also Baba Yaga; Kuz'ma-Dem'yan
sleep, *see* dreams; sleepers; 'sleeping preachers'
sleepers, 10: 2613–15
Seven, of Ephesus, **9: 2536, 10:** 2615
'sleeping preachers' (Finland), **3:** 828
Sleipnir (horse of Odin), **6:** 1642, **8:** 2043, *2044*
smith, 10: 2616–20
Greek god, *see* Hephaestus
see also Goibniu; tinkers; Wayland the Smith
Smith, Emma (Mormonism), **7:** 1889
Smith, G. A. (hypnotist), **5:** 1190, **8:** 2275
Smith, Joseph (founder of Mormons), **6:** 1622, **7:** 1886ff
Smithers, Alan, (statistics in astrology), **1:** 182
Freemasonry and, **7:** 1890
Smithfield (London), ghost of, **4:** *1099*
smoke:
disease and, **8:** 2166
divination by, *see* capnomancy; empyromancy
of tobacco, **11:** 2858
Smyth, Charles Piazzi (pyramidologist), **9:** 2313, 2314
Smyth-Pigott, John Hugh (leader of Agapemonites), **7:** 1828, 1830, **8:** 2258, *2258,* 2259
snail, 10: 2620
warts cured by, **10:** 2620
snake, *see* serpent
snake-charmer, Indian, **10:** *2621*
snake-handling cults, 1: 196, **10: 2621–4**
snake-stone (jewel), **6:** 1511
snakeweed (plant), *see* bistort
sneezing, 10: 2625
in augury, **1:** 194
'bless you', reason for saying, **3:** 648, **10:** 2625
demons enter the body during, **10:** 2625
as omen, **10:** 2625
soul leaves the body in, **3:** 648
snow, 11: 3039–40
snowshoe dance, of Chippewa Indians, **8:** *2011*
Soal, S. G. 3: *879,* 881, **7:** 1785, **8:** 2278
Socharis (Egyptian god), *see* Seker
Societas Rosicruciana in Anglia (Soc. Ros.), **9:** *2427,* 2430
Society of Dependants, *see* Cokelers
Society Islands (Polynesia), **8:** 2230f
Society for Psychical Research, 9: 2273, 2274ff
apparitions and, **9:** 2275, **11:** 2962
  phantasms of the living, **5:** 1190, **8:** 2275
Mme Blavatsky and, **1:** 293
Borley Rectory and, **1:** 311f
cross-correspondences and, **2:** 553, **7:** 1787, **11:** 3030
Edmund Gurney and, **5:** 1190, **7:** 1919, **8:** 2274
mediums and, *see* mediums, Society for Psychical Research and
F. W. H. Myers and, **7:** 1919, **8:** 2274
'Palm Sunday' case, **11:** 3030
poltergeists and, **8:** 2275
telepathy and, **8:** 2275
Socrates, 5: 1282
Soc. Ros., *see* Societas Rosicruciana in Anglia

Sodom and Gomorrah, 10: 2625
Sogbo (Dahomean spirit), 2: 586
Soka Gakkai (Japanese religious sect), 6: 1498
soldier's woundwort (plant), *see* yarrow
Sol Invictus (Roman sun cult), 10: 2722
solistry, *see* foot reading
Solomon, King, 10: 2626
Ethiopia and, 3: 843
hoopoe and, 1: 271
jinn commanded by, 6: 1516
as magician, 1: 167, 5: 1181, 10: 2626
peacock and, 8: 2153
Queen of Sheba and, 3: 843, 9: 2316f
Temple built by, 10: 2626, 11: 2906, 3065
Solomon's seal (herb), 5: *1275*, 1276
soma (sacred plant), 3: 711, 5: 1272, 1434, 7: 1908, 9: 2458, 10: 2626
haoma the Iranian equivalent of, 11: 3103
Somerset, meaning of the name, 4: 1110
Somerset witches, 10: 2626
see also Cox, Julian
song, singing, 10: 2627–31
of dying swan, 10: 2738
in magic, 5: 1419
see also carol; hymn; psalms; Scottish and Border ballads; Sirens
sorcery, *see* witchcraft
sortes (lots; Rome), 6: 1647, 9: 2418–19
sortilege, *see* lots, divination by
soteriology (definition), 10: 2636
see also salvation
Sothis (star), *see* Sirius, in Egypt
soul, 9: 2366–8
animism and, 1: 132, 10: 2636
astral body distinguished from 1: 171
Australian aborigines' beliefs concerning, 2: 576, 8: *2145*, 11: 2860
blood and, 11: 294f
Brazilian beliefs concerning, 2: 329f
breath and, 2: 333, 10: 2636
in Tibet, 2: 336
butterfly and, 2: 380, 6: 1447
in children's games, 2: 454
Chinese beliefs concerning, 2: 459, 460
in Christianity, *see* Christianity, soul in
double and, 3: 672, 3: 2636
dualism and, 3: 859
Egyptian beliefs concerning, 3: 791, 5: 1413, 6: *1704*, 9: *2346*, 10: *2637*
see also Egypt, life after death
Eskimo beliefs concerning, 3: 834f
Finnish beliefs concerning, 4: 959
Gnostic view of, 4: 1116f
Gonds and, 10: 2637f
Greek views of, 5: 1413
Orphic myth of Dionysus and, 3: 859
Plato on, 1: 172–3, 5: 1413
see also pneuma; Psyche; reincarnation, in Greece
see also reincarnation, in Hinduism
in Islam, 6: 1708
Jains and, 6: 1481f
in Judaism, 6: 1535, 8: 2135
more than one 'soul', or spiritual component of the personality, 10: 2636f
in Egypt, 3: 791
Naga beliefs concerning, 7: 1939
Neoplatonist view of, 1: 173, 7: 1967f, 8: 2208
Parsee beliefs concerning, 8: 2141
Polynesian beliefs concerning, 8: 2231f
rebirth of, *see* reincarnation
reflection in mirror as, 7: 1855
sale of, to the Devil, *see* pact, Satanic
shadow and, 3: 672, 9: 2543, 10: 2636
shamans and, 8: 2549
in Voodoo (*gros bon ange*), 11: 2969ff
wandering of, in primitive belief, 3: 648, 9: 2543, 10: 2636, 2638
will-o'-the-wisp as, 11: 3031
see also self
soul cakers (Hallowe'en mumming plays), 4: 1004
soul-catcher, of Pacific North-West Indian shamans, 8: 2108, 2109
south, 3: 640
South America, modern:
ashes in, 1: 164, 166
body-painting in, 10: 2804
Christianity in, 10: 2645
baptism, 2: *513*
Pentecostalist movement, 8: 2162
coca in, 3: 714
death, myths of origin of, 3: 612f
head trophies in, 5: *1233*, 1237
jaguar and, 6: 1480
tattooing in, 10: 2800
weather magic in, 1: 164
see also Brazil; Desana; El Dorado; Guarayo Indians
South America, pre-Columbian, *see* Incas
Southcott, Joanna, 10: 2645–6
J. J. Jezreel and, 6: 1514f, 10: 2646
supposed pregnancy of, 9: 2521, 10: 2646
Southeast Asia, 10: 2646–8
Sowthern, Elizabeth (Old Demdike; witch), 6: 1591ff
space, visitors from, *see* flying saucers
Spain, witchcraft in, 1: 233ff
Spanish fly (cantharides), 6: 1660
Spanish Inquisition, 5: 1283f, 1444
Basque witchcraft and, 1: 233ff
Spare, Austin (artist), 1: *183*, 183–4, *185*, 4: *995*, 5: *1406*, 8: *2056*
sparrow, sacred to Aphrodite, 3: 522
Spartas, Reuben, 11: 2989–90
speaking in tongues (glossolalia), 4: 1115, 10: 2649–53
New Testament references to, 10: 2649
Pentecostalist movement and, 8: 2159, 2162, 10: 2649, 2651ff
spear:
of Cu Chulainn, 2: 565
in Germanic mythology, 4: 1086
of Lugh, 6: 1640
of Odin (Gungnir), 3: 737, 4: 1086, 8: 2047
spectacle idols (eye idols), 4: 888
spectral evidence (witch trials), 3: 672, 11: 3043
spectre (definition), 10: 2653
see also apparition; Brocken spectre of
Spee, Friedrich von, 1: 228, 4: 1080
spell, spells, 10: 2653
poetry and, 8: 2210ff
Spencer, Philipp Jakob (pietist), 8: 2191
spheres, heavenly, 4: 1020–1, 6: 1685f, 10: 2653
in the Cabala, *see* sefiroth
Copernican theory and, 2: 352
Lull and, 5: *1291*, 6: *1666*
music of, 8: 2024, 10: 2653
17th cent. diagram of, 11: *2949*
see also firmament
Sphinx 10: 2653
Egyptian, 10: 2653
of Giza, 3: 704
Greek, 10: 2653
Oedipus and, 9: *2385*
spider, 10: 2653–5
in Japan, 10: *2654*, *2655*
see also Ananse; tarantella; Yiyi
Spina, Alphonsus de, 4: 1044
spine, (body), 1: 299
Kundalini and, 6: 1586f
spinning, 10: 2655
Spinoza, Benedict, 7: 1849
spiral, as maze, 7: 1774
spirit, spirits, 4: 931ff, 10: 2655
in Africa, 1: 73
Ashanti, 1: 162, 163
Dahomey, *see vodun*
Ethiopia, 3: 845f
fetishes and, 4: 938
guardian spirits, 5: 1183–6
Kikuyu, 6: 1561f
Nuer, 8: 2020ff
in Melanesia, 7: 1796, *1796*, 1797
in New Guinea, 5: *1236*, 7: *1797*, 1974, 1976
in Mesopotamia, 7: 1823f
Nagas and, 7: 1939f
Roman, of food, *see* Penates
Slav, 10: 2607, *2608*, 2612
in Southeast Asia, 10: 2646ff
summoning of, *see* ritual magic
Veddas and, 11: 2936–8
see also angels; animism; demons; double; elementals; ghosts; guardian spirits; jinn; keres; poltergeists; soul; Spiritualism
spiritism (or spiritualism) in Brazil, 7: 1981, 10: 2639–45, 2660
spirit photography, 10: 2663
spiritual churches (West Africa), 7: 1981
Spiritualism, 10: 2656–63
American origin of, 10: 2656
automatic art/writing and, 1: 205, 209
Mme Blavatsky and, 1: 290
in Brazil, *see* spiritism
Britain, Spiritualism, introduced to, 10: 2658–9
Christianity and, 10: 2659f
Sir William Crookes and, 2: 547f, 8: 2274
Davenport brothers and, 3: 606
Sir Arthur Conan Doyle and, 3: 686ff, 10: 2659
enthusiasm in, 3: 828
extra-sensory perception and, 3: 877
healing and, 4: 909
Sir Oliver Lodge and, 10: 2659
non-Christian sources of, 10: 2656
mesmerism, 7: 1817, 8: 2273f
psychical research and, 8: 2273f
seven planes of existence, 10: 2660
Shakers and, 3: 828, 9: 2545
table-tilting and, 8: 2090, 2092
theurgy compared with, 10: 2823f
vibration and, 11: 2949
see also mediums
Spiritualists' National Union Ltd (formerly the Spiritualists' National Federation), 10: 2659, 2660
spiritual wives, Oneida community and, 2: 502
spittle, 10: 2664
in Mesopotamian magic, 7: 1824
as protection against the Evil Eye, 4: 890, 10: 2664
Splendor Solis, 1: 96, 3: *803*, 6: *1628*, 10: *2717*
split personality, mediumistic controls seen as instances of, 7: 1783
spontaneous psi experiences, 10: 2665–76
see also extra-sensory perception; psychokinesis
spriggans (Cornish fairies), 2: 519
spring (season), 10: 2677–83
cuckoo and, 2: 566
sword dances and, 10: 2750f
see also carnival; May Day
springs, 10: 2684ff
in Brittany, 2: 349, 10: 2685
curative, 10: 2684f
of Lourdes, 6: 1653
of the Pyrenees, 6: 1650
future foretold by, 10: 2684
nymphs of, *see* Naiads
springwort (herb), 11: 3060
Spurzheim, J. K. (phrenologist), 8: 2188f
sputnik, on Chinese textile, 9: *2494–5*
squassation (torture), 1: 92
Sraosha (Zoroastrian god), 11: 3102
Srosh (Parsee deity), 8: 2138
stag, 10: 2687–91
Artemis and Actaeon and, 3: 630, 10: 2687, *2689*, *2690–1*
Celts and, 1: 129, 2: 443, 5: 1350f, 10: 2687–9

in Christian symbolism, **10:** 2687
Hittites and, **10:** 2687
shape-shifting and, **10:** 2687–9
stag-beetle, 6: 1447, *1447*
stairs, *see* steps and ladders
Stallo (Lapp giant), **6:** 1607–8
standing stones:
in Brittany, **2:** *348,* 348–9, 572, **3:** *718*
in Cornwall, **2:** 519–20, *520,* **10:** *2706*
see also dolmen; megaliths; stone circles
Stanton, Mary Olmsted (physiognomist), **8:** 2190
star, stars, **10: 2692–3**
Christianity and, **10:** 2693
divination by, *see* astrology
in Egypt, *see* Egypt, stars in
eyes and, **4:** 886
five-pointed, *see* pentagram
Ishtar, symbol of, **6:** *1459,* **10:** 2692
in Mexican mythology, **1:** 217, 218f
North American Indians and, **8:** 2008f
shooting stars, *see* meteors
six-pointed, *see* hexagram
Slavs and, **10:** 2610
see also Algol; circumpolar stars; constellations; Copernican theory; Evening Star; Milky Way; Morning Star; planets; Pole Star; Sirius
Star(s) (Tarot card), **8:** 2146, **10:** *2792,* 2794
Star of David, 5: 1300, *1300,* **6:** *1538*
Starkey, George (alchemist), **7:** 1808, **8:** 2180
star-sapphire (jewel), **6:** 1512, **10:** 2773
stations of the cross, 10: 2693
Stauff, Philipp, 4: 1081, **6:** 1636
Steiner, Rudolf, 10: 2693–5
Anthroposophy and, **10:** 2693ff
Rosicrucianism and, **9:** 2433
Theosophy and, **1:** 258, **10:** 2693f
Stella Matutina (esoteric order), **4:** 1132f, **9:** 2433
Stephen, St, 3: 767, **7:** 1747
steps and ladders, stairs, 5: 1364, **6:** *1547,* **1589, 10: 2695–7**
Sthaviras (Buddhist sect), *see* Elders
Stheno (Gorgon), **4:** 1141
stigmata, and other physical phenomena of mysticism, **7:** 1971, **10: 2697–703**
blood and, **10:** 2698
St Catherine of Siena and, **2:** 426, **10:** 2701
distortion of the body, **10:** 2701
ecstasy and, **10:** 2697–8
St Francis of Assisi and, **4:** *1031,* 1032, **10:** 2698, *2700*
hysteria and, **10:** 2698, 2700, 2701
incendium amoris, **10:** 2700
incombustibility, **10:** 2700–1
incorruptibility of the body, **10:** 2701
inedia, **10:** 2701
miracles of abundance, **10:** 2702
mystic ring, **10:** 2697, 2699
odour of sanctity, **10:** 2701
psychokinesis and, **10:** 2702
see also Forgione, Father Pio; levitation
stilt dance, Nigerian, **2:** *587*
stockings, 10: 2703
Stoicism, 6: 1707, **9:** 2523
Athene and, **1:** 187
death and, **3:** 858, **6:** 1707
  Prometheus, **8:** 2263
pantheism in, **8:** 2240
see also Posidonius
stone, stones, **10: 2705–8**
on altars, **10:** 2707
Celts and, **10:** 2706, 2788
flint tools of Stone Age, **10:** 2707
  see also elf-bolts
see also omphalos; standing stones
Stone Age, *see* Neolithic (New Stone Age); Paleolithic (Old Stone Age)
see also Bushmen; Veddas
stone circles, 2: 487
at Castlerigg (Cumberland), **3:** *718*
in Co. Meath (Ireland), **2:** *486*
see also Stonehenge
Stonehenge, 10: 2703–4
aerial view of, **3:** *718*
Apollo and, **3:** 721
astronomical aspects of, **3:** 722, **10:** 2704
Druids and, **3:** 721f, **10:** 2703
  modern, **3:** *717,* 721, 722, **7:** *1845,* **8:** *2034,* **10:** 2703
Merlin and, **7:** 1810, 1811, *1811,* **10:** 2703
Stoney, J. B. (leader of Exclusive Brethren), **3:** 868
stork, 10: 2708–9
storm, 10: 2709
Baal as god of, **1:** 222, **10:** 2604
crow and, **2:** 556
death of king heralded by, **8:** 2064
eagle and, **3:** 746
Harpies and, **5:** 1212
Indra as god of, **10:** 2602
Japanese god of (Susa-no-o), **3:** 695, **10:** 2562
protection against:
  acorn, **5:** 1368
  bells, **1:** 251
  owl, **8:** 2098
see also thunder and lightning
Strachan, Isobel (witch), **1:** 63
Strang, James J. (Mormon leader), **7:** 1888–9
strappado (torture), **1:** 91, 92
strega (Italian witch), **6:** 1474
Strength (Tarot card), **8:** 2147, **10:** *2792,* 2793
Strindberg, August, New Templars and, **7:** 1983
string, 10: 2709–12
Eskimo string figures, **3:** *837*
see also cat's cradle; knot
strix (Roman witch), **6:** 1474
Struwwelpeter (children's book), **1:** 85
Stubb (Stump), Peter (werewolf), **11:** 3010
Stukeley, William, on the Druids, **3:** 721
Stump, Peter (werewolf), see Stubb, Peter
stupa (Buddhism), **9:** 2366–7, **10:** 2587, *2840*
Dhamek *stupa* at Sarnath, **9:** *2359*
Sturgess, E. M., 9: *2285*
Sturluson, Snorri, 1: 226, **4:** 1103, **9:** 2483, 2484
Style, Elizabeth (witch), **10:** 2626
stylites (pillar saints), **6:** 1678–9, **10:** 2578
see also Simeon Stylites
Stymphalian lake, Hercules and birds of, **5:** 1279
Styx (river), **2:** 448, **5:** 1260
Suarez, Francis, 10: 2703
subconscious, the, *see* unconscious
submerged towns and villages, legends of, *see* lost lands
subterranean race, 10: 2712–13
Bulwer Lytton and, **6:** 1670
Succoth (Judaism), *see* Feast of Tabernacles
succubus, *see* incubus and succubus
Sucellos (Celtic god), **2:** 443, **5:** 1205
Sudan, *see* Dogon; Nilotes
Sudras (caste; Hinduism), **2:** 415f
Sufis (Islam), **3:** 775, 778, **6:** 1469, **7:** 2004, **10: 2713–16**
meditation and, 7: 1778
Omar Khayyam and, **8:** 2063
see also dervish; Ghazali; Ibn Arabi; Mansur al-Hallaj; Rumi, Jalalu'd-Din
suggestion, in healing, **7:** 1854
see also faith-healing; hypnotism, in medicine
Suibne Gelt (Irish legend), **11:** 3028
suicide:
buried at crossroads, **2:** 374, 555
ghosts of suicides, **5:** 1225
see also hara-kiri; kamikaze; suttee
sulphur, 10: 2716
mercury and, in alchemy, **4:** 1129, **7:** 1807f
Sumatar Harabesi (Mesopotamia), **5:** 1213
Sumer, Sumerians (Mesopotamia), **1:** 223, **3:** 690, **7:** 1818, **10: 2716**
bull and, **2:** 365, **5:** 1347
creation myths of, **2:** 535f, **3:** 750
demoness of, **6:** *1631*
flood legend of, **4:** 993f, 1106
gods of, **7:** 1818ff
  iconography of, **5:** 1394
  see also An; Enlil; Inanna; Ninhursag; Nisaba
hell and, **5:** 1266
hero myth of, *see* Gilgamesh
kingship in **6:** 1570
owl and, **8:** 2096
see also Eannatum (of Lagash); Eridu; Gudea (of Lagash)
Summers, Montague, on Baphomet, **1:** 229
sun, 10: 2717–25
in alchemy, see *Splendor Solis*
in astrology, **1:** 175, 180, **10:** 2725
churches, etc., built facing the **2:** 361, **3:** 640
cock and, **2:** 490f
correspondences with, **2:** 522
crane and, **2:** 532
in Crete, moon and, **5:** 1271
cross as symbol of, **2:** 550
eclipse of, **3:** 771f, **10:** 2725
in Egypt, *see* Egypt, sun and
Eskimo and, **3:** 833, *837,* **5:** 1428
Ethiopian god of, *see* Dhat Himyam
first man and, **4:** 979
folktales as solar myths, **4:** 1009
gold and, **2:** 522, **4:** 1129, **6:** *1628*
goose and, **4:** 1138–9
Greek gods of, *see* Apollo; Helios
Great Beast 666 and, **6:** 1691–2
hawk and, **5:** 1227
Hittite gods of, **5:** 1323f
hoopoe and, **1:** 271
horse and, **10:** 2720
Ibo cult of, **5:** 1387f
Incas and, **5:** *1411,* 1424f
Indian gods of, **10:** 2722
see also Surya
jewels associated with, **6:** 1511
lizards and, **6:** 1638
magical papyri contain invocation to, **6:** 1689
megaliths and, **10:** 2724–5
Mesopotamian gods of, *see* Ninurta; Shamash
Mexican god of, *see* Tonatiuh
Mithras and, **7:** 1862, 1863f
moon and, **10:** 2719, 2720
  in Australia, **10:** 2719–20
  in Crete, **5:** 1271
  in Eskimo incest myth, **3:** 833, **5:** 1428
  in Rumanian incest myth, **7:** 1877
North American Indians and, **8:** *2006*
see also Sun Dance
phoenix and, **8:** 2185
Rome and, **10:** 2722
  Mithras, **7:** 1862, 1863f
in Scandinavia, **10:** 2720–1
Shinto goddess of, **10:** 2652
Slavs and **10:** 2610
wheels as symbols of, **11:** 3014ff
see also disk; Sunday
Sun (Tarot card), **8:** 2146, **10:** *2793,* 2794
Sun dance (of Great Plains Indians), **4:** 1162ff, **10:** 2721
Sunday, 3: 606f, **10: 2725**
eight and, **3:** 795
magical operations suited to, **2:** 522
Whit Sunday, **11:** 3022
see also Palm Sunday
Sunnites (Islam), **6:** 1465, **10: 2725**
Mahdi and, **6:** 1699
Mohammed, Sunnite view of, **7:** 1873
Sunyavada (Buddhism), **10: 2726**
Suovetaurilia (Roman festival), **7:** 1863
superego (Freudian term), **4:** 1049
superstitions, 10: 2726–32
Surrealism (art movement), **1:** 148ff
see also Dali, Salvador; Ernst, Max; Magritte, René

Surt (giant; Scandinavian mythology), **9:** 2486
Surya (Indian sun god), **5:** *1306, 1315,* 1435, **10:** *2720,* 2722
Susa-no-o (Japanese god), **3:** 695, **9:** 2562
Suso, Heinrich (mystic), **3:** 634, 769
suttee, 10: 2733–4
Sutton Hoo ship burial, 1: *253,* 254, 297, **4:** *1086*
Svafilfari (horse; Scandinavian mythology), **6:** 1642
svami, *see* swami
Svantovit (Slav god), see Svetovit
Svarozhich (Slav god), **10:** 2611
Svetambaras (Jain sect), **6:** 1481
Svetovit (Svantovit; Slav god), **10:** 2610–11, *2611*
Swaffer, Hannen, Spiritualism and, **10:** 2659
swallow (bird), **10: 2735–6**
in Babylonian flood legend, **4:** 993
in legends of Christ, **6: 1696: 10:** 2736
in Greece, **10:** 2735
Philomela myth, **7:** 2000, **10:** 2735
in medicine, **10:** 2735
Swami (svami), **10: 2736**
swan, 10: 2736–8
Celts and, **2:** 444
Zeus as, *see* Leda
swastika, 2: 550, **10: 2739**
Ludwig Fahrenkrog and, **7:** *1965,* **10:** 2739
in Greece, **10:** *2739*
Guido von List and, **6:** 1636, **10:** 2739
National Socialism and, **2:** 550, *551,* **10:** 2739, *2739*
Navaho Indians and, **10:** 2739
New Templars and, **7:** 1983
Pictish, **2:** *551*
völkisch movement and, **10:** 2739
Swazi, first fruits ceremonies of, **9:** 2393
swearing, 2: 579
in oath-taking, *see* oath
Swedenborg, Emanuel, 10: 2740–1, 11: 2962–3
reincarnation rejected by, **9:** 2350
Swedish witchcraft, 3: 855, **4:** 998, **10: 2742–3**
Swifte, Edmund Lenthal, ghost seen by, **5:** 1227
swimming of witches, *see* floating of witches
Swinburne, Algernon Charles, on Christianity, **9:** 2477
swine, *see* pig
Swithin, St, 10: 2605
sword, 10: 2744–53
of Arthur, *see* Excalibur
Beowulf and, **10:** 2744, 2746, 2748
of Charlemagne (Joyeuse), **10:** 2748
crusaders and, **10:** 2748, *2752*
of Damocles, **10:** 2744
Galahad and, **4:** 1057
in Grail legend, **4:** 1071f, 1146, **10:** 2750
of Hoder (Mimingus), **1:** 226
in Japanese imperial symbolism, **9:** 2563
knighthood and, **10:** 2749
oldest known, **10:** 2744
of Roland (Durandal), **10:** 2748
of Siegfried (Balmung), **10:** 2744
of State, English, **10:** *2744*
sword dances, **10:** *2746, 2747,* 2750–3
Theseus and, **10:** *2750*
of the Vikings, **10:** 2748
see also Trfing
Sybaris, Sybarites, **9:** 2526
sycamore (tree), Helston furry dance and, **5:** 1268
sycomore (Egyptian sacred tree), **11:** 2874
sylphs (elementals), **2:** 334, **3:** 802f
Sylvester II (pope), Satanic pact and, **8:** 2112
symbolism, 8: 2173–4, **10: 2754–60**
in art, **1:** 146
of the centre, **10:** 2758
Christian, *see* Christianity, symbolism in
of dreams, Freud on, **4:** 1049
of the hero, **10:** 2759
Jung on, **10:** 2759
of the key, **5:** 1364, **6:** 1561, **10:** 2756
of the moon, **10:** 2758
of the net, **7:** 1970, **10:** 2756
Oswald Wirth on, **10:** 2790
see also inverted symbols; landscape symbolism; path symbolism; phallic symbolism; Rose Cross
Symonds, John Addington, 8: 2239
Symondsbury (Dorset), mumming play at, **4:** 1004–5
sympathetic magic, 3: 642f, **5:** 1409, **10: 2760**
in the Ozarks, **8:** 2102
see also imitative magic
synagogue (Judaism), **6:** 1531, *1534*
synchronicity, Jung's principle of, **6:** 1552, 1648, **11:** 2950
syncretism (definition), **10: 2760**
Synod of Whitby, 2: 396
Syon Cope, 8: *2070,* 2071
Syria, *see* Phoenicians and Canaanites
Syrianus (Neoplatonist), **8:** 2259, 2260

T

T (letter), as magical protection, **2:** 552
Tabernacle, Ark of the Testimony in, *see* Ark, of Yahweh
table-tilting, 8: 2090, *2091,* 2092, **10: 2767**
D. D. Home and **5:** 1333f
Willi Schneider and, **9:** 2489
taboo (tabu), **10: 2767–71**
in Africa, **1:** 78
Bushmen, **2:** 380
Congo, **10:** 2770
beans, **5:** 1213
flood and, **1:** 294f
Eskimos and, **3:** 833–4, 835, **9:** 2515f
hunting, in Brazil, **5:** 1374
incest, **5:** 1428f
Brazil, **2:** 326, 327f
among the Maori (tapu), **7:** *1730,* 1731f, 1733
in Micronesia, **8:** 2232
Navaho Indians and, **7:** 1952
in the Ozarks, **8:** 2102–3
in Polynesia, **8:** 2230f, **10:** 2769
Tabor, Mount, 7: 1899–1900
Taborites (adventist sect), **9:** 2520
tabu, *see* taboo
Tagaro (Melanesian spirit), **7:** 1799
Tages (Etruscan deity), **6:** 1637
Tagore, Rabindranath, 5: 1317, 1321, *1321*
Gandhi and, **6:** 1698
Tahaki (Polynesian hero), **8:** 2232
Tahiti (Polynesia), **8:** 2230f, *2231*
Taigheirin (Highland ceremony), **2:** 419
Taigi, Blessed Anna Maria, 10: 2701
Taiping rebellion, 7: 1827, *1835*
Taj Mahal, 2: *375*
Taka Shima Kaemon (Japanese seer), **6:** 1648
Taliesin, 9: 2551
talismans, 10: 2772–5
Agrippa on, **1:** 300, **9:** 2374
amulets distinguished from, **10:** 2772
of Great Plains Indians, **5:** 1164
see also magic squares; mezuzah
Tallmadge, Emily (automatic artist), **7:** *1785*
Talmud (Judaism), **6:** 1532
Tammuz (Dumuzi; Mesopotamian god), **3:** 739, **10: 2776**
Inanna/Ishtar and, **7:** 1820, 1822, **10:** 2776
Tanchelm, 3: 825, **9:** 2518
Tane (Polynesian god), **8:** 2230
Tangaroa (Tangaloa, Ta'aroa; Polynesian god), **8:** 2230, *2230*
Tanit Pene Baal (Carthaginian goddess), **8:** 2184
Tannhaüser, 11: 2978
tansy (herb), Easter associations of, **3:** 760
Tantalus, bones of, preserved at Argos, **9:** 2351
Tantrism (Shaktism), **5:** 1314, **9:** 2540, **10: 2778–83**
alchemy and, **10:** 2780
diamond and, **6:** 1513
magic in, **10:** 2779
mandala and, **6:** 1716
mantras and, **9:** 2540, **10:** 2780
sex and, **5:** 1314, **10:** 2778, 2780, 2782f
Tantric Buddhism, **2:** 360
yoga and, **10:** 2778
Tao, Taoism, **2:** 457ff, **10: 2784–7**
meditation in, **7:** 1778
***Tao Te Ching,* 10:** 2526, 2784, 2785
Tapiola (Finland), **4:** 958
Tara (Ireland), **4:** *965,* 966, **10: 2787–8**
Taranis (Celtic god), **2:** 442
tarantella, tarantism, **2: 600, 10:** 2655
Taresque (dragon of Tarascon), **7:** 1892
Tarhun (Luwian weather god), **5:** 1323
Tarot, 2: 403, 405–6, *407,* **10: 2789–94**
Cabalist Tree of Life and, **2:** 387, **8:** 2146–7, **10:** 2789
Crowley and, **2:** *562–3,* **8:** *2068*
Fate and, **4:** 920
in fortune-telling, **2:** 406–7, **10:** 2789, *2794*
four Hallows of Grail legend and, **10:** 2750
Hebrew alphabet and, **1:** 112, **2:** 406, **10:** 2789
individual trumps of, **2:** *407,* **8:** 2146–7, **10:** 2791–4
see also Chariot; Death; Devil; Fool; Hanged Man; High Priestess; Lovers; Moon; Pope; Universe; Wheel of Fortune
Eliphas Levi and, **6:** 1619
origin of, legend of, **2:** 407–8
Papus and, **8:** *2125,* 2125f, **10:** 2791
path symbolism and, **2:** 387, **8:** 2146–7
A. E. Waite and, **2:** 406, **10:** *2790–3,* 2791
Waldenses and, **11:** 2982
wheel and, **10:** 2791
Tarquiup Inua (Eskimo moon spirit), **3:** 833
tarragon (herb), **5:** 1276
Taru (Hattic weather god), **5:** 1323
Tashmishu (Hittite god), **5:** 1324
task (double), **3:** 672
tattooing, 2: 526, **5:** *1253,* **7:** 1917–18, **10: 2795–804**
Tau (Hebrew letter), **10: 2805**
Tauler, Johann (mystic), **9:** 2318
Pseudo-Dionysius and, **3:** 634
Eckhart and, **3:** 769
Taurobolium (bull rite of Cybele and Attis), **1:** 230, **10: 2805**
Taurt (Egyptian goddess), **1:** *127,* 128
Taurus (the Bull; zodiac sign, in astrology), **1:** 144, 175, 181, **10: 2805**
Taylor, John (pyramidologist), **9:** 2313, 2314
Taylor, Thomas (Platonist), **10: 2805–9**
taziya (Islam), **7:** 1873–4
tea, in Japan, **11:** 3085
Tea Ceremony, **6:** 1492, *1494, 1498,* **11:** 3080–1
Tea (Irish goddess), **10:** 2787
tea-leaf reading, 10: 2810
Tears of Juno/Isis (plant), *see* vervain
teeth, *see* Tooth, temple of the; toothache
tefillin (Judaism), **6:** 1537
Tefnut (Egyptian goddess), **2:** 534, **3:** 791
Teilhard de Chardin, 10: 2811–12
Telchines (Greek mythology), **2:** 523
Telegonus (son of Odysseus and Circe), **2:** 486
telekinesis, *see* psychokinesis
Telemachus (son of Odysseus and Penelope), **2:** 486
telepathy, 2: 487, **3:** 875, 877ff, **10:** 2665f, 2673, **2812**
automatic art/writing and, **1:** 207f
cross-correspondences, **2:** 554
clairvoyance and, **3:** 878
Sir Arthur Conan Doyle's experiments with,

3: 686
mediums and, **7:** 1785ff
Mrs Piper, **8:** 2200
Gilbert Murray and, **8:** 2277–8
object reading and, **8:** 2039
phantasms of the living and, **5:** 1190, **8:** 2275
Society for Psychical Research and, **8:** 2275
in twins, **11:** 2904
Telephus (son of Hercules), **10:** 2689
Telipinu (Hittite god), **5:** 1325
teleportation, *see* apportation
Tellus (Roman deity), **9:** 2412f
Temperance (Tarot card), **8:** 2147, **10:** *2792,* 2793
Templars, *see* Knights Templar
Templars of the East, *see* Order of the Templars of the East
Temple of Health (James Graham), **7:** 1854
ten, 2: 487, **8:** 2068
eleven and, **3:** 808
as the Tetractys, **8:** 2025, **9:** 2316
Tendai (Japanese Buddhist sect), **6:** 1486, 1489, 1492
Ten (later Fifteen) Men for Sacrificing (Roman priests), **9:** 2413, 2417
Tenochtitlan (Aztec capital, now Mexico City), **1:** 216, **2:** 361
Tenri-kyo (Japanese religious sect), **1:** 117, **6:** 1495
Tensho Kotai Jingu-kyo (Japanese religious sect), **6:** 1495–6
Teotihuacan (Mexican city), **1:** 214, **10:** *2721*
Teresa of Avila, St, 10: 2812–14, 11: 2965
ecstasy and, **3:** 773
John of the Cross and, **6:** 1524
levitation of, **10:** 2703
on the untrustworthiness of visions, **11:** 2965
Teresa of Lisieux, St, 9: 2462, **10:** 2701
Tereus, Philomela and (Greek mythology), **7:** 2000, **10:** 2735
Terpsichore (Muse), **7:** 1905, *1905*
Tertullian (Christian writer), **7:** 1873
on the absurdity of Christianity, **6:** 1680
on the Christian cross, **2:** 550
on Pontius Pilate, **8:** 2234
on the evilness of woman, **4:** 980
Teshik-tash, cave of (Uzbekistan), Neanderthal burial in, **5:** 1343–5
Teshub (Hittite/Hurrian weather god), **1:** 223, **5:** 1323, 1324f, 1347
***Testament of Solomon,* 5:** 1181
testicles, 5: 1276
see also castration
Tetractys, 8: 2025, **9:** 2316
Tetragrammaton (YHWH, name of Yahweh), **2:** *386,* **7:** 1942, **10: 2814, 11:** 3063
Iao as variant of, **7:** 1944
Teutates (Celtic god), **2:** 428, 442, 443
Teutonic mythology, *see* Germanic mythology
Tewa Indians (Pueblo), **9:** 2300f
Tezcatlipoca (Mexican god), **1:** 217, 219
colours of, **3:** 640
as jaguar, **1:** *131*
maize and, *see* Xipe Totec
mirror symbol of, **8:** 2042
skull representing (?), **1:** 217
Thales of Miletus, eclipse predicted by, **3:** 772
Thalestris (Amazon), **1:** 119
Thalia (one of the Graces), **4:** 1145
Thalia (Muse), **7:** 1905
Thanatos (Greek god of death), **3:** 617, *710*
Thanksgiving Day, 5: 1214
Thebes (Egypt):
Amun-Re and, **3:** 789f, **5:** 1402
creation myth of priesthood of, **2:** 535
Thebes (Greece), Dionysus and, **3:** 635f
Thecla, St, 7: 1922
martyrdom of, **7:** *1986*
theism, 7: 1849
Themiscyra (now Terme; Turkey), Amazons and, **1:** 117
Theodore (7th cent. archbishop of Canterbury), **1: 130**
Theodosius I, Emperor, Olympic Games abolished by, **4:** 1067
theogony (definition), **10: 2814**
theology, mystical and speculative distinguished, **7:** 1930
Theophilus of Adana, Satanic pact and, **8:** 2110
Theophilus of Antioch (Christian writer), on immortality, **5:** 1415
theophoric names, 7: 1940–1
theosophy, Theosophical Society, **1:** 258f, 291ff, **10: 2814–16**
Mrs Besant and, **1:** 258, **10:** 2814, 2815, 2816
Mme Blavatsky and, **1:** 258, 291ff, **10:** 2814
Golden Dawn and, **4:** 1131, 1132
Krishnamurti and, **1:** 258, 259, **10:** 2815–16
Papus and, **8:** 2125
G. W. Russell and, **9:** 2442
St-Germain and, **9:** 2461
Rudolf Steiner and, **1:** 258, **10:** 2693f
Thomas Taylor and, **10:** 2809
A. E. Waite and, **11:** 2979
Yeats and, **11:** 3067
Theravada (Buddhism), **2:** 358
in Ceylon, **2:** 358, **10:** 2585ff
in Conjeeveram, **2:** 360
in Southeast Asia, **10:** 2585, 2648
Thérèse, *see* Teresa
Thermes (Lapp god), **6:** *1606*
Thersites, killed by Achilles, **1:** 119
Theseus (Greek hero), **10: 2817–21**
Amazons and, **1:** 119, **10:** 2819
Athens and, **9:** 2351, **10:** 2817f, 2821
Dioscuri and, **10:** 2820
Helen of Troy and, **10:** 2819–20
Minos and, **10:** 2820
Minotaur, **10:** 2818, *2818*
Pirithous and, **8:** 2170, **10:** 2819
sword and, **10:** *2750*
underworld visited by, **5:** 1266, **8:** 2168–70, **10:** 2819
Thesmophoria (festival of Demeter), **3:** 621, **4:** 968
Thespiae (Greece), cult of Eros at, **3:** 829, 830
Thespis (Greek drama), **3:** 697
Thessalonians, St Paul's epistles to, **8:** 2148
Thetis (nereid, mother of Achilles), **1:** 65, 66, **8:** 2031
on Portland Vase, **3:** *830*
theurgy, 10: 2821–4
Neoplatonism and, **7:** 1968, **8:** 2259, 2260, **10:** 2821ff
Thibault, Julie, 1: 240f, *240*
Thinite Period (Egyptian history), **3:** 788
thirteen, 8: 2026, **10: 2824–5**
as baker's dozen, **10:** 2825
Friday and, **3:** 606
twelve and, **10:** 2825
witchcraft and, **10:** 2825
Thjazi (giant; Scandinavian mythology), **6:** 1642
Tholen, W., object reading and, **8:** 2042
Thomas, John (founder of the Christadelphians), **9:** 2521
Thomas, St (Didymus; apostle), **7:** 1989, **11:** 2903
Thomas à Kempis, 9: 2318, 2526
Thomas the Rhymer, 9: 2503f
Thompson, Frederic L. (automatic painter), *see* Thompson-Gifford case
Thompson, Sir Henry, cremation and, **2:** 541
Thompson, Stith (student of folktales), **4:** 1009
Thompson-Gifford case (automatic art), **1:** 206-7
Thor (Scandinavian god), **9:** 2483, **10: 2825–8**
Bifrost not crossed by, **9:** 2333–4
birch tree sacred to, **1:** 265
earth and, **10:** 2825
giants and, **4:** 1103, **10:** 2826–8
Geirrod, **6:** 1642, **10:** 2826
Hrungnir, **10:** 2826
Hymir, **10:** 2826
Skrymir, **4:** 1103, **10:** 2828
Thrym, **5:** 1205, **6:** 1642
hammer of (Mjölnir), **3:** 737, **5:** 1205, **6:** 1641–2, **10:** 2826, *2827*
Loki and, **6:** 1641, 1642, **10:** 2826–8
Midgard Serpent and, **9:** 2486, **10:** 2826, *2827*
oak and, **10:** 2826
sons of, **9:** 2486
thunder and lightning and, **10:** 2826
wife of (Sif), **3:** 737, **10:** 2825
thorn, holy of Glastonbury, **4:** *1113,* 1114, *1114,* **5:** 1229
Thoth (Egyptian god), **3:** 791, *792*
baboon and, **1:** 129
Book of the Dead and, **9:** 2377
Hermes identified with, **5:** 1290
Hermes Trismegistus identified with, **3:** 791
Horus and, **5:** 1359
ibis and, **3:** 791
in judgement of the dead, **3:** 791, **6:** 1541
Thothmes IV (pharaoh), Sphinx of Giza and, **3:** 704
thought transference, *see* telepathy
Thracian Rider god, 10: 2828–9
thread, 10: 2709
three, 8: 2025, **10: 2830–3**
Celts and, **2:** 443, **4:** 965–6, **6:** 1639
see also triple deities, Celtic, *below*
completeness of, **8:** 2026, **10:** 2831f
fifteen and, **4:** 939
in Greece, *see* Cerberus; Geryon; triple deities, Greek, *below*
luckiness of, **1:** 113, **10:** 2830, 2831
names adding to, **1:** 113, **8:** 2023, 2024, **10:** 2830
in the New Testament, **10:** 2832
one and, **10:** 2830
in Pythagoreanism, **9:** 2316
Renaissance humanism and, **9:** 2372–3, **10:** 2832
in Scottish and Border ballads, **9:** 2503ff
three-headed dog, in Greek mythology, *see* Cerberus
three heads of Thracian Rider god, **10:** 2828
three magi, **6:** 1680, **10:** *2833*
triple deities, **10:** 2832
Celtic, **2:** 345, 443, **4:** 966, **5:** 1239
Christian, *see* Trinity
Greek, **10:** 2832
Hecate as, **5:** 1257
see also Fates; Furies; Gorgons; Graces
Hindu (Brahman), **10:** 2832–3
Scandinavian, *see* Norns
two and, **10:** 2830
see also triangle
threshold, doorway, **5:** 1364, 1365, **9:** 2389f, **10: 2833–4**
Janus and, **6:** 1483f
see also key
throne mysticism (Merkabah), **2:** 382f, **4:** 895, **10: 2834–5**
Thrym (giant), Thor and, **5:** 1205, **6:** 1642
Thugs (Indian secret society), **6:** 1556, **10: 2835–6**
thumb:
in baptism, **4:** 1089
of Finn, **4:** 966
in palmistry, **5:** 1201
as phallic symbol, **4:** 1089
in Trinity symbol, **4:** *1087*
see also mano cornuta
Thumb, Tom (dwarf), **3:** *738*
thunder-beard (plant), *see* houseleek
thunderbird, 8: *2106,* **10: 2836–7, 11:** 3105
thunderbolt:
Donar and, **4:** 1086
Jupiter and, **10:** *2602*

Thunor and, **4:** 1086
Zeus and, **5:** 1205, *1301,* **11:** 3089, *3089*
Zulus and, **11:** 3105
'Thunderbolt Vehicle' (Tantric Buddhism), *see* Buddhism, Tantric
thunder and lightning:
in augury, **1:** 194, **3:** 848, **11:** 3004–5
Australian spirit of, **11:** *3003*
Jupiter and, **6:** 1552
mushroom and, **7:** 1908
protection against:
acorn, **5:** 1368, **8:** 2035
hazel, **8:** 2203
houseleek, **5:** 1369
laurel, **6:** 1610–11
oak, **8:** 2034–5, **10:** 2604
olive, **8:** 2060
owl, **8:** 2098
palm, **8:** 2116
plants, various, **10:** 2604
prehistoric stone axes, etc. ('thunder weapons'), **4:** 1086
Thor and, **10:** 2826
woodpecker and, **11:** 3060
Zeus and, **11:** 3093
Zulus and, **11:** 3105
see also storm; thunderbird; thunderbolt
'thunder weapons', **4:** 1086
Thunor (Anglo-Saxon god), **4:** 1086
Thursday, **3:** 606, 607, **4:** 1086
see also Maundy Thursday
thyrsos, 10: 2837
Tiahuanaco (Peru), **5:** 1424
Tiamat (Mesopotamian mythology), **2:** 536–7, **3:** 690, **7:** 1734, 1821, 1822–3, **10: 2837**
Tibet, 10: 2838–44
breath, as the soul, in, **2:** 336
Buddhism in, **10:** 2839ff
Buddha, **5:** *1397*
see also lamas, Tibetan
China and, **10:** 2838, 2843
drum, made of skulls, from, **3:** *726*
exorcizing dagger of, **11:** *3021*
harvest festival in, **5:** 1218
judgement of the dead and, **5:** 1266
mandalas of, **6:** *1551, 1716*
masks of, **7:** *1762,* 1763
oracles of, **11:** 2867
prayer wheel in, **10:** *2843,* **11:** 3015
pre-Buddhist religion of (Bon), **10:** 2839
priests of, *see* lamas, Tibetan
reincarnation and, **6:** 1589f, **9:** 2348, **10:** 2841–2
rosary in, **9:** 2420
wheel of life in, **6:** *1558, 1559,* **11:** *3015*
see also Book of the Dead (Tibet)
Tigari cult (Africa), **7:** 1979–80
tiger, 10: 2844
white, in China, **11:** 3018
Tiglath-Pileser III (king of Assyria), **6:** 1644, *1644*
Tijani Order (Sufism), **10:** 2716
tiki *(hei-tiki;* Polynesian amulet), **6:** *1478,* 1480, **10:** *2595,* **2844**
Tilea, M. Virgil, National Socialism and, **7:** 1946
time, 11: 2845–52
St Augustine on, **11:** 2845
Indian beliefs concerning, **11:** 2846–7, 2848
Mithraism and, **11:** 2848
Rome and, **9:** 2479, **11:** 2848
wheel as symbol of, **11:** 3014f
in Zoroastrianism, *see* Zurvan
see also calendar; cycles of time; Dunne, J. W.; Father Time; Golden Age; history
tin (metal), **2:** 522
Tinia (Tin; Etruscan god), **3:** 849
tinkers, 11: 2853–5
Tintagel (Cornwall), **1:** 156, **2:** 390, *390,* 391
Tipitaka (Buddhism), **10:** 2585
Tiruvannamalai (India), *see* Arunachala
Tiryns (Greece), excavation of, **5:** 1167
Tisiphone (Greek mythology), **4:** 918, 1054
Titans (Greek mythology), **2:** 546, **3:** 751
Dionysus killed by, **3:** 742, 859, **8:** 2085
see also Cronus
Tityroi, 9: 2482
Tiw (Anglo-Saxon god), **4:** 1084
Tiwa Indians (Pueblo), **9:** 2300
Tiwat (Luwian sun god), **5:** 1323
Tiwaz (Germanic god), **4:** 1084
Tiyat (Palaic sun god), **5:** 1323
Tiye, Queen (of Egypt), **8:** 2070
Tlaloc (Mexican god), **1:** 219, 220, **7:** 1909, 1910, **11:** 3006
Tlazolteotl (Aztec goddess), **1:** 273
Tloque Nahuaque (Mixtec god), **2:** *538*
toad, 7: 1910, **11: 2855–7**
basilisk and, **11:** 2856
bear sacrifice and, **11:** 2856
evil eye and, **4:** 889
horses controlled by toadmen, **11:** 2856
jewel in head of, **6:** 1514, **11:** 2856
Tlaloc and, **7:** 1909, 1910
as witches' familiar, **3:** 755, 866, **4:** 914, **10:** 2626, **11:** 2855
toadstone, 6: 1514, **11:** 2856
toadstool, 7: 1910
tobacco, 8: 2166–7, **11: 2858**
in medicine, **11:** 2858
North American Indians and, **8:** 2010, **11:** 2858
shamanism and, **3:** 712
Tobias and Sarah, 1: 167, **3:** 870
Todaiji Temple (Japan), **6:** 1488, *1497*
toe:
healing by, King Pyrrhus and, **4:** 908
of Vishnu, as source of Ganges, **4:** 1068
Toland, John (Druidic organizer), **3:** 722
Toledo, Council of (AD447), Devil defined by, **5:** 1348
Tollund, hanged man of, **9:** 2453, *2453*
Tolpudddle martyrs, 8: 2038
Tolstoyans (communistic religious movement), **2:** 497
Toltecs, 1: 214, 216
carved figures of, at Tula, **1:** 190
fire god of, *see* Xiuhtecuhtli
Maya and, **7:** 1772
tomato, 6: 1660, 1718
tombstone, gravestone, **10:** 2706
Ethiopian, **10:** *2707*
in London cemetery, **2:** *373*
Tomlinson, A. J., 8: 2161
Tomlinson, Dr H. (physician and radiesthetist), **9:** 2331, **11:** 2950–1
Tomlinson, Homer, 5: 1332, **8:** 2161
Tomlinson, Milton, 5: 1332, **8:** 2161
Tomzcyk, Stanislawa (Hon. Mrs Everard Feilding; medium), **7:** 1792
Tonatiuh (Mexican sun god), **1:** 214–15, *216, 217,* 218
Tonga (Polynesia), **8:** 2230f
Tongs (Chinese secret society), **11: 2858**
tonton macoute, **11:** 2969
Tooth, Temple of the (Ceylon), **8:** 2196, *2198,* **10:** *2585, 2586,* 2587
toothache, St Apollonia and, **3:** 648, **9:** *2464*
topaz, 6: 1511, *1513*
top hat, 5: 1244
topheth, **8:** 2184, *2184*
topping out (building ceremony), **2:** 362
Torah (Judaism), **6:** 1531, 1532, 1536, **11: 2858**
Torquemada, Tomas de, 5: 1286
tortoise:
in China, **3:** 693, **8:** 2188
hare and, **5:** *1211*
invention of lyre and, **5:** 1289
Vishnu incarnate as, **5:** 1420, *1421,* **11:** 2960
torture:
of heretics, **5:** 1283, *1284–5*
by squassation, **1:** 92
by strappado, **1:** *92,* 92
of witches, **3:** 853, 854, *854, 855,* **4:** *1077,* 1079
at Bamberg, **1:** 227f, *227, 228*
Louis Gaufridi, **1:** 92
totem, totemism, **1:** 128, **11: 2859–63**
in Australia, **1:** 128, 198, **4:** 1012, **11:** 2859–60
Durkheim on, **9:** 2358
in Egypt, doubts concerning existence of, **1:** 128, **3:** 790
Europe, ancient, totemism, not discernible in, **11:** 2863
exogamy and, **5:** 1429
in Melanesia, **11:** 2863
Nilotic, **7:** 2002
North American Indians and, **7:** 2012, **11:** 2859, 2861, *2861, 2862*
origin of the word, **11:** 2861
Touareg, 11: 2863–5
touch, 4: 908, 956
see also king's evil; 'touching the bun'
'touching the bun', 9: 2510
tourmaline, 6: 1511
tower, symbolism of, **6:** 1603
see also Tower Struck by Lightning (Tarot card)
Tower of Babel, 3: 799, **11: 2866–7**
by Breughel, **2:** 341, *341*
French, 15th cent., **10:** *2650*
Nimrod as builder of, **11:** 2867
seven and, **11:** 2867
ziggurat as original of, **11:** 2867
Tower of London:
building of, **2: 454**
haunting of, **4:** 1099, **5:** *1224,* 1227
ravens at, **2:** 557
towers of silence (Parsees), **8:** 2139, *2139,* 2140–1, **11:** *3099*
Tower Struck by Lightning (Falling Tower, Fire of Heaven, House of God; Tarot card), **8:** 2146–7, **10:** 2792, 2793
trance, 11: 2867–70
St Catherine of Siena and, **2:** 425
drugs and, **11:** 2867
ecstasy and, **3:** 778, **10:** 2697–8
in magic, **10:** 2868f
mediums and, **7:** 1783f, **11:** 2869f
in theurgy, **10:** 2823
oracular, **8:** 2073
at Delphi, **11:** 2867
in Tibet, **11:** 2867
in Voodoo, **11:** 2867f, 2870
in yoga, **11:** *2869,* 2870
see also hypnotism
transcendent (definition), **5:** 1412
Trancendentalists (philosophical group), **7:** 1993, **10:** 2809
transmigration of souls, *see* reincarnation
transubstantiation, 7: 1768, **9:** 2450, **11: 2870**
trataka (yoga), **11:** 3074
treasure:
dwarfs and, **3:** 735f
giants and, **6:** 1477 1478
sleeping heroes and, **10:** 2614–15
see also El Dorado; treasure magic
treasure magic, 7: 1954, **11: 2870–2**, 2986
tree, trees, **11: 2873–80**
in Cinderella stories, **2:** 484–5
cross of Jesus and, *see* Crucifixion, tree as the cross
May Day and, *see* May Day, trees and
in the Old Testament, **11:** 2874f, 2878
as oracle, **11:** 2878
worship of trees, *see* tree spirits
see also almond; apple; arbutus; ash; banyan; bay; beech; birth; bo-tree; cedar; Christmas tree; cypress; elder; elm; fig; fir; hawthorn; hazel; holly; laurel; myrrh; myrtle; oak; olive; palm; pine; rowan; sycamore; thorn, holy, of Glastonbury; vine; willow; yew
also evergreens; forest; garden; grove; resin; Tree of Life; world tree

tree of Jesse, 11: *2874*
Tree of the Knowledge of Good and Evil and Tree of Life (Christianity), **2:** 538, **3:** 859–60, **4:** 979f
Crucifixion and, **2:** 552, **6:** *1707*
in Mexico, **11:** *2874*
in 13th cent. MS, **6:** *1706*
Tree of Life, 11: 2872, 2879
Cabalist (sefirotic tree), **2:** *384,* 384f, *385,* **8:** 2146
  in modern magic, **2:** 387
  Tarot and, **10:** 2789
Christian, *see* Tree of the Knowledge of Good and Evil
Lull and, **5:** *1291*
see also world tree
tree spirits, gods; tree worship, **11:** 2874ff, 2878–9, 2942
Ashanti, **1:** 162
in Egypt, **9:** *2346,* **11:** 2874
  Osiris as, **4:** 967
Greek, **11:** 2876f, 2878–9
  see also dryads
Indian, **1:** 132, **5:** 1436, **8:** *2243,* **11:** 2875
Roman, **11:** 2876, 2878–9
see also Green Man
Trent, Council of (1545–63), **2:** 474
Trfing (magic sword), **3:** 737
Triad Society (Chinese secret society), **2:** *461,* 463
trial by ordeal, 8: 2037, 2079
bread in, **2:** 331
Congolese, **2:** 509
host in, **8:** 2036
Masai, **7:** 1754
triangle, 10: 2830f
magic circle and, **9:** 2399
see also hexagram
trickster, 11: 2881–5
Loki as, **6:** 1643, **11:** 2883
North American Indians and, **4:** 1161–2, **11:** 2881–2, 2884f
  see also Coyote; raven, as trickster
spider, West African, *see* Ananse
Triglav (Slav god), **10:** 2611
trinity, 11: 2885
in Christianity, *see* Trinity, the
in Hinduism (Brahma, Vishnu, Shiva), **1:** 324, **11:** 2960
see also three, triple deities
Trinity, the (Christianity), **10:** 2831, 2832
in baptism, **1:** 231
fingers symbol of, **4:** *1087,* 1089
in 14th cent. MS, **5:** *1396*
Eliphas Levi on, **10:** 2830
Virgin Mary and, **7:** 1750
rejected by Judaism, **6:** 1531
triple head representing the, **5:** *1236*
see also Holy Ghost; Jesus
Triptolemus (Greek mythology), **3:** 621, *804, 806,* **7:** 1909
Trismosin, Salomon, on the panacea, **3:** 811
Tristan (Tristram), **11: 2885–9**
in Arthurian legend, **1:** 154, **11:** 3025
Brittany and, **2:** 347
dragon killed by, **11:** 2886
Wagner and, **11:** 2885–6, 2889, 2978
Trita (Hindu god), **3:** 691
Trithemius (abbot of Spanheim), **3:** 618
Triton (Greek merman), **11:** 2897
Troano Manuscript, 6: *1615*
Trobriand Islands, yam harvest festival in, **5:** *1215*
Trogenburg, Trogin (maze), **7:** 1775
Trojan War, 11: 2890f, *2891, 2892–3*
Achilles and, **1:** 65–6
Aphrodite and, **1:** 136
Athene and, **1:** 142, 186, **1:** 2890
catalogue of ships, **11:** 3090
origin of, **1:** 66, 142
Penthesilea and, **1:** 119
see also Agamemnon; Helen of Troy; Troy
troll, 11: 2889
trough eyes, 4: 888
trout, 11: 2890
Troy (Ilion), **11: 2890–5**
Carl Blegen and, **11:** 2891ff
founding of, by Dardanus, **4:** 995
mazes and, **7:** 1775
Schliemann and, **5:** 1167, **11:** 2894
see also Cassandra; Hesione; Misenus; Trojan War
Troy Towns (mazes), **7:** 1775
Trude, Frau, 11: 3024
True Black Magic (*The Secret of Secrets;* grimoire), **3:** 607, **5:** 1182, **9:** 2397f
True Cross (Christianity), **2:** 550f, **9:** 2353
trumpet, 11: 2895–7
in Nepal, **10:** *2840*
Truth (cosmic order), in Zoroastrianism, **1:** 3100f
see also Ahura Mazdah; Ohrmazd
tsaddikism (Hasidism), **5:** 1220
T-shaped cross (*crux commissa,* St Anthony's cross, Tau cross), **2:** 550, 552, **10:** 2805
Tsimshian Indians, moon and, **5:** 1287
Tsou Yen (Chinese philosopher), **1:** 69
Tu (Ku; Polynesian god), **8:** 2230
Tuesday, 3: 606, 607, **4:** 1084
see also Shrove Tuesday
Tugdual, Archbishop, 11: 2987, *2988*
Tugdual, St, 2: 349
Tulouff, Martin (witch), **2:** 350, 447
Tunstead Farm (Derbyshire), skull at, **5:** 1226
Tuonela (Finnish land of the dead), **4:** 959–60
Turan (Etruscan goddess), Venus identified with, **3:** 849
turkey, at Christmas, **2:** 480
Turms (Etruscan god), Mercury identified with, **3:** 849
Turner, Victor W., ritual studied by, **9:** 2394ff
Turner, William (herbalist), on mandrake, **6:** 1717, 1720
turquoise, 6: 1511, *1513*
Turin shroud, 11: 2897–98
turtle, Vishnu incarnate as, *see* tortoise, Vishnu incarnate as
Tutankhamen (pharaoh), **3:** 790, **5:** 1402
amulets of meteoric iron in tomb of, **6:** 1454
corn-mummy from tomb of, **11:** 2939–40
gold coffin of, **3:** *786–7*
gold sarcophagus of, **4:** *1129*
Nefertiti and, **5:** 1400
scarab jewel from tomb of, **9:** *2488*
Twelfth Night, 2: 483, **11:** 2900
bean cake and, **1:** 242
twelve, 1: 112, **8:** 2026, **10:** 2831, **11: 2898–900**
completeness of, **11:** 2897
eleven and, **3:** 808
in Revelation, **11:** 2897, 2898–900
seven and, **11:** 2897
thirteen and, **10:** 2825
twelve apostles of Jesus, **11:** 2898
twelve days of Christmas, **11:** *2898, 2899,* 2900, *2900*
twelve Imams, *see* Imams
twelve Labours of Hercules, **5:** 1279, **11:** 2897–8
twelve Olympian gods of Greece, **5:** 1168, **11:** 2898
twelve tribes of Israel, **6:** 1643, **11:** 2898
twenty-two, 8: 2026
Hebrew alphabet and, **1:** 112, **2:** 383
Tarot pack and, **1:** 112, **2:** 387
Twilight of the Gods (Scandinavian mythology), *see* Ragnarok
twins, 11: 2901–5
birth of, **1:** 275, **11:** 2902
Brazilian myth of, **2:** 329
Kwakiutl Indians and, **9:** 2474
Mani, twin self of, **4:** 1115, **11:** 2903
in Nigeria, **11:** 2902, *2905*
Nuer and, **11:** 2902
Ohrmazd and Ahriman as, **11:** 3107
in the Old Testament, **11:** 2902–3
salmon and, **9:** 2474
telepathy and, **11:** 2904
St Thomas as twin of Jesus, **11:** 2903
twin gods, **11:** 2903
  Germanic and Scandinavian, **4:** 1086–7
  Greek, *see* Dioscuri
  Indian, *see* Asvins
zodiac sign of the Twins, *see* Gemini
see also Hercules, Iphicles and; Romulus and Remus
two, 1: 113, **8:** 2025, **11: 2905–6**
Devil and, **11:** 2906
eleven and, **3:** 808
evil and, **1:** 113, **8:** 2068, **11:** 2905f
names adding to, **1:** 113, **8:** 2023, **11:** 2905
one and, **8:** 2068, **10:** 2830
pairs of animals in Noah's ark, **11:** 2906
in Pythagoreanism, **9:** 2316
three and, **10:** 2830
two-faced god, *see* Janus
woman and, **11:** 2905f
Two Brothers, Tale of the, **4:** 1007
Twrch Trwyth (boar; Arthurian legend), **1:** 130, 153, **4:** 966, **6:** 1674
Tyburn (London), gallows at, **2:** 555
Tylor, Sir Edward (anthropologist), **1:** 132, *132,* **4:** 1009
Tylwyth Teg (Welsh fairies), **4:** 902
Tyno Helig (Welsh lost land legend), **4:** 995–6
Typhon, 4: 1103, **9:** 2529
Etna and, **5:** 1269
Set identified with, **3:** 790, **9:** 2529, 2533
Tyr (Scandinavian god), **4:** 1084, **9:** 2483, **11: 2906**
Fenris wolf bound by, **4:** 1084, **11:** *3048*
at Ragnarok, **9:** 2486
Tyre (Phoenician city), **8:** 2114, 2180, 2183
Tyrnoc (Dyrnawg; giant), cauldron of, **4:** 1149
Tyrrell, G.N.M., on ghosts, **4:** 1101
Tzara, Tristan, 1: 147

U

Ubaydallah (Mahdi), **6:** 1699
Ueueteotl (Mexican god), **1:** 217
Uffington, white horse of, **1:** 128
UFOs, *see* flying saucers
Ugarit (Phoenician city, near modern Ras Shamra), texts from, **1:** 168f, 222f, **3:** 704, **8:** 2180, **10:** 2761ff
Uggae (Babylonian death god), **3:** 616
Uighurs, Mu and, **6:** 1614f
Ukko (Ilmarinen, Jumala; Finnish god), **4:** 958
rainbow and, **9:** 2333
salt and, **9:** 2475
Ukobach (demon), **3:** *861*
Ullikummi (Hittite monster), **5:** 1324
***Ulster Cycle*, 2:** 565f
Ulysses (Greek hero), *see* Odysseus
Uma (wife of Shiva; Hinduism), **5:** 1314, **10:** 2573
Umall (Irish legend), *see* Cumall
Umbanda (Macumba; Brazilian spiritism), **7:** 1981, **10:** *2640, 2642,* 2644–5, **11:** *2974, 2975*
umbilical cord, 11: 2907
umbrella, 10: 2605, **11: 2907**
in Cruikshank cartoon, **10:** *2605*
in Ethiopia, **3:** *841*
of peacock feathers, **8:** 2153
umra (Islam), **6:** 1468
Unas (pharaoh), **9:** 2489
unconscious, the (subconscious):
art and, **1:** 148f
J. W. Dunne's view of, **8:** 2269

Freud and, **4:** 1048ff
Jung and, **11:** 3002
  collective unconscious, **6:** 1549
psi and, **10:** 2665
revealed through automatisms, **8:** 2090
  see also automatic art; automatic writing; mediums
water as symbol of, **11:** 3002
see also collective unconscious
unction, anointing, **8:** 2049f, **11: 2907**
anointing of Jesus, **8:** *2049,* 2050
anointing of kings, **6:** *1572,* **8:** 2049–50
unction of the sick (Catholic sacrament), **8:** 2050
  see also extreme unction
Uncumber, St (Santa Liberata, St Wilgeforte), **11: 2907**
undines (elementals), 3: 802f
unguents, witches', *see* flying ointment
Uni (Etruscan goddess), **3:** 849
unicorn, 11: 2908–10
in alchemy, **11:** 2910
bear and, **1:** 243
in the Bible, **11:** 2909
captured by virgin, **11:** *2908,* 2909
in China *(ki-lin),* **3:** 693, **8:** 2188, **11:** 2910
in Christian symbolism, **11:** 2909
horn of, **11:** 2908f, 2909–10
lion and, **11:** 2909, *2910*
of Mohenjo-daro, **5:** *1434, 1435*
opposites, combination of, symbolized by, **11:** 2910
unidentified flying objects, *see* flying saucers
United States of America:
Divine Principles sect in, **3:** 663
extra-sensory perception studied in, **8:** 2278
  see also Duke University
first saint of, *see* Cabrini, St Frances
folklore of, **11:** 2911–20
  American Indians and, **11:** 2917
  hero legends in, **11:** 2919f
  Negroes and, **11:** 2917–18
  pig in weather lore, **8:** 2192
Negroes in, **7:** 1959, **11:** 2917–18
Rosicrucianism in, **9:** 2433
witchcraft in, *see* Salem witches
see also Black Muslims; Mardi Gras; North American Indians; Ozarks; snake-handling cults; Washington, George
Unity School of Christianity, 7: 1994
universe, cosmos, nature of:
Chinese view of, **6:** 1712
  see also Yin and Yang
god's role in, Graeco-Roman views on, **8:** 2240
man as copy of, *see* macrocosm and microcosm
the sex act and, **8:** 2177
see also cosmic order; cosmogony; great chain of being; one, the One, as divine principle; spheres, heavenly
Universe (World, Tarot card), **8:** *2094,* 2146, **10:** *2793,* 2794
unknowing, in Christian mysticism, **3:** 634
see also Cloud of Unknowing
'unknown gods', 4: 896
unleavened bread, at Passover, **6:** 1536
untouchables (India), **2:** 416, **5:** 1321
Upanishads (Hindu sacred texts), **5:** 1307, 1309ff, **11:** 2930–1
Brahman in, **1:** 323, **5:** 1309ff
dualism in, **3:** 731
mysticism and, **7:** 1933ff
Upelluri (Hittite giant), **5:** 1324
Up-helly-aa (Shetland fire festival), **4:** *969,* **7:** *1996*
Uppsala, *see* Old Uppsala
Ur (Mesopotamia):
Chaldeans and, **2:** 446
goat and, **10:** *2761*
moon god of, **6:** 1459
Urania (Muse), **7:** 1905
Uranus (Greek god), **1:** 135, **10:** 2601, **11: 2921**
Uranus (planet), in astrology, **1:** 175, 180, **11:** 2921
Urban II (pope), First Crusade preached by, **11:** 2993, *2996*
Urban VI (pope), **2:** 427
Urban VIII (pope), **6:** *1474*
eclipse feared by, **6:** 1686
on exorcism, **3:** 873
attempt on life of, **6:** 1476
Uriel (angel), north and, **3:** 640
urine, 2: 380, **8:** *2128,* **11: 2921**
see also witch bottle
urn, funerary:
Ashanti, **1:** 162
Brazilian, **3:** 571
Zapotec, **7:** *1838*
Urnfield culture, Celts and, **2:** 437
Ursula, St, and the 11,000 virgins, **11:** 2907
Uruk (Mesopotamian city), *see* Erech
ushabti (Egypt), **1:** *300,* **7:** 1904
Utnapishtim (Babylonian flood legend), **3:** 817, **4:** 992, 1106, **9:** 2456
Utu (Mesopotamian sun god), *see* Shamash

V

Vafthrudnir (giant; Scandinavian mythology), **11:** 3035
Vaikuntha (paradise of Vishnu), **8:** *2132*
Väinämoinen (Finnish hero), **4:** 958, 960f
Vairocana (Buddha), **2:** 360
Vaisheshika (Hinduism), **11:** 3070
Vaisyas (caste; Hinduism), **2:** 415f
Vajrapani (Bodhisattva), **10:** *2839*
Vajrayana (Tantric Buddhism), *see* Buddhism, Tantric
Valdesi, *see* Waldenses
Valencia, Pedro de, on Basque witchcraft, **1:** 236
Valentine card, 5: *1249, 1253,* **8:** *2204,* 2205
Valentinus (Gnostic), **3:** 730, **4:** 1115, 1116ff
Valhalla (Scandinavian mythology), **8:** 2047, 2134, **9:** 2346, **11: 2922**
Valkyries, 4: 920, 1086, **8:** 2043, 2047
see also Brynhild
valley, symbolism of, **6:** 1602
Vallin, Pierre (witch), **4:** 1043
vampire, 11: 2922–8
see also Dracula
Vandy, Edgar, 7: 1786–7
van Helmont, Jan Baptist, 3: 810, **8:** 2180
Vanir (Scandinavian deities of fertility), **4:** 1051f, **9:** 2483
in Germanic mythology, **4:** 1086
see also Freyja; Freyr
Varaha (Vishnu), **1:** 129, **9:** *2349,* **11:** 2960
Varney the Vampire, **11:** *2923*
Varuna (Indian god), **4:** 886, **5:** 1435, **10:** 2602
Vasudeva (Hinduism), **11:** 2960
Vasudhara (Buddhist earth goddess), **6:** *1715*
Vaudois, *see* Waldenses
Vayu (Iranian god), **11:** 3103
Vedanta, 7: 1937, **11: 2929–35,** 3070
Buddhism and, **2:** 360
as a dualist system, **3:** 731
Vedas (Hindu sacred texts), **1:** 323, **5:** 1307ff, 1434ff, **11:** 2930–1, **2936**
creation myth of Purusha in, **2:** 415–16
dragon myths of, **3:** 691
eagle in, **3:** 746
god of the dead in, **3:** 616
sacrifice in, **5:** 1307f, 1435, **9:** 2456
social divisions in, **2:** 415
yoga study of (jnana yoga), **11:** 3071
see also Upanishads; Vedanta
Veddas (forest tribe of Ceylon), **11: 2936–8**
vegetation spirits, deities, 11: 2938–43
Adonis as, **1:** 138, **3:** 739
Attis as, **1:** 193, **2:** 583, **4:** 967, **11:** 2941
Baal as, **1:** 222, 223, **8:** 2182–3, **10:** 2762, **11:** 2940–1
Janus as, **6:** 1484
king and, **6:** 1566ff, **11:** 2941
Osiris as, **4:** 967, **8:** 2088, **11:** 2939
Tammuz as, **10:** 2776
see also Demeter; tree spirits
Veles (Slav god), *see* Volos
Vena (wicked king; Hindu mythology), **3:** *732*
Veneration of the Cross ('Creeping to the Cross'; Good Friday ritual), **3:** 766
Venice, Doge of, sea married to, **9:** *2513*
Venner, Thomas (preacher), **9:** 2521, *2522*
Venus (goddess), **7:** *1898,* **9:** 2412, **11: 2943–7**
Aphrodite identified with, **1:** 135, **11:** 2943
birth of, **1:** 135, *136*
copper and, **2:** 522
Cupid and Psyche and, **3:** 831
dove and, **3:** *681,* 682
emerald and, **3:** 813
Erycina, **11:** 2943–4
gardens and, **11:** 2943
green and, **2:** 522
  see also emerald *above*
Hadrian and, **11:** 2944
Julian Caesar and, **11:** 2944
Lancelot and, **6:** *1595*
Libra and, **6:** 1620
Mars and, **11:** *2946*
meaning of the name, **11:** 2943
of Milo, **1:** 138
myrtle and, **11:** 2946
pearl and, **8:** 2157
of Rhodes, **11:** *2943*
Rokeby Venus (Velazquez), **9:** *2539*
rose and, **9:** 2421
sewers and, **11:** 2946
Venus asleep (Delvaux), **1:** 137
Venus (planet), **11:** 2947
in astrology, **1:** 175, 180, **11:** 2947
jewels associated with, **3:** 813, **6:** 1511
in Mesopotamia, **6:** 1460, **10:** 2692
Mother Goddess and, **7:** 1895
see also Evening Star; Morning Star
Venuses, prehistoric, *see* faceless goddesses, Paleolithic
Verminus (Roman god of cattle worms), **9:** 2414
Veronica, St, veil of, **9:** *2352*
Verrall, Mrs, cross-correspondences and, **2:** 553f, **7:** 1787
Verrall, Helen (later Mrs W. H. Salter), cross-correspondences and, **2:** 553f
Versailles adventure (Moberly and Jourdain), **11: 2947–8**
verse, *see* poets, poetry
vervain (Cerealis, Demetria, Mercury's Blood, Persephonion, Tears of Juno/Isis), **11: 2948**
vessels of plenty, Celtic, **4:** 1147f
Vesta (Roman goddess), **5:** 1254, **9:** 2418, **11: 2949**
Hestia identified with, 5: 1300, **11:** 2949
Vestal Virgins, 2: 345, **5:** 1254, **11: 2949**
Vianney, Jean-Marie-Baptiste, *see* Curé of Ars
Vibhajyavadins (Distinctionists; Buddhist sect), **2:** 358
vibration, 11: 2949–51
see also radiesthesia; spheres, music of
Vidar (son of Odin), **9:** 2486
Vienna, Council of (1311), 9: 2318
vigil, 11: 2951
Vikar, King, Odin and, **8:** 2045
Vikings, 8: 2043, 2045
ship burials of, **4:** 1051
swords of, **10:** 2748
see also berserkers
Villa of the Mysteries (Pompeii), **3:** *636, 637,* **4:** *989, 1016,* **7:** *1926–7,* **11: 2951**
Villate, Joseph Rene, 11: 2988, *2988,* 2989
Vinalia (Roman festivals), **11:** 2943

Vincent, St, raven and, **2:** 557
vine, 11: 2952
Dionysus and, **3:** *634,* 635
viper's bugloss (herb), **5:** *1275,* 1276
Viracocha (Peruvian creator), **5:** 1424, 1425
Virgil, 11: 2952
in Dante's *Divine Comedy,* **2:** 602ff
on the Golden Age, **11:** 2851–2
magical reputation of, **8:** *2211*
see also Aeneid
Virgin (zodiac sign), *see* Virgo
virgin births, 11: 2952–6
of Jesus, **5:** 1420, **7:** 1747ff, **11:** 2952ff
virginity, 11: 2956
of Hera, annually restored, **4:** 1029
unicorn captured by a virgin, **11:** *2908, 2909*
white as symbol of, **11:** 3017
see also Mary, the Virgin; Vestal Virgins; virgin births
Virgin Mary, *see* Mary, the Virgin
Virgo (the Virgin; zodiac sign, in astrology), **1:** 175, 181, **11: 2957**
Vishnu (Indian god), **5:** 1313, 1314, 1435, **6:** 1629, **11: 2958–60**
asleep, on the serpent Ananta, **10:** *2614*
cosmic serpent Shesha and, **11:** 2960
Ganges and, **4:** 1068
Garuda and, **1:** 269, **5:** *1310*
incarnations of, **5:** 1420, **11:** 2960
as a boar (Varaha), **1:** 130, **9:** *2349,* **11:** 2960
as Buddha, **11:** 2960
as a dwarf, **11:** 2960
as a fish, **11:** 2960
as a man-lion, **11:** *2959,* 2960
as a tortoise (or turtle), **5:** *1421,* **11:** 2960
as a white horse, **9:** *2550–1*
see also Krishna; Rama; Vishvarupa
Indra and, **11:** 2958
lotus and, **11:** 2960
in mandala, **6:** *1714*
Narayana and, **5:** 1420, **11:** 2958
paradise of, **8:** *2132*
as sustainer of the universe, **1:** 324, **11:** 2960
time and, **11:** 2847
in trinity with Brahma and Shiva, **1:** 324, **11:** 2960
wife of, *see* Lakshmi
Vishvamitra (yogi), **9:** 2524
Vishvarupa (Vishnu), **6:** *1705*
visions, 11: 2961–6
apparitions, hallucinations, compared with, **11:** 2961f
of St Bernadette of Lourdes, **6:** 1653
of Blake, **1:** 283ff, **11:** 2963
Great Plains Indians and, **3:** 775, **4:** 1162f
of St Hildegard of Bingen, **5:** 1302, **11:** 2965
Virgin Mary seen in, **11:** 2965f, 2983
see also St Bernadette *above*
Visitation, Order of the, 4: 1033
visual illusions (optical illusions), **9:** *2292, 2293*
Visvarupa (serpent; Indian myth), **3:** 691
Vitus, St, dancing mania and, **2:** 600
Vivekananda, Swami (Hindu reformer), **5:** 1316, 1317, **9:** 2361
Vix (France), cauldron of, **2:** 428
vodun (spirits; Dahomey), **2:** 584ff, **11:** 2967
Vodyanoy (Slav water spirits), **10:** 2612
volantica (Roman witch), **6:** 1474
volcanoes:
St Brendan and, **2:** 339
as giants' burial-places, **4:** 1103
Hephaestus associated with, **5:** 1268, 1269f, **10:** 2620
origin of the word, **5:** 1270
see also Etna; obsidian; Santorin
Volcanus (Roman god), *see* Vulcan
völkisch movement, **7:** 1964ff, **10:** 2739
Vollrath, Hugo (occultist), **7:** 1945, *1946*
Volos (Veles; Slav god), **10:** 2610
Volsungs (Scandinavian heroes), **5:** 1298
Frigg and, **4:** 1051
shape-shifting and, **9:** 2553–6
Volta, La (witches' dance), **6:** 1476
Voltumna (Etruscan god), **3:** 849
Völuspá, end of the world in, **3:** 817, **9:** 2484f
Von Däniken, Erich, 11: 2966
Voodoo, 7: 1961, **11: 2967–76**
Dahomey and, **2:** 584, **11:** 2882–3
initiation of, **11:** 2972ff, 3096
magic and, **11:** 2967ff
marriage and, **11:** 2974f
obeah and, **11:** 2967f
origin of, **2:** 584, **11:** 2967
possession in, **3:** 713, **7:** 1961, **8:** 2239, **11:** 2867f, 2870, 2973–4
priests of, **11:** 2972ff
sex and, **11:** 2974f
Sirens in, **10:** *2588–9*
soul (*gros bon ange*), in, **11:** 2969ff
trance in, **11:** 2867f, 2870
see also Damballa; zombies
Voorthuizen, Louwrens van, *see* Lou
Vril Society (the Luminous Lodge), **6:** 1670
Vulcan (Volcanus; Roman god), **5:** 1270
Vulcano (island), Hephaestus and, **5:** 1270
vulture:
in augury, **1:** 194
founding of Rome and, **4:** 1027
in the Bible, **8:** 2158
in Egypt, **1:** *271*

W

Wachler, Dr Ernst, 7: 1964
waft (double), **3:** 672
Wagner, Richard, 11: 2977–9
Nibelungenlied and, **7:** 1999, **1:** 2978
Tristan and, **11:** 2885–6, 2889, 2978
Wahhabi sect (Islam), Sufism banned by, **10:** 2715
Wailing Wall (Jerusalem), **6:** *1501,* **8:** *2194*
Waite, A. E., 11: 2979
Cabala and, **2:** 387, **11:** 2979
Golden Dawn and, **4:** 1131, 1132, **11:** 2979
Tarot and, **2:** 406, **10:** *2790–3,* 2791
theosophy and, **11:** 2979
wake (burial), dancing at, **2:** 598
Wakefield, mystery play cycle of, **7:** 1922, 1923–4
Wakley, Thomas, magnetism and, **6:** 1695
Waldenses (Valdesi, Vaudois, Poor Men of Lyons), **2:** 473, **11: 2979–82**
phoenix in bestiary of, **8:** 2186
Waldo, Peter, 11: 2979–80
Waldorf School, 10: 2694
wallaby, 1: 128
Walpurgisnacht, witches and, **3:** 853
Walsingham, 11: 2983–4
Walworth Jumpers (Girlingites, Bible Christians, Children of God, English Shakers), **4: 1108, 11: 2984**
wampum beads, 6: 1456, *1458*
wand, 11: 2985–7
in magic, *see* magic wand
wandering bishops *(episcopi vagantes),* **11: 2987–90**
Wandering Jew (Ahasuerus), **11: 2990–1**
war:
Christian attitudes to, **2:** 470, 472
holy, *see* holy war
Mars as god of, **7:** 1743f
superstitions revived in time of, **10:** 2731
see also armies
Warboys, witches of, **5:** *1379,* 1382
Wardley, James (Shaker), **9:** 2545
Warminster (Wilts), flying saucers and, **4:** 1001
warts, cure of:
ash tree, **1:** 160
cat's tail, **2:** 420
knotted string, **10:** 2711
Lord's Prayer, **5:** 1418
pebbles, **10:** 2708
pins, **8:** 2102
snails, **10:** 2620
spider's web, **10:** 2655
tobacco juice, **11:** 2858
Washington, George, Freemasonry and, **4:** 1038, *1038–9*
Waste Land (Arthurian legend), **4:** 1147, 1152f
Watchers, the, 3: 628, **4:** 1102, 1121
Watchman movement (Africa), **9:** 2522
water, 11: 2997–3002
in alchemy, **11:** 3002
chaos and, **11:** 3001
in creation myths, **1:** 229, **2:** 533, 535, 536
the dead, their need of, *see refrigerium*
divination by (hydromancy), **9:** 2506
dragon and, **3:** 690
in Easter customs, **3:** 763
in Egypt, **1:** 229, 231, **9:** 2345, *2346*
see also Nile
as element, **3:** 801f
end of the world and, **3:** 815
evil spirits and, **3:** 872
fertility and, **4:** 936
green and, **3:** 813
harvest and, **2:** 518, **5:** 1214, 1215, 1217
in Mesopotamian mythology, *see* Apsu; Tiamat
as mirror, **7:** 1855f
moon and, **11:** 3002
New Year and, **7:** 1995–7
in the Old Testament, **11:** 2998
Roman god of, *see* Neptune
Slavs and, **10:** 2612
spirits of, *see* kelpies; Lorelei; Naiads; Nereids; nixies; Oceanides; Rusalki; Vodyanoy
symbolism of, **6:** 1602
as symbol of the unconscious, **11:** 3002
turned to wine by Jesus, *see* marriage of Cana
witches and, *see* floating of witches
woman and, **11:** 3002
see also baptism; flood; fountain; lakes; rain; rivers; sea; springs; wells
Water-carrier (zodiac sign), *see* Aquarius
water divining, 3: 683
Waterhouse, Agnes (witch), **3:** 753, **4:** 916
water-lily, as the lotus of mythology, **6:** 1649
Wathatotaro (American Indian chief), **6:** 1456
Watts, Mrs Alaric (automatic painter), **1:** *205, 207*
wax images, *see* image magic
way, the, as symbol, *see* path symbolism
Wayland the Smith, 4: *1084,* **10:** 2620, 2744
weather:
birds and, **10:** 2836f
at funerals, **10:** 2604–5
gods of:
Hittite, *see* Teshub
Indian, *see* Indra
Phoenician, *see* Baal, as weather god
see also sky, gods of
lore of:
diver, **3:** 651
oak and ash, **8:** 2035
in the Ozarks, **8:** 2102
pig, **8:** 2192
rainbow, **9:** 2335
'red sky at night, shepherd's delight', **6:** 1664
robin, **9:** 2403
rook, **6:** 1696, **9:** 2419
wolf in descriptive terms for, **11:** 3049
see also frost; ice; rain; snow; storm; thunder and lightning; weathercock; weather magic
also sky
weathercock, 2: 491
weather magic, 11: 3003–7
ashes and, **1:** 164

see also rain-making
wedding, *see* marriage; wedding-cake; wedding ring
wedding-cake, 7: 1738
wedding ring, 9: 2387–9
Wednesday, 3: 606f
week, 3: 607
see also days
Wei Po-Yang (Chinese alchemist), **3:** 809
Weir, Helen (automatic artist), **7:** *1784, 1785*
Weir, Thomas, 11: 3007–8
Weira, Waldo (psychic writer), **1:** 208
Weishaupt, Adam (founder of the Illuminati), **5:** 1402ff, *1403*
Welling, Georg von, 4: *1125*
wells, 10: 2684ff
cursing well of St Aelian, **2:** 581, **10:** 2685–7
dragons and, **3:** 690
well-dressing, **4:** 936, **10:** *2684*
holy, **10:** 2684–5
Celts and, **5:** 1240
hawthorn and, **5:** 1229
saints and, **10:** 2685
symbolism of, **6:** 1602
wishing-well, **10:** 2687, **11: 3040**
Wells, H. G., 9: 2498–500
Welsh Revival (1904–5), **8:** 2160, **10:** 2651
Wenham, Jane (witch), **2:** 419, **5:** 1385, **8:** 2247
werewolf *(loup-garou),* **6: 1650, 11: 3008–12**
Bertrand, **1: 257**
of Eschenbach, **11:** *3010*
Gilles Garnier, **11:** 3010, 3011
of Gévaudan, **11:** *3011*
Jean Grenier, **5: 1174, 11:** 3011
necrophilia and, **1:** 257
in Petronius' Satyricon, **9:** 2552
revenants as, **11:** 3011
silver bullet used to kill, **11:** 3012
Peter Stubb, **11:** 3010
witches as, **11:** 3010f
were-animals other than wolves, **11:** 3008
Wesley, John (preacher), **2:** 514, **3:** 826, 828, **5:** 1328, **8:** 2236
Wessex people, 10: 2704
west, 3: 640
Westcott, Dr Wynn, Golden Dawn and, **4:** 1131, 1132, **9:** 2430f, **11:** 2951
Westmorland, Lady (altar frontal), **10:** *2824*
Weyer, Johann (demonologist), *see* Wier, John
whale, 11: 3013–14
in the bestiary, **1:** 259, **11:** 3013
St Brendan and, **1:** *337,* 338
Eskimo and, **11:** 3014
Jonah and, **6:** 1526, *1526,* 1527, *1527,* 1528, *1528,* **11:** 3013, *3013*
mermaid and, **11:** 3014
North American Indians and, **11:** 3014
see also killer whale
wheat, *see* corn
wheel, 11: 3014–17
in Ezekiel's vision, **11:** 3016–17
of fortune, **11:** 3015
in fortune-telling (cards), **2:** 404–5
in medieval symbolism, **11:** 3015, *3016*
Tarot card, *see* Wheel of Fortune (Tarot card)
in Greece, **11:** 3015
as Jain symbol of time, **11:** 3014f
of life (Buddhism and Hinduism), **6:** *1558,* 1559, *1559,* **11:** *3015*
midsummer and, **11:** 3015f
as symbol of the sun, **11:** 3014ff
see also disk
Tarot and, **10:** 2791
see also Wheel of Fortune (Tarot card)
wheel dances, *see* ring dances
wryneck and, **11:** 3063
see also prayer wheel
Wheel of Fortune (of Life; Tarot card), **8:** 2147, **10:** 2793, *2793,* **11:** 3015
whipping, *see* flagellation
Whiro (Maori god), **3:** 691
Whitby, Daniel, 9: 2520
Whitby, Synod of, *see* Synod of Whitby
white, 2: 494ff, **11: 3017–18**
in Christian symbolism, **4:** 1059, **11:** 3017
death and, **11:** 3018
moon and, **2:** 522
Philosophers' Stone and, **7:** 1808
in race myths, **11:** 3018
in ritual magic, **9:** 2399
silver and, **2:** 522
as symbol of purity, **2:** 495, **4:** 1059, **11:** 3017
as symbol of virginity, **11:** 3017
white animals, **11:** 3018
white birds, **1:** 271, **2:** 494
white flowers, **4:** 996
White, John (artist), Algonquin Indians painted by, **1:** 105, *105,* 106, 107
White Book of Rhydderch (Welsh tales), **6:** 1671–2
White Boys (Manx mummers), **4:** 1004
Whitehead, A. N. on religion, **9:** 2359
Whitehead, Paul, 5: 1253, **7:** 1794
white horse of Uffington, 1: 128
Whitehouse, Mrs Mary, Moral Rearmament and, **7:** 1884
White Jews (Cochin Jews), **8:** 2081
white magic, 11: 3018–21
distinguished from black magic, **1:** 115, **3:** 617
in Africa, **1:** 81f
witchcraft and, **11:** 3021, 3042
see also cunning men; evil eye, protection against; witch bottle
whitethorn, *see* hawthorn
Whitsun, 11: 3022
see also Pentecost
Whittle, Anne (Old Chattox; witch), **6:** 1591ff, **8:** 2112
Wicca (modern witchcraft), **7:** 1866
wicken (tree), *see* rowan
Wickland, Dr Carl, 9: 2350
Wicliffe, John, *see* Wyclif, John
widdershins (anticlockwise), **2:** 487, **11: 3022**
widows, Hindu, suicide of, *see* suttee
Wiedemann, Jacob, 5: 1376
Wienholt, Arnold, 8: 2274
Wier, John (Johann Weyer; demonologist), **1:** 249, **5:** 1381–2
on Faust, **4:** 923
on Satan, **3:** 862
Wihio (Cheyenne trickster), **4:** 1161
Wild Edric, 4: 904–5, **11:** 3022
wilderness, *see* desert
Wild Hunt, 1: 144, **11: 3022**
Arthur associated with, **11:** 3022
the Devil as leader of, **11:** 3022
Holda as leader of, **5:** 1327
Odin as leader of, **4:** 1086, **11:** 3022
wildwood, 11: 3023–7
see also Lailoken; woodwouse
Wilfrid, St, of Ripon, **7:** 1750
Wilgeforte, St, *see* Uncumber, St
Wilkes, John, 7: 1794, *1794*
Willermoz, Jean-Baptiste, Order of the Holy City founded by, **7:** 1747
Willett, Mrs (Mrs Coombe Tennant), **11: 3030**
cross-correspondences and, **2:** 553, **11:** 3030
William II (William Rufus), death fetch of, **3:** 674
William III, King's Evil and, **6:** 1573
William with the little flame, *see* will-o'-the-wisp
William of Malmesbury (chronicler):
on King Arthur, **1:** 154
Gawain, **4:** 1071
on Glastonbury, **4:** 1111
William, Charles Edward (medium), Sir William Crookes and, **2:** 548
Williams, Edward (Iolo Morganwg), Druids and, **3:** 721, 723
Williamson, Hugh Ross, witchcraft theory of Margaret Murray and, **1:** 248
will-o'-the-wisp (corpse candle, corpse light, elf light, fairy fire, fetch candle, fetch light, foolish fire, fox fire, friar's lantern, *ignis fatuus,* Jack of the Bright Light, jack-o'-lantern, William with the little flame), **4:** 901, **5: 1400, 9:** 2297, **11: 3031,** 3069
see also ghul; St Elmo's Fire
willow, 11: 3031–2
Hasidism and, **5:** *1219*
Wilson, John (peyote cults), *see* Nishkuntu
wind, 10: 2601
controlled by knotted string, **10:** 2712
Enlil and, **10:** 2604
from the four quarters of the compass, **10:** *2600*
Varuna and, **10:** *2602*
see also storm
window, 5: 1363
wine:
invented by Dionysus, **3:** *634,* 635
'good wine needs no bush', **5:** 1329
wings, 11: 3032–4
of Daedalus and Icarus, **10:** *2724,* **11:** 3033
disk, winged, as sun symbol, **5:** 1395, *1398,* **11:** 3014, *3034*
of dragons, **11:** 3033
of fairies, **11:** 3033, *3034*
horses, winged, **11:** 3032
of divine messengers, **1:** 268
of angels, **11:** 3033
see also bat; birds; Harpies
Winifrid, St, 10: 2685
Winnebago Indians, trickster of, **11:** 2881, 2884
Winner, Anna Kennedy, on the Masters, **7:** 1769
Winstanley, Gerrard (leader of the Diggers), **9:** 2520
winter, 11: 3035–40
bonfires lit at onset of, **8:** 2166, **11:** 3035
festivals of, **11:** 3035
see also Christmas; midwinter; New Year; Saturnalia
Winther, Dr Christian, Anna Rasmussen and, **7:** 1792
Wirth, Oswald (occultist), **1:** 241, **2:** 405, **8:** 2126, **10:** 2790
wisdom literature, 11: 3040
wish, 11: 3040
see also wish-bone; wishing-well
wish-bone, 4: 1139, **11: 3040**
Wish Hounds (Wild Hunt), **11:** 3022
wishing-well, 10: 2687, **11: 3040**
witch balls, 4: 890, **5:** 1363
'Witch Bishop', *see* Dornheim, Prince-Bishop Gottfried von
witch bottle, 1: 296, **2:** *582,* **8:** *2219,* **11:** 2921, 3021
in East Anglia, **3:** 755, 757
at Canewdon, **2:** 401
James Murrell and, **7:** 1904
witchcraft, sorcery, **11: 3041–6**
in Africa, *see* Africa, witchcraft in
in America:
in New England, *see* Salem witches
in the Ozarks, **8:** 2100
Pueblo Indians, **9:** 2302f
black magic and, **1:** 115
in European history, *see* European witchcraft
finding of witches, **3:** 853–4, **4: 951–5**
see also pricking of witches
hysterical possession and witchcraft, **5: 1379–85**
modern, *see* modern witchcraft
old age and witchcraft, **8: 2051–7**
in primitive societies and in European history, comparison of, **4:** 951, 953ff, **10:** 2631ff, **11:** 3042ff
psychology of witches and witchcraft accusations, **5:** 1379

mental disorder, **5:** 1379ff, **8:** 2053ff, 2280, **10:** 2634
sexual repression, **5:** 1381
social tension relieved by accusations, **4:** 954–5, **8:** 2053ff, **10:** 2631ff, **11:** 3043, 3045–6
sorcery and witchcraft distinguished, **1:** 115, 211, **11:** 3041–2, 3105
in Southeast Asia, **10:** 2648
women, witches seen as typically, **8:** 2051, **10:** 2634, **11:** 3045
witch-doctor, African, **1:** 76, 78, **11:** *3045*
Azande, **1:** 212, **4:** 953, *953, 954–5*
Bushmen, **2:** 378f
Congo, **2:** *503, 504,* 509
divination by, **8:** 2078–9
witch dolls, *see* image magic
witchety grub (Australian totem), **4:** 1012
witches' mark, 4: 916, **8:** 2247
witch-wood (tree), *see* rowan
Witte, Alfred (astrologer), **1:** 182
Wodan (Wotan; Germanic god), **4:** 1084f
eagle and, **4:** *1086*
meaning of the name, **4:** 1086
neo-pagan Germanic cults and, **7:** 1964ff
Odin and, **4:** 1084f
Wild Hunt and, **4:** 1086
Woden (Anglo-Saxon god), **4:** 1086
wodewose, *see* woodwouse
wolf, 11: 3047–9
the Devil and, **11:** 3049
Eskimo and, **3:** 834
Evil Eye averted by skin of, **11:** 3049
Greek gods and, **11:** 3047
Apollo, **1:** 129, 139, **11:** 3047
of Gubbio, St Francis and, **11:** *3047,* 3049
in the *Rig-Veda,* **11:** 3047
Romulus and Remus suckled by, **4:** *1025,* 1026f, **11:** *2903*
in Scandinavian mythology:
Odin and, **4:** 1086, **8:** *2043*
sun and, **10:** 2721
see also Fenris wolf
shape-shifting and, **9:** 2552, 2553f, **11:** 3049
see also werewolf
war gods and, **1:** 129
weather, wolf in descriptive terms for, **11:** 3049
witchcraft and, **11:** 3049
werewolf, **11:** 3010f
Wolfdietrich (Teutonic hero), **4:** 1029
Wolfram von Eschenbach, 8: 2142–3
Wagner and, **11:** 2978
Wolsey, Cardinal, 9: 2387
woman, 11: 3050–9
Berbers and, **1:** 255
Christian attitudes to, **11:** 3057f
see also Adam, Eve and
in the Congo, **2:** 505
in Egyptian tomb painting, **11:** *3051*
evilness of, **4:** 980, **11:** 3050ff
Zulu, **11:** 3105–6
see also Pandora
Hindu view of, **11:** 3050
Kikuyu and, **6:** 1563
in the *Mahabharata,* **11:** 3053
Virgin Mary as ideal woman, **7:** 1752
moon and, **7:** 1877
in Peru, **5:** 1427
Pueblo Indians and, **9:** 2300
pygmies and, **9:** 2309f
in Tantrism, **10:** 2779
Three Ages of (Baldung Grien), **3:** *613*
Touareg and, **11:** 2863
two and, **11:** 2905f
uncleanness of, **11:** 3053
water and, **11:** 3002
witches seen as typically women, **8:** 2051, **10:** 2634, **11:** 3045
Zulu view of, **11:** 3105f
see also birth; first woman; marriage; menstruation; mother; Mother Goddess; pregnancy; prostitution; virginity
Wood, Ernest (Theosophist), **10:** 2814, 2815
woodhouse (wild man), *see* woodwouse
Woodman, Dr, Golden Dawn and, **4:** 1131
woodpecker, 11: 3060
in augury, **1:** 194
in Borneo, **1:** 314–15
fertility and, **11:** 3060
as oracle of Mars, **7:** 1744, **11:** 3060
ploughing and, **11:** 3060
rain and, **10:** 2837, **11:** 3060
springwort and, **11:** 3060
thunder and, **11:** 3060
woodwouse (wodewose, woodhouse; wildman of the woods), **4:** 968, **11:** 3025
woody nightshade (plant), *see* bittersweet nightshade
words, language:
in magic, **8:** 2279
see also incantation; Mass, in magic; names, in magic; spell
music and, in religion, **7:** 1911
see also alphabet; mantra; names; poets; posies (mottoes); riddles; song; speaking in tongues; writing
World, the (Tarot card), *see* Universe
world mountain, 10: 2758
Eurasian, **8:** 2262
see also Atlas
Hindu, **7:** 1899, **9:** 2366, **10:** 2758
world tree and, **11:** 2879
world serpent, cosmic snake, **9:** 2529
in Hinduism, *see* Shesha
in Scandinavian mythology, *see* Midgard Serpent
world tree, cosmic tree, **10:** 2758, **11:** 2879
in Scandinavian mythology, *see* Yggdrasill
shamans and, **9:** 2547, 2548
world mountain and, **11:** 2879
see also Crucifixion, tree as the cross; Tree of Life
Wotan, *see* Wodan
Wotan Society (Wachler), **7:** 1964
Wovoka (North American Indian prophet), **4:** 1091f
wraith, *see* phantasms of the living
wreath, 11: 3060
as crown, **2:** 564, **6:** 1610
death and, **2:** 564
wren, 11: 3061
fire brought from heaven by, **11:** 3061
killing of, on St Stephen's Day, **8:** 2026, **11:** 3061
St Malo and, **9:** 2468, **11:** 3061
owl and, **8:** 2098
robin and, **9:** 2402, **11:** 3061
wrestling, Japanese, **6:** *1486–7*
writing, 1: 111f
see also alphabet; hieroglyphs; papyrus; parchment; runes
Wroe, John, 10: 2646
Wronski, Joseph Maria Hoëne-, 6: 1618, **11: 3062–3**
wryneck (bird), **11: 3063**
Wulff, Wilhelm (astrologer), National Socialism and, **7:** 1948
Wulfstan, St, beards shaved by, **5:** 1204
Wundt, Wilhelm (psychologist), on dreaming, **6:** 1679
Wurusemu (Hattic goddess), **5:** 1323
Würzburg, witch trials of, **4:** 1079
Wu Ti (Chinese emperor), **11:** 3083–4
Wyclif (Wicliffe), John, 2: 473, **5:** 1286
wyvern, 1: 297

X

X, Malcolm (Black Muslim), **1:** 279, 280
Xanthus (horse of Achilles), **5:** 1212
Xaphan (demon), **3:** *861*
Xavier, Chico, (spiritist writer), **1:** 208
Xavier, St Francis, 9: 2462
Xenophanes of Colophon, 9: 2354
Xerxes (Persian king), **11:** 3103
Xipe Totec (Tezcatlipoca), **1:** 219, **11:** *2941*
Xiuhtecuhtli (Toltec fire god), **4:** *970*
Xolotl (Evening Star; Mexican deity), **1:** 218
X-shaped cross (*crux decussata;* St Andrew's cross), **2:** 550

Y

Yahweh (YHWH, Jehovah), **11: 3063–6**
Gnostic view of, **9:** 2477
as High God, **5:** 1302
Israelites as chosen people of, **3:** 798f, **5:** 1322, **11:** 3063ff
name of, **11:** 3063–4, *see also* Tetragrammaton
promised land and, **3:** 798f, **5:** 1322, **11:** 2992, 3064ff
sacrifice of the first-born to, **4:** 976
as storm god, **3:** 691
temple of, at Jerusalem, *see* Jerusalem, temple of Yahweh at
as war god, **11:** 3064
Zealots and, **11:** 3077f
yakku (spirits, Ceylon), **11:** 2936
Yama (Indian god):
as first man, **3:** 616, **11:** 2902
as god of the dead, **8:** 2134, **11:** 2902
Yama (Tibetan god), **5:** 1266
yama (yoga), **11:** 2934–5, 3072–3
Yang and Yin (China), *see* Yin and Yang
yantra (mandala), **6:** 1716
yarrow (bloodwort, knight's milfoil, soldier's woundwort), **5:** 1276, **7:** 1846, **8:** 2203
Yarthkins (Fenland fairies), **4:** 903
Yathrib (Medina), **7:** 1872
see also Medina
Yeats, W. B., 4: *1133,* **11: 3066–8**
Blake and, **11:** 3067
on Mme Blavatsky, **1:** 293
collective unconscious and, **11:** 3068
Golden Dawn and, **1:** 284, **4:** 1131, 1132, **11:** 3067
S. L. Mathers and, **11:** 3067
G. W. Russell and, **9:** 2442f
Theosophical Society and, **11:** 3067
Yee King, *see* I Ching
yellow, 1: 271, **2:** 496, 522, **3:** 642
see also bile, yellow
Yellow Emperor, *see* Huang Ti
Yellow Hats (dGe-lug-pa; Tibetan religious order), **10:** 2842–3
Yeth Hounds (Wild Hunt), **11:** 3022
yeti, *see* abominable snowman
yew, 11: *2879,* **11: 3069–70**
Yezidi (sect; Iraq), **3:** 730
Yggdrasill (ash tree, the World Tree; Scandinavian mythology), **1:** 160, *160,* **9:** 2484, 2486, **11: 3070**
YHWH (Yahweh), *see* Tetragrammaton
Yin and Yang, 1: 68–9, **2:** 457ff, **6:** 1712, **11: 3070**
dragons and, **3:** 694
I Ching and, **5:** 1390
Taoism and, **10:** 2786–7
Yiyi (West African spider myth), **3:** 615
Ymir (giant; Scandinavian mythology), **3:** 530, *537,* **4:** 1103, **9:** 2484
Ynys-witrin (Isle of Glass), **4:** 1109, 1110
yoga, 7: 1777–8, **9:** 2525–6, **10:** 2839–40, **11: 3070–6**
astral body and, **1:** 172
breath control *(pranayama)* in, **2:** 335f, **6:** 1586, **7:** 1777, **11:** 3073–4
concentration (*dharana*) in, **7:** 1777, **11:** 3074
drug experiences compared with, **11:** 3076
magical feats and yoga powers distinguished, **11:** 3075–6
meditation (*dhyana*) in, **7:** 1777, **11:** 3074
sex and, **11:** 3073
see also Vishvamitra
siddhis in **11:** 3076

Tantrism and, **10:** 2778
trance and, **11:** *2869,* 2870
see also samadhi
types of, **11:** 2932–4, 3070–1
in Vedanta, **11:** 2932–5
see also Kanphata; Kundalini
Yoga-Vedanta Forest Academy, 10: 2591
Yom Kippur, *see* atonement, Jewish day of
yoni (female symbol; India), **5:** 1288, **6:** 1633, **10:** 2782–3, **11: 3076**
lotus and, **6:** 1650
York, mystery play cycle of, **7:** 1922, 1923, 1924
Yorke, Gerald, 4: 1133
Young, Brigham, 7: 1888f, *1889*
Ys, Ville d', 2: 349
Yucatan (Mexico), Maya in, **7:** 1772
Yugas (world ages; Hinduism and Buddhism), **3:** 817
Yuki-onne (Japanese snow woman), **11:** 3039
Yule, 2: 480, **11: 3076**
boar and, **1:** 297
Yule log, **2:** 480, **5:** *1254,* 1254f, **11:** 3076
oak and, **8:** 2035
olive and, **8:** 2060
Yves, St, 2: 348

Z

Zachary (pope), anathema and, **2:** 582
Zagreus (Greek mythology), **3:** 650, 859, **8:** 2170, **11:** 3089
Zambia, Lumpa Church in, **7:** 1979
Zamurrad (Persian giant), **10:** *2686*
Zapata (Mexican hero), **5:** *1298*
Zapotecs, 1: 214, **7:** *1838*
Zar (Ethiopian spirit), **3:** 845, **8:** 2239
Zarathushtra, *see* Zoroaster
Zealots (Jewish history), **2:** 466, **11: 3077–8**
Jesus and, **2:** 467, **6:** 1508ff, **11:** 3077, 3078
zebu, *see* East indian humped zebu
Zedler, Johann Heinrich, 3: 809, 810, **7:** 1808
Zen Buddhism, 6: 1486, 1489f, **11: 3079–88**
Bodhisattvas in, **11:** 3081
enlightenment (*satori*) in, **7:** 1932, **11:** 3079
meditation in, **7:** 1778, **11:** 3084
origin of the name, **11:** 3080
riddles (koan) in, **11:** 3085–6
Samurai and, **6:** 1492
tea and, **6:** 1492, *1494, 1498,* **11:** 3080–1
Zend-Avesta, *see Avesta*
Zener cards, 8: 2278
Zeno (philosopher), **8:** 2240
Zenobius, St, 3: *872*
Zeno of Verona, on possession, **8:** 2238
Zephaniah (Old Testament prophet), **8:** 2267
Zeus, 5: *1166,* 1167f, **11: 3089–94**
altar of, at Pergamon, **1:** 117
Aphrodite and, **1:** 136, 137, 138
Apollo and, **1:** 139
Artemis and, **3:** 630
Athene and, **1:** 185f, **8:** *2260*
Baal and, **1:** 223
bear and, **1:** 246
bees and, **8:** 2032
birth of, in Crete, **2:** 435, 523, **5:** 1167, **8:** 2032, **9:** 2482, **11:** *3094*
birth of, elsewhere, **5:** 1168
bull and, **5:** 1167, 1271, 1348, **11:** 3090
see also Europa *below*
Callisto and, **1:** 246, **3:** 630f
Capricorn (constellation) and, *see* Amalthea
Celeus and, **11:** 3060
centre of the world sought by, **7:** 1952
Chiron and, **2:** 445
cock and, **1:** 309f
Crete and, **5:** 1167f, **11:** 3089ff
see also birth of, in Crete, *above*
Cronus and, **2:** 546f
Cybele, Attis, and, **2:** 583
Danae and, **10:** *2604,* **11:** *2954*
Dionysus and:
Cretan Zeus compared with Dionysus, **5:** 1167, 1168
Zeus as father of Dionysus, **3:** 635, 650, 859, **5:** 1329, **7:** 1908, **8:** 2170
dryads and, **3:** 728
as dying god, **5:** 1167, 1168
eagle and, **3:** 746, **11:** 3090, *3092,* 3093, *3093*
Eleusis and, **3:** 807
Eros and, **3:** 829, 830
Europa and, **2:** 365, **10:** 2805, **11:** 3090
Ganymede abducted by, **11:** *3092*
gold, Zeus as shower of, *see* Danae *above*
Hades as the subterranean Zeus, **8:** 2208, 2209
Hecate and, **5:** 1256f
Hephaestus and, **5:** 1205, 1268f
Hera and, **2:** 523, **3:** 635, **5:** *1270,* 1271
Hercules his son, **5:** 1279
as High God, **5:** 1302, **10:** 2601
honey of, stolen by Celeus, **11:** 3060
Io and, **5:** 1271
Ixion and, **2:** 445, **11:** 3015
Jupiter the counterpart of, **6:** 1552
Leda and, **1:** 270, **10:** *2737, 2738*
Lycaeus (Lykaios), **9:** 2552, **11:** 3008
Melissa and, **8:** 2032
Minos and, **5:** 1168
Minotaur and, **11:** 3090
Olympian and Cretan forms distinguished, **5:** 1167
Olympic Games and, **8:** 2060, **11:** 3093
oracle of, *see* Dodona
Persephone and, **8:** 2168, 2170
Philomela and, **7:** 2000
Prometheus and, **8:** 2262ff
ram and, **9:** 2556, **11:** 3090
Sagittarius and, **2:** 445
Semele and, **3:** 635, **7:** 1908
shape-shifting by, **9:** 2550
see also Danae *above;* Europa *above;* Ganymede *above;* Leda *above*
as sky god, **10:** 2601
statue of, by Pheidias, **5:** 1396, **11:** 3093
subterranean (*katachthonios*), *see* Hades *above*
thunder and lightning, thunderbolts, and, **5:** *1301,* **11:** 3089, *3089,* 3093
Zagreus and, **3:** 650, 859, **8:** 2170
Zevi, Sabbatai, 5: 1219
Cabala and, **2:** 386
Lost Tribes of Israel and, **6:** 1645
Zhob valley, clay figurines from, **3:** 750
ziggurat, 9: 2362–3
Tower of Babel based on, **11:** 2867
Zinzendorf, Count, 3: 827, **5:** 1328
Zion (Sion), hill of (Jerusalem), **6:** 1502, **7:** 1899, 1900, **11: 3094**
Zion Christian Church, 7: 1831–2
Zionism, 6: 1531, **11:** 3094
Star of David the emblem of, **6:** *1538*
Zion's Watch Tower Tract Society (later the Jehovah's Witnesses), **6:** 1499
zircon (jewel), **6:** *1513*
Ziusudra (Sumerian flood legend), **3:** 817, **4:** 993, 1100
Zizka, John, 9: 2520
zodiac, 1: *174,* 175ff, *177,* **11: 3094**
Golden Dawn and, **4:** *1130*
medieval calendar with, **3:** *838*
precession of the Equinoxes and, **1:** 143
signs of, *see* Aquarius; Aries; Cancer; Capricorn; Gemini; Leo; Libra; Pisces; Sagittarius; Scorpio; Taurus; Virgo
Zohar (Book of Splendour; Cabala), **2:** 383ff
zombies, 8: 2078, **11: 3095–6**
Zoroaster (Zarathushtra), **7:** 1862, **8:** 2048, 2138, **11:** 3098, 3100
in 15th cent. Flemish miniature, **11:** *3102*
writings of (the *Gathas*), **4:** 1070, **8:** 2048, **11:** 3103
see also Zoroastrianism
Zoroastrianism, 11: 3097–3103
angels in, **1:** 126
bridge to the land of the dead in, **2:** 345, **6:** 1545, **11:** 3100
creation myths of, **8:** 2048, **11:** 3100, 3107
death and, **3:** 616, **8:** 2048
dualism in, **1:** 86ff, **3:** 729–30, 859, **11:** 3099–3100, 3103, 3107
end of the world in, **8:** 2048
evil principle, darkness, in, *see* Ahriman
fire temple of, **11:** *3098*
first man myth of, *see* Gayomart
free will in, **1:** 86, **11:** 3100
good principle, light, in, *see* Ohrmazd
heaven in, **11:** 3100–3101
hell in, **5:** 1261, **11:** 3100–3101
judgement of the dead in, **2:** 345, **6:** 1545–6, **11:** 3100–3101
life after death in, **6:** 1712
see also hell *above;* judgement of the dead *above*
Mani as Zoroastrian heretic, **5:** 1282
monotheism in, **11:** 3039–3100
Parthians and, **8:** 2144
sacred plant (haoma) in, **11:** 3102
sacred text of, *see Avesta*
soul in, **6:** 1712
time personified in, *see* Zurvan
see also Parsees
Zoser (pharaoh), **5:** 1404, 1405
Zosimus, homunculus and, **5:** 1338
Zu (Anzu; Mesopotamian deity), **3:** 690, **7:** 1821
Zugrun, Eleonore (medium), *2223*
Zulu, 11: 3103–6
rainbow and, **9:** 2333, **11:** 3105
Zuni Indians (Pueblo), **8:** *2010,* **9:** 2300ff
Zurvan (Zoroastrianism), **1:** 86–8, **3:** 729–30, **11:** 2487–8, 3100, 3103, **3107**
Zwingli, Ulrich, 8: 2242

BIBLIOGRAPHY

This bibliographical section of *Man, Myth and Magic* is specially devised to provide teachers, students and general readers with a convenient and comprehensive means of access to the full scope of the volume set.

The major thematic areas of the encyclopedia can be explored by following the classified subject guides. In addition, an excellent range of books for further reading is provided for in-depth study.

MAGIC—ITS MANY FORMS

"The question of magic is a question of discovering and employing hitherto unknown forces in Nature."

It is impossible to know precisely when human beings first tried to harness these forces—certainly the impulse to do so is expressed in prehistoric cave paintings depicting hunting scenes. From these early examples of imitative hunting magic, the whole history of magical rituals has developed, with its appendages of circles and pentagrams, chants and spells, all building up towards an identifiable tradition.

CLASSIFIED SUBJECT GUIDE

Abracadabra
Alchemy
Ashes
Astral body
Atavisms
Battle of Bewitchment
Black Mass
Blood
Body
Builders' Rites
Candle
Circle
Clophill
Colours
Correspondences
Crossroads
Curse
Days and Hours
Disease
Elixir of Life
Emerald
Evil
Eye
Fingers
Forces
Gematria
Gesture
Gold
Golem
Green
Grimoire
Hair
Hand of Glory
Hexagram
House
Hunting Magic
Imitative Magic
Incantation
Invisibility
Iron
Jade
Jewels
Kundalini
Lead
Love Magic
Macrocosm and Microcosm
Magic
Magical Papyri
Magic Squares
Magnetism
Mandala
Mantra
Mercury
Mirror
Names
Necromancy
Opposites
Pearl
Pentagram
Perfume
Philosophers' Stone
Psychic Attack
Red
Renaissance
Sacred Magic of Abra-Melin
Salt
Satanism
Sex
Shadow
Shape-Shifting
Sin-Eater
Skull
Smith
Sorcery
Spittle
String
Sword
Talisman
Tarot
Threshold
Treasure Magic
Vibration
Voodoo
Wand
Weather Magic
White Magic

FURTHER READING

Alford, Violet, *Sword Dance and Drama,* Dufour, 1963.
— and **Gallop, Rodney,** *The Traditional Dance,* Methuen, London, 1935.

Baldick, R., *The Life of J.-K. Huysmans,* Oxford University Press, 1955.
Bell, H. I., *Cults and Creeds in Graeco-Roman Egypt,* Ares, 1975.
Blau, J. L., *The Christian Interpretation of the Cabala in the Renaissance,* Columbia University Press, 1944.
Blavatsky, H. P., *The Secret Doctrine,* Theosophical Publishing House, 1980.
Bonner, C., *Studies in Magical Amulets,* University of Michigan Press, 1950.
Bonser, W., *The Medical Background of Anglo-Saxon England,* Wellcome Institute, London, 1963,
Bowra, C. M., *Primitive Song,* Weidenfeld, London, 1962.
Brandon, S. G. F., *Creation Legends of the Ancient Near East,* Verry, Lawrence, 1963.
— *Man and His Destiny in the Great Religions,* Univ. of Toronto Press, 1962.
— *The Judgement of the Dead,* Scribner, 1969.
Burland, C. A., *The Arts of the Alchemists,* Macmillan, 1967.
— *The Magical Arts,* Barker, London, 1966.
Butler, C., *Number Symbolism,* Routledge & Kegan Paul, 1970.
Butler, E. M., *Ritual Magic,* Cambridge University Press, 1979.

Camp, L. Sprague de, *The Ancient Engineers,* Doubleday.
Case, P. F., *The Tarot,* Macoy, 1977.
Cavendish, R., *The Black Arts,* Capricorn, 1968.
— *The Tarot,* Harper and Row, 1975.
Clark, R. T. Rundle, *Myth and Symbol in Ancient Egypt,* Thames & Hudson, 1978.
Clodd, E., *Magic in Names,* Gale, 1968.
Coudert, A., *Alchemy, The Philosopher's Stone,* Wildwood House, 1980.
Coulton, G. G., *Life in the Middle Ages,* Cambridge Univ. Press, 1967 reprint.
Crawford, O. G. S., *The Eye Goddess,* Macmillan, 1958.
Crookall, R., *The Study and Practice of Astral Projection,* Wehman, 1961.
— *The Techniques of Astral Projection,* Wehman, 1964.
Crow, W. B., *Precious Stones,* Weiser, 1980.
Crowley, Aleister, *Magick in Theory and Practice,* Dover, 1976.
— *Liber 777,* Weiser, 1976.

Davidson, T., *Rowan Tree and Red Thread,* Clarke, Irwin, 1950.
Dawson, W. R., *The Bridle of Pegasus,* Methuen, London, 1930.
Deren, Maya, *Divine Horsemen,* Dell Publishing, 1972.
Dodds, E. R., *The Greeks and the Irrational,* University of California Press, 1951.
— *Pagan and Christian in an Age of Anxiety,* Norton, 1970.
Donnelly, Dorothy, *The Golden Well,* Sheed and Ward, 1950.
Dundes, A., *Evil Eye,* Garland Publishing, 1981.

Eliade, Mircea, *The Forge and the Crucible,* University of Chicago Press, 1979.
Ellis Davidson, H. R., *The Sword in Anglo-Saxon England,* Oxford University Press, 1962.
Elworthy, F. T., *The Evil Eye,* Julian Press, 1958.
Evans, E. E., *Irish Folkways,* Routledge & Kegan Paul, 1966.
Evans, Joan, *English Posies and Posy Rings,* Oxford University Press, 1931.
Evans-Pritchard, E. E., *Essays in Social Anthropology,* Free Press, 1963.
Ewen, C. L'Estrange, *Witchcraft and Demonianism,* Barnes and Noble, 1970 reprint.

Flew, A., *A New Approach to Psychical Research,* Watts, 1953.
Fortune, Dion, *The Mystical Qabalah,* Weiser.
— *Psychic Self-Defence,* Weiser.
Fox, Oliver, *Astral Projection,* Citadel Press, 1974.
Frazer, J. G., *The Golden Bough,* St. Martin's Press, 1980.
— *Folklore in the Old Testament,* Macmillan, 1918.

Gaster, M. ed., *The Sword of Moses,* Weiser, 1970 reprint.
Gennep, A. van, *The Rites of Passage,* University of Chicago Press, 1961.
Ghalioungi, P., *Magic and Medical Science in Ancient Egypt,* Barnes and Noble, 1965.
Graves, C., *Alchemist,* Ace Books, 1981.
Gray, W. G., *Magical Ritual Methods,* Weiser.
Green, Celia, *Out-of-the-Body Experiences,* Institute of Psychophysical Research, Oxford, 1968.

Guazzo, *Compendium Maleficarum,* AMS Press reprint.
Guthrie, W. K. C., *The Greeks and Their Gods,* Beacon Press, 1968.

Hand, W. P., *Magical* Medicine, University of California Press, 1981.
Hart, H., *The Enigma of Survival,* C. C. Thomas, 1959.
Hartmann, Franz, *Magic White and Black,* Borgo Press, 1980.
Hole, Christina, ed., *Encyclopaedia of Superstitions,* Merrimack, 1979.
Hollander, Lee M., ed., *The Poetic Edda,* University of Texas Press, 1964.
Huxley, Francis, *The Invisibles,* Humanities, 1966.
Huysmans, J.-K., *Down There (Là Bas),* French and European Publications.

Inglis, B., *A History of Medicine,* World Publishing, 1965.

Jones, Barbara, *Design for Death,* Bobbs-Merrill, 1967.
Jones, William, *Finger-Ring Lore,* Chatto and Windus, London, 1877.
Jung, C. G., *Archetypes and the Collective Unconscious,* Princeton University Press, 2nd Edition, 1969.
— *Psychology and Alchemy,* Princeton University Press, 1968.
— *Mysterium Conjunctionis,* Princeton University Press, 1970.

Kennedy, Douglas, *England's Dances,* Clarke, Irwin, 1949.
King, F., *Ritual Magic in England,* Spearman, London, 1970.
Kittredge, G. L., *Witchcraft in Old and New England,* Atheneum Pubs., 1972.
Knight, Gareth, Practical Guide to Qabalistic Symbolism, Weiser.
Kunz, G. F., *The Magic of Jewels and Charms,* Lippincott, Philadelphia, 1915.

Laguerre, M. S., *Voodoo Heritage,* Sage Publications, 1980.
Langton, E., *Essentials of Demonology,* AMS Press reprint.
Leadbeater, C. W., *The Astral Plane,* Theosophical Publishing House, 1973 reprint.
Lefebure, F., *Expérientes Initiatiques,* Omnium Littéraire, Paris, 1956.
Levi, Eliphas, *Transcendental Magic,* Weiser.
Lockhart, J. G., *Curses, Luck and Talismans,* Gale, 1968.

MacGregor Mathers, S. L., *Astral Projection, Ritual Magic and Alchemy,* Spearman, London, 1971.
Mallowan, M. E. L., *Early Mesopotamia and Iran,* McGraw-Hill, 1965.
Maple, Eric, *Deadly Magic,* Weiser, 1976.
— *The Realm of Ghosts,* American Book Co.
— *Magic, Medicine and Quackery,* A. S. Barnes, 1968.
Mayananda, S., *The Tarot Today,* Weiser.
Mayne, W., *Ghosts,* Elsevier-Nelson, 1971.
Metraux, A., *Voodoo in Haiti,* Schocken, 1972.
Meyer-Meyrink, *The Golem,* translated by Madge Pemberton, Ungar, 1964.
Middleton, J., ed., *Magic, Witchcraft and Cursing,* University of Texas Press, 1976.

Nilsson, M. P., *Greek Popular Religion,* Columbia University Press, 1940.
Nock, A. D., *Conversion,* Oxford University Press, 1961 reprint.
Nurnburg, Walter, *Hands at Mass,* Sheed and Ward, 1951.

Oakeshott, R. E., *The Archaeology of Weapons,* Praeger, 1963.

Papus, *Tarot of the Bohemians,* Weiser.
Pevsner, N., *An Outline of European Architecture,* Penguin, London, revised edition, 1968.
Phillips, D. G., *White Magic,* Scholarly, 1981.
Podmore, F., *From Mesmer to Christian Science,* University Books.
Powell, A. E., *The Etheric Double,* Theosophical Publishing House, 1925.
Powell-Williams, Norman, *The Ideas of the Fall and of Original Sin,* Longmans, London, 1927.
Precope, J., *Medicine, Magic and Mythology,* Heinemann, London, 1954

Read, J., *Prelude to Chemistry: An Outline of Alchemy,* M.I.T. press.
Rees, B. R., *The Use of Greek,* University of Wales Press, Cardiff, 1960.
Regardie, Israel, *The Tree of Life,* Llewellyn Publications, 1970.
Rhodes, H. T. F., *The Satanic Mass,* Citadel, 1975.
Robbins, R. H., *Encyclopedia of Witchcraft and Demonology,* Crown, 1959.

Sanford, E., *Psychical Research & Spiritualism,* American classical college, 1980.
Scholem, Gershom G., *On the Kabalah and its Symbolism,* Schocken, 1969.
Seeman, B., *The River of Life,* Norton, 1961.
Sepharial, W. G. O., *Book of Charms and Talismans,* Wehman, 1965.
Seznec, J., *The Survival of the Pagan Gods,* Princeton University Press, 1972.
Shah, Idries, *The Secret Lore of Magic,* Citadel Press, 1970.
Sigerist, H. E., *History of Medicine,* Oxford University Press, 1951.
Sudre, R., *Treatise on Parapsychology,* Fernhill House, 1960.
Sumner, W. G., *Folkways,* Dover, 1959.

Thronger, R., *A Calendar of German Customs,* Dufour, 1968.
Trachtenberg, J., *Jewish Magic and Superstition,* Atheneum Pubs., 1970 reprint.
Tucci, G., *The Theory and Practice of the Mandala,* Wehman.
Turner, V. W., The Forest of Symbols, Cornell University Press, 1968.

Waite, A. E., *The Book of Ceremonial Magic,* Citadel Press, 1970.
— *The Holy Kabbalah,* University Books reprint.
— *The Pictorial Key to the Tarot,* Wehman.
Walker, Benjamin, *Hindu World,* Praeger, 1968.
— *Sex and the Supernatural,* Macdonald, London, 1971.
Walker, D. P., *Spiritual and Demonic Magic from Ficino to Campanella,* Notre Dame Press, 1975.
Wind, E., *Pagan Mysteries of the Renaissance,* Barnes and Noble, 1968
Wymer, N., *English Town Crafts,* C. River Books, 1976.

Yates, F. A., *Giordano Bruno and the Hermetic Tradition,* Random, 1969.

Zaehner, R. C., *The Dawn and Twilight of Zoroastrianism,* Putnam, 1961.
Zoete, Beryl de and **Spies, Walter,** *Dance and Drama in Bali,* Harper and Row, 1938.

WITCHCRAFT

CLASSIFIED SUBJECT GUIDE

Aberdeen Witches
All Hallows' Eve
Bamberg Witches
Basque Witchcraft
Broomstick
Canewdon
Channel Islands
East Anglian and Essex Witches
European Witch Persecutions
Familiars
Finding of Witches
Flying Ointment
French Witchcraft
German Witchcraft
Gowdie, Isabel
Hysterical Possession and Witchcraft
Italian Witchcraft
Kyteler, Alice
Lancashire Witches
Modern Witchcraft
North Berwick Witches
Nudity
Old Age and Witchcraft
Poisoning
Pricking
Sabbath
Salem Witches
Somerset Witches
Swedish Witchcraft
Weir, Thomas
Witchcraft

Since supernatural forces have always been regarded with a mixture of fear and respect, these attitudes have carried over to those special people who put forward claims to being able to manipulate the natural world—for good or evil. Although we often think of witches as female, in fact many cultures have male witches. Witches have traditionally carried great authority—as healers, as seers and as wise advisors to people with problems. The fear that witches inspired led to such appalling reactions as the witch hunts in Europe and America, in which thousands of witches were put to death. Witchcraft continues to thrive in many cultures around the world—in recent years there has been a revival in Europe and America.

FURTHER READING

Apuleius, *The Golden Ass,* Indiana Univ. Press, 1962.

Baroja, J. C., *The World of Witches,* University of Chicago Press, 1973.

Cavendish, Richard, *The Black Arts,* Putnam, 1967.

Davies, R. Trevor, *Four Centuries of Witch Beliefs,* Methuen, London, 1947.
Dingwall, E. J., *Some Human Oddities,* Home and Van Thal, 1947.

Evans-Pritchard, E. E., *Witchcraft, Oracles and Magic among the Azande,* Oxford University Press, 1976.
Ewen, C. L'Estrange, Witchcraft and Demonianism, AMS Press reprint.
— *Witch Hunting and Witch Trials,* Dial Press, 1929.

Gardner, G., *Witchcraft Today,* Citadel Press, 1970.
Gluckman, M., *Custom and Conflict in Africa,* Barnes and Noble, 1969.
— *Politics, Law and Ritual in Tribal Society,* New American Library, 1968.
Guazzo, *Compendium Maleficarum,* Universal Books, 1975.

Hansen, Chadwick, *Witchcraft at Salem,* New American Library.
Hole, Christina, *A Mirror of Witchcraft,* Rowman, 1977.
— *Witchcraft in England,* Rowman, 1977.
Hoyt, C. A., *Witchcraft,* Southern Illinois University Press, 1981.

Johnson, R., *Witches & Demons in History & Folklore,* Johnson, N.C., 1978.

Kittredge, G. L., *Witchcraft in Old and New England,* Atheneum, 1972.

Lea, H. C., *Materials Toward a History of Witchcraft,* AMS Press reprint.

MacFarlane, A. D. J., *Witchcraft in Tudor and Stuart England,* Harper and Row, 1970.
Malleus Maleficarum, Hogarth Press, London, 1969 reprint.
Maple, Eric, *The Dark World of Witches,* A. S. Barnes, 1964.
Marwick, M. G., *Sorcery in its Social Setting: A Study of the Northern Rhodesian Cewa,* Humanities, 1965.
— *Witchcraft and Sorcery,* Penguin, London, 1971.
Middleton, J., *Lugbara Religion,* Oxford University Press, 1961.
— and **Winter, E. H., ed.,** *Witchcraft and Sorcery in East Africa,* Praeger, 1963.
Mitchell, J. C., *The Tao Village,* Manchester University Press, 1957.
Murray, Margaret A., *The God of the Witches,* Oxford University Press, 1970.
— *The Witch-Cult in Western Europe,* Oxford University Press, 1967 reprint.

Oesterreich, T. K., *Possession,* Citadel Press, 1974.

Peel, E. and **Southern, P.,** *The Trials of the Lancashire Witches,* Taplinger, 1970.

Revesz, T. R., *Witches,* Raintree Pubs., 1977.
Remy, Nicholas, *Demonolatry,* Universal Books, 1975.
Robbins, R. H., *Witchcraft: An Introduction to the Literature of Witchcraft,* Kraus Intl., 1978.
Roberts, *Witches and Witch Hunters,* Folcroft, 1973.
Rose, Elliot, *A Razor for a Goat,* University of Toronto Press, 1962.
Rush, J. A. *Witchcraft and Sorcery,* C. C. Thomas, 1974.

Scot, Reginald, *Discoverie of Witchcraft,* Illinois University Press, 1964.
Smyth, Frank, *Modern Witchcraft,* Macdonald, London, 1970.
Starkey, Marion, L., *The Devil in Massachusetts,* Doubleday, 1952.
Summers, Montague, *History of Witchcraft and Demonology,* Routledge & Kegan Paul, 1973.

Trevor-Roper, H. R. *Crisis of the Seventeenth Century: Religion, the Reformation and Social Change,* Harper and Row, 1967.
Turner, V. W., *Schism & Continuity in an African Society,* Humanities, 1972.

Wedeck, H. E., *A Treasury of Witchcraft,* Cidadel Press, 1966.

Zilboorg, G. and **Henry, G. W.,** *A History of Medical Psychology,* Norton, 1941.

GOOD AND EVIL

Many cultures have regarded the supernatural world in what can be described as a dualistic manner. The world becomes divided into extremes; good and evil are personified as God and the Devil in various forms, depending on the culture. A divided universe implies conflict—an interminable war between the powers of light and darkness, the spirits of Heaven and Hell. Many writers and thinkers have found this divided world an accurate mirror of the conflict that rages within their own selves, the inspiration for the great debate on the nature of the universe.

CLASSIFIED SUBJECT GUIDE

Ahriman	**Baphomet**	**Exorcism**	**Lilith**
Aix-en-Provence Nuns	**Beelzebub**	**Grandier, Urbain**	**Lucifer**
Angels	**Belial**	**Great Beast**	**Pact**
Antichrist	**Devil**	**Guardian Spirits**	**Possession**
Armies	**Directions**	**Headless Spirits**	**Renata, Sister Maria**
Asmodeus	**Dualism**	**Herne the Hunter**	**Revelation**
Astarte	**Elements and Elementals**	**Incubus and Succubus**	**Wild Hunt**
Auxonne Nuns	**Evil**	**Jinn**	**Zombies**

FURTHER READING

Butler, E. M., *The Myth of the Magus,* Cambridge University Press, 1979.

Caird, G. B., *The Revelation of St John the Divine,* Harper and Row, 1966.
Cavendish, R., *Visions of Heaven & Hell,* Orbis, 1977.

Davidson, Gustav, *Dictionary of Angels,* Macmillan, 1967.

Eliade, Mircea, *Shamanism,* Pantheon Books, 1964.
Evans-Pritchard, E. E., *Witchcraft, Oracles and Magic among the Azande,* Oxford University Press, 1937.

Farrer, Austin, *The Revelation of St John the Divine,* Oxford University Press, 1964.

Gibson, J. C., *Canaanite Myths & Legends,* Attic Press, 1978.
Gluckman, M., *The Allocation of Responsibility,* Manchester University Press, 1970.
Guillaume, A., *Prophecy and Divination,* Harper and Row, 1938.

Harrison, M. W., *Angels Then & Now,* Branch-Smith, 1975.
Hole, Christina, *Haunted England,* British Books, 1951.
Hughes, T. P., *A Dictionary of Islam,* International Publications Service, 1976.
Hurston, Zora, *Tell My Horse,* Lippincott, 1938.
Huxley, Aldous, *The Devils of Loudun,* Harper & Row, 1979.
Huxley, Francis, *The Invisibles,* Humanities, 1966.

Johnson, F. R., *Witches & Demons in History and Folklore,* Johnson N.C., 1978.

Lea, H. C., *Materials Towards a History of Witchcraft,* AMS Press reprint.
Lhermitte, Jean, *True and False Possession,* Hawthorn Books, 1963.

Maple, Eric, *The Realm of Ghosts,* American Book Co.

— *The Domain of Devils,* A. S. Barnes, 1966.
Metraux, Alfred, *Voodoo in Haiti,* Schocken, 1972.
Middleton, J., ed., *Magic, Witchcraft and Curing,* University of Texas Press, 1976.

Navman, E., *Exorcism Through The Ages,* Citadel press, 1974.

Oesterreich, T. K., *Possession,* R. R. Smith, 1930.

Remy, Nicholas, *Demonolatry,* Muller, London, 1970 reprint.
Risedorf, G., *Ghosts & Ghouls,* Raintree Pubs., 1977.
Robbins, R. H., *Encyclopedia of Witchcraft and Demonology,* Crown, 1959.

Sargant, William, *Battle for the Mind,* Greenwood, 1975.
— *The Unquiet Mind,* Little, Brown, 1967.
— *The Mind Possessed,* Harper & Row, 1974.
Summers, M., *The History of Witchcraft and Demonology,* Routledge & Kegan Paul, 1973.
— ed., *Malleus Maleficarum,* Weiser.
Swete, H. B., *The Apocalypse in the Ancient Church,* Macmillan, 1911.

Tenney, M. C., *Interpreting Revelation,* Eerdmans, 1957.
Thurston, H., *Ghosts and Poltergeists,* Regnery, 1955.
Tritton, A. S., *Islam, Beliefs and Practices,* Hutchinson: Hillary House, 1966.
Turner, V. W., *The Drums of Affliction,* Cornell University Press, 1981.

Westermarck, E., *Ritual and Belief in Morocco,* Universal Books, 1968.

Zaehner, R. C., *The Dawn and Twilight of Zoroastrianism,* Putnam, 1961.

FORETELLING THE FUTURE

"Today is tomorrow's yesterday, but who knows what tomorrow brings?" The urge to look ahead into the future is buried deep in the human consciousness. Perhaps it is a way of controlling events, or imposing a known pattern on time, even a way of expressing hope and faith in better times. Whatever the reasons for its existence, fortune-telling has myriad forms, each with its individual rules and rituals.

CLASSIFIED SUBJECT GUIDE

Alphabet	**Four**	**Nine**	**Scrying**
Aquarius	**Gemini**	**Numerology**	**Seven**
Aries	**Geomancy**	**Omens**	**Six**
Astrology	**I Ching**	**One**	**Sneezing**
Augury	**Jupiter**	**Oracles**	**Stars**
Cancer	**Leo**	**Palmistry**	**Sun**
Capricorn	**Libra**	**Phrenology and Physiognomy**	**Taurus**
Cards	**Liver**	**Pisces**	**Tea-Leaf Reading**
Divination	**Lots**	**Pluto**	**Thirteen**
Dreams	**Luck**	**Prophecy**	**Three**
Eight	**Mars**	**Pyramidology**	**Twelve**
Eleven	**Mercury**	**Sagittarius**	**Two**
Fate	**Moon**	**Saturn**	**Uranus**
Five	**Necromancy**	**Scorpio**	**Venus**
Forty	**Neptune**		**Virgo**

FURTHER READING

Abbott, A. E., *Encyclopaedia of Numbers,* Emerson Press.
Anderson, M., *Palmistry,* Weiser, 1980.

Bellamy, H. S., *Moons, Myths and Man,* Faber, London, 2nd revised edition, 1950.
Besterman, T., *Crystal-Gazing,* Rider, London, 1924.
Blofeld, John, *The Book of Change,* Allen & Unwin, London, 1968.
Butler, C., *Number Symbolism,* Routledge, London, 1970.

Caird, G. B., *The Revelation of St John the Divine,* Harper and Row, 1966.
Case, P. F., *The Tarot,* Macoy, 1947.
Cavendish, Richard, *The Black Arts,* Capricorn, 1968.
— *The Tarot,* Harper & Row, 1975.
Cheiro's Language of the Hand, Arco Books, 1968 reprint.

Davidson, D. and **Aldersmith, H.,** *The Great Pyramid, its Divine Message,* Williams & Norgate, 1924.
Dickey, J., *Zodiac,* Doubleday, 1976.
Diringer, D. & F., *A History of the Alphabet throughout the ages and in all lands,* Gresham, England, 1978.
— *Writings, Its Origins and Early History,* Praeger, 1962.
Doresse, J., *The Secret Books of the Gnostics,* AMS Press reprint.
Dunne, J. W., *An Experiment with Time,* Faber, London, 3rd edition, 1934.

Edgar, J. and **M.,** *The Great Pyramid,* Bone and Hulley, 1910.
Elliot, Ralph W. V., *Runes,* Philosophical Library, 1959.
Evans-Pritchard, E. E., *Witchcraft, Oracles and Magic among the Azande,* Clarendon Press, Oxford, 1976.

Frazer, J. G., *The Golden Bough,* St. Martin's Press, 1980.

Gettings, Fred, *The Book of the Hand,* Paul Hamlyn, London, 1965.
Gibson, W. R. and **L. R.,** *The Psychic Sciences,* Pocket Books, 1968.
Gleadow, R., *The Origin of the Zodiac,* Atheneum, 1969.

Hawkes, J., *Man and the Sun, Solpub, 1978.*
Hone, M. E., *The Modern Textbook of Astrology,* Weiser.
Hopper, V. F., *Medieval Number Symbolism,* Cooper Sq. Pubs., 1969.
Howe, E., *Astrology: The Story of its Role in World War II,* Walker and Co., 1968.

Innes, Brian, *Tarot,* Arco, 1978.

Jung, C. G. and **Wilhelm, R.,** *The I Ching,* Princeton University Press, 3rd revised edition, 1979.
— *The Secret of the Golden Flower,* Harcourt, Brace and World, revised edition, 1970.

Leek, Sybil, *Book of Fortune-Telling,* W. H. Allen, London, 1970.

Mayo, J., *How to read the Ephemeris,* Llewellyn Publications.
McIntosh, C., *The Astrologers and Their Creed,* Praeger, 1969.
Melville, John, *Crystal Gazing,* Weiser, 1970 reprint.
Michell, John, *View over Atlantis,* Garnstone Press, 1969.

Papus, *The Tarot of the Bohemians,* Wilshire Books.
Parke, H. W., *Greek Oracles,* Hutchinson, London, 1967.
— *Oracles of Zeus,* Blackwell, Oxford, 1967.

Rakoczi, Basil Ivan, *The Painted Caravan,* Brucher, London, 1954.

Seward, A. F., *Zodiac and its Mysteries,* Wehman, 1967.
Sharpe, E. F., *Dream Analysis,* Brunner-Hazel, 1978.
Smyth, C. Piazzi, *Our Inheritance in the Great Pyramid,* Steiner Books, 1978.

Waite, A. E., *The Pictorial Key to the Tarot,* Wehman.
Williams, John Alden, ed., *Islam,* Braziller, 1961.
Wilcox, L. H., *Astrology, Mysticism & the Occult,* Editorial Research Services, 1980.
Wilson, Mona, *The Life of William Blake,* Oxford, 1950.
Wind, E., *Pagan Mysteries in the Renaissance,* Norton, 1969.

Zaehner, R. C., *Mysticism, Sacred and Profane,* Oxford University Press, 1967 reprint.

NATURE MYSTERIES

The origin of all religious systems derives from man's early questionings of nature. Why do the tides ebb and flow? Why is there day and night? What explanation is there for the succession of the seasons—for springtime and the harvest, for rain and sun? In the richness of the earth and the immensity of the skies, human beings found the symbolic forms for these mysteries—they made powerful creatures in the zodiac; created holy places and legends. They told stories about the creation of the world and its peoples, all inspired by the variety and beauty of the natural world.

CLASSIFIED SUBJECT GUIDE

Bread
Breath
Creation Myths
Death
Dying God
Earth
Eclipse
Egg
End of the World
Evil
Fertility
Fire
First Man
Flood
Food and Drink
Ganges
Harvest
Head
High Gods
Honey
Horns
Light
May Day
Midsummer Eve
Moon
Mother Goddess
Mountain
New Year
Night
Rainbow
Sea
Sky
Spring
Springs and Wells
Stars
Stones
Sun
Time
Twins
Vegetation Spirits
Water
Winter

FURTHER READING

Abetti, G., *Solar Research,* Macmillan, 1962.

Baillie, J. *The Belief in Progress,* Scribner, 1921.
Bellamy, H. S., *Moons, Myths and Man,* Faber London, 2nd revised edition, 1950.
Brandon, S. G. F., *Creation Legends of the Ancient Near East,* Verry, Lawrence, 1963.
— *History, Time and Deity,* Barnes and Noble, 1965.
— *Man and His Destiny in the Great Religions,* Univ. of Toronto Press, 1962.
— *The Judgement of the Dead,* Scribner, 1969.

Cirlot, J. E., *A Dictionary of Symbols,* Philosophical Library, 1962.
Conrad, Jack, *The Horn and the Sword,* Greenwood, 1973.
Cumont, F., *Astrology and Religion among the Greeks and Romans,* Peter Smith.

Daniel, Glyn, *The Idea of Prehistory,* C. A. Watts, 1964.
Doresse, J., *The Secret Books of the Egyptian Gnostics,* AMS Press reprint.

Eliade, Mircea, ed., *From Primitives to Zen,* Harper and Row, 1978.
— *Patterns in Comparative Religion,* New American Library.
— *The Forge and the Crucible,* University of Chicago Press, 1979.
— *The Sacred and the Profane,* Harcourt, Brace and World, 1968.
— *The Two and the One,* University of Chicago Press, 1979.
Evans, J., ed., *The Flowering of the Middle Ages,* McGraw-Hill, 1966.

Frankfort, H., *Ancient Egyptian Religion,* Harper and Row, 1961.
— *Kingship and the Gods,* University of Chicago Press, 1978.
Fraser, J., ed., *Voices of Time,* Braziller, 1965.
Frazer, J. G., *Folk-lore in the Old Testament,* abridged edition, Macmillan, London, 1923.
— *The Golden Bough,* St. Martin's Press, 1980.

Gaster, T., *New Year,* Abelard-Schumann, 1955.
Gedda, Luigi, *Twins in History and Science,* C. C. Thomas, 1961.
Gibson, J. C., *Canaanite Myths & Legends,* Attic Press, 1978.
Graves, Robert and **Patai, Raphael,** *Hebrew Myths,* McGraw-Hill, 1966.
Guthrie, W. K. C., *The Greeks and Their Gods,* Beacon Press, 1968.

Harris, J. Rendle, *The Cult of the Heavenly Twins,* Cambridge University Press, 1906.
Hawkes, Jacquetta, *Man and the Sun,* Solpub, 1978.
Hays, H. R., *In the Beginning: Early Man and His Gods,* Putnam, 1963.
Hick, John, *Evil and the God of Love,* Harper and Row, rev. ed., 1977.
Hiers, R. H., *Jesus and the Future,* John Knox, 1981
Hole, Christina, *Easter and Its Customs,* Barrows and Co., 1961.
—ed., *Encyclopaedia of Superstition,* Merrimack Book Services, 1979.
— *English Folklore,* Scribner, 1940.
— *English Shrines and Sanctuaries,* Batsford, 1954.
Hooke, S. H., ed., *Myth, Ritual and Kingship,* Clarendon Press, Oxford, 1958.

James, E. O., *Seasonal Feasts and Festivals,* Barnes and Noble, 1961.
— *The Cult of the Mother Goddess,* Praeger, 1959.
— *The Tree of Life,* Brill, Leiden, 1966.
— *The Worship of the Sky-God,* Athlone Press, 1963.
Jensen, A. E., *Myth and Cult among Primitive Peoples,* University of Chicago Press, 1973.
Jones, Francis, *The Holy Wells of Wales,* University of Wales Press, 1964.
Jones, T. Gwynn, *Welsh Folklore and Folk Customs,* Rowman, rev. ed., 1979.

Laborde, Errol, *Mardi Gras!,* Picayune Press, 1981.
Leeuw, G. van der, *Religion in Essence and Manifestation,* Allen and Unwin, London, 1938.

MacLagan, D., *Creation Myths,* Thames & Hudson, 1977.
Maple, Eric, *The Domain of Devils,* A. S. Barnes, 1966.
Moore, P., *Suns, Myths and Men,* Norton.
Mylonas, G. E., *Eleusis and the Eleusinian Mysteries,* Princeton University Press, 1961.

Neumann, E., *The Great Mother,* Princeton University Press, 1972.
Nock, A. D., *Early Gentile Christianity and its Hellenistic Background,* Harper and Row, 1964.
North, F. J., *Sunken Cities,* University of Wales Press, Cardiff, 1957.

Perry, W. J., *The Children of the Sun,* Methuen, London, 1923.
Pettazzoni, R., *The All-Knowing God,* Ryerson Press, 1956.
Powell-Williams, Norman, *The Ideas of the Fall and of Original Sin,* Longmans, London, 1927.

Rad, Gerhard von, *Old Testament Theology,* Harper and Row.
Rahner, Karl, *On the Theology of Death,* Nelson, London, 1961.
Regardie, Israel, *The Tree of Life,* Weiser, 1969.
Rohde, E., *Psyche,* Harper Torchbooks, 1966 reprint.
Rose, H. J., *Handbook of Greek Mythology,* Dutton, 1959.
Ross, Anne, *Pagan Celtic Britain,* Columbia University Press, 1968.

Scheinfeld, Amram, *Twins and Supertwins,* Lippincott, 1967.
Schmidt, W., *High Gods in North America,* Oxford University Press, 1933.
Scroggs, Robin, *The Last Adam,* Fortress Press, 1966.
Seznec, J., *The Survival of the Pagan Gods,* Harper Torchbooks, 1961.
Sheppard, Ronald and **Norton, Edward,** *The Story of Bread,* Fernhill, 1957.
Spencer, Sidney, *Mysticism in World Religion,* Peter Smith.

Watson, P. *Twins,* Viking Press, 1982.
Watts, Alan W., *Easter, Its Story and Meaning,* Schuman, 1950.
Wickiser, R. and others, *Mardi Gras Day,* Henry Holt, 1948.
Woolley, Sir Leonard, *Excavations at Ur,* Barnes and Noble, 1963.

PLANTS AND ANIMALS IN MYTHOLOGY

Human beings have always been fascinated by other living things on earth. In an all-embracing urge to perceive magic in everything, we have included plants and animals into our belief systems and folk tales, and this has provided us with a precious heritage. Flowers, herbs and trees have accumulated some wonderful stories—they can heal, lull you to sleep, bring you luck, ward off witches—and you can be enchanted in the uncanny forest. A similar tradition applies to animals—they have sometimes shared man's life on the most intimate terms. "The magical mimicry by which a man turns himself into a beast may also be the magic by which he transforms himself into a god."

CLASSIFIED SUBJECT GUIDE

Animals	Elder	Lizard	Scarab
Apple	Elephant	Lotus	Scorpion
Ash	Fig	Magpie and Rook	Seal
Bat	Fir	Mandrake	Serpent
Bean	Fish	Mistletoe	Sheep
Bear	Frog	Mushroom	Spider
Birds	Garlic	Nightingale	Stag
Boar	Goat	Oak	Stork
Bull	Goose	Olive	Swallow
Cat	Hare	Ostrich	Swan
Cock	Hawthorn	Owl	Toad
Corn	Hazel	Palm	Trees
Cow	Herbs	Peacock	Trout
Crane	Holly and Ivy	Pelican	Vervain
Crow	Horse	Pig	Whale
Cuckoo	Houseleek	Plants and Flowers	Wildwood
Diver	Hyena and Jackal	Robin	Willow
Dog	Insects	Rose	Woodpecker
Dolphin	Laurel	Rowan	Wren
Dove	Lily	St John's Wort	Wryneck
Eagle	Lion	Salmon	Yew

FURTHER READING

Altheim, F., *A History of Roman Religion,* Dutton, 1938.
Armstrong, E. A., *The Folklore of Birds,* Dover, 1969.
— *The Wren,* Macmillan, 1955.

Campbell, Joseph, *The Masks of God: Primitive Mythology,* Viking Press, 1968.
Carpenter, Rhys, *Folk Tale, Fiction and Saga in the Homeric Epics,* University of California Press, 1974.
Conrad, J. R. *The Horn and the Sword,* Greenwood, 1973
Cottrell, L., *The Bull of Minos,* Evans, London, 1953.

Dale-Green, Patricia, *Cult of the Cat,* Houghton Mifflin, 1963.
— *Dog,* Houghton Mifflin, 1967.

Eliade, Mircea, *Patterns in Comparative Religion,* New American Library.
Evans, Sir A., *The Palace of Minos,* Biblo and Tannen, 1921.
Evans, G. E., *Ask the Fellows Who Cut the Hay,* Faber, London, 1966.
Evans-Pritchard, E. E., The Nuer, Oxford University Press, 1969.

Frankfort, Henri, *Before Philosophy,* Penguin, London, 1949.
— *Ancient Egyptian Religion,* Harper & Row.
Frazer, J. G., *The Golden Bough,* St. Martin's Press, 1980.

Glueck, N., *Deities and Dolphins,* Farrar, Straus and Giroux, 1965.
Guthrie, W. K. C., *The Greeks and their Gods,* Beacon Press, 1968.

Harter, W. *Birds: In Fact & Legend,* Stirling, 1979.
Heron-Allen, E., *Barnacles in Nature and Myth,* Oxford University Press, 1928.
Hole, Christina, ed., *Encyclopaedia of Superstitions,* Book Services, 1979.
Howey, M. Oldfield, *The Horse in Magic and Myth,* Castle Books, 1958.

Ingersoll, E., *Birds in Legend, Fable and Folklore,* Gale, 1968.

Jung, E. and **Von Franz, M.-L.**, *The Grail Legend,* Sigo Press.

Keen, M., *The Outlaws of Medieval Legend,* Univ. of Toronto Press, 1961.

Lack, David, *Robin Redbreast,* Oxford University Press, 1950.
— *The Life of the Robin,* Beekman, 1970.

Mabinogion, The, translated by G. and T. Jones, Biblio Distributors, 1976.

Opie, I. and **P.**, *The Oxford Dictionary of Nursery Rhymes,* Oxford University Press, 1957.

Ross, Anne, *Pagan Celtic Britain,* Columbia University Press, 1967.

Sheppard, R. and **Newton, E.**, *The Story of Bread,* Fernhill, 1957.
Spence, L., *Myths and Legends of Ancient Egypt,* Harrap, London, 1949.
Stenuit, R., *The Dolphin,* Dent, London, 1969

Thompson, D'Arcy, *A Glossary of Greek Birds,* Oxford University Press, 1936.

Vernon, A., *History & Romance of the Horse,* Gale, 1975.

Wilkins, E., *The Rose-Garden Game,* Gollancz, London, 1969.

ORIGINS OF MYTHOLOGY, RELIGION AND MAGIC

The human race has occupied areas of the earth as sharply contrasted as Scandinavia and Egypt; Finland and India; Africa and America; China and Australia. Yet, wherever cultures have grown up, there are common universal themes running through their major religions and mythologies. These explore the mysteries of birth and death, the progression of the seasons, the riddle of the creation of the earth. In addition to these major themes there are also specific, national influences at work. It is this interweaving of the huge variety of local customs and experiences that makes up the marvellous tapestry of the world's religious systems.

FURTHER READING

Albright, W. F., *From the Stone Age to Christianity,* John Hopkins Press, 1957.
Allen, T. C., *The Egyptian Book of the Dead,* Chicago University Press, 1960.
Allen, T. W., **Halliday, W. R.**, and **Sikes, E. E.**, *The Homeric Hymns,* AMS Press reprint.
Altheim, F., *A History of Roman Religion,* Dutton, 1938.

Bailey, C., *Phases in the Religion of Ancient Rome,* Greenwood Press, 1972.
Bailey, D. S., *The Sexual Relation in Christian Thought,* Harper and Row, 1959.
Behr, C. A., *Aelius Aristides and the Sacred*

Tales, Hakkert, 1968.

Bosi, Roberto, *The Lapps,* Greenwood Press, 1976.

Brandon, S. G. F., *Creation Legends of the Ancient Near East,* Verry, Lawrence, 1963.

— *History, Time and Deity,* Barnes and Noble, 1965.

— *The Judgement of the Dead,* Scribner, 1969.

— *Man and His Destiny in the Great Religions,* University of Toronto Press, 1962.

— ed., *The Saviour God,* Barnes and Noble, 1963.

Breasted, J. H., *Development of Religion and Thought in Ancient Egypt,* Peter Smith, 1959.

Budge, E. A. W., *The Book of the Dead,* Universal Books Company, 1960.

— *Osiris and the Egyptian Resurrection,* P. L. Warner, 1911.

Burland, C. A., *The Ancient Maya,* John Day, 1967.

— *The Gods of Mexico,* Putnam, 1967.

— *Magic Books from Mexico,* Penguin, London, 1955.

— *The Incas,* Silver, 1979.

Bushbell, G. H. S., *Ancient Arts of the Americas,* Praeger, 1965.

Cavendish, R., *The Great Religions,* Contact, 1980.

Cerny, J., *Ancient Egyptian Religion,* Greenwood, 1979.

Clark, K., *The Nude,* Princeton University Press, 1972.

Colledge, M. A. R., *The Parthians,* Praeger, 1967.

Cook, A. B., *Zeus,* Biblo & Tanner.

Cotterell, A., *Minoan World,* Scribner, 1980

Crosher, J., *Aztecs,* Silver, 1977.

Cross, T. P. and **Slover, C. H.,** *Ancient Irish Tales,* Barnes and Noble, 1966.

Cunliffe, B., *Celtic World,* McGraw, 1973.

Dennis, G., *The Cities and Cemeteries of Etruria,* Dent, London, 1907.

De Waal Malefijt, A., *Religion and Culture,* Macmillan, 1968.

Dodds, E. R., *The Greeks and the Irrational,* Univ. of California Press, 1951.

Driver, Miles J. C., *The Babylonian Laws,* Oxford University Press, 1952–55.

Durkheim, E., *The Division of Labour in Society,* Free Press, 1947.

Duthie, A., *Greek Mythology,* Greenwood, 1979.

Edelstein, E. and **L.,** *Asclepius,* Arno, 1976.

Eliade, Mircea, *Cosmos and History: The Myth of the Eternal Return,* Harper and Row Torchbooks, 1959.

— *Patterns in Comparative Religion,* New American Library.

— *Gods, Goddesses & Myths of Creation,* Harper & Row, 1974.

Ellis Davidson, H. R., *Gods and Myths of Northern Europe,* Penguin, London, 1965.

— *Pagan Scandinavia,* Thames & Hudson, London, 1967.

— *Scandinavian Mythology,* Hamlyn, London, 1969.

Engnell, I., *Studies in Divine Kingship in the Ancient Near East,* Allenson, 2nd edition, 1967.

Evans, J. D., *Malta,* Praeger, 1959.

Evans-Pritchard, E. E., *The Divine Kingship*

CLASSIFIED SUBJECT GUIDE

Amazons	**Egypt**	**Ishtar**	**Carthaginians**
Animism	**Eros**	**Isis**	**Poseidon**
Aphrodite	**Eternal Return**	**Janus**	**Prehistoric Religion**
Apollo	**Etruscans**	**King**	**Priests**
Astarte	**Finland**	**Lapland**	**Prostitution**
Athene	**Founding of Rome**	**Lares**	**Religion**
Aztecs	**Freyr**	**Loki**	**Ritual**
Baal	**Germanic Mythology**	**Mabinogion**	**Rome**
Balder	**Great Chain of Being**	**Malta**	**Sacrifice**
Book of the Dead	**Greece**	**Man**	**Scandinavia**
Bran	**Grimm**	**Marduk**	**Serapis**
Brigit	**Harranian Religion**	**Mars**	**Seth**
Brittany	**Healing Gods**	**Maya**	**Sibyls**
Cauldron	**Hecate**	**Mesopotamia**	**Slavs**
Caves	**Hephaestus**	**Mithras**	**Stonehenge**
Celts	**Hera**	**Nibelungenlied**	**Syria and Palestine**
Circe	**Hermes**	**Oath**	**Tammuz**
Crete	**History**	**Odin**	**Tara**
Cronus	**Hittites**	**Ohrmazd**	**Thor**
Cybele	**Horus**	**Osiris**	**Venus**
Demeter	**Ikhnaten**	**Pan**	**Woman**
Diana	**Imhotep**	**Parthians**	**Zeus**
Dionysus	**Incas**	**Persephone**	**Zoroastrianism**
Dualism	**India**	**Phoenicians and**	**Zurvan**

of the Shilluk of the Nilotic Sudan, Macmillan, 1948.

Farnell, L. R., *The Cults of the Greek States,* Caratzas Bros, 1977.

Frankfort, H., *Kingship and the Gods,* University of Chicago Press, 1978.

Frazer, J. G., *The Golden Bough,* St. Martin's Press, 1980.

Frye, R. N., *The Heritage of Persia,* World Publishing, 1962.

Galinsky, G. K., *Aeneas, Sicily and Rome,* Princeton University Press, 1969.

Gardner, A. H., *Egypt of the Pharaohs,* Oxford University Press, 1966.

Ghirshman, R., *Iran,* Penguin, 1978.

Gibson, J. C., *Canaanite Myths & Legends,* Attic Press, 1978.

Gluckman, M., *Custom and Conflict in Africa,* Barnes and Noble, 1969.

— *Politics, Law and Ritual in Tribal Society,* Aldine, 1965.

The Golden Ass of Apuleius, translated by W. Aldington, Century Bookbindery, 1981.

Gordon, C. H., *Ugaritic Literature,* Argonaut.

Grant, M., *Myths of the Greeks and Romans,* New American Library, 1964.

Grant, R. M., *Gnosticism and Early Christianity,* Harper and Row, 1966.

Graves, Robert, *The Greek Myths,* Braziller, 1959.

Gray, G. B., *Sacrifice in the Old Testament,* Ktav Publishing, 1970.

Gray, J., *The Canaanites,* Praeger, 1964.

— *The Legacy of Canaan,* Humanities, 1967.

— *Near Eastern Mythology,* Paul Hamlyn, London, 1970.

Gray, L. J., ed., *Mythology of All Races,* Cooper Square Publishers, 1964.

Greer, Germaine, *The Female Eunuch,* McGraw-Hill, 1980.

Griffiths, J. G., *The Origins of Osiris,* Argonaut.

Gurney, O. R., *The Hittites,* Penguin, London, revised edition, 1969.

Guthrie, W. K. C., *The Greeks and Their Gods,* Beacon Press, 1968.

— *Orpheus and Greek Religion,* Norton, 1967.

Hallow, W. W. and **Van Dijk, J. J. A.,** *The Exaltation of Inanna,* AMS Press, 1979.

Harden, Donald, *The Phoenicians,* Praeger, 1962.

Harrison, J., *Prolegomena to the Study of Greek Religion,* Merlin, 1981.

Hawkes, J., *Dawn of the Gods,* Random House, 1968.

Hawkins, Gerald S., *Stonehenge Decoded,* Dell, 1966.

Hays, H. R., *The Dangerous Sex,* Putnam, 1964.

Henning, M., tr. by, *The Hymns of Zarathustra,* Hyperion, 1980.

Hesiod, *Loeb edition,* Harvard University Press.

Hesiod & Theogius, trs. by P. Werder, Penguin, 1976.

Hodgkin, R., *History of the Anglo-Saxons,* Oxford University Press, 3rd edition, 1953.

Hogg, A. G., *The Christian Message to the Hindu,* Macmillan, 1947.

Hooke, S. H., *Middle Eastern Mythology,* Penguin, London, 1963.

— ed., *Myth, Ritual and Kingship,* Oxford University Press, 1958.

Huergon, J., *Daily Life of the Etruscans,* Macmillan, 1964.

Hurry, J. B., *Imhotep,* Ares Publishers, 1978.

Hyams, E. and **Ordish, G.,** *The Last of the Incas,* Simon and Schuster, 1963.

Jackson, K. H., *The International Popular Tale and Early Welsh Tradition,* Oxford University Press, 1961.

James, E. O., *The Ancient Gods,* Putnam, 1964.

— *The Worship of the Sky-God,* Athlone Press, 1963.

— *Christian Myth and Ritual,* Peter Smith.

— *Comparative Religion,* Methuen, Barnes and Noble, 1961.

— *The Cult of the Mother Goddess,* Barnes and Noble, 1961.

— *The Nature and Function of Priesthood,* Barnes and Noble, 1955.

— *The Origin of Sacrifice,* John Murray, London, 1933.

— *Prehistoric Religion,* Barnes and Noble, 1961.

Jayne, W. A., *The Healing Gods of Ancient Civilizations,* AMS Press reprint.
Johnson, A. R., *Sacral Kingship in Ancient Israel,* Verry, revised edition.
Jonas, Hans, *The Gnostic Religion,* Peter Smith, rev. ed.
Jones, Gwyn and **Thomas**, *The Mabinogion,* Biblio Distributors, 1976.

Kerenyi, C., *Asklepios,* Thames & Hudson, London, 1960.
— *Eleusis: Archetypal Image of Mother and Daughter,* Princeton University Press, 1967.
Kramer, S. N., *Sumerian Mythology,* University of Pennsylvania Press, 1972.
— *The Sumerians,* University of Chicago Press, 1971.

Langdon, S., *The Babylonian Epic of Creation,* Clarendon Press, Oxford, 1923.
Levy, G. R., *The Gate of Horn,* Humanities, 1968.
Licht, H., *Sexual Life in Ancient Greece,* Greenwood, 1976.
Livy, *History of Rome,* Loeb edition, Harvard University Press.

Mackenzie, D. A., *Egyptian Myth & Legend,* Longwood Press, 1976.
Magoun Jr., F. P., *Kalevala,* Harvard University Press.
Manker, Ernest, *People of the Eight Seasons,* Studio Publications, 1964.
Maringer, J., *The Gods of Prehistoric Man,* Knopf, 1960.
Massignon, G., ed., *Folktales of France,* University of Chicago Press, 1968.
Mercer, S. A. B., *The Religion of Ancient Egypt,* Luzac, London, 1949.
— *The Pyramid Texts,* Longmans, Toronto, 1952.
Michaelis-Jena, R., *The Brothers Grimm,* Praeger, 1970.
— *New Tales from Grimm,* Smithers, 1960.
Michels, A. K., *The Calendar of the Roman Republic,* Greenwood Press, 1978.
Moscati, S., *The World of the Phoenicians,* Praeger, 1968.
Moule, C. F. D., *The Sacrifice of Christ,* Fortress, 1964.

Nibelungenlied, translated by A. T. Hatto, Penguin, London, 1964, with commentary.
Nicholson, Irene, *Firefly in the Night,* Faber, London, 1959.
Nilsson, M. P., *Greek Popular Religion,* Harper and Row, 1940.
— *History of Greek Religion,* Greenwood, 1980.
— *The Minoan-Mycenaean Religion,* Lund, Sweden, 1950.
— *The Mycenaean Origin of Greek Mythology,* University of California Press, 1973.

Ogilvie, R. M., *The Romans and Their Gods,* Norton, 1970.
Oppenheim, A. L., *Ancient Mesopotamia, Portrait of a Dead Civilization,* University of Chicago Press, 1977.
Otto, E., *Egyptian Art and the Cults of Osiris and Amon,* Abrams, 1967.

Palmer, R. E. A., *The Archaic Community of the Romans,* Cambridge University Press, 1970.
Panniker, R., *The Unknown Christ of Hinduism,* Orbis Books, 1981.
Panofsky, D. and **E.**, *Pandora's Box,* Harper Torchbooks, 1965 reprint.
Piggott, Stuart, *Ancient Europe,* Aldine Publishing, 1966.
— *The Druids,* Praeger, 1968.
Plutarch, *Lives,* translated by E. Cary, Loeb edition, Harvard University Press.
Powell, T. G. E., *The Celts,* Praeger, 1958.

Radhakrishnan, S., *East and West Religion,* Macmillan, 1933.
— and **Raju, P. T., ed.**, *The Concept of Man,* Johnsen, 1966.
Raymond, E., *Stonehenge & Druidism,* Artisan Sales, 1979.
Richardson, E., *Etruscans,* Univ. of Chicago Press, 1976.
Ringgren, H., *The Messiah in the Old Testament,* Allenson, 1956.
Rose, H. J., *Ancient Roman Religion,* Hutchinson: Hillary House, 1948 reprint.
— *A Handbook of Greek Mythology,* Dutton, 1959.
Ross, Anne, *Everyday Life of the Ancient Celts,* Batsford, London, 1970.
— *Pagan Celtic Britain,* Columbia University Press, 1968.
Rossiter, S., *Blue Guide to Malta,* Rand McNally, 1979.
Rostovtzeff, M. I., *Caravan Cities,* AMS Press reprint.

Saggs, H. W. F., *The Greatness that was Babylon,* Praeger, 1969.
Savoy, G., *Vilcabamba: Lost City of the Incas,* R. Hale, 1971.
Scholem, G. G., *On the Kabbalah and its Symbolism,* Schocken, 1969.
Scullard, H. H., *The Etruscan Cities and Rome,* Cornell Univ. Press, 1967.
Seltman, Charles, *The Twelve Olympians: Gods and Goddesses of Greece,* Apollo Editions.
Sharpe, E. J., *Not to Destroy but to Fulfil,* Gleerup, 1965.
Soustelle, Jacques, *Daily Life among the Aztecs,* Macmillan, 1962.
Stern, J., *Grimm's Fairy Tales,* Routledge, London, 1948.

Thompson, J. E., *The Rise and Fall of Maya Civilization,* University of Oklahoma Press, 1977.
Thomson, G., *The Prehistoric Aegean,* Beekman Publishers, 1978.
Turner, V. W., *Forest of Symbols,* Cornell University Press, 1967.
— *The Ritual Process,* Cornell University Press, 1977.
Turville Petre, E. O. G., *Myth and Religion of the North,* Greenwood Press, 1975.

Vaillant, G. C., *The Aztecs of Mexico,* Doubleday, 1962.
Vaughan, A. C., *The House of the Double Axe,* Doubleday, 1959.
Virgil, *Aenid,* edited by K. W. Grangden, Cambridge University Press, 1976.

Wagenvoort, H., *Roman Dynamism,* Greenwood Press, 1976.
Wach, J., *The Comparative Study of Religion,* Columbia University Press, 1958.
Walker, B., *Hindu World,* Praeger, 1968.
Webster, T. B. L., *From Mycenae to Homer,* Praeger, 1959.
Wheeler, Sir Mortimer, *Early India and Pakistan,* Praeger, 1968.
— *The Indus Civilization,* Cambridge University Press, 3rd edition, 1968.
Willets, R. F., *Ancient Crete: A Social History,* University of Toronto Press, 1965.
— *Cretan Cults and Festivals,* Greenwood, 1980.

Zaehner, R. C., *The Dawn and Twilight of Zoroastrianism,* Putnam, 1961.
— *The Teachings of the Magi,* Oxford University Press, 1976.
— *Zurvan, a Zoroastrian Dilemma,* Biblo & Tanner, 1973.

SYMBOLS AND MEANINGS IN MYTHOLOGY AND RELIGION

Men employ symbols because they invoke powerful associations. We have only to think of our national flag to be aware of how strongly this can represent our feelings about our country—of love, nostalgia, awe, longing, pride, shame—a host of feelings. In the same way, we have used symbols in religion and mythology, again to express powerful emotions in a kind of shorthand. The cross must be one of the best known of all religious symbols. It brings to mind the mystery of the crucifixion and the resurrection which lies at the heart of Christianity. Other symbols are found in art, in drama and in dance—"Through symbols, dances, pictures, man has given shape to the intangible, form to the invisible, flesh to the shadow."

FURTHER READING

Alexander, M. trans., *The Earliest English Poems,* Penguin, London.
Alford, Violet, *Sword Dance and Drama.* Dufour, 1963.
— and **Gallop, R.**, *The Traditional Dance,* Methuen, London, 1935.
Amis, K., *New Maps of Hell,* Arno, 1975.
Atkins, S., *Goethe's Faust,* Harvard University Press, 1958.

Baughman, E., *Type and Motif Index of the Folktales of England and North America,* Mouton, The Hague, 1966.
Bergin, O., *Bardic Poetry,* Dolmen Press, Dublin, 1967.
Bevan, E., *Holy Images,* AMS Press reprint.

CLASSIFIED SUBJECT GUIDE

Art	**Drum**	**Iconography**	**Riddles**
Bells	**Ensor**	**Landscape**	**Rossetti, D. G.**
Blake	**Feather**	**Masks**	**Science Fiction**
Bosch	**Films**	**Milton**	**Scottish and Border Ballads**
Breughel	**Folkplays**	**Morris Dances**	**Ship**
Carole	**Folktales**	**Music**	**Song**
Cave Art	**Fool**	**Mystery Plays**	**Steps and Ladders**
Children's Games	**Games**	**Navel**	**Swastika**
Costume	**Goethe**	**Nursery Rhymes**	**Sword**
Cross	**Hammer**	**Oil**	**Symbolism**
Dance	**Head-Dress**	**Path Symbolism**	**Trumpet**
Dance of Death	**Helston Furry Dance**	**Phallic Symbolism**	**Wagner**
Dancing Mania	**Hermaphrodite**	**Poets**	**Wheel**
Dante	**Hobby-Horse**	**Redon, Odilon**	**Wings**
Drama	**Horseshoe**	**Religion**	

Blackstone, Bernard, *English Blake;* Shoe String Press, 1966.
Blunt, A., *The Art of William Blake,* Columbia, 1959.
Bourguet, P. du, *Early Christian Painting,* Viking Press.
Brandel, Rose, *The Music of Central Africa,* Norton, 1976.
Brandon, S. G. F., ed., *A Dictionary of Comparative Religion,* Scribner, 1970.
Briggs, K. M., *Dictionary of British Folktales,* Routledge, London, 1970.
Butler, E. M., *The Fortunes of Faust,* Cambridge University Press, 1979.
Butler, Ivan, *The Horror Film,* A. S. Barnes, 1967.

Campbell, L. A., *Mithraic Iconography and Ideology,* Brill, Leiden, 1968.
Carney, J., *The Irish Bardic Poets,* Dufour, 1968.
Carter, L., *Dragons, Elves and Heroes,* Ballantyne Books, 1971.
— *The Young Magicians,* Ballantyne Books, 1971.
Case, P. F., *The Tarot,* Macoy, 1977.
Cavendish, R., *The Black Arts,* Putnam, 1967.
Chamberlain, Houston Stewart, *Richard Wagner,* Dutton, 1909.
Chambers, Sir Edmund, *The English Folk-Play,* Russell, 1964 reprint.
— *The Mediaeval Stage,* Clarendon, Oxford, 1903.
Chase, Gilbert, *America's Music,* McGraw-Hill, 1966.
Chevalier, J., *Dictionnaire des Symboles,* French European Publications, 1973.
Child, Francis James, ed., *The English and Scottish Popular Ballads,* Peter Smith.
Cirlot, J. E., *A Dictionary of Symbols,* Philosophical Library, 1972 2nd ed.
Clarens, Carlos, *Illustrated History of Horror Movies,* Putnam, 1967.
Clark, J. M., *The Dance of Death in the Middle Ages and the Renaissance,* Jackson, Glasgow, 1950.
Clark, K., *Landscape into Art,* Harper and Row, 1978.
Clarke, W. K. L., ed., *Liturgy and Worship,* Allenson, 1932.
Crawley, A. C., ed., *Everyman and Medieval Plays,* Everyman Library, Dutton, 1956.
Cutner, H., *A Short History of Sex Worship,* Watts, 1940.

Dante, *Inferno,* translated by L. Binyon, St Martin's Press, 1933.
— *Paradise,* translated by L. Binyon, St Martin's Press, 1943.
— *Purgatory,* translated by L. Binyon, St Martin's Press, 1938.
Davies, J. G., *The Theology of William Blake,* Oxford University Press, 1948.
Digby, G. W., *Symbol and Image in William Blake,* Oxford Univ. Press, 1957.
Donington, Robert, *Wagner's 'Ring' and its Symbols,* Merrimack Book Services, 1974.
Dorson, R. D., *The British Folklorists,* University of Chicago Press, 1969.
Douglas, Mary, *Natural Symbols,* Pantheon Books, 1970.

Eliade, Mircea, *Patterns in Comparative Religion,* New American Library.
Elliott, R. C., *The Power of Satire,* Princeton University Press, 1960.
Ellis Davidson, H. R., *The Sword in Anglo-Saxon England,* Oxford University Press, 1962.

Ferguson, G., *Signs and Symbols in Christian Art,* Oxford Univ. Press, 1966.
Foote, Henry W., *Three Centuries of American Hymnody,* Shoe String Press, 1968 reprint.
Franger, Wilhelm, *The Millennium of Hieronymus Bosch,* University of Chicago Press, 1952.
Frankfort, H., *The Art and Architecture of the Ancient Orient,* Penguin, 1978.
Franklin, H. B., *Future Perfect,* Oxford University Press, 1966.
Friedenthal, R., *Goethe: His Life and Times,* World Publishing, 1965.
Fryre, N., *Fearful Symmetry,* Princeton University Press, 1947.

Goethe, Johann Wolfgang von, *Faust,* translated by Sir Theodore Martin, Dutton.
— *Faust,* translated by Bayard Taylor, Collier-Macmillan, 1962.
Gorer, G., *Africa Dances,* Norton, revised edition, 1962.
Grabar, A., *Early Christian Art,* Braziller, 1967.
Graves, Robert, *The White Goddess,* Octagon Books, 1972.
Gray, R. D., *Goethe the Alchemist,* AMS Press reprint.
Graziosi, P., *Palaeolithic Art,* McGraw-Hill, 1960.

Hadow W. H., *Richard Wagner,* AMS Press reprint.
Harrison, M., *The History of the Hat,* Herbert Jenkins, 1960.
Hatfield, H., *Goethe: A Critical Introduction,* Harvard University Press, 1964.
Hirst, D., *Hidden Riches: Traditional Symbolism from the Renaissance to Blake,* Barnes and Noble, 1964.
Hole, Christina, ed., *Encyclopedia of Superstitions,* Hutchinson, London, 1961.
— *British Folk Customs,* Hutchinson, London, 1971.
Huet, M., *Dance, Art & Ritual of Africa,* Pantheon, 1978.

Ingram, T., *Bells in England,* Saunders.

Jung, C. G., *Symbols of Transformation,* Princeton University Press 2nd edition, 1967.
— ed., *Man and His Symbols,* State Mutual Books, 1981.

Kemper, R. H., *Costume,* Newsweek, 1978.
Kennedy, D., *England's Dances,* Clarke, Irwin, 1949.
Keynes, Geoffrey, ed., *The Complete Writings of William Blake,* Random House, 1957.
Kracauer, Siegfried, *From Caligari to Hitler,* Dobson, London, 1947.
Krappe, A. H., *The Science of Folklore,* Norton, 1964.
Kurath, Gertrude P., *Michigan Indian Festivals,* Ann Arbor Publishers, 1966.

Laming, A., *Lascaux,* Penguin, London.
Lang, Andrew, *Custom and Myth,* 2nd rev. ed. AMS Press.
Lawler, L. B., *The Dance in Ancient Greece,* Columbia University Press, 1978.
Leroi-Gourhan, A., *Treasures of Prehistoric Art,* Abrams, 1967.
Lewes, H. G., *The Life of Goethe,* ed. V. Lange, Ungar, 1965.
Lewis, C. S., *Of Other Worlds,* Harcourt, Brace and World, 1966.
Liddell, L. A., *Clothes & Your Appearance,* Goodheart, 1981.

Male, E., *The Gothic Image,* Harper & Row, 1973.
Mallowan, M. E. L., *Early Mesopotamia and Iran,* McGraw-Hill, 1965.
Maringer, J. and **Bandi, H.,** *Art in the Ice Age,* Praeger, 1953.
Mellaart, J., *Earliest Civilisations of the Near East,* McGraw-Hill, 1966.
Mills, G., *The Neoplatonism of William Blake,* Harper and Row, 1961.
Montgomerie, Norah and **William,** *The Hogarth Book of Scottish Nursery Rhymes,* Clarke, Irwin, 1964.
Moore, P., *Science and Fiction,* Norwood Editions, 1980.
Murray, Gilbert, *A History of Ancient Greek Literature,* Folcroft reprint.
Mylonas, G. E., *Eleusis and the Eleusinian Mysteries,* Princeton University Press, 1961.

Nettle, Bruno, *Music in Primitive Culture,* Harvard University Press, 1956.
Newell, W. W., *Games and Songs of American Children,* Dover, 1903.
Nicholls, P., *Science Fiction at Large,* Harper & Row, 1977.
Nicholson, M. Hope, *Voyages to the Moon,* Collier-Macmillan, 1960.

Nicoll, Allardyce, *English Drama: a Modern Viewpoint,* Barnes and Noble, 1968.
— *Masks, Mimes and Miracles,* Cooper Square, 1964.
— *World Drama,* Harcourt, Brace and World, 1949.
Nicholson, Alexander, *Gaelic Riddles and Enigmas,* Folcroft, 1976.
Nketia, J. H. Kwabena, *Drumming in Akan Communities of Ghana,* Humanities, 1963.

Oakeshott, R. E., *The Archaeology of Weapons,* Praeger, 1963.
Opie, Iona and **Peter,** *Children's Games in Street and Playground,* Oxford University Press, 1969.
— *The Oxford Dictionary of Nursery Rhymes,* Oxford University Press, 1951.

Parrot, A., *The Temple of Jerusalem,* Philosophical Library, 1957.
Parsons, Elsie C., *Pueblo Indian Religion,* University of Chicago Press, 1939.
Pollard, A. W., ed., *English Miracle Plays, Moralities and Interludes,* Richard West.

Raine, K., *Blake and Tradition,* Princeton University Press, 1968.
Raphael, A., *Goethe and the Philosophers' Stone,* Routledge, London, 1965.
Reymond, A. E., *The Mythical Origin of the Egyptian Temple,* Barnes and Noble, 1969.
Routley, E., *Church Music & the Christian Faith,* Hope, 1979.
Ruse, F., *Dance in Society,* Routledge and Kegan Paul, London, 1969.

Sachs, C., *World History of the Dance,* Norton, 1978.
Sayers, D. L., *Hell, Purgatory,* Penguin, London, 1962.
Sieveking, A., *Cave Artists,* Thames & Hudson, 1979.
Sisson, C. H., *The Divine Comedy,* Regnery-Gateway, 1981.
Speck, Frank G. and **Broom, L.,** *Cherokee Dance and Drama,* University of California Press, 1951.
Strindberg, A., tr. by A. Paulson, *Dance of Death,* Norton, 1976.

Taylor, Archer, *English Riddles from Oral Tradition,* Octagon Books, 1977.
— and **Hull, Vernam,** *A Collection of Irish Riddles,* University of California Press.
Thompson, Stith, *The Folk-Tale,* University of California Press, 1977.
Tolnay de C., *Hieronymus Bosch,* Reynal.
Toulmin Smith, Lucy, ed., *The York Plays,* Russell.

Ucko, P. J. and **Rosenfeld, R.,** *Palaeolithic Cave Art,* McGraw-Hill, 1967.
Van der Leeuw G., *Sacred and Profane Beauty,* Abingdon, 1968.
Von Simpson, O., *The Gothic Cathedral,* Princeton University Press, 1973.

Waite, A. E., *The Pictorial Key to the Tarot,* Citadel, 1979.
Walker, B., *Hindu World,* Praeger, 1968.
— *Sex and the Supernatural,* Macdonald, London, 1970.
Watson, D., *Richard Wagner,* Schirmer Books, 1981.
Webster, H., *Primitive Secret Societies,* Octagon Books, 1968 reprint.
Wells, Evelyn Kendrick, *The Ballad Tree,* Ronald Press, 1950.
Welsford, E., *The Court Masque,* Russell, 1962 reprint.
Weston, Jessie L., *The Legends of the Wagner Drama,* Nutt, 1896.
Wilkins, E., *The Rose-Garden Game,* Herder and Herder, 1969.
Wilkinson, E. M. and **Willoughby, L. A.,** *Goethe: Poet and Thinker,* Barnes and Noble, 1962.
Wimberley, Lowry C., *Folklore of the English and Scottish Ballads,* University of Chicago Press, 1928.

Zambrano, A. L., *Horror,* Gordon Press, 1975.

THE HERO'S QUEST

Human experience has mainly been turbulent and full of struggle. We have felt small and insignificant when ranged against the immensity of the universe about us. Yet, human beings have always displayed a remarkable capacity for imagination and expansiveness; the miracles of survival in the face of flood and famine could be translated into superhuman courage and valour—the slaying of the dragons that the universe pits against us. The other side of impotence is unlimited strength—the daring of Hercules; the valour of Galahad; the vision of the knight in search of the Grail. The vast majority of the human race may be weak and vulnerable, but heroic figures do emerge to echo our braver dreams.

CLASSIFIED SUBJECT GUIDE

Achilles
Alexander the Great
Arthur
Attila
Beowulf
Brendan, St
Camelot and Arthurian Britain
Cu Chulainn
Finn
Galahad
Gawain
Gilgamesh
Glastonbury
Grail
Gwydion
Hercules
Hero
Jack
Lancelot
Lleu
Merlin
Morgan le Fay
Parsifal
Prometheus
Robin Hood
Theseus
Tristan
Troy
Wandering Jew

FURTHER READING

Ashe, Geoffrey, *From Caesar to Arthur,* Collins, London, 1960.
— *King Arthur's Avalon,* Dutton, 1958.
— *Land to the West: St Brendan's Voyage to America,* Viking Press, 1962.
— ed., *The Quest for Arthur's Britain,* Granada Publishing Ltd., 1980.

Barber, R. W., *Arthurian Legends,* State Mutual Bks., 1981.
Beowulf, translated by M. Alexander, Penguin, London, 1973.
Beroul, *Romance of Tristan,* Penguin.
Blegen, C. W., *Troy and the Trojans,* Praeger, 1963.
— and others, *Troy,* Princeton University Press, 1950-58.
Bowra, C. M., *Heroic Poetry,* St Martin's Press, 1969.
Bromwich, Rachel, *Trioedd Yns Prydein, The Welsh Triads,* University of Wales Press, Cardiff, 1961.

Campbell, J., *The Hero with a Thousand Faces,* Princeton Univ. Press, 1968.
Cary, G., *The Medieval Alexander,* Cambridge University Press, 1967.
Cavendish, R., *King Arthur and the Grail—The Arthurian Legends and their Meaning,* Taplinger, 1979.
Chadwick, H. M. and **N. K.,** *The Growth of Literature,* Cambridge University Press, 1969.
Chambers, R. W., ed., *Beowulf: An Introduction,* Cambridge Univ. Press, 1959.
Chretien de Troyes, *Yvain,* Everyman, London.
— *Erec et Enide,* Everyman, London.
— *Lancelot,* Everyman, London.
Eliade, Mircea, *Patterns in Comparative Religion,* New American Library.
Epic of Gilgamesh, The, translated by R. C. Thompson, AMS Press, 1979.

Farnell, L. R., *Cults of the Greek States,* 5 Vols, Caratzas Bros., 1977.
Finley, M. I., *The World of Odysseus,* Revised edition, Viking Press, 1978.
Forrest, M., ed., *Troy & the Early Greeks,* Cambridge University Press, 1973.
Frazer, J. G., *Apollodorus,* Loeb Library, 1921.
— *Myths of the Origin of Fire,* Hacker, reprint.

Garmonsway, G. N., Simpson, J. and **Ellis Davidson, H. R.,** *Beowulf and Its Analogues,* Dutton.
Geoffrey of Monmouth, *History of the Kings of Britain,* Penguin, London.
Gottfried von Strassburg, *Tristan,* Penguin, London.
Grant, M., *Myths of the Greeks and Romans,* New American Library, 1964.
Graves, Robert, *The White Goddess,* Octagon Books, 1972.
— *The Greek Myths,* Braziller, 1959.

Hammond, N. G., *Alexander the Great:*

King, Commander & Statesman, Noyes, 1981.
Harris, P. Valentine, *The Truth about Robin Hood,* P. V. Harris, 7th edition, 1959.
Homer, *Iliad,* translated by R. Fitzgerald, Doubleday, 1975.
— *Odyssey,* translated by E. V. Rieu, Penguin, London, 1946.

Keen, Maurice, *The Outlaws of Mediaeval Legend,* Routledge, London, 1961.
Kramer, S. N., *Sumerian Mythology,* American Philosophical Society, 1944.

Lambert, W. G. and **Millard, A. R.,** *The Babylonian Story of the Flood,* Oxford University Press, 1969.
Lehane, Brendan, *The Quest of Three Abbots,* Viking Press, 1968.
Little, George A., *Brendan the Navigator,* Gill and Son, Dublin, 1945.
Loomis, R. S., *The Grail: From Celtic Myth to Christian Symbol,* Columbia University Press, 1963.
— ed., *Arthurian Literature in the Middle Ages,* Oxford University Press, 1959.

Mabinogion, The, translated by Gwyn and Thomas Jones, Biblio Dist., 1976.
MacNeill, Maire, *The Festival of Lughnasa,* Oxford University Press, 1962.
Malory, Sir Thomas, *Morte D'Arthur,* Everyman, London.
Matarasso, P. M., trans. *The Quest of the Holy Grail,* AMS Press.
Murray, Gilbert, *Greek Studies,* Clarendon Press, Oxford, 1946.

Nibelungenlied, edited by A. T. Hatto, Penguin, London, 1965.

O'Rahilly, T. F., *Early Irish History and Mythology,* Dublin Institute, 1946.
Owen, D. D. R., *The Evolution of the Grail Legend,* Oliver and Boyd, London, 1968.

Parzival, translated by A. T. Hatto, Penguin, 1980.

Rose, H. J., *A Handbook of Greek Mythology,* Methuen, London, 6th edition, 1958.
Ross, Anne, *Pagan Celtic Britain,* Columbia University Press, 1967.

Severin, Tim, *Brendan Voyage,* McGraw-Hill, 1978.
Stone, B., trans. *Sir Gawain and the Green Knight,* Penguin, London, 1959.

Treharne, R. F., *The Glastonbury Legends,* Fernhill House, 1967.

Waite, A. E., *The Holy Grail,* University Books reprint.
Walker, J. W., *The True History of Robin Hood,* Rowman, 1973.
Weston, Jessie L., *From Ritual to Romance,* Anchor Books, 1957 reprint.
Whitelock, D., *The Audience of Beowulf,* Oxford University Press, 1951.

MYSTERIOUS BEASTS AND LANDS IN MYTHOLOGY

Who has not shivered slightly at the thought of a vampire or a werewolf, or thrilled to the idea of visiting a completely new world, such as the legendary island of Atlantis, which is reputed to have disappeared beneath the sea. The creation of other lands and fabulous creatures to inhabit them is a natural extension of magical thinking. Fairy tales are rich in such ideas, and they represent some very powerful archetypes of human experience. Dragons, fairies, dwarfs and harpies all impinge on us in their different ways, showing us a glimpse of the terror, helplessness and enchantment that lurks inside us all.

CLASSIFIED SUBJECT GUIDE

Abominable Snowman	**Dwarfs**	**Lemuria and Mu**	**Sirens**
Atlantis	**Fairies**	**Mermaids and Mermen**	**Sleepers**
Centaur	**Furies**	**Nymphs**	**Thunderbird**
Changeling	**Giants**	**Phoenix**	**Trolls**
Chimaera	**Gorgons**	**Puck**	**Unicorn**
Cinderella	**Harpy**	**Roc**	**Vampire**
Dragon	**Kraken**	**Satyrs**	**Werewolf**

FURTHER READING

Apollodorus, *Library of Mythology,* Loeb edition, Harvard University Press.
Arrowsmith, William, ed., 'The Bacchae', in *Complete Greek Tragedies,* Chicago University Press, 1958.

Baring-Gould, Sabine, *Curious Myths of the Middle Ages,* Oxford University Press, 1978.
Bischoff, D., *Vampires of the Night World,* Ballantine, 1981.
Briggs, K. M., *The Anatomy of Puck,* Arno, 1977.
— *The Fairies in English Tradition and Literature,* Chicago University Press, 1967.

Churchward, James, *The Lost Continent of Mu,* Crown.
Cooper, B., *The Vampire in Legend, Fact and Art,* Robert Hale, 1973.

Dodds, E. R., ed., *The Bacchae,* Oxford University Press, 2nd edition, 1960.

Eisler, Robert, *Man into Wolf,* Ross-Erikson, 1978.
Ellis Davidson, H. R., *Gods and Myths of Northern Europe,* Penguin, London, 1965.

Galanopoulos, A. G. and **Bacon, E.,** *Atlantis: The Truth Behind the Legend,* Bobbs-Merrill, 1969.
Graves, Robert, *The Greek Myths,* Braziller, 1959.

Hartland, E. S., *The Science of Fairy Tales,* Gale, 1968.
Hunt, Robert, *Popular Romances of the West,* Blom, 1968 reprint.

Jung, C. G., *Psychology and Alchemy,* Princeton University Press, 1968.

Keightley, Thomas, *The Fairy Mythology,* Bohn's Antiquarian Library Series, Gale.

Ley, Willie, *The Lungfish, the Dodo and the Unicorn,* Viking Press, 1948.

Ramage, E. S., ed., *Atlantis—Fact or Fiction,* Indiana University Press, 1978.

Schefold, K., *Myth and Legend in Early Greek Art,* Abrams, 1966.
Shepard, Odell, *The Lore of the Unicorn,* Harper and Row, 1979.
Summers, Montague, *The Vampire, his Kith and Kin,* Dutton, 1928.
— *The Vampire in Europe,* Universal Books, 1961.
— *The Werewolf,* Citadel Press, 1973.

BELIEFS AND RELIGIONS WORLDWIDE

One of the most astonishing features of the modern world is the sheer diversity of religious activity and belief that is still thriving in the shadow of space exploration and technology. It could be said that as we explore the outer limits of the physical universe with science, we seem to have a corresponding impulse to explore our inner universe with faith. Mythology, magic and folklore are still alive in different parts of the world, as are the so-called "primitive" beliefs of peoples in remote lands. The following articles demonstrate the wide range of religions, both in their major forms and more localized aspects.

CLASSIFIED SUBJECT GUIDE

Africa
Algonquin Indians
Altar
Amida
Ashanti
Atonement
Australia
Azande
Bahais
Baptism
Berbers
Bhagavad Gita
Borneo
Brahman
Brazil
Buddhism
Bushmen
Cargo Cults
Caste
China
Christianity
Christmas
Congo
Dahomey
Dead Sea Scrolls
Druzes
Easter and Holy Week
Election
Eskimo
Ethiopia
Fasting
Gautama Buddha
Ghost Dance
Great Plains Indians
Gypsies
Head
Heresy
Hinduism
Ibo
Incest
Iroquois
Islam
Jains
Japan
Jerusalem
Jesus
Judaism
Kali
Karma
Kikuyu
Krishna
Lamas
Madness
Mahatmas
Mana
Manitou
Maori
Mary
Masai
Mass
Mecca and Medina
Meditation
Melanesia
Menstruation
Mexico and Central America
Mohammed
Mutilation
Nagas
Navaho
Negroes
New Guinea
New Religious Movements
Nilotes
Nirvana
North American Indians
Nuer
Ozarks
Pacific North-West Indians
Parsees
Peyote Cults
Pilgrimage
Polynesia and Micronesia
Pueblo Indians
Pygmies
Race Myths
Sacraments
Saints
Self-Denial
Shaman
Shinto
Shiva
Sikhs
Sinhalese Buddhism
South America
Southeast Asia
Taboo
Taoism
Tattooing
Tibet
Tinkers
Totem
Touareg
Trickster
United States of America
Vedanta
Veddas
Vishnu
War, Holy
Yahweh
Yoga
Zealots
Zen
Zulu

FURTHER READING

Adams Beck, L., *Life of the Buddha,* Collins, London, 1959.
Albright, W. F., *Yahweh and the Gods of Canaan,* Eisenbrauns, 1978.
Alexander, H. B., *North American Mythology,* Cooper Square, 1964.
Allegro, J. M., *The Dead Sea Scrolls,* Penguin, London, 1959.
Anesaki, M., *History of Japanese Religion,* Tuttle, 1963.
Archer, J. C., *The Sikhs,* Russell, 1971.
Archer, W. G., *The Loves of Krishna,* Grove Press, 1958.
Argyle, W. J., *The Fon of Dahomey,* Oxford University Press, 1966.
Ashe, Geoffrey, *Gandhi: a Study in Revolution,* Stein and Day, 1969.
Attwater, D., *The Penguin Dictionary of Saints,* Penguin, London, 1965.
Aung, Maung Htin, *Burmese Buddhism,* Oxford University Press, 1966.

Baeck, Leo, *This People Israel: The Meaning of Jewish Existence,* Holt, Rinehart and Winston, 1965.
Bainton, R. H., *The Horizon History of Christianity.* American Heritage Publ., 1964.
Basham, A. L., *The Wonder that Was India,* Taplinger, 1968.
Baxter, P. T. W. and **Butt, Audrey**, *The Azande and Related Peoples of the Anglo-Egyptian Sudan and Belgian Congo,* International African Institute, 1953.
Bell, Sir Charles, *The Religion of Tibet,* Oxford University Press, 1969 reprint.
— *Tibet Past and Present,* Krishna Press.
Bernard, Theos, *Hatha Yoga,* Wehman.
Berndt, R. M., *Kunapipi,* Cheshire, Melbourne, 1951.
— *Djanggawul,* Routledge, London, 1952.
Bevan, Edwin R. and **Singer, Charles, ed.**, *The Legacy of Israel,* Oxford University Press, 1927.
Bhagavad Gita, translated by W. D. P. Hill, with notes, Oxford Univ. Press, 1967.
Bhagavad Gita, translated by Christopher Isherwood and Swami Prabhayananda, with introduction by Aldous Huxley, Vedanta Press, 1972.
Bhagavad Gita, translated by Juan Mascar Penguin, London, 1962.
Black, M., *The Scrolls and Christian Origins,* Scribner, 1969.
Bouquet, A. C., *Hinduism,* Hutchinson, London, 1966 reprint.
Brandon, S. G. F., *The Trial of Jesus of Nazareth,* Stein and Day, 1979.
— *History, Time and Deity,* Barnes and Noble, 1965.
— *Jesus and the Zealots,* Scribner, 1968.
— *Man and His Destiny in the Great Religions,* University of Toronto Press, 1962.
— *The Fall of Jerusalem and the Christian Church,* Allenson, revised edition, 1957.
— ed., *Dictionary of Comparative Religion,* Scribner, 1970.
Brewster, E. H., *The Life of Gotama the Buddha,* AMS Press reprint.
Bruce, F. F., *Second Thoughts on the Dead Sea scrolls,* Eerdmans, 1956.
Buck, Sir Peter, *The Coming of the Maori,* Tri-Ocean, 1950.
Buday, G., *The History of the Christmas Card,* Gale, 1972.
Budge, E. A. W., *Amulets and Superstitions,* Dover Press, 1978.
— *A History of Ethiopia, Nubia and Abyssinia,* B. Franklin, 1969 reprint.
— *Legend of Our Lady Mary, the Perpetual Virgin, and her Mother Hanna,* Medici Society, 1922.
Burland, C. A., *North American Indian Mythology,* Hamlyn, London, 1967.
Burness, D., *Shaka, King of the Zulus,* Three Continents, 1976.
Burridge, K. O. L., *Mambu,* Barnes and Noble, 1960.
— *New Heaven, New Earth,* Biblio Dist., 1980.
Burton, Sir Richard, *Personal Narrative of a Pilgrimage to Al-Madinah and Mecca,* Peter Smith.

Campbell, Joseph, *The Masks of God: Primitive Mythology,* Penguin, 1976.
Carson, A., *Baptism,* Kregel, 1981.
Caughlin, L., *Yoga: The Spirit of Union,* Kendall-Hunt, 1981.
Chaucer, *Canterbury Tales,* Biblio Dist., 1977.
Clark, E. E., *Indian Legends of the Pacific North-West,* University of California Press, 1958.
Clebert, Jean-Paul, *The Gypsies,* Penguin, London, 1969.
Codrington, R. H., *The Melanesians. Studies in their Anthropology and Folklore,* Dover, 1972.
Coedes, C., *The Making of South East Asia,* University of California Press, 1969.
Coffin, Tristram Potter, ed., *Our Living Traditions,* Basic Books, 1968.
Collier, J., *The Indians of the Americas,* NAL, 1952.
Conze, E., *Buddhism: Its Essence and Development,* Harper and Row.
— *Buddhist Texts through the Ages,* Cassirer, Oxford, 1954.
— *Buddhist Thought in India,* University of Michigan Press, 1967.
Copleston, F. C., *Medieval Philosophy,* Harper and Row, 1961.
Coulson, N. J., *A History of Islamic Law,* Columbia University Press.
Coulton, G. G., *Inquisition and Liberty,* Peter Smith.
Cranstone, B. A. L., *Melanesia: A Short Ethnography,* British Museum, London.
Crawley, E., *The Mystic Rose,* Arden Library, 1976.
Crippen, T. G., *Christmas & Christmas Lore,* Gale, 1976.
Cross, F. L., ed., *Oxford Dictionary of the Christian Church,* Oxford University Press, 1974.

Danielou, A., *Hindu Polytheism,* Princeton University Press, 1964.
Dasgupta, S. N., *A History of Indian Philosophy,* Humanities, 1975.
David-Neil, Alexandra, *Initiations and Initiates in Tibet,* Rider, London, 1958.
— *With Mystics and Magicians in Tibet,* University Books, 1958.
Davies, J. G., *The Early Christian Church,* Baker Books, 1980.
De la Vallee Poussin, Louis, *The Way to Nirvana,* Cambridge University Press, 1917.
Desideri, I., *An Account of Tibet,* Routledge, London, 1937.
Dorson, R. M., *American Folklore,* University of Chicago Press, 1971.
— *Buying the Wind,* University of Chicago Press, 1964.
Douglas, Mary, *Purity and Danger,* Praeger, 1966.
Drower, E. S., *Water into Wine,* AMS Press reprint of 1956 ed.
Duchesne, L., *Christian Worship,* S.P.C.K., London, 1931.
Dukes, Paul, *The Yoga of Health, Youth and Joy,* Harper and Row, 1960.
Dumoulin, S. J., Heinrich, *A History of Zen Buddhism,* Pantheon Books, 1963.

Eliade, Mircea, *Shamanism: Archaic Techniques of Ecstasy,* Princeton University Press, 1964.
— *Yoga, Immortality and Freedom,* Princeton University Press, 1970.
Eliot, Sir C., *Japanese Buddhism,* Barnes and Noble, 1935.
Elkin, A. P., *The Australian Aborigines,* Doubleday, 1964.
— *Aboriginal Man of High Degree,* St Martin's Press, 1978.
Encyclopaedia of Islam, Humanities, 1960–78.
Epstein, Isadore, *Judaism,* Penguin, London, 1959.
Esslemont, J. E., *Baha-Ullah and the New Era,* Bahai, 4th rev. ed., 1980.
Evans, Nanamoli, *The Path of Purification (Visuddhi-magga),* distributed by Luzac, London.
Evans-Pritchard, E. E., *Essays on Social Anthropology,* Free Press, 1963.
— *Azande: History & Political Institutions,* Oxford University Press, 1971.
— *Kinship and Marriage among the Nuer,* Oxford University Press, 1951.
— *The Nuer,* Oxford University Press, 1940.
— *Nuer Religion,* Oxford University Press, 1956.
— *The Position of Women in Primitive Societies,* Free Press, 1965.
— *Witchcraft, Oracles and Magic among the Azande,* Oxford University Press, 1967.
— *The Zande Trickster,* Oxford University Press, 1967.
Evans-Wentz, W. Y., ed., *Tibetan Yoga and Secret Doctrines,* Oxford University Press, 2nd edition, 1958.
— ed., *The Tibetan Book of the Dead,* Oxford University Press, 3rd edition, 1957.

Farah, C. E., *Islam—Beliefs & Observances,* Barrons, 1982.
Farb, Peter, *Man's Rise to Civilization: The Cultural Ascent of the Indians of North America,* 2nd rev. ed., Dutton, 1978.
Fedden, Robin, *Syria and Lebanon,* Macmillan, 1966.
Ferraby, John, *All Things Made New,* Bahai, 1960.
Fisher, J. D. C., *Christian Initiation: Baptism in the Medieval West,* Allenson, 1965.
Forde, Daryll, ed., *African Worlds,* International African Institute, 1954.
— and **Jones, J. I.,** *The Ibo and Ibo Speaking Peoples of South Eastern Nigeria,* International Publishing Services, 1962.
Fortune, R. F., *Manus Religion,* Nebraska University Press, 1965.
Fox, Robin, *Kinship and Marriage,* Penguin, London, 1968.
Frazer, J. G., *The Golden Bough,* St Martin's Press, 1980.
— *Totemism and Exogamy,* Barnes and Noble, 1968.
Freud, Sigmund, *Totem and Taboo,* Norton, 1952.
Fromm, Erich, Suzuki, D. T. and **De Martino, Richard,** *Zen Buddhism and Psychoanalysis,* Harper and Row, 1970.

Geddes, W. R., *Nine Dayak Nights,* Oxford University Press, 1968.
Gibb, H. A. R., *Mohammedanism,* Oxford University Press, 2nd edition, 1962.
Giles, L., *The Sayings of Lao Tzu,* Paragon.
Gluckman, M., *Analysis of a Social Situation in Modern Zululand,* Manchester University Press, 1958.
— *Custom and Conflict in Africa,* Barnes and Noble, 1969.
— *Order and Rebellion in Tribal Africa,* Free Press, 1963.
— *Politics, Law and Ritual in Tribal Society,* Biblio Dist., 1977.
Grabar, A., *Christian Iconography,* Princeton University Press, 1980.
Green, M. M., *Ibo Village Affairs,* Praeger.

Hadfield, P., *Traits of Divine Kingship In Africa,* Greenwood reprint.
Hambly, W. D., *History of Tattooing,* Gale, 1975.
Handy, E. S. C., *Polynesian Religion,* Kraus reprint.
Hare, W. L., *Systems of Meditation in Religion,* Saunders, 1937.
Hastings, J., ed., *Dictionary of the Bible,* Scribner, revised edition, 1963.
— ed., *Encyclopaedia of Religion and Ethics,* Scribner, 1961.
Hawthorn, A., *Art of the Kwakiutl Indians and Other Northwest Coast Tribes,* University of Washington Press, 1967.
Herbert, J., *Shinto,* Stein and Day, 1967.
Hernton, Calvin C., *Sex and Racism in America,* Grove Press, 1966.
Herrigel, Eugene, *Zen in the Art of Archery,* Random, 1971.
Herskovits, M. J., *Dahomey,* J. J. Augustin, 1938.
Hiatt, L. R., ed., *Aboriginal Mythology,* Humanities, 1975.
Hodge, F. W., ed., *Handbook of American Indians North of Mexico,* Scholarly Press, 1968.
Holtom, D. C., *Modern Japan and Shinto Nationalism,* Paragon, 1963.
— *The National Faith of Japan,* Paragon, 1965.
Hourani, A. H., *Minorities in the Arab World,* AMS Press reprint.
Howell, P. P., *A Manual of Nuer Law,* Oxford University Press, 1954.
Huffman R., *Nuer Customs and Folklore,* Biblio Distributors, 1970.
Jackson, A., *The Bushmen of South Africa,* Oxford University Press, 1957.
Jacobs, L., *Principles of the Jewish Faith,* Basic Book, 1964.
James, E. O., *Christian Myth and Ritual,* Peter Smith.
— *Seasonal Feasts and Festivals,* Barnes and Noble, 1963.
Jarvie, I. C., *The Revolution in Anthropology,* Regnery-Gateway, 1969.
Johnson, F. R., *Algonquians, The Indians of the Part of the New World first visited by the English,* Vols. 1 & 2, Johnson, 1972.

Kamal, Ahmad, *The Sacred Journey,* Duell, 1961.
Kapleau, P., *Zen East & West,* Doubleday, 1980.
Kehoe, A. B., *North American Indians,* Prentice-Hall, 1981.
Kelly, J. N. D., *Early Christian Doctrines,* Harper & Row, 1978.
Korel, Joel, *White Racism: A Psychohistory,* Pantheon Books, 1970.
Krige, E. J., *The Social System of the Zulus,* Tri-Ocean.

La Barre, Weston, *The Peyote Cult,* Schocken, 4th ed. 1976.
Lacarriere, J., *The God Possessed,* Fernhill, 1963.
La Forge, O., *Pictorial History of the American Indians,* Spring Books, 1962.
Lambert, H. E., *The Kikuyu: Social and Political Institutions,* Oxford University Press, 1956.
Lantenari, C., *The Religions of the Oppressed,* Knopf, 1963.
Lawrence, Peter, *Road Belong Cargo,* Humanities, 1967.
— and **Meggitt, M. J., ed.,** *Gods, Ghosts and Men in Melanesia,* Oxford University Press, 1965.
Leakey, L. S. B., *Mau Mau and the Kikuyu,* AMS Press reprint.
Leff, G., *Heresy in the Later Middle Ages,* Manchester University Press, 1967.
Lemarchand, R., *Political Awakening in the Belgian Congo,* University of California Press, 1964.
Levi-Strauss, Claude, *Totemism,* Beacon Press, 1963.
Levy, R., *The Social Structure of Islam,* Cambridge University Press, 1957.
Loomis, C. Grant, *White Magic,* Medieval Academy of America, 1967.
Lounsbery, G. C., *Buddhist Meditation in the Southern School,* Knopf, 1936.
Luomala, Katharine, *Voices on the Wind,* Bishop Museum Press, Honolulu, 1955.

MacCulloch, J. A., *Medieval Faith and Fable,* R. West, 1978.
MacQuarrie, J., *Twentieth Century Religious Thought,* Harper and Row, 1963.
Majumdar, S. K., *Introduction to Yoga: Principles and Practice,* University Books, 1967.
Malinowski, B., *Argonauts of the Western Pacific,* Dutton, 1961.

— *Coral Gardens and their Magic,* Dover, 1978.
Marsh, G. H., *A Comparative Study of Eskimo - Aleut Religion,* University of Alaska Press, 1954.
Martin, P. S., *Indians Before Columbus,* University of Chicago Press, 1947.
Masani, Sir R. P., *The Religion of the Good Life, Zoroastrianism,* Macmillan, 1968.
Mascaro, J., ed., *The Upanishads,* Penguin, London, 1965.
Masters, R. E. L. and **Houston, Jean,** *The Varieties of Psychedelic Experience,* Holt, Rinehart and Winston, 1966.
McConnel, Ursula, *Myths of the Mungkan,* Melbourne University Press, 1957.
McCormick, A., *Tinker-Gypsies,* Norwood Edns.
McFarland, H. Neill, *The Rush Hour of the Gods,* Macmillan, 1967.
Metge, Joan, *The Maoris of New Zealand,* Routledge & Kegan Paul, 1976.
Meyer, R., *Baha'i: Follower of the Light,* Baha'i, 1979.
Middleton, J. and **Winter, E. H., ed.,** *Witchcraft and Sorcery in East Africa,* Praeger, 1963.
Montagne, R., *Berbers: Their Social & Political Organization,* Biblio Dist., 1973.
Mookerji, R. K., *Hindu Civilization,* Bharatiya Vidya Bhuan Bombay, 1950.
Morgan, K. W., ed., *The Religion of the Hindus,* Ronald Press, 1953.
Murdock, G. P., *Africa, Its People and their Culture History,* McGraw-Hill, 1959.
Mylonas, G., *Eleusis and the Eleusinian Mysteries,* Princeton Univ. Press, 1961.

Nabil, *The Dawnbreakers,* Baha'i, 1932.
Narayan, B. K., *Mohammed,* Verry, 1980.
Nibblelink, C., *Gypsies,* Green River Press, 1978.
Nicholson, R. A., *The Mysteries of Islam,* Dufour, 1962.
Noth, M., *History of Israel,* Harper and Row, 2nd edition, 1960.
Nukariya, K., *The Religion of the Samurai,* Rowman, 1973.

Oceania, a quarterly published by the University of Sydney.
Offner, C. B. and **Van Straelen, H.,** *Modern Japanese Religions,* Twayne, 1963.
Owen Cole, W. and **Sambhi, P. S.,** *Sikhs,* Routledge & Kegan Paul, 1978.

Parkyns, Mansfield, *Life in Abyssinia,* Barnes and Noble, 1966.
Parrinder, Geoffrey, *African Mythology,* Hamlyn, London, 1968.
— *African Traditional Religion,* Greenwood, 1976.
Parsons, Elsie C., *Pueblo Indian Religion,* Univ. of Chicago Press, 1939.
Peel, J. D. Y., *Aladura,* Oxford University Press, 1968.
Poignant, Roslyn, *Oceanic Mythology,* Cooper Square Pubs., 1967.

Quick, O. C., *The Christian Sacraments,* Nisbet, London, 1927.

Radhakrishnan, S., *Eastern Religions and Western Thought,* Oxford University Press, 1975.
— *The Hindu View of Life,* Allen and Unwin, London, 1980 reprint.
— *Indian Philosophy,* Orient Book Dist., 1977.
Radin, Paul, *The Story of the American Indian,* Tudor/Liveright, 1944, revised edition.
— *The Trickster,* Schocken, 1972.
Rahman, F., *Islam,* Univ. of Chicago Press, 1979.
Rahula, W., *History of Buddhism in Ceylon: The Anuradhapura Period,* Intl. Publications Serv. 1966.
Randolph, Vance, *Ozark Magic and Folklore,* Dover, 1947.
Reining, Conrad C., *The Zande Scheme,* Northwestern University Press, 1966.
Renou, L., *Religions of Ancient India,* Schocken, 1968.
Reynolds, U., *Tibet: A Lost World,* Am. Fed. Arb., 1978.
Richards, A., *Chisungu,* Humanities.
Richmond, Sonya, *Common Sense about Yoga,* Arc Books, 1971.
Ritter, E. A., *Shaka Zulu,* Longmans, Toronto, 1955.
Robinson, R. H., *The Buddhist Religion,* Dickenson, 1969.
Rodd, Francis Rennell, *People of the Veil,* Humanities, 1966.
Ronen, D., *Dahomey: Between Tradition & Modernity,* Cornell University Press, 1975.
Ross, Anne, *Pagan Celtic Britain,* Columbia University Press, 1968.
Ross, Nancy Wilson, *Three Ways of Asian Wisdom: Hinduism, Buddhism and Zen,* Simon and Schuster, 1966.
— *Buddhism: A Way of Life & Thought,* Knopf, 1980.
Rowley, H. H., *The Biblical Doctrine of Election,* Ryerson Press, 1950.
— *From Joseph to Joshua,* Oxford University Press, 1950.
— *Worship in Ancient Israel,* Fortress, 1967.
Runciman, S., *A History of the Crusades,* Cambridge University Press, 1954.
— *The Medieval Manichee,* Cambridge University Press, 1955.

St Clair, David, *Drum and Candle,* Doubleday, 1970.
St J. B. Philby, H., *A Pilgrim in Arabia,* Golden Cockerell, 1946.
Salibi, Kamal S., *The Modern History of Lebanon,* Caravan Books, 1977.
Sandin, Benedict, *The Sea Dayaks Before White Rajah Rule,* Michigan State University Press, 1968.
Saunders, E. Dale, *Buddhism in Japan,* University of Pennsylvania Press, 1977.
Savoy, G., *Vilcabamba: Last City of the Incas,* R. Hale, 1971.
Schebesta, Paul, *Among Congo Pygmies,* AMS Press reprint.
— *My Pygmy and Negro Hosts,* AMS Press reprint.
Schechter, S., *Studies in Judaism,* Atheneum, 1970.
Schwimmer, Erik, ed., *The Maori People in the 1960's,* Humanities, 1969.
— *The World of the Maori,* Redd, Wellington, 1963.
Sen, K. M., *Hinduism,* Gannon.
Sharpe, E. J., *Not to Destroy but to Fulfil,* Lund, Sweden, 1955.
Siers, J. and **Ngata, W. T.,** *Maori People of New Zealand,* Intl. Pubs. Serv., 1976.
Singer, M., ed., *Krishna: Myths, Rites and Attitudes,* Greenwood Press, 1981.
Singh, Khushwant, *A History of the Sikhs,* Princeton University Press, 1963.
Siu, R. G. H., *The Tao of Science,* M.I.T. Press, 1958.
Slater, R. L., *Paradox and Nirvana,* Chicago University Press, 1951.
Smith, B. *Meditation: The Inward Art,* McClelland, 1963.
Smith, Edwin W. ed., *African Ideas of God,* Friendship Press, 1950.
Snellgrove, David L., *Four Lamas of Dolpo,* Harvard University Press, 1967.
— and **Richardson, H. E.,** *A Cultural History of Tibet,* Praeger, 1968.
Southall, Aidan W., *Alur Society: a Study in Processes and Types of Domination,* Cambridge University Press, 1956.
Spiro, Melford E., *Burmese Supernaturalism,* Inst. for the Study of Human Issues, 1978.
Steiner, Franz, *Taboo,* Penguin, 1967 reprint.
Steinilber-Oberlin, E. and **Matsuo, K.,** *The Buddhist Sects of Japan,* Gordon Press, 1977.
Strehlow, T. G. H., *Aranda Traditions,* Johnson, 1968 reprint.
Suzuki, D. T., *Zen and Japanese Buddhism,* Japan Publications, 1962.
Symonds, John, *Lady of the Magic Eyes, Madame Blavatsky Medium and Magician,* Yoseloff, 1960.

Thomas, E., *The Harmless People,* Knopf, 1959.
Thomas, E. J., *The Life of Buddha in Legend and History,* Routledge & Kegan Paul, 1969.
Thomsen, Harry, *The New Religions of Japan,* Greenwood, 1978.
Thrupp, S., *Millennial Dreams in Action,* Humanities, 1962.
Trevor, J. C., *Dead Sea Scrolls,* Eerdmans, 1978.
Trimmingham, J. S., *Islam in Ethiopia,* Barnes and Noble, 1965.
Turnbull, Colin M., *The Forest People,* Simon and Schuster, 1961.
— *Wayward Servants, the Two Worlds of the African Pygmies,* Greenwood, 1976.
Turner, V. W., *The Drums of Affliction,* Cornell University Press, 1981.
— *History of an African Independent Church,* Oxford University Press, 1967.
— *Continuity in an African Society,* Manchester University Press, 1958.

Ullendorf, E., *The Ethiopians,* Oxford University Press, 1973.
— *Ethiopia and the Bible,* Oxford University Press, 1968.
Underhill, Ruth M., *Red Man's Religion,* Univ. of Chicago Press, 1972.
Unwin, J. D., *Sex and Culture,* Oxford University Press, 1934.

Vermes, G., *The Dead Sea Scrolls in English,* Heritage Press.

Waley, Arthur, *The Way and its Power,* Grove Press, 1958.
Walker, Benjamin, *Hindu World,* Praeger, 1968.
Watt, W. Montgomery, *Muhammad,*

Prophet and Statesman, Oxford University Press, 1974.
Watts, Alan W., *The Way of Zen,* Random, 1974.
Weiser, F. X., *The Easter Book,* Harcourt, Brace and World, 1955.
Welch, Holmes, *The Parting of the Way,* Beacon Press, 1966 reprint.
Wellard, James, *Lost Worlds of Africa,* Dutton, 1967.
Weyer, E. M., *The Eskimoes: Their Environment and Folkways,* Shoestring Press, 1962.
Whistler, L., *The English Festivals,* Heinemann, London, 1947.
Willey, B., *Christianity Past & Present,* Hyperion, 1980.
Williams, F., *Drama of the Orokolo,* Oxford University Press, 1940.
Williamson, R. W., *Religion and Social Organization in Central Polynesia,* AMS Press reprint.
Worsley, Peter, *The Trumpet Shall Sound,* Schocken, 1968.
Wright, A. F., *Buddhism in Chinese History,* Stanford University Press, 1959.

Yadin, Y., *Masada: Herod's Fortress and the Zealots Last Stand,* Random House, 1966.
Yang, C. K., *Religion in Chinese Society,* University of California Press, 1961.
Young, Wayland, *Eros Denied,* Grove Press, 1964.

Zaehner, R. C., *The Concise Encyclopaedia of Living Faiths,* Beacon Press.
— *Hinduism,* Oxford University Press, 1962.
— *Hindu and Muslim Mysticism,* Schocken, 1969.
— ed., *Hindu Scriptures,* Biblio Dist., 1976.
Zernov, N., *Eastern Christendom,* Putnam, 1961.
Zimmer, H., *Myths and Symbols of Indian Art and Civilization,* Princeton University Press, 1971.

PARANORMAL RESEARCH

As interest in the paranormal has grown, a number of psychical researchers and psychologists have been investigating ways in which modern techniques of investigation can be used to explore this area. Statistics, double blind tests, laboratory neutrality have all been employed to examine such disparate experiences as ESP (extra-sensory perception); trance states; poltergeist activity; mediumistic powers; dreams; psychokinesis and faith healing. Some of the most fascinating work has been applied to astrology by statisticians and psychologists in an attempt to measure the impact on personality type of planetary positions at the time of birth.

CLASSIFIED SUBJECT GUIDE

Automatic Art
Conversion
Crookes, Sir William
Cross Correspondences
Davenports
Double
Dowsing
Doyle, Sir A. Conan
Dreams
Extra-Sensory Perception
Faith Healing
Freud
Gurney, Edmund
Home, D. D.
Homoeopathy
Jung, C. G.
Leonard, Mrs
Lourdes
Mediums
Miracles
Myers, F. W. H.
Object Reading
Ouija Boards
Out-of-the-Body Experiences
Palladino, Eusapia
Piper, Mrs
Poltergeists
Psychical Research
Psychokinesis
Psychology
Radiesthesia
Schneider Bros.
Spiritualism
Spontaneous psi Experiences
Superstitions
Trance
Visions
Willett, Mrs

FURTHER READING

Bagnall, O., *The Origin and Properties of the Human Aura.* Weiser, 1975.
Bakan, David, *Sigmund Freud and the Jewish Mystical Tradition,* Schocken Books, 1965.
Barbanell, M., *This is Spiritualism,* Smithers, 1959.
Bauer, Paul, *Christianity and Superstition,* Marshall, Morgan and Scott, London, 1966.
Becker, R. de, *The Understanding of Dreams,* Hawthorn Books, 1968.
Beevers, John, *The Sun and Her Mantle,* Newman Press, 1953.
Blunsdon, N., *Popular Dictionary of Spiritualism,* Fernhill, 1961.
Borland, D. M., *Homeopathy in Practice,* State Mutual Books, 1980.
Broad, C. D., *Lectures on Psychical Research,* Humanities, 1962.
Bruce, A. B., *Miracles of Christ,* Klock & Klock, 1980.

Carr, John Dickson, *Life of Sir Arthur Conan Doyle,* Murray, London, 1949.
Carrington, H., *Eusapia Palladino and her Phenomena,* T. Werner Laurie, London, 1910.
Coates, S. E., *Psychical Research,* Am Classical College Press, 1980.
Conan Doyle, Sir Arthur, *Memories and Adventures,* Modern Library, 1946.

Deren, M., *Divine Horsemen,* Dell Publishing, 1972.
Dingwall, E. J., *The Critics' Dilemma,* privately published, London, 1966.
— *Some Human Oddities,* University Books, 1962.
— *Very Peculiar People,* Rider, London, 1950.
Dodds, E. R., *The Greeks and the Irrational,* Univ. of California Press, 1951.
Dunne, J. W., *An Experiment with Time,* Macmillan, 1938.

Fordham, F., *An Introduction to Jung's Psychology,* Gannon.
Fox, Oliver, *Astral Projection,* Citadel Press, 1974.
Freud, Martin, *Sigmund Freud, Man and Father,* Vanguard, 1958.
Freud, Sigmund, *Collected Works,* translated by James Strachey in 24 vols., Macmillan, 1953 and Norton 1963–1977.
— *The Interpretation of Dreams,* Avon, 1967.

Gauld, Alan, *The Founders of Psychical Research,* Schocken Books, 1968.
— and **Cornell, A. D.,** *Poltergeists,* Routledge & Kegan Paul, 1979.
Green, Celia, *Lucid Dreams,* Institute of Psychophysical Research, Oxford, 1980.
— *Out-of-the-Body Experiences,* Institute of Psychophysical Research, Oxford, 1980.
— and **McCreery, C.,** *Apparitions,* State Mutual Books, 1977.
Groddeck, G. W., *The Unknown Self,* translated by V. M. E. Collins, Funk and Wagnalls, 1951.
Guillaume, A., *Prophecy and Divination among the Hebrews and Semites,* Harper and Row, 1939.
Hall, T. H., *The Spiritualists,* Garrett-Helix, 1963.
Hansel, C. E., *ESP & Parapsychology: A Critical Re-evaluation,* Prometheus Books, 1980.
Hart, Bernard, *Psychopathology,* Cambridge University Press, 1927.
Hart, H., *The Enigma of Survival,* C. C. Thomas, 1959.
Heywood, Rosalind, *Beyond the Reach of Sense,* Dutton, 1961.
Home, D. D., *Some Incidents in My Life,* Universal Books, 1973.
Howels, J. G., ed., *Modern Perspectives in World Psychiatry,* Brunner-Hazel, 1975.

Inglis, B., *Natural and Supernatural,* Abacus, 1979.
Iremonger, Lucille, *The Ghosts of Versailles,* Faber and Faber, London, 1957.

Jahoda, Gustav, *The Psychology of Superstition,* Aronson, 1974.
James, William, *The Varieties of Religious Experience,* Collier-Macmillan, 1961.
— *The Will to Believe,* Harvard University Press, 1979.
Jung, C. G., *Memories, Dreams and Reflections,* Random House, 1965.

Keller, Werner, *The Bible as History,* Morrow, 1981.
Kilner, W. J., *The Human Atmosphere,* University Books, reprint.
Kinshaw, F., *Future Tense,* Pendulum, 1980.

MacKenzie, Andrew, *The Unexplained,* Abelard Schuman, 1968.
MacKenzie, Norman, *Dreams and Dreaming,* Vanguard, 1965.
Maple, Eric, *The Realm of Ghosts,* A. S. Barnes, 1964.
— *Superstition and the Superstitious,* W. H. Allen, London, 1971.
Martindale, C. C., *The Message of Fatima,*

Kenedy, 1950.
Masters, R. E. L. and **Houston, J.,** *The Varieties of Psychedelic Experience,* Holt, Rinehart and Winston, 1966.
McCreery, Charles, *Science, Philosophy and ESP,* Shoe String Press, 1967.
Medhurst, R. G. and **Goldney, K. M.,** *William Crookes and the Physical Phenomena of Mediumship,* Proceedings of the S.P.R., vol. 54, London, 1964.
Mermet, Abbé A., *Principles and Practice of Radiesthesia,* State Mutual Books, 1981.
Miller, G. A., *Psychology: The Science of Mental Life,* Harper and Row, 1962.
Miller, Paul, *Born to Heal,* Spiritualist Press, London, 1962.
Mitchell, E. D., *Psychic Exploration,* Paragon, 1979.
Moses, W. S., *Spirit Teachings,* Arno, 1976.
Moule, C. F. D., ed., *Miracles,* Allenson, 1965.
Murphy, Gardner, *The Challenge of Psychical Research,* Greenwood Press, 1979.
Myers, F. W. H., *Human Personality and its Survival of Bodily Death,* Arno Press, 1975.

Neame, Alan, *The Happening at Lourdes,* Simon and Schuster, 1968.
Nelson, G. K., *Spiritualism and Society,* Schocken, 1969.

Olaner, F. E., *Superstition,* Horizon, 1981.
Owen, A. R. G., *Can We Explain the Poltergeist?,* Garrett, 1964.
— *Hysteria, Hypnosis and Healing,* Garrett-Helix, 1969.

Piper, Alta L., *The Life and Work of Mrs Piper,* Routledge, London, 1929.
Playfair, Lyon Guy, *The Indefinite Boundary,* Souvenir Press, 1976.
Podmore, F., *Modern Spiritualism,* republished as *The Mediums of the 19th Century,* ed. E. J. Dingwall, University Books, 1963.
Pollack, J. H., *Croiset, the Clairvoyant,* Doubleday, 1964.
Powell Davies, A., *The Ten Commandments,* Signet Key Books, 1956.
Price, Harry, *Poltergeist Over England,* Country Life, London, 1945.
Prince, Morton, *The Unconscious,* Macmillan, 1914.

Rao, K. Ramakrishna, *Experimental Parapsychology,* C. C. Thomas, 1966.
Read, H., Fordham, F. and **Adler, G., ed.,** *The Collected Works of C. G. Jung,* Princeton University Press, 1960–1979.
Rhine, J. B., *The Reach of the Mind,* Apollo Editions, 1961.
— and **Pratt, J. G.,** *Parapsychology: Frontier Science of the Mind,* C. C. Thomas, 1962, revised edition.
— and others, *Extrasensory Perception After Sixty Years,* Branden.
— ed., *Progress in Parapsychology,* Parapsychology Press, Durham, North Carolina, 1971.
Rhine, Louisa E., *ESP in Life and Lab,* Collier-Macmillan, 1969.
— *Hidden Channels of the Mind,* Apollo, 1966.
— *Mind Over Matter,* Macmillan, 1970.
Richardson, Alan, *The Miracle Stories of the Gospels,* Allenson, 1941.
Richet, C., *Thirty Years of Psychical Research,* Arno, 1975.
Rose, Louis, *Faith Healing,* Gollancz, London, 1968.

Salter, W. H., *The S.P.R.: An Outline of its History,* S.P.R., London, 1948.
— *Zoar: The Evidence of Psychical Research Concerning Survival,* Arno, 1975.
Saltmarsh, H. F., *Evidence of Personal Survival from Cross Correspondences,* Arno, 1975.
Sargant, William, *Battle for the Mind,* Doubleday, 1957.
— *The Unquiet Mind,* Little, Brown, 1967.
Sharp, W. and **Macleod, F.,** *The Wilfion Scripts,* Wilfion Books, 1980.
Sharpe, E. F. *Dream Analysis,* Brunner-Hazel, 1978.
Sitwell, Sacheverell, *Poltergeists,* Faber, London, 1940.
Sladek, J., *The New Apocrypha,* Granada, 1978.
Smith, Robert D., *Comparative Miracles,* Herder, 1965.
Soal, S. G. and **Bateman, F.,** *Modern Experiments in Telepathy,* Greenwood.
Steadman, R., *Sigmund Freud,* Paddington Press, 1979.
Stewart, R., *The Sixth Sense,* Delacorte.

Thompson, C. J. S., *Magic and Healing,* Gale, 1973.
Thouless, R. H. *Experimental Psychical Research,* Penguin, London, 1963.
Thurston, Herbert, *Beauraing and Other Apparitions,* Folcroft, 1977.
— *Ghosts and Poltergeists,* Regnery, 1955.
— *Surprising Mystics,* Regnery, 1955.
Tomlinson, Dr H., *Medical Divination,* State Mutual Books, 1980.
Trilling, Lionel, *Freud and the Crisis of Our Culture,* Patterson, 1966.
Trochu, Francis, *Saint Bernadette Soubirous,* Pantheon Books, 1958.
Tromp, S. W., *Psychical Physics,* Elsevier, London, 1949.
Tyrrell, G. N. M., *The Personality of Man,* Pelican, London, 1947.
— *Science and Psychical Phenomena,* Arno.

Vogt, E. Z. and **Hyman, R.,** *Water Witching USA,* University of Chicago Press, 1979.

Watson, Dr R. T. B., *Radiesthesia and Some Associated Phenomena,* Markham House Press, London, 1957.
Wavell, Stewart, *Trance,* Dutton, 1967.
Wethered, V. D., *Introduction to Medical Radiesthesia and Radionics,* C. W. Daniel and Co., 1957.
Whiteman, J. H. M., *The Mystical Life,* Humanities, 1961.

APPROACHES TO THE AFTER-LIFE

CLASSIFIED SUBJECT GUIDE

Birth	**Hell**	**Judgement of the Dead**	**Purgatory**
Burial	**Immortality**	**Marriage**	**Reincarnation**
Cremation	**Incarnation**	**Mummification**	**Relics**
Cult of the Dead	**Initiation**	**Paradise**	**Rites of Passage**
Ghosts	**Interrogation of the Dead**	**Predestination**	**Soul**
Haunted Houses			**Suttee**

"Where do we come from, and where are we going?" The central issues concerning the meaning of our existence on earth always raise questions about the possibility of an after-life. The major landmarks of human experience—birth, marriage and death—are surrounded with rituals of powerful emotional resonance. They dramatize the recurring cycle of the renewal and destruction of life. As human beings we are uniquely concerned with the quality of our consciousness. Do we have a soul, a spirit? Can this part of the self survive the body's death? If so, to what purpose—are we reincarnated as so many people firmly believe? Every religion and mythology tries to explore these questions in some form or other.

FURTHER READING

Addison, J. T., *Life Beyond Death,* Houghton Mifflin, 1933.
Allen, M. R., *Male Cults and Secret Initiation in Melanesia,* Cambridge University Press, 1967.

Bardens, Dennis, *Ghosts and Hauntings,* Taplinger, 1968.
Bendann, E., *Death Customs,* Gale, 1971.
Bennett, E., *Apparitions and Haunted Houses,* Gale reprint.
Boettner, L., *The Reformed Doctrine of Predestination,* Presby and Reformed.
Brandon, S. G. F., *The Judgement of the Dead,* Scribner, 1969.
Briggs, Katharine M., *The Fairies in English Tradition,* University of Chicago Press, 1967.
Budge, E. A. W., *The Mummy,* Macmillan, 1972.
Burnet, J. *The Socratic Doctrine of the Soul,* Oxford University Press, 1916.

Calvin, John, *Concerning the Eternal Predestination of God,* Attic Press, 1961 reprint.

Clark, G. and **Piggott, S.,** *Prehistoric Societies,* Knopf, 1965.
Copleston, F., *History of Philosophy,* Doubleday, 1944–66.
Crawley, Ernest, *The Mystic Rose,* Gale, 1971.
Cumont, Franz, *Afterlife in Roman Paganism,* Yale University Press, 1922.

Daniel, Glyn, *The Megalith Builders of Western Europe,* Penguin, London, 1963.
Davies, H. F., ed., *Catholic Dictionary of Theology,* Nelson, 1967.
Dawson, W. R., *The Customs of Couvade,* Manchester Univ. Press, 1929.
Douglas, M. R., Purity and Danger, Routledge, 1978.
Ducasse, C. J., *A Critical Examination of the Belief in Life After Death,* C. C. Thomas, 1974.

Eliade, Mircea, *The Myth of the Eternal Return,* Princeton Univ. Press, 1954.
— *Rites and Symbols of Initiation,* Peter Smith.

Farrelly, M. J., *Predestination, Grace and Free Will,* Newman Press, 1964.
Forde, Daryll, ed., *African Worlds,* Oxford University Press, 1954.
Fortes, M. and **Dieterlen, G.,** *African Systems of Thought,* Oxford University Press, 1965.

Gennep, A. van, *The Rites of Passage,* University of Chicago Press, 1961.
Gluckman, M., ed., *Essays on the Ritual of Social Relations,* Humanities, 1962.
Goody, Jack, *Death, Property and the Ancestors,* Stanford University Press, 1962.
Green, C. and **McCreery, C.,** *Apparitions,* State Mutual Books, 1977.
Grillmeier, A., *Christ in Christian Tradition,* Sheed and Ward, 1965.

Hartland, E. S., *Primitive Paternity,* Arno Press, 1972.
Head, J. and **Cranston, S. L., ed.,** *Reincarnation: An East-West Anthology,* Theos. Pub. House, 1968.
— *Reincarnation: The Phoenix Fire Mystery,* Julian Press/Crown, 1977.
Hole, Christina, *Haunted England,* Scribner, 1941.
HSU, Francis, *Under the Ancestors' Shadow,* Routledge, London, 1948.
Hughes, T. P., *A Dictionary of Islam,* Gordon Press, 1980.

James, E. O., *The Ancient Gods,* Putnam, 1964.
— *Prehistoric Religion,* Praeger, 1957.
Jones, Barbara, *Design for Death,* Bobbs-Merrill, 1967.

Leslie, Shane, *St Patrick's Purgatory,* Burns and Oates, London, 1932.
Lutoslawski, W., *Pre-Existence and Reincarnation,* Allen and Unwin, London, 1926.

MacCulloch, J. A., *The Harrowing of Hell,* AMS Press reprint.
Maple, Eric, *The Realm of Ghosts,* A. S. Barnes, 1964.
Marcel, G., *The Mystery of Being,* Regnery.
Maringer, J., *The Gods of Prehistoric Man,* Knopf, 1960.
Middleton, John, *Lugbara Religion,* Oxford University Press, 1960.
Morgan, C., *Liberties of the Mind,* Century, 1979.
Myths and Symbols: Studies in Honor of Mircea Eliade, Chicago University Press, 1969.

Norman, D., *The Stately Ghosts of England,* Muller, 1963.

Risedorf, G., *Ghosts & Ghouls,* Raintree, 1977.

Smyth, F., *Ghosts & Poltergeists,* Aldus, 1976.
Sutcliffe, E. F., *The Old Testament and the Future of Life,* Newman Bookshop, 1947.

Tritton, A. S., *Islam, Beliefs and Practices,* Hyperion Press, 1981.
Turner, V. W., *Forest of Symbols,* Cornell University Press, 1967.
Tyrrell, G. N. M., *Apparitions,* Collier-Macmillan, 1963.
— *The Personality of Man,* Penguin, London, 1946.

Walker, D. P., *The Decline of Hell,* University of Chicago Press, 1964.
West, D. J., *Psychical Research Today,* Hillary House, 1954.
Westermarck, Edward, *Short History of Marriage,* Humanities, 1969.
Wilson, M., *Rituals of Kinship among the Nyakyusa,* Oxford Univ. Press, 1957.
— *Communal Rituals among the Nyakyusa,* Oxford University Press, 1959.

Zaehner, R. C., *The Dawn and Twilight of Zoroastrianism,* Putnam, 1961.

VISIONARY PIONEERS

Orthodox religious beliefs and observances do not satisfy everyone. There are thousands of people all over the world who express their spiritual needs outside the mainstream religions. These individuals include mystics, gnostics, occultists, magicians, spiritualists and students of the Cabala, and they either practise alone or in small groups and sects. These explorers of untrodden paths and unusual spiritual techniques are often pioneers of new ways of thinking about the world. Their constant questioning and willingness to consider new issues makes their contribution to the spiritual life of the human race both fascinating and inherently valuable.

FURTHER READING

Amadeo, Fr., *Blessed Gemma Galgani,* Burns and Oates, London, 1935.
Ancelet-Hustache, J., *Master Eckhart and the Rhineland Mystics,* Harper and Row, 1957.
Andrews, E. D., *The People Called Shakers,* Peter Smith, revised edition.
Arberry, A. J., *Omar Khayyam,* Yale University Press, 1952.
— *Sufism: An Account of the Mystics of Islam,* Allen and Unwin, 1979.
— ed., *Religion in the Middle East,* Cambridge University Press, 1969.
— ed., *Tales from the Masnavi,* Allen and Unwin, London, 1961.
— ed., *More Tales from the Masnavi,* Hillary House, 1963.
Armstrong, A. H., *The Architecture of the Intelligible Universe in the Philosophy of Plotinus,* Macmillan, 1940.
Arndt, K. J. R., *George Rapp's Harmony Society, 1785–1847,* University of Pennsylvania Press, 1965.
Auclair, Marcelle, *St Teresa of Avila,* Doubleday.

Baldwin, James, *The Fire Next Time,* Dell, 1970.
Barrett, W. P., *The Trial of Joan of Arc,* Gotham House, 1932.
Bates, Ernest and **Dittermore, J. V.,** *Mary Baker Eddy: The Truth and the Tradition,* Knopf, 1932.
Beasley, Norman, *The Cross and the Crown,* Duell, 1952.
— *Mary Baker Eddy,* Duell, Sloan and Pearce, 1963.
Bell, H. Idris, *Cults and Creeds in Graeco-Roman Egypt,* Ares Publishers, 1977.
Besant, Annie, *Man: Whence, How and Whither,* Theosophical Publishing House, 1913.
Bharati, Agehananda, *The Tantric Tradition,* Greenwood, 1977.
Bihalji-Merin, Oto and **Benac, Alojz,** *The Bogomils,* Thames and Hudson, London, 1962.
Blavatsky, Mme., *Isis Unveiled,* Theosophical Publishing House.
— *Key to Theosophy,* Theosophical Publishing House, 1980 reprint.
— *The Secret Doctrine,* Theosophical Publishing House.
Bloch-Hoell, N., *The Pentecostal Movement,* Humanities Press, 1965.
Boehme, Jacob, *Aurora,* Hillary House, 1960.
— *Of Heaven and Hell,* Everyman, 1934.
— *Mysterium Magnum,* John M. Watkins, London, 1965.
— *Signatura Rerum,* Everyman, 1912.
— *Supersensual Life,* Everyman, 1926.
Bourdeaux, Michael, *Opium of the People,* Bobbs-Merrill, 1966.
Boyd, Ernest, *Ireland's Literary Renaissance,* Barnes and Noble, revised edition, 1968.
Braden, C. S., *Christian Science Today,* Southern Methodist Univ. Press, 1958.

CLASSIFIED SUBJECT GUIDE

Acupuncture
Agrippa
Anandamayi Ma
Apollonius of Tyana
Besant, Annie
Black Muslims
Blavatsky, Mme
Boehme
Bogomils
Bruno, Giordano
Cabala
Cagliostro
Camisards
Cathars
Catherine of Siena
Cayce, Edgar
Christian Science
Cloud of Unknowing
Cokelers
Coleridge
Communistic Religious Movements
Conselheiero, Antonio
Convulsionaries
Crowley, Aleister
Daniel
Dee, John
Dervish
Dionysius the Areopagite
Divine Principles
Doukhobors
Druids
Ebionites
Eckhart, Meister
Ecstasy
Eddy, Mary Baker
Eleusis
Enthusiasm
Exclusive Brethren
Ezekiel
Fakir
Faust
Flagellation
Fludd, Robert
Flying Saucers
Fortune, Dion
Fox, George
Francis of Assisi, St
Freemasonry
Germanen Order
Ghazali
Gilles de Rais
Gnosticism
Golden Dawn
Gurdjieff
Guyon, Mme
Hasidism
Hermetica
Hildegard of Bingen
Hilton, Walter
Holiness Movement
Holy Rollers
Hutterian Brethren
Ibn Arabi
Illuminati
Irving, Edward
Jehovah's Witnesses
Jezreel, J. J.
Joan of Arc
John of the Cross
Julian of Norwich
Knights Templar
Lavater, J. K.
Law, William
Levi, Eliphas
List, Guido von
Lost Tribes of Israel
Lull, Raymond
Luria, Isaac
Lytton, Bulwer
Mahdi
Manicheans
Mankind United
Martinists
Masters
Medmenham Monks
Mesmer
Messianic Movements
Montanists
Moral Rearmament
Mormons
Mystery Religions
Mysticism
National Socialism
Neo-Pagan German Cults
Neoplatonism
Neumann, Teresa
New Templars
New Thought
Nostradamus
Old Believers
Omar Khayyam
Oriental Jewish Communities
Orpheus and Orphism
Ouspensky
Paracelsus
Peculiar People
Pentecostalist Movement
Plato's Myths
Plotinus
Prince, H. J.
Proclus
Pythagoras
Quietism
Ramakrishna
Ramana Maharshi
Rasputin
Rosicrucians
Rumi
Russell, G. W.
Sai Baba
St Germain, Comte de
Second Coming
Shakers
Simeon Stylites
Simon Magus
Sivananda
Skoptsy
Snake-Handling Cults
Southcott, Joanna
Speaking in Tongues
Steiner, Rudolf
Stigmata
Sufis
Swedenborg
Tantrism
Taylor, Thomas
Teilhard de Chardin
Teresa of Avila
Theosophy
Theurgy
Throne Mysticism
Thugs
Waite, A. E.
Waldenses
Walworth Jumpers
Wronski
Yeats, W. B.

— *Spirits in Rebellion,* Southern Methodist University Press, 1980.

Brodie, Fawn M., *No Man Knows My History: The Life of Joseph Smith,* Knopf, 1971.

Brumbach, C., *What Meaneth This?,* Gospel Publishing House.

Burckhardt, Titus, *Introduction to Sufi Doctrine,* Orientalia Art Ltd., 1971.

Burkitt, F. C., *The Religion of the Manichees,* AMS Press reprint.

Burland, C. A., *The Arts of the Alchemists,* Macmillan, 1968.

Burton, Sir Richard, *The City of the Saints,* Knopf, new edition, 1963.

Butler, E. M., *The Fortunes of Faust,* Cambridge University Press, 1979.

Butler, W. E., *Magic and the Qabalah, Llewellyn Publications.*

Calley, M. J. C., *God's People: West Indian Pentecostal Sects in England,* Oxford University Press, 1965.

Carty, Charles M., *The Two Stigmatists: Padre Pio and Teresa Neuman,* Radio Replies Press, 1956.

Cavendish, R., *The Black Arts,* Putnam, 1967.

— *A History of Magic,* Taplinger, 1977.

Celano, Thomas of, *The Lives of St Francis,* translated by A. G. Ferrers-Howell, Franciscan Herald, 1962.

Clark, James M., *The Great German Mystics,* Russell, 1970.

— and **Skinner, J. V.,** *Meister Eckhart: Selected Treatises and Sermons,* Harper and Row, 1958.

Clyde, William, *'A. E.',* Grant and Murray, 1935.

Clymer, R. Swinburne, *The Rosicrucian Fraternity in America,* Rosicrucian Foundation, Quakerstown, Pennsylvania, 1935.

— *The Book of Rosicruciae,* Philosophical Publishing Co., Quakerstown, 1946–49.

Cohn, Norman, *The Pursuit of the Millennium,* Oxford University Press, 1970.

Copleston, F., *History of Philosophy,* 8 vols, Doubleday, 1946–63.

Craven, J. B., *Doctor Robert Fludd – Robertus de Fluctibus – the English Rosicrucian,* William Peace and Son, London, 1902.

Cumont, Franz, *The Oriental Religions in Roman Paganism,* Peter Smith, 1958 reprint.

Cunha, E. Da, *Rebellion in the Backlands,* Chicago University Press, 1957.

Cunningham, L., *Saint Francis of Assisi,* Harper and Row, 1981.

Curtayne, Alice, *Saint Catherine of Siena,* Tan Books, 1980.

Daraul, Arkon, *Secret Societies,* Fernhill House, 1961.

Dasgupta, S. B., *An Introduction to Tantrik Buddhism,* Calcutta University Press, 1950.

Deacon, Richard, *John Dee,* Muller, London, 1968.

D'Epinay, Christian L., *Haven of the Masses,* Lutterworth, London, 1969.

Dewar, J., *The Unlocked Secret,* Kimber, London, 1969.

Dewitt, J., *Christian Science Way of Life,* Christian Science, 1971.

Dingwall, E. J., ed., *Abnormal Hypnotic Phenomena: a Survey of Nineteenth Century Cases,* Barnes and Noble, 1968.

Dodds, E. R., ed., Proclus: The Elements of Theology, Clarendon Press, Oxford, 1923.

Donaldson, D. M., *The Shi'ite Religion,* AMS Press.

Dresser, Horatio W., ed., *The Quimby Manuscripts,* Citadel Press, 1976.

Driberg, Tom, *The Mystery of Moral Re-Armament,* Knopf, 1964.

Eglington, John, *A Memoir of A. E.,* Macmillan, 1937.

Endersby, Victor A., *The Hall of Magic Mirrors,* Carlton Press, 1969.

Fauset, A., *Black Gods of the Metropolis,* University of Pennsylvania Press, 1971.

Flannery, M. C., *Yeats & Magic: The Earlier Works,* Barnes & Noble, 1977.

Fortune, Dion, *Psychic Self Defence,* Aquarian Press, London, 1967.

— *Applied Magic,* Aquarian Press, London, 1967.

— *Sane Occultism,* Aquarian Press, London, 1967.

— *The Mystical Qabalah,* Weiser.

— *Moon Magic,* Aquarian Press, London, 1957.

— *The Sea Priestess,* Weiser, 1981.

Fox, George, *Journals,* edited by N. Penney, Octagon Books, 1976.

Gasquet, C., ed., *Letters of St Teresa,* Gordon Press, 1977.

Gee, D., *Why Pentecost?,* Elim Publishing House, 1944.

Gibbon, Monk, ed., *The Living Torch: A Selection from A. E.'s Writings,* Arno reprint.

Gie, F., *Joan of Arc,* Harper & Row, 1981.

Goss, F. L., ed., *The Jung Codex,* Morehouse-Barlow, 1955.

Goudge, H. L., *The British Israel Theory,* Mowbray, 1933.

Graef, Hilda, *The Case of Therese Neumann,* Newman Press, 1951.

— *The Story of Mysticism,* Doubleday, 1965.

Grant, K., *Aleister Crowley & The Hidden God,* Weiser, 1974.

Grant, R. M., *Gnosticism and Early Christianity,* Harper and Row, 1966.

Gurdjieff, G. I., *All and Everything,* Dutton, 1964.

— *Meetings With Remarkable Men,* Dutton, 1963.

Guthrie, W. K. C., *Orpheus and Greek Religion,* Methuen, London, 2nd edition, 1952.

Happold, F. C., *Mysticism,* Peter Smith.

Harris, S. and **Crittenden, H.,** *The Incredible Father Divine,* Doubleday, 1953.

Hartmann, F., *Jacob Boehme,* Steinerbooks, 1981.

Heer, F., *The Medieval World: Europe 1100–1350,* NAL, 1964.

Henson, H., *Oxford Group Movement,*

Oxford University Press, 2nd edition 1934.
Hirst, D., *Hidden Riches,* Barnes and Noble, 1964.
Hobhouse, S., ed., *Selected Mystical Writings of William Law,* Rockcliff, London, 4th edition, 1949.
Hodgson, G. E., *English Mystics,* Gordon Press, 1977.
Hoekema, A. A., *The Four Major Cults,* Eerdmans, 1963.
Holloway, Mark, *Heavens on Earth,* Smithers, 1951.
Hone, Joseph, *W. B. Yeats 1865–1939,* St Martin, 2nd edition, 1962.
Hoornaert, R., *Saint Teresa in her Writings,* Sheed and Ward, 1931.
Howard, P., *Frank Buchman's Secret,* Doubleday, 1961.
Howarth, Herbert, *The Irish Writers,* Hull and Wang, 1939.
Howe, Ellic, *Astrology: The Story of its Role in World War II,* Walker and Co., 1968.
Howland, J. B., *Acupuncture Principles & Your Health,* Auricle Press, 1981.
Hulme, K. *Undiscovered Country,* Little, Brown, 1972.
Huidobro, U., *Cagliostro,* Gordon Press, 1974.
Hunt, D., *Exploring the Occult,* Pan Books, London, 1964.

Inglis, *Natural and Supernatural,* Abacus, 1979.

Johnston, Julia, *Mary Baker Eddy: Her Mission and Triumph,* Christian Science Publishing Society.
Jonas, H., *The Gnostic Religion,* Beacon Press, 1963.
Jones, B. E., *Freemason's Guide and Compendium,* Verry, Lawrence, 1965.
Judge, W. Q., *The Ocean of Theosophy,* Theosophical Publishing House, reprint.

Kavanaugh, K., trans., *The Collected Works of St John of the Cross.* ICS Publications, 1979.
Kelsey, M. T., *Speaking With Tongues,* Epworth Press, London, 1965.
Kendrick, T. D., *The Druids,* Biblio Dist., 1966.
Kennedy, H. A. S., *Mrs Eddy,* Mitre Press, London, 1947.
Kerkhofs, J., ed., *Catholic Pentecostals Now,* Alba Books, 1977.
Knowles, M. D., *The English Mystical Tradition,* Burns and Oates, London, 1961.
— *What is Mysticism?,* Hawthorn Books, 1966.
Knox, Ronald, *Enthusiasm,* Oxford University Press, 1961.
Kolarz, Walter, *Religion in the Soviet Union,* St Martin, 1962.

La Barre, Weston, *They Shall Take Up Serpents,* Schocken Books, 1974.
Laski, Marghanita, *Ecstasy,* Greenwood, 1978.
Lavier, J., *Points of Chinese Acupuncture,* Weiser.
Lea, Henry Charles, *A History of the Inquisition,* AMS Press reprint.
Leroy, O., *Levitation,* Burns and Oates, London, 1928.
Levi, Eliphas, *Transcendental Magic,* Weiser, 1980.
— *The History of Magic,* translated by A. E. Waite, Weiser, 1980.
— *The Key of the Mysteries,* translated and edited by A. Crowley, Weiser, 1980.
Lewin, Lewis L., *Phantastica: Narcotic and Stimulating Drugs,* Dutton, revised edition, 1964.
Lewis, H. Spencer, *Rosicrucian Questions and Answers,* Rosicrucians Library, California, 1932.
Lewy, Hans, *Chaldaean Oracles and Theurgy,* Cairo Institut Français, 1956.
Linforth, I. M., *The Arts of Orpheus,* Arno reprint.
Lings, Martin, *A Sufi Saint of the Twentieth Century, Shaikh Ahmad al-Alawi,* University of California Press, 1972.
Linn, W. A., *Mormons and Mormonism,* Gordon Press, 1973.
Lloyd, A., *Quaker Social History, 1669–1738,* Greenwood, 1979.
Lomax, Louis E., *When the Word is Given,* Greenwood Press, 1979.
Lutyens, Mary, ed., *The Krishnamurti Reader,* Penguin, London, 1970.
Lytton, Earl of, *The Life of Edward Bulwer, First Lord of Lytton,* Macmillan, 1913.

MacKenzie, N., ed., *Secret Societies,* Macmillan, 1971.
Madaule, J., *The Albigensian Crusade,* Fordham, 1967.
Mann, Felix, *Acupuncture: The Ancient Chinese Art of Healing,* International Ideas, 1978.
— *The Meridians of Acupuncture,* Heinemann, London, 1964.
— *The Treatment of Disease by Acupuncture,* Heinemann, London, 2nd edition, 1964.
Martensen, H. L., *Jacob Boehme,* Rockcliff, London, 1949.
Martin, E. J., *The Trial of the Templars,* AMS Press reprint.
— *Mary Baker Eddy, An Appraisal,* Christian Science, 1968.
Massie, Robert K., *Nicholas and Alexandra,* Dell Publishing, 1978.
McCann, J., ed., *The Cloud of Unknowing,* Burns and Oates, London, 1952.
McCormick, Donald, *Temple of Love,* Nelson, Scott and Foster, 1962.
McLoughlin, William G., *Modern Revivalism,* Ronald Press, 1959.
Meade, M., *Madame Blavatsky,* Putnam, 1980.
Meek, M. G., *Johann Faust: the Man and the Myth,* Oxford University Press, 1930.
Meister Eckhart, *Mystic & Philosopher,* tr. by R. Shermann, Indiana Univ. Press, 1978.
Mesmer, F. A., *Mesmerism,* tr. by G. Bloch, W. Kaufmann, 1980.
Molinari, P., *Julian of Norwich,* Longmans, London, 1958.
Moore, George, *Hail and Farewell,* Humanities, 1980.
Mylonas, G. E., *Eleusis and the Eleusinian Mysteries,* Princeton Univ. Press.

Neilson, F., *Teilhard de Chardin's Vision of the Future,* Revisionist Press, 1979.
Nethercot, A. H., *The First Five Lives of Annie Besant,* University of Chicago Press, 1960.
— *The Last Four Lives of Annie Besant,* University of Chicago Press, 1963.
Nicholson, Reynold A., *The Mathnawi Jalalu'd-Din Rumi,* Lazuc, London, 1925–40.
— *Selected Poems from the Divani Shamsi,* Cambridge University Press, 1977.
Nilsson, M. P., *Greek Popular Religion,* Harper and Row, 1940.
— *History of Greek Religion,* Greenwood, 1980.
Nock, A. D., *Early Gentile Christianity and its Hellenistic Background,* Harper and Row, 1964.
— and **Festugiere, A.-J., ed.,** *Corpus Hermeticum,* Budé Series, Paris, 1945–54.
Nordhoff, C., *The Communistic Societies of the United States,* Peter Smith.
Norris, Katrina, *Jamaica: The Search for an Identity,* Oxford University Press, 1962.
Nott, S. C., *Teachings of Gurdjieff,* Routledge, London, 1961.
Nye, Robert, *Faust,* Putnam, 1981.

Obolensky, D., *The Bogomils: A Study in Balkan Neo-Manicheism,* AMS Press.
O'Brien, Kate, *Teresa of Avila,* Max Parrish, London, 1951.
Oesterreich, T. K., *Possession,* R. R. Smith, 1930.
Oldenbourg, Z., *Massacre at Montségur,* Funk and Wagnall, 1968.
Osborne, Arthur, *The Collected Works of Ramana Maharshi,* Rider, London, 1959.
— *The Incredible Sai Baba,* Rider, London, 1958.
Otto, Rudolf, *Mysticism East and West,* Meridian Books, 1957 reprint.
Ouspensky, P. D., *Tertium Organum,* Random, 1970.
— *A New Model of the Universe,* Knopf, 1934.
— *In Search of the Miraculous,* Harcourt, Brace and World, 1947.
— *Psychology of Man's Possible Evolution,* Random, 1973.
Owen, A. L., *The Famous Druids,* Greenwood, 1979.

Palmer, P. M. and **More, R. P.,** *The Sources of the Faust Tradition from Simon Magus to Lessing,* Haskell House, 1959.
Papasogli, G., *St Teresa of Avila,* Daughters of St Paul, 1973.
Paracelsus, *Selected Writings,* Princeton University Press, 2nd edition 1958.
Peers, E. A., *Ramon Lull,* Gordon Press, 1980.
— ed., *The Complete Works of St Teresa of Jesus,* Sheed and Ward, 1946.
Pernoud, R., *Joan of Arc,* Stein and Day, 1969.
Peters, F., *Boyhood with Gurdjieff,* Capra Press, 1980.
Pick, F. L., *History of Freemasonry,* Wehman Brothers, Inc.
Piggott, S., *The Druids,* Praeger, 1968.
Podmore, F., *From Mesmer to Christian Science,* Univ. Books, 1963.
Poppelbaum, H., *Man and Animal,* Anthroposophical Publishing Co., London, 1960.
Powell, Lyman P., *Mary Baker Eddy: A Life Size Portrait,* Christian Science

Publishing Society, revised edition.
Preece, Harold and **Kraft, Celia,** *Dew on Jordan,* Dutton, 1946.
Puech, H.-C., *Le Manichéisme,* Paris, 1969.

Regardie, Israel, *The Golden Dawn,* Llewellyn Publications, 4th edn. 1978, 2 vols.
Ribadeau Dumas, F., *Cagliostro - Scoundrel or Saint?,* Orion Press, 1967.
Rogers, P. G., *The Fifth Monarchy Men,* Oxford University Press, 1966.
Rogerson, Alan, *Millions Now Living Will Never Die,* Constable, London, 1969.
Rubai'yat of Omar Khayyam, translated by A. J. Arberry, Emery Walker, 1949.
Runciman, S., *The Medieval Manichee,* Cambridge University Press, 1947.

Scholem, G. G., *Major Trends in Jewish Mysticism,* Schocken, 1969.
— *On the Kabbalah and its Symbolism,* Schocken, 1969.
Schuon, Frithjof, *Understanding Islam,* Allen and Unwin, 1976.
Scott, W., *Hermetica,* Oxford University Press, 1924–36.
Scott Davidson, Ellen, *Forerunners of St Francis,* Houghton and Mifflin, 1927.
Scudder, V. D., *St Catherine as Seen in Her Letters,* Dent, London, 1905.
Shah, Idries, *The Sufis,* Doubleday, 1971.
— *Tales of the Dervishes,* Dutton, 1969.
— *The Way of the Sufi,* Dutton, 1970.
Shaikh Ad-Darqawi, *Letters of a Sufi Master,* Weiser, 1970.
Sharma, Major-General A. N., *Swami Sivananda, The Sage of Practical Wisdom,* The Yoga-Vedanta Forest Academy, Rishikesh, 1959.
Shepherd, A. P., *A Scientist of the Invisible,* Musson, 1954.
Sherley-Price, L., ed., *St Francis of Assisi, his Life and his Writings,* Harper and Row, 1959.
Silberger, J., *Mary Baker Eddy: An Interpretative Biography,* Little, 1980.
Simon, E., *The Piebald Standard,* AMS Press reprint.
Sitwell, G., *Medieval Spiritual Writers,* Burns and Oates, London, 1961.
Sivananda, Swami, *Autobiography,* The Yoga-Vedanta Forest Academy, Rishikesh.
Siwek, Paul, *The Riddle of Konnersreuth,* Bruce Publishing Co., 1953.
Smith, Robert D., *Comparative Miracles,* Herder, 1965.
Speaight, Robert, *Teilhard de Chardin,* Harper and Row, 1968.
Spencer, S., *Mysticism in World Religion,* Peter Smith.
Steiner, Rudolf, *Christianity as Mystical Fact,* Rudolf Steiner Press, 1981.
— *The Philosophy of Spiritual Activity,* Rudolf Steiner Press, 1963.
— *Knowledge of the Higher Worlds and its Attainment,* Rudolf Steiner Press, 1969.
— *The Threefold Commonwealth,* Rudolf Steiner Press, 1966.
— *The Course of My Life,* Rudolf Steiner Press, 1970.
— *Occult Science - An Outline,* Rudolf Steiner Press, 1969.
Stewart, C. N., *Bulwer Lytton as Occultist,* Theosophical Press, 1927.
Stoudt, J. J., *Sunrise to Eternity,* AMS Press.
Strizower, S., *Exotic Jewish Communities,* Yoseloff, 1962.
Summers, Montague, *The Physical Phenomena of Mysticism,* Barnes and Noble, 1950.
Sumption, J., *Albigensian Crusade,* Merrimack Book Services, 1978.
Sundkler, Bengt, *Bantu Prophets in South Africa,* Oxford University Press.
Symonds, John, *Madame Blavatsky, Medium and Magician,* Yoseloff, 1960.
— *Thomas Brown and the Angels,* Hutchinson, London, 1961.
— *The Great Beast,* Roy Publishers, 1952.
— *The Magic of Aleister Crowley,* Saunders.
— and **Grant, K., ed.,** *The Confessions of Aleister Crowley,* Hill and Wang, 1970.

Taylor, P. A. M., *Expectation Westward,* Cornell University Press, 1966.
Teilhard de Chardin, Pierre, *Hymn of the Universe,* Harper and Row, 1964.
— *Le Milieu Divin,* Harper and Row, 1960.
— *The Phenomenon of Man,* Harper and Row, 1959.
— *Letters to Two Friends 1926–1952,* World Publishing, 1969.
Thorndike, L., *History of Magic and Experimental Science,* Columbia University Press, 1923–58.
Thorold, A., *The Dialogue of the Seraphic Virgin, Catherine of Siena,* Tan Books.
Thurston, Herbert, *The Physical Phenomena of Mysticism,* Regnery, 1952.
— *Surprising Mystics,* Regnery, 1955.
Trimmingham, J. S., *Islam in Ethiopia,* Biblio Distributors, 1965.
— *Islam in the Sudan,* Barnes and Noble.
Trowbridge, W. H. R., *Cagliostro,* Chapman and Hall, London, 1910.

Underhill, Evelyn, *Mysticism,* World Publishing, 1955.

Veith, I., *The Yellow Emperor's Classic of Internal Medicine,* Univ. of California Press.

Waite, A. E., *The Real History of the Rosicrucians,* Redway, 1887.
— *The Brotherhood of the Rosy Cross,* University Books reprint.
Walker, B., *Hindu World,* Praeger, 1968.
— *Sex and the Supernatural,* Macdonald, London, 1970.
Walker, D. P., *Spiritual and Demonic Magic,* University of Notre Dame Press.
Walker, K., *Venture with Ideas,* Clarke, Irwin, 1951.
Watt, W. M., *The Faith & Practice of Al Ghazali,* Orientalia, 1967.
Weatherford, W. D. and **Brewer, E. D. C.,** *Life and Religion in Southern Appalachia,* Friendship Press, 1962.
Wild, R., *Enthusiasm in the Spirit,* Ave Maria, 1975.
Weitzenhoffer, A., *Hypnotism,* Wiley, 1953.
West, R. B., *The Kingdom of the Saints,* Viking Press, 1957.
Whalen, William J., *Armageddon Round the Corner,* John Day, 1962.
White, W. C., *Chinese Jews,* Paragon, 1966.
Widengren, G., *Mani and Manichaeism,* Harcourt, Brace and World, 1966.
Williams, George H., *The Radical Reformation,* Westminster Press, 1962.
Wilson, B. R., *Sects and Society,* Greenwood, 1978.
— *Religious Sects,* World University Library, London, 1970.
— ed., *Patterns of Sectarianism* Humanities.
Wilson, F. A. C., *W. B. Yeats and Tradition,* Macmillan, 1958.
— *Yeats's Iconography,* Macmillan, 1960.
Wilson, R. M., *The Gnostic Problem,* AMS Press reprint.
Winner, Anna Kennedy, *The Basic Ideas of Occult Wisdom,* Theosophical Publishing House, 1970.
Wolters, C., ed., *Revelations of Divine Love,* Dynamic Learning Corp., 1980.
— tr. by, *Cloud of Unknowing,* & other works, Penguin, 1978.

Yates, F. A., *Giordano Bruno and the Hermetic Tradition,* Random House, 1969.
Yeats, W. B., *Autobiography,* Collier-Macmillan, 1966.
— *The Collected Poems,* Macmillan, 2nd edition, 1956.
— *The Collected Plays,* Macmillan, 2nd edition, 1952.
— *Mythologies,* Macmillan, 1959.
— *A Vision,* Collier-Macmillan, revised edition, 1961.
— *Essays and Introductions,* Macmillan.

Zaehner, R. C., *Mysticism, Sacred and Profane,* Oxford University Press, 1961.
— *Hinduism,* Oxford Univ. Press, 1962.
— *Hindu and Muslim Mysticism,* Schocken.
— *Concordant Discord,* Oxford Univ. Press.
Zilboorg, G. and **Henry, E. W.,** *A History of Medical Psychology,* Norton, 1941.